80x86

Architecture and

Programming

80x86

Architecture and

Programming

Volume II: Architecture Reference

Covers implementations from the 8086 to the i486,
and includes the 80x87 processor extension

Rakesh K. Agarwal

PRENTICE HALL, ENGLEWOOD CLIFFS, NEW JERSEY 07632

Library of Congress Cataloging-in-Publication Data

Agarwal, Rakesh K.
    80x86 architecture and programming / Rakesh K. Agarwal.
        p.   cm.
    Includes bibliographical references.
    Contents: -- v. 2. Architecture reference.
    ISBN 0-13-245432-7 (v. 2)
        1. Intel 80x86 (Microprocessor)   I. Title. II. Title:
    Architecture and programming.
    QA76.8.I2929A36   1991
    005.265--dc20   90-7111
                                                                CIP

Editorial/production supervision: *Brendan M. Stewart*
Cover design: *Bruce Kenselaar*
Manufacturing buyer: *Margaret Rizzi*
Cover slide photo: *Reginald Wickham*

Published by Prentice-Hall, Inc.
A Division of Simon & Schuster
Englewood Cliffs, New Jersey 07632

This book can be made available to businesses
and organizations at a special discount when
ordered in large quantities. For more information
contact:

Prentice-Hall, Inc.
Special Sales and Markets
College Division
Englewood Cliffs, N.J. 07632

Printed in the United States of America
10 9 8 7 6 5 4 3 2 1

ISBN 0-13-245432-7

Prentice-Hall International (UK) Limited, *London*
Prentice-Hall of Australia Pty. Limited, *Sydney*
Prentice-Hall Canada Inc., *Toronto*
Prentice-Hall Hispanoamericana, S.A., *Mexico*
Prentice-Hall of India Private Limited, *New Delhi*
Prentice-Hall of Japan, Inc., *Tokyo*
Simon & Schuster Asia Pte. Ltd., *Singapore*
Editora Prentice-Hall do Brasil, Ltda., *Rio de Janeiro*

To Vineeta,
who helped start this book,
and to Ashwin,
who helped finish it

Contents

Chapter 1 Introduction   **1**

    1.1 Implementation variations   *3*
    1.2 How to use this book   *4*
    1.3 Notation   *5*
        1.3.1 Notational extensions to C   *5*
        1.3.2 Undefined and reserved fields   *7*
        1.3.3 Problems with procedural description   *8*

Chapter 2 The 80x86 Machine   **11**

    2.1 The 80x86 machine   *11*
        2.1.1 Instruction overlap   *13*
    2.2 Chapter organization   *14*
    2.3 Data representation   *15*
        2.3.1 Data alignment rules   *15*
        2.3.2 Little Endian, Big Endian, and integer
             representation   *16*
        2.3.3 Representing strings   *17*
        2.3.4 Representing unpacked BCD data   *18*
        2.3.5 Representing packed BCD data   *18*
        2.3.6 Floating point   *19*
    2.4 Register set   *20*
        2.4.1 Programmer visible registers   *20*
        2.4.2 General registers   *21*
        2.4.3 Flags register   *23*
        2.4.4 Segment registers   *25*
        2.4.5 Control registers   *26*
        2.4.6 Debug registers   *28*
        2.4.7 Test registers   *29*

2.4.8 Programmer invisible registers   *30*

2.4.9 Restartability registers   *31*

2.4.10 Segment descriptor registers   *32*

2.4.11 Miscellaneous registers   *33*

2.5 Execution modes   *36*

2.6 Protection and memory management concepts   *40*

2.6.1 CPL and privileged mode   *41*

2.6.2 I/O access and IOPL   *41*

2.6.3 I/O port access control   *42*

2.6.4 Memory access control   *43*

2.6.4.1 Protected segment access rules   *44*

2.6.4.2 Paged memory access rules   *48*

2.6.4.3 Priority of memory access rules   *51*

2.7 Memory access   *51*

2.7.1 Loading segment registers in REAL and VM86 modes   *53*

2.7.2 Loading segment registers in PROTECTED mode   *55*

2.7.2.1 The GDT and LDT descriptors   *59*

2.7.2.2 The read_descr routine   *62*

2.7.2.3 Setting the Accessed flag   *66*

2.7.2.4 The role of the null SELECTOR   *67*

2.7.2.5 Segment descriptor loading rules   *68*

2.7.3 Switching from PROTECTED to REAL mode   *72*

2.7.4 Reading memory   *72*

2.7.4.1 Reading data segments   *73*

2.7.4.2 Reading segment descriptor tables   *74*

2.7.4.3 Reading task state segments   *75*

2.7.4.4 Reading interrupt descriptor tables   *77*

2.7.4.5 Checking segment limits   *78*

2.7.5 Writing memory   *78*

2.7.5.1 Writing data segments   *79*

2.7.5.2 Writing segment descriptor tables   *80*

2.7.5.3 Writing into task state segments   *81*

2.7.6 Fetching instructions   *82*

2.7.7 Translation and protection via paging   *83*

2.7.7.1 Handling page faults   *90*

2.7.7.2 Reading linear memory   *91*

2.7.7.3 Writing linear memory   *94*

2.7.8 Alignment checks on the i486   *98*

2.7.9 Caching on the 80*x*86   *99*

2.7.9.1 Memory caching on the i486   *103*
2.7.9.2 Deactivating the cache   *106*
2.7.9.3 Memory mapped I/O locations   *107*
2.7.9.4 Second-level caches   *107*
2.7.10 Paging and TLBs   *108*
2.7.10.1 Processing TLB misses   *110*
2.7.10.2 Setting the Dirty bit   *110*
2.7.10.3 TLB replacement policy   *110*
2.7.11 Atomic transactions, and the lock function   *111*
2.8 Stack operations   *113*
2.8.1 Big stacks, SS, and expand-down segments   *115*
2.8.2 Push and pop definitions   *116*
2.9 I/O access   *118*
2.9.1 I/O space protection checks   *119*
2.10 Gates and privilege level transitions   *121*
2.10.1 Using call gates in JMP instructions   *127*
2.10.2 Conforming segments   *127*
2.11 Task switches   *128*
2.11.1 Returning from a nested task   *141*
2.11.2 Direct task switch via TSS descriptors   *143*
2.11.3 Setting up the first TSS via LTR   *143*
2.12 Interrupts and exceptions   *143*
2.12.1 Servicing interrupts and exceptions   *145*
2.12.2 Error codes   *146*
2.12.3 Simultaneous interrupts   *149*
2.12.4 Simultaneous exceptions   *149*
2.12.5 Software interrupts, hardware interrupts, and
       NMI   *150*
2.12.6 Exception handling   *151*
2.12.6.1 Double faults and benign and contributory
         exceptions   *152*
2.12.7 The signal_*xxxx* routines   *153*
2.12.8 The handle_intr_xcp routine   *159*
2.13 Instruction interruptability   *165*
2.14 Instruction restartability   *167*
2.15 Halt and shutdown   *168*
2.16 Software debug features   *169*
2.16.1 Instruction single step   *169*
2.16.2 Instruction breakpoints via INT 3   *170*
2.16.3 Breakpoint register usage   *171*
2.16.3.1 The debug status register   *172*
2.16.3.2 The debug control register   *173*

2.16.3.3 Checking for data breakpoints   *174*
2.16.3.4 Reporting breakpoints   *175*
2.16.3.5 Use of the RF flag   *176*
2.17 Processor initialization   *177*
2.17.1 Initializing the 8086   *178*
2.17.2 Initializing the 80286   *180*
2.17.3 Initializing the 80386 and i486   *181*
2.17.4 Initializing the 80376   *184*
2.18 Instruction decoding   *185*
2.18.1 Encoding structure   *187*
2.18.2 Instruction prefixes   *190*
2.18.3 Instruction opcodes and operands   *191*
2.18.3.1 Default segment register selection   *194*
2.18.3.2 Overriding the default segment selection   *195*
2.18.3.3 The address size attribute   *195*
2.18.3.4 OFFSET wraparound vs. data wraparound   *196*
2.18.3.5 Linear address wraparound   *198*
2.18.3.6 Physical address wraparound, and MS-DOS   *198*
2.18.4 The operand size attribute   *198*
2.19 Differences between 80x86 implementations   *200*
2.19.1 The 8086 and 8088   *200*
2.19.2 The 80186 and 80188   *202*
2.19.3 The 80286   *203*
2.19.4 The 80386 and 80386SX   *205*
2.19.5 The 80376   *206*
2.19.6 The i486   *207*

Chapter 3 The 80x87 Processor Extension   **209**

3.1 The IEEE floating point standard and the 80x87   *209*
3.2 Organization of this chapter   *211*
3.3 80x87 data representation   *211*
3.3.1 Floating point data   *212*
3.3.1.1 Unnormalized values   *214*
3.3.1.2 Denormalized values   *215*
3.3.1.3 Zero and pseudozero representation   *216*
3.3.1.4 Infinity representation   *218*
3.3.1.5 NaN representation   *220*
3.3.2 Integer data representation   *222*

3.3.3 Packed BCD data representation   *223*
3.4 IEEE floating point arithmetic principles   *225*
   3.4.1 Rounding   *226*
   3.4.1.1 Round to integer   *226*
   3.4.2 Floating point comparison   *227*
   3.4.3 Floating point exceptions   *228*
   3.4.3.1 Invalid operation   *228*
   3.4.3.2 Division by zero   *228*
   3.4.3.3 Overflow   *229*
   3.4.3.4 Underflow   *229*
   3.4.3.5 Loss of precision   *230*
   3.4.3.6 Denormal operand   *230*
3.5 Overview of the 80x87   *230*
3.6 80x87 registers   *232*
   3.6.1 The FTAG register   *232*
   3.6.2 The status and control registers   *234*
   3.6.3 Exception address registers   *237*
   3.6.4 Saving and restoring 80x87 state   *238*
   3.6.4.1 Mixing environment formats   *245*
3.7 80x87 stack operations   *246*
3.8 Coordinating an 80x86 with an 80x87   *248*
   3.8.1 8086 coordination with an 8087   *249*
   3.8.2 Saving processor extension state on a task switch   *250*
3.9 80x87 exception reporting   *251*
   3.9.1 The PE_OVERRUN exception   *256*
3.10 Emulating the numerics processor extension   *257*
3.11 80x87 initial state   *257*
3.12 80x87 instruction encoding   *259*
3.13 80x87 detection method   *260*

Chapter 4 The Instruction Set   **261**

4.1 Instruction mnemonics by function   *262*
4.2 Notation   *267*
4.3 Instructions sorted by mnemonic   *274*

References   589

Appendix A Instructions Sorted by Opcode   591
Index   607

Figures

Figure 1.1: Main features of major 80x86 implementations   *2*

Figure 2.1: Big Endian and Little Endian representations   *16*

Figure 2.2: Revised Little Endian representation of
1,000,000   *17*

Figure 2.3: String storage in memory   *17*

Figure 2.4: Unpacked BCD representation of 213,600   *18*

Figure 2.5: Packed BCD representation of 213,600   *19*

Figure 2.6: The 80x86 general registers   *22*

Figure 2.7: The 80x86 flags register   *24*

Figure 2.8: The 80x86 segment registers   *26*

Figure 2.9: The 80x86 control registers   *27*

Figure 2.10: The 80x86 debug registers   *29*

Figure 2.11: The 80x86 test registers   *30*

Figure 2.12: Logical contents of a segment descriptor
register   *34*

Figure 2.13: Differences between REAL, PROTECTED, and
VM86 modes   *39*

Figure 2.14: How to set execution modes   *38*

Figure 2.15: Memory access overview   *43*

Figure 2.16: Expand-up segment access   *47*

Figure 2.17: Expand-down segment access   *48*

Figure 2.18: Linear memory and physical memory   *49*

Figure 2.19: Mapping a linear address to a physical
address   *50*

Figure 2.20: Physical memory sizes of 80x86
implementations   *52*

Figure 2.21: Memory access in REAL and VM86 modes   *54*

Figure 2.22: The format of a PROTECTED mode
SELECTOR   *56*

Figure 2.23: PROTECTED mode segment descriptor
access   *57*

Figure 2.24: Loading the GDT descriptor   *61*

Figure 2.25: Loading the LDT descriptor   *62*

Figure 2.26: Classification of 80x86 descriptors *64*

Figure 2.27: Format of the (PROTECTED mode) null
SELECTOR *67*

Figure 2.28: Linear address structure when paging is
enabled *84*

Figure 2.29: Format of directory table base address register
(CR3) *84*

Figure 2.30: Format of directory table and page table
entries *85*

Figure 2.31: Page protection via U_S, W_R, and WP flags *89*

Figure 2.32: Combining directory table and page table access
rights *90*

Figure 2.33: Natural boundaries of 80x86 application data
types *99*

Figure 2.34: The structure of a set associative cache *101*

Figure 2.35: The 80386/i486 TLB *109*

Figure 2.36: An 80x86 system with mulitple masters *111*

Figure 2.37: Stack accesses in the 80x86 *114*

Figure 2.38: 80x86 gate descriptor formats *122*

Figure 2.39: 80286-style task state segments (TSS16) *130*

Figure 2.40: 80386-style task state segments (TSS32) *131*

Figure 2.41: PROTECTED/VM86 mode 80x86 interrupt vector
entry formats *146*

Figure 2.42: PROTECTED mode error code formats *147*

Figure 2.43: Page fault error code interpretation *148*

Figure 2.44: 80x86 exception attributes *154*

Figure 2.45: Breakpoint register type and length
encodings *174*

Figure 2.46: General structure of nonbranching
instructions *188*

Figure 2.47: Branch format and miscellaneous other
formats *189*

Figure 2.48: Summary of 80x86 instruction prefixes *190*

Figure 2.49: 16-bit effective address (OFFSET)
generation *192*

Figure 2.50: 32-bit effective address (OFFSET)
generation *193*

Figure 3.1: 80x87 floating point data representation *213*

Figure 3.2: Attributes of 80x87 floating point formats *215*

Figure 3.3: 80x87 denormal data representation *217*

Figure 3.4: 80x87 zero representation *218*

Figure 3.5: 80x87 representation of infinity *220*

Figure 3.6: Representing NaNs in the 80*x*87   *221*
Figure 3.7: 80*x*87 integer data representation   *223*
Figure 3.8: 80*x*87 packed BCD data representation   *224*
Figure 3.9: The relation between real numbers and floating
         point   *225*
Figure 3.10: The relationship between an 80*x*86 and an
         80*x*87   *231*
Figure 3.11: 80*x*87 register stack and status register   *233*
Figure 3.12: The 80*x*87 control register (FCW)   *235*
Figure 3.13: REAL and VM86 mode environment
         formats   *239*
Figure 3.14: PROTECTED mode environment formats   *238*
Figure 3.15: Memory image of stack used by 80*x*87
         state   *241*
Figure 3.16: The Intel-recommended processor extension
         interface   *252*
Figure 3.17: The PC/AT processor extension interface   *253*
Figure 3.18: The i486 processor extension interface   *254*
Figure 3.19: Encoding of 80*x*87 instructions   *259*

Copyrights and Trademarks

Preface

About the '86 family

The IBM® Corporation ushered in a new era in the history of computing when it introduced the IBM PC in 1981. The microprocessor chosen to power the PC was Intel® Corporation's 8088, a variant of Intel's flagship microprocessor of the day, the 8086. Although the 8086 enjoyed substantial market share in its own right, the popularity of the PC immensely increased the total market size for microprocessors, and cemented the 8086's future as an industry standard computer architecture.

Keeping in mind that Intel introduced the 8086 at a time when 8-bit microprocessors set the standard, the fact that its view of memory was a generalization of memory bank switching (using 64-kilobyte banks) did not seem a problem. However, increasing memory densities and the popularity of the 8086 in general-purpose programming applications soon made its architectural advances look like architectural warts. These deficiencies largely went unfixed in the 80186 and 80286, the successors to the 8086.

By the time the 80386 design process began, Intel had enough time to think through the architectural enhancements needed to fix the '86 family's memory addressing problems. The 80386 also benefited from emerging software standards, especially the C programming language and the UNIX® operating system. These standards made clear the importance of a "flat" view of memory, where memory addresses can be manipulated as easily as integers. The net result was an architecture that allowed the construction of demand-paged operating systems where a single integer could directly address up to 4 gigabytes of memory. A side effect of the fixes, required in its own right, was the introduction of a full suite of 32-bit operations.

The dominant PC operating system, MS-DOS®, had already accommodated the 8086's shortcomings. Customer feedback helped shape support for virtualized MS-DOS support (in the form of the 80386's VM-86 mode). These factors, along with the stability of the software standards just mentioned, allowed the architecture of the '86 family of processors to stabilize also. Thus we see that the follow-on to the 80386, the i486, has only minor software architecture enhancements. This architectural stability provides the motivation for this reference manual: to provide a definition of the *80x86*, the architecture of the family of processors that has evolved from the original 8086.

About this book series

This is the second of a two-volume series of books describing the software architecture of the 80*x*86 family of processors. The titles of the two volumes are

Volume I: Tutorial and Cookbook

Volume II: Architecture Reference

The first volume presents the main features of the architecture, making extensive use of assembly language examples to motivate concepts. The examples are self-contained and, whenever possible, can be assembled and executed. This volume focuses on presenting the complete architecture in a reference format. Cross-referencing (using page and section numbers) is used in the text to help the reader locate interrelated concepts in different parts of the book. An extensive index is also included.

Feedback

Although the manuscript has been reviewed for accuracy, errors or ambiguities in the descriptions may remain. Your feedback in this regard will be greatly appreciated. Please send your correspondence addressed to

Prentice-Hall, Inc.
Englewood Cliffs, NJ 07632
Attn: Karen Gettman

Acknowledgments

This book has benefited from the help of many people. Richard Simone and Gene Hill at Intel Corporation provided enough workplace flexibility to allow me to complete large parts of an early draft of the book. This draft benefited from the comments of Heinz Breu, Richard Simone, and Raj Shah. Bo Ericsson's review of later drafts of the book resulted in many error fixes and structural improvements. Bo also suggested the format for Appendix A. Piyush Patel and Jim Picard helped by providing missing information about the architecture.

Thanks go to Karen Gettman and Bernard Goodwin at Prentice-Hall for their seemingly infinite patience. And, finally, my gratitude goes to Vineeta for helping when help was needed most.

Palo Alto, California   R.K.A.

80x86

Architecture and

Programming

Chapter 1

Introduction

This book is a reference manual for the 80*x*86, the processor architecture that is embodied in the PC and PS/2® family of microcomputers. There are many implementations of the 80*x*86, not all of which support the complete architecture described here. Indeed, the architecture as it stands today has evolved over a decade of developments in silicon design capability. The latest member of the 80*x*86 family, the i486, is a 32 bit machine that offers extensive memory management and protection facilities. Floating point arithmetic support is built-in, as is a memory cache. This contrasts with the original 80*x*86 member, the 8086, which supports a 16 bit software architecture and no memory management or protection features. Floating point is available on the 8086 via a separate coprocessor (the 8087). The 8086 has no integrated cache; there is little need for it since commonly available memories are fast enough to keep up with it. The i486 is about 30 to 40 times faster than the 8086. Both the 8086 and the i486, as well as most other implementations of the 80*x*86 architecture are products of Intel Corporation.

As the foregoing discussion suggests, the 80*x*86 architecture has evolved over time as a series of upward-compatible extensions to the architecture that was initially embodied in the 8086. To date, the flagship processors following the 8086 have been the 80286, the 80386, and the i486. The major features of each of these processors are shown in Figure 1.1. Each successive generation of the 80*x*86 family, up to the 80386, has added numerous architectural features to its predecessor. In particular, the 80286 added extensive segment-oriented memory management and protection features to the basic 8086 architecture, and the 80386 extended the architecture to 32 bits and added page-based memory management and protection.

This trend of enhancing function with each successive generation ended with the 80386. The i486, the 80386's successor, focuses on performance improvements and integration, rather than architectural enhancements. The only new

instruction of general interest in the i486 is BSWAP, an instruction that reverses
the ordering of bytes in a (32-bit) double word. We can expect the successors of
the i486 to follow this new trend.

Processor	Date introduced	Main features
8086	1978	16-bit software architecture 16-bit direct (offset) address 8087 coprocessor for floating point Approximately 0.33 MIPS
80286	1982	8086 features + Extensive segment-based protection mechanisms 80287 coprocessor for floating point Approximately 1 MIPS
80386	1985	80286 features + 32-bit software architecture 32-bit direct (offset) address Page-based memory management and protection 80387 coprocessor for floating point Approximately 3.5 MIPS
i486	1989	80386 features + Integrated 80387-style coprocessor Integrated 8 KB instruction/data cache Multiprocessor support Approximately 12 MIPS

Figure 1.1: Main features of major 80*x*86 implementations

1.1 Implementation variations

Although only four implementations of the 80x86 are listed in Figure 1.1, at present there are nine different 80x86 family members marketed by Intel. For the most part, these additional processors are variants of the major implementations listed. Each of these variants is briefly described in the paragraphs that follow.

The 8086, which has a 16-bit-wide interface to memory, has a variant called the 8088 that has an 8-bit-wide memory interface. Reducing the width of the memory interface reduces the number of components needed to build a microcomputer and, hence, reduces complexity and system cost. It is the 8088 that was used in the original IBM PC.

The 80286 and i486 have no variants. However, the 80386 has two variants: the 80386SX and the 80376. The 80386SX can be viewed as the 8088 counterpart of the 80386. The normal width of the interface between the 80386 and memory is 32 bits. In the 80386SX this width has been reduced to 16 bits. In terms of software features and datapath design, the 80386SX is identical to the 80386. The 80376 is kind of an oddball. It is similar to the 80386SX in that it has a 16-bit bus; however, it has been defeatured to disallow its use in MS-DOS and general programming applications. The main use of the 80376 is in 32-bit controller applications. By retaining a subset of the full 80386 architecture, 80376 programs are able to use a subset of programming tools intended for the 80386. See §2.19.5 on page 206 for details on what has been omitted from the 80376.

We have discussed three variants of the major 80x86 family members. Another family member, the 80186, is not really a variant but an separate design that improves on the 8086 and as well integrates peripheral devices like interrupt controllers and DMA. Because the details of how the peripherals are configured do not match the system architecture of the IBM PC, the 80186 has not been used commonly in PC-compatible designs. Like the 80376, its main market is controller applications. The 80186 (which has a 16-bit-wide memory interface) also has a variant, the 80188, that has a 8-bit-wide memory interface.

In addition to the differences between differing implementations, it is worthwhile noting that most implementations are available at a variety of frequency ratings. For example, the maximum operating frequency of an 8086 can be anywhere between 5 MHz and 10 Mhz, the maximum operating frequency of an 80286 can be anywhere from 6 Mhz to 20 Mhz, and the maximum operating frequency of an 80386 can be anywhere from 16 Mhz to 33 Mhz. At present, the i486 is

available only as a 25 MHz part, with 33 Mhz parts to follow. Within a
particular implementation, a part's frequency rating directly corresponds with
CPU performance. However, structural differences between implementations
also affect CPU performance; for example, a 25 Mhz i486 has about twice the
performance of a 25 Mhz 80386. Furthermore, performance at the system level
(i.e., performance as perceived by the user of a computer) is affected by the
speed of the memory system attached to the CPU, and the performance of its I/O
devices.

1.2 How to use this book

Although this book is primarily a reference manual, it is organized so that it can
be of use to both the occasional assembly language programmer seeking the
definition of a particular instruction and to the systems software programmer
wanting to understand some detail about the architecture. Both these objectives
are attained by relying heavily on a modified C language notation to describe
virtually all aspects of the architecture. The user wanting the definition of a
simple instruction can simply refer to the alphabetic listing of instruction in
Chapter 4. (The first-time reader is encouraged to read the introductory sections
of the chapter.) The definitions in Chapter 4 are usually kept brief. If a
particular instruction performs a complex control sequence, its description is
invariably encapsulated in a subroutine invocation. The definitions of all such
subroutines are given in Chapter 2. This chapter also describes noninstruction-
related architecture concepts, such as interrupt and exception handling.

Chapter 4 provides the definitions of both 80x86 and 80x87 instructions.
However, many aspects of the 80x87 are best described outside the the context of
instruction definitions. Examples are the 80x86 — 80x87 interface, and the
general principles governing floating point arithmetic, as specified by the 80x87.
These details are given in Chapter 3.

The linear nature of text descriptions does not correspond well with the
architecture of the 80x86, which consists of a network of interrelated concepts.
This book tries to alleviate this problem by providing extensive cross-referencing
of related (but nonconsecutive) descriptions. The reader is also encouraged to
look up the index to locate a subject whose description might be spread over
different parts of the book.

1.3 Notation

Both for reasons of precision and conciseness, the C programming language is used to describe the bulk of the architecture. Even though C language notation is sometimes cryptic, we have resisted the temptation to change it in any way. However, standard C notation has been enhanced somewhat; for example, bit field selection is permitted. The reader unfamiliar with the basics of C language should consult one of the many excellent texts on the language; see, for example, [Kernighan and Ritchie, 1978]. The subsection below describes the extensions to C language notation used in this book.

1.3.1 Notational extensions to C

The C language is extended to allow manipulation of fields of bits within an elementary C type. For example, in

```
int i;
char b;

b = i⟨9:7⟩;
b = signex(i⟨9:7⟩);
i⟨20:15⟩ = b⟨6:1⟩;
```

the first assignment copies the value of the 3-bit field in *i* starting at bit index 7 and ending at bit index 9 to the character *b*. The high-order bits of *b* (i.e., bits 3 through 7) are cleared to zeros. The second line does the same assignment, except it assumes two's complement values (i.e., it sign extends the source before copying to the destination). The third line copies bits 1 through 6 of *b* to bits 15 through 20 of *i*; the remaining bits of *i* are left undisturbed. Note that all values are encoded in Little Endian notation;[1] hence, the least significant bit of a value always has the smallest bit index.

Another area of difference is in how arithmetic and relational operators are used. In standard C the actual operation performed depends on the type of the operands. For example, the program fragment

```
int i1, i2, i3;
unsigned int u1, u2;
```

---

[1] Little Endian data representation is discussed in §2.3.2 on page 16.

```
if (i1 > i2)
   i1 = i2 / i3;
if (u1 <= u2)
   u2 = u1-1;
```

compares i1 and i2 as signed values (since int is a signed integer), and u1 and u2 as unsigned values. Furthermore, the quotient of i2 divided by i3 is generated assuming signed division. For flexibility, we require explicit specification of the type of the operation. In particular, unsigned operators have a subscript "u", whereas signed operators are unadorned. So, the unsigned comparison above is modified to

```
if (u1 <=u u2)
   u2 = u1-1;
```

whereas the signed division operation is left as is.

The complete list of unsigned operators used in this book is as follows:

- $/_u$: Unsigned divide (yields nonnegative quotient)
- $\%_u$: Unsigned modulus (yields nonnegative modulus)
- $>_u$: Unsigned "greater than"
- $<_u$: Unsigned "less than"
- $<=_u$: Unsigned "less than or equal to"
- $>=_u$: Unsigned "greater than or equal to"
- $*_u$: Unsigned multiply
- $>>_u$: Logical right-shift; vacated bits are filled with zeros. (The arithmetic right shift operator ">>" fills vacated bits with the sign of the original shift operand.)

All expressions are evaluated assuming infinite precision. This is done for notational convenience. An infinitely large expression evaluator allows easy detection of overflow conditions which occur in the finite-sized expression evaluator (i.e. the ALU) of an 80x86 implementation. Also, double precision products from two single precision values are easily generated. The result of an expression is always truncated to match the number of bits available in the destination (if any). Occasionally, it is useful to have an infinitely precise destination. The special variable *result* is used for this purpose. For example, in

result = dst − src
OF = *result* $< -2^{os-1}$ || *result* $> 2^{os-1}$-1

the infinitely precise difference between the variables *dst* and *src* is assigned to *result*. The flag OF is set TRUE if the *result* cannot fit into the destination, when viewed as a signed quantity. If *result* were not treatable as a value of infinite precision, the expression defining OF's value would be a lot more complicated. Of course, if *result* is assigned to a finite-sized object, only its least significant bits are copied. For example,

EAX = *result*

copies the least significant 32 bits of *result* to EAX, assuming EAX is a DWORD storage location.

Occasionally, the extended C notation described above is inadequate to describe a certain concept. Whenever this happens, the extra-C concept is described in prose, and is enclosed in « ... ». For example,

```
if ( « NMI pin active » )
    handle_intr_xcp(2, FALSE);
```

denotes that activating the NMI pin results in the actions specified by handle_intr_xcp.

Finally, note that a minor liberty is taken with C language notation in the area of declarations of temporary variables. Occasionally, such variables (used to store intermediate results) are not declared. This sloppiness is of little consequence since the type of the temporary is apparent from the context.

1.3.2 Undefined and reserved fields

Sometimes, the architecture does not specify how certain state gets modified. For example, the architecture specifies that the zero flag's (ZF's) value is unknown after a multiply operation. This is signified by assigning it the special value *undefined*; for example,

ZF = *undefined*

Programs should never compare a value against an undefined value, even though the "undefined" value may yield the same bit pattern in a given implementation of the 80x86 architecture. For example, let us say that ZF is always set to 0 after a multiply operation in some implementation of the 80x86. If the value of the EFLAGS register (which contains ZF) is now compared against some constant (e.g. to check the OF flag) unpredictable results may occur between different

80x86 architecture implementations. The only safe way to compare EFLAGS here is to mask out the *undefined* values prior to the comparison.

In addition to *undefined* expressions, the architecture sometimes marks the following items as ***reserved***:

- a complete register (e.g., the control register CR4)

- one or more fields within a register (e.g., the high-order 13 bits of the EFLAGS register)

- specific values of a field (e.g., type 8 of a control descriptor's Type field)

Reserved items are thus marked for purposes of future expandability. They may also be used by a particular 80x86 implementation for features not useful to the usual user of the part, for example, for implementing internal testability features. Therefore, reserved registers should never be read from or written into. When reading a register containing a reserved field, the value of the reserved field should be treated as *undefined*. When updating a field in a register that also contains reserved fields, use the following steps:

1. read the register into a temporary register. (In most cases the temporary register is a general-purpose register like EAX.)

2. update the bits in the temporary register corresponding to the field to be updated in the original register.

3. write back the temporary register in its entirety into the original register.

These steps help ensure that all reserved field values are left unmodified.

1.3.3 Problems with procedural description

Pseudo-C language is used in this book to describe the 80x86 architecture because the notation is both familiar and relatively precise. However a serious shortcoming in any procedural notation (like C) is that descriptions take the form of a sequence of actions. The ordering imposed by the sequence need not be a part of the specification. Rather than use alternate notation, the approach taken in this book is to use C language, but with the following caveats:

- If I_1 and I_2 are 80x86 instructions that execute in sequence, an implementation must ensure that I_1 completes before I_2 is started. The instruction completion requirement is only with respect to software operation. In particular, this rule does not preclude the use of overlapped instruction processing techniques such as pipelining.

- If an 80x86 instruction makes more than one memory reference, the order in which the memory references are specified in the C language description of the instruction's behavior is not necessarily the order in which a particular implementation of the 80x86 would perform the references. Note, however, that the ordering of memory references made is always preserved at the instruction level. In particular, assume that I_1 makes memory references m_{11} and m_{12}, and I_2 makes memory references m_{21}, m_{22}, and m_{23}. Assuming they do not interact, memory references m_{11} and m_{12} can be performed in any order, as can m_{21}, m_{22}, and m_{23}. However, memory references in the group m_{21}-m_{22}-m_{23} are guaranteed to be performed after memory references in m_{11}-m_{12}.

- The ability of an 80x86 implementation to choose the order in which memory references are performed within an instruction can lead to differing exception reporting. For example, if both memory locations a and b are referenced in an instruction, and reference to both locations cause PAGE faults, the page fault address reported by a particular implementation can be either that of a or of b.

Chapter 2

The 80x86 Machine

Our objective is to specify the 80x86 architecture as a program. To do so we have to specify the 80x86 data structures (i.e., 80x86 registers and memory) and the algorithms that operate on these data structures. The algorithms constitute the definition of instructions and the method by which interrupts and exceptions are handled. But for the description of instructions (see Chapter 4), all other aspects of the 80x86 architecture are described in this chapter. The description of floating point support, which is available via a separate coprocessor in all 80x86 implementations other than the i486[2] is deferred to Chapter 3.

2.1 The 80x86 machine

For starters, let us examine the top-level execution loop of the 80x86 architecture.

```
x86_cpu()
{   reset_cpu();                          /* see page 178 */

    while (1) { /* do forever */
        checkpoint();                     /* see page 168 */
        instr = decode_instruction();     /* see page 185 */
        execute(instr);                   /* see page 259 */

    NEXT_INSTR:
        report_brkpts();                  /* see page 175 */
        check_interrupts();               /* see page 151 */
    }
}
```

80x86 operation begins with the reset_cpu routine. This routine initializes most of the 80x86 registers to a state that is sufficient for program execution to begin.

---

[2] The numerics coprocessor is integrated on-chip in the i486.

11

The reset_cpu routine is described in §2.17 on page 178. After the 80x86 CPU is initialized, the instruction interpretation loop is entered. This is an infinite loop; it terminates only when the CPU is reset.

80x86 instruction interpretation is done in five parts. First, a snapshot is taken of the registers visible to the programmer. This snapshot, taken by the checkpoint routine, is saved in a set of background registers. Since it is taken before the current instruction is executed, it reflects the state of the CPU registers just after the previous instruction completed execution. The snapshot allows for recovery from faults that might occur while executing the current instruction. Fault recovery, and the checkpoint routine are both discussed in detail in §2.14 on page 168. Note that applications programs typically do not need to worry about fault recovery. The operating system software, in conjuction with actions taken by the 80x86, make fault recovery transparent.

Processing of the current instruction begins after checkpointing is done. Instructions are stored in memory in a compact, encoded representation. The current instruction is fetched from memory and decoded by the decode_instruction routine (described in §2.18 on page 185). This routine also advances the current instruction pointer (called EIP) to point at the next instruction. The decode_instruction routine determines the type of operation to be performed and its parameters. Parameters include the instruction operands (i.e., register name and/or memory address), if any, the size of the operation (8, 16, or 32 bits), and whether or not the the memory access (if specified) should be done atomically (i.e., as a LOCKed transaction). The operation type and parameters are fed to the execute routine, which actually performs the specified operation on the operands. If some type of exception is detected while performing the operation, the appropriate exception handler is invoked. Since the description of instructions forms the bulk of this book, a separate chapter, Chapter 4, is devoted to it.

The 80x86 architecture supports a variety of features useful in the construction of software debuggers. These are

1. instruction single stepping

2. instruction address breakpoints

3. data address breakpoints

Single stepping allows a user specified routine to be invoked after every instruction executes successfully. Instruction breakpoints and data breakpoints allow a user-specified routine to be invoked when one of a set of instructions is about to be executed or one of a set of data addresses is accessed. Checks for these conditions done by the report_brkpts routine. This routine is described fully in §2.16.3.4 on page 175. Note that only single stepping is supported by all implementations of the 80x86 architecture. Instruction and data breakpoints are available only on the 80376, 80386, and i486.

The last action taken in the interpretation of an instruction is a check for externally generated interrupts (also called *hardware interrupts*). The procedure for servicing them is specified by the check_interrupts routine, described in §2.12.5 on page 151.

After checking interrupts, the entire five-step process is repeated for the next instruction. It is important to note that the "next" instruction is not necessarily the instruction in memory that follows the current instruction. For example the current instruction pointer will get changed by the execute routine if a branch is taken. Also, the report_brkpts routine will update the instruction pointer to the first instruction of the debug services routine if a breakpoint is detected. Similarly, the check_interrupts routine will point the instruction pointer at the entry of the appropriate interrupt handler if an interrupt occurs. In the latter two cases, the address of the instruction pointer following the execute routine's completion is saved on the program stack so that the thread of execution prior to the breakpoint or interrupt can be resumed after the debug service routine or interrupt handler has completed.

2.1.1 Instruction overlap

The 80x86 architecture requires all its implementations be such that (from a software point of view) a given instruction should complete before the next instruction begins. However, this requirement is relaxed when it comes to memory and I/O access completion, and breakpoint reporting. In particular, an 80x86 implementation is allowed to start a new instruction before memory (or I/O) references resulting from the previous instruction have completed. (All memory *fault checks* are still required to complete before the next instruction can start. This ensures that the instruction address reported by a fault always matches the address of the instruction in which the memory reference occurred.)

A consequence of allowing deferment of the physical completion of a memory or I/O reference is that it is not possible for an agent outside the CPU to affect program behavior reliably. In particular, assume that a system based on an 80x86 family processor watches I/O addresses and generates a hardware interrupt when certain I/O addresses are recognized. (This might be done, for example, to

simulate the I/O permission bit map of the 80386 and i486 on the 80286.) In
such a system the interrupt handler will not necessarily be entered with the return
address pointing at the instruction following the instruction issuing the I/O
command. This is because by the time the I/O address is made visible to the
external system, the 80x86 may have begun the next instruction.

A situation similar to that just described can occur when data breakpoint
detection is enabled. Data breakpoints are normally reported as traps; that is,
they are reported just before executing the instruction following the instruction
causing the data breakpoint. If, however, a breakpoint is detected because of a
memory reference that occurs near the end of an instruction, the following
instruction may complete before the breakpoint is reported. Providing this
flexibility simplifies memory access pipelining in certain implementations. To
inform an implementation that correct detection of data breakpoints is desired,
the 80x86 requires the user to set the "exact" debug flags. If these flags
(described in §2.16) are set, the implementation is required to report data
breakpoints for an instruction before executing the next one. Of course,
instruction execution rate may suffer as a result. Keep in mind that breakpoints
are only supported on the 80376, 80386, and i486.

2.2 Chapter organization

Many of the sections of this chapter have just been described, using a top-level
description of the instruction execution loop as a starting point. To complete the
picture, numerous background algorithms need to be described. As well, the
80x86 data structures need to be specified.

Data structures recognized by the 80x86 take the form of CPU registers (e.g., the
general registers) and structures in memory that the 80x86 operates on directly
(e.g., segment descriptors). The basic data types supported by the 80x86 are
described in §2.3 and the 80x86 register set is described in §2.4 on page 20. Data
structures used by the 80x86 in the memory address generation process are
described in §2.7 on page 51. This section also describes the memory address
generation algorithm. In addition to memory, the 80x86 architecture supports the
notion of an I/O address space. I/O addresses are associated with I/O
(peripheral) devices. I/O space reads and writes are used to control the
peripherals. I/O access is described in §2.9 on page 118.

2.3 Data representation

Since raw memory is merely a string of bits, it is important to establish conventions for representing different types of data. In general, the 80x86 represents integer data using binary arithmetic. If signed quantities are to be represented, two's-complement notation is used.

The smallest addressable unit of memory is the **BYTE**. A BYTE consists of eight consecutive bits of storage. Therefore it can represent an unsigned value in range 0 to 2^8 (i.e. 256) inclusive or a signed (two's complement) value in the range -2^7 to $+2^7$-1 (i.e., -128 to $+127$) inclusive. Furthermore, using the ASCII or EBCDIC collating sequence, a BYTE can represent one character of text. Each BYTE of memory has a unique address.

A **WORD** is two consecutive BYTEs (i.e., 16 bits), and a **DWORD** is four consecutive BYTEs (i.e., 32 bits). To address a WORD or a DWORD, the address of the least constituent BYTE in the WORD or DWORD is used. In other words, a WORD at address a occupies byte addresses a and a+1, and a DWORD at address a occupies byte addresses a through a+3 inclusive.

Note that the 80376, 80386, and i486 can operate on 32 bits of data at a time. Hence it may make more sense to call a 32 bit quantity a "WORD" on these machines. However, for notational consistency with early, 16 bit implementations of the 80x86 architecture (e.g. the 80286), the term "WORD" will always refer to a 16 bit quantity. The term "DWORD" will be used to denote a *d*ouble*word* (i.e. 32 bit) quantity.

2.3.1 Data alignment rules

Some architectures require that a data item be aligned on its **natural boundary** in physical memory; that is, the data should be stored at an address that is a multiple of the size of the data type. On such a machine a WORD can only appear at even byte addresses, and a DWORD at addresses that are multiples of four. There are no such restrictions in the 80x86 architecture. A DWORD, for example, can appear at address 5 (not a multiple of 4) or at address 100 (a multiple of 4). A data item that is not stored on its natural boundary is termed **unaligned** or **misaligned**. Misaligned data accesses take longer to process; therefore they should be avoided whenever possible. See §2.7.8 on page 98 for further discussion of issues related to data alignment on natural boundaries.

2.3.2 Little Endian, Big Endian, and integer representation

As long as values fit within a the smallest addressable unit (i.e. a BYTE), there is
no problem. However, if a single data item requires more than one BYTE of
storage (e.g., a string of five characters, or a DWORD integer) the question of
byte ordering arises. For example, assume we want to store the integer 1,000,000
(i.e., 0F4240 in hexadecimal) as a 32-bit quantity in the DWORD at addresses 4,
5, 6, and 7. Should the least significant byte (with value 0x40) be stored at
address 4 or at address 7? Either scheme is sensible, as shown in Figure 2.1.
The storage scheme where the least significant byte is stored in the least
numbered address is called the **Little Endian** scheme; the scheme where the
least significant byte is stored at the highest address is called the **Big Endian**
scheme. The 80*x*86 architecture uses the *Little Endian* scheme to store numeric
quantities.

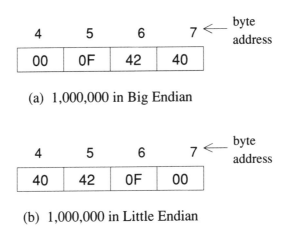

(a) 1,000,000 in Big Endian

(b) 1,000,000 in Little Endian

Figure 2.1: Big Endian and Little Endian representations

The Little Endian storage scheme has the disadvantage that memory images
shown on paper appear in backward order, if increasing memory addresses are
shown from left to right. This can be corrected if addresses are shown instead
from right to left. For example, the revised Little Endian representation of

0x0F4240 shown above is as depicted in Figure 2.2. In this book we will always employ this right-to-left convention for showing memory images.

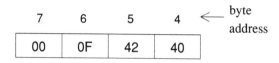

Figure 2.2: Revised Little Endian representation of 1,000,000

If numeric data that was generated on a Big Endian[3] computer is read in on an 80x86 computer, the byte order must be reversed by software. For a WORD data item, the XCHG instruction can be used to do the swap. For a DWORD data item, the BSWAP instruction (available only on the i486) can be used.

2.3.3 Representing strings

We have examined integer representation so far. What about character strings? For example, if the five-character string "Hello" is to be stored at addresses 6 through 10 should the 'H' be stored at address 6 or at address 10? Most machines, regardless of whether they use Little Endian or Big Endian schemes to store integers, will store the 'H' at address 6; that is, the head of a string is always stored at the least numbered address.[4] A pictorial depiction of how "Hello" appears in 80x86 memory is shown in Figure 2.3. Note that the string characters

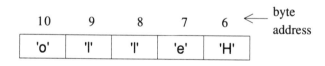

Figure 2.3: String storage in memory

appear backward on the printed page. This is because we write increasing byte

---

[3] Examples of Big Endian architectures are the Motorola 68000, the RT/PC, and the IBM 3090. Little Endian machines include the National Semiconductor 32000 and the DEC VAX.

[4] There is an exception to this rule: PDP-11 software swaps the byte order of every pair of bytes in a string. This improves the performance of routines that operate on strings, but makes strings very hard to read.

addresses from right to left. This is unnatural for strings, but works well for Little Endian integers.

2.3.4 Representing unpacked BCD data

Some applications prefer to represent data in decimal, rather than in binary. This can be done by encoding each decimal digit in four bits (i.e., in a **nibble**). Each nibble stores a value between 0 and 9; encodings for 10 through 15 are not used. Such a scheme is known as **binary coded decimal**, or **BCD**. If only the low nibble of each BYTE is used to store a decimal digit, the representation is called **unpacked** or **zone-format** BCD. Figure 2.4 shows the representation of the decimal value 213,600 in unpacked BCD form. In this representation, ordinary ASCII characters have been used to for the digits. This works because the ASCII representations of the digits '0' through '9' are 0x30 through 0x39 respectively. Since the number is stored as a string, it appears to be stored backwards in our right-to-left writing scheme.

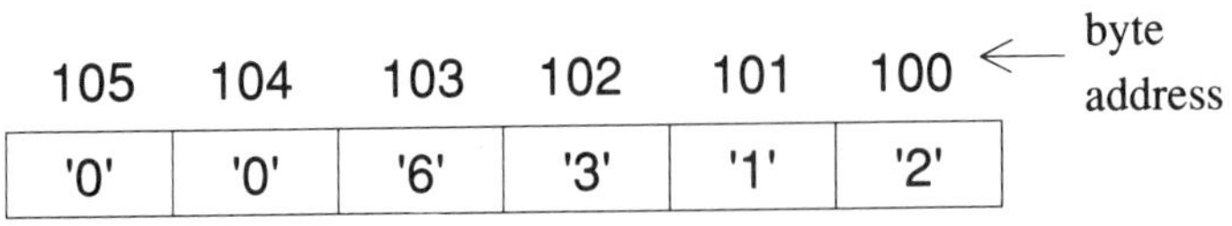

Figure 2.4: Unpacked BCD representation of 213,600

The 80x86 architecture does not support unpacked BCD arithmetic directly. Rather it provides instructions that can be used in conjunction with the normal binary arithmetic instructions to perform single digit BCD arithmetic. These primitive functions need to be repeated to perform general unpacked BCD arithmetic. The instructions for unpacked BCD support are as follows.

- AAA: ASCII Adjust AL after Add
- AAD: ASCII Adjust AX before Divide
- AAM: ASCII Adjust AX after Multiply
- AAS: ASCII Adjust AL after Subtract

2.3.5 Representing packed BCD data

Packed BCD is very similar to unpacked BCD. However, two digits are stored in each BYTE instead of one. This is done by making use of the high nibble of each BYTE that went unused in unpacked BCD: the high nibble stores the more significant digit in the BYTE. Figure 2.5 shows the representation of the decimal value 213,600 in packed BCD form. Reading numbers is rather awkward when written in the right-to-left scheme: each pair of digits appears in forward order, but the pairs themselves appear in backward order! Of course, other representation formats are possible. For example, the PACKED_BCD data type supported by the 80x87 processor extension stores the least significant digit in the least significant nibble of the first operand byte. See Figure 3.6 on page 223 for the format.

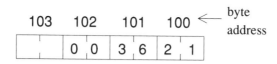

Figure 2.5: Packed BCD representation of 213,600

As with unpacked BCD arithmetic, the 80x86 architecture does not support packed BCD arithmetic directly. Rather, two instructions are provided to perform adjust the result of binary addition and subtraction so that they simulate two-digit packed decimal addition and subtraction. These primitive instructions need to be executed repeatedly to perform packed BCD arithmetic on multiple digits. The instructions are

- DAA: Decimal Adjust AL after Add
- DAS: Decimal Adjust AL after Subtract

If the 80x87 floating point processor extension is used, conversion instructions between packed BCD and floating point become available. These instructions can be used in conjunction with the extensive floating point support provided by the 80x87 to provide packed BCD arithmetic. See page 222 in Chapter 3 for more details.

2.3.6 Floating point

Floating point support is not an integral part of the 80x86 architecture. Rather, it is provided via the 80x87 processor extension. On all implementations of the 80x86 other than the i486, this coprocessor is a separate chip. On the i486, the 80x87 instruction set is integrated on-chip. To highlight the fact that floating point support is an extension to the basic architecture, all floating point discussion is deferred to Chapter 3.

2.4 Register set

This section defines all the registers supported by the 80x86 architecture. The registers are shown both as C language declarations and schematically as memory diagrams. Most registers are defined as 32 bit (DWORD) wide. On 16-bit implementations of the architecture (i.e., the 8086, 80186, and 80286 these registers are usually truncated to 16 bits. Furthermore, some registers (or bit-fields within them) are only available on certain implementations. All registers (and fields within registers) that are not available uniformly across all implementations are identified in the register declarations. In the memory diagrams this fact is shown by using differing background shadings.

2.4.1 Programmer visible registers

The 80x86 has two classes of registers: *programmer visible* and *programmer invisible*. **Programmer visible registers** are those that the programmer can directly manipulate using the 80x86 instruction set. For reasons that will become apparent later, let us group all the visible registers into a structure, as shown.

```
typedef struct {
    DWORD       genReg[8];      /* Eight general registers */
    SELECTOR    segReg[8];      /* Eight segment registers */
    DWORD       flags;          /* EFLAGS */
    DWORD       ctrlReg[4];     /* Control registers */
    DWORD       debReg[8];      /* Debug registers */
    DWORD       testReg[8];     /* Testability registers */
} X86_REGISTERS;
```

In addition to the registers shown, the instruction pointer is a part of the programmer visible CPU state. Its is a DWORD quantity that points to the next instruction to be executed.

```
DWORD EIP;                      /* Instruction pointer */
```

The EIP register is shown separately since it is sometimes convenient to group together all visible registers *except* for EIP.

The fields of the structure name the various types of registers available in the 80x86. For example, *genReg* defines the eight DWORD-size general-purpose registers and *segReg* the eight segment registers. A SELECTOR is a WORD sized quantity; see page 56 for its definition. The X86_REGISTERS are instantiated as follows.

```
X86_REGISTERS curr;              /* Current instruction's state */
```

This structure stores the *current* instruction's state. (As we shall soon see, there is need for a background copy of the visible registers called *prev*. prev stores the state of the visible registers at the end of execution of the *previous* instruction.)

The fields of the X86_REGISTERS structure *curr* have commonly used concrete register names. The subsections that follow use C language #define directives to map the fields of curr to their common 80x86 names.

2.4.2 General registers

The most heavily used of the 80x86 registers are the **general-purpose registers**. The term "general-purpose register" is usually shortened to **general register**. General registers are used for storing variables, computing expression values, computing memory addresses, et cetera; that is, they are used for general programming.

There are eight general registers in the 80x86, as shown below. On the 80376, 80386, and i486 the general registers are 32 bits (DWORD) wide; on the remaining versions of the 80x86, they are 16 bits (WORD) wide. Since BYTE, WORD, and DWORD operations are supported, it is necessary to have 8-, 16-, and 32-bit general registers. Rather than provide separate storage for each, the shorter registers are overlaid on the longer ones, as shown in Figure 2.6. The WORD general registers are simply truncated versions of the DWORD general registers. Two BYTE registers are mapped onto each of the WORD registers AX, BX, CX, and DX. The name of the BYTE register occupying the high-order bits of the WORD register is suffixed with an "H"; the BYTE register occupying the low bits is suffixed with an "L."

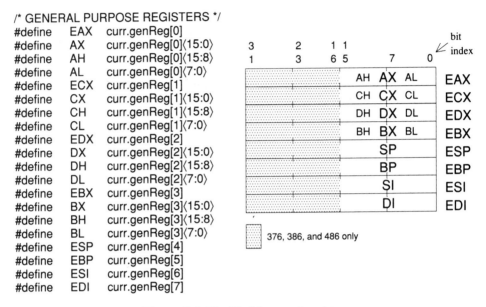

/* GENERAL PURPOSE REGISTERS */
#define   EAX   curr.genReg[0]
#define   AX   curr.genReg[0]⟨15:0⟩
#define   AH   curr.genReg[0]⟨15:8⟩
#define   AL   curr.genReg[0]⟨7:0⟩
#define   ECX   curr.genReg[1]
#define   CX   curr.genReg[1]⟨15:0⟩
#define   CH   curr.genReg[1]⟨15:8⟩
#define   CL   curr.genReg[1]⟨7:0⟩
#define   EDX   curr.genReg[2]
#define   DX   curr.genReg[2]⟨15:0⟩
#define   DH   curr.genReg[2]⟨15:8⟩
#define   DL   curr.genReg[2]⟨7:0⟩
#define   EBX   curr.genReg[3]
#define   BX   curr.genReg[3]⟨15:0⟩
#define   BH   curr.genReg[3]⟨15:8⟩
#define   BL   curr.genReg[3]⟨7:0⟩
#define   ESP   curr.genReg[4]
#define   EBP   curr.genReg[5]
#define   ESI   curr.genReg[6]
#define   EDI   curr.genReg[7]

Figure 2.6: The 80*x*86 general registers

Note the seemingly awkward ordering of general register names; for example, instead of assigning index 1 of *genReg* to EBX, it has been assigned to ECX. This has been done so that the index reflects the value used to encode the register name in an instruction. For example, the binary value 010 is used to specify the EDX register in an instruction. 010_2 also encodes DX and DL; the instruction opcode selects the register size. This encoding scheme does not work for the high-order BYTE registers (e.g., DH) since each such register has a corresponding low-order register (e.g., DL). The solution adopted is to offset the encoding values of the high-order BYTE registers by 4. So, since DL's encoding is 010_2, DH's encoding is 110_2. Instruction encoding is discussed fully in §2.18 (starting on page 185).

2.4.3 Flags register

Most arithmetic and logical operations set flags indicating the type of result; for example, was there an overflow, is the result equal to zero, et cetera. These flags are grouped together in a 16-bit register called FLAGS. FLAGS also stores other control and status bits. For example, the "interrupt enable" flag IF is stored here, as is the IOPL field. On the 80376, 80386, and i486 the FLAGS register has been extended to 32 bits to accommodate new flags. The extended version of FLAGS is called EFLAGS.

The location of each of the flags in this register, as well as their definitions and availability, is shown in the C definitions below, and in Figure 2.7. Flags marked as **all** are available on all implementations of the 80*x*86. Some bit positions are marked either as 0 or 1. These positions are permanently set to the specified value. Writing into the EFLAGS register does not alter these bits' values. The bits marked "reserved" are set aside for future expansion, and should not be accessed. See page 8 (§1.3.2) for a discussion of how to handle reserved fields.

```
/* [E]FLAGS register and individual flags */
#define  EFLAGS   curr.flags
#define  FLAGS    curr.flags⟨15:0⟩
#define  AC       EFLAGS⟨18⟩        /* Alignment check enable [486] */
#define  VM       EFLAGS⟨17⟩        /* Virtual-86 mode enable [386, 486] */
#define  RF       EFLAGS⟨16⟩        /* Restart flag [376, 386, 486] */
#define  NT       EFLAGS⟨14⟩        /* Nested task [286, 376, 386, 486] */
#define  IOPL     EFLAGS⟨13:12⟩     /* I/O priv. lev. [286, 376, 386, 486] */
#define  OF       EFLAGS⟨11⟩        /* Overflow flag [all] */
#define  DF       EFLAGS⟨10⟩        /* String op direction flag [all] */
#define  IF       EFLAGS⟨9⟩         /* Interrupt enable [all] */
#define  TF       EFLAGS⟨8⟩         /* Trap (single-step) enable [all] */
#define  SF       EFLAGS⟨7⟩         /* Sign flag [all] */
#define  ZF       EFLAGS⟨6⟩         /* Zero-result flag [all] */
#define  AF       EFLAGS⟨4⟩         /* Auxiliary carry flag [all] */
#define  PF       EFLAGS⟨2⟩         /* Even parity flag [all] */
#define  CF       EFLAGS⟨0⟩         /* Carry flag [all] */
```

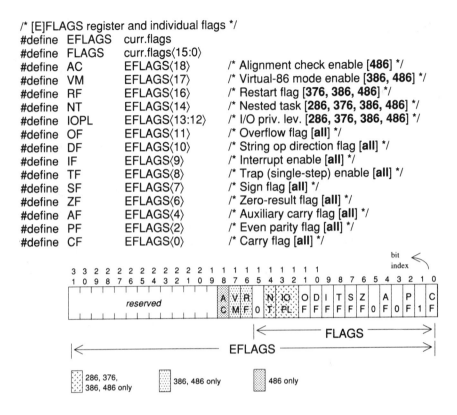

Figure 2.7: The 80*x*86 flags register

The CF, PF, AF, ZF, SF, and OF flags are collectively called the **arithmetic flags**. These flags are set by instructions that perform arithmetic and logical operations. Their settings are shown in Chapter 4 as a part of the definition of each of the instructions.

The trap flag (TF) enables single stepping of instructions. Single stepping is discussed in §2.16 on page 169. The interrupt flag (IF), if set, enables hardware interrupts. (Software interrupts are always enabled.) The direction flag (DF) is used by string instructions to control whether the string should be processed from low address to high address (DF set to 0) or from high address to low address (DF set to 1). The string instructions are CMPS*x*, INS*x*, LODS*x*, MOVS*x*, OUTS*x*, SCAS*x*, and STOS*x*. See their descriptions in Chapter 4 for more details.

All flags described thus far are supported by all versions of the 80x86 architecture. The remaining flags are only available in certain versions. The IOPL field is not a flag in the strict sense. Rather it is a two-bit numeric value (in the range 0 to 3) that determines the minimum privilege level needed before I/O instructions can be executed. The IOPL field is only available on the 80286, 80376, 80386, and i486 processors. For more details on this field, see §2.6.

Like the IOPL field, the NT flag is only available on the 80286 and later processors. The flag is set automatically set on entry to a *nested task* and cleared on exit. However, the (systems) programmer is free to update its value explicitly. The concept of a nested task is discussed in §2.11.

The RF flag is only available on the 80376, 80386, and i486. It is used in conjunction with breakpoints that allow instruction restart to ensure that the restarted instructions do not signal a breakpoint repeatedly. This flag is described in §2.16.

The VM flag determines whether or not the processor is in VM86 mode. VM86 mode is an execution mode (see §2.5) that allows application programs to run with 8086 semantics in the context of a PROTECTED mode operating system. To activate VM86 mode both the VM flag and the PE flag (stored in the CR0 register) need to be set to 1. The VM flag is only available on the 80386 and i486.

The AC flag is unique to the i486. In conjunction with the AM flag in CR0, it determines whether or not misaligned accesses to memory are trapped. See §2.7.8 on page 98 for more information on the i486's alignment feature.

2.4.4 Segment registers

As we shall see later (§2.7), all memory accesses in the 80x86 are relative to a *segment*. A segment is a contiguous region of memory; a SELECTOR is a WORD-sized quantity that identifies a segment. An instruction making a memory access never references a SELECTOR directly. Rather, it references one of a set of **segment selector registers**.[5] (The term "segment selector register" is usually truncated to **segment register**.) The register stores the SELECTOR to be used by the memory access. Since SELECTORs are WORD-sized, segment registers are WORD-sized also. Figure 2.8 show the segment registers defined by the 80x86. Note that the FS and GS segment registers are only available on the

---

[5] Far CALLs and JMPs are exceptions to this rule. However, they load the SELECTOR value specified in the instruction into the CS segment register as a consequence of performing the call or jump.

80376, 80386, and i486. Furthermore, the local descriptor table (LDT) and task state segment (TSS) are only useful in PROTECTED mode. Since PROTECTED mode is unavailable on the 8086 and 80186, these processors do not have the LDTS and TSS registers either.

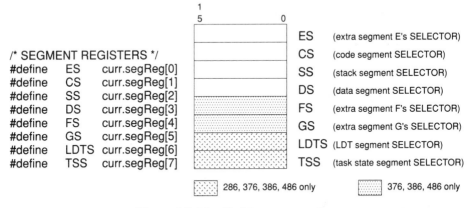

Figure 2.8: The 80x86 segment registers

2.4.5 Control registers

The 80x86 allocates eight **control registers** named CR0 through CR7. These registers store the bits that control its execution mode. They also store information needed to support paging, and a variety of other miscellaneous information. Of the eight control registers only CR0, CR2, and CR3 are defined at present. The remaining five are reserved, and cannot be read from or written into.

Control registers are a relatively new concept in the evolution of the 80x86 architecture. CR0 is only available on the 80376, 80386, and i486. The lower half of CR0 is also found on the 80286. This 16-bit register is called MSW (for *M*achine *S*tatus *W*ord). CR2 and CR3 relate to paging, so they are only available on the 80386 and i486. The C language definition of the control registers is shown below. An equivalent diagrammatic representation is given in Figure 2.9.

```
/* Control register CR0 */
#define   CR0   curr.ctrlReg[0]      /* Machine status word */
#define   MSW   CR0⟨15:0⟩            /* an alias for the low WORD of CR0 */
#define   PG    CR0⟨31⟩              /* Paging enable (see §2.7.7) [386, 486] */
#define   CD    CR0⟨30⟩              /* Caching disable (see §2.7.9.1) [486] */
#define   NW    CR0⟨29⟩              /* Writes-transparent control (see §2.7.9.1) [486]
                                        */
#define   AM    CR0⟨18⟩              /* Alignment check mask (see §2.7.8) [486] */
#define   WP    CR0⟨16⟩              /* Supervisor write protect (see §2.7.7) [486] */
#define   NE    CR0⟨5⟩               /* Numerics exception control (see §3.9) [486] */
#define   ET    CR0⟨4⟩               /* Processor extension [see text below] */
#define   TS    CR0⟨3⟩               /* Task switch occurred (see §3.8.2) [286, 376,
                                        386, 486] */
#define   EM    CR0⟨2⟩               /* Emulate processor extension (see §3.10) [286,
                                        376, 386, 486] */
#define   MP    CR0⟨1⟩               /* Monitor coprocessor (see §3.10) [286, 376,
                                        386, 486] */
#define   PE    CR0⟨0⟩               /* Enable segmented protection (see §2.7.2)
                                        [286, (376), 386, 486] */

/* Control register CR2: page fault address [386, 486] */
#define   CR2   curr.ctrlReg[1]

/* Control register CR3: page directory base [386, 486] */
#define   CR3   curr.ctrlReg[3]
#define   DirTabBase CR3⟨31:12⟩     /* Directory table base address [386, 486] */
#define   UCD   CR3⟨4⟩               /* Unpaged access caching disable [486] */
#define   UWT   CR3⟨3⟩               /* Unpaged access write through control [486] */
```

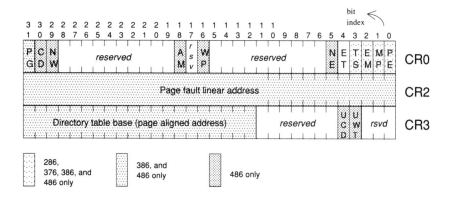

Figure 2.9: The 80x86 control registers

As shown in the figure, CR0 is a collection of bits that control various aspects of machine behavior. The section discussing each flag in detail is referenced next to the flag's declaration. The ET flag, however, is discussed here since it is a bit of an oddity: it is available only in early manufacturing lots of the 80386. Its purpose is to distinguish between whether a 80287 or a 80387 is attached to the 80386. If ET (which denotes "processor *extension type*") is set to 1, a 80387 is attached; if a 80287 (or no coprocessor) is attached, it is set to 0. ET's setting is done automatically by the hardware on reset. For a variety of reasons, this feature was removed from the 80386 after the B-stepping;[6] all following versions only support the 80387. For the sake of software compatibility, the ET bit position in CR0 is permanently set to 1 in post-B-step 80386's, 80376's, and in the i486.

CR2 and CR3 are used strictly for paging. Therefore, they are only available on the 80386 and i486. Their use is described in §2.7.7 on page 83. On the i486, two previously unused bits in the low part of CR3 are assigned for external cache control. These flags are defined in §2.7.9.1 on page 103.

2.4.6 Debug registers

A unique aspect of the 80x86 architecture is its ability to detect memory address breakpoints. This feature can be used to build software debuggers that can trap accesses to user-specified data locations. As shown in the C definitions below and in Figure 2.10, there are six registers defined to support the debug features. How these registers are used is the subject of §2.16 on page 169. Debug registers are only available on the 80376, 80386, and i486.

```
/* Debugging registers */
#define    DR0    curr.debReg[0]      /* Break address 0 */
#define    DR1    curr.debReg[1]      /* Break address 1 */
#define    DR2    curr.debReg[2]      /* Break address 2 */
#define    DR3    curr.debReg[3]      /* Break address 3 */
#define    DR6    curr.debReg[6]      /* Breakpoint status */
#define    DR7    curr.debReg[7]      /* Breakpoint control */
```

---

[6] A "stepping" is a way of identifying the revision level of a part. A0-step is the initial version. Major version changes increment the letter in the stepping id; for example, B0-step is the first major revision of A-step. Minor revisions increment the number; for example, B2-step is a minor revision of B1-step.

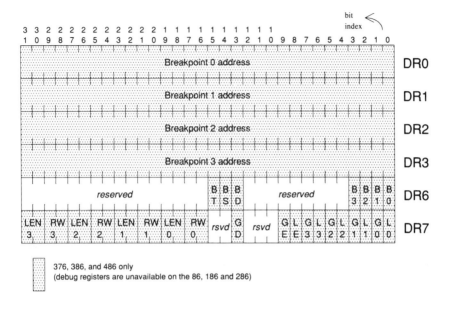

Figure 2.10: The 80x86 debug registers

2.4.7 Test registers

Like the debug registers, test registers are unique to the 80376, 80386, and i486. These registers are of limited use to programmers. Their main purpose is to allow testing of the TLB[7] and, on the i486, the on-chip cache. These features are used by Intel in its manufacturing tests. They can also be used for incoming inspection test at customer sites, and as a part of the power-on, self-test (POST) sequence executed by systems based on these processors.

More details on testability features are provided in the description of the test register MOV instruction (see page 509). The C definitions below and Figure 2.11 show the structure of the test registers. Note that only TR3 through TR7 are defined. The remaining registers, TR0, TR1, and TR2, are not defined and should not be read or written.

---

[7] A TLB, or *t*ranslation *l*ookaside *b*uffer, is a type of cache used to implement paging efficiently. The TLB concept and its use in the 80x86 are discussed in §2.7.10.

```
/* Testability registers (TR0, TR1, and TR2 are undefined) */
#define    TR3    curr.testReg[3]       /* Cache test data [486] */
#define    TR4    curr.testReg[4]       /* Cache test status [486] */
#define    TR5    curr.testReg[5]       /* Cache test control [486] */
#define    TR6    curr.testReg[6]       /* TLB test control [386, 486] */
#define    TR7    curr.testReg[7]       /* TLB test control [386, 486] */
```

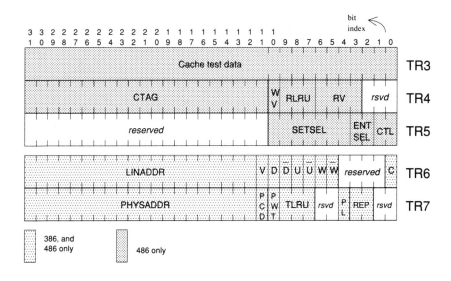

Figure 2.11: The 80x86 test registers

2.4.8 Programmer invisible registers

The 80x86 architecture has a number of registers that are not directly
manipulable; that is, they do not appear as operands of instructions. These
registers, called **programmer invisible registers**, fall into one of the following
categories:

1. registers required to support instruction restart

2. registers required by the memory access mechanism

3. miscellaneous flags that help simplify the architecture description

Since these registers are not directly accessible, their representations shown here should be viewed as an abstraction of what actually appears in the various 80x86 implementations. In fact, some registers may not even be present. This is because the organization of registers as shown here is done with readability rather that implementation efficiency in mind. Now let us review the registers in each category.

2.4.9 Restartability registers

Instruction **restartability** is the ability of a CPU to undo the effects of an instruction if its execution results in some error condition (e.g. if the instruction accesses invalid memory). More details on this feature are found in §2.14 on page 167. For the moment note that the 80x86 architecture requires all instructions to be restartable (except in certain cases where severe operating system programming errors are present). Restartability of programmer visible state can be described by creating a copy of X86_REGISTERS as follows

```
X86_REGISTERS prev;     /* State at end of previous instruction */
```

Just as the instruction pointer EIP was stored outside the curr structure, so too a background copy of EIP called prevEIP is stored outside of prev, as follows

```
DWORD prev_EIP;
```

The assignments

```
prev = curr;
prev_EIP = EIP;
```

are done before any instruction is executed. Thus, if an erroneous condition occurs during instruction execution, the state of the CPU prior to the offending instruction's start can be restored by the assignment

```
curr = prev;
```

If the erroneous condition is potentially fixable it is also desirable to restore EIP to the start of the instruction, so that it may be retried after the fix is made. This is done by the assignment

EIP = prevEIP;

2.4.10 Segment descriptor registers

We have already noted that memory accesses are always relative to some
segment (see §2.4.4). The name of the segment, that is, its SELECTOR, is stored
in a segment register. How is a particular SELECTOR associated with a segment
of memory? A set of registers called a **segment descriptor registers** make the
association. These descriptor registers contain information like the starting and
ending addresses of the segment in memory and the types of accesses that are
allowed. Whenever an access is requested via a particular *segment register* the
associated *segment descriptor register* is interrogated to determine the actual
memory address to be accessed. Segment descriptor registers are special in that
they cannot be loaded directly. Rather, whenever a segment register is loaded, its
corresponding descriptor register is automatically loaded with information
describing the segment. This information is determined either by looking up a
table in memory (if in PROTECTED mode), or by manipulating the value of the
SELECTOR itself. This procedure is described in detail in §2.7.1 on page 53 for
REAL and VM86 modes and in §2.7.2 on page 55 for PROTECTED mode.

Conceptually, the format of a segment descriptor register is as shown below.
Figure 2.12 shows a DESCR pictorially. Keep in mind that the structure
definition shows a decoded view of a segment descriptor. Many of the fields are
mutually exclusive, so a particular implementation of the 80x86 may not provide
storage for all of the fields. This does not not matter, since the fields are only
used to describe the behavior of instructions; normally, they are not directly
readable or writable by the programmer.

```
typedef struct {
    DWORD Base;                /* Segment's base address */
    DWORD Limit;               /* Segment's max valid offset */
    short DPL;                 /* 2 bit descriptor privilege level */
    BOOLEAN  Valid,            /* Is segment valid? */
             CDSeg,            /* TRUE if code or data segment descriptor */
             Readable,         /* Is segment readable? */
             Writable,         /* Is segment writable? */
             Executable,       /* Is segment executable? */
             Conforming,       /* Is segment conforming? (valid if Executable) */
             ExpandDown;       /* Is segment expand-down? (valid if not Executable)
                                  */
    short Type;                /* Four bit descriptor type; valid if CDSeg FALSE */
    BOOLEAN DefaultAttr;       /* "Default" attribute */
```

```
/* Following two fields used only by LAR instruction */
short GDField;                    /* G, D, Intel-reserved, and User-available bits */
short Accessed;                   /* descriptor Accessed flag */

/* Following two fields only meaningful for gate descriptors */
SELECTOR Selector;                /* Selector named by gate */
DWORD Offset;                     /* Offset within segment named by Selector */

/* Following Field only meaningful for CALLGATE16 and CALLGATE32. */
short ParamCount;
} DESCR;
```

The segment descriptor registers are instantiated as follows

```
DESCR descrVec[10];               /* Descriptor information */
```

As with segVec's elements, each element of descrVec has a common name. The #defines which follow show this mapping.

```
/* SEGMENT DESCRIPTORS CORRESPONDING TO SEGMENT REGISTERS */
#define ES_desc    descrVec[0]
#define CS_desc    descrVec[1]
#define SS_desc    descrVec[2]
#define DS_desc    descrVec[3]
#define FS_desc    descrVec[4]
#define GS_desc    descrVec[5]
#define LDT_desc   descrVec[6]
#define TSS_desc   descrVec[7]
#define GDT_desc   descrVec[8]
#define IDT_desc   descrVec[9]
```

Note that there are eight segment registers but ten descriptors. GDT_desc and IDT_desc are special descriptors which do not have associated SELECTORs.

2.4.11 Miscellaneous registers

prev and descrVec are the two main sets of programmer invisible storage. A number of global flags (i.e., of type BOOLEAN) are also needed to describe various fine points of the architecture. An overview of the flags is given here. More details can be found in the section referenced next to each flag's declaration below.

One group of flags denotes that a certain action is in progress. For example, NMI_handler_active is set TRUE whenever an NMI handler starts to execute and is set FALSE when the handler exits. This is done so that a panic condition in the system (which is what NMI ususally signals) does not cause the $80x86$ to

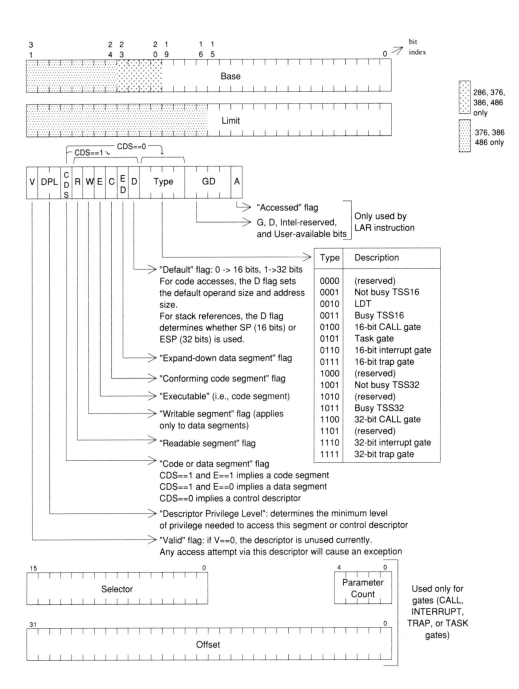

Figure 2.12: Logical contents of a segment descriptor register

repeatedly enter the NMI handler. Similarly, task_switch_in_progress indicates that the 80x86 is attempting to perform a task switch and XH_flag indicates that it is attempting to enter an exception or hardware interrupt handler. These latter two flags get set because both actions are composed of numerous subactions, many of which can generate exceptions. An exception under these circumstances has special significance; hence the flags.

```
BOOLEAN   task_switch_in_progress,    /* see §2.11 on page 134 */
          NMI_handler_active,         /* see §2.12.5 on page 151 */
          XH_flag;                    /* see §2.12.2 on page 146 */
```

The 80x86 supports single stepping. When in single-step mode the processor signals an exception after executing each instruction. Single step mode is activated by setting the TF flag. We want the exception to be signaled one instruction *after* the instruction that set TF. This is done in the instruction descriptions by creating a one-instruction-delayed copy of TF. This flag is called prev_TF.

Some implementations of the 80x86 (the 80376, 80386, and i486) have breakpoint registers that allows the programmer to detect reads and writes of memory locations. The 80x86 architecture says that breakpoints are not reported until after the instruction has completed execution. For purposes of description, we define a brkpt_active vector which contains one flag for each breakpoint register. These flags accumulate breakpoint matches during instruction execution for reporting when the instruction terminates. The single-step delay flag and the breakpoint accumulation flags are declared below.

```
BOOLEAN   prev_TF,                    /* see §2.16.1 on page 169 */
          brkpt_active[4];            /* see §2.16.3.3 on page 175 */
```

The last flag that is needed is used when defining a new stack. One way to do this is to load the SS and ESP registers using two MOV instructions. Regardless of which register is loaded first, there is the danger that an interrupt (or breakpoint) may occur between the first and second instructions. This can cause problems, since servicing the interrupt (or breakpoint) requires a valid stack (assuming a same-level service routine is used). The solution adopted by the 80x86 is to disable hardware interrupts and debug traps for one instruction period whenever an instruction only loads SS. The flag prev_insr_loaded_SS keeps track of this fact.

```
BOOLEAN   prev_instr_loaded_SS;       /* see §2.12.5 on page 151 */
```

This solution assumes, of course, that ESP is always loaded after the SS load. (An alternate approach, available in the 80376, 80386, and i486, is to use the LSS instruction. This instruction loads SS and ESP atomically, thus guaranteeing that no exception can intervene between the the two register loads.)

In addition to these flags a two-bit-wide register, called *CPL*, controls the current privilege level of the 80*x*86 processor. CPL can have a value between 0 and 3 inclusive. To allow proper recovery from an error in an instruction that updates CPL, a backup copy of it is kept in prev_CPL.

```
int     CPL,                           /* see §2.6.1 on page 41 */
        prev_CPL;
```

Finally, a counter and a flag are used in the architecture definition to count the number of exceptions encountered while trying to enter an exception handler. Normally, there should be no errors in this situation. However, if there are errors, a serious systems software integrity problem has occurred. The flag and counter are used to make this determination. Used only when describing 80*x*86 exception handling, they have the following declarations.

```
int         exception_count;           /* see §2.12.6 on page 151 */
BOOLEAN     first_page_fault_seen;     /* see §2.12.6 on page 151 */
```

To ensure that only exception counts within an instruction are counted, exception_count is initialized to 0, and first_page_fault_seen is set to FALSE prior to every instruction's execution.

2.5 Execution modes

At any given instant, the 80*x*86 operates in one of three modes: REAL, PROTECTED, or VM86. Most application instructions operate identically in all three modes. Virtually all of the differences pertain to systems software aspects of the architecture. The differences are as follows:

1. *segments:* in REAL and VM86 modes, the base address of a segment named by a selector *s* is *s* * 16. In PROTECTED mode, the segment base is determined by using *s* as an index into one of two segment descriptor tables. Also, normal REAL and VM86 mode operation permits both read and write access to segments, and fixes the accessible region of memory at 64 kilobytes (starting from the segment base). In PROTECTED mode

access to a segment can be restricted based on privilege level and access type (i.e. data read, data write, or code fetch). Furthermore, the accessible region of memory can be restricted via a "limit" value. References beyond this limit are disallowed.

2. *privilege level:* an 80*x*86 program executes at one of four privilege levels, numbered 0 through 3. A REAL mode program runs only with a privilege level of 0, and a VM86 mode program is constrained to run at privilege level 3. A PROTECTED mode program, however, can switch between any of the four levels (under operating system control). Privilege levels are fully discussed in §2.6 below.

3. *I/O privilege sensitivity:* instructions that affect I/O device access (e.g. the IN and OUT instructions) have restricted access in VM86 and PROTECTED modes. Furthermore, in VM86 mode, instructions that reference the "interrupt enable" flag IF) are also sensitive to I/O privilege. Programs executing in REAL mode always have the privilege to perform I/O accesses. Instructions that I/O privilege to execute are called *IOPL-sensitive*. This notion is discussed in §2.6 on page 40.

4. *interrupt and exception handling:* interrupts and exceptions are serviced via a memory-based data structure called an *interrupt vector*. The interrupt vector can be in one of two formats: REAL-mode format, or PROTECTED-mode format. If an interrupt/exception occurs while in REAL mode, the REAL-mode vector format is assumed by the processor; in PROTECTED and VM86 modes the PROTECTED-mode vector format is assumed. See §2.12 on page 143 for more details.

5. *address translation and protection mechanisms:* the 80*x*86 translates a programmer-specified address (called *logical addresses*) to an intermediate form (called a *linear address*) via the *segment translation mechanism*. The linear address is converted to a *physical address* via the *paging mechanism*. The segment translation mechanism supported in REAL and VM86 modes is a subset of the segment translation mechanism supported in PROTECTED mode. Furthermore, the paging mechanism is only supported in VM86 and PROTECTED modes. More details can be found in §2.7 on page 51.

Processor modes were added to the 80*x*86 processor family as a way of improving functionality while retaining backward compatibility. For example, the 8086 only features the REAL mode of operation. The 80286 introduces PROTECTED mode, but does not support paging. The 80386 adds VM86 mode and paged memory management. The i486 is fully compatible with the 80386 in this area; it does not add any new features. A summary of the differences between the various modes is shown in Figure 2.13.

How are mode switches between the three modes accomplished? First, note from Figure 2.13 that not all implementations support all modes. REAL mode, the most basic mode, is available to all implementations of the 80x86 except the 80376. For the 8086 and the 80186, REAL mode is the only available mode. So the question of mode switching does not arise. The 80286 supports REAL mode and PROTECTED mode. The current mode is determined by the setting of the PE (Protection Enable) flag stored in the MSW register: if this flag is set to 1, PROTECTED mode is enabled. The MSW is loaded using the LMSW instruction. Note, however, that once the 80286 enters PROTECTED mode it can cannot go back to REAL mode; that is, once set, the PE flag cannot be reset.

The 80386 and i486 support all three modes. PROTECTED mode is enabled by setting PE, as before, and VM86 mode is enabled by setting the VM flag in the EFLAGS register. Note, also, that these two processors can switch back to REAL mode from PROTECTED mode; that is, they allow the PE flag to be reset. The 80376 is an oddity in that it only supports PROTECTED mode; REAL and VM86 modes are unavailable on it. Furthermore, the paging mechanism has been disabled on the 80376. Figure 2.14 summarizes the relationship between modes and flags settings.

MODE	FLAG SETTINGS		COMMENTS
	PE	VM	
REAL	0	don't care	8086 and 80186 are permanently in REAL mode
PROTECTED	1	0	available only on the 286, 376, and 486
Virtual-86 (VM86)	1	1	available only on 386, 486

Figure 2.14: How to set execution modes

Attribute	REAL mode [all versions]	PROTECTED mode [286, 376, 386, 486 only]	virtual-86 (VM86) mode [386 and 486 only]
segments	Base address is seg# * 16. All segments are readable and writable	Base address, limit, and read/write access determined via table lookup	Base address is seg# * 16. All segments are readable and writable
privilege levels	0 only	0, 1, 2 or 3	3 only
I/O privilege sensitivity	none (all I/O instructions available)	IN, OUT are IOPL-sensitive and use I/O permission map. CLI, STI are IOPL-sensitive. IRET, POPF, PUSHF update IF only if executed with I/O privilege	IN, OUT are IOPL-sensitive and use I/O permission map. CLI, STI, IRET, POPF, PUSHF are all IOPL-sensitive.
hardware interrupts, INT3 & INTO instructions, and exceptions	serviced via REAL-mode interrupt vector	serviced via PROTECTED-mode interrupt vector	serviced via PROTECTED-mode interrupt vector
software interrupts (INT n)	serviced via REAL-mode intr. vector	serviced via PROTECTED-mode intr. vector	serviced via PROT mode intr. vec. but IOPL-sensitive
address translation & protection	No protection in segment-ation scheme. Paging not available	Protected segmentation available; 80386 and 80486 provide paging also	No protection in segment-ation scheme; but full paging available

Figure 2.13: Differences between REAL, PROTECTED, and VM86 modes

The C language descriptions of instructions use the variable *mode* as a shorthand for the settings of the PE and VM86, and for specifying the processors on which a particular action is supported. For example, the code fragment

```
if ( mode == PROTECTED )
   d1 = IDT_read4(vecnum, vecnum*8);
```

says that the call to function IDT_read4 should be made only if the PE flag is set and the VM flag is clear. The code fragment also implies that this action is not implemented on the 8086 and 80186 processors (since PROTECTED mode is unavailable in them).

2.6 Protection and memory management concepts

This section provides an overview of resource protection facilities provided by the 80*x*86 architecture. As implied by the discussion in the previous section, not all implementations of the 80*x*86 support protection. In particular, the 8086, and 80186 have no protection facilities. Therefore, none of the features discussed here are available on these processors. The 80286 and 80376 offer different subsets of the overall 80*x*86 protection facilities. The 80386 and i486 fully support all the 80*x*86 protection features.

Four types of resources are protected by the 80*x*86:

1. the ability to execute instructions that access certain control bits or data structures useful to an operating system kernel. This is called **privileged instruction access**.

2. the ability to execute instructions that control and access I/O devices. This is called **I/O-privilege-level sensitive instruction access**, or more simply **IOPL-sensitive instruction access**.

3. access to particular I/O addresses (i.e., PORTs).

4. access to regions of memory. All memory locations belong to either a segment, a page, or both a segment and a page. Both segments and pages can be protected in a variety of ways.

How is resource protection provided? Each protected resource has an associated **access rule**. The access rule typically compares one or more access rights available to the instruction requesting the resource against the access rights needed for the request to succeed. Let us introduce some types of access rights and see how they are used.

2.6.1 CPL and privileged mode

A basic concept in implementing resource protection is that of **current privilege level**, abbreviated as **CPL**. The CPL is a value between 0 and 3 (inclusive) that participates in all protected resource access decisions. At any given point in its execution a program always has a CPL value; that is, it has a specified level of privilege. A CPL value of 0 denotes greatest privilege, whereas a CPL value of 3 denotes the least privilege. Most protected resources are tagged with a number between 0 and 3 that indicates the minimum level of privilege needed to access them. For example, a privileged instruction can only be performed when CPL is 0. An example of a privileged operation is the ability to switch between execution modes. Hence LMSW, an instruction that can be used to switch between certain execution modes, is a privileged instruction and can only be executed when CPL is 0. A program executing with a CPL of 0 is said to be in **privileged mode**. (Do not confuse this "mode" with the execution modes discussed earlier.)

In general, the four protection levels define a hierarchy of trust. If CPL is c, all resources tagged as requiring a privilege level p, where $p \geq c$, are accessible. Therefore, when the CPL is 0 any resource is accessible, provided additional access rules requirements (if any) for the resource are met.

The CPL value is stored in a register named CPL. CPL cannot be directly manipulated by the programmer. CPL changes can only occur at certain subroutine call or task transition boundaries. A (protectable) data structure called a *gate* mediates transitions to greater privilege levels, thus allowing control over access to privileged routines. See §2.10 on page 121 for a descriptions of gates, and the related concept of a *conforming code segment*.

2.6.2 I/O access and IOPL

The 80x86 defines a separate privilege category for I/O access. Therefore, a program may be configured so that it can access I/O devices, but not perform other kernel functions (e.g., switching execution modes). To execute an instruction related to I/O access, CPL must be at least as privileged as the privilege level stored in the **IOPL** (*I/O Privilege Level*) register field. (IOPL is a field in the EFLAGS register.) So, for example, if IOPL is set to 2, CPL would have to be 2, 1, or 0 for an I/O access instruction to execute. See §2.9 on page 118 for complete details.

Instructions that access I/O PORTs are IN, OUT, INSx, and OUTSx; so these instructions execute if CPL ≤ IOPL. The ability to enable and disable hardware interrupts is also an I/O privilege. Hence, CLI and STI require I/O privilege to execute. Since the instructions IRET[D], POPF[D], and PUSHF[D] update the IF (interrupt enable) flag, these instructions execute in VM86 mode only if CPL ≤ IOPL. In PROTECTED mode IRET[D], POPF[D], and PUSHF[D] are allowed to execute regardless of the CPL value. However, the IF flag is not updated if the instructions are executed in an environment where CPL > IOPL.

2.6.3 I/O port access control

Restricting access to I/O devices is a necessary feature of any high-quality multitasking computer system. But the IOPL access rule is perhaps too restrictive: it either permits or prohibits access to all I/O ports. In some cases it makes sense to allocate a device (i.e., the small subset of I/O addresses used to communicate with the device) to a particular task. This is especially true for devices that cannot be meaningfully shared between processes; for example, a keyboard or a serial port. In such a scenario the task can write to the device's hardware registers directly (rather than asking the operating system to do it). The reason such a feature is important is twofold:

1. some devices require a high density of I/O commands to operate efficiently. In such cases passing each command through an operating system service call is very inefficient.

2. software written for MS-DOS often talks directly to I/O registers, either because MS-DOS does not provide a device driver for the partcular device or because of reason (1.) above. Since a goal of the 80x86 architecture is to provide a virtualized MS-DOS environment, selective I/O port allocation based on the needs of a particular virtual MS-DOS machine is desirable.

The 80x86 supports selective I/O port access on a per task basis via a bit map called the *I/O permission map*. The bit map is a vector of 65,536 bits; there is one bit for each PORT address in the I/O address range. I/O instructions executed without I/O privilege use the permission map to determine whether the I/O addresses referenced are accessible. Note that the I/O permission map is only available on the 80376, 80386, and i486. See §2.9 on page 118 for more details.

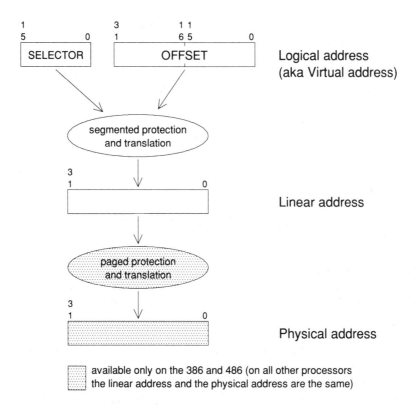

Figure 2.15: Memory access overview

2.6.4 Memory access control

The memory access mechanism of the 80x86 features the most elaborate access rules. This section discusses the relevant concepts; an algorithmic specification of how the 80x86 performs memory access is provided in §2.7 (starting on page 51). Readers interested in an historical perspective should note that many of the memory management and protection concepts and terminology embodied in the 80x86 architecture find their origins in the Multics operating system and the General Electric 645 computer.

Two separate sets of access rules are applied to memory accesses: *segmentation* access rules and *paging* access rules. A global view of how memory access rules are applied is shown in Figure 2.15.

A programmer's view of a memory address has two components: an **offset** and a
segment, where the segment is a contiguous region of memory named by a
WORD sized quantity called a SELECTOR. In its most general form, the offset
(also called an **effective address**) is a DWORD quantity. This allows segments
that are 2^{32} (or over 4 billion) bytes in size. For compatibility with the 80286 and
its predecessors offsets can also be WORD-sized. This effectively reduces the
segment size to 2^{16} bytes (i.e. 64 kilobytes). Whether an offset is viewed as a
WORD or DWORD quantity depends on the address size attribute of the
instruction generating the offset. The address size attribute, and the way offsets
are specified is further discussed in the section on instruction decoding (see §2.18
on page 185). The C language definitions use the type OFFSET to denote a
offset quantity. Keep in mind that an OFFSET can either be WORD sized or
DWORD sized.

Because consecutive instruction and data references are often within the same
segment, the 80*x*86 instruction set favours an instruction format where only the
OFFSET component of a memory address is specified. The SELECTOR
component is implicitly fetched from one of a set of registers called segment
registers. Such an OFFSET-only address is called a **near pointer**, whereas a full
SELECTOR:OFFSET is called a **far pointer** or **logical address**.

The 80*x*86 converts a logical address to a *linear address* via the segmentation
mechanism. Then, the linear address is converted into the *physical address* via
the paging mechanism. Both the segmentation and paging mechanisms translate
one type of address to another (e.g., logical to linear) and as well, apply access
rules. If either the segment access rule or the page access rule for a memory
reference fails, the reference is inhibited and a memory access fault is signaled.

Segmentation access rules are only implemented in the 80286, 80376, 80386, and
i486, whereas paging is only available in the 80386 and i486. The remaining
processors (the 8086 and 80186) do not enforce any memory access rules; that is,
memory is unprotected on these processors. Note, however, that segmented
address translation in some form is available on all versions of the 80*x*86; see
§2.7 for details.

2.6.4.1 Protected segment access rules

What are the rules for segment access? Recall from §2.4.10 (page 32) that a
segment is described by a segment descriptor register. This register stores
various attributes of the segment. One of the attributes is the descriptor's
privilege level, or DPL. The DPL specifies the minimum privilege level needed
to access the memory segment pointed at by the descriptor. Hence, if a segment

descriptor's DPL is 2, an instruction accessing the segment will only succeed if executed with CPL ≤ 2. Notice the similarity between this rule and the CPL ≤ IOPL rule for I/O accesses. The main difference is that there is only one IOPL value that applies to all I/O addresses, whereas each memory segment has its own DPL value.

In addition to a *current* privilege level check memory accesses must also pass a *requestor's* privilege level check. The difference between the requestor's privilege level and the current privilege level is as follows. Let us say an application program operating with CPL set to 3 makes a request to an I/O device driver to fill an I/O buffer. Since the I/O device driver accesses restricted resources (e.g., the I/O device), it operates with CPL set to 1 (say). So, the driver can access segments whose DPL is 1, 2, or 3. Normally, the application program can only gain access to segments with a DPL of 3. But let's say the application passes a SELECTOR of a segment whose DPL is 2, or even 1, to the device driver. The driver takes this parameter SELECTOR to be the SELECTOR of the "I/O buffer" to be loaded. Since the driver's CPL is 1, it will successfully write into this "I/O buffer," even though it is supposedly protected from the application. Gaining access to a protected address by "hiding" the access in a call to a privileged routine is known as the *Trojan horse problem.*

To solve the Trojan horse problem, the 80x86 distinguishes between the privilege level of a routine actually accessing memory (the CPL), and the privilege level of the originating requestor of the memory access. The originator's privilege level is formally called the **requestor's privilege level**, or **RPL**. The RPL of a memory access is treated like an alternate CPL. Hence, for the access to succeed, RPL must be at least as privileged as the DPL of the accessed segment; that is, RPL ≤ DPL. In summary, for a memory access to succeed, it must be that

CPL ≤ DPL and RPL ≤ DPL

The expression can be restated as

max(CPL, RPL) ≤ DPL

The term max(CPL, RPL) is sometimes called the *effective privilege level*, or *EPL*. This book, however, will not introduce this additional terminology; all privilege level checks will be described in terms of CPL, DPL, and RPL only.

Where is the RPL value stored? Since a RPL is specific to a given memory access, it is most convenient to associate it with the memory address for the access. In fact, the RPL is stored in the two least significant bits of a SELECTOR. The format of a SELECTOR is shown on page 56.

One last issue remains with the use of RPL. We have just stated that the RPL is stored in the SELECTOR of a memory reference. Since the SELECTOR is generated by the requestor, it would seem easy for a malicious requestor to always specify an RPL of 0, thereby effectively bypassing the RPL vs. DPL check. To help solve this problem the 80*x*86 provides the ARPL (Adjust *RPL*) instruction. This instruction (described fully on page 283) can be used to update the RPL field of SELECTOR parameters so that they never exceed the privilege level of the caller.

There are two more checks that are a part of the segment access rules:

1. read/write/execute access

2. segment limit check

An access can be of one of three types: a memory read, a memory write, or an instruction fetch (from memory). Every descriptor register stores the flags Readable, Writable, and Executable that indicate whether the corresponding type of access is allowed for the segment associated with the descriptor. For all access made via a particular descriptor, the type of access is validated against the allowed set of access types. If the corresponding access flag is not set, the access is suppressed and a fault is signaled. For example, if a memory write is attempted via a descriptor where the Writable flag is not set, the write does not take place. Instead, a fault is signaled.

In addition to the access type check, the offset of the location accessed is compared against the maximum allowed offset. This maximum value, called the Limit, is also stored in the descriptor register. If the comparison fails, the access is suppressed and a fault is signaled. A summary of all memory access rules, as

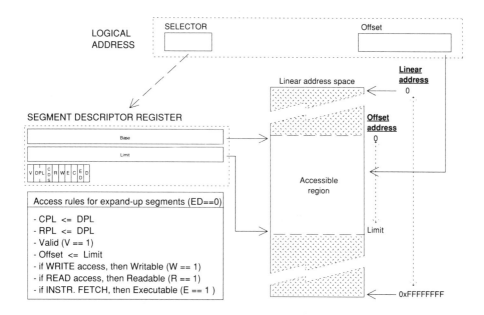

Figure 2.16: Expand-up segment access

well as a diagrammatic representation of memory access, is shown in Figure 2.16.

In the diagram notice that the valid offsets in a segment range from 0 through to the Limit value, inclusive. Sometimes it makes sense to do the opposite: have offsets in the range 0 to Limit be invalid, and offsets in the range Limit+1 to 0xFFFFFFFF be valid. This is useful for allocating space for stacks because, in the 80x86, stacks start at a high address and grow toward smaller addresses. Such segments are called **expand-down segments**. Correspondingly, segments where the valid range of offsets is 0 to Limit are sometimes called **expand-up segments**. Whether or not a segment is expand-down is controlled by the setting of the ED flag in the segment's descriptor. Figure 2.17 gives a diagrammatic view of expand-down memory access. Further discussion of stacks and expand-down segments can be found in §2.8 on page 113.

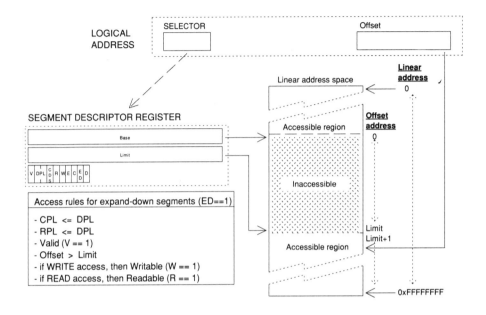

Figure 2.17: Expand-down segment access

2.6.4.2 Paged memory access rules

On all versions of the 80x86 other than the 80386 and i486 the linear address is the address used to access physical memory. (In other words, the linear address and the physical address are one and the same on these processors.) However, on the 80386 and i486, the linear address space and physical address space can optionally be viewed as sequence of **pages**, where a page is a 4-kilobyte block of memory whose starting byte address is multiple of 4,096 (i.e., a page is an aligned 4-KB memory block). A page in linear memory can be mapped to any page in physical memory. Furthermore, not all linear memory pages need be mapped; some of these pages can be marked "not present." Both linear addresses and physical addresses are 32 bits wide. Since all pages are aligned on 4,096 byte (i.e., 0x1000 byte) boundaries, the least significant 12 bits of these addresses are used as the byte index within a page. The remaining 20 bits form the page number. Thus, both linear and physical page numbers range from 0 to 0xFFFFF,

inclusive. The relationship between linear memory and physical memory is
shown in Figure 2.18.

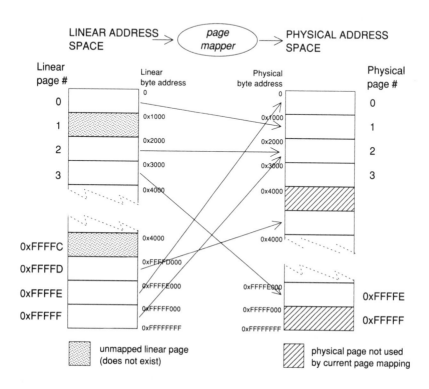

Figure 2.18: Linear memory and physical memory

In the diagram, linear page 0 is mapped to physical page 1, and both linear pages
2 and 0xFFFFF are mapped to physical page 2. Linear pages 1 and 0xFFFFC are
not mapped; that is, they are not present in physical memory. A linear memory
address that falls on a page that is not present generates a *page fault*; furthermore,
execution of the instruction that generated the faulty address is suppressed.

From the description just given, it is apparent that each linear page must have
information stored about it somewhere, describing whether or not it is present,
and if present, what physical page it corresponds to. This information is stored in
a *page table entry*. A page table entry also contains a bit (called the W_R bit)
signifying whether or not the page is writable and another bit (called the U_S bit)
that specifies the minimum CPL needed to access the page.

The W_R flag is a simplification of the Readable, Writable, and Executable flags found in segment descriptor registers. Paging access rules always allow a page to be read and executed from (assuming all other access rules pass). Similarly, U_S (denoting "*U*ser / *S*upervisor)") is a simplification of the segment descriptor's DPL field. A U_S setting of 1 is analogous to a DPL setting of 3; that is, a linear page whose U_S flag is set is accessible at any privilege level. Setting U_S to 0 is analogous to a CPL setting of 2; that is, a linear page whose U_S flag is clear is accessible only when CPL ≤ 2.

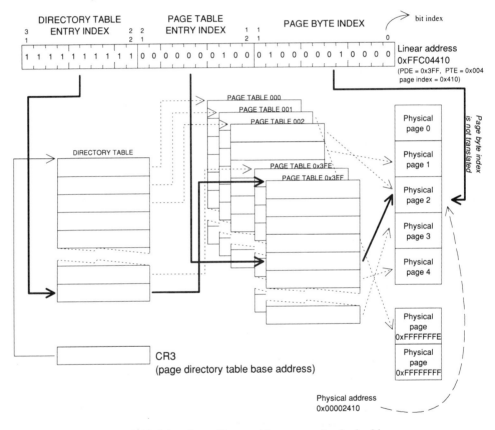

Figure 2.19: Mapping a linear address to a physical address

How is the page table entry accessed? This is best explained via the diagram in Figure 2.19. A 32-bit linear address has three components: a **directory table entry index** (**DTE**), a **page table entry index** (**PTE**), and a **page byte index**. The 10 most significant bits form the DTE value, the next 10 bits constitute the PTE, and the remaining 12 bits form the byte index into the page. In the figure the linear address shown is 0xFFC04410; that is, its PTE value is 0x3FF, its DTE value is 0x4, and its page byte index is 0x410. The DTE is used as an index into a memory resident table called the **directory table**. (The directory table's base address is stored in control register CR3.) Each entry in the directory table points to a **page table**. In the example shown in the figure, DTE is set to 0x3FF; that is, it selects the last page table. The selected page table is indexed using PTE, the page table entry index. In our case PTE is set to 0x4, so the page table entry 0x4 of page table 0x3FF is selected. Each entry in the page table points at a page in physical memory. The pointer in the figure shows the selected page table entry pointing at physical page 2. The page byte index is 0x410. Hence, with the directory and page tables arrangement shown in the diagram, linear address 0xFFC04410 translates to physical address 0x00002410.

For an algorithmic specification of the paging mechanism, as well as a description of the formats of the directory table base (CR3), DTEs, and PTEs, see §2.7.7 (starting on page 83).

2.6.4.3 Priority of memory access rules

A segmented memory access rule violation signals a *segment fault*, whereas a paged memory access rule signals a *page fault*. Since segment faults and page faults use distinct exception handlers (see §2.12) it is important to note that segment faults take priority over page faults. In other words, if both the segment descriptor and the page table entry corresponding to a logical address contain access rule violations, only the segment fault is reported.

2.7 Memory access

This section builds on the memory access principles outlined in §2.6.4 by providing concrete, algorithmic descriptions of how a memory address is translated from a logical address to a physical address. How memory access rules are applied (for both the segmentation and paging cases) is also described.

The 80*x*86 view of physical memory is as an array of up to 2^{32} BYTEs (i.e., 4,294,967,296 bytes) of storage. This memory array is used to store instructions (i.e., program code) and data. In C language notation, the array can be denoted as

```
BYTE mem_vec[4294967296];      /* Main memory */
```

Not all versions of the 80*x*86 support full, 32-bit physical memory addressing. Figure 2.20 shows the maximum physical memory size allowed by each of the available implementations. The figure also shows the number of wires that connect the processor to the memory subsystem. This quantity is called the **bus size**.[8] This book usually only discusses the major versions of the 80*x*86 family; for example, the 8086 (rather than the 8088) and the 80386 (rather than the 80386SX). The principal difference between these minor versions (e.g., the 8088) and their major counterparts (e.g., the 8086) is the bus size. Processors up to the 80386 typically provide a fixed bus size. However, the 80386 allows both 16-bit-wide and 32-bit-wide memories to be attached to it. The i486 extends this notion and allows 8-, 16-, or 32-bit wide memories to be attached.

PROCESSOR	BITS IN PHYSICAL ADDRESS	PHYSICAL ADDRESS SIZE (in bytes)	PHYSICAL MEMORY WIDTH (in bits) [aka BUS SIZE]
8086	20	1,048,576	16
8088	20	1,048,576	8
80186	20	1,048,576	16
80188	20	1,048,576	8
80286	24	16,777,216	16
80376	24	16,777,216	16
80386SX	24	16,777,216	16
80386	32	4,294,967,296	32 / 16
i486	32	4,294,967,296	32 / 16 / 8

Figure 2.20: Physical memory sizes of 80*x*86 implementations

---

[8] A more consistent term for this quantity might be "bus width." However, the commonly used term is "bus size."

Except for performance differences, the impact of differing bus sizes is hidden from the applications programmer: e.g. a DWORD access on the 80386SX automatically results in (usually) two 16-bit memory accesses. However, systems programmers need to be aware of the bus size. This is because an instruction making an *n*-bit access to memory actually makes *n*÷bus_size physical memory accesses if the access is aligned, and *n*÷bus_size + 1 accesses if the access is misaligned. Splitting one logical reference into two or more physical references may cause problems in multiprocessor situations, especially if more than one processor happen to access the same memory location simultaneously.

2.7.1 Loading segment registers in REAL and VM86 modes

In the previous section we saw that a programmer specifies a memory address using a *logical address*. A logical address is translated into a linear address with the help of a segment descriptor register. Although a segment descriptor register is general enough to describe segmentation in all three execution modes (REAL, VM86, and PROTECTED), recall from §2.5 (on page 36) that the meaning of a segment when in REAL and VM86 modes is different from its meaning when in PROTECTED mode. In particular, in REAL and VM86 modes the starting linear address of a segment (i.e., its base) is the SELECTOR naming the segment multiplied by 16. Therefore, given a segment SELECTOR *sel* and an OFFSET *off*, the linear address corresponding to it is as follows:

lin_addr = sel * 16 + off

In REAL mode there is no paged translation mechanism, so the linear address *lin_addr* is also the physical address. This address is used to access system memory. In VM86 mode *lin_addr* is also the physical address if paging is disabled (i.e., if the PG flag is set to 0). However, if paging is enabled, *lin_addr* is checked for validity and translated to the physical address using the current

page tables. REAL and VM86 mode address translation is depicted in
Figure 2.21.

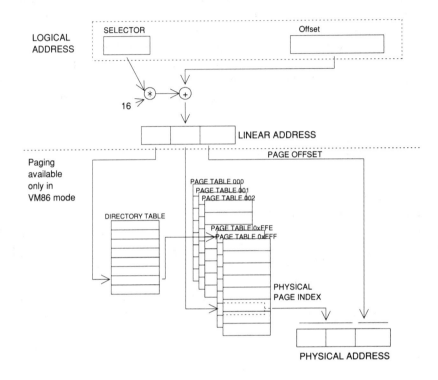

Figure 2.21: Memory access in REAL and VM86 modes

How does scheme of multiplying a SELECTOR by 16 to get the segment base fit
in with the use of segment descriptor registers and the segment access rules
discussed in §2.6.4.1? To reference a segment, the user needs to load a segment
register with the SELECTOR naming the segment. (Segment registers are
described in §2.4.4 on page 25.) Whenever an instruction or event occurs that
loads a segment register with some SELECTOR value *sel*, the segment register is
loaded and as well, the Base field of the corresponding segment descriptor
register is initialized to Base * 16. As an example, the following instruction
sequence can be used to load register BX with the WORD at linear address
0x1BD15.

```
mov     ax, 1AC9h          ; load segment register DS with SELECTOR 0x1AC9,
mov     ds, ax             ; and load DS_descr.Base with 0x1AC90
```

```
; access WORD at 0x1AC9:0x1085 (linear address = 0x1AC90+0x1085 = 0x1BD15)
mov     bx, ds:[1085h]
```

Why have this restrictive form of segment access when the more general PROTECTED mode segment access (described in the following subsection) is also available? The answer is that not all implementations of the 80x86 support PROTECTED mode. In particular, the original member of the 80x86 family, the 8086, does not have PROTECTED mode. Nor does the 80186. PROTECTED mode was introduced in the 80286 as a way to support the construction of (relatively) secure operating systems, and as a way of increasing the available physical memory size from 1 megabyte to 16 megabytes. In fact, the 8086 and 80186 do not have segment descriptor registers in the form described thus far. Since they operate in REAL mode only, specialized hardware simply adds the shifted contents of a segment register to an offset value to generate a linear address. Since paging is not available on these processors either, the linear address is used as the physical address.

Because this book is about all 80x86 processors, memory segment accesses is described using segment descriptor registers, regardless of the execution mode. The reader interested only in the 8086 or 80186 should keep in mind only REAL mode is available on them. Consequently, all program fragments gated by the conditional statement

if (**mode** == PROTECTED) ...

or

if (**mode** == VM86) ...

do not apply to these processors.

The following subsection describes how segment descriptor registers are loaded in PROTECTED mode. The subsections after that (§2.7.4 through §2.7.6) use C language to describe memory access. For REAL and VM86 modes, keep in mind the way in which segment registers are loaded. But for this difference, memory access in PROTECTED mode is the same as memory access in REAL and VM86 modes.

2.7.2 Loading segment registers in PROTECTED mode

A generalization (well almost) of the memory addressing scheme shown in Figure 2.21 is as follows. Instead of multiplying the SELECTOR by 16, use it as an index into a (memory-based) descriptor table. Each entry in the descriptor table stores information about a segment (i.e., its **Base** address, **Limit** value and access rights). Loading a segment register now results in loading the selected descriptor table entry into the segment descriptor register associated with the segment register. At the expense of having to store the descriptor table in memory, this scheme allows the user to load any segment base address and limit value into the segment descriptor register. This scheme is used when segment register are loaded in PROTECTED mode.

How does the SELECTOR index into the descriptor table? In REAL and VM86 modes, a SELECTOR is simply a WORD-sized integer. In PROTECTED mode it is a structure with three fields, as shown in the C declaration below.

```
typedef struct {
    unsigned Index : 13;
    unsigned TI : 1;
    unsigned RPL : 2;
} SELECTOR ;
```

An equivalent diagrammatic representation is given in Figure 2.22.

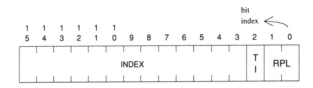

Figure 2.22: The format of a PROTECTED mode SELECTOR

The two least significant bits of a SELECTOR are its RPL (or *Requestor's Privilege Level*) field, the next bit is its **TI** (or *Tables Indicator*) field, and the most significant 13 bits constitute the **table index**. The RPL field was described in §2.6.4.1 on page 44; this field does not play a role in indexing into the descriptor table. The two remaining fields, TI and Index are used to access the memory descriptor as follows. TI selects one of two descriptor tables: the **global descriptor table (GDT)** or the **local descriptor table (LDT)**. If TI is set to 0, the GDT is used; otherwise (if it is set to 1), the LDT is used. The 13 Index bits

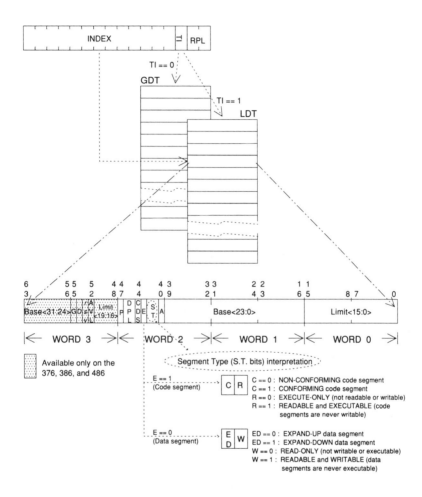

Figure 2.23: PROTECTED mode segment descriptor access

select one of 2^{13} (i.e., 8,192) descriptors stored in the chosen table. This process is diagrammed in Figure 2.23.

Two tables are supported so that segment descriptor information private to a task can be stored separately from descriptor information that is globally applicable. As suggested by the table names, task-specific descriptors are stored in the LDT whereas globally applicable descriptors are stored in the GDT. The systems programmer can switch to a new LDT by issuing the LLDT instruction. A new

LDT is also loaded whenever a task switch occurs. (See §2.11 (starting on page 128) for a description of tasks.) In contrast, a system typically only has one GDT.

Now, compare the memory image of a descriptor table entry (shown in the figure), with the format of the segment descriptor register (shown in Figure 2.12 on page 34). The memory image does not match the register format; the most notable difference is the way in which the Base and Limit fields have been split apart in the memory image. The main reason for this is historical: the 80286, the first implementation of the 80x86 to support descriptor tables, only supports a 24-bit Base address and a 16-bit Limit. Since an extension to 32 bits was not envisioned when the 80286 was architected, the Base and Limit fields are packed together in a five-byte area. Segment access rights occupy another byte, giving a total descriptor size of six bytes. However, the 80286 allocates eight bytes for each descriptor and marks the two extra bytes as *reserved*. (The *reserved* area, WORD #3 of the memory descriptor, is shaded in the figure.) This WORD is used by the 32-bit members of the 80x86 (i.e., the 80376, 80386, and i486) to encode the addressability extensions as follows.

Since the 80286-style descriptor has a 24-bit Base and a 16-bit Limit, 8 additional Base bits and 16 additional Limit bits are needed to extend both fields to 32 bits. The 8 Base bits are stored in the most significant BYTE of WORD #3. This leaves 8 unused bits; however, 16 additional bits are needed to extend the Limit field. To solve this problem, only 4 of the 8 free bits are used to extend the Limit; we now have a 20-bit Limit. An additional bit, the **limit granularity flag** (shown in Figure 2.23 as the **G** flag) determines whether or not the Limit value stored in the descriptor table specifies the maximum BYTE index or page index for the segment. If G is set to 0 the Limit value is BYTE-granular; otherwise, it is page-granular.

There are a couple of fine points to consider regarding the use of the G flag. Firstly, note that a BYTE-granular Limit value of 5 (say) means that bytes 0 through 5 of the segment are accessible.[9] Analogously, a page-granular Limit of 5 implies that *pages* 0 through 5 (inclusive) of the segment are accessible. What is the equivalent BYTE-granular address for this range of pages? Since a page is 0x1000 BYTEs in size, pages 0 through 5 span BYTE addresses 0 through 0x5FFF. Therefore, the BYTE-granular limit *bg_limit* corresponding to a page-granular Limit is

bg_limit = (Limit * 0x1000) + 0xFFF

---

[9] For simplicity, let us assume that the segment is expand-up. The description for expand-down segments is similar, except that the accessible and inaccessible regions are reversed.

Another factor regarding page-granular Limits is alignment rules. A page is normally an aligned object; that is, the starting BYTE address of a page is always a multiple of 0x1000 (the page size). However, the use of the term "page" in the context of Limit granularity does not imply any alignment requirements. This is useful since the base address of a segment can be any BYTE address; that is, there are no segment alignment requirements. So, for example, if Base of a segment is 0x23 and it has a page-granular Limit of 0x17, its ending BYTE address in the linear address space is 0x23 + x17FFF, that is, 0x18022.

Three unused bits remain in the descriptor. One of these bits is shown as the **D** flag in Figure 2.23. This flag determines the default address size and operand size attributes of instructions that are fetched (hence the name D). These attributes are discussed in §2.18 (starting on page 185). For stack operations, the flag determines whether SP or ESP should be used. Furthermore, for expand-down segments, the D flag determines whether the segment limit is 0xFFFF or 0xFFFFFFFF. The SP/ESP and expand-down segment limit selection is done for compatibility with the 80286. On the 80286 the maximum segment limit is 0xFFFF, and only SP is used to access the stack (the general registers are only 16 bits wide). See §2.8 (starting on page 113) for more on 80x86 stacks. Note that the D flag is also called the DefaultAttr flag or the Big flag. The name "DefaultAttr" is used usually in the context of the code segment descriptor register CS_desc, whereas the name "Big" is used in the context of stack segment descriptors.

The two remaining bits have no architecture defined function. One bit is reserved by Intel for future expansion. It is marked *rsv* in Figure 2.23. The remaining bit, marked **AVL**, is available for use by the programmer.

2.7.2.1 The GDT and LDT descriptors

Since the GDT and LDT each store up to 2^{13} (i.e., 8,192) descriptors, and since each descriptor occupies 8 bytes of memory, both the GDT and LDT each occupy up to $8,192 \times 8$ bytes (i.e., 64 kilobytes) of memory. How are these tables initialized? We noted earlier that *all* programmer generated memory addresses are logical addresses: that is, they are composed of a SELECTOR and an OFFSET. But how can a logical address be used to set up a GDT (say) if the table that the SELECTOR indexes into is not initialized? The answer is that the very first time the GDT is initialized, it is done in REAL mode. Since a segment descriptor register load does not use a table lookup in REAL mode, a GDT can be set up while in this mode and then a transition can be made to PROTECTED mode.[10] GDT setup is done via the LGDT instruction. This instruction takes a logical address that points to a specially formatted 6-byte structure. The low-order WORD of this structure is the limit value for the GDT area, and the DWORD that follows forms its base address in linear memory. This base address and limit value is loaded into the GDT_desc register. Figure 2.24 shows the format of the operand to LGDT. It also shows how the LGDT instruction operates. The GDT limit is only a 16-bit value because the maximum table size can never exceed 64 kilobytes. However, by setting the limit to some value less than 0xFFFF a GDT that is smaller than 64 kilobytes can also be defined. Such a GDT has fewer than 8,192 entries. If an attempt is made to load a segment register with a SELECTOR that selects a descriptor that is beyond the GDT limit, a segmentation (GP) fault is signaled. Note that since the GDT addresses are linear addresses, the GDT itself can be paged (on the 80386 and i486). If this is done, care must be taken to ensure that the page storing certain critical

---

[10] The 80376 is an oddball: it operates only in PROTECTED mode. However, on reset the data segment descriptor registers are initialized to point at the first 64 kilobytes of physical memory. This allows a GDT to be set up in this memory region. The only special requirement for the proper operation of the 80376 is that the GDT has to be initialized (via a LGDT instruction) before the first segment register load instruction is executed.

descriptors (e.g., the descriptor for the code segment containing the page fault handler) is always present when accessed.

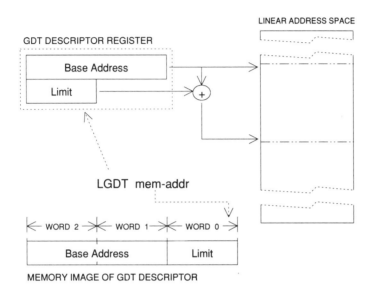

Figure 2.24: Loading the GDT descriptor

Just like the GDT, the LDT is a table that resides in the linear address space. Like the GDT, LDT memory can be demand-paged on the 80386 and i486. The main difference between a LDT and a GDT is in their respective descriptor formats. Unlike the GDT descriptor, which is a specially formatted descriptor, the LDT descriptor format looks very much like a special segment descriptor. The LDT descriptor can be loaded either via the LLDT instruction or as the result of a task switch. The format of the memory image of the LDT descriptor, and the corresponding LDT descriptor register is shown in Figure 2.25.

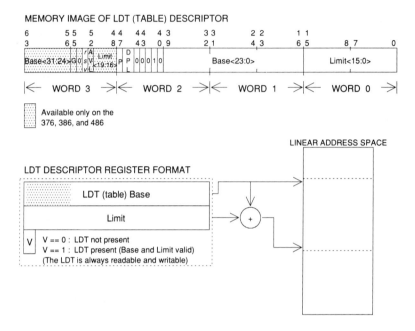

Figure 2.25: Loading the LDT descriptor

2.7.2.2 The read_descr routine

It is apparent from the discussion of the last few subsections that a descriptor that is stored in a descriptor table needs to be decoded before it can be loaded into a descriptor register. This decoding is done by the read_descr function, described below. This function accepts a SELECTOR *sel* as a parameter. *sel* is used to select a descriptor in the GDT or LDT (as specified by *sel*'s TI flag). This descriptor is decoded into a DESCR structure. The structure forms the return value of the function.

read_descr is invoked in the C language architecture descriptions whenever a descriptor is to be read. We have already seen two different classes of descriptors: a code/data segment descriptor and an LDT segment descriptor. In fact, there are three descriptor classes in all:

1. code and data segment descriptors

2. special segment descriptors (used for LDT_SEG and TSS segments)

3. control descriptors (used for all gates)

The first two descriptor classes define regions of memory in the linear address space. In contrast, control descriptors in general are pointers to memory locations within segments defined by descriptors of the first two types. Therefore, a valid control descriptor contains a SELECTOR for a code/data or special segment descriptor and an offset into the segment.[11]

The memory storage format of all three classes of descriptors is shown in Figure 2.26. Rather than have three separate routines to load each class of descriptor, read_descr is able to read all three classes. The definition of DESCR accommodates all three descriptor fields also. (Of course, in actual implementations of the 80x86 descriptor registers only store what is needed; for example, a data segment descriptor like DS_desc does not have the Selector and Offset fields associated with control descriptors.) A generalized read_descr routine is useful for instructions that perform different actions based on the type of descriptor used. For example, the SELECTOR to a far CALL instruction can point either to a code segment descriptor, a call gate, a TSS descriptor or a task gate. The description of the far CALL instruction simply loads the descriptor specified by its SELECTOR using read_descr (see page 295). The DESCR that is returned is analyzed to determine whether a normal far CALL, a privilege level switch (gated CALL), or task switch should be performed.

```
DESCR read_descr(sel, TSS_load)
SELECTOR sel;
BOOLEAN TSS_load;
{  DESCR    tableDesc,          /* Points at GDT or LDT */
            desc;               /* Temp used to construct descriptor */
   DWORD d1, d2;
   WORD erc = (sel & 0xFFFC);   /* Error code that is reported in case descriptor read
                                   fails */

   /* == Select descriptor table == */
   if ( sel⟨2⟩ == 0 )           /* TI points at GDT */
     tableDesc = GDT_desc;
   else                         /* TI points at LDT */
     tableDesc = LDT_desc;

   /* == Read descriptor data (DTAB_read accesses memory with CPL set to 0) == */
```

---

[11] The only exception is the TASKGATE control descriptor. This descriptor merely points at a TSS descriptor. The Offset field of TASKGATE descriptors is unused.

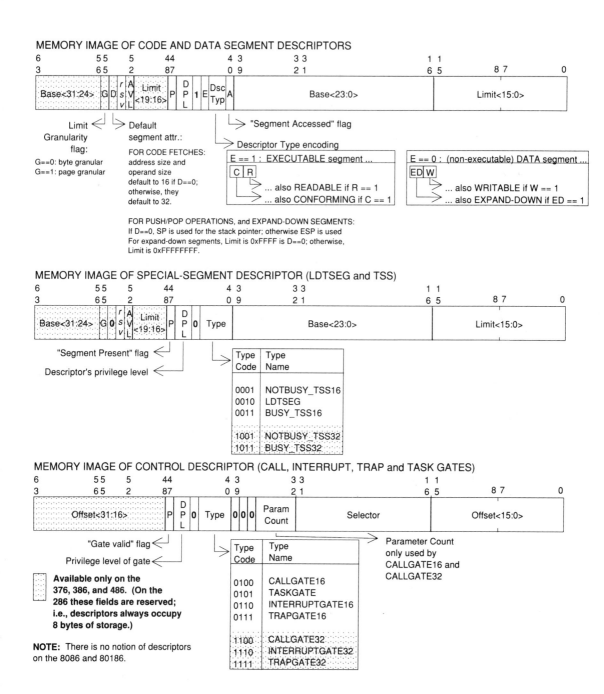

Figure 2.26: Classification of 80x86 descriptors

```
d1 = DTAB_read4(erc, tableDesc, sel⟨15:3⟩*8, TSS_load);        /* Read 1st DWORD */
d2 = DTAB_read4(erc, tableDesc, sel⟨15:3⟩*8 + 4, TSS_load);    /* Read 2nd DWORD */
```

/* == Initialize _Valid_, _DPL_, and _CDSeg_ fields. If _CDSeg_ is 1, descriptor is for code/data
        segment: initialize _Base_, _Limit_, _DefaultAttr_ and access rights fields. If _CDseg_ is 0,
        descriptor is either for a special segment, or for a control gate. If special segment
        (_Type_ is either LDT_SEG, TSS16 or TSS32) initialize _Type_, _Base_ and _Limit_ fields;
        otherwise, initialize _Type_, _Selector_ and _Offset_ fields. == */

```
desc.Valid = d2⟨15⟩;                         /* "Present" flag of descriptor */
desc.DPL = d2⟨14:13⟩;                        /* DPL field */
desc.CDSeg = d2⟨12⟩;                         /* "Code/data descriptor" flag */
if ( desc.CDSeg )        /* == Descriptor is for code or data segment == */
{   /* == Piece together Base fields into one 32 bit quantity == */
    desc.Base = ( d2⟨31:24⟩ << 24 ) | ( d2⟨7:0⟩ << 16 ) | d1⟨31:16⟩;

    /* == Piece together Limit fields == */
    desc.Limit = ( d2⟨19:16⟩ << 16 ) | d1⟨15:0⟩ ;
    if ( d2⟨23⟩ == 1 ) /* Page granular limit: convert page address to byte address */
        desc.Limit = ( desc.Limit << 12 ) + 0xFFF ;

    /* == Initialize DefaultAttr and Executable flags and, depending on Executable value,
    initialize the Readable, Writable, Executable, expandDown and Conforming flags ==
    */
    desc.DefaultAttr = d2⟨22⟩;
    desc.Executable = d2⟨11⟩;
    if ( desc.Executable )                    /* Code segment descriptor */
    {   desc.Conforming = d2⟨10⟩;
        desc.Readable = d2⟨9⟩;
        desc.Writable = FALSE;                /* Code segment is never writable */
        desc.ExpandDown = FALSE;              /* "ExpandDown" is a data seg attribute */
    }
    else                                      /* Data seg. descr. */
    {   desc.ExpandDown = d2⟨10⟩;
        desc.Writable = d2⟨9⟩;
        desc.Readable = TRUE;                 /* Data segment is always readable */
        desc.Conforming = FALSE;              /* "Conforming" is a code seg attribute */
    }
    desc.Type = 0;                            /* Type field not defined for code/data seg */
}

else                      /* == Control segment or gate descriptor == */
{   /* == Setup type of descriptor, and selector and offset it points at == */
    desc.Type = d2⟨11:8⟩;
    desc.Selector = d1⟨31:16⟩;
    desc.Offset = (d2⟨31:16⟩ << 16) | d1⟨15:0⟩;

    /* == Gates and special segments are never executable, but special segments can
        be read and written.  CALL gates have a ParamCount field that specifies the
        number of WORDs (CALLGATE16) or DWORDs (CALLGATE32) to be copied
        from the caller's stack to the called routine's stack. == */
    desc.Executable = FALSE;
```

```
if ( desc.Type == LDT_SEG || desc.Type == NOTBUSY_TSS16 ||
     desc.Type == BUSY_TSS16 || desc.Type == NOTBUSY_TSS32 ||
     desc.Type == BUSY_TSS32 )
{  desc.Readable = TRUE;
   desc.Writable = TRUE;
}
else
{  desc.Readable = FALSE;
   desc.Writable = FALSE;
   desc.ParamCount = d2⟨4:0⟩;  /* used by CALL gates only */
}
}

/* == Save Accessed flag.  Also save the 4 bit GD0A field (that stores the Granularity,
      Default, Intel-reserved, and Available bits).  GD0A and Accessed are saved solely
      for the purpose of describing the LAR instruction. == */
desc.Accessed = d2⟨8⟩;
desc.GDField = d2⟨23:20⟩;

return (desc);
}
```

2.7.2.3 Setting the Accessed flag

Operating systems often find it useful to know whether or not a specific segment of code or data has been accessed. The 80*x*86 helps out by providing an Accessed flag in code and data segment descriptors. Rather than set this flag at the time a segment is actually read or written, the 80*x*86 architecture assumes that whenever a code or data segment descriptor is loaded the corresponding segment will get accessed. Therefore, the Accessed flag (i.e., the A bit) of code or data segment descriptor is set whenever the corresponding SELECTOR is loaded into a segment register. The routine mark_accessed, defined below, performs this function.

```
mark_accessed(sel)
SELECTOR sel;
{  DESCR  tableDesc,      /* Points at GDT or LDT */
           desc;          /* Temp used to construct descriptor */
   unsigned d2;

   /* == Select table == */
   if ( sel⟨2⟩ == 0 )                /* TI points at GDT */
      tableDesc = GDT_desc;
   else                              /* TI points at LDT */
      tableDesc = LDT_desc;
```

```
/* == Set the "Accessed" bit to 1 == */
d2 = DTAB_read1(sel, tableDesc, sel.Index*8 + 5, FALSE);          /* see page 74 */
DTAB_write1(sel, tableDesc, sel.Index*8 + 5, d2 | 1, FALSE);      /* see page 81 */
}
```

Note that the architecture simply requires that the **Accessed** field be set to 1; it does not require that the byte containing it be (re)read as shown in the mark_accessed routine.

2.7.2.4 The role of the null SELECTOR

Any segment register can be used at any time to access data in the segment it points at. Sometimes, however, it is convenient to disable a segment register; that is, to mark the segment register "not associated with any segment." This can be done using the **null SELECTOR**. The format of a null SELECTOR is as shown in Figure 2.27; that is, it is the index of the first entry (Index == 0) of the GDT. The RPL field value is not looked at in a null SELECTOR. Viewed another way, a null SELECTOR is any SELECTOR whose value is in the range 0x0000 to 0x0003 inclusive.

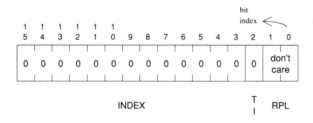

Figure 2.27: Format of the (PROTECTED mode) null SELECTOR

Whenever a SELECTOR is loaded into a segment register it is checked to see if it is null. If so, the descriptor is not read; instead, the segment descriptor register's **Valid** flag is set to 0. Keep in mind that null SELECTORs only make sense in PROTECTED mode. In REAL and VM86 modes the usual "multiply the SELECTOR by 16" rule is applied to all SELECTORs. So, the instruction sequence

```
; Load segment register DS with SELECTOR 0x0002
mov     ax, 0002h
mov     ds, ax
```

sets the Base of the descriptor register DS_desc to 0x020 if executed in REAL or VM86 modes. If the same sequence is executed in PROTECTED mode however, DS_desc is invalidated (i.e., its Valid flag is set to 0).

Whenever a null SELECTOR check is made in the C language descriptions, a call to the nullSel routine is made. nullSel returns TRUE if the SELECTOR passed to it is null; otherwise it returns FALSE. The function's definition is as follows.

```
BOOLEAN nullSel(sel)
SELECTOR sel;
{
    return ( sel.Index == 0  &&  sel.TI == 0 );
}
```

2.7.2.5 Segment descriptor loading rules

The past few subsections have provided the background material necessary to describe how segment descriptor registers are loaded in PROTECTED mode on an 80x86 processor. In general, given a SELECTOR and a segment register that is to be loaded with the SELECTOR, the steps taken are as follows.

1. Check if SELECTOR is null. If so, load segment register with SELECTOR value, and invalidate segment descriptor register corresponding to the segment register. For the null SELECTOR case, only these actions are taken. For the non-null case, the segment register is loaded with the SELECTOR value and processing continues with step 2.

2. Read the descriptor named by the SELECTOR and make sure the segment access rules for it pass. If they do not, signal a segmentation (GP) fault. If they do, continue with step 3.

3. Check the Present flag. If the segment is not present, signal a not-present (NP) fault. This can be used to implement demand segmentation. Note that NP is signaled only if the descriptor is valid in all other respects. (In a descriptor register, the Present flag is called the "descriptor valid", or Valid flag.)

4. Load the descriptor register corresponding to the loaded segment register with the segment information fetched from the descriptor table.

5. Set the Accessed flag in the memory image of the selected descriptor to 1.

Each of these steps is performed in a similar way regardless of the segment register being loaded. However, some differences arise because two of the segment registers, CS and SS, have specialized uses. The instruction stream is fetched from the segment pointed at by CS.[12] Therefore, a rule specific to CS loads is that the segment descriptor of any SELECTOR that is loaded into it must be executable.   Also, it never makes sense to invalidate CS_desc (e.g., by loading a null SELECTOR). Similarly, the segment pointed at by SS is used as the segment where the stack is stored. Therefore, it must always be writable, and SS_desc should never be invalid. The remaining segment registers ES and DS, and on the 80376, 80386, and i486, FS and GS reference general data segments and have no special requirements.

The special rules for loading CS are defined in the load_CS function, and those pertaining to loading SS are defined in the load_SS function. ES, DS, FS, and GS loads are done via load_data_seg. Each of these functions, defined below, accepts a SELECTOR (*sel*) and a flag *TSS_load* as parameters. Assuming the access rules pass, the segment register is loaded with *sel*, and the descriptor corresponding to *sel* is loaded into the descriptor register corresponding to the loaded segment register. The *TSS_load* flag is used solely if an error is detected during the load (e.g., if an access rule fails, or if the descriptor in memory is inaccessible). If *TSS_load* is TRUE, an error is reported as a TASK fault; if FALSE, it is reported as a general protection (GP) fault. *TSS_load* is only set true when a segment register is loaded during a task switch operation. Task switches are discussed in §2.11 (starting on page 128).

```
DESCR load_CS(sel, TSS_load)
SELECTOR sel;
BOOLEAN TSS_load;
{  DESCR desc;

    /* == If sel is null, signal error (a code segment must always be present) == */
    if ( nullSel(sel) )
       signal_fault( (TSS_load ? TASK : GP),  (sel & 0xFFFC) );

    /* == Disallow descriptor table access to other system agents.  See §2.7.11 == */
    lock(DESCR_TABLE);
```

---

[12] The offset of the instruction is the contents of the instruction pointer EIP; see §2.18 for more.

```
    /* == Read raw descriptor.  For non-task-switch invocations of load_CS the descriptor
          being loaded can usually point to either a code segment or a gate.  The following
          check signals a fault if a non-code/data segment descriptor is encountered in the
          context of a task switch (TSS_load set to TRUE).  If a non-code/data segment is
          seen outside a task switch, further checking to see whether the descriptor is valid
          is left to the caller. == */
    desc = read_descr(sel, TSS_load);
    if ( !desc.CDSeg && !TSS_load )
       return( desc );
    else
       signal_fault(TASK, (sel & 0xFFFC));

    /* == Now ensure that the code/data segment is in fact an executable segment with the
          right protection attributes == */
    if ( desc.Executable  &&  ( (desc.Conforming && CPL >= desc.DPL )  ||
       ( !desc.Conforming && CPL == desc.DPL && sel.RPL <= desc.DPL ) ) )
    {  if ( ! desc.Valid )
          signal_fault(NP, (sel & 0xFFFC));
    }
    else
       signal_fault( (TSS_load ? TASK : GP),  (sel & 0xFFFC) );

    /* == Mark the descriptor "accessed" and reallow other agents to access descriptor
          tables == */
    mark_accessed(sel);
    unlock(DESCR_TABLE);

    return (desc) ;
}




DESCR load_SS(sel, TSS_load)
SELECTOR sel;
BOOLEAN TSS_load;
{  DESCR desc;

    /* == If sel is null, signal error (a stack segment must always be present).  Also ensure
          that the new SSes RPL matches the CPL. == */
    if ( nullSel(sel)  ||  sel.RPL != CPL )
       signal_fault((TSS_load ? TASK : GP),  (sel & 0xFFFC));

    /* == Disallow descriptor table access to other system agents.  See §2.7.11 == */
    lock(DESCR_TABLE);
```

```
/* == Read raw descriptor and perform stack segment checks == */
desc = read_descr(sel, TSS_load);
if ( desc.Writable  &&  desc.DPL == CPL )
{   if ( !desc.Valid )
        signal_fault(STACK, (sel & 0xFFFC));
}
else
    signal_fault((TSS_load ? TASK : GP),  (sel & 0xFFFC));

/* == Mark the descriptor "accessed" and reallow other agents to access descriptor
        tables == */
mark_accessed(sel);
unlock(DESCR_TABLE);

return (desc) ;
}




DESCR load_data_seg(sel, TSS_load)
SELECTOR sel;
BOOLEAN TSS_load;
{ DESCR desc;

    /* == If sel is null, invalidate the descriptor and exit. == */
    if ( nullSel(sel) )
    {   desc.Valid = FALSE;
        return (desc) ;
    }

    /* == Disallow descriptor table access to other system agents.  See §2.7.11 == */
    lock(DESCR_TABLE);

    /* == Read raw descriptor and perform data segment checks == */
    desc = read_descr(sel, TSS_load);
    if ( ( (desc.Readable || desc.Writable) && !desc.Conforming && desc.DPL >= CPL &&
        desc.DPL >= sel.RPL ) || ( desc.Readable && desc.Conforming ) )
    {   if ( !desc.Valid )
            signal_fault(NP, (sel & 0xFFFC));
    }
    else
        signal_fault((TSS_load ? TASK : GP),  (sel & 0xFFFC));

    /* == Mark the descriptor "accessed" and reallow other agents to access descriptor
            tables == */
    mark_accessed(sel);
    unlock(DESCR_TABLE);
```

```
    return (desc);
}
```

2.7.3 Switching from PROTECTED to REAL mode

As mentioned earlier, it is possible on the 80386 and i486 to switch back from
PROTECTED mode to REAL mode. When this is done, the only action taken by
the 80x86 is to clear the PE flag. In particular, the current state of the descriptor
registers is left undisturbed. Therefore, it is possible to switch back to REAL
mode but have the segment descriptor register base and limit be non-REAL-mode
values. Such a pseudo REAL, or UNREAL, execution mode can cause a REAL
mode system to crash, unless used very carefully. Also keep in mind that entry
to VM86 mode always sets all descriptor register limits to 0xFFFF and bases to
SELECTOR * 16.

UNREAL mode is easily avoided by loading the descriptor registers with values
that "look" like REAL descriptors. See the description of the control register
MOV instruction (page 501) for a possible instruction sequence that switches
back to REAL mode.

2.7.4 Reading memory

We have just completed looking at descriptions of how descriptor registers are
loaded. Now let us see how memory is read. Memory reads during normal
instruction execution are done via the readx routines. read1 is used if a BYTE is
to be read, and read2 and read4 are used for WORDs and DWORDs, respectively.
In the C language instruction descriptions in Chapter 4 the readx calls are not
made directly. Rather, a specialized notation is used that calls to the readx
functions. This use of notation is discussed in §4.2 (starting on page 265).

In addition to the readx routines, there are three other classes of routines used in
special circumstances:

  1. DTAB_readx : these are used to read descriptor table entries.
  2. TSS_readx : these are used when reading memory data during a task
                  switch.
  3. IDT_readx : these are used when reading an interrupt vector.

The main difference between these specialized routines and their readx
counterparts is in the way that access rule violations are handled. These
differences are detailed later in this subsection.

2.7.4.1 Reading data segments

Now let us look at the definition of read*x*. Parameters to these routines specify a descriptor register, and an OFFSET *off*. Instead of passing the descriptor register directly, its *index* value in the descriptor registers vector is passed.[13] Passing the index allows easy detection of the name of descriptor register. This is needed because, in case of an access rules violation, the STACK fault exception handler is invoked if the access was via SS_desc (i.e., descrVec[2]); in all other cases the general protection fault (GP fault) handler is used.

Apart from access rule checks, the primary purpose of read*x* is to compute the access' linear address. This is done adding the segment base referenced by *desc_ind* to *off*. A segment limit check is performed via the call to the in_limits function (see page 78) to make sure that all bytes accessed are within the segment's range. Also, the Valid and Readable flags are checked. If any of these checks fail a segmentation fault is signaled as previously discussed. If the checks pass, the linear address is passed to the LA_read*x* routine. This group of routines performs breakpoint checking and paged address translation and protection. See §2.7.7 on page 83 for a definition of the LA_read*x* routines.

```
BYTE read1(desc_ind, off)
int desc_ind;
OFFSET off;
{   DESCR desc = descrVec[desc_ind];

    /* == Verify access rules: read BYTE in linear memory if rules pass. == */
    if ( desc.Valid && desc.Readable && in_limits(desc, off, 1) )
        return ( LA_read1(desc.Base + off) );              /* see page 91 */

    /* == If there is an access rules violation, signal STACK fault if access was via
          SS_desc; in all other cases signal GP fault.  The error code reported is always 0.
          == */
    signal_fault((desc_ind == SS_INDEX ? STACK : GP), 0);   /* see page 155 */
}

WORD read2(desc_ind, off)
int desc_ind;
OFFSET off;
{   DESCR desc = descrVec[desc_ind];

    /* == Verify access rules: read WORD in linear memory if rules pass. == */
    if ( desc.Valid && desc.Readable && in_limits(desc, off, 2) )
        return ( LA_read2(desc.Base + off) );              /* see page 92 */
```

---

[13] Segment descriptor register indexes are defined in §2.4.10 on page 32.

```
    /* == If there is an access rules violation, signal STACK fault if access was via
          SS_desc; in all other cases signal GP fault.  The error code reported is always 0.
          == */
    signal_fault((desc_ind == SS_INDEX ? STACK : GP),  0);     /* see page 155 */
}

DWORD read4(desc_ind, off)
int desc_ind;
OFFSET off;
{   DESCR desc = descrVec[desc_ind];

    /* == Verify access rules: read DWORD in linear memory if rules pass. == */
    if ( desc.Valid && desc.Readable && in_limits(desc, off, 4) )
        return ( LA_read4(desc.Base + off) );                  /* see page 92 */

    /* == If there is an access rules violation, signal STACK fault if access was via SS_desc
          (desc_ind == 2); in all other cases signal GP fault.  The error code reported is
          always 0. == */
    signal_fault((desc_ind == SS_INDEX ? STACK : GP),  0);     /* see page 155 */
}
```

2.7.4.2 Reading segment descriptor tables

Now let us look at the definitions of the specialized read routines starting with DTAB_readx. The sole purpose of DTAB_readx is to read segment descriptor table entries, that is, entries in the GDT and LDT. The routines have four parameters: an error code (err_code), a descriptor register desc, an offset value off, and a flag TSS_load that is set to TRUE whenever the descriptor table is being read during a task switch. The error code is actually a SELECTOR value that is passed to the fault handler in case an access rule violation is detected. Unlike the readx routines, exception reporting is handled in the same way regardless of whether the GDT or the LDT is being read. Therefore, the descriptor register value is passed as a parameter directly.

Another difference in the DTAB_readx routines is that the reads are done with CPL set to 0. If this were not done, an application program (executing with CPL set to 3) would not be able to access the descriptor tables if paged protection were enabled and the pages belonging to the descriptor table were marked "supervisor access only." The C language definitions of DTAB_read1 and DTAB_read4 follow. DTAB_read2 is not used; accordingly, it is not defined.

```
BYTE DTAB_read1(err_code, desc, off, TSS_load)
SELECTOR err_code;
DESCR desc;
OFFSET off;
BOOLEAN TSS_load;
{   int saveCPL = CPL;
```

```
    /* == Verify access rules, signal GP fault with err_code if violation occurs.  NOTE:
           Readable flag check is not done because LDT_desc and GDT_desc are always
           readable == */
    if ( ! desc.Valid  ||  ! desc.Readable  ||  ! in_limits(desc, off, 1) )
       signal_fault(TSS_load ? TASK : GP,  (err_code & 0xFFFC));    /* see page 155 */

    /* == If access checks pass, read linear address with CPL temporarily set to 0 ==
    CPL = 0;
    return ( LA_read1(desc.Base + off) );                            /* see page 91 */
    CPL = saveCPL;
}

DWORD DTAB_read4(err_code, desc, off, TSS_load)
SELECTOR err_code;
DESCR desc;
OFFSET off;
BOOLEAN TSS_load;
{   int saveCPL = CPL;

    /* == Verify access rules, signal GP fault with err_code if violation occurs.  NOTE:
           Readable flag check is not done because LDT_desc and GDT_desc are always
           readable == */
    if ( ! desc.Valid  ||  ! desc.Readable  ||  ! in_limits(desc, off, 4) )
       signal_fault(TSS_load ? TASK : GP,  (err_code & 0xFFFC));    /* see page 155 */

    /* == If access checks pass, read linear address with CPL temporarily set to 0 ==
    CPL = 0;
    return ( LA_read4(desc.Base + off) );                            /* see page 92 */
    CPL = saveCPL;
}
```

2.7.4.3 Reading task state segments

As implied by the name the TSS_read*x* routines are used when reading the task state segment. (Task state segments and their role in task switches are discussed in §2.11 (starting on page 128).) These routines are very similar to DTAB_read*x*. The main difference is that if an error is encountered during the access a TASK fault rather than a GP fault is signaled. The routines are invoked with two parameters: an error code (*err_code*) that is typically the SELECTOR of the task state segment being read and an offset into TSS_desc (the task state segment's descriptor register). There is no need to specify the descriptor since it is always TSS_desc.

```
BYTE TSS_read1(err_code, off)
SELECTOR err_code;
OFFSET off;
{   short saveCPL = CPL;
    BYTE result;

    if ( TSS_desc.Valid && in_limits(TSS_desc, off, 1 ) )
    {   CPL = 0;
        result = LA_read1(desc.Base + off);
        CPL = saveCPL;
        return(result);
    }

    signal_fault(TASK, (err_code & 0xFFFC));
}

WORD TSS_read2(err_code, off)
SELECTOR err_code;
OFFSET off;
{   short saveCPL = CPL;
    BYTE result;

    if ( TSS_desc.Valid && in_limits(TSS_desc, off, 2 ) )
    {   CPL = 0;
        result = LA_read2(desc.Base + off);
        CPL = saveCPL;
        return(result);
    }

    signal_fault(TASK, (err_code & 0xFFFC));
}

DWORD TSS_read4(err_code, off)
SELECTOR err_code;
OFFSET off;
{   short saveCPL = CPL;
    BYTE result;

    if ( TSS_desc.Valid && in_limits(TSS_desc, off, 4 ) )
    {   CPL = 0;
        result = LA_read4(desc.Base + off);
        CPL = saveCPL;
        return(result);
    }
```

```
    signal_fault(TASK, (err_code & 0xFFFC));
}
```

2.7.4.4 Reading interrupt descriptor tables

The final category of specialized read routines is IDT_read*x*. This catgeory is
used to read entries in the interrupt descriptor table (IDT). Only the WORD and
DWORD variants are needed; hence only IDT_read4 and IDT_read2 are defined.
These routines are like TSS_read*x* except that a vector number is passed as the
error code rather than a SELECTOR. Also, the IDT flag in the error code gets set
if a fault is reported.

```
WORD IDT_read2(vecnum, off)
int vecnum;
DWORD offset;
{   short saveCPL = CPL;
    WORD result;

    /* == If IDT access within IDT segment limits, read linear memory with CPL temporarily
          set to 0. == */
    if ( in_limits(IDT_desc, off, 2 ) )
    {   CPL = 0;
        result = LA_read2(desc.Base + off);
        CPL = saveCPL;
        return(result);
    }

    /* == If limit check failed, construct error code by combining vector number and IDT flag
          (set to 1), and signal segmentation fault == */
    err_code = ( vecnum << 3 ) | 2;
    signal_fault(GP, err_code);
}


DWORD IDT_read4(vecnum, off)
int vecnum;
DWORD offset;
{   short saveCPL = CPL;
    DWORD result;

    /* == If IDT access within IDT segment limits, read linear memory with CPL temporarily
          set to 0. == */
    if ( in_limits(IDT_desc, off, 4 ) )
    {   CPL = 0;
        result = LA_read4(desc.Base + off);
        CPL = saveCPL;
        return(result);
    }
```

```
/* == If limit check failed, construct error code by combining vector number and IDT flag
       (set to 1), and signal segmentation fault == */
err_code = ( vecnum << 3 ) | 2;
signal_fault(GP, err_code);
}
```

2.7.4.5 Checking segment limits

All the read routines just described check the read access offset against the the
segment's Limit. This check is done by the in_limits function, defined below.
This function reads the Limit field of the specified descriptor register and converts
it into a the actual limit by factoring in whether or not the descriptor is for an
expand-down segment.

```
BOOLEAN in_limits(desc, off, size)
{   DWORD edLimit;

    if ( desc.ExpandDown )
    {   edLimit = desc.DefaultAttr ? 0xFFFFFFFF : 0xFFFF;
        return ( off > desc.Limit  &&  (off + size-1) <= edLimit );
    }
    else /* Normal (expand-up) segment */
        return ( (off + size-1) <= desc.Limit );
}
```

The in_limits routine is also used for checking segment limits of memory write
transactions. These are now described.

2.7.5 Writing memory

Memory writes on the 80x86 can be described via a set of routines that are
virtually identical to the read routines just described. The main difference with
writes is that a parameter specifying the value to be written is supplied, and that
protection checks verify that the segment being written is writable. (In addition,
of course, the memory vector is written rather than read.)

Memory reads during normal instruction execution are done via the writex
routines. write1, write2, and write4 are used for BYTE, WORD, and DWORD
writes, respectively. As with the readx routines, the C language instruction
descriptions in Chapter 4 do not make writex calls directly. Rather, an
assignment like

```
dst = AX;
```

implies that a write*x* call is being made. (In the example, register AX is written to memory location *dst*.) The use of this notation is discussed in §4.2 (starting on page 265).

In addition to the read*x* routines, there are two other classes of routines used in special circumstances:

1. DTAB_write1 : this is used to update the Accessed flag in descriptor table entries.
2. TSS_write*x* : these are used to save task state when performing a task switch.

The main difference between these specialized routines and their write*x* counterparts is in the way that access rule violations are handled. These differences are detailed later in this subsection. Note that there are no IDT_write*x* routines corresponding to the IDT_read*x* routines. This is because the 80*x*86 never needs to write the interrupt descriptor table when servicing an interrupt or exception. Initialization of the IDT (as well as other tables like the GDT, LDT, and page tables) is done by accessing the memory occupied by them via a data segment descriptor.

2.7.5.1 Writing data segments

The write1, write2, and write4 routines describe how the 80*x*86 writes a BYTE, WORD or DWORD, respectively. Each routine takes three parameters: an *index* into the descriptor register vector (*desc_ind*), an offset *off*, and the *value* to be written. A descriptor index and offset specify the logical address of the data to be written. (See the section on "reading data segments", §2.7.4.1, for more.) The value of the data to be written is passed in the *value* parameter. All three routines only perform segmentation checks and compute the linear address. This address is passed to the LA_write*x* routines that perform paged translation and protection checks, and also, check for data breakpoints. Paged translation is discussed further in §2.7.7 (starting on page 83).

```
write1(desc_ind, off, value)
int desc_ind;
OFFSET off;
BYTE value;
{  DESCR desc = descrVec[desc_ind];

    /* == Verify access rules: write BYTE to linear memory if rules pass. == */
    if ( desc.Valid && desc.Writable && in_limits(desc, off, 1) )
        LA_write1(desc.Base + off,  value);        /* see page 95 */
```

```
    /* == If there is an access rules violation, signal STACK fault if access was via
          SS_desc; in all other cases signal GP fault.  The error code reported is always 0.
          == */
    signal_fault((desc_ind == SS_INDEX ? STACK : GP), 0);     /* see page 155 */
}


write2(desc_ind, off, value)
int desc_ind;
OFFSET off;
WORD value;
{  DESCR desc = descrVec[desc_ind];

    /* == Verify access rules: write WORD to linear memory if rules pass. == */
    if ( desc.Valid && desc.Writable && in_limits(desc, off, 2) )
       LA_write2(desc.Base + off,  value);          /* see page 95 */

    /* == If there is an access rules violation, signal STACK fault if access was via
          SS_desc; in all other cases signal GP fault.  The error code reported is always 0.
          == */
    signal_fault((desc_ind == SS_INDEX ? STACK : GP), 0);     /* see page 155 */
}


write4(desc_ind, off, value)
int desc_ind;
OFFSET off;
DWORD value;
{  DESCR desc = descrVec[desc_ind];

    /* == Verify access rules: write DWORD to linear memory if rules pass. == */
    if ( desc.Valid && desc.Writable && in_limits(desc, off, 4) )
       LA_write4(desc.Base + off,  value);          /* see page 96 */

    /* == If there is an access rules violation, signal STACK fault if access was via
          SS_desc; in all other cases signal GP fault.  The error code reported is always 0.
          == */
    signal_fault((desc_ind == SS_INDEX ? STACK : GP), 0);     /* see page 155 */
}
```

2.7.5.2 Writing segment descriptor tables

The only time when the GDT and LDT are written via GDT_desc and LDT_desc
is when the Accessed flag is updated (see, for example, the mark_accessed
routine on page 66). This is done by reading the BYTE containing the flag,
setting the bit, then writing it back. Since only a BYTE needs to be written, only
DTAB_write1 is defined.

```
DTAB_write1(err_code, desc, off, value)
SELECTOR err_code;
DESCR desc;
OFFSET off;
BYTE value;
{   int saveCPL = CPL;
```

   /* == *Verify access rules, signal GP fault with* err_code *if violation occurs. NOTE:*
         Writable flag check is not done because LDT_desc and GDT_desc are always
         writable == */
```
   if ( ! desc.Valid  ||  ! in_limits(desc, off, 1) )
      signal_fault(GP,  (err_code & 0xFFFC));    /* see page 155 */
```

   /* == *If access checks pass, read linear address with CPL temporarily set to 0* ==
```
   CPL = 0;
   LA_write1(desc.Base + off,  value);              /* see page 95 */
   CPL = saveCPL;
}
```

2.7.5.3 Writing into task state segments

The descriptions of the task switch operations use BYTE, WORD, and DWORD
writes into the TSS defined by TSS_desc. The routines TSS_write1,
TSS_write2, and TSS_write4 describe how these writes occur.

```
TSS_write1(err_code, off, value)
SELECTOR err_code;
OFFSET off;
BYTE value;
{   short saveCPL = CPL;
```

   /* == *Verify access rules, signal TASK fault with* err_code *if violation occurs. NOTE:*
         Writable flag check is not done because TSS_desc is always writable. If access
         rules pass, the linear address and value to be written are passed to LA_write1 ==
         */
```
   if ( TSS_desc.Valid  &&  in_limits(TSS_desc, off, 1 ) )
   {   CPL = 0;
      LA_write1(desc.Base + off,  value);           /* see page 95 */
      CPL = saveCPL;
   }

   signal_fault(TASK, err_code);
}
```

```
TSS_write2(err_code, off, value)
SELECTOR err_code;
OFFSET off;
WORD value;
{   short saveCPL = CPL;

    /* == Verify access rules, signal TASK fault with err_code if violation occurs.  NOTE:
            Writable flag check is not done because TSS_desc is always writable.  If access
            rules pass, the linear address and value to be written are passed to LA_write2 ==
            */
    if ( TSS_desc.Valid && in_limits(TSS_desc, off, 1 ) )
    {   CPL = 0;
        LA_write2(desc.Base + off, value);         /* see page 95 */
        CPL = saveCPL;
    }

    signal_fault(TASK, err_code);
}


TSS_write4(err_code, off, value)
SELECTOR err_code;
OFFSET off;
DWORD value;
{   short saveCPL = CPL;

    /* == Verify access rules, signal TASK fault with err_code if violation occurs.  NOTE:
            Writable flag check is not done because TSS_desc is always writable.  If access
            rules pass, the linear address and value to be written are passed to LA_write4 ==
            */
    if ( TSS_desc.Valid && in_limits(TSS_desc, off, 1 ) )
    {   CPL = 0;
        LA_write4(desc.Base + off, value);         /* see page 96 */
        CPL = saveCPL;
    }

    signal_fault(TASK, err_code);
}
```

2.7.6 Fetching instructions

Instruction (i.e. code) fetches are a specialized form of memory read. The next instruction to be executed is always pointed at by CS:EIP; that is, the next instruction is fetched from the offset specified by the EIP register within the CS segment. (On the 8086, 80186, and 80286 the offset within a segment is a WORD quantity. Thus on these implementations, only the 16-bit subset of EIP, that is, IP, is used as the instruction offset pointer.)

For the purposes of description fetching an instruction is broken down into a sequence of single-byte reads. The fetch_code1 routine, defined below, performs this read.

```
BYTE fetch_code1()
{
   if ( in_limits(CS_desc, EIP, 1) )
      return ( mem_vec[LA_rdChk(desc.Base + off)] );

   signal_fault(GP, 0);
}
```

Note that there is no check is made to validate that CS_desc is executable. This is permissible because the Executable flag is checked whenever CS (and hence, CS_desc) is loaded in PROTECTED mode. In REAL and VM86 modes all segments are executable; so here too no check is required.

2.7.7 Translation and protection via paging

The paging mechanism of the 80x86 maps a linear address into a physical address, and as well, makes sure that the page access rules pass. An overview of paged translation and page access rules was provided in §2.6.4.2 (starting on page 48). This section gives an algorithmic description of paging. In particular, the LA_readx and LA_writex routines used in the previous sections are defined here. These routines accept a linear address and convert it into a physical address. If paging is disabled (flag PG==0 and flag PE==1) the physical address *is* the linear address; that is, no translation or page protection checks are performed. If paging is enabled (flag PG==1 and flag PE==1) the linear address is converted into a physical address based on the directory table and page tables that are active currently. The reader is reminded that paging is only available on the 80386 and i486; in the context of the C language description, PG can be thought of as permanently set to 0 on the 8086, 80186, 80286, and 80376.

Figure 2.19 on page 50 gave a pictorial view of how the directory table and page tables are used to translate a linear address to a physical address. Although the linear address is a DWORD quantity generated by adding the base address of a segment to an offset value, it is interpreted as having three component fields: these fields are used to index into the directory table, a page table, and a physical page (see Figure 2.19). A linear address can be cast formally as the C language type LIN_ADDR, as follows.

```
typedef struct {
    unsigned DTE : 10;       /* Directory table entry index */
    unsigned PTE : 10;       /* Page table entry index */
    unsigned PageInd : 12;   /* Offset within a page */
} LIN_ADDR;
```

An equivalent diagrammatic representation is given in Figure 2.28. Keep in mind that a LIN_ADDR is interpreted in this way only when paging is enabled. With paging disabled, a linear address is the same as a physical address; that is, a byte index into the physical memory vector mem_vec.

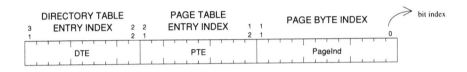

Figure 2.28: Linear address structure when paging is enabled

The directory table and each of the (up to) 1,024 page tables contain 1,024 entries each. Each entry is a DWORD, so the directory and page tables are each fixed-size, 4,096-byte (1,024 × 4 bytes) objects. The base address of the directory table is stored in CR3. The format of CR3, shown in Figure 2.29, indicates that the directory table is page aligned. Also note that the address is a physical address.

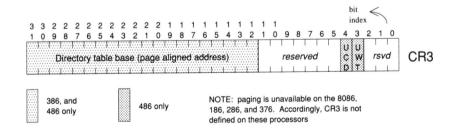

Figure 2.29: Format of directory table base address register (CR3)

The format of directory table and page table entries is shown as the C language type declarations DIR_TAB_ENT and PAGE_TAB_ENT below. It is also shown as a diagram in Figure 2.30.

```
/* DIRECTORY TABLE ENTRY */
typedef struct {
    unsigned PTBase: 20;              /* Page table base address */
    unsigned Available : 3;           /* These bits are available to user */
    unsigned Rsvd1: 3;                /* Intel-reserved bits */
    unsigned PTAcc: 1;                /* "Page table accessed" flag */
    unsigned PTCD : 1;                /* Page table caching disable [486] */
    unsigned PTWT : 1;                /* Page table write-through control [486] */
    unsigned U_S : 1;                 /* USER/SUPERVISOR attribute */
    unsigned R_W : 1;                 /* "Page writable" flag */
    unsigned PTPresent : 1;           /* "Page table present" flag */
}   DIR_TAB_ENT;


/* PAGE TABLE ENTRY */
typedef struct {
    unsigned PBase: 20;               /* Page base address */
    unsigned Available : 3;           /* These bits are available to user */
    unsigned Rsvd1: 2;                /* Intel-reserved bits */
    unsigned PDirty: 1;               /* "Page written" flag */
    unsigned PAcc: 1;                 /* "Page accessed" flag */
    unsigned PCD : 1;                 /* Page caching disable [486] */
    unsigned PWT : 1;                 /* Page write-through control [486] */
    unsigned U_S : 1;                 /* USER/SUPERVISOR attribute */
    unsigned R_W : 1;                 /* "Page writable" flag */
    unsigned PPresent : 1;            /* "Page present" flag */
}   PAGE_TAB_ENT;
```

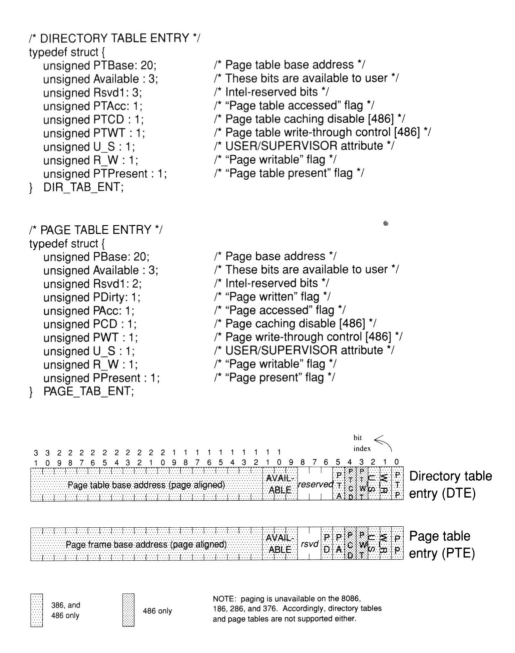

Figure 2.30: Format of directory table and page table entries

Each directory table entry stores (among other things) the base address of a page table. A page table entry is very similar to a directory table entry, except that it stores the base address of a physical page. Both these addresses are physical addresses.

In the process of converting a linear address to a physical address one directory table entry and one page table entry is used. In addition to the translation address, both these entries contain usage statistics flags and protection flags. On the i486, they also contain caching policy flags. With the exception of the "page dirty" flag, a copy of each flag appears in both the directory entry and page table entry. The statistics and protection flags are described in turn below. Discussion of the cache management flags (PTCD, PTWT, PCD and PWT, and UCD and UWT in CR3) is deferred to §2.7.9.1 (starting on page 103).

The two statistics flags are "accessed" and "dirty". If set to 1, the "accessed" flag indicates that the corresponding entry has been used to translate a linear address. For a directory table entry (i.e., DTE), this flag is called PTAccessed; for a page table entry (i.e., PTE), it is called PAccessed. The "dirty" flag is only available for PTEs; it is called PDirty. If set to 1 it indicates that the corresponding physical page has been written to. PTAccessed, PAccessed, and PDirty flags are set by the 80x86 as specified; they are not cleared automatically, however. It is up to system software to clear these flags as it sees fit. These flags' main use is in the implementation of page replacement policy in a demand paged operating system.

There are three protection flags: the "present" flag, the "write protect" flag, and the "user access" flag. The DTE "present" flag is called PTPresent (for *Page Table Present*), and the PTE "present" flag is called PPresent (for *Page Present*). If PTPresent is set to 1, the remaining fields of the DTE are valid; in particular, PTBase specifies the physical address of the page table corresponding to the DTE. If PTPresent's value is 0, the entire page table corresponding to the DTE is not present. Since a page table maps 22 bits of the linear address, marking a DTE "not present" invalidates a 2^{22} byte region (i.e., 4-megabyte region) of the linear address space. The PPresent flag, if set to 0 says that there is no physical page associated with the page table entry; thus, a PTE that is marked "not present" invalidates a 4,096-byte region of memory.

Before we leave the "present" flag, let us point out an important difference between it and the "Present" flag of segment descriptors. (See §2.7.2.5 on page 68 for a review of the segment descriptor Present flag.) PPresent and PTPresent not only indicate the absence or presence of a page or page table; they also validate the remaining bits in the PTE or DTE. In other words, the fields of a PTE are looked at only if PPresent is 1, and the fields of a DTE are looked at only if PTPresent is 1. In contrast, all fields of a segment descriptor are required to be valid, regardless of whether the segment is marked Present. This difference has the following consequence. Say we are about to load a data segment descriptor register. If the Present flag of the descriptor selected from the GDT or LDT is set to 0 the "segment not present" (NP) fault is signaled only if the remaining descriptor attributes show it to be a data segment descriptor or a readable code segment descriptor. If, for example, the descriptor were for a "not present" TSS a general protection (GP) fault would be signaled.

Now let us look at the "user access" and "write protect" flags. The "user access" flag, called the U_S flag in both a DTE and a PTE, encodes the minimum level of privilege needed to access a specific page. If U_S is 0, the CPL must be less than 3; that is, the application layer is denied read, write, and execute access. If U_S is 1, there is no CPL restriction: any layer inlcuding the application layer (with CPL == 3) can access the associated page. Assuming the CPL access rule passes, the "write protect" flag (called W_R for both DTEs and PTEs) is checked to limit the allowed type of access. If W_R is 1 all access type (read, write and execute) are permitted. If W_R is 0, only read and execute accesses are allowed.

To reduce hardware complexity, the 80386 simplifies the U_S and W_R rules as follows: the W_R flag is checked only when an access is made with CPL set to 3 (i.e., only for a User-mode access). This is reasonable from a protection point of view, since Supervisor-mode code (that executes with CPL less than 3) can be considered trusted code. However, it disallows forking in kernel code using copy-on-write techniques.[14] The i486 corrects this situation: it checks the W_R flag regardless of the CPL at the time of access. For complete compatibility, a separate control flag is needed to specify whether or not W_R should be checked in Supervisor mode. This flag, called WP (for *Write Protect*), is stored in bit position 16 of register CR0. If WP is 1, i486-style checks of the W_R flag are performed. If it is 0, W_R is only checked in User-mode (i.e., 80386 compatibility is retained.) The bit position for WP is marked *reserved* on the 80386; so 80386 software should initialize the bit explicitly. Since the i486 implementation initializes this bit position of CR0 to 0, 80386 software that follows the rules regarding *reserved* fields will run without modification on the

---

[14] The use of copy-on-write is not covered in this volume. See Volume I of this book, or an operating system textbook (e.g., [Bach, 1986]) for details.

i486. The combined effect of U_S and W_R flags and the WP mode flag is shown in Figure 2.31. Keep in mind that WP is always 0 on the 80386.

WP flag	DTE/PTE access rights		Allowed access types	
	U_S	W_R	User mode (CPL==3)	Sup mode (CPL <= 2)
0	0	0	None	Read, Write, Execute
0	0	1	None	Read, Write, Execute
0	1	0	Read, Execute	Read, Write, Execute
0	1	1	Read, Write, Execute	Read, Write, Execute
1	0	0	None	Read, Execute
1	0	1	None	Read, Write, Execute
1	1	0	Read, Execute	Read, Execute
1	1	1	Read, Write, Execute	Read, Write, Execute

486 only (on the 386 the WP flag is permanently 0)

Figure 2.31: Page protection via U_S, W_R, and WP flags

The U_S and W_R flags appear in both DTEs and PTEs. Since one DTE and one PTE always participate in a successful linear address to physical address mapping, how are the two U_Ses and two W_Rs combined to determine whether the page is in fact accessible by User-mode code, and whether it is writable? The answer is that the most restrictive of the two U_S flags and the most restrictive of the two W_R flags determine the actual access rights. To be precise, Supervisor-mode-only access (U_S == 0 is more restrictive than User-mode access; and read/execute-only access (U_S == 0 is more restrictive than read/write/execute access. The effect of the combined flags is shown in Figure 2.32.

DTE U_S	PTE U_S	Effective User/Supervisor page access
0	0	Accessible only if CPL <= 2
0	1	Accessible only if CPL <= 2
1	0	Accessible only if CPL <= 2
1	1	Accessible at any CPL

DTE W_R	PTE W_R	Effective Write/Read, Exec. page access
0	0	Read and Execute only
0	1	Read and Execute only
1	0	Read and Execute only
1	1	Read, Write and Execute

Figure 2.32: Combining directory table and page table access rights

2.7.7.1 Handling page faults

If one of the page access rules described does not pass during a memory access, a page fault is signaled. A special exception handler, the **PAGE** fault handler, is invoked when this occurs. The error code pushed onto the stack prior to entering the page fault service routine records the type of access that caused the fault. Additionally, a dedicated control register, CR2, is loaded with the faulty linear address. CR2 is a DWORD register that simply stores a linear address; for a diagram of the register see Figure 2.9 on page 27. The LA_read$x$ and LA_write$x$ routines described in the following subsections show error code generation, and the conditions under which a fault is signaled. CR2 initialization is also shown. For more on error codes and how a page fault (and, in general, any exception) is serviced, see §2.12 (starting on page 143).

2.7.7.2 Reading linear memory

The linear memory read functions LA_read1, LA_read2, and LA_read4 specify how a read of a BYTE, WORD, or DWORD from a specified address in the linear address space is performed. The LIN_ADDR value *laddr* passed to the functions is also compared against the four breakpoint registers DR0 through DR3. If there is a match, it is recorded and reported after the instruction completes. (Breakpoint registers are only available on the 80376, 80386, and i486.) The linear address BYTE read function LA_read1, described below, shows this sequence of actions.

```
BYTE LA_read1(laddr)
LIN_ADDR laddr;
{   /* == Compute physical address corresponding to laddr, and check page read access
        rules == */
    DWORD phys_addr = LA_rdChk(laddr);    /* function defined later in this section */

    /* == Check for data breakpoint; record address matches but defer reporting them to
        end of instruction's execution.  This check is only done on the 80376, 80386, and
        i486. == */
    check_brkpt(READ, laddr);                    /* see page 175 */

    /* == Access physical memory, returning value of BYTE read.  Note that phys_addr
        wraps around in physical memory without warning if its value exceeds the
        maximum physical memory size (i.e., 2^ADDR_BITS bytes).  ADDR_BITS is 20 for the
        8086 and 80186, 24 for the 80286, 80376 and 80386SX, and 32 for the 80386 and
        i486. == */
    return ( mem_vec[phys_addr % 2^ADDR_BITS] );
}
```

For a WORD or DWORD access, the linear address might be close enough to the end of a page that the access strides more than one page. For example, a DWORD at linear address 0x0002AFFD occupies addresses 0x0002AFFD through 0x0002B000, inclusive; that is, the first three BYTEs of the DWORD are in linear page 0x0002A, but the last BYTE is in linear page 0x0002B. This raises the possibility that DWORD may actually span two noncontiguous physical pages. Another possibility is that linear page 0x0002A is accessible, whereas linear page is inaccessible. In such a condition, the DWORD access is disallowed: all BYTEs of a data item must be accessible for the overall access to succeed.

To handle the contingencies just discussed, LA_read2 and LA_read4 are defined in terms of single BYTE LA_read1 calls. Actual implementations, of course, handle WORD and DWORD reads in a single access to physical memory whenever possible. The number of bytes read at once is determined by the bus size. (See page 52 for a discussion of bus size.)

```
WORD LA_read2(laddr)
LIN_ADDR laddr;
{  BYTE b1, b0;

   /* == Check if access address is on its natural boundary; i.e. WORD-aligned. If not,
         signal an alignment fault. This check is only done on the i486; on all other
         processors the alignment check control flags, AM and AC, are permanently set to
         0. See §2.7.8 for more details. == */
   if ( CPL == 3 && AM && AC && laddr⟨0⟩ != 0 )
      signal_fault(ALIGN);          /* see page 155 */

   /* == Get each BYTE in WORD and assemble together.  Note that laddr+1 is computed
         modulo-2^lm, where lm is 20 for the 8086 and 80186, 24 for the 80286, and 32 for
         the 80376, 80386SX, 80386, and i486. == */
   b1 = LA_read1(laddr);
   b0 = LA_read1(laddr+1);

   return ( (b1 << 8) | b0 );
}


DWORD LA_read4(laddr)
LIN_ADDR laddr;
{  BYTE b3, b3, b1, b0;

   /* == Check if access address is on its natural boundary; i.e., DWORD-aligned. If not,
         signal an alignment fault. This check is only done on the i486; on all other
         processors the alignment check control flags, AM and AC, are permanently set to
         0. See §2.7.8 for more details. == */
   if ( CPL == 3 && AM && AC && laddr⟨1:0⟩ != 0 )
      signal_fault(ALIGN);          /* see page 155 */

   /* == Get each BYTE in DWORD and assemble together.  Increments off laddr are
         done modulo-2^lm, where lm is 20 for the 8086 and 80186, 24 for the 80286, and
         32 for the 80376, 80386SX, 80386, and i486. == */
   b0 = LA_read1(laddr);
   b1 = LA_read1(laddr+1);
   b2 = LA_read1(laddr+2);
   b3 = LA_read1(laddr+3);

   return ( (b3 << 24) | (b2 << 16) | (b1 << 8) | b0 );
}
```

The LA_readx routines just described defer the linear address (LIN_ADDR) to physical address (PHYS_ADDR) mapping to the LA_rdChk function. This function, whose name denotes "linear address read check," maps the LIN_ADDR parameter laddr passed to it into a PHYS_ADDR. If paging is disabled, the function simply returns laddr as the physical address; that is, it operates as an identity map. (Keep in mind that paging is permanently disabled on versions of

the 80*x*86 other than the 80386 and i486.) If paging is enabled, *laddr* is
converted into a physical address by consulting the currently active directory
table and page tables. All page access rules for memory read are applied as the
table entries are looked up. If any access rule fails a PAGE fault is reported.
Also, if the "accessed" flag in either the directory table entry or the page table
entry used for the translation is not set to 1, action is taken to do so. This update
is done atomically, so that shared page tables (in a multiprocessor configuration)
can be used.

```
PHYS_ADDR LA_rdChk(laddr)
LIN_ADDR laddr;
{   DTE *dir_table;             /* Pointer to directory table */
    DTE dte;                    /* Temp storage for selected directory table entry */
    PTE *page_table;            /* Pointer to selected page table */
    PTE dte;                    /* Temp storage for selected page table entry */
    WORD err_code;

    /* == Check CR0⟨31⟩ (PG flag); if clear (i.e., paging disabled), simply return laddr as the
          physical address.  Otherwise, translate via directory table and page table lookup
          into a physical address. == */
    if ( PG == 0 )                      /* Paging disabled: PHYS_ADDR is LIN_ADDR */
        return( laddr );

    /* == Setup tentative error code: indicate read access and U_S based on CPL == */
    err_code = ( (CPL == 3) ? 4 : 0 ) ;

    /* == Read directory table entry; signal fault if selected entry marked "not present".
          PDB field of CR3 contains directory table's base address == */
    dir_table = &mem_vec[CR3 & 0xFFFFF000];
    lock(DIR_TABLE);                    /* see page 111 */
    dte = dir_table[laddr.DTE];
    if ( !dte.PTPresent )               /* Page table is not present */
    {   CR2 = laddr;
        signal_fault(PAGE, err_code);   /* Report "not present" error */
    }

    /* == If USER-mode (CPL==3) access, ensure that DTE's U_S flag is set to 1 == */
    if ( CPL == 3  &&  dte.U_S == 0 )   /* USER-mode access of SUPERVISOR page
                                           table */
    {   CR2 = laddr;
        signal_fault(PAGE, err_code | 1);
    }

    /* == Set "page table accessed flag", if not already set == */
    if ( !dte.PTAcc )
        dir_table[laddr.DTE] = dte | 0x20;  /* Set PTAcc bit */
    unlock(DIR_TABLE);                  /* see page 111 */

    /* == Read page table entry based on selected dte.  Signal fault if selected page is
          marked "not present" == */
```

```
    page_table = &mem_vec[dte & 0xFFFFF000];    /* get dte.PTBase */
    lock(PAGE_TABLE);                            /* see page 111 */
    pte = page_table[laddr.PTE];
    if ( !pte.PPresent )                         /* Page is not present */
    {  CR2 = laddr;
       signal_fault(PAGE, err_code);             /* Report "not present" error */
    }

    /* == If USER-mode (CPL==3) access, ensure that PTE's U_S flag is set to 1 == */
    if ( CPL == 3  &&  pte.U_S == 0 )
    {  CR2 = laddr;
       signal_fault(PAGE, err_code | 1);
    }

    /* == Set "page table accessed flag", if not already set == */
    if ( !pte.PAcc )                             /* Set "PAcc" bit, if clear */
        page_table[laddr.PTE] = pte | 0x20;      /* Set PAcc bit */
    unlock(PAGE_TABLE);                          /* see page 111 */

    /* == Checks pass: return PHYS_ADDR corresponding to laddr == */
    return ( (pte & 0xFFFFF000) | laddr.PageInd );
}
```

Note that LA_rdChk makes a minimum of two memory accesses (i.e. mem_vec references) when paging is enabled. LA_rdChk is itself called by the LA_readx routines, each of which make a minimum of one memory reference also. Thus, the memory read description given implies that each memory read request by the programmer of the 80x86 results in a minimum of three physical memory references (if paging is enabled.) Memory references are frequent enough that if the 80386 and i486 implemented the paging function as described, throughput would suffer severely. The common solution to this problem (also adopted by the 80386 and i486) is to store frequently used directory table entries and page table entries in high-speed registers within the CPU. This collection of registers, called a *TLB*, is described in §2.7.10 (starting on page 108).

2.7.7.3 Writing linear memory

Writing into the linear address space is very similar to reading from it. The differences are as follows:

1. the W_R flag is checked in the directory table entry and the page table entry. Both must be set to 1 for the write to succeed. Note that on the 80386, the W_R is only checked if a User-mode access (an access done with CPL set to 3) is made; Supervisor-mode accesses are always granted write access. On the i486 the WP flag in CR0 determines whether

Supervisor-mode writes should be done like the 80386 (WP == 0), or whether write protection should be allowed (WP == 1).

2. the "page dirty" flag (PDirty) in the page table entry used for the write is set to 1, if it is not already set. (There is no "page table dirty" flag.)

Of course, the direction of data traffic is also reversed: the LA_write*x* routines accept the value of the data to be written; they do not return any value.

The definition of LA_write1 is as follows.

```
LA_write1(laddr, value)
LIN_ADDR laddr;
BYTE value;
{   /* == Compute physical address corresponding to laddr, and check page write access
        rules == */
    DWORD phys_addr = LA_wrChk(laddr);    /* function defined later in this section */

    /* == Check for data breakpoint; record address matches but defer reporting them to
        end of instruction's execution.  This check is done only on the 80376, 80386, and
        i486. == */
    check_brkpt(WRITE, laddr);              /* see page 175 */

    /* == Write BYTE to physical memory address.  Note that phys addr wraps around in
        physical memory without warning if its value exceeds the maximum physical
        memory size (i.e., 2^ADDR_BITS bytes).  ADDR BITS is 20 for the 8086 and 80186,
        24 for the 80286, 80376 and 80386SX, and 32 for the 80386 and i486. == */
    mem_vec[phys_addr % 2^ADDR_BITS] = value;
}
```

As with multiple BYTE reads, multiple BYTE writes have to handle the case where the write spans more than one page. This is done by individually translating each BYTE address in the WORD or DWORD to be written, as shown in the descriptions of LA_write2 (used for WORD writes) and LA_write4 (used for DWORD writes).

```
LA_write2(laddr, value)
LIN_ADDR laddr;
WORD value;
{
    /* == Check if access address is on its natural boundary; i.e. WORD-aligned.  If not,
        signal an alignment fault.  This check is only done on the i486; on all other
        processors the alignment check control flags, AM and AC, are permanently set to
        0.  See §2.7.8 for more details. == */
    if ( CPL == 3 && AM && AC && laddr⟨0⟩ != 0 )
        signal_fault(ALIGN);             /* see page 155 */
```

```
    /* == Write each BYTE in WORD using  LA_write1  calls.  Note that laddr+1 is
            computed modulo-2ᵖᵐ, where pm is 20 for the 8086 and 80186, 24 for the 80286,
            80376, and 80386SX, and 32 for the 80386 and i486. == */
    LA_write1(laddr,  value⟨7:0⟩);
    LA_write1(laddr+1,  value⟨15:8⟩);
}


LA_write4(laddr, value)
LIN_ADDR laddr;
DWORD value;
{
    /* == Check if access address is on its natural boundary; i.e., DWORD-aligned.  If not,
            signal an alignment fault.  This check is only done on the i486; on all other
            processors the alignment check control flags, AM and AC, are permanently set to
            0.  See §2.7.8 for more details. == */
    if ( CPL == 3  &&  AM  &&  AC  &&  laddr⟨1:0⟩ != 0 )
        signal_fault(ALIGN);            /* see page 155 */

    /* == Write each BYTE in DWORD using  LA_write1  calls.  Note that increments off
            laddr (e.g. laddr+3) are computed modulo-2ᵖᵐ, where pm is 20 for the 8086 and
            80186, 24 for the 80286, 80376, and 80386SX, and 32 for the 80386 and i486. ==
            */
    LA_write1(laddr,  value⟨7:0⟩);
    LA_write1(laddr+1,  value⟨15:8⟩);
    LA_write1(laddr+2,  value⟨23:16⟩);
    LA_write1(laddr+3,  value⟨31:24⟩);
}
```

The **LA_wrChk** is like **LA_rdChk** except that it ensures that the DTE and PTE used in the write have their **W_R** flags set. It also updates the "page dirty" flag in the DTE, if needed.

```
PHYS_ADDR LA_wrChk(laddr)
LIN_ADDR laddr;
{   DTE *dir_table;                     /* Pointer to directory table */
    DTE dte;                            /* Temp storage for selected directory table entry */
{   PTE *page_table;                    /* Pointer to selected page table */
    PTE dte;                            /* Temp storage for selected page table entry */
    WORD err_code;

    /* == Check CR0⟨31⟩ (PG flag); if clear (i.e., paging disabled), simply return laddr as the
            physical address.  Otherwise, translate via directory table and page table lookup
            into a physical address. == */
    if ( PG == 0 )                      /* Paging disabled: PHYS_ADDR is LIN_ADDR */
        return( laddr );

    /* == Setup tentative error code: indicate write access and U_S based on CPL == */
    err_code = ( (CPL == 3) ? 4 : 0 ) | 2;
```

```
/* == Read directory table entry; signal fault if selected entry marked "not present".
       PDB field of CR3 contains directory table's base address == */
dir_table = &mem_vec[CR3 & 0xFFFFF000];
lock(DIR_TABLE);                          /* see page 111 */
dte = dir_table[laddr.DTE];
if ( !dte.PTPresent )                     /* Page table is not present */
{   CR2 = laddr;
    signal_fault(PAGE, err_code);         /* Report "not present" error */
}

/* == If USER-mode (CPL==3) access, ensure that DTE's U_S flag is set to 1 == */
if ( CPL == 3  &&  dte.U_S == 0 )
{   CR2 = laddr;
    signal_fault(PAGE, err_code | 1);
}

/* == If USER-mode (CPL==3) access, or (for the i486) the "supervisor write protect"
       flag (WP) is set, ensure that DTE's W_R flag is set to 1 == */
if ( (CPL == 3 || WP)  &&  dte.W_R == 0 )
{   CR2 = laddr;
    signal_fault(PAGE, err_code | 1);
}

/* == Set "page table accessed flag", if not already set == */
if ( !dte.PTAcc )
    dir_table[laddr.DTE] = dte | 0x20;    /* Set PTAcc bit */
unlock(DIR_TABLE);                        /* see page 111 */

/* == Read page table entry based on selected dte.  Signal fault if selected page is
       marked "not present" == */
page_table = &mem_vec[dte & 0xFFFFF000];          /* get dte.PTBase */
lock(PAGE_TABLE);                         /* see page 111 */
pte = page_table[laddr.PTE];
if ( !pte.PPresent )                      /* Page is not present */
{   CR2 = laddr;
    signal_fault(PAGE, err_code);         /* Report "not present" error */
}

/* == If USER-mode (CPL==3) access, ensure that PTE's U_S flag is set to 1 == */
if ( CPL == 3  &&  pte.U_S == 0 )
{   CR2 = laddr;
    signal_fault(PAGE, err_code | 1);
}

/* == If USER-mode (CPL==3) access, or (for the i486) the "supervisor write protect"
       flag (WP) is set, ensure that PTE's W_R flag is set to 1 == */
if ( (CPL == 3 || WP)  &&  pte.W_R == 0 )
{   CR2 = laddr;
    signal_fault(PAGE, err_code | 1);
}

/* == Set "page table accessed" flag, if not already set == */
```

```
    if ( !pte.PAcc )
        pte = pte | 0x20;                      /* Set PAcc bit */

    /* == Set "page written" flag, if not already set == */
    if ( !pte.PDirty )
        pte = pte | 0x40;                      /* Set PDirty bit */

    page_table[laddr.PTE] = pte;               /* Store updated PTE */

    unlock(PAGE_TABLE);                        /* see page 111 */

    /* == Checks pass: return PHYS_ADDR corresponding to laddr == */
    return ( (pte & 0xFFFFF000) | laddr.PageInd );
}
```

2.7.8 Alignment checks on the i486

A data item is said to be aligned on its natural boundary if its byte address in the physical address space is a multiple of the number of BYTEs in the data type. Although the 80x86 does not require that data be aligned, doing so has the advantage that a reference to the data item results in a minimum number of memory references. To allow a user to determine whether or not a particular application makes data references that are not aligned, the i486 can be configured so that all nonaligned accesses made by an application are trapped.

Alignment checks can also be used to improve the efficiency of some programming environments, as follows. In languages like LISP, Smalltalk, and REXX the type of arguments to an operation can, in general, only be determined at runtime. In particular, in an expression such as

a + b

a and b might be any combination of integers, floating point values, or numeric strings. Furthermore, their types might change as the program containing the expression executes. One way to translate programs in such languages into 80x86 code is to check the operand types at run time and activate the appropriate operation routine. But this can be very time consuming. Fortunately, studies of execution-time behavior of programs in these languages have shown that the operands to arithmetic operators are almost always integers. This observation can be used in conjunction with alignment checks to speed up expression evaluation as follows: store all integers (stored in DWORDs) on their natural boundary, and store all other types at misaligned addresses. If an operation (e.g. the addition shown above) is attempted on an operand, it will succeed only if the operand is aligned. If it is misaligned, an alignment fault will be taken. The fault

Access Type	Alignment factor (in bytes)
BYTE	1 (no alignment)
WORD	2
DWORD	4
Bit string	4
Single precision REAL	4
Double precision REAL	8
Extended precision REAL	8
SELECTOR	2
48-bit FAR pointer	4
32-bit FAR pointer	2
Pseudodescriptor (48 bits)	4
14-byte FLDENV/FSTENV operand	2
28-byte FLDENV/FSTENV operand	4
94-byte FRESTOR/FSAVE operand	2
108-byte FRESTOR/FSAVE operand	4

Figure 2.33: Natural boundaries of 80x86 application data types

handler can examine the operand to determine its type and execute the appropriate routine.

The natural boundary for some data types is easily deduced; for example, it is apparent that the address of an aligned WORD is a multiple of two. But what about a bit string? A far pointer? The alignment of all operands that the application instruction set of the 80x86 can operate on is shown in Figure 2.33. Note that only BYTE operands have no alignment; for all other operand types performance is maximized (and physical memory references minimized) if the operand is stored on its natural boundary.

2.7.9 Caching on the 80x86

A cache is a small, fast memory that stores a copy of the most frequently used areas of main memory. A memory reference made by a processor containing a cache interrogates the cache first. If the reference is to a data item that is currently in the cache, a reference to the larger (but slower) main memory is avoided. If the item is not found in the cache, a normal memory reference is

made. In most instances, this memory data item is also loaded into the cache so
that a future reference to it (which is a likely event) can avoid a memory
reference. Caching is done for two main reasons:

1. main memory can be made relatively slow (and hence, relatively
   inexpensive) because most references go to the (fast) cache.

2. the number of accesses to main memory is drastically reduced. This helps
   in tightly coupled multiprocessor systems, where several CPUs try to access
   a single memory. (This assumes that each processor has its own cache.)

There are a number of issues in cache design. For example, the **replacement
policy** issue addresses which data item should be removed from a (full) cache
when a new data item is brought in from main memory. The **cache coherency**
issue addresses how consistency is retained if a data item stored in a given
processor's cache is updated in main memory, or in another cache. Since caches
contain copies of data items, a given copy of a modified data item must be
updated (or deleted) before a reference to it is made. Other issues relate to the
organization of the cache; that is, how many elements should it have, should it
store only instructions, only data, or both, and so on. Enough of an overview of
these concepts is provided here so that caches used in 80x86 implementations can
be described. The reader interested in a more complete discussion is referred to
[Smith, 1982].

Caches are implemented only in the 80386 and i486. It is worthwhile noting that
they are not strictly a part of the 80x86 *architecture*. In particular, it is possible
that the cache organizations described here may be changed in future
implementations of the 80x86. However, systems programmers need to be aware
of caches, since their presence may affect system program behavior.

The type of cache implemented in the 80x86 is called a **set associative cache**. A
set associative cache can be thought of as a two-dimensional array of
CACHE_ELEMENTs, as shown in Figure 2.34 and in the C language declarations
below.

```
typedef struct {
   BOOLEAN Valid;
   unsigned tag;
   BYTE data_line[LINE_SIZE];
} CACHE_ELEMENT;
```

CACHE_ELEMENT cache[NUM_SETS][SET_SIZE];

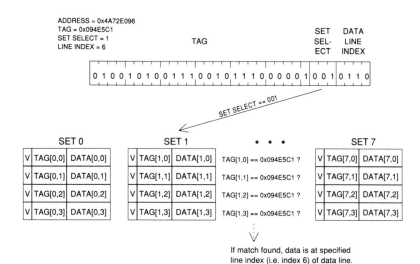

Figure 2.34: The structure of a set associative cache

Each cache element consists of a *tag* and an associated *data_line*. The *tag* consists of the most significant bits of the memory address of the *data_line*. (Since only portions of main memory are in the cache, each *data_line* needs to have an associated memory address.) The *data_line* contains a copy of the LINE_SIZE bytes of data stored at the address mapped by the cache element. Since a cache element may have no data in it an additional flag, called Valid, is used. This flag is TRUE only when the cache entry has valid data in it.

To check whether an address *addr* is mapped by the cache, it is divided into three components, as follows:

1. a *data line index* : this field indexes into the data line within the cache that contains the data being accessed. The data line to use is determined by using the following two components of *addr*.

2. a *set select* value : this field selects the cache set that is to be used to look up the data.

3. a *tag* value : each of the tags in the set selected by the *set select* field is
   compared with the tag field of *addr*. If a match occurs, the associated data
   line is indexed using the data line index component of *addr*. Since cache
   access needs to be fast, the tag comparisons are done in hardware in
   parallel.

In the example cache of Figure 2.34 the data line index uses the 4 least
significant bits of *addr*, implying that the cache's line size is 16 bytes. The set
select occupies the next 3 address bits, implying that there are eight sets in the
cache. The remaining 25 bits of the address form the tag value that is compared
against the selected set's tag's. Note that the number of sets (NUM_SETS) and
the data line size (LINE_SIZE) need to be of the form 2^n, where *n* is an integer.
However, there can be an arbitrary number of tags in a set. (Figure 2.34 happens
to show four tags per set.) The number of tags per set in a cache is called its **set
size**. Another term the set size is **associativity**. Hence, the example cache's
associativity (or set size) is four.

It is well to keep in mind that an access to a cache does not guarantee that the
data being sought will be located there. In particular, the cache is completely
empty initially (i.e., all the "cache entry valid" (Valid) bits are cleared).
Therefore, no match will occur between the tag component of the very first
address used to access the cache and the tag elements in the set selected by the
address. If data cannot be located in the cache, a **cache miss** is said to occur; if it
is found, a **cache hit** is said to occur. When this happens, the address used to
access the cache is used instead to access normal memory. The data thus fetched
is used by the program requesting it, as usual. Furthermore, the data (and its
associated address tag) is usually also stored in the cache in the set specified by
the address. Subsequent accesses to the same address are serviced by the cache.
One of the metrics used to measure the efficacy of a cache is the number of
accesses that result in cache hits in relation to the total number of accesses made.
This value, usually represented as fraction, is called the cache's **hit rate** or **hit
ratio**. Since the maximum hit rate is 1 (i.e., the case where all accesses are cache
hits), the **miss rate** or **miss ratio** is simply 1 − «hit rate».

After a large enough number of cached memory accesses have been made, the
cache will reach a state where all elements of a given set are filled with data. At
this point a decision has to be made as to how to service the next access whose
address selects the full set, but for which none of the tags in the set match the
address' tag (i.e., if there is a cache miss). If the access is a memory read, the
usual strategy is to read external memory (as usual) and *replace* one of the

existing set element's contents with the data read. The algorithm used to choose which element to replace is called the cache's **replacement policy**.

2.7.9.1 Memory caching on the i486

The preceding discussion provides enough background information to describe the cache implemented on the i486.[15] This cache has 128 sets, with each set containing 4 elements. Furthermore, the data line of each element is 16 bytes long. Since each set can store up to 64 bytes of main memory data (at 4 lines × 16 bytes per line) and there are 128 sets in all, the total i486 cache size is 8,192 bytes (i.e., 8 kilobytes). C notation for this structure is as follows:

```
typedef struct {
    BOOLEAN Valid;
    unsigned tag;
    BYTE data_line[16];
} CACHE_ELEMENT;

CACHE_ELEMENT cache_486[128][4];
```

Since LINE_SIZE is 16, a line index is 4 bits wide. Since NUM_SETS is 128, there are 7 set select bits. Since the cache is referenced using physical addresses, each address is 32 bits wide. The least significant 4 bits of this address form the line index, the next 7 bits are used for set select, and the remaining 21 bits form the tag. It is worthwhile noting that the cache could have been designed to use linear addresses, or even logical addresses, for tags. Since virtually all addresses generated by an 80x86 program start out as logical addresses, doing so would have the advantage that cache access times would improve (since the address needed to access the cache could be computed sooner). However, linear and logical address tags can give rise to a situation where two distinct linear addresses (or logical addresses) can point to the same physical memory location. This problem is known as address **aliasing**. Similarly, it is possible for two distinct physical addresses to have the same linear (or logical) address in two separate tasks. This is known as the **synonyms** problem. Additionally, using physical addresses also simplifies cache address cross-checks from external device. (Cross-checking is described below.) For all these reasons the i486 implementation chooses to use physical addressing for its cache.

---

[15] Of course, other 80x86 computer systems may implement caches external to the microprocessor; in fact, many 80386 systems do just that. What sets the i486 apart is the fact that the cache is integrated into the microprocessor chip. This integration also allows the cache to be substantially faster than it could have been if it were outside the processor.

In the i486, *all* memory references and instruction fetches lookup the cache. If the reference results in a cache hit, the data are read from, or written to the cache, as appropriate. Additionally, in the case of a write, the data are also written out to main memory if the NW flag (the "*not-w*rites-transparent" flag) in CR0 is disabled (i.e., set to 0). This policy of transferring all writes to main memory, known as **write-through** ensures that the i486's cache state is always known to system components outside the i486. Write-through also simplifies the work needed to be done when a cache line needs to be replaced. To make sure that data in all caches in a system (e.g., one with multiple i486s) are up-to-date, the i486 also watches the memory bus to ensure that no system agent (e.g., a DMA channel or another i486) performs a write to an address that is currently mapped by the cache. If such a write does occur, the i486 simply invalidates the cache line containing the address. This feature is called **cross-checking**, or **bus watch**.[16] Bus watch is only enabled when the NW flag is clear; that is, when writes are transparent.

Note that the alternative to write-through is **write-back**. Writes are accumulated in the cache in this scheme. When a cache line needs to be replaced its contents are checked to verify whether they have been updated. If so, the line is written back to main memory. This strategy defers the (slow) external memory writes that the write-through scheme performs. The drawback is that cache and memory images get synchronized only when a cache line is removed. The write-back scheme is not supported by the i486. See [Goodman, 1983] and [Smith, 1982] for further discussion of this issue.

What happens if the memory reference results in a cache miss? The answer depends on whether the reference was a read or a write, and whether or not caching is enabled. If caching is disabled, the reference is simply transferred to the external memory system; the cache's contents are not changed in any way. (Keep in mind that cache *lookup* is *always* enabled; enabling caching only determines what happens when the lookup results in a cache miss.) If caching is enabled and the reference is a memory write, the effect is just as if caching were disabled: the external memory is updated, but the cache is not altered in any way. If caching is enabled and the reference is a memory read, external memory is read to satisfy the request (just as in the case where caching is disabled). Additionally, the data line in main memory that stores the referenced item is brought into the cache. Since a data line is always aligned on a boundary of

---

[16] The i486 cannot simultaneously cross-check whether an external system write collides with its current cache contents, and perform an internal cache access. In particular, the cache is unavailable for internal accesses while an external access cross-check is performed. Since external writes can be quite frequent, the system designer has the option to perform cross-checks (called **invalidate cycles**) only on selected memory addresses. System software has to ensure that there can be no possibility of two system agents writing to non-cross-checked addresses.

LINE_SIZE bytes (in this case, 16 bytes), it is possible that a memory reference of two or more bytes may span two cache lines. Hence a single memory read may actually bring in two cache lines.

A number of factors "conspire" to determine whether or not caching is enabled for a particular memory access. First, the global caching disable flag CD (stored in control register CR0) must be set. If this flag is set when a cache miss occurs, no cache fill occurs. Additionally, the system components outside the i486 have a say in whether caching should occur. This is achieved via the KEN (suggestive of "caching enable") pin of the i486. In the time slot that a data item is returned to the i486, the system also activates or deactivates the KEN pin. If KEN is deactivated the data item returned is not loaded into the cache, regardless of the state of the CD flag.

CD and KEN are global factors that control caching. In addition, a third flag, call it the "local caching disable" or lCD flag, provides localized control over caching. lCD is not a fixed flag; rather it is one of the UCD, PTCD, or PCD flags (stored in CR3, directory table entries, or page table entries, respectively). Which flag is used depends on the nature of the transaction. If paging is disabled, directory tables and page tables do not come into the picture. Hence, the local caching disable flag used is UCD (the *u*npaged-access *c*ache *d*isable flag stored in CR3). With paging enabled, the lCD choice rules are as follows. UCD is used when the i486 reads the directory table to service a paged memory request. When the i486 reads a page table entry (to service a paged memory request), the PTCD flag in the directory table that points to the page table used is used. Finally, when a normal page is read, the PCD flag in the page table entry corresponding to the page is used.

We have seen three factors, the CD flag, the KEN input pin, and one of the lCD flags that control caching. One final factor, whether or not the memory read is done with the bus locked, also affects caching. All locked memory reads are done with caching disabled, regardless of the setting of the other caching control flags or KEN pin. The list below summarizes the conditions under which caching (i.e. cache line fills) is disabled.

1. all writes: if a memory write's address is located in the cache, the cache value is updated as is the copy of the written location in main memory. If the write results in a cache miss, only main memory is updated: the cache line corresponding to the write is *not* brought into the cache.

2. all reads done with the CD flag set.

3. all reads done where the memory access results in the activation of the KEN pin.

4. all locked reads: a locked read can result either because of a LOCK prefix or because of a system data structure update (see uses of the lock function in the C language descriptions of the architecture). A locked read is always part of a read-modify-write transaction.

5. an unlocked read transaction performed to refresh the TLB that results in a read of a directory table entry, where CD is clear and KEN is active, and the UCD flag (stored in CR3) is cleared.

6. an unlocked read transaction performed to refresh the TLB that results in a read of a page table entry, where CD is clear and KEN is active, and the PTCD flag of the directory table entry pointing at the page table is cleared.

7. any other unlocked read transaction performed with paging enabled (i.e., PG set) where CD is clear and KEN is active, and the PCD flag of the page table entry pointing at the page accessed is cleared.

8. any other unlocked read transaction performed with paging disabled (i.e., PG clear) where CD is clear and KEN is active, and the UCD flag in CR3 is also clear.

2.7.9.2 Deactivating the cache

The i486 cache is always "on"; that is, memory references are always passed by the cache. Sometimes, however, it may be desirable to deactivate the cache entirely. The way to achieve this is by preventing cache line fills (i.e., disabling caching) and making sure that there are no valid cache entries. Disabling caching was discussed in the previous subsection; the most straightforward way of doing so is by setting the CD flag. Invalidating all cache entries can be done either by writing to the cache registers (via test registers TR4 and TR5; see the test register MOV instructions defined on page 509), or by issuing the INVD or WBINVD instructions. Use of the INVD or WBINVD instructions is recommended, as they provide an invalidation mechanism that is independent of the cache size.

2.7.9.3 Memory mapped I/O locations

Although the 80x86 architecture recommends the use of I/O instructions to communicate with I/O devices, it does no prevent the system designer from building peripherals that respond to memory accesses. Such memory-mapped peripheral access can fail if caching is enabled. For example, assume that a peripheral device is controlled via reads and writes to physical address 0xFC000004. The very first read to 0xFC000004 will result in a cache miss; so the read request will be sent outside the i486, as desired. However, the read data will be loaded into the on-chip cache and subsequent reads will access the cache data. To prevent this from happening, caching should be disabled when accessing memory-mapped peripheral addresses. The easiest way to achieve this is to activate the KEN pin when returning data from the peripheral device.

2.7.9.4 Second-level caches

A key component that helps the i486 achieve its performance level is its on-chip cache. However, it still makes sense to add cache externally (at the system level) to help improve performance in the cases when there is an on-chip cache miss. The design of this **second-level cache** needs to address all the caching issues that arose in the first-level, on-chip cache. The i486 says nothing about these issues; however, it does transmit any caching and write-through attributes that it knows whenever it makes an external memory request. This is done as follows.

Recall that the i486 makes an external memory reference whenever there is a memory write, a cache miss, or a read with caching disabled. The request is accompanied by the state of the lCD ("local caching disable") and lWT ("local write-through") flags. Recall that lCD is either one of the UCD, PTCD, or PCD flags, depending on the type of access being made. Similarly, lWT is either one of the UWT, PTWT, or PWT flags, and is chosen based on the access type. The basis on which the choice is made is reiterated below.

Access Type	ICD chosen	IWT chosen
any memory access done with + paging disabled	UCD	UWT
Directory table entry read (DTEs are never written)	UCD	UWT
Page table entry read/write	PTCD	PTWT
Paged memory read/write	PCD	PWT

It is worthwhile reemphasizing that the i486 on-chip cache always operates in write-through mode (assuming that the nontransparent-writes flag (NW) is disabled.) The IWT flags should be configured by software to reflect data that can safely be stored in a write-back cache. Since write-back caches are potentially more efficient, the second-level cache can make use of the IWT information to improve it efficiency. Future implementations of the 80x86 can also enhance their on-chip caches to include a write-back mode of operation. Software that configures the IWT flag to "write-back" could then make use of this feature.

2.7.10 Paging and TLBs

The paging capabilities of the 80386 and i486 (see Figure 2.19 on page 50) lead to an interesting observation: since translating a linear address to a physical address requires a directory table and page table lookup, it follows that every program-generated memory access should result in at least three actual memory references (one for the directory table entry, one for the page table entry, and one for the accessed data). This 3:1 increase in memory access time is too high a penalty to be acceptable. The 80386 and i486 (and other paged processors) solve this problem by utilizing a specialized cache called a **translation lookaside buffer**, or **TLB**. The TLB's tags contain linear page frame addresses that have been recently accessed by the 80386 (or i486). The "data line" corresponding to each tag is the *physical* page frame address corresponding to the linear page frame address stored in the tag. As with the data cache, each tag has a Valid bit indicating whether it stores a valid value. The 80386 and i486 TLB is a set associative cache with a set size of four and three set select bits (i.e., the TLB has

eight sets). This is depicted in Figure 2.35. A C language declaration of the TLB
(call it TLB_x86) can be found on page 510.

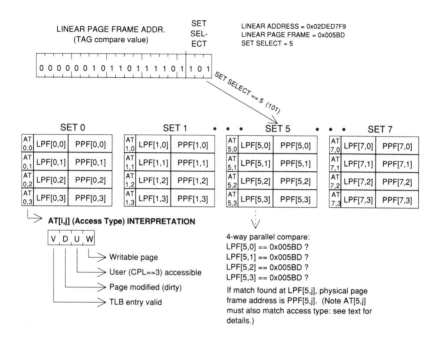

Figure 2.35: The 80386/i486 TLB

On reset, all TLB Valid bits are clear; that is, no linear address mapping
information is stored in the TLB. Now let us see what happens when a memory
access is made with paging enabled. The linear address of the memory access,
say at address 0x02DED7F9, is stripped of its page index bits. (Recall that these
low-order 12 bits do not participate in the linear address to physical address
translation.) The remaining 20 bits, the linear page frame address (0x02DED in
the example), are used to look up the TLB. Since the TLB has eight sets, the
low-order three bits of the linear page frame address selects one of the eight sets.
The remaining 17 bits (whose value is 0x005BD for the example) is compared
simultaneously against all four page frame tags in the selected set. Since the set
select value is 5 for the example, 0x005BD is compared against each of the four
tags LPF[5,*j*] (see Figure 2.35). Note that a comparison is performed only if the
Valid bit for the corresponding flag is set. Additionally, for the comparison to
succeed, the type of access (User/Supervisor mode and read vs. write) must also

match. For example, if a frame address match were found at LPF[5,2] and CPL was 3 (i.e., the 80*x*86 was in User mode), U[5,2] would have to be set, indicating that the page mapped by the TLB was a User-mode-accessible page. Furthermore, if the access were a write, W[5,2] (the "page writable" flag) would also have to be set.

2.7.10.1 Processing TLB misses

What happens if no tag match is found, or if a tag matches but the access type bits (U and W) do not match? In the latter case, a linear to physical address match has been found in the TLB, but the access is invalid; hence, a PAGE fault is signaled. If no tag match (known as a **TLB miss**) occurs, the directory table and a page table is looked up according to the paging address translation rules (see §2.7.7 (starting on page 83), and Figure 2.19). If the requested linear address is mapped by the directory/page tables, the new linear to physical mapping is stored in the TLB. Subsequent references to the page containing the linear address will match in the TLB, and avoid a directory/page table lookup.

2.7.10.2 Setting the Dirty bit

The paging mechanism specifies that if a physical page is written, the PDirty flag of the page table entry corresponding to the page should get set. This requirement is handled via the D[*i,j*] bit stored in each TLB entry. Whenever a TLB lookup is performed because of a memory write, the TLB entry comparisons also check to see that the D[*i,j*] flag of the matching entry is set. If a match occurs but the D[*i,j*] bit is found clear, a directory/page table lookup is initiated, just as if there were a TLB miss. However, the PDirty flag of the accessed page table entry is set in the process.

2.7.10.3 TLB replacement policy

What happens if a TLB miss occurs, but all entries in the accessed TLB set are filled? As with any cache, one of the set elements needs to be replaced. The element to be replaced is chosen "randomly." The choice is not truly random: rather the current value of a counter that counts between 0 and 3 is used as the index of the set element that is replaced. This counter is incremented every time a memory reference is made. Since it is unlikely that there is a correlation between the number of accesses made between TLB element replacement requests, the counter exhibits a degree of randomness.

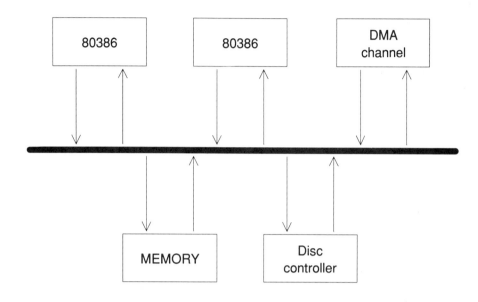

Figure 2.36: An 80x86 system with mulitple masters

2.7.11 Atomic transactions, and the lock function

In a typical 80x86-based system, the 80x86 processor, memory, and other devices that access memory, communicate over a common bus. This situation is depicted in Figure 2.36. Here the system consists of two CPUs, a DMA channel, a disk controller, and some memory. The CPUs and the DMA channel can both initiate requests to either memory or to the disk controller. Devices that can initiate bus transactions are called **masters**. Devices that respond to requests are called **slaves**. Thus, the figure shows a system with three masters and two slaves.

Now consider an instruction that increments a memory location m

INC m

This instruction reads the value of m, increments it, then writes back the updated value to memory. In a system that has only one master, this read-modify-write operation is guaranteed to complete uninterrupted. However, in a system like the one depicted in Figure 2.36 it is conceivable that more than one master (e.g. the two 80386s) may try to perform read-modify-write operations to the same location simultaneously. In such a situation *m* might get incremented by 1 or by 2, depending on the way in which the reads and writes get interleaved. To avoid such problems, the 80x86 allows the user to **lock** together all memory references generated by an instruction that performs a read-modify-write operation to memory. This atomic operation request is specified by placing the LOCK prefix byte immediately before the instruction to be locked. This prefix is discussed in Chapter 4 on page 482.

The notation used to lock memory, operate on it, then unlock it is

```
lock(MEM);
«perform locked operations»
unlock(MEM);
```

80x86 implementations indicate that a locked operation is in progress by activating the LOCK pin. Since it is possible for an exception to occur while performing the locked operations, the 80x86 automatically issues an

```
unlock(MEM);
```

prior to servicing any interrupt. Note that a lock can be held only for the duration of an instruction. It is not possible to lock more than one instruction. To achieve a similar effect, the sequence of instructions to be locked should be placed in a critical section. The critical section can be protected using semaphores that are implemented using the LOCK prefix.

In addition to allowing the user to lock read-modify-write instructions, there are occasions when accesses that are internally generated by the 80x86 need to be locked. An example is a segment descriptor table access resulting from a PROTECTED mode SELECTOR load. The two DWORDs in the descriptor table entry need to be read atomically. Otherwise, it is conceivable that another master might update the descriptor's contents while it is being read (or its Accessed flag is being set). Similarly, updating the PDirty flag in a page table entry is done as a locked operation. The complete list of lockable entities is as follows:

- DESCR_TABLE: Segment descriptor table access to update "accessed" flag
- DIR_TABLE: Paging directory table access to update PTAccessed flag
- PAGE_TABLE: Page table access to update PAccessed flag
- IDT: Interrupt descriptor table access
- MEM: Programmer generated locked access (LOCK prefix)

The distinction between lockable entities is made solely for the purpose of architectural description. All existing implementations of the 80x86 activate the LOCK pin whenever any of the entities is locked. A locked operation on any of these entities is denoted as with the MEM case, as follows:

```
lock(entity);
«perform locked operations»
unlock(entity);
```

where *entity* is any of the lock group mentioned above. Note that only memory accesses are lockable; I/O accesses are never locked.

2.8 Stack operations

A number of 80x86 instructions make use of a stack. The stack is stored in memory. 80x86 stacks start in high memory and grow toward low memory. The region of memory available to the stack is defined by the *stack segment*, the extents of which are defined by the SS segment register (and the SS_desc descriptor register).

As with any stack, we need to know how stack element addresses are generated, and the width of elements pushed onto the stack. As shown in Figure 2.37, either SP or ESP is used as the stack pointer (i.e., the offset within the stack segment that corresponds to the current top-of-stack). The width of elements pushed is determined by the instruction's operand size.

How do we determine whether SP or ESP should be used for stack addressing? For the 80286 and its predecessors (the 8086 and 80186) the answer is easy: SP is used since only SP is available. In the 80386 and i486, however, either ESP or SP can be used. At first sight, it may make sense to use the instruction's address size attribute to make the choice. However, it is possible to issue an instruction such as

PUSH mvar

where *mvar* is a memory-based variable. Using normal conventions (see §2.18 for more on the address size attribute), the instruction's address size attribute is used to generate *mvar*'s offset. Hence, another source of information is needed for selecting the stack offset size (i.e., SP vs. ESP). The solution adopted is to use the DefaultAttr flag in SS_desc. If this flag is 0, SP is used; otherwise, ESP is used. As a consequence, the stack pointer offsets wraparound at 0xFFFF when

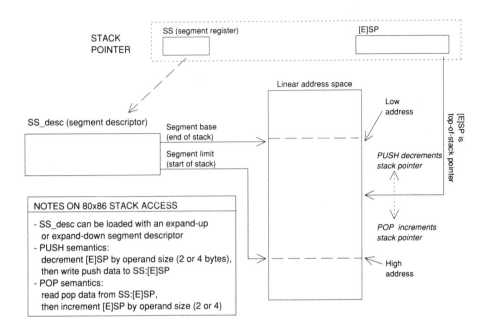

Figure 2.37: Stack accesses in the *80x86*

SP is used and at 0xFFFFFFFF when ESP is used. When used in this way, the DefaultAttr flag is sometimes called the Big flag (suggesting that a "big stack" is active if Big is set to 1). Note that when SP is used in the 80386 and i486, the upper half of ESP is left unmodified. This can matter if a transition is made from a stack where Big is 0 to a stack where Big is 1, but the stack pointer is not changed. Care must be taken to ensure that ESP's upper half is initialized to zero before the first stack reference. Also note that on the 80376, the Big flag is permanently set to 1; hence, on this machine, stack addressing is always done using ESP.

We have seen how the *80x86* determines the stack-top address. Now let us look at how the width of the item pushed onto the stack is determined. The general rule is that the stack operation instruction's operand size matches the width of the push or pop. For example, an instruction that pushes a WORD memory location has an operand size of 16 bits. Therefore, [E]SP is decremented by 2 when the instruction is executed. Similarly, an instruction that pops into a DWORD general register adds 4 to [E]SP. Although the operand size rule is easy to follow, the operand size of an instruction is not always obvious. The operand

size attribute is discussed further in §2.18 (starting on page 185). For the
moment, note that for the stack operation class of instructions, the stack operand
size can be determined as follows:

1. if a general register or memory location is being pushed or popped, the
   operand size matches that of the operand.

2. if a CALLGATE16 is used to mediate a privilege level transfer, stack data is
   pushed as WORDs (i.e. with an operand size of 16); if a CALLGATE32 is
   used, DWORDs are pushed. Privilege level transitions are further discussed
   in §2.10.

3. if a segment register is pushed or popped using the PUSH *seg-reg* or
   POP *seg-reg* instructions, the operand size always matches the the
   DefaultAttr setting of the code segment in which the instruction appears.

By using the set of rules outlined, the 80x86 stack invariably keeps the stack
pointer aligned on a WORD boundary when executing 16-bit code, and on a
DWORD boundary when executing 32-bit code. This assumes, of course, that the
stack pointer is initialized to an aligned address. Note that it is never possible to
push or pop a BYTE quantity.

2.8.1 Big stacks, SS, and expand-down segments

We just saw how DefaultAttr (the Big flag) of SS_desc controls stack pointer
generation. It is important to note that Big only has an effect on stack operations.
In particular, the Big attribute does not affect offset generation if the SS segment
override is applied to an instruction. For example, in all three instructions

```
MOV  AX, SS:[EDX+4]
MOV  AX, [EBP+2]
MOV  AX, [ESP+24]
```

the WORD at the *32-bit offset* within the SS segment that is stored in EDX+4 (or
EBP+2 or ESP+24) is moved to the AX register. The Big flag is not consulted for
offset wraparound; rather, wraparound occurs based on the instruction's address
size attribute (which is 32 bits for all three instructions).

Independent of the use of the DefaultAttr flag to determine a stack's "bigness,"
recall from §2.7.4.5 that DefaultAttr also controls the (implied) limit of expand-
down segments. If it is 1, the limit value used is 0xFFFFFFFF; if it is 0 the limit
is 0xFFFF. This rule works well since expand-down segments are usually used

for stacks. Note, however, that the rule also applies if an expand-down segment descriptor is loaded into a nonstack segment descriptor register (e.g., DS_desc).

In summary, the Big/DefaultAttr flag is used in the following ways:

1. if Big is 1, ESP is used; if Big is 0, SP is used.

2. if Big is 1 wraparound occurs at offset 0xFFFFFFFF; otherwise wraparound occurs at offset 0xFFFF.

3. if the descriptor is for an expand-down segment Big determines the segment's limit: it is 0xFFFFFFFF is Big is 1, otherwise it is 0xFFFF.

2.8.2 Push and pop definitions

We end the discussion of 80*x*86 stack operations by giving formal descriptions of the push and pop operations. The operations are of the form push*x* and pop*x*, where *x* is either 2 or 4, depending on whether the operation is on a WORD or a DWORD.

```
push2(value)
WORD value;
{  /* == Use ESP if SS_desc.DefaultAttr == 1 (i.e. "Big" stack); else use SP == */
   DWORD stack_ptr = SS_desc.DefaultAttr ? (ESP – 2) : (DWORD) (SP – 2) ;

   /* == Use decremented stack pointer to write to stack == */
   write2(SS_INDEX, stack_ptr, value);

   /* == Set SP or ESP to new stack pointer value == */
   if ( SS_desc.DefaultAttr == 1 )
      ESP = stack_ptr;
   else
      SP = (WORD) stack_ptr;
}


push4(value)
DWORD value;
{  /* == Use ESP if SS_desc.DefaultAttr == 1 (i.e. "Big" stack); else use SP == */
   DWORD stack_ptr = SS_desc.DefaultAttr ? (ESP – 4) : (DWORD) (SP – 4) ;

   /* == Use decremented stack pointer to write to stack == */
   write2(SS_INDEX, stack_ptr, value);
```

```
/* == Set SP or ESP to new stack pointer value == */
if ( SS_desc.DefaultAttr == 1 )
    ESP = stack_ptr;
else
    SP = (WORD) stack_ptr;
}
```

It is worthwhile considering what happens when SP or ESP is itself pushed onto the stack. Is the value pushed the decremented value, or the nondecremented value? The definition above suggests that the nondecremented value is used. This is what occurs on the 80286 and its successors. The 8086, however, pushes the value after decrementing SP.

Now let us look at the pop operations.

```
WORD pop2()
{   DWORD stack_ptr = SS_desc.DefaultAttr ? ESP : (DWORD) SP ;
    WORD pop_val = read2(SS_INDEX, stack_ptr);

    /* == Set SP or ESP to new stack pointer value == */
    if ( SS_desc.DefaultAttr == 1 )
        ESP = stack_ptr+2;
    else
        SP = (WORD) (stack_ptr+2);

    /* == Return popped value == */
    return( pop_val );
}


DWORD pop4()
{   DWORD stack_ptr = SS_desc.DefaultAttr ? ESP : (DWORD) SP ;
    DWORD pop_val = read4(SS_INDEX, stack_ptr);

    /* == Set SP or ESP to new stack pointer value == */
    if ( SS_desc.DefaultAttr == 1 )
        ESP = stack_ptr+4;
    else
        SP = (WORD) (stack_ptr+4);

    /* == Return popped value == */
    return( pop_val );
}
```

As a notational convenience, the function calls **pushOS** and **popOS** are often used in much of the C language architecture descriptions. These translate to their respective function calls with *OS* replaced by the operand size. In C notation they can be defined as

```
#define pushOS(x)  ( (os == 16) ? push2(x) : push4(x) )
#define popOS(x)    ( (os == 16) ? pop2(x) : pop4(x) )
```

2.9 I/O access

I/O access is substantially simpler than memory access. It differs from memory access in the following respects:

1. an I/O access is not subject to translation: the address specified by an I/O instruction is directly presented (as the physical address) to the I/O subsystem.

2. since there is no notion of a "logical I/O address," there is no notion of an "I/O segment" either.

3. the I/O address is substantially smaller than the memory address space: only 2^{16} (or 65536) byte-sized I/O ports are supported.

4. unlike memory segments and memory pages, groups of I/O addresses cannot be made selectively read-only. On the 80286, however, the IOPL *facility* can be used to completely disable both reads and writes to all I/O ports. Furthermore, on the 80376, 80386, and i486 any subset of I/O ports can be totally disabled; both reads and writes are disabled to this subset of ports. Selective disabling of ports is done using a task-specific bit map called an *I/O permission map*. IOPL is described in §2.6.2 on page 41; the I/O permission map is described later in this section.

5. the only instructions provided for I/O access are those that move data between an I/O port and register (instructions IN and OUT), or an I/O port and a string of memory locations (instructions INSx and OUTSx.)

As the name suggests, the purpose of the I/O address space is to store control and status ports of I/O devices. To accommodate C language notation, the I/O space is defined as a vector of BYTEPORTs.

```
BYTEPORT io_vec[65536];
```

Each BYTEPORT is an 8-bit quantity. Two consecutive BYTEPORTs make a WORDPORT, and two consecutive WORDPORTs make a DWORDPORT. WORDPORT and DWORDPORT addresses are usually aligned at multiples of 2 and 4, respectively. Misaligned accesses are permitted by the architecture. However, just as with misaligned memory references, more than one physical I/O access is generated. Note that the order in which the the low and high addresses of the misaligned reference is generated is not specified by the architecture. This can cause unpredictable I/O device behavior, since port access sequencing is typically important when communicating with a peripheral device.

The IN, OUT, INS*x*, and OUTS*x* instructions operate in two steps:

1. check protection attributes of I/O port being accessed; signal a GP fault if access disallowed. (No protection checks are done on the 8086 and 80186; accordingly, faults are never signaled on them.)

2. if access allowed, perform read or write of specified I/O port

In the instruction descriptions in Chapter 4 the following shorthand is used for I/O accesses. A sample I/O port read is

```
/* == Read the BYTEPORTs port and port+1 into reg AX == */
AX = *( (WORDPORT *) port );      /* AL = io_vec[port]; */
                                  /* AH = io_vec[port+1]; */
```

and a sample I/O port write is

```
/* == Store EAX into BYTEPORTs port, port+1, port+2 and port+3 == */
*( (DWORDPORT *) port ) = EAX;  /* io_vec[port] = EAX & 0xFF; */
                                /* io_vec[port+1] = (EAX >> 8) & 0xFF;
                                /* io_vec[port+2] = (EAX >> 16) & 0xFF;
                                /* io_vec[port+3] = (EAX >> 24) & 0xFF;
```

2.9.1 I/O space protection checks

The protection attribute of an I/O port either enables or disables access to the port. If a port is disabled, a general protection fault is signaled when an access is attempted.

The algorithm used to check whether a port is enabled or disabled is based on settings in a bit map called the **I/O permission map**. The bit map is a contiguous area of upto 8,193 bytes that is stored in the highest addresses of a TSS32.[17] To check if a BYTEPORT *port* is accessible, *port* is used as a bit index into the I/O bit map. If the extracted bit's value is 0 the access is allowed, if it is

---

[17] The format of a 32-bit TSS TSS32 and its usage is described in §2.11 on page 128.

1 the access is denied. If *port* is a WORDPORT, the bits at index *port* and *port*+1 must both be 0 for the access to succeed. For a DWORDPORT whose address is *port*, all four bits starting at bit index *port* must be 0 for the access to succeed.

Note that an I/O bit map of 8,192 bytes is sufficient to map all 65,536 addresses in the I/O address space. However, an additional byte that is initialized to 0xFF must be allocated at the end of the table. This byte handles the boundary case where an access to WORDPORT 0xFFFF or DWORDPORT 0xFFFD (or beyond) is attempted.

If a particular system does not support all 65,536 I/O ports, the bit map can be truncated by reducing the size of the Limit field in the TSS32. For example, if a system only supports I/O addresses 0 through 0xFFF (i.e., 4,096 BYTEPORTs) a 513-byte I/O bit map suffices. This can be achieved by storing the I/O map starting at byte offset Limit-(4096/8), or Limit-512. Regardless of whether the I/O bit map is truncated using a reduced Limit value, it must be the case that a full-sized bit map consisting of 0x2001 bytes (i.e., 8,192 bytes + 1 boundary byte) does not exceed the maximum TSS limit of 0xFFFF. More precisely, if IOBase is the offset of the I/O permission map in a TSS32, the following relation must hold

IOBase + 0x2000 ≤ 0xFFFF, that is,

IOBase ≤ 0xDFFF

If this relation does not hold, I/O permission checks may succeed when they should fail.

The algorithm described above is reiterated below as a C language function. This function, called IOPermission, accepts two parameters: an I/O port address *port* and a port size *os*. *os* is set to 1 for a BYTEPORT, to 2 for a WORDPORT, and to 4 for a DWORDPORT. It returns TRUE if access to the specified port is valid; if invalid, it returns FALSE.

```
BOOLEAN IOPermission(port, os)
PORT port;
int os;
{   WORD IOBase;            /* I/O bit map base address */
    WORD permbits;          /* buffer for permission bits */
    unsigned bi;            /* port bit index into permbits buffer */
    short saveCPL;          /* CPL save area while reading permission map */

    /* == Make sure current TSS is a TSS32.  If not, disallow access. == */
    if ( TSS_desc.Type == NOTBUSY_TSS16 )
        return(FALSE);
```

```
/* == Read offset of I/O permission map into IOBase.  The offset is relative to the base
      of the TSS == */
saveCPL = CPL;
CPL = 0;
IOBase = read2(TSS_INDEX, 0x66);  /* see page 73 */

/* == Read WORD containing the permission bits for the accessed port(s).  Note that an
implementation is required not to read more than a WORD of data.  However, it is free
to read only a BYTE if the permission bits to be checked fit within a BYTE. == */
permbits = read2(TSS_INDEX, IOBase + port/8);  /* see page 73 */
CPL = saveCPL;

/* == Check permission bits for selected port(s): all must be 0 for the access to
      succeed. == */
bi = port & 0x7;  /* get bit index into permbits */
if ( permbits⟨(bi+os-1) : bi⟩ == 0 )
   return(TRUE);
else
   return(FALSE);
}
```

2.10 Gates and privilege level transitions

One issue that has not been covered yet is how privilege level transitions are made. A program cannot simply issue a "load CPL" instruction to change its privilege level, for doing so would allow a program to subvert the entire notion of privilege-level-based protection. In the 80x86, a transition to a greater level of privilege (i.e., to a numerically smaller CPL value) is mediated through a descriptor called a **gate**. A transition to a lesser privilege level does not require any special data structures: it is accomplished by executing the "subroutine return" instruction RETF, where the return address is the address at the lesser level of privilege.

Now let us look at the main features of gates. A gate always points to an entry point of a routine. Thus, all gate types (except for a TASKGATE) contain a SELECTOR and an offset value. The entry point of the gate is at the specified offset within the segment named by the SELECTOR. As shown in Figure 2.38, there are four types of gates:

1. *call gates:* used to transition to a routine that executes at the same, or greater, privilege level (i.e. the CPL at the call gate target is numerically less than or equal to the CPL at the time the gate is referenced.) Call gates can only reside in the local descriptor table (LDT) or the global descriptor table (GDT).

2. *interrupt gates:* used mostly to enter a hardware interrupt service routine. Interrupt gates can reside only in the interrupt descriptor table (IDT).

3. *trap gates:* used mostly to enter an exception or software interrupt service routine. Like interrupt gates, trap gates can only reside in the IDT.

4. *task gates:* used to transition to a new task. Instead of containing an entry point (i.e. a SELECTOR and offset), a task gate contains a SELECTOR that

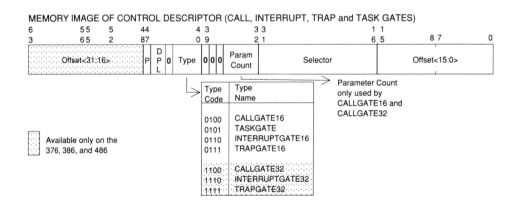

Figure 2.38: 80x86 gate descriptor formats

names a special kind of segment called a *task state segment*. A task gate can reside in the GDT, LDT, or the IDT.

This section will only examine the use of call gates. The control transfer mechanism discussed applies to interrupt and trap gates also. However there are enough minor operational differences that their description is deferred to §2.12.8 (starting on page 159). Task gates are used to switch processor context. Although such a context switch can result in a privilege level change, the intent behind task switches is completely different from (intratask) privilege transitions. Tasks and task switches are described in §2.11 on page 128.

As was shown in Figure 2.38, a call gate stores a SELECTOR and an OFFSET. Since the call gate is a descriptor stored in the LDT or GDT, it is itself referenced using a SELECTOR. If a far CALL uses a SELECTOR that names a call gate, the SELECTOR and OFFSET specified by the gate is used as the branch target. The OFFSET specified in the far CALL itself is ignored.

To allow selective access to the routines pointed at by call gates, the privilege level of the gate (i.e., the DPL field of the gate's descriptor) is compared against CPL. Similarly, the RPL field of the gate's SELECTOR is also compared against CPL. Both privilege indicators must be at least as privileged (i.e., no greater numerically) than CPL. If this check fails, a GP fault is signaled.

Assuming the check passes, the descriptor named by the SELECTOR stored in the gate is read in. This descriptor *must* be for an executable segment; any other descriptor type results in a GP exception. Assuming this is true, the new code segment is defined by this descriptor. Furthermore, the branch target offset (i.e., the new EIP value) is set to the OFFSET value specified in the gate. In addition to performing a branch, CPL is also updated to the DPL of the new code segment descriptor.

The issue of privilege level change requires further study. For a particular CPL value prior to a gated CALL, the new privilege level after the CALL, call it *new_cpl*, is restricted to be no greater than the (old) CPL. This makes sense since the purpose of call gates is to mediate access to privileged services. (Routines that perform non-sensitive services (e.g., compute square root) but need to be shared by many different privilege levels can be stored in conforming code segments. Conforming segments are described in the next section.)

There still are two possibilities to consider: *new_cpl* == CPL and *new_cpl* < CPL. If new_cpl == CPL no change in privilege level occurs. The CALL is processed normally in this case; that is, the address of the instruction following the CALL is pushed onto the stack, and control is transferred to the SELECTOR and OFFSET named in the gate. If new_cpl < CPL, the following six actions are taken:

1. The current stack pointer is stored in a temporary location, and the stack pointer corresponding to the new privilege level is stored in SS:ESP (if the new SS points at a "Big" stack segment), or in SS:SP (if the new SS points at a stack segment that is not "Big").

2. the old stack pointer value is pushed onto the new stack.

3. a number of parameters are copied from the top of the old stack to the new stack. The number copied is specified by the ParamCount field in the call gate. If the call gate is a CALLGATE16, ParamCount WORDs are copied; if it is a CALLGATE32, ParamCount DWORDs are copied.

4. the instruction address (CS:EIP) of the instruction following the CALL is pushed onto the new stack.

5. the privilege level (CPL) is changed to the DPL of the new code segment.

6. control is transferred to the SELECTOR and OFFSET named in the gate; that is, CS:EIP is updated.

The gated call procedure discussed so far is formally described in the far CALL instruction definition on page 295. The description there invokes the routine priv_lev_switch_CALL to perform the interlevel transfer of control. This routine, whose main features are outlined in the list above, is now defined in C language. The routine accepts three parameters. The first parameter, *os*, is set based on the type of call gate used: if the call gate is a CALLGATE16, *os* is set to 16; if it is a CALLGATE32, *os* is set to 32.[18] The *os* value determines whether data pushed onto the stack (e.g., the stack pointer, the return address) are WORDs or DWORDs. The remaining two parameters are the new CS descriptor new_CS_desc, and *parm_count*, a count of the number of parameters to be copied from the old stack to the new stack. Note that *param_count* is in units of WORDs if *os* is 16, and in units of DWORDs if *os* is 32.

```
priv_lev_switch_CALL(os, new_CS_desc, parm_count)
int os; /* Set to 16 for CALLGATE16, 32 for CALLGATE32 */
DESCR new_CS_desc;
int parm_count;
```

---

[18] Note that the 80286 only supports CALLGATE16s, the 80386 and i486 support both CALLGATE16s and CALLGATE32s. The 80386 and i486 support CALLGATE16s and CALLGATE32s for backward compatibility with the 80286. The 80376, which is "sideways compatible" with the 80386, only supports CALLGATE32s.

```
{  short new_CPL;
   short save_CPL;
   SELECTOR new_SS;
   DWORD new_ESP;
   DESCR new_SS_desc;

   /* == Set the new CPL to the new code segment descriptor's DPL == */
   new_CPL = new_CS_desc.DPL;

   /* == Read in new privilege level's stack pointer.  Note that the high order WORD of
         new_ESP is undefined if the current TSS is TSS16.  The TSS_read routines are
         defined on page 76 == */
   if ( TSS_desc.Type == TSS16 )
   {  new_ESP⟨15:0⟩ = TSS_read2( TSS, (new_CPL*4 + 2) );
      new_ESP⟨31:16⟩ = undefined;
      new_SS = TSS_read2( TSS, (new_CPL*4 + 4) );
   }
   else /* TSS_desc.Type == TSS32 */
   {  new_ESP = TSS_read4( TSS, (new_CPL*8 + 4) );
      new_SS = TSS_read2( TSS, (new_CPL*8 + 8) );
   }

   /* == Load new SS, temporarily setting CPL to new_CPL.  This is done so that that the
         load_SS can be used to load the new descriptor. == */
   save_CPL = CPL;
   CPL = new_CPL;
   new_SS_desc = load_SS(new_SS, TRUE);  /* see page 70 */
   CPL = save_CPL;

   /* == If in VM86 mode, push REAL-mode GS, FS, DS, ES, and invalidate them.  The
      push routine new_stk_push is defined below. == */
   if ( mode == VM86 )
   {  new_ESP = new_stk_push(os, new_SS, new_SS_desc, new_ESP, GS);
      new_ESP = new_stk_push(os, new_SS, new_SS_desc, new_ESP, FS);
      new_ESP = new_stk_push(os, new_SS, new_SS_desc, new_ESP, DS);
      new_ESP = new_stk_push(os, new_SS, new_SS_desc, new_ESP, ES);
      DS = ES = FS = GS = 0;
      DS_desc.Valid = ES_desc.Valid = FS_desc.Valid = GS_desc.Valid = 0;
   }

   /* == Now push old SS and [E]SP, ... */
   new_ESP = new_stk_push(os, new_SS, new_SS_desc, new_ESP, SS);
   new_ESP = new_stk_push(os, new_SS, new_SS_desc, new_ESP, ESP);

   /* ... copy parameters, ... */
   stack_ptr = ESP + (parm_count * (os / 8));
   for ( i = 1;  i <= parm_count;  i++ )
   {  stack_ptr = SS_desc.DefaultAttr ? (ESP – (os/8)) : (DWORD) (SP – (os/8)) ;
      if ( os == 2 )
         tmp = read2(SS_INDEX, stack_ptr);           /* see page 73 */
      else  /* os == 4 */
         tmp = read4(SS_INDEX, stack_ptr);           /* see page 74 */
```

```
      new_ESP = new_stk_push(os, new_SS, new_SS_desc, new_ESP, tmp);
   }

   /* ..., and push old CS and [E]IP == */
   new_ESP = new_stk_push(os, new_SS, new_SS_desc, new_ESP, CS);
   new_ESP = new_stk_push(os, new_SS, new_SS_desc, new_ESP, EIP);

   /* == Clear VM in case it was set, and setup SS:[E]SP, and CPL == */
   VM = 0;
   SS = new_SS;
   SS_desc = new_SS_desc;
   if ( SS_desc.Default == 1 ) /* "Big" stack */
      ESP = new_ESP;
   else /* 64KB stack */
      SP = new_ESP⟨15:0⟩;

   CPL = new_CPL;
}
```

Since the normal push*x* and routines push*x* routines operate assuming SS:[E]SP is the stack pointer, they cannot be used to copy parameters from the new stack to the old stack. A specialized routine, new_stk_push, does the job of pushing data onto the new stack. The parameters passed to the routine are the operand size (*os*), the new stack's SELECTOR (new_SS), descriptor (new_desc), and stack offset (new_ESP), and the value to be pushed. If *os* is 16, *value* is interpreted as a WORD; that is, only a WORD is pushed. If *os* is 32, a DWORD is pushed.

```
DWORD new_stk_push(os, new_SS, new_desc, new_ESP, value)
int os;
DESCR new_desc;
DWORD new_ESP;
DWORD value;
{  int saveCPL = CPL;
   DWORD stack_ptr = new_ESP – os;

   /* == Use only the low order WORD of the new stack's pointer if DefaultAttr (i.e., "Big"
        flag) is set to 0 == */
   if ( new_desc.DefaultAttr == 0 )
      stack_ptr = stack_ptr⟨15:0⟩;
```

```
/* == Use decremented stack pointer to write os bytes to stack.  Note that the linear
       address of the write is computed inline to accommodate specialized error
       reporting.  == */
if ( new_desc.Valid  &&  new_desc.Writable  &&  in_limits(new_desc, new_ESP, os) )
{   /* == Write to new stack with CPL set to 0.  Thus, the push succeeds even if an
           application makes a call to a kernel routine, where the kernel routine's stack
           occupies privileged pages == */
    CPL = 0;
    if ( os == 2 )
      LA_write2(new_desc.Base + stack_ptr,  value);
    else  /* os == 4 */
      LA_write4(new_desc.Base + stack_ptr,  value);
    CPL = saveCPL;
}
else
    /* == Access rule violation: signal STACK fault and report SELECTOR of faulty SS as
           error code == */
    signal_fault(STACK, new_SS);

/* == Function returns decremented stack pointer value == */
return( stack_ptr );
}
```

2.10.1 Using call gates in JMP instructions

The only use of call gates shown so far is in the context of the far CALL
instruction. Call gates are usable by one other instruction: far JMPs. However,
far JMPs through gates are only allowed if the gated transfer of control does not
result in a change in privilege level. This can happen if the code descriptor
pointed at by the gate has a DPL whose value matches CPL. The other
possibility is that a transfer is made to a conforming code segment.

2.10.2 Conforming segments

All the fuss made about privilege levels by the $80x86$ architecture is done
presumably because such code operates on sensitive data, or because it has direct
access to shared resources (e.g., a printer's communication port). A system may
have numerous service routines, however, that do not perform sensitive
operations. These routines may just be a packaging of commonly used functions;
for example, a string copy routine or math library functions. One way to
implement such functions is to store in a code segment that has a DPL of 0. This
way, all privilege levels can access the routine via a call gate. This approach is
valid, but has the following problems:

1. gated calls take substantially longer to execute than normal far calls through a code segment descriptor.

2. since the service routine operates with a CPL of 0, care must be taken to ensure that no parameter passed to it (either directly or indirectly) points to data stored in a segment that is inaccessible to the caller. This is simply the Trojan horse problem discussed on page 45.

3. the mechanics of installing a service routine is complicated. In particular, the casual (nonprivileged) user will not be allowed to install such routines.

To address these performance and convenience-of-use issues, the 80x86 introduces the notion of a **conforming segment**. A far CALL or far JMP to a conforming segment does not result in CPL change (or a stack change). Since there is no change in CPL, the routine invoked in the conforming segment has access to exactly the same data that the caller had. Furthermore, a transfer to a conforming segment occurs in roughly the same number of clocks as a transfer to a same-level segment. Since a conforming segment contains code, it can never be written to. However, code executing at *any* privilege level is allowed to read data stored in a conforming segment. Hence a conforming segment is a good place to store globally used constants (e.g., system configuration information).

For a formal description of conforming segment access rules for code fetch, see the load_CS routine described on page 69. For similar access rules for data access, see the load_data_seg routine definition (described on page 71). Note that a conforming segment can never be loaded into the stack segment descriptor register since stacks must always be writable.

2.11 Task switches

When a task switch occurs in an operating system, all context related to the currently executing task is saved away, and a new context is brought in. Context information not only includes the CPU registers, but also the memory occupied by the task, opened file handles, and access ports to other devices. The 80x86 notion of a task switch is small subset of all these context elements: here only major CPU registers of the current context are saved and a new one brought in. In this sense an 80x86 task is more akin to the notion of a "thread" in Mach or OS/2, than to a full task context. This section discusses how the 80x86 task switch mechanism operates.

Before starting, note that the task switch function can be performed without the aid of the 80x86 task switch mechanism. In fact, the 8086 and 80186 do not implement any task switch in hardware (and so, none of the features described in this section is available on them). Multi-tasking systems implemented on these low-end 80x86 implementations perform task switches using a sequence of (simple) 80x86 instructions. For the remainder of this section, the terms "task" and "task switch" will refer to the corresponding features explicitly defined by the 80x86 architecture and implemented by the 80286 and its successors.

A task switch can occur as a result of one of many actions

1. by executing a far CALL or far JMP, where the SELECTOR of the CALL or JMP names a task gate or TSS. (Task gates and TSSes are described below.)

2. by executing a software interrupt instruction (INT).

3. as a consequence of entering an exception, or hardware interrupt handler.

4. by executing an IRET instruction: a successful task switch can set the "nested task" flag (NT). If an IRET is executed with NT set, the current task state is saved and a task switch is performed to the task that invoked the current task.

These actions have one factor in common: they reference a descriptor in either the GDT or LDT (in the case of CALLs and JMPs) or a descriptor in the IDT (in the case of interrupts and exceptions). If the descriptor's type is a TASKGATE the transfer of control is done as a task switch. (The action taken for non-TASKGATE entries such as call gates is discussed in §2.10; the action taken for interrupt gates is discussed in §2.12.8.)

The TASKGATEs Selector field (see Figure 2.38 on page 122) points to another descriptor called the **task state segment** (**TSS**). For reasons that will become apparent soon, the TSS descriptor must reside in the GDT. If it doesn't (or if it is not a TSS descriptor) an error is signaled. The TSS descriptor defines a *special segment*. Recall (from §2.7.2.2 on page 62) that special segment descriptors are similar to data segment descriptors in that they have Base and Limit fields that define a region in the linear address space. However, they store data that are only accessed under special circumstances. In the case of TSSes, the data stored is the state of the registers of a particular task. In particular, the TSS pointed at by a TASKGATE's Selector field contains the register state of a (new) task.

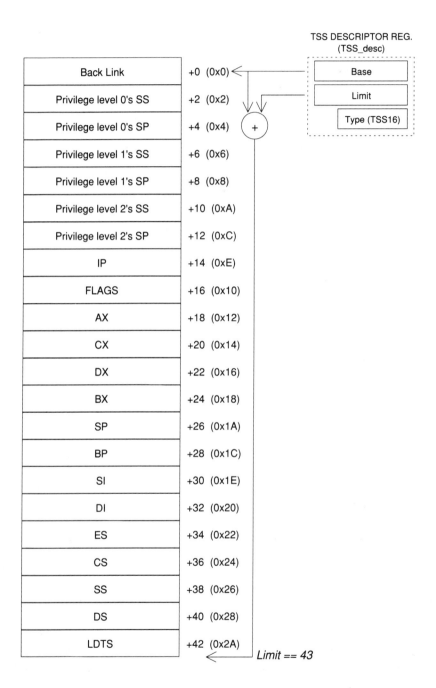

Figure 2.39: 80286-style task state segments (TSS16)

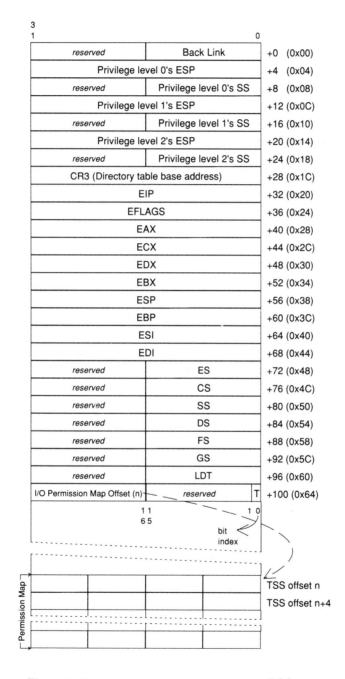

Figure 2.40: 80386-style task state segments (TSS32)

There are two types of task state segments: TSS16 and TSS32. TSS16, shown in Figure 2.39, stores an image of the 80x86 registers in their 16-bit forms. TSS32, shown in Figure 2.40, stores a complete 32-bit image of major 80x86 registers. TSS16, which originated in the 80286, does not store the upper halves of registers. TSS32s are unavailable on the 80286. This corresponds with the fact that it is a 16-bit processor. Note that a TSS16 is often called a 80286-style TSS, whereas a TSS32 is often called a 80386-style TSS. TSS32s are only supported on the 80376, 80386, and i486. For backward compatibility, the 80386 and i486 also support TSS16s. In the figures, note that both TSS structures are pointed at by the TSS_desc descriptor register. This register stores the currently active TSS descriptor information on-chip. Any successful task switch updates the register.

A TSS16 is differentiated from a TSS32 by the Type field of its descriptor. TSSes are always either "not busy" or "busy." Software that creates a TSS descriptor invariably initializes it to be "not busy." If a task switch is initaited using the TSS, the 80x86 automatically marks the TSS "busy". This ensures that no further activations of the task corresponding to the TSS are possible while the task is still active. The Type field of a TSS descriptor not only indicates whether it is a TSS16 or TSS32, but also indicates whether or not it is busy. In particular, there are four Types of TSSes: NOTBUSY_TSS16, BUSY_TSS16, NOTBUSY_TSS32, and BUSY_TSS32. See Figure 2.26 on page 64 for their bit encodings.

Now let us see the steps taken to transfer control from the current task to a new task. The discussion assumes that *tg_desc* is the descriptor of task gate of the task to be transferred to.

1. Ensure *tg_desc.Selector* is valid (i.e., not a null SELECTOR and resident in the GDT).

2. Read descriptor named by *tg_desc.Selector* and validate it. Validity checks include a test to make sure that the descriptor is a "not busy" TSS descriptor (i.e., a NOTBUSY_TSS16 or NOTBUSY_TSS32); for task returns (i.e., task switches via IRETs) the test ensures the opposite, that is, that the descriptor is a "busy" TSS (a BUSY_TSS16 or BUSY_TSS32). A TSS descriptor is marked "busy" the task corresponding to it gets invoked. It is marked "not busy" when the task is terminated (via an IRET).

3. Mark the TSS descriptor "busy." This prevents repeated invocations of a task while it is still active.

4. Save the task state of the *current* task in its task state segment.

5. If this is a nested task switch, save the SELECTOR of the current TSS in the new BackLink field of the new TSS.

6. Establish the new task state by loading it from the new task state segment. Since the task state includes the instruction pointer, loading the new task state results in a transfer of control to the entry point of the new task.

The steps outlined above leave out some of the details that the task switch mechanism addresses. For example, on the 80376, 80386, and i486, the debug address match enable flags are disabled by a task switch. This is necessary since address maps (i.e., the page tables) can change when a task switch occurs. These details are covered in the formal definition of task switch, shown below.

The definition of the first step, reading the SELECTOR stored in the task gate and validating it, is shown in the definitions of the actions where a task switch is allowed. For example, see the definition of the task JMP (page 458) and task CALL (page 301) instructions to see how the task gate is validated by these instructions. As a sample, the task gate analysis routine for task switches that are invoked using an interrupt vector entry is shown below. This routine, int_via_task_gate, accepts three parameters: a SELECTOR *sel*, a flag *err_flag*, and an error code *err_code*. *sel* names the TSS SELECTOR found in the task gate. The other two parameters are peculiar to control transfers initiated via the interrupt vector. They signal whether or not an error code should be pushed onto the new task's stack, and if so, the value of the error code. Error codes are discussed in the section on interrupts and exceptions; see, in particular, subsection §2.12.2 (starting on page 146).

```
int_via_task_gate(sel, err_flag, err_code)
SELECTOR sel;
BOOLEAN err_flag;
WORD err_code;
{
    /* == Ensure selector named in task gate is not NULL, nor in the LDT == */
    if ( nullSel(sel) || sel.TI == 1 )
        signal_fault(GP, (sel & 0xFFFC));        /* see page 155 */

    /* == Ensure task gate selector names an available TSS16 or TSS32, and if so, that the
    TSS is present (i.e., Valid flag is set) == */
    desc = read_descr(sel, FALSE);
    if ( desc.Type != NOTBUSY_TSS16  &&  desc.Type != NOTBUSY_TSS32 )
        signal_fault(GP, (sel & 0xFFFC));        /* see page 155 */
```

```
if ( !desc.Valid )
    signal_fault(NP, (sel & 0xFFFC));       /* see page 155 */

/* Do the task switch as a nested switch ("TRUE" parameter).  See the definition of
    enter_new_task below for the semantics of a task switch. */
enter_new_task(desc.Selector, desc, TRUE, err_flag, err_code);
}
```

The primary task switch routine is the enter_new_task routine, defined below.
The first two parameters to the routine, a SELECTOR *sel* and a DESCR *desc*,
specify the SELECTOR and corresponding descriptor of the new TSS. (All
callers of this routine verify that the descriptor belongs to a TSS and that the TSS
is "not busy.") The third parameter, *nested_task*, is set to TRUE by the caller if
the current task is to be left active.[19] Doing so sets the NT flag in the EFLAGS
image of the new task and also saves the current task's TSS SELECTOR in the
new TSS's BackLink field. This allows the task return instruction (IRET) to
resume execution of the calling task once the called task completes. Note that
the current task's SELECTOR is not passed as a parameter to enter_new_task.
This is because this SELECTOR (as well as the current task's descriptor
contents) are stored in the special segment register TSS and the descriptor
register TSS_desc, respectively. The remaining parameters to enter_new_task
are *err_flag* and *err_code*. As discussed above, their use is in reporting error
codes when servicing exceptions.

```
enter_new_task(sel, desc, nested_task, err_flag, err_code)
SELECTOR sel;
DESCR desc;
BOOLEAN nested_task;
BOOLEAN err_flag;
WORD err_code;
{ BOOLEAN trapAfterSwitch;

    /* == Set the "Busy" bit atomically in the new TSS == */
    lock(DESCR_TABLE); /* gain exclusive access to descr. tables */
    d2 = DTAB_read1(sel, GDT_desc, sel.Index*8 + 5, TRUE);      /* see page 74 */
    DTAB_write1(sel, GDT_desc, sel.Index*8 + 5, d2 | 2, TRUE);  /* see page 81 */
    unlock(DESCR_TABLE); /* release descriptor tables */

    /* == Save current task state if feasible.  Disable further "save_task_state" invocations
        (caused by faults while saving state, etc.) until load of new context is complete. ==
        */
    if ( ! task_switch_in_progress )
    {   task_switch_in_progress = TRUE;
        save_task_state();
    }
```

---

[19] This is done when the task switch is initiated via a CALL instruction, or because of an interrupt or exception.

```
/* == Don't carry over single stepping from task invoker's environment == */
prev_TF = 0;

/* == Load new TSS descriptor; save back link if chained task switch == */
TSS_desc = desc;   /* TSS_desc now points at new TSS */
if (nested_task)   /* save caller's TSS selector */
   TSS_write2(sel, 0, TSS);              /* see page 82 */

/* == Read in new task state values; push error code if needed == */
if ( TSS_desc.Type == NOTBUSY_TSS16 )  /* 80286-style TSS (TSS16) */
{  read_TSS16(sel, TSS_desc, nested_task);  /* see page 137 */
   trapAfterSwitch = FALSE;
   if ( err_flag )  /* push WORD-sized error code */
      push2(err_code);      /* see page 116 */
}
else  /* 80386/i486-style TSS TSS32 */
{  trapAfterSwitch = read_TSS32(sel, TSS_desc, nested_task);  /* see page 138 */
   /* == Push error code as a DWORD (to retain stack alignment).  The value of the
         high-order WORD of the error code is undefined. == */
   if ( err_flag )
      push4(err_code);      /* see page 116 */
}

/* == Reset debugging "local enable" flag (L0, L1, L2, and L3), and the "local exact" flag
      (LE) stored in DR7.  This is only done on the 80376, 80386, and i486 == */
DR7⟨8⟩ = DR7⟨6⟩ = DR7⟨4⟩ = DR7⟨2⟩ = DR7⟨0⟩ = FALSE;

/* == If TSS32, raise debug fault if T bit set in TSS == */
if ( trapAfterSwitch )
{  /* Set "Because" code to "T bit set in TSS" (i.e. set BT flag) */
   DR6⟨15⟩ = 1;
   signal_fault(DEBUG);          /* see page 155 */
}

/* == Clear XH_flag in case this invocation of enter_new_task was because of an
      exception or hardware interrupt.  (See §2.12.2 on page 146 for more on the
      XH_flag) == */
XH_flag = FALSE;
}
```

The enter_new_task routine makes calls to the subordinate routines
save_task_state, read_TSS16, and read_TSS32. Save_task_state writes the
contents of the major 80x86 registers to the TSS belonging to the current task.
There is no need to pass parameters to this routine, since both the current TSS's
SELECTOR and descriptor are in the task state segment register TSS and the
descriptor register TSS_desc, respectively. Examining the Type field of
TSS_desc allows save_task_state to determine whether 16-bit registers (TSS16)
or 32-bit registers (TSS32) should be saved.

```
save_task_state
{
    /* == Save general register, segment registers, flags, EIP == */
    if ( TSS_desc.Type == NOTBUSY_TSS32 )  /* 80386/i486-style TSS */
    {   TSS_write4(sel, 32, EIP);
        TSS_write4(sel, 36, EFLAGS);
        TSS_write4(sel, 40, EAX);
        TSS_write4(sel, 44, ECX);
        TSS_write4(sel, 48, EDX);
        TSS_write4(sel, 52, EBX);
        TSS_write4(sel, 56, ESP);
        TSS_write4(sel, 60, EBP);
        TSS_write4(sel, 64, ESI);
        TSS_write4(sel, 68, EDI);
        TSS_write2(sel, 72, ES);
        TSS_write2(sel, 76, CS);
        TSS_write2(sel, 80, SS);
        TSS_write2(sel, 84, DS);
        TSS_write2(sel, 88, FS);
        TSS_write2(sel, 92, GS);
    }
    else  /* 80286-style TSS (TSS16): save low-order WORDs */
    {   TSS_write2(sel, 14, EIP);
        TSS_write2(sel, 16, EFLAGS);
        TSS_write2(sel, 18, EAX);
        TSS_write2(sel, 20, ECX);
        TSS_write2(sel, 22, EDX);
        TSS_write2(sel, 24, EBX);
        TSS_write2(sel, 26, ESP);
        TSS_write2(sel, 28, EBP);
        TSS_write2(sel, 30, ESI);
        TSS_write2(sel, 32, EDI);
        TSS_write2(sel, 34, ES);
        TSS_write2(sel, 36, CS);
        TSS_write2(sel, 38, SS);
        TSS_write2(sel, 40, DS);
    }
}
```

The read_TSS16 and read_TSS32 routines are used to load the contents of a TSS into the 80*x*86 registers. The TSS's SELECTOR and descriptor contents are passed as the parameters *sel* and *desc* to the routines. The difference between the two routines is that read_TSS16 loads only the WORD component of registers, whereas read_TSS32 loads all register bits. Several other actions are taken by read_TSS32. For example, it loads the page directory base register, CR3. It also has the capability to enter VM86 state; doing so requires loading the segment descriptor registers with REAL-mode-style descriptor values. Another feature available only in TSS32's is the ability to generate a DEBUG exception whenever a task switch occurs. This exception occurs if the new task's TSS has its T flag set; see Figure 2.40 for the flag's location.

```
read_TSS16(sel, desc, nested_task)
SELECTOR sel;
DESCR desc;
BOOLEAN nested_task;
{   DESCR oldTSSDescTable = ( TSS⟨2⟩ ? LDT_desc : GDT_desc );

    /* == Read in register state, but first make sure that the last BYTE of the TSS is
         accessible. == */
    if ( TSS_desc.Limit < 43 )                /* new TSS16 is too small: segmentation fault */
        signal_fault(TASK,  (sel & 0xFFFC));
    LA_rdChk(TSS_desc.Base + 43);     /* verify page access rules (see page 93) */

    IP = TSS_read2(sel, 14);
    EFLAGS = TSS_read2(sel, 16);
    AX = TSS_read2(sel, 18);
    CX = TSS_read2(sel, 20);
    DX = TSS_read2(sel, 22);
    BX = TSS_read2(sel, 24);
    SP = TSS_read2(sel, 26);
    BP = TSS_read2(sel, 28);
    SI = TSS_read2(sel, 30);
    DI = TSS_read2(sel, 32);
    ES  = TSS_read2(sel, 34);
    CS  = TSS_read2(sel, 36);
    SS  = TSS_read2(sel, 38);
    DS  = TSS_read2(sel, 40);
    LDT = TSS_read2(sel, 42);

    /* == Zero out FS and GS (80376, 80386, and i486 only) since they are not supported
         by a TSS16 == */
    FS  = 0;
    GS  = 0;

    /* == Set NT bit in FLAGS if nested task switch == */
    if ( nested_task )
        NT = 1;  /* set FLAGS⟨14⟩ */

    /* == New TSS completely read in: OK to handle faults in new context == */
    prev = curr;

    /* == Clear caller's "Busy" bit if non-nested task switch == */
    if ( ! nested_task )
    {   lock(DESCR_TABLE);     /* disallow descr. table access to other system agents */
        temp = DTAB_read1(TSS, oldTSSDescTable, sel.Index*8 + 5);
        DTAB_write1(TSS, oldTSSDescTable, TSS.Index*8 + 5, temp & 0xFD);
        unlock(DESCR_TABLE); /* reallow other agents to access descriptor tables */
    }
```

```
    /* == Initialize TSS and set "task switched" (TS) bit == */
    TSS = sel;                    /* Set current TSS selector. */
    TS = 1;                       /* Set CR0⟨3⟩ */

    /* == Safe to reallow state saves; clear  task_switch_in_progress  flag. == */
    task_switch_in_progress = FALSE;

    /* == Finally, load in segment descriptor register contents == */
    load_protected_descr();          /* see page 140 */
}



BOOLEAN read_TSS32(sel, desc, nested_task)
SELECTOR sel;
DESCR desc;
BOOLEAN nested_task;
{   DESCR oldTSSDescTable = ( TSS⟨2⟩ ? LDT_desc : GDT_desc );
    char trapByte;

    /* == Read in register state, but first make sure that the last BYTE of the TSS is
          accessible. == */
    if ( TSS_desc.Limit < 100 )          /* new TSS32 is too small: segmentation fault */
       signal_fault(TASK,  (sel & 0xFFFC));
    LA_rdChk(TSS_desc.Base + 100);    /* verify page access rules (see page 93) */

    /* == Read in register state == */
    EIP = TSS_read4(sel, 32);
    EFLAGS = TSS_read4(sel, 36);
    EAX = TSS_read4(sel, 40);
    ECX = TSS_read4(sel, 44);
    EDX = TSS_read4(sel, 48);
    EBX = TSS_read4(sel, 52);
    ESP = TSS_read4(sel, 56);
    EBP = TSS_read4(sel, 60);
    ESI = TSS_read4(sel, 64);
    EDI = TSS_read4(sel, 68);
    ES  = TSS_read2(sel, 72);
    CS  = TSS_read2(sel, 76);
    SS  = TSS_read2(sel, 80);
    DS  = TSS_read2(sel, 84);
    FS  = TSS_read2(sel, 88);
    GS  = TSS_read2(sel, 92);
    LDT = TSS_read2(sel, 96);
    trapByte = TSS_read1(sel, 100);

    /* == Set NT bit in EFLAGS if nested task switch == */
    if ( nested_task )
       NT = 1;  /* set EFLAGS⟨14⟩ */

    /* == New TSS completely read in: OK to handle faults in new context == */
    prev = curr;
```

```
/* == Clear caller's "Busy" bit if nonnested task switch == */
if ( ! nested_task )
{   lock(DESCR_TABLE);      /* disallow descr. table access to other system agents */
    temp = DTAB_read1(TSS, oldTSSDescTable, sel.Index*8 + 5);
    DTAB_write1(TSS, oldTSSDescTable, TSS.Index*8 + 5, temp & 0xFD);
    unlock(DESCR_TABLE);  /* reallow other agents to access descr. tables */
}

/* == Initialize CR3 if paging enabled.  NOTE: The new TSS is read in using the old
      page table, but the new task's descriptors are read in using the new page table.
      == */
if ( PG )
    CR3 = TSS_read4(sel, 28);

/* == Initialize TSS and set "task switched" (TS) bit == */
TSS = sel; /* Set current TSS selector. */
TS = 1;    /* Set CR0⟨3⟩ */

/* == Safe to re-allow state saves == */
task_switch_in_progress = FALSE;

/* == Initialize descriptors and CPL based on execution mode == */
if ( VM ) /* VM-86 mode: simulate 8086-style segments (80386 and i486 only) */
{   /* == Load descriptors for ES, CS, SS, DS, FS, GS with REAL-mode values == */
    init_VM_desc(); /* see below */

    /* == VM-86 code executes at level 3 == */
    CPL = 3;

    /* == Load LDT segment register and descriptor == */
    LDT_desc.Valid = FALSE;
    LDT_desc = load_LDT(LDT);
}
else /* == PROTECTED-386 mode: protected mode descriptor load == */
    load_protected_descr();      /* see page 140 */

/* == Return TRUE if T flag set in TSS32.  (This will cause a DEBUG exception with the
      BT flag in DR6 set to 1) == */
return ( trapByte⟨0⟩ == 1 );
}
```

When the new TSS32's VM flag is set, the new task is activated using VM86 mode semantics. In particular, all segment descriptor registers are initialized as in REAL mode (i.e., with the Base set to the segment register contents multiplied by 16). This initialization is done by the init_VM_desc routine shown below. This routine is also used by IRET if an interrupt is returning to a VM86 execution environment.

```
init_VM_desc()
{
    /* == Initialize ES_desc, CS_desc, SS_desc, DS_desc, FS_desc, GS_desc == */
    for (i = 0; i <= 5; i++)
    {   descrVec[i].Valid = TRUE;
        descrVec[i].Base = curr.segReg[i] * 16;
        descrVec[i].Limit = 0xFFFF;
        descrVec[i].DPL = 3;
        descrVec[i].DefaultAttr = FALSE;
        descrVec[i].Readable = TRUE;
        descrVec[i].Writable = TRUE;
        descrVec[i].Executable = FALSE;
        descrVec[i].ExpandDown = FALSE;
    }

    /* == Make CS's segment executable == */
    CS_desc.Executable = TRUE;
}
```

The load_protected_descr routine is a service routine used by read_TSS16 and *read_TSS32*. It loads all descriptors corresponding to segment registers (except for GDT and IDT) using protected mode descriptor checks. Faults, if any, are reported.

```
load_protected_descr()
{
    /* == Get new CPL.  In PROTECTED mode, CPL is always in CS.RPL == */
    CPL = CS.RPL;

    /* == Invalidate all task-specific descriptors before loading them.  This way, if a fault
          occurs while loading them, the fault handler will not have spurious access to the
          segments pointed at by the registers. == */
    for ( i = 0; i <= 6; i++ )
        descrVec[i].Valid = FALSE;

    /* == Now load all task-specific descriptors == */
    LDT_desc = load_LDT(LDT);               /* see below */
    SS_desc = load_SS(SS, TRUE);            /* see page 70 */
    CS_desc = load_CS(CS, TRUE);            /* see page 69 */
    ES_desc = load_data_seg(ES, TRUE);      /* see page 71 */
    DS_desc = load_data_seg(DS, TRUE);      /* see page 71 */
    /* == FS and GS, and their descriptors, are only loaded for TSS32s. == */
    FS_desc = load_data_seg(FS, TRUE);      /* see page 71 */
    GS_desc = load_data_seg(GS, TRUE);      /* see page 71 */
}
```

The load_LDT function is used by load_protected_descr to initialize the new task's LDT_desc. This routine is also used when loading a TSS32 that is currently in VM86 mode; that is, it is used directly by the read_TSS32 routine. The function itself returns the descriptor (DESCR) corresponding to the SELECTOR *sel* passed as a parameter. Protection checks pertaining to descriptors pointing at LDTs are made. Since the load_LDT routine is only used by the task switch function all faults are reported as TASK faults.

Note that a new LDT can be established via the LLDT instruction also. The checks made by LLDT (described on page 478) match the checks made by load_LDT, except that a "not present" LDT segment signals the "not present" (NP) fault. Note that there is no Accessed flag in an LDT descriptor, and hence none is set.

```
DESCR load_LDT(sel)
SELECTOR sel;
{ DESCR desc;

    /* == An LDT descriptor can only reside in the GDT.  Otherwise, during a task switch,
          there would be ambiguity as to whether to load the descriptor from the new task's
          LDT or the old task's LDT == */
    if ( sel.TI == 1 )
      signal_fault(TASK,  (sel & 0xFFFC));              /* see page 155 */

    /* == Loading a null LDT SELECTOR is allowed.  However, the LDT has to be
          invalidated in this case. == */
    if ( nullSel(sel) )
      desc.Valid = FALSE;
    else
    {  lock(DESCR_TABLE);     /* disallow descriptor table access to other system agents
                                 */

      desc = read_descr(sel, TRUE);
      if ( desc.Type != LDT_SEG || !desc.Valid )
        signal_fault(TASK,  (sel & 0xFFFC));            /* see page 155 */

      unlock(DESCR_TABLE); /* reallow other agents to access descriptor tables */
    }

    /* == Checks pass: return loaded descriptor register == */
    return (desc);
}
```

2.11.1 Returning from a nested task

The enter_new_task routine, described on page 134, is used to activate a task. The exit_task routine defined in this section is used to save the current state of a task and reactivate the task that called the current task. Since the calling task's

SELECTOR is saved in the BackLink field of the current TSS, and current TSS information is stored in the registers TSS and TSS_desc, there is no need to pass any parameters to the enter_new_task routine.

```
exit_task()
SELECTOR sel;
{   BOOLEAN trapAfterSwitch;
    SELECTOR backlink;  /* caller's TSS selector */

    /* == Clear the "nested task" flag (EFLAGS⟨14⟩), and save current task state == */
    NT = 0;
    save_task_state();                                    /* see page 136 */

    /* == Don't carry back single step to previous task == */
    prev_TF = 0;

    /* == Read caller's backlink and check its validity == */
    backlink = TSS_read2(TSS, 0);                         /* see page 76 */
    lock(DESCR_TABLE);     /* disallow descr. table access to other system agents */
    desc = read_descr(backlink, TRUE, FALSE);        /* see page 63 */
    if ( desc.Type == NOTBUSY_TSS16 || desc.Type == NOTBUSY_TSS32 )
    {   if ( ! desc.Valid )
            signal_fault(NP,  (backlink & 0xFFFC));       /* see page 155 */
    }
    else
        signal_fault(TASK, (backlink & 0xFFFC));          /* see page 155 */
    unlock(DESCR_TABLE);  /* reallow other agents to access descriptor tables */

    /* == Load new TSS descriptor == */
    TSS_desc = desc;

    /* == Read in new task state values == */
    if ( TSS_desc.Type == NOTBUSY_TSS16 ) /* 80286-style TSS */
    {   read_TSS16(sel, TSS_desc);                        /* see page 137 */
        trapAfterSwitch = FALSE;
    }
    else  /* 80386/i486-style TSS */
        trapAfterSwitch = read_TSS32(sel, TSS_desc);  /* see page 138 */

    /* == Reset debugging "local enable" flag (L0, L1, L2, and L3), and the "local exact" flag
          (LE) stored in DR7.  This is only done on the 80376, 80386, and i486 == */
    DR7⟨8⟩ = DR7⟨6⟩ = DR7⟨4⟩ = DR7⟨2⟩ = DR7⟨0⟩ = FALSE;

    /* == If TSS32, raise debug fault if T bit set == */
    if ( trapAfterSwitch )
    {   /* Set "Because" code to "T bit set in TSS" (i.e., set BT flag) */
        DR6⟨15⟩ = 1;
        signal_fault(DEBUG);              /* see page 155 */
    }
}
```

Note that the only way to return from the current task is via the IRET instruction. If this instruction is executed with the NT flag in the EFLAGS register set, a task return is initiated.

2.11.2 Direct task switch via TSS descriptors

The entire discussion of task switching thus far has assumed that a task gate is used to initiate a task switch. Why not use a TSS descriptor directly? For this to be allowed, TSS descriptors would have to appear in IDT entries, LDT entries, and GDT entries. We know that TSS descriptors can (and must) reside as GDT entries. If they were allowed as LDT entries, it would not be possible to reliably save their SELECTOR value in the BackLink field of a TSS. (This is because the LDT can change as the result of a task switch.) Allowing them as IDT entries is safe in that the IDT does not change when a task switch occurs. However, there is no way to encode an IDT entry as a SELECTOR! (The notion of a task gate is introduced for these reasons.)

The only remaining possibility is to allow task switches via TSS descriptors stored in the GDT. This special case is in fact permitted. Since GDT SELECTORs can only be referenced by the JMP and CALL instructions, only these instructions can make use of this shortcut.

2.11.3 Setting up the first TSS via LTR

All successful task switches save the state of the current task before invoking the new task. However, when the very first task switch is performed there is no task state segment established; that is, the TSS_desc descriptor register and TSS segment register have invalid state. The LTR instruction, which accepts a WORD value as its operand, is used to resolve this problem. The WORD value is assumed to be a valid TSS SELECTOR. It is loaded into TSS, and the corresponding descriptor is loaded into TSS_desc. However, no task switch is performed. See page 495 for details.

2.12 Interrupts and exceptions

Any change in the sequential flow of control of a program that is not initiated by a branch or subroutine call is either due to an interrupt or an exception. **Interrupts** can be raised either explicitly by software (via the INT or INTO instructions) or by a source external to the 80x86. Software-generated interrupts are called **software interrupts**, and external interrupts are often called **hardware interrupts**. Interrupts are only serviced at the end of an instruction, or at certain well-defined points within the execution of potentially long-running instructions (namely, a REPeated string copy or a coprocessor instruction; see §2.13 for more details.)

Exceptions are similar to software interrupts in that they usually occur as the result of an instruction's execution. However, they are used to report abnormal events (e.g., an attempt to divide by zero or an attempt to write into a read-only segment). There are four classes of exceptions in the 80x86. These classes specify the effect of the exception on the instruction that was executing when it occurred.

1. **faults**: the instruction is nullified: in general, all actions taken by the instruction up to the exception are undone.[20] The fault handler points at the instruction. Thus the fault handler can repair the fault and retry the instruction.

2. **traps**: the instruction completes before the trap handler is entered. The trap handler points at the instruction that would execute next had the trap not occurred. The only exceptions that are traps are DEBUG exceptions caused by single step or a data breakpoint activation. Since software interrupt handlers always point at the instruction following the software interrupt, they may be viewed as traps also. Note that a DIVIDE exception on a 8086 is a trap: the exception handler always points at the instruction following the divide instruction. (On the 80286, 80376, 80386, and i486, DIVIDE exceptions are faults.)

3. **imprecise exceptions**: the instruction completes before the trap handler is entered. However, there is no guarantee that that the exception handler points at the instruction following the one that caused the exception. In particular, several instructions may execute before the exception is recognized. Imprecise exceptions can occur because of one of the following reasons:

   a. an error while communicating with a coprocessor (exceptions PE_OVERRUN, and PE_ERROR).
   b. a data breakpoint (signaled via a DEBUG exception) that occurs with the "exact" flags (in DR7) not set.

---

[20] See §2.14 on page 167 for exemptions from this rule.

Although it is not possible to detect the instruction that caused the imprecise exception based on the information provided by the exception handler, auxiliary information is sometimes available that makes such detection possible. For example, the coprocessor error exception is imprecise; however, the instruction and data address of all coprocessor instructions are saved in special registers that allow identification of the source of the error.

4. **aborts**: aborts are imprecise exceptions that are generated by very severe system errors. Examples are a DOUBLE_FAULT or a SHUTDOWN condition. Note that aborts can also be caused by protection violations when accessing certain regions of a task-state segment. Such errors are reported as TASK faults.

2.12.1 Servicing interrupts and exceptions

Both interrupts and exceptions are serviced via entries in an **interrupt vector**. If interrupt number *n* occurs, the entry at index *n* in the vector is used. If an exception occurs, it is serviced using a specific vector entry. The entry depends on the type of exception. Note that some entries, such as the GP fault entry, are shared by a variety of exceptions.

Each entry in the interrupt vector is a (software programmable) specification of the address of the routine to be used to handle the interrupt or exception. The format of the entry depends on whether or not the processor is in REAL mode when the interrupt/exception occurs.

In REAL mode each entry is simply a far pointer (i.e., a segment and offset) to the interrupt/exception handler, as follows:

```
typedef struct {
    WORD Offset;        /* relative byte index +0 */
    WORD Selector;      /* relative byte index +2 */
} REAL_INT_VEC ;
```

In VM86 and PROTECTED modes, each entry specifies either an interrupt gate, a trap gate, or a task gate. A task gate contains the SELECTOR of a TSS; this TSS is used to service the exception or interrupt. A trap gate or interrupt gate names a protected selector and offset value, much like a call gate. The only difference between a trap gate and an interrupt gate is that an interrupt gate disables the interrupt enable flag IF before entering the handler; a trap gate leaves IF unmodified.

Interrupt and trap gates use the stack to save data about the environment in which the interrupt/exception occurred. To support both 16-bit (pre-80386) and 32-bit environments there are 16-bit and 32-bit variants of each type of gate. They are called INTERRUPT_GATE16 and TRAP_GATE16, and INTERRUPT_GATE32 and TRAP_GATE32, respectively. The format of a TASKGATE, INTERRUPT_GATE16, TRAP_GATE16, INTERRUPT_GATE32, and TRAP_GATE32 is shown in Figure 2.41.

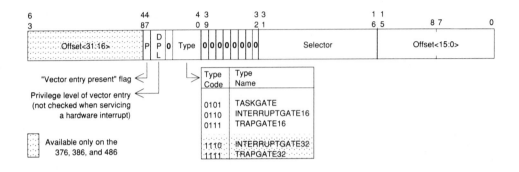

Figure 2.41: PROTECTED/VM86 mode 80x86 interrupt vector entry formats

2.12.2 Error codes

When operating in PROTECTED or VM86 modes certain exceptions have error codes associated with them. These error codes usually signify two things:

1. the selector that caused the exception, or, if the exception was because of a defective interrupt vector (IDT) entry, the index of the interrupt.

2. was the exception signaled while trying to enter a hardware interrupt or exception handler?

There are two exceptions to this general rule:

1. the PAGE fault handler's error code only specifies the nature of the access (read or write? user or supervisor? page present?) that caused the fault to occur.

2. the DOUBLE_FAULT abort always has an error code of zero.

The exceptions that have an associated error code are DOUBLE_FAULT, INVALID_TSS, NP, STACK, GP, and PAGE faults. These (and other) exceptions are elaborated on below.

Error codes have the format shown in Figure 2.42.   For non-page-fault

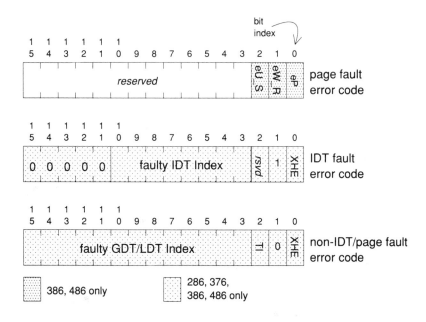

Figure 2.42: PROTECTED mode error code formats

exceptions, the IDT flag, if set to 1, indicates that the error occurred while accessing the IDT, that is, during a IDT_read or IDT_write. The IDT vector entry number is stored in the IDTIndex field. If the IDT flag is 0, bits 15 through 2 of the error code stores the selector Index and table index (TI) much as in a normal SELECTOR. This names the defective selector.

If a nonpage fault exception occurs while trying to invoke an interrupt or exception, the **XHE** flag[21] (suggestive of "*e*xception or *h*ardware interrupt *e*rror") is also updated.   This flag is set to 1 if the exception was caused while trying to invoke an exception or hardware interrupt handler.   In all other cases, it is set to 0.   In other words, this flag is set to 1 only if the IDT entry of a hardware

---

[21] The XHE flag is sometimes called the EXT flag.

interrupt or exception handler, or the control gate, TSS, or selector stored in the
IDT entry is found to be defective. In the C language descriptions that follow a
global flag, XH_flag is set TRUE whenever a hardware interrupt or exception is
processed. This flag is interrogated whenever a fault is signaled; if TRUE, the
XHE flag in the error code reported is set to 1. XH_flag is cleared (i.e., set to
FALSE) just before dispatching the first instruction of an exception handler.

The page fault exception has associated with it a special error code, as shown in
Figure 2.41. The error code has three flags eP, eW_R, and eU_S stored in a
format similar to the three least significant bits of a page table entry. Their
interpretation is somewhat different though, as shown in Figure 2.43. Page faults
are also special in that the linear address that caused the fault is stored in control
register CR2.

FIELD	VALUE	DESCRIPTION
eP	0	The page fault was caused by a not-present page
	1	The page fault was caused because of a read/write or user/supervisor violation
eW_R	0	The page fault was caused by a read access
	1	The page fault was caused by a write access
eU_S	0	The page fault was signaled when making a supervisor mode access
	1	The page fault was signaled when making a user mode access

Figure 2.43: Page fault error code interpretation

Error codes are pushed onto the stack of the exception handler, just before the
exception handler is invoked. Thus, handlers for exceptions that have error
codes can simply pop it off the stack. A procedural description of the steps in
exception handling, including error code storage, is given in §2.12.8 on
page 159.

2.12.3 Simultaneous interrupts

Interrupts have no associated priority, except that software interrupts are always taken; that is, they cannot be disabled by clearing the IF flag. Furthermore, if a hardware interrupt occurs after a software interrupt instruction has begun execution, the software interrupt is posted (i.e., the software interrupt's handler is entered) before the hardware interrupt is recognized.

It is not possible for more than one software interrupt to occur simultaneously. Furthermore, the 80x86 architecture says nothing about the relative priorities of simultaneous hardware interrupts. It is up to the hardware external to the processor to prioritize among the interrupts and present the appropriate interrupt number to the processor.[22]

2.12.4 Simultaneous exceptions

Unlike interrupts, several exceptions can occur simultaneously. The priority of exceptions in relation to each other and in relation to interrupts is as follows.

1. instruction breakpoint   *HIGHEST PRIORITY*
2. nonmaskable interrupt (NMI)
3. hardware interrupt
4. instruction fetch segmentation fault
5. instruction fetch page fault
6. IOPL, LOCK, and privileged instruction violations

---

7. faults and traps during instruction execution
8. software interrupts

---

9. data breakpoints and/or single step   *LOWEST PRIORITY*

The exceptions are categorized into three groups (shown separated by horizontal lines). The first group includes exceptions that are checked before an instruction is executed. The second group identifies exceptions that can occur during the execution of an instruction. The third group identifies exceptions that can occur after an instruction completes. Note that for all memory references, segmentation faults always take precedence over page faults.

---

[22] An exception is the 80186: this single chip part incorporates an 8259-like interrupt controller.

2.12.5 Software interrupts, hardware interrupts, and NMI

Now let us look at interrupt handling in greater detail. Software interrupts are signaled via the INT class of instructions. Their formal definitions invoke the software_interrupt routine, described below. Hardware interrupts are externally generated events that the 80*x*86 detects only at instruction boundaries or at other well-defined points in certain long-running instructions called *interruptable instructions*. (See §2.13 on page 165 for more on interruptable instructions.) Normal hardware interrupts are enabled only if the interrupt enable flag IF is set. A special type of hardware interrupt, called a non-maskable interrupt, or **NMI**, is enabled regardless of IF's setting. The formal definition of how both normal hardware interrupts and NMIs are detected is shown in check_interrupts routine, defined below. Check_interrupts is activated by the main instruction interpretation loop; see page 11.

Both the software_interrupt and check_interrupts routines function very similarly in that they ultimately activate the central interrupt and exception handling routine handle_intr_xcp. There are two principal differences in the way that handle_intr_xcp handles software interrupts and hardware interrupts, as follows:

1. When invoking a software interrupt, CPL must be at least as privileged as the selected IDT entry's DPL (i.e., CPL ≤ IDT entry's DPL). Hardware interrupts do not make this check.

2. If an exception occurs while trying to invoke a hardware interrupt handler (or a benign exception handler), the XHE flag is set in the error code pushed for the exception handler. The flag is cleared in all other cases (including the case where an exception occurs while trying to service a software interrupt).

```
software_interrupt( vecnum )
int vecnum;
{
    /* == Clear global XH_flag, indicating that a software interrupt is being processed.  Then
          invoke interrupt with no error code ("FALSE" parameter). == */
    XH_flag = FALSE;
    handle_intr_xcp(vecnum, FALSE);          /* see page 160 */
}
```

```
check_interrupts()
{
    if ( ! prev_instr_loaded_SS )
    {  /* == Check for non-maskable interrupts (NMI) == */
       if ( « NMI pin active »  &&  ! NMI_handler_active )
       {  /* Lock out further NMIs until this one has been serviced.²³  Use vector entry #2 to
             service the NMI. */
          NMI_handler_active = TRUE;
          XH_flag = TRUE;
          handle_intr_xcp(2, FALSE);          /* see page 160 */
       }

       else /* == Check for normal hardware interrupts if IF is set == */
       if ( IF  &&  « INTR pin active » )
       {  int_num = « hardware interrupt vector entry number (see text) » ;
          /* Invoke interrupt handler with no error code ("FALSE" parameter). */
          XH_flag = TRUE;
          handle_intr_xcp(int_num, FALSE);    /* see page 160 */
       }
    }
}
```

2.12.6   Exception handling

Since exceptions occur during the course of an instruction's execution, the
conditions under which they occur are a part of the instruction's description.
These descriptions use the following routines to signal that an exception has
occurred:

---

[23] NMIs are not locked out on the 8086: repeated NMI signals will result in the NMI handler being entered
repeatedly.

- signal_fault(int vecnum, WORD error_code)

- signal_trap(int vecnum, WORD error_code)

- signal_imprecise(int vecnum, WORD error_code)

- signal_abort(int vecnum, WORD error_code)

The list shows one routine for each of the exception classes discussed on page 144. From the point of view of the architecture, all these routines have the same specification; that is, they all use the number specified by the vecnum parameter to index into the interrupt vector. The reason for categorizing them is to document the nature of the exception.

2.12.6.1 Double faults and benign and contributory exceptions

Consider the situation where an exception occurs while trying to enter an exception handler; for example, let us say that the IDT entry of the "segment not present" (NP) fault handler is erroneous. This is a catastrophic error, potentially. In particular, if the error is one where the IDT entry is *itself* marked "not present," an infinite loop would occur.

To address this problem, the 80x86 architecture categorizes exceptions in two groups: **benign** and **contributory**. In general, benign exceptions are allowed to occur repeatedly. For example, the integer overflow exception OVERFLOW and the DEBUG exception are both benign. Therefore, if a breakpoint is detected while attempting to enter the OVERFLOW exception handler, the DEBUG exception handler is entered instead (as desired). Contributory exceptions, however, are those that signal a structural failure in the operating system software, if they occur more than once. For example, NP faults are contributory. Therefore, in the erroneous IDT scenario just mentioned, two successive contributory exceptions are detected by the 80x86.

What happens when more than one contributory exception occurs in sequence? Rather than service the second such exception via its exception handler, a special exception, called **double fault** is signaled. User supplied code in the DOUBLE_FAULT exception handler can process this severe condition as it sees fit. A special case in which two successive contributory exceptions are allowed is when the second such exception is a PAGE fault, but the first one is not. In this case the PAGE fault handler is invoked as usual. This permits most exception handlers to be stored in demand paged memory.

A final situation to consider is what happens if the DOUBLE_FAULT handler cannot be activated also. If this happens, the 80x86 gives up and signals a shutdown condition. Shutdown is discussed in §2.15 on page 168. A routine that encapsulates the exception counting is defined below. A call to this routine, called double_fault, is a part of the definition of how any contributory exception is processed by the 80x86. The routine returns FALSE if the double fault (or shutdown) condition has not occurred. Otherwise, it signals a DOUBLE_FAULT or enters the shutdown state, as appropriate.

```
BOOLEAN double_fault()
{  /* == Take care of double fault and shutdown conditions == */
   exception_count = exception_count + 1;
   if ( exception_count == 2 )
   {  signal_abort(DOUBLE_FAULT, 0);
      return(TRUE);
   }
   else if ( exception_count == 3 )
   {  shutdown();
      return(TRUE);
   }

   return(FALSE);
}
```

For ease of reference Figure 2.44 lists all 80x86 exception types along with its attributes.

2.12.7 The signal_*xxxx* routines

As pointed out earlier, the definition of how exceptions are processed is encapsulated in the four routines signal_fault, signal_trap, signal_imprecise, and signal_abort. Each of these routines operates very similarly, except that only signal_fault restores the instruction pointer EIP. The operation of the signal routines have a lot in common with the check_interrupts and software_interrupt routines described earlier. In fact, the definition of how the exception is dispatched is encapsulated in the subroutine handle_intr_xcp. This routine is activated by all the signal routines (and also by the hardware and software interrupt routines).

EXCEPTION	INT. VEC#	ERR. CODE?	EXCEPTION CLASS	EXCEPTION TYPE
DIVIDE	0	no	fault	contributory
DEBUG	1	no	data breakpoints and single step are traps, all others are faults	benign
NMI	2	no	(hardware intr. - trap)	—
INT3	3	no	(software intr. - trap)	—
OVERFLOW	4	no	(software intr. - trap)	—
BOUND	5	no	fault	benign
INVALID_INSTR	6	no	fault	benign
PE_UNAVAILABLE	7	no	fault	benign
DOUBLE_FAULT	8	yes (0)	abort	contributory
PE_OVERRUN	9	no	imprecise	contributory
TASK	10	yes	fault	contributory
NP	11	yes	fault	contributory
STACK	12	yes	fault	contributory
GP	13	yes	fault	contributory
PAGE (386, 486 only)	14	yes	fault	benign or contributory; see text
PE_ERROR	16	no	imprecise	benign
ALIGN (486 only)	17	no	fault	benign

Figure 2.44: 80x86 exception attributes

```
signal_fault(xcptype, error_code)
int xcptype;
WORD error_code;
{
    /* == Restore register state prior to the instruction's execution.  See §2.14 on page 167
          for more information. == */
    curr = prev;
    EIP = prev_EIP;
    CPL = prev_CPL;

    /* == Clear any breakpoints sensed so far.  The DEBUG fault has already recorded the
          breakpoints in DR6, so all is well. == */
    clear_active_brkpts();  /* see page 176 */

    /* == Set "restart" flag (RF) so that multiple debug faults do not occur. == */
    if ( xcptype != DEBUG )
        RF = 1;

    /* == Check fault type and activate appropriate handler == */
    switch ( xcptype )
    {   case DIVIDE:24 /* div by 0 or div overflow: use vector #0 */
            if ( ! double_fault() )
            {   XH_flag = TRUE;
                handle_intr_xcp(0, FALSE);          /* see page 160 */
            }
            break;

        case DEBUG: /* code breakpoint, debug register access fault (available only on the
                          80376, 80386, and i486): use vector #1 */
            DR7⟨13⟩ = 0;  /* clear GD flag to reallow DR access */
            XH_flag = TRUE;
            handle_intr_xcp(1, FALSE);              /* see page 160 */
            break;

        case BOUND: /* BOUND instruction trap: use vector #5 */
            XH_flag = TRUE;
            handle_intr_xcp(5, FALSE);              /* see page 160 */
            break;

        case INVALID_INSTR: /* undefined opcode or operand: use vector #6 */
            XH_flag = TRUE;
            handle_intr_xcp(6, FALSE);              /* see page 160 */
            break;
```

---

[24] On a 8086, the DIVIDE exception is a *trap*: on entry to the exception handler, the return address points at the instruction following the [I]DIV. Also, a BYTE or WORD IDIV where the quotient is the smallest negative number (0x80 for BYTE IDIV or 0x8000 for WORD IDIV) generates a DIVIDE exception on the 8086. On other 80*x*86 implementations, the correct quotient is produced (and no exception is generated).

```
case PE_UNAVAILABLE: /* processor extension disabled: use vector #7 */
    XH_flag = TRUE;
    handle_intr_xcp(7, FALSE);          /* see page 160 */
    break;

case TASK: /* defective TSS or descriptor within TSS: use vector #10 */
    if ( ! double_fault() )
    {   if ( XH_flag )
            error_code⟨0⟩ = 1;   /* Set XHE indicator */
        XH_flag = TRUE;
        handle_intr_xcp(10, TRUE, error_code);     /* see page 160 */
    }
    break;

case NP: /* segment not present: use vector #11 */
    if ( ! double_fault() )
    {   if ( XH_flag )
            error_code⟨0⟩ = 1;   /* Set XHE indicator */
        XH_flag = TRUE;
        handle_intr_xcp(11, TRUE, error_code);     /* see page 160 */
    }
    break;

case STACK: /* invalid stack: use vector #12 */
    if ( ! double_fault() )
    {   if ( XH_flag )
            error_code⟨0⟩ = 1;   /* Set XHE indicator */
        XH_flag = TRUE;
        handle_intr_xcp(12, TRUE, error_code);     /* see page 160 */
    }
    break;

case GP: /* general protection violation: use vector #13 */
    if ( ! double_fault() )
    {   if ( XH_flag )
            error_code⟨0⟩ = 1;   /* Set XHE indicator */
        handle_intr_xcp(13, TRUE, error_code);     /* see page 160 */
    }
    break;
```

```
      case PAGE: /* page fault: use vector #14 */
         /* == Take care of double fault and shutdown conditions specially for PAGE faults
               == */
         if ( exception_count != 1 || first_page_fault_seen )
            exception_count = exception_count + 1;
         if ( exception_count == 2 )
            signal_abort(DOUBLE_FAULT, 0);
         else if ( exception_count == 3 )
            shutdown();
         else /* no DOUBLE_FAULT: handle page fault */
         {  XH_flag = TRUE;
            first_page_fault_seen = TRUE;
            handle_intr_xcp(13, TRUE, (error_code & 0xFFFC));
         }
         break;

      case ALIGN: /* data alignment check (i486-only): use vector #17 */
         XH_flag = TRUE;
         handle_intr_xcp(17, FALSE);          /* see page 160 */
         break;
   }
}


signal_trap(xcptype, error_code)
int xcptype;
WORD error_code;
{  /* == Restore CPL of instruction that was executing when trap occurred, and clear any
         breakpoints sensed thus far. == */
   CPL = prev_CPL;
   clear_active_brkpts(); /* see page 176 */

   /* == Activate trap handler without restoring EIP.  == */
   switch ( xcptype )
   {  case DEBUG: /* single step, or task switch trap (task switch trapping is available only
                      on the 80376, 80386, and i486): use vector #1 */
         DR7<13> = 0;  /* clear GD flag to reallow DR access */
         XH_flag = TRUE;
         handle_intr_xcp(1, FALSE);           /* see page 160 */
         break;
   }
}

signal_imprecise(xcptype, error_code)
int xcptype;
WORD error_code;
{
   /* == Restore CPL of instruction that was executing when exception occurred, and clear
         any breakpoints sensed thus far. == */
   CPL = prev_CPL;
   clear_active_brkpts(); /* see page 176 */
```

```
       switch ( xcptype )
       {   case DEBUG: /* inexact data breakpoint:²⁵ use vector #1 */
              DR7⟨13⟩ = 0;  /* clear GD flag to reallow DR access */
              XH_flag = TRUE;
              handle_intr_xcp(1, FALSE);            /* see page 160 */
              break;

           /* == Memory access error while transferring data to/from processor extension. On
                 the 80286 this exception is imprecise; however, on the 80376 and 80386, this
                 exception is a fault (i.e. the exception handler points at the offending
                 instruction). == */
        case PE_OVERRUN: /* PE transfer error; use vector #9 */
           if ( ! doubleFault() )
           {   RF = 1;
               XH_flag = TRUE;
               handle_intr_xcp(9, FALSE);           /* see page 160 */
           }
           break;

           /* == Error signaled by processor extension. == */
        case PE_ERROR: /* use vector #16 */
           EIP = prev_EIP;
           CPL = prev_CPL;
           if ( ! doubleFault() )
           {   RF = 1;
               XH_flag = TRUE;
               handle_intr_xcp(16, FALSE);          /* see page 160 */
           }
           break;
       }
}


signal_abort(xcptype, error_code)
int xcptype;
WORD error_code;
{   /* == Restore CPL of instruction that was executing when abort occurred, and clear any
         breakpoints sensed thus far. == */
    CPL = prev_CPL;
    clear_active_brkpts(); /* see page 176 */
```

---

[25] Imprecise DEBUG exceptions are caused by data breakpoints that occur with the Exact flag in DR7 clear.
Such breakpoints may not even be detected; hence, when setting data breakpoints, setting the Exact flag is
highly recommended.

```
    /* Activate handler associated with abort type */
    switch ( xcptype )
    {   case DOUBLE_FAULT: /* severe error: use vector #8, errorcode = 0 */
            handle_intr_xcp(8, TRUE, 0);                    /* see page 160 */
            break;
    }
}
```

2.12.8 The handle_intr_xcp **routine**

All interrupts and exceptions are processed by the 80x86 architecture via a
common set of actions, as follows:

1. Release all locks on resources. This is done in case the exception being
   processed occurred while a resource was still locked.

2. Check the current execution mode. If in REAL mode, push the current
   FLAGS, CS, and IP values onto the stack, and branch to the address at the
   requested interrupt vector element entry. In REAL mode, each interrupt
   vector element consists of two WORD-sized entries. The low-order WORD
   stores the interrupt entry point's IP value, and the high-order WORD stores
   it CS value. If not in REAL mode, continue with following step.

3. If in PROTECTED mode or VM86 mode, interpret the interrupt vector as a
   sequence of descriptors. (Each descriptor occupies eight bytes of memory;
   hence the interrupt vector in PROTECTED or VM86 modes is twice as large
   as in REAL mode.) Check the type of the descriptor corresponding to the
   requested interrupt or exception. If it is a TASKGATE, initiate a task switch.
   Otherwise, if it is a TRAP_GATE or INTERRUPT_GATE, switch to the
   privilege level indicated by the gate's code segment, and push the
   [E]FLAGS, CS, and [E]IP onto the new privilege level's stack. Note that if
   an interrupt or exception is serviced via a TRAP_GATE16 or
   INTERRUPT_GATE16 WORD-sized quantities (i.e., FLAGS, CS, and IP)
   are pushed; otherwise, if a TRAP_GATE32 or INTERRUPT_GATE32 is
   used, DWORD-sized quantities (i.e., EFLAGS, CS padded out to a DWORD,
   and EIP) are pushed.

These actions are encapsulated in C language notation in the handle_intr_xcp
routine, described below. This routine is called by all signal_*xxxx* routines, as
well as the hardware_interrupt and software_interrupt routines. The parameters
to it specify the interrupt vector element number to use, *vecnum*, a flag (*err_flag*)

indicating whether or not an error code should be pushed, and an error code
value *err_code*. The *err_code* parameter is used only when *err_flag* is TRUE.

```
handle_intr_xcp(vecnum, err_flag, err_code)
int vecnum;
BOOLEAN err_flag;
WORD err_code;
{
    /* == Unlock all locked resources, just in case exception occurred in the middle of a
          locked operation == */
    unlock(DESCR_TABLE);
    unlock(DIR_TABLE);
    unlock(PAGE_TABLE);
    unlock(IDT);
    unlock(MEM);                    /* release lock from any LOCK instructions */

    /* == Check execution mode and dispatch interrupt/exception accordingly == */
    if ( mode == REAL ) /* use REAL mode interrupt handling */
    {   /* == Store flags and address of instruction causing exception on stack == */
        push2(EFLAGS);              /* Push low WORD of EFLAGS only */
        push2(CS);                  /* Push segment selector of instruction causing exception
                                       */
        push2(IP);                  /* and push its offset (low WORD of EIP) */
        IF = 0;                     /* Enter handler with interrupts disabled */
        TF = 0;                     /* Enter handler with single stepping disabled */
        prev_TF = 0;

        /* == Read REAL mode IDT vector jump address, and set up jump to it == */
        lock(IDT);
        EIP = IDT_read2(vecnum, vecnum*4); /* High WORD of EIP set to 0 */
        CS = IDT_read2(vecnum, vecnum*4+2);
        /* == Instruction execution resumes at CS:IP, the exception handler entry == */
        unlock(IDT);

        /* == Longjump to main instruction loop.  This is done in case an exception that
              occurred in the middle of an instruction's execution is being serviced.  See
              page 11. == */
        goto NEXT_INSTR;
    }

    /* == mode is VM86 or PROTECTED: use PROTECTED mode interrupt handling == */
    else
    {   DWORD d1, d2;               /* Temp storage for IDT vector entry */
        DWORD xcpEFLAGS;            /* Save area for EFLAGS state in environment of
                                       exception/interrupt */

        lock(IDT);
        d1 = IDT_read4(vecnum, vecnum*8);     /* Selector and lo offset */
        d2 = IDT_read4(vecnum, vecnum*8+4);   /* Hi offset and gate type */
        unlock(IDT);
```

```
/* == If software interrupt (i.e., global flag XH_flag set to FALSE), make sure that CPL
      is privileged enough to read IDT entry (i.e., CPL <= DPL) == */
if ( ! XH_flag  &&  CPL > d2⟨14:13⟩ ) /* CPL > descriptor's DPL: error */
   signal_fault(GP, ( (vecnum << 3) | 2 ));

/* == Save EFLAGS, in case interrupt/exception is handled via a interrupt/trap gate
      == */
xcpEFLAGS = EFLAGS;

/* == Handle interrupt via interrupt gate or task gate protocol, based on type of
      descriptor.  Report error if invalid descriptor == */
if ( d2⟨12⟩ == 1 ) /* descriptor is a code/data segment: error */
   signal_fault(GP, ( (vecnum << 3) | 2 ));
switch ( d2⟨11:8⟩ ) /* Make selection based on Type field */
{  /* == Interrupt/trap gates: 16 bits wide == */
   case INTERRUPT_GATE16:
      IF = 0;  /* Enter handler with interrupts disabled */

   case TRAP_GATE16:
      if ( d2⟨15⟩ == 0 ) /* descriptor marked "not present": error */
         signal_fault(NP, ( (vecnum << 3) | 2 ));

      /* == Handle as 16 bit interrupt/trap gate == */
      int_xcp_gate(16, d1, d2, xcpEFLAGS, err_flag, err_code);
      break;

   /* == Interrupt/trap gates: 32 bits wide == */
   case INTERRUPT_GATE32:
      IF = 0;  /* Enter handler with interrupts disabled */

   case TRAP_GATE32:
      if ( d2⟨15⟩ == 0 ) /* descriptor marked "not present": error */
         signal_fault(NP, ( (vecnum << 3) | 2 ));

      /* == Handle as 32 bit interrupt/trap gate == */
      int_xcp_gate(32, d1, d2, xcpEFLAGS, err_flag, err_code);
      break;

   /* == Task gate == */
   case TASKGATE:
      if ( d2⟨15⟩ == 0 ) /* descriptor marked "not present": error */
         signal_fault(NP, ( (vecnum << 3) | 2 ));
      /* Task switch via selector named in task gate */
      int_via_task_gate(d1⟨31:16⟩, err_flag, err_code);  /* see page 133 */
      break;
```

```
        /* == None of the above: signal error == */
        default:
            signal_fault(GP, ( (vecnum << 3) | 2 ));
            break;
    }
  }
}
```

Handle_intr_xcp only goes so far as to show how different types of descriptors are processed. If a TASKGATE is seen, the int_via_task_gate routine, described on page 133, is invoked. If an interrupt or task gate is seen, the int_xcp_gate routine, described below, is used. This routine's operation has numerous similarities with the operation of a PROTECTED mode far CALL. Like the CALL instruction, it switches privilege levels (and stacks) if the code segment named in the gate is of a higher privilege. However, unlike a CALL, it does not copy any parameters from the old stack to the new stack. Also, a FLAGS (for 16-bit descriptor types) or EFLAGS (for 32-bit descriptor types) image is pushed onto the stack.

```
int_xcp_gate(os, d1, d2, oldEFLAGS, err_flag, err_code);
int os;                    /* Push 16 or 32 bit parameters */
DWORD d1, d2;              /* Contents of IDT vector descriptor */
DWORD oldEFLAGS;          /* EFLAGS when interrupt/exception occurred */
BOOLEAN err_flag;         /* Push err_code if TRUE */
WORD err_code;
{   SELECTOR IDT_sel = d1⟨31:16⟩;
    DWORD IDT_offset = (d2⟨31:16⟩ << 16) | d1⟨15:0⟩;

    /* == Enter handler with single stepping disabled == */
    TF = 0;
    prev_TF = 0;

    /* == Clear NT flag so that IRET used to exit handler does not do a task switch == */
    NT = 0;

    /* == Make sure new CS SELECTOR is not null == */
    if ( nullSel(IDT_sel) )
        signal_fault( GP, ( IDT_sel & 0xFFFC ) );

    /* == Read new CS descriptor and verify its type. Mark the descriptor as "accessed". If
          there is no change in privilege level perform a same level transfer; otherwise
          perform an inter-level transfer. == */
    lock(DESCR_TABLE);
    desc = read_descr(IDT_sel, FALSE);
    if ( desc.Executable )
    {   if ( !desc.Valid )
            signal_fault(NP, ( IDT_sel & 0xFFFC ) );
```

```
      if ( mode != VM86  &&  ( ( desc.Conforming && CPL >= desc.DPL ) ||
           ( !desc.Conforming && CPL == desc.DPL ) ) )
      {   mark_accessed(IDT_sel);
          unlock(DESCR_TABLE);
          goto SAME_LEVEL_INTR;
      }

      else if ( desc.Executable && !desc.Conforming  &&
              ( (mode == VM86  &&  desc.DPL == 0) ||
                (mode != VM86  &&  desc.DPL < CPL) ) )
      {   mark_accessed(IDT_sel);
          unlock(DESCR_TABLE);
          goto INTER_LEVEL_INTR;
      }

      else  /* erroneous IDT_sel descriptor */
          signal_fault( GP, ( IDT_sel & 0xFFFC ) );
  }

  /* == Process interrupt/exception transfer as a "same level" transfer; i.e. no privilege
  level (or stack) change occurs. == */
SAME_LEVEL_INTR:
  IDT_sel.RPL = CPL; /* set new CS's RPL bits */

  /* == Reset RF (it was set on entry to signal_fault to prevent multiple DEBUG faults);
      also, do not single step into handler == */
  RF = 0;
  prev_TF = TF = 0;

  /* == Push [E]FLAGS, CS, [E]IP, and optional error code == */
  pushOS(xcpEFLAGS);
  pushOS(CS);
  pushOS(EIP);
  if ( err_flag )
      pushOS(err_code);

  /* == Clear XH_flag since exception or interrupt handler is about to be invoked.  (See
      §2.12.2 on page 146 for more on the XH_flag) == */
  XH_flag = FALSE;

  /* == Set CS, EIP and blast out to top-level instruction loop == */
  CS = IDT_sel;
  EIP = IDT_offset;
  goto NEXT_INSTR;  /* longjump to main instruction loop */


  /* == Process interrupt/exception transfer as an "interlevel" transfer; i.e., change
  privilege level and stack. == */
INTER_LEVEL_INTR:
  new_CPL = desc.DPL;  /* new CPL is the new code segment descriptor's DPL */
  IDT_sel.RPL = new_CPL; /* set new CS's RPL bits to handler's CPL */
```

```
/* == Read in new privilege level's stack pointer.  Note that the high order WORD of
       new_ESP is undefined if the current TSS is TSS16. == */
if ( TSS_desc.Type == TSS16 )
{   new_ESP⟨15:0⟩ = TSS_read2( TSS, (new_CPL*4 + 2) );
    new_ESP⟨31:16⟩ = undefined;
    new_SS = TSS_read2( TSS, (new_CPL*4 + 4) );
}
else /* TSS_desc.Type == TSS32 */
{   new_ESP = TSS_read4( TSS, (new_CPL*8 + 4) );
    new_SS = TSS_read2( TSS, (new_CPL*8 + 8) );
}

/* == Load new SS, temporarily setting CPL to new_CPL so that load_SS can be used
   == */
save_CPL = CPL;
CPL = new_CPL;
new_SS_desc = load_SS(new_SS, TRUE);
CPL = save_CPL;

/* == If in VM86 mode, save REAL-mode GS, FS, DS, ES, and invalidate them == */
if ( mode == VM86 )
{   new_ESP = new_stk_push(os, new_SS, new_SS_desc, new_ESP, GS);
    new_ESP = new_stk_push(os, new_SS, new_SS_desc, new_ESP, FS);
    new_ESP = new_stk_push(os, new_SS, new_SS_desc, new_ESP, DS);
    new_ESP = new_stk_push(os, new_SS, new_SS_desc, new_ESP, ES);
    DS = ES = FS = GS = 0;
    DS_desc.Valid = ES_desc.Valid = FS_desc.Valid = GS_desc.Valid = 0;
}

/* == Now push old SS and [E]SP, ... */
new_ESP = new_stk_push(os, new_SS, new_SS_desc, new_ESP, SS);
new_ESP = new_stk_push(os, new_SS, new_SS_desc, new_ESP, ESP);

/* ..., and push old CS and [E]IP == */
new_ESP = new_stk_push(os, new_SS, new_SS_desc, new_ESP, CS);
new_ESP = new_stk_push(os, new_SS, new_SS_desc, new_ESP, EIP);

/* == Push error code, if required == */
if ( err_flag )
    new_ESP = new_stk_push(os, new_SS, new_SS_desc, new_ESP, err_code);

/* == Clear VM in case it was set; also, reset RF (it was set on entry to  signal_fault  to
       prevent multiple DEBUG faults), and disable single stepping in case it was
       enabled when exception occurred == */
RF = 0;
VM = 0;
prev_TF = TF = 0;

/* == Setup SS:[E]SP, CS:[E]IP, and CPL == */
SS = new_SS;
SS_desc = new_SS_desc;
if ( SS_desc.Default == 1 ) /* "Big" stack */
```

```
      ESP = new_ESP;
   else /* 64KB stack */
      SP = new_ESP⟨15:0⟩;

   CPL = new_CPL;
   CS = IDT_sel;
   EIP = IDT_offset;
```

   /* == Since exception or interrupt handler has been entered successfully, the XH_flag
      can be reset. (See §2.12.2 on page 146 for more on the XH_flag) == */
   XH_flag = FALSE;

   /* == Blast out of nested routines to top-level instruction execution loop. This is done in
      case an exception that occurred in the middle of an instruction's execution is
      being processed. See page 11. == */
   goto NEXT_INSTR;
}

2.13   Instruction interruptability

Since hardware interrupts are only recognized on instruction boundaries, the lag between the time that an interrupt occurs and the time that it is recognized by the 80x86 can be as long as the running time of the longest running instruction. This lag is called **interrupt latency**. Because some instructions in the 80x86 repertoire can run potentially for a long time (i.e., several hundred or even thousands of cycles), the interrupt latency can be correspondingly long. To prevent this situation, most long-running instructions are made interruptable. An interruptable instruction is defined in a way such that its execution is suspendable at well-defined points in it execution. This allows an interrupt service routine to be invoked. Once the interrupt service is complete, the instruction is resumed.

There are two broad categories of interruptable instructions in the 80x86. The first is string operations; that is, operations which use a REPx prefix. Recall (from page 542) that a REPx prefixes one of the instructions CMPx, INSx, LODSx, MOVSx, OUTSx, SCASx, or STOSx. For example, MOVSB copies the BYTE at memory address DS:ESI (the source address) to the BYTE at memory address ES:EDI (the destination address). It then increments (or decrements) ESI and EDI. The "repeated move string" instruction REP MOVSB issues MOVSB the number of times specified by the value of the ECX register. After each repetition, ECX is decremented. In summary, REP MOVSB copies ECX BYTEs from the source to the destination. If a hardware interrupt occurs while a REP MOVSB is in progress the currently active MOVSB operation is completed, and the interrupt handler is entered. The CS:EIP value pushed onto the stack (when entering the interrupt service routine) points at the REP MOVSB. Hence, after the interrupt is serviced, execution resumes at the REP MOVSB. Since each MOVSB increments/decrements ESI and EDI, and decrements the loop counter ECX, the BYTE string copy resumes where it left off. Therefore, the interrupt latency of a REP MOVSB is no greater than the time taken to execute the component of the instruction. Note that data breakpoints that occur in a particular iteration are also recognized (and serviced) immediately after the iteration.

The other category of interruptable instructions is processor extension (i.e., 80*x*87) operations. Since 80*x*87 operations, including floating point operations of the i486, can operate in parallel with 80*x*86 instruction execution, most 80*x*87 operations initiated by an 80*x*86 first wait to make sure that the previous 80*x*87 instruction (if any) has completed. If this previous instruction is long-running,[26] the wait to initiate the current 80*x*87 instruction can be correspondingly long. Rather than hold up interrupt service during this waiting period, the 80*x*86 services any active interrupt. As with string operations, the CS:EIP pushed onto the stack when entering the interrupt service routine is that of the interrupted 80*x*87 operation. Hence, when interrupt service is complete, execution resumes at the interrupted instruction.

In the description of string and 80*x*87 instructions, the function external_interrupt is used to detect whether or not an interrupt has occurred. The function, defined below, returns TRUE if an interrupt is active and interrupt detection is enabled.

```
BOOLEAN external_interrupt()
{
   if ( ! prev_instr_loaded_SS && ( ( ! NMI_handler_active && «NMI pin active» ) ||
      ( IF && «INTR pin active» ) ) )
   {  /* == Set restart flag so that instruction breakpoints are not doubly reported. == */
      RF = 1;
      return( TRUE );
   }
   else
      return( FALSE );
}
```

In addition to external_interrupt, the brkpt_detected predicate is used to detect whether a data breakpoint occurred during the last iteration of a REP instruction. This predicate is TRUE if any of the breakpoint accumulation flags brkpt_active are set.

---

[26] Many 80*x*87 instructions take hundreds of clocks to complete execution

```
BOOLEAN brkpt_detected()
{
   return( brkpt_active[0] || brkpt_active[1] || brkpt_active[2] || brkpt_active[3] )
}
```

2.14 Instruction restartability

Assume that a variable *var* is stored in a read-only region of memory, and that the instruction

ADC   var, 2   ; var = var + 2 + CF (CF is the carry flag)

is executed. The ADC (add with carry) instruction operates as follows:

1. the value of *var* is read from memory.
2. the value read is incremented by 2. It is also incremented by 1 if the carry flag CF is set.
3. the arithmetic flags (including CF) are updated to reflect the result of the addition.
4. the incremented value is written back to memory.

The first three steps operate normally. However, step 4 signals a fault since an attempt is made to write back to a write-protected location. Let us say that the location is write protected not because the user has no write privileges to it but because the operating system wants notification whenever the location is written.[27] In such cases the exception handler would make the page writable, and then reattempt the instruction. The problem in doing so, of course, is that CF has been updated already. Therefore the retry of the instruction will likely produce a different result from its initial execution (had it completed successfully).

The solution adopted by the 80x86 (and many other architectures) is to require that instructions be **restartable**; that is, all registers, flags, and memory and I/O locations read by an instruction must be restored to their original state in the case of an exception. Note that restoration of locations that are written but not read is optional.

Now let us look at how restartability is described in the C language notation used by this book. To describe it in its strictest terms, every instruction would have to save only the operands that were read by it, and restore them in case of an error.

---

[27] This might be done by a kernel that implements address space forks using copy-on-write, or by a debugger that wants to know when a particular page is written.

This is too cumbersome to denote, and also does not capture the fact that an implementation can restore operands that are only written to, at its discretion. For both these reasons, the approach taken is to show that all major registers are saved prior to the execution of any instruction. If a fault is detected during the instruction, the saved state is restored. These actions are encapsulated in the following routine:

```
checkpoint()
{
    /* == Save current state, in case of error == */
    prev = curr;
    prev_EIP = EIP;
    prev_CPL = CPL;

    /* == Reset miscellaneous flags and counters == */
    exception_count = 0;
    first_page_fault_seen = FALSE;
}
```

Checkpointing is done before each instruction's execution.

2.15 Halt and shutdown

A 80x86 ceases program execution under one of two conditions:

1. if a HLT instruction is executed successfully.

2. if a fault is detected between the time a double fault is detected and the first instruction of the double fault handler is fetched.

The 80x86 enters the **halt** state when a HLT instruction is executed. The state entered if a fault occurs when trying to service a double fault is called **shutdown**. All implementations of the 80x86 can halt. However, since fault detection only occurs on the 80286, 80376, 80386, and i486, only these processors can enter a shutdown condition. In either case, the halt (or shutdown) is signaled by issuing a special type of bus cycle called a **halt cycle**. The "address" associated with the halt cycle is set to 0 if the processor has entered the halt state. The address is set to 2 if it has entered the shutdown state. Therefore, system components surrounding the 80x86 can decide what action to take to release the processor from its inactive state.[28]

---

[28] PC/AT systems reset the processor whenever a shutdown is detected. In the case of a halt, it does nothing; the next system timer tick automatically releases the processor from the halt state.

For both halts and shutdowns, any locked resources (i.e. DESCR_TABLE, DIR_TABLE, PAGE_TABLE, IDT, and MEM) are released and the 80x86 waits for an external interrupt to occur. The interrupt is serviced as usual; the return address for the interrupt handler is set to the instruction following the HLT. Normal rules apply for interrupt detection. In particular, if normal interrupts are disabled, only a nonmaskable interrupt (or system reset) will release the processor from the halt or shutdown condition.

2.16   Software debug features

The 80x86 architecture supports three primary mechanisms to aid the construction of software debuggers:

1.   instruction single step

2.   instruction breakpoint via instruction replacement

3.   instruction and data breakpoints via address breakpoint registers

In addition to these features, I/O port access breakpoints can also be implemented via the I/O permission map. This section describes the three main debug features in turn; use of the I/O permission map is described in §2.9 on page 118. Note that the first two features are supported by all 80x86 implementations. Breakpoint registers and the I/O permission map, however, are only available on the 80376, 80386, and i486.

2.16.1   Instruction single step

If an instruction is executed with the trap flag (TF) set a DEBUG exception is generated after the instruction completes successfully. TF is reset automatically prior to executing the first instruction of the DEBUG exception handler; however, the [E]FLAGS image pushed onto the stack keeps TF set. Therefore, the debug handler executes without further DEBUG exceptions (caused by TF). When the IRET to leave the handler is executed, TF is set once again (since the restored [E]FLAGS image has it set). This generates another DEBUG trap after the instruction at the target of the IRET completes. The mechanism activated by setting TF allows a body of code to be executed instruction by instruction. This **single-stepping** feature is used primarily by program debuggers.

There are a couple of issues to consider in the context of single stepping. First, what happens if an instruction's execution is started with TF set, but a fault is detected during the execution? To avoid single stepping into the fault handler, TF is cleared prior to entering it. However, the TF image pushed onto the stack is left set, so that a retry of the faulty instruction (with the fault presumably repaired) resumes single stepping.

Another issue deals with the details of how the single step operation is described formally. Since the DEBUG exception caused by single step occurs after an instruction completes, it makes sense to check TF after an instruction has completed successfully. However, this presents a problem when describing instructions that modify TF; for example, IRET or POPF. In particular, consider an IRET that has just set TF. Although TF appears set after the IRET completes, the DEBUG trap should be deferred till after the instruction at the target of the IRET completes. In other words, the effect of setting TF should be delayed by one instruction. This is achieved by introducing the invisible flag prev_TF. This flag tracks the value of TF, delayed by one instruction. If prev_TF is set upon an instruction's completion, a DEBUG trap is signaled. This flag is updated at the end of an instruction, after all DEBUG exceptions have been checked. See the function report_brkpts for details.

2.16.2 Instruction breakpoints via INT 3

In addition to single stepping, a common feature found in debuggers is the ability to breakpoint on the execution of a particular instruction. A way this can be done on the 80x86 is by replacing the breakpointed instruction by a special "trap" instruction and saving the replaced instruction in a buffer. Now execution of the program under debug is begun. If the "trap" instruction is executed control flow is diverted to the debugger. The debugger can now report that an instruction breakpoint has occurred. To resume normal execution, the original instruction (saved in the buffer) is copied back over the "trap" instruction.

The 80x86 "trap" instruction is called INT3. If executed, this instruction simply signals a software interrupt via interrupt 3; that is, its behavior is identical to that of the software interrupt instruction INT 3. However, this instruction takes two bytes to encode, whereas INT3 is a one-byte instruction. This special encoding is provided so that the shortest 80x86 instructions (which occupy only a single byte) can be replaced without having to increase the size of the program being debugged.

Note that the use of vector entry 3 for instruction breakpoints precludes its use for other purposes. Also note that the INT 3 handler points at the instruction following it. This makes it impossible to predict reliably the address of the instruction that signaled the interrupt. (This is because the interrupt 3 handler can be entered by more than one instruction, and because it is not possible to determine the instruction that precedes the current instruction in a variable instruction length machine like the 80x86.) Therefore, for a debugger to operate properly, it has to keep track of the addresses where breakpoints have been set, and determine the breakpoint address accordingly.

2.16.3 Breakpoint register usage

Setting instruction breakpoints via INT 3 is invasive. Unless used carefully, it can lead to problems when debugging shared, multitasking code. Also, the method cannot be used to set instruction breakpoints in ROM memory. To solve these problems, and to allow setting memory reference breakpoints as well, the 80376, 80386, and i486 introduce four linear address breakpoint registers, DR0 through DR3, a status register, DR6, and a control register, DR7. DR0 through DR4 store up to four distinct breakpoint addresses. The debug control register contains bits that allow any subset of the four registers to be enabled. It also specifies whether a breakpoint address refer to an instruction or to data. For data breakpoints it further specifies whether the breakpoint should occur on a write only, or whether it should occur on a read or a write. Furthermore, it specifies the breakpoint region, that is, the number of bytes (starting at a given breakpoint address) that should be monitored.

The starting address of an instructions about to execute is always compared against all breakpoint registers that are configured as instruction breakpoints. Similarly, the address of all bytes of memory that participate in a memory access are compared against breakpoint registers configured as data breakpoint regions. If any byte falls within a breakpoint region, or if an instruction breakpoint is active, a DEBUG exception is signaled.

To ensure reliable instruction operation, all checks for DEBUG exceptions are done after an instruction completes. This works well for single stepping (described earlier). It also works well for instruction breakpoints, since CS:EIP always points at the next instruction. Therefore, instruction breakpoints are signaled *before* the breakpointed instruction begins execution; that is, they are processed as faults. (Note that this is different from the way INT 3 instruction breakpoints are reported.) However, data breakpoint handling is somewhat messy.

Data breakpoints that occur during an instruction's execution are recorded in a breakpoint vector (brkpt_active). By only recording data breakpoints (and not reporting them) completion of instructions that make multiple memory references is ensured. The data breakpoints vector is checked at the end of an instruction, and any active breakpoints are reported. However, since the instruction has completed execution, the DEBUG exception handler is invoked pointing at the instruction *following* the instruction in which the data breakpoint occurred; that is, data breakpoints are serviced as traps, rather than faults. Because the 80*x*86 instruction encoding is such that it is not possible to determine the instruction that precedes the current instruction, it is not possible (in general) to determine the instruction that caused a data breakpoint simply by referencing the instruction pointed at by a DEBUG exception handler. Partial solutions to this problem entail keeping track of a disassembled set of instructions. If a data breakpoint occurs, the disassembled instruction list can be examined to determine the instruction preceding the instruction where the breakpoint was reported. This assumes, however, that the instruction that caused the breakpoint is not a branch instruction.

In addition to instruction and data breakpoints the 80376, 80386, and i486 also introduce the notion of trapping on a task switch. This is done by examining the T flag of the new task's task state segment. (Since the T flag is available only in a TSS32, task switch traps are only possible when the new task's TSS is a TSS32.) If T is set, a DEBUG exception is reported.

Since debug register access is via normal 80*x*86 instructions (see the MOV instructions described on pages 507 through 510), it is possible that a program being debugged by a debugger that uses the breakpoint registers may itself try to update the debug registers. To disallow such "nested" debug register access, it is possible to disable debug register access by setting a specific flag (GD) in DR7 (the debug control register). If an instruction references a debug register when GD is set, a DEBUG fault is signaled.

2.16.3.1 The debug status register

Many combinations of instruction breakpoints, data breakpoints, single-step, task trap, and debug register access fault can occur at the end of an instruction. Since all invoke the DEBUG exception handler, a mechanism for specifying the cause of the DEBUG exception is needed. The debug status register DR6, shown diagrammatically in Figure 2.10 on page 29, fills this need. The flags in this register indicate the exception cause, as shown in the C language defintions below.

```
#define BT    DR6⟨15⟩         /* Because of Task switch */
#define BS    DR6⟨14⟩         /* Because of Single step */
#define BD    DR6⟨13⟩         /* Because of debug register access */
#define B3    DR6⟨3⟩          /* Because of DR3 match */
#define B2    DR6⟨2⟩          /* Because of DR2 match */
#define B1    DR6⟨1⟩          /* Because of DR1 match */
#define B0    DR6⟨0⟩          /* Because of DR0 match */
```

The "Because" flags are only set by the 80*x*86, they are not cleared. It is up to the DEBUG exception handler to clear them. (If left uncleared, DR6 will accumulate all DEBUG exception causes.)

2.16.3.2 The debug control register

We have discussed a number of uses of DR7, the debug control register. Let us examine its structure more closely. Figure 2.10 on page 29 presents a diagrammatic view of the register; the definitions below do the same in C language notation.

```
#define LEN3 DR7⟨31:30⟩       /* DR3 match length */
#define RW3  DR7⟨29:28⟩       /* DR3 match type */
#define LEN2 DR7⟨27:26⟩       /* DR2 match length */
#define RW2  DR7⟨25:24⟩       /* DR2 match type */
#define LEN1 DR7⟨23:22⟩       /* DR1 match length */
#define RW1  DR7⟨21:20⟩       /* DR1 match type */
#define LEN0 DR7⟨19:18⟩       /* DR0 match length */
#define RW0  DR7⟨17:16⟩       /* DR0 match type */
#define GD    DR7⟨13⟩         /* Global Disable */
#define GE    DR7⟨9⟩          /* Global Exact flag */
#define LE    DR7⟨8⟩          /* Local Exact flag */
#define G3    DR7⟨7⟩          /* Global DR3 enable flag */
#define L3    DR7⟨6⟩          /* Local DR3 enable flag */
#define G2    DR7⟨5⟩          /* Global DR2 enable flag */
#define L2    DR7⟨4⟩          /* Local DR2 enable flag */
#define G1    DR7⟨3⟩          /* Global DR1 enable flag */
#define L1    DR7⟨2⟩          /* Local DR1 enable flag */
#define G0    DR7⟨1⟩          /* Global DR0 enable flag */
#define L0    DR7⟨0⟩          /* Local DR0 enable flag */
```

Note that enable flags (except GD) have "global" and "local" variants. Both variants need to be set before the corresponding check is enabled. For example, to enable matching on the address stored in DR1, both LE1 and GE1 must be set

RW setting	Breakpoint type
00	Instruction execution only (LEN must be set to 00)
01	Data writes only
10	*reserved*
11	Data reads or writes

LEN setting	Size of breakpoint region
00	1 byte (this is the only valid setting for instruction breakpoints)
01	2 bytes
10	*reserved*
11	4 bytes

NOTE: A data breakpoint address register's contents must be a multiple of the breakpoint region's size.

Figure 2.45: Breakpoint register type and length encodings

to 1. Also note that task switch traps occur whenever the T flag in a new TSS is set; there is no enable flag corresponding to it.

The LENx and RWx fields in DR7 control whether or not the corresponding debug registers (DR0 through DR3) are configured for instruction or data breakpoints. In the case of a data breakpoint the LENx field indicates the size of the breakpoint region. The encodings used for both fields are summarized in Figure 2.45. As shown in the figure, all breakpoint regions are required to be region-size aligned. For example, if LEN2 is set to 01 (i.e., the region size is a WORD), the address in DR2 must be a multiple of 2. In fact, the least significant bit of the breakpoint address register is ignored if the region is WORD-sized, and the two least significant bits are ignored if the region is DWORD-sized.

2.16.3.3 Checking for data breakpoints

Data breakpoints are only accumulated during an instruction's execution, and reported after the instruction completes successfully. This requires that every memory data reference be compared against the breakpoint registers. This is done in the linear memory read and write routines (see §2.7.7.2 and §2.7.7.3, respectively) via calls to the check_brkpt routine. The definition of this routine is as follows.

```
check_brkpt(type, laddr)
{
    /* == Accumulate (but do not report) breakpoint matches in brkpt active vector. == */
    if ( (G0 || L0) && !brkpt_active[0] )
        brkpt_active[0] = ( (type==WRITE && RW0==1) || RW0==3 ) &&
                          DR0 <=ᵤ laddr && laddr <=ᵤ DR0+LEN0 ;
    if ( (G1 || L1) && !brkpt_active[1] )
        brkpt_active[1] = ( (type==WRITE && RW1==1) || RW1==3 ) &&
                          DR1 <=ᵤ laddr && laddr <=ᵤ DR1+LEN1 ;
    if ( (G2 || L2) && !brkpt_active[2] )
        brkpt_active[2] = ( (type==WRITE && RW2==1) || RW2==3 ) &&
                          DR2 <=ᵤ laddr && laddr <=ᵤ DR2+LEN2 ;
    if ( (G3 || L3) && !brkpt_active[3] )
        brkpt_active[3] = ( (type=WRITE && RW3==1) || RW3==3 ) &&
                          DR3 <=ᵤ laddr && laddr <=ᵤ DR3+LEN3 ;
}
```

2.16.3.4 Reporting breakpoints

Single-step conditions, instruction breakpoints on the instruction that will execute next, and data breakpoints for the instruction just executed are all reported at the end of every instruction. The definition of this function is shown below.

```
report_brkpts()
{
    /* == Check for instruction breakpoints, by comparing against address of instruction
          about to execute == */
    linEIP = CS_desc.Base + EIP;
    B0 = brkpt_active[0] || ( ! RF && (G0 || L0) && RW0 == 0 && LEN0 == 1 &&
                          (DR0 == linEIP) );
    B1 = brkpt_active[1] || ( ! RF && (G1 || L1) && RW1 == 0 && LEN1 == 1 &&
                          (DR1 == linEIP) );
    B2 = brkpt_active[2] || ( ! RF && (G2 || L2) && RW2 == 0 && LEN2 == 1 &&
                          (DR2 == linEIP) );
    B3 = brkpt_active[3] || ( ! RF && (G3 || L3) && RW3 == 0 && LEN3 == 1 &&
                          (DR3 == linEIP) );

    /* == Reset all brkpt active flags (set by data breakpoints), since they have all been
          checked.  Also, clear the restart flag (RF), since the current instruction has just
          completed successfully. == */
    clear_active_brkpts(); /* see below */
    RF = 0;

    /* == Check if single stepping is active.  If so set BS flag (DR6⟨14⟩) == */
    if ( prev_TF )
        BS = 1;
```

```
/* == Make the TF setting from this instruction the new prev_TF == */
prev_TF = TF;

/* == Report any active breakpoints, or single step condition. Note that if an instruction
      breakpoint is active, it is in reference to the current EIP value; i.e. in reference to
      the instruction about to be executed. Hence, instruction breakpoints are more
      properly viewed as faults. == */
if ( B0 || B1 || B2 || B3 || prev_TF )
   signal_trap(DEBUG);
}
```

In the case of data breakpoints, the temporary accumulation vector active_brkpts
needs to be cleared after all breakpoints have been reported. This is also done
whenever a fault is detected (so that partially detected data breakpoints don't get
reported). The clear_active_brkpts routine, described below, performs this
function.

```
clear_active_brkpts()
{
   brkpt_active[0] = FALSE;
   brkpt_active[1] = FALSE;
   brkpt_active[2] = FALSE;
   brkpt_active[3] = FALSE;
}
```

2.16.3.5 Use of the RF flag

We know from the discussion above that if an instruction breakpoint is set, it is
signaled just before the instruction begins execution. Since breakpoints do not
indicate a defect in a program, it is very likely that the debugger setting the
breakpoint will attempt to execute the instruction after servicing a breakpoint on
it. To do so would require that the breakpoint be removed. This can be
undesirable if the intent of the debugger is to have a permanent breakpoint set at
the instruction.

The 80x86 solves this problem by allowing DEBUG faults to be inhibited for the
duration of a single instruction. This happens whenever the RF (i.e., **restart
flag**) is set. Since RF is a part of the EFLAGS image, it is loaded whenever a
32-bit IRET is performed. The general method for using the flag is as follows:

1. Set up a DEBUG exception handler so that it determines whether or not a
    debug fault has occurred. This can be done by examining the debug status
    register DR6.

2. If the exception is a debug fault, set the RF flag bit position in the EFLAGS image that was pushed onto the stack (when the DEBUG exception handler was entered).

3. Complete execution of the DEBUG exception handler. When the IRETD to leave the handler is executed, the RF flag will get set.

4. The IRETD will reattempt execution of the instruction that caused the debug fault. However, since RF is set, no exception will be reported.

5. Just after checking for breakpoints, RF is automatically cleared by the 80x86. Thus, debug faults on subsequent instructions are enabled once more.

An important point to note in all this is that RF is stored in the upper half of EFLAGS; that is, it is unavailable in the FLAGS image. Therefore, for the restart flag function to operate correctly, the DEBUG exception handler must exit using an IRETD.

Another issue is what happens if a nondebug fault (e.g., a PAGE fault) is detected when executing an instruction that had an instruction breakpoint. If the fault is repaired and the instruction reattempted, the instruction breakpoint will be reported once again. The same situation would occur if an interruptable instruction were resumed (after an interrupt service). Rather than require that all handlers of such faults and interrupts set the RF flag, it is done automatically. That is, when entering a nondebug fault handler, or an interrupt service routine that suspended an interruptable instruction, the RF flag image pushed onto the stack is automatically set. Keep in mind that RF is only pushed if the interrupt is serviced via an INTERRUPT_GATE32 or TRAP_GATE32. In particular, in REAL mode, the RF flag has to be set explicitly by software.

2.17 Processor initialization

This section describes the state of 80x86 registers upon reset. The reset state of the 80x87 processor extension's registers is described in §3.11 (starting on page 257). Note that 80x86 programs using the 80x87 should not assume that the processor extension is self-initializing. To guarantee that an 80x87 is initialized, the FNINIT instruction must be issued.

Since some registers (e.g., CR0) are not present in all implementations of the 80x86, and since some implementations only support 16-bit registers, it is cumbersome to try to capture all initialization actions in a single routine. Instead, the reset_cpu routine (referenced by the main instruction loop on page 11) is defined in terms of four distinct routines, as follows:

- reset_86: defines the reset state for the 8086 and 80186
- reset_286: defines the reset state for the 80286
- reset_386_486: defines the reset state for the 80386 and i486
- reset_376: defines the reset state for the 80376

The routines may initialize register state that does not exist on a given processor. This is done so that the C language descriptions make sense for the subset implementations. For example, the PG (paging enable) flag is set to 0 by the reset_86 routine, to indicate that paging features are unavailable on the 8086. Such "permanent" flag settings are marked with comments indicating their nature.

2.17.1 Initializing the 8086

The 8086 (and 80186) are 16-bit processors with no segment protection or paging facilities. The initial state of their registers are as follows.

```
reset_86()
{
    /* == Initialize FLAGS.  Flags in the upper half of EFLAGS are not available. == */
    EFLAGS⟨31:16⟩ = undefined;              /* AC, RF, VM unavailable */
    FLAGS⟨15:2⟩ = 0;
    FLAGS⟨1⟩ = 1;                           /* Permanently set to 1 */
    FLAGS⟨0⟩ = 0;

    /* == Setup segment registers and segment descriptor registers to have REAL mode
          values.  An 8086 does not implement descriptor registers, and does not have flags
          such as  Readable  and  Writable.  The initial values given here are done so that
          the memory access algorithms shown in this book are meaningful.  == */
    ES = 0;
    ES_desc.Base = 0;
    /* Following ES_desc settings are permanent */
    ES_desc.Readable = ES_desc.Writable = TRUE;
    ES_desc.Executable = FALSE;
    ES_desc.Limit = 0xFFFF;
    ES_desc.DefaultAttr = 0;

    SS = 0;
    SS_desc.Base = 0;
    /* Following SS_desc settings are permanent */
```

```
SS_desc.Readable = SS_desc.Writable = TRUE;
SS_desc.Executable = FALSE;
SS_desc.Limit = 0xFFFF;
SS_desc.DefaultAttr = 0;

DS = 0;
DS_desc.Base = 0;
/* Following DS_desc settings are permanent */
DS_desc.Readable = DS_desc.Writable = TRUE;
DS_desc.Executable = FALSE;
DS_desc.Limit = 0xFFFF;
DS_desc.DefaultAttr = 0;

CS = 0xF000;
CS_desc.Base = 0xF0000;
/* Following CS_desc settings are permanent */
CS_desc.Readable = CS_desc.Writable = CS_desc.Executable = TRUE;
CS_desc.Limit = 0xFFFF;
CS_desc.DefaultAttr = 0;

/* == Initialize IP register.  (The upper half of EIP is unavailable.) == */
IP = 0xFFF0;  /* start address is F000:FFF0; i.e., 0xFFFF0 */

/* == Initialize miscellaneous invisible state == */
prev_TF = 0;
prev_instr_loaded_SS = FALSE;

/* == General registers are not initialized == */
AX = undefined;   CX = undefined;  DX = undefined;  BX = undefined;
SP = undefined;   BP = undefined;  SI = undefined;  DI = undefined;


/* === All remaining initializations are permanent === */

/* == Setup interrupt table descriptor, starting at address 0 == */
IDT_desc.Base = 0;
IDT_desc.Limit = 0x3FF;  /* 256 4-byte entries */
IDT_desc.Readable = TRUE;

/* == Set flags to indicate REAL mode.  Also, disable alignment checks (available only
on the i486) == */
CPL = 0;
PE = 0;
PG = 0;
AM = AC = 0;

/* == In the 8086, an NMI is always serviced, even if it occurs while in the NMI handler.
     This is indicated by permanently clearing NMI_handler_active. == */
NMI_handler_active = FALSE;

/* == Clear brkpt_active vector, since breakpoints are not supported.  Also set restart
     flag (RF) to permanently disable debug faults. == */
```

```
    brkpt_active[0] = FALSE;  brkpt_active[1] = FALSE;
    brkpt_active[2] = FALSE;  brkpt_active[3] = FALSE;
    RF = 1;
}
```

2.17.2 Initializing the 80286

Although the 80286 is a 16-bit microprocessor, it features segment-based
memory protection. It also has a machine status word (MSW) that stores the PE,
MP, TS, and EM flags. The initial state of the 80286 is very similar to the 8086;
however, state related to memory protection is actually present. For example, the
Limit field of segment descriptor registers is an actual (invisible) register.

```
reset_286()
{
    /* == Initialize FLAGS.  Flags in the upper half of EFLAGS are not available. == */
    EFLAGS⟨31:16⟩ = undefined;            /* AC, RF, VM unavailable */
    FLAGS⟨15:2⟩ = 0;
    FLAGS⟨1⟩ = 1;                          /* Permanently set to 1 */
    FLAGS⟨0⟩ = 0;

    /* == Setup segment registers and segment descriptor registers.  Unlike the 8086, the
          80286 Limit and access rights are programmable.  However, the Limit field's value
          is constrained to be no greater than 0xFFFF, and the Base field's value can be no
          greater than 0xFFFFFF. == */
    ES = 0;
    ES_desc.Base = 0;
    ES_desc.Readable = ES_desc.Writable = TRUE;
    ES_desc.Executable = FALSE;
    ES_desc.Limit = 0xFFFF;
    ES_desc.DefaultAttr = 0; /* permanent 0 */

    SS = 0;
    SS_desc.Base = 0;
    SS_desc.Readable = SS_desc.Writable = TRUE;
    SS_desc.Executable = FALSE;
    SS_desc.Limit = 0xFFFF;
    SS_desc.DefaultAttr = 0; /* permanent 0 */

    DS = 0;
    DS_desc.Base = 0;
    DS_desc.Readable = DS_desc.Writable = TRUE;
    DS_desc.Executable = FALSE;
    DS_desc.Limit = 0xFFFF;
    DS_desc.DefaultAttr = 0; /* permanent 0 */

    CS = 0xF000;
    CS_desc.Base = 0xF0000;
    CS_desc.Readable = CS_desc.Writable = CS_desc.Executable = TRUE;
    CS_desc.Limit = 0xFFFF;
```

```
CS_desc.DefaultAttr = 0;  /* permanent 0 */

/* == Setup interrupt table descriptor, starting at address 0 == */
IDT_desc.Base = 0;
IDT_desc.Limit = 0x3FF;  /* 256 4-byte entries (REAL mode) */
IDT_desc.Readable = TRUE;

/* == Initialize IP register.  (The upper half of EIP is unavailable.) == */
IP = 0xFFF0;  /* start address is F000:FFF0; i.e. 0xFFFF0 */

/* == Set flags to indicate REAL mode, and set other MSW bits.  Also set CPL to 0 to
      reflect REAL mode. == */
MSW = undefined;  /* all MSW flags except PE, MP, EM, and TS are undefined */
PE = MP = EM = TS = 0;

CPL = 0;

/* == Initialize miscellaneous invisible state == */
prev_TF = 0;
prev_instr_loaded_SS = FALSE;
NMI_handler_active = FALSE;

/* == General registers are not initialized == */
AX = undefined;   CX = undefined;  DX = undefined;  BX = undefined;
SP = undefined;   BP = undefined;  SI = undefined;  DI = undefined;


/* === All remaining initializations are permanent === */

/* == Disable paging and alignment checks permanently (since they are unavailable) ==
      */
PG = 0;
AM = AC = 0;

/* == Clear brkpt_active vector, since breakpoints registers are not supported.  Also set
      restart flag (RF) to permanently disable debug faults. == */
brkpt_active[0] = FALSE;  brkpt_active[1] = FALSE;
brkpt_active[2] = FALSE;  brkpt_active[3] = FALSE;
RF = 1;
}
```

2.17.3 Initializing the 80386 and i486

The 80386 is the earliest implementation of the 80x86 family that features 32-bit registers, and paging-based memory protection. This is the reason for some of the differences between the 80286 and 80386 initialization sequences. The 80386 also introduces the following initialization-related concepts.

1. built-in self-test (BIST): this feature tests most of the logic implemented in regular arrays (i.e., PLAs) and the control ROM for defects introduced

either at the time of manufacture, or in field use. A successful self-test sequence is indicated if EAX is set to 0 after reset. Any other value indicates a defect.

2. part identifier: this is a pair of numbers stored in the DH and DL registers after reset. The number in DH identifies the 80*x*86 implementation (e.g., the 80386 is specified by setting DH to 3). The number in DL is related to the revision level (i.e., stepping id) of the part. Intel does not guarantee any correspondence between DL values and part revisions. However, the general intention is to increment DL values as newer steppings appear. System initialization software can utilize DL values published by Intel to take into account bugs and features that might be specific to a particular stepping.

The i486 implements all 80386 features, including self-test.[29] Additionally, it defines certain flags related to the control of its on-chip cache and alignment check features. The reset_386_486 routine below describes the reset state for both the 80386 and i486. i486-specific flags are clearly marked.

```
reset_386_486()
{
    /* == Perform optional self-test.  Self-test is selected on the 80386 by activating the
          BUSY pin on RESET.  On the i486 it is selected by activating the AHOLD pin in
          the clock cycle prior to deactivating RESET. == */
    if ( « self test » )
    {   if ( « self test passed » )
            EAX = 0;
        else
            EAX = undefined;
    }

    /* == Identify device == */
    if ( « CPU is 80386 » )
        DH = 0x03;  DL = « stepping id »;
    else if ( « CPU is 80386SX » )
        DH = 0x23;  DL = « stepping id »;
    else /* « CPU is i486 » */
        DH = 0x04;  DL = « stepping id »;

    /* == Initialize EFLAGS.  Unused bits 15, 5, and 3 are permanently set to 0.  Unused bit
       1 is permanently set to 1. == */
    EFLAGS⟨31:19⟩ = undefined;
    /* Define alignment check flag (AC) */
    if ( « CPU is 80386 » )
        EFLAGS⟨18⟩ = undefined;
```

---

[29] The i486's self-test checks PLAs and the control ROM and also tests the TLB and the on-chip cache.

```
else /* « CPU is i486 » */
   EFLAGS⟨18⟩ = 0;
/* Clear all active flags */
EFLAGS⟨17:2⟩ = 0;
EFLAGS⟨1⟩ = 1;
EFLAGS⟨0⟩ = 0;

/* == Initialize machine status word CR0.  The state of all unused bits in this register are
       undefined. == */
CR0 = undefined;
PG = 0;  TS = 0;  EM = 0;  MP = 0;  PE = 0;
if ( « CPU is i486 » )  /* initialize CD, NW, AM flags */
{   CD = 0;  /* enable caching */
    NW = 0;  /* writes are transparent */
    AM = 0;  /* disable AC (the alignment check flag) */
}

/* == Setup segment registers and segment descriptor registers using a loop.  Note that
       both the Limit and Base fields of 80386 and i486 descriptors can store 32-bit
       values.  Also note that the FS and GS segment and descriptor registers are
       available, in addition to ES, CS, SS, and DS. == */
for (i = 0; i <= 5; i++)
{   /* Set all segment registers to 0 */
    curr.segReg[i] = 0;

    descrVec[i].Valid = TRUE;
    descrVec[i].Base = 0;
    descrVec[i].Limit = 0xFFFF;
    descrVec[i].DPL = 0;
    descrVec[i].DefaultAttr = FALSE;
    descrVec[i].Readable = TRUE;
    descrVec[i].Writable = TRUE;
    descrVec[i].Executable = FALSE;
    descrVec[i].ExpandDown = FALSE;
}
/* == Make CS's segment executable, and set it at high memory == */
CS = 0xF000;
CS_desc.Executable = TRUE;
CS_desc.Base = 0xFFFF0000;
/* Set initial code fetch address */
EIP = 0x0000FFF0;

/* == Setup initial interrupt descriptor table (IDT) == */
IDT_desc.Base = 0;
IDT_desc.Limit = 2047;     /* 256 entries */
IDT_desc.Readable = TRUE;  /* Write/Exec attributes never used */

/* == Initialize CPL and miscellaneous state == */
CPL = 0;
prev_TF = 0;
prev_instr_loaded_SS = FALSE;
task_switch_in_progress = FALSE;
```

```
    NMI_handler_active = FALSE;
    brkpt_active[0] = FALSE;  brkpt_active[1] = FALSE;
    brkpt_active[2] = FALSE;  brkpt_active[3] = FALSE;
}
```

2.17.4 Initializing the 80376

From the point of view of programming compatibility, the full-blown 80*x*86 architecture has four execution modes: REAL, 16-bit PROTECTED, 32-bit PROTECTED, and VM86. The 80376 is a defeatured 80386 that can only execute in 32-bit PROTECTED mode. Furthermore, paging is unavailable on the part. Therefore, the initialization for the 80376 is very similar to that of the 80386, except that some flags are permanently set.

```
reset_376()
{
    /* == Perform optional self-test.  Self-test is selected on the 80376 by activating the
          BUSY pin on RESET. == */
    if ( « self test » )
    {   if ( « self test passed » )
            EAX = 0;
        else
            EAX = undefined;
    }

    /* == Identify device (the 0x33 identifies a 80376) == */
    DH = 0x33;  DL = « stepping id »;

    /* == Initialize EFLAGS.  Unused bits 15, 5, and 3 are permanently set to 0.  Unused bit
       1 is permanently set to 1. == */
    EFLAGS⟨31:18⟩ = undefined;
    /* Clear all active flags.  Note that the VM flag is permanently set to 0 on the 80376. */
    EFLAGS⟨17:2⟩ = 0;
    EFLAGS⟨1⟩ = 1;
    EFLAGS⟨0⟩ = 0;

    /* == Initialize machine status word CR0.  The state of all unused bits in this register are
          undefined.  The settings for PG and PE are permanent; i.e. the 80376 is always in
          PROTECTED mode, and can never enable paging. == */
    CR0 = undefined;
    PG = 0;
    PE = 0;
    TS = 0;  EM = 0;  MP = 0;

    /* == Setup segment registers and segment descriptor registers using a loop.  Note that
          both the Limit and Base fields of 80386 and i486 descriptors can store 32 bit
          values.  Also note that the FS and GS segment and descriptor registers are
          available, in addition to ES, CS, SS, and DS.  The DefaultAttr flag is permanently
          1 for all descriptors. == */
```

```
for (i = 0; i <= 5; i++)
{   /* Set all segment registers to 0 */
    curr.segReg[i] = 0;

    descrVec[i].Valid = TRUE;
    descrVec[i].Base = 0;
    descrVec[i].Limit = 0xFFFF;
    descrVec[i].DPL = 0;
    descrVec[i].DefaultAttr = 1;  /* permanently set (indicating 32 bit mode) */
    descrVec[i].Readable = TRUE;
    descrVec[i].Writable = TRUE;
    descrVec[i].Executable = FALSE;
    descrVec[i].ExpandDown = FALSE;
}
/* == Make CS's segment executable, and set it at high memory == */
CS = 0xF000;
CS_desc.Executable = TRUE;
CS_desc.Base = 0xFFFF0000;
/* Set initial code fetch address */
EIP = 0x0000FFF0;

/* == Setup initial interrupt descriptor table (IDT) == */
IDT_desc.Base = 0;
IDT_desc.Limit = 2047;     /* 256 entries */
IDT_desc.Readable = TRUE;  /* Write/Exec attributes never used */

/* == Initialize CPL and miscellaneous state == */
CPL = 0;
prev_TF = 0;
prev_instr_loaded_SS = FALSE;
task_switch_in_progress = FALSE;
NMI_handler_active = FALSE;
brkpt_active[0] = FALSE;  brkpt_active[1] = FALSE;
brkpt_active[2] = FALSE;  brkpt_active[3] = FALSE;
}
```

2.18 Instruction decoding

The main instruction interpretation loop (see page 11) uses the decode_instruction routine to determine an instruction's operation, and its operands (e.g., the name of a register operand or the offset and segment register that participate in a memory reference). Another (perhaps more useful) way to view decode_instruction's function is that it defines the format and encoding of 80x86 instructions. This section takes the latter view and describes 80x86 instruction encoding using diagrams and prose rather than as a C language routine.

80x86 instructions have three general categories of operands: registers, memory locations, and immediates. Based on these categories, a broad grouping of 80x86 instructions is as follows:

1. instructions with no operands (e.g., HLT).

2. instructions with a single operand: the operand is usually either a general register or memory operand (e.g., PUSH EAX pushed the value of EAX onto the stack).

3. instructions with two operands: one operand is either a general register or memory operand, the other operand is a general register. In most cases, the two operands are combined using a binary operator and the result is stored back into one of the operands (e.g., ADD AX, var increments AX by the value of the memory-based variable *var*).

4. move operations (with two operands): one operand is a general register, whereas the other is another general, segment, control, test, or debug register. This allows data to be copied between the various register classes. For the segment register and general register cases, the other operand can be a general register or a memory location (e.g., MOV CR0, EDX loads control register CR0 with the contents of general register EDX).

5. instructions with three operands: one operand is a general register, another is a general register or memory operand, and the third is an immediate. The only three operand instructions are the funnel shift instructions SHLD and SHRD and the three-operand multiply instruction IMUL.

6. jump/call instructions with an EIP-relative displacement: these instructions transfer control to a location within the current code segment that is relative to the current instruction pointer (EIP).

7. jump/call instructions with an OFFSET-only target: these instructions transfer control to the instruction at the offset specified by the operand within the current code segment. OFFSET-only operands are often called "near" operands. Correspondingly, the operand's address is called a near pointer.

8. jump/call instructions with a SELECTOR:OFFSET target: these instructions transfer control to the instruction at the OFFSET within the segment named by the SELECTOR. Such operands are often called "far" operands. Correspondingly, the operand's address is called a far pointer.

Many instructions have implied operands. For example, the IDIV instruction, which divides a signed DWORD by a signed WORD, always fetches the dividend from the register pair DX:AX. Another group of instructions with implied registers are the string operations. In general, these instructions fetch one operand from the offset within the DS segment specified by ESI and another operand from the offset within the ES segment specified by ESI. Since such instructions uniquely identify a register, they are said to **characterize** the register(s) involved. Characterized register use increases instruction encoding efficiency, but reduces programming flexibility.

In general, an instruction's operand field either encodes all possible registers of a given class, or it assumes an implied register: there are no instructions that allow only a subset of registers (with size greater than one) as operands. Note, however, that the registers that can participate in the generation of 16-bit offset addressing is limited: only combinations of BP, BX, SI, and DI are allowed. Most of these restrictions disappear when using 32-bit addressing; the only restriction that remains is that ESP cannot be used as an index register.

2.18.1 Encoding structure

80x86 instructions are variable in length and can start at any byte address in memory; that is, there are no alignment requirements. (Note, however, that aligning the target of a branch to a DWORD, and preferably a 16-byte boundary, can improve performance.) The shortest instruction is 1 byte in size. Because of the possibility of prefixes (described below) an instruction can be made arbitrarily long. However, the longest instruction without redundant prefixes is 10 bytes in the case of the 80286 and its predecessors and 15 bytes for the 80376, 80386, and i486. Attempting to execute an 11-byte or longer instruction on the

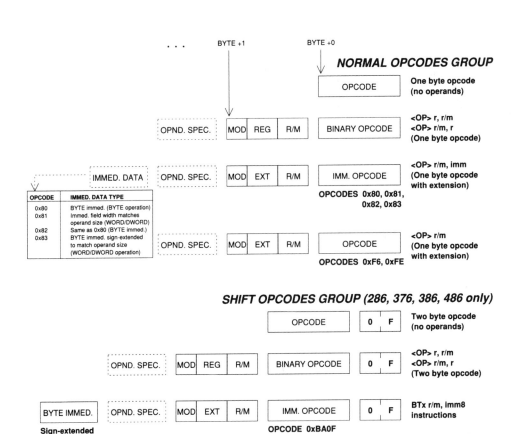

Figure 2.46: General structure of nonbranching instructions

80286, or a 16-byte or longer instruction on the 80376, 80386, or i486 signals a GP fault with an error code of 0.

An instruction has three possible components: a prefix list, an opcode specification, and a list of operands. An instruction always begins with its prefixes (if any). That is, the prefixes occupy the least numbered memory addresses. These are followed by the opcode. The opcode can occupy either one or two bytes. Most opcodes are one byte in size. However, since all single-byte opcodes are assigned, an "overflow" opcode space is defined using the byte value 0x0F as a shift; that is, if the first opcode byte is 0x0F the "shifted" opcode map is looked up using the second opcode byte. In some cases, the opcode only specifies a category of operations: the actual operation is specified by the "extension" field in the byte following the last opcode byte. A diagrammatic representation of most non-branching instructions is shown in Figure 2.46. The branching instructions' formats, and the formats of assorted special cases are shown in Figure 2.47. Keeping with the convention used throughout this book, the instruction data is shown right to left in both figures; that is, bytes occupying smaller addresses appear on the right.

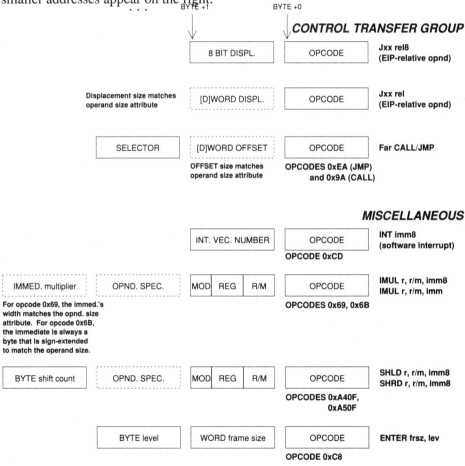

Figure 2.47: Branch format and miscellaneous other formats

PREFIX	ENCODING (in hex)	DESCRIPTION
ES:	26	Override default, and use ES_desc for mem. opnd.
CS:	2E	Override default, and use CS_desc for mem. opnd.
SS:	36	Override default, and use SS_desc for mem. opnd.
DS:	3E	Override default, and use DS_desc for mem. opnd.
FS:	64	Override default, and use FS_desc for mem. opnd. (376, 386, 486 only)
GS:	65	Override default, and use GS_desc for mem. opnd. (376,386,486 only)
LOCK	F0	Perform memory read-modify-write in instruction that follows atomically
REP/REPE	F3	Repeat following string instruction (see text below)
REPNE	F2	Repeat following string instruction (see text below)
opnd. size	66	Make operand size attrib. the inverse of the default
addr. size	67	Make address size attrib. the inverse of the default

Figure 2.48: Summary of 80*x*86 instruction prefixes

2.18.2 Instruction prefixes

Prefixes are optional single-byte entities that modify the behavior of the instruction they precede. Figure 2.48 lists all instruction prefixes, along with the effects they have. Prefixes may appear in any order, as long as they all immediately precede the instruction they are meant for. Not all prefixes make sense in all contexts. For example, the REP prefix can only appear in front of string element instructions; that is, the instructions CMP*x*, INS*x*, LODS*x*, MOVS*x*, OUTS*x*, SCAS*x*, STOS*x*. 80*x*86 implementations up to the 80286 ignore nonmeaningful prefixes. However, invalid uses of the REPx and LOCK prefixes are flagged by the 80376, 80386, and i486. This is done by signaling an INVALID_INSTR fault. All other prefixes, if used nonmeaningfully, are ignored without warning on all 80x86 implementations.

2.18.3 Instruction opcodes and operands

Figure 2.46 and Figure 2.47 showed the formats of 80x86 instructions. The opcode field's interpretation is straightforward; it is simply unique byte value assigned to each instruction. (This byte value is shown in opcode heading of each instruction described in Chapter 4.) Some opcodes name instruction groups; for example, opcode 0x80 names a group of operations that have an immediate operand, and a register or memory operand. Group opcodes use the opcode extension field in the following byte (also called the MOD/RM byte) to resolve the operation type. (Chapter 4 shows extension fields using a "/" notation; for example, 80 /7, an encoding for a form of CMP instruction, denotes that the opcode byte is set to 0x80, whereas the extension field in the MOD/RM byte following is set to 7.)

Operand encoding is not as simple as opcode encoding. To understand the encoding, keep in mind that there can be many classes of operands. Each operand class is encoded differently. Furthermore, multiple encoding methods may exist for the same (commonly used) operand. Some operand classes are numeric quantities (represented in Little Endian notation). These numeric quantities may be unsigned (as in the case of the interrupt vector number operand of the INT instruction) or may be signed (as in the case of the EIP-relative displacement value in conditional jump instructions. As always, signed values are represented in two's complement. Usually, the size of a numeric field is fixed. In some cases, however, it is controlled by either the address size attribute or the operand size attribute of the instruction. (These attributes are described in §2.18.3.3 and §2.18.4, respectively.) In these cases, the numeric field is either a WORD or a DWORD, matching the size of the applicable attribute. Variable-size fields are shown enclosed in dashed boxes in the instruction format figures.

The most complex operand encoding is that which begins with the MOD/RM byte. This byte has three fields: mode ("MOD"), register ("REG"), and register/memory ("R/M"). Instruction formats that have an opcode extension use the REG field to store the extension. In all other cases the REG field stores the encoding for a register of a particular type; the type of register used is implied by the opcode. REG is a three bit field. This is sufficient since each register type has eight registers in it, at most; for example, there are eight general registers, and three defined control registers. It is worthwhile noting that the general

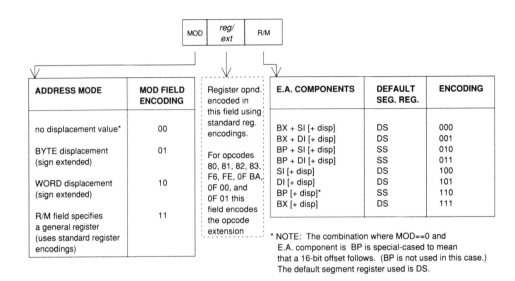

Figure 2.49: 16-bit effective address (OFFSET) generation

registers can be BYTE-sized, WORD-sized, or DWORD-sized. The general register size used always matches the operand size attribute (described later). (There are some implied register operands that are fixed in size. For example, CL is used by shift instructions to store the shift count.)

The MOD and R/M fields encode either a general register or a memory operand. In almost all cases size of the register or memory operand matches the operand size attribute of the instruction. The only exceptions are in the case of precision conversion instructions (e.g., MOVSX, which sign-extends a BYTE operand to a WORD or DWORD, or a WORD operand to a DWORD).

How are the MOD and R/M fields decoded? A general register operand is encoded by setting MOD to 3 (i.e., 11_2). In this case the three-bit-wide R/M field encodes the general register name, using normal general register encodings (see Figure 2.6 on page 22). To understand memory operand encoding, first recall that memory addresses in the 80x86 have two components, a SELECTOR and an OFFSET, and that the SELECTOR used is stored in a segment register. OFFSETs come in two sizes: WORD and DWORD. WORD-sized OFFSETs are used when the address size attribute of an instruction is 16; when it is 32, the OFFSETs are DWORD-sized. The way the MOD and R/M fields are interpreted

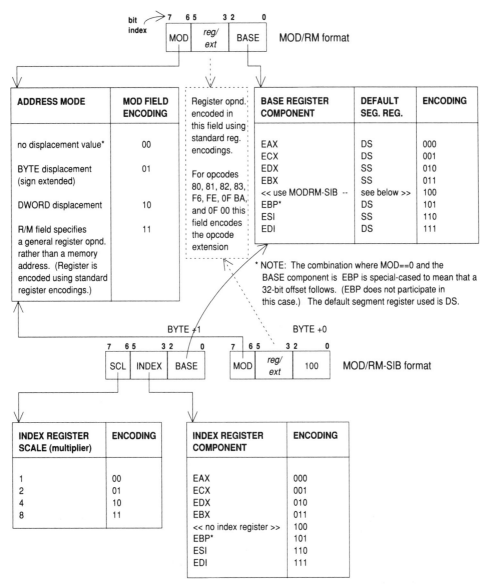

Figure 2.50: 32-bit effective address (OFFSET) generation

for WORD-sized OFFSETs is shown in Figure 2.49; for DWORD-sized OFFSETs the scheme used is shown in Figure 2.50.

As shown in the figures, an OFFSET is generated by summing three components: a **base register**, an **index register**, and a **displacement**. The base and index registers are both general registers, whereas the displacement is a numeric quantity that is a part of the instruction. The choice of base and index registers in WORD-sized OFFSET generation is very limited. In particular, only the BP and BX registers can be used as bases, and only SI and DI can be used as indices. Most of these restrictions are lifted when using DWORD OFFSETs. The only restriction that remains is that ESP cannot be used as an index register.

The displacement field is either a BYTE or a WORD when using WORD-sized OFFSETs and is a BYTE or a DWORD when using DWORD-sized OFFSETs. The size used depends on the value of the MOD field. Setting MOD to 0 indicates that no displacement field is present, that is, that the displacement value is zero.

Sometimes it is useful to have only a displacement component in the OFFSET. In such cases neither the base nor index register components are present. For 16-bit OFFSETs, this is done by selecting the encoding where the base register is BP, and there is no index or displacement; that is, with MOD set to 0 and R/M set to 6. This situation is special-cased to mean that a WORD-sized OFFSET value follows the MOD/RM byte. The same technique is used for 32-bit OFFSETs; that is, the encoding where only the base register EBP is present is used. Since the base register encodings used are different, the MOD is to 0, but the R/M field (i.e. BASE) is set to 5. This encoding implies that a DWORD-sized OFFSET follows the MOD/RM byte.

It is worthwhile noting that, under certain circumstances, the additional addressing flexibility of DWORD OFFSETs entails the use of a second byte following the MOD/RM byte. In particular, if an index component is present, the base and index registers are specified in this second byte. The index can also be scaled (i.e., multiplied) by 2, 4, or 8 before being added. The scale value, and the index and base registers are encoded in the **SIB byte**, as shown in Figure 2.50. (SIB is an abbreviation for scale-index-base; it also suggests that it is MOD/RM's "sibling.")

2.18.3.1 Default segment register selection

Earlier we noted that the SELECTOR component of a memory address is fetched from a segment register. How is this segment register specified? The answer is that it is implied. For memory addresses generated via a MOD/RM operand specification, the segment register implied depends on the base register used by the OFFSET. If it is BP (in the case of 16-bit addressing) or it is EBP or ESP (in the case of 32-bit addressing), the SS segment register (and SS_desc segment descriptor register) applies. For all other base registers, and for the special case where a direct numeric offset is specified, the DS segment register is used.

For the string operation instructions, the (up to) two memory operands are specified using DS:ESI and ES:EDI. Stack references resulting from the push(es) or pop(s) in the instructions PUSH, PUSHA, POP, POPA, PUSHF, POPF, CALL, RET, INT, and IRET) always use the SS segment register.

2.18.3.2 Overriding the default segment selection

If the default chosen by a MOD/RM memory operand is inappropriate, it can be overridden via a segment override prefix. There are as many override prefixes as there are segment registers; see §2.18.2 for their encodings. In addition to MOD/RM operands, string instructions with an implied DS:ESI operand can also override the DS segment register by using the appropriate prefix. The use of SS in stack operations (see the list above) cannot be overridden. Nor can the ES register be overridden in the ES:EDI operand of string operations.

2.18.3.3 The address size attribute

The discussion of MOD/RM and SIB bytes made use of the notion of an **address size attribute**. On the 8086, 80186, and 80286 is always 16. (This implies, in particular, that OFFSETs are only 16 bits wide on these processors.) On the 80386 and i486 there is the notion of a *default address size attribute*. This attribute is determined by the DefaultAttr flag in the code segment descriptor register CS_desc. If CS_desc.DefaultAttr is 0, the default address size attribute is 16; otherwise, it is 32. Whenever VM86 mode is entered DefaultAttr is automatically cleared; that is, the address size is set to 16 bits. The same is true when these machines are reset. This keeps both REAL and VM86 modes of the 80386 and i486 compatible with the REAL mode of the 80286 (and 80186 and 8086). Note, however, that a transition from PROTECTED mode to REAL mode (possible only on the 80386 and i486) does not change the DefaultAttr setting. The programmer has to do so explicitly, if true REAL mode operation is desired.

Address size handling on the 80376 deserves special mention. Rather than have DefaultAttr be a programmable flag, it is permanently set to 1. This means the default address size attribute is always 32 bits on this part. Sixteen bit addressing is possible, but only if an address size prefix is used. Therefore 16 bit code is executable on the 80376, but its encoding is incompatible with that of the 16 bit code that executes on the 80286.

Situations may arise where the default address size attribute is inappropriate. In such cases the address size override prefix (encoded as 0x67) changes the address size attribute to the inverse of the default. Therefore, if an instruction with an address size override prefix is executed with the DefaultAttr set to 1, the address size attribute for the instruction is 16. As Figures 2.49 and 2.50 show, the address size attribute value changes the interpretation of the MOD/RM byte substantially. Therefore, the programmer cannot insert an address size prefix in front of an instruction encoded using 16-bit rules and except to get 32-bit addressing.

Other than changing the interpretation of the MOD/RM byte (an the operand bytes that follow it), the address size attribute also controls the size of addressing related registers whose use is implied by string instructions. In particular, SI, DI, and CX are used by string instructions executed with an address size of 16; if the address size is 32, ESI, EDI, and ECX are used. On occasion, this variability is denoted in this book by placing the "E" in brackets; that is, by using [E]SI, [E]DI, and ECX. Note that the stack pointer offset is SP or ESP depending on the setting of the Big flag, and not the address size attribute. (The Big flag is discussed in §2.8 on page 113.) Also note that control over whether IP or EIP is used is determined by the *operand size* attribute rather than the address size attribute.

The instruction descriptions in Chapter 4 use the variable *as* to denote the current instruction's address size attribute. Most 80x86 assemblers that support the 80386 and i486 use the segment directive USE16 to specify a segment whose default address size is 16, and USE32 to specify a segment whose default address size is 32.

2.18.3.4 OFFSET **wraparound vs. data wraparound**

In both 16-bit and 32-bit effective address (OFFSET) generation, it is possible that the sum of the OFFSET components overflow the number of bits in the effective address. In such cases, the overflow bits are discarded without warning. This results in OFFSET **wraparound**. For example, if the base register's value in a 16-bit OFFSET computation is 0xFF02, the index register's value is 0xFF, and the displacement is 0x10, the sum is 0x10011. Only the least significant 16 bits of the result constitute the OFFSET; that is, its value is 0x11.

OFFSET wraparound can occur either from the highest offset value to zero, or from zero to the highest offset value. A common use of low-to-high OFFSET wraparound is in stack initialization. If the first byte of a stack (which grows toward smaller addresses) is to be at OFFSET 0xFFFF (or 0xFFFFFFFF for a big stack), it is initialized by setting SP (resp. ESP) to 0. Now, if a DWORD is pushed onto the stack, SP (resp. ESP) is decremented to 0xFFFC (resp. 0xFFFFFFFD), and the DWORD is written at SS:SP (resp. SS:ESP). Thus, OFFSET wraparound allows use of all bytes up to offset 0xFFFF (resp. 0xFFFFFFFF).

Now consider what happens if the OFFSET of a multibyte memory operand is such that wraparound occurs within the bytes of the operand. For example, if a WORD operand's OFFSET if 0xFFFF, its first BYTE is at OFFSET 0xFFFF whereas its second BYTE is at offset 0x0000. Checking the memory rules (see §2.7) we see that the in_limits check (see page 78) would fail, so signaling a GP fault. This is true for all 80x86 implementations except for the 8086 and 80186: on these early implementations the WORD is constructed using the BYTEs at offsets 0xFFFF and 0x0. This type of wraparound is called **data wraparound**.

Yet another issue to consider is the behavior of data wraparound in instructions that access multiple items in memory. For example, the LDS instruction reads a far pointer. Such a pointer consists of a WORD-sized SELECTOR, and a WORD- or DWORD-sized OFFSET. If data wraparound occurs within the SELECTOR or the OFFSET, an error is signaled as discussed above. However, if data wraparound occurs at the boundary between the SELECTOR and the OFFSET, no exception occurs. Similar behavior occurs in string operands. If data wraparound occurs with a string element, a GP fault is reported (on the 80286 and its successors). However, if wraparound occurs at the boundary of a string element, no exception is reported. (All this assumes, of course, that segment limit checks and access rights checks have passed.)

In general, data wraparound exceptions can be avoided by keeping operands aligned on their natural boundaries. The alignment requirements for all multi-element operands is given in Figure 2.33 on page 99. Note that these data wraparound rules are not incorporated in the C language descriptions of instructions. Doing so would involve computing all displacements from a particular OFFSET using modulo-2as arithmetic, where *as* is the address size attribute. This is not done to minimize descriptive clumsiness.

2.18.3.5 Linear address wraparound

Recall that a linear address is computed by adding an OFFSET to a segment base value. It is possible for this addition to overflow the maximum linear address. Since the linear address and the physical address are the same on all implementations of the 80x86 except the 80386 and i486, linear address wraparound is usually the same as physical address wraparound (described below). For the 80386 and i486, however, note that linear address wraparound occurs without warning. Since linear addresses are always 32 bits wide, such wraparound only occurs near linear address 0xFFFFFFFF.

2.18.3.6 Physical address wraparound, and MS-DOS

Except when paging is enabled, the physical address and the linear address are the same. Since the number of physical address bits is never greater than the number of bits in a segment's base address, the possibility of physical address overflow exists. As with linear addresses, overflow is handled by wraparound; that is, the overflow bits are ignored. Figure 2.20 on page 52 shows the physical address size of all 80x86 implementations.

It should be noted that by default, systems based on MS-DOS enable only the 20 least significant physical address bits. This limits physical memory to a maximum of one megabyte (2^{20} bytes) and is done for compatibility with programs that were developed for the original IBM PC that relied on physical address wraparound. (The IBM PC is based on the 8088 microprocessor, and only has 20 physical address bits.) Since the high-address inhibition is done by system logic external to the microprocessor, most 80x86 implementations are not aware of this wraparound. However, the i486 needs to be aware of it since it has an internal memory system (namely, its cache). Access to the cache (which is performed using physical addresses) is done using only the low-order 20 bits whenever the A20M pin is active. Addresses presented to the system memory are also truncated to 20 bits when this occurs. This pin, whose name suggests "mask address lines 20 and above," is unique to the i486. MS-DOS software that wants to use physical memory above 1 megabyte has to send an "enable A20" message to the system logic. On i486-based systems, the system logic responds by disabling A20M. On other MS-DOS systems, the system address pins above address pin 19 are enabled.

2.18.4 The operand size attribute

The address size attribute is introduced was introduced in the 80386 for compatibility with existing 16-bit code. The **operand size attribute**, also

introduced in the 80386, is no more than an encoding trick for representing
DWORD operations. To understand its function, observe first that in the 80286
(and its predecessors), it is an instruction's opcode that encodes whether a BYTE
operation or a WORD operation is to be performed. Since the 80386 supports
BYTE, WORD, and DWORD operations, the question arises of how the (new)
DWORD operations should be encoded. Rather than introduce a whole new set
of opcodes the 80386 expands the meaning of a WORD operations to mean
"WORD or DWORD operation." A WORD operation is performed if the operand
size attribute is 16, if it is 32 a DWORD operation is performed.

In the absence of any other indicator, a WORD/DWORD operations operand size
is determined by the *default operand size attribute*. Like the default address size
attribute, this attribute is simply the value of the DefaultAttr flag in CS_desc: if
the flag is set to 0, the default operand size is 16; otherwise, it is 32. Keep in
mind that this flag has no effect on the operand size attribute of instructions that
operate on BYTEs. A BYTE operation's operand size is always 8.

The effect of the default operand size attribute is to configure an 80386 (or i486)
as a machine that performs BYTE and WORD operations, or as a machine that
performs BYTE and DWORD operations. The first configuration is useful for
code that does not manipulate large numbers, and for code that is compatible
with the 80286 (and its predecessors). The second configuration is useful for
programs (and programming environments) that manipulate 32-bit data and
addresses. The absence of directly encoded WORD operations in the latter
configuration is all right, as studies show that in the presence of 32-bit
operations, the usefulness of 16-bit operations is limited. However, BYTE
operations are always useful (because characters are usually represented as BYTE
strings).

Even if the default operand size is not the one desired, it can be overridden by
using the *operand size prefix*. Much like the address size prefix, this prefix
(encoded as 0x66) inverts the sense of the default operand size. Therefore, if
DefaultAttr is 0 (i.e., WORD operations are the default) and a WORD/DWORD
instruction is executed with the operand size prefix, the instruction performs a
DWORD operation.

Unlike the address size prefix, it is frequently possible to convert a WORD
operation to a DWORD (and conversely) simply by placing an operand size
override prefix in front of it. This is because the encoding for a WORD-sized
general register matches that of the corresponding DWORD-sized register.
Furthermore, for memory operands, note that memory address generation is

unaffected by an instruction's operand size attribute. The only difference is in the number of bytes in memory that are accessed.

The instruction descriptions in Chapter 4 use the variable *os* to denote the current instruction's operand size attribute. Most 80*x*86 assemblers that support the 80386 and i486 use the segment directive USE16 to specify a segment whose default operand size is 16, and USE32 to specify a segment whose default operand size is 32. Since the DefaultAttr flag applies to both the operand size and the address size, the USE16 and USE32 directives apply to both attributes also.

2.19 Differences between 80*x*86 implementations

Figure 1.1 (see page 2) summarized the differences between the major implementations of the 80*x*86. However, there are nine implementations of the 80*x*86 family in all. This section discusses the differences between each of these implementations from a global software perspective.

The differences between the differing implementations can be categorized based on the following attributes:

1. The available execution modes

2. The sizes of operations and segment offsets supported

3. The list of instructions supported

4. The types of exceptions supported

5. The number of bits (i.e., data pins) connecting the 80*x*86 to its (external) memory and I/O subsystem

Let us examine each in turn.

2.19.1 The 8086 and 8088

The 8086 is the original member of the 80*x*86 family. It has its roots in the 8-bit 8080 processor family, but does not try to maintain binary compatibility with it. The 8086 is a 16-bit processor; that is, its registers are WORD-wide, and computations are done using a 16-bit data path (i.e., its ALU is 16 bits wide). The 8086 implements only the REAL mode of execution.

Since it is a 16-bit processor, the operand size of instructions is either 8 or 16; 32-bit operations are unavailable. Moreover, the address size is fixed at 16 bits. So, OFFSET computations are done using 16-bit arithmetic. An implication is that OFFSET arithmetic is done modulo-2^{16}. Futhermore, data wraparound (described in §2.18.3.4) does not result in an exception on the 8086. Normal REAL mode memory access rules apply; however, the only segment registers defined are ES, CS, SS, and DS. Segment registers FS and GS are unavailable; also, LDT and TSS are not needed because no protection or hardware task switch features are present.

There are no memory or I/O space protection features on the 8086, nor is their any notion of expand-down or conforming segments. This follows from the fact that only REAL mode is available on it. The 8086 registers are the WORD-sized general registers, the segment registers, and FLAGS. Debug, control, and test registers are not available. Not all application instructions are supported by the 8086 either. The unsupported instructions are BOUND, BSWAP, POPA, PUSHA, SHLD, SHRD, INS*x*, OUTS*x*, ENTER, LEAVE, PUSH of an immediate (constant) value, the three operand variant of IMUL, and all shift and rotate instructions that specify a constant shift amount that is greater than 1. Therefore, all of

```
SHL    AX, 1
RCR    WORD PTR [BX], CL
PUSH   BX
```

are valid on the 8086, but both

```
SHR    AX, 3
PUSH   12
```

are invalid. Also unavailable are all instructions that deal with protection concepts (e.g., LMSW and VERR) or instructions that access the TLB and/or cache.

A minor difference in the operation of the 8086 is in the effect of the instruction

```
PUSH   SP
```

The 8086 pushes the value of SP after the stack pointer is decremented, whereas the 80286, 80376, 80386, and i486 push the original SP value. This quirk is often used by software to determine whether a program is executing on an 8086.

The 8086 supports a numerics processor extension, the 8087. This is a separate chip that may or may not be present in a system. Errors in floating point operations are reported via a system-specific hardware interrupt rather than via the PE_ERROR exception. On MS-DOS systems, 8087 errors are reported via the NMI interrupt. Also, most floating point operations issued by the 80x86 need to be preceded by a WAIT instruction. This instruction ensures that the 80x87 is free to accept a command. (WAITs are unnecessary on the 80286 and its successors.)

Because of the limited number of features in the 8086, only a subset of all possible 80x86 exceptions can occur. The exceptions possible are DIVIDE and DEBUG. The only reason the DEBUG exception can arise is because of a single-step condition; data and instruction breakpoints are unsupported. Any of the software and hardware interrupts can be signaled, including the software interrupts generated by the INTO and INT3 instructions. The NMI pin can be activated to signal a nonmaskable interrupt. However, NMIs that occur while executing an NMI handler are serviced. (Other 80x86 implementations inhibit NMI service within an NMI handler.) Note also that the INVALID_INSTR exception cannot occur on the 8086. The machine state resulting from executing an unused opcode is *undefined*.

The 8086 memory interface has 20 address lines and 16 data lines. Therefore, maximum memory size is 1 megabyte and can be read and written a WORD at a time. The 8088 is identical to the 8086 in terms of the software architecture. Internally, its implementation is very similar to the 8086 also. The primary difference between the 8086 and 8088 is in the memory bus size: instead of 8 data lines, it has 16 data lines. Physical memory addressability is still 1 megabyte. The 8088 is the processor used in the original IBM PC. Unless otherwise specified, all discussion of the 8086 in this book applies equally to the 8088.

2.19.2 The 80186 and 80188

The 80186 programming model is an extension of the 8086's (and 8088's) programming model. It features almost all 80x86 application-level instructions; the only ones missing are BSWAP, SHLD, and SHRD. Being a 16-bit processor, it only supports BYTE and WORD operations and, like the 8086, does not support DWORD operations. Also, since the 80186 operates only in REAL mode, none of the PROTECTED mode instructions (e.g., LAR, or VERW) is supported. As with the 8086, the only available segment registers are ES, CS, SS, and DS. The 80186 does not have debug, control, or test register support.

In addition to the core CPU, the 80186 also integrates DMA channels, programmable timers, and an 8259-like interrupt controller onto a single chip. These peripheral devices are accessed by reading and writing specific WORDs in a *control block*. This control block can be located at any 256 byte boundary in either the memory or I/O space. Location selection is done by programming a *relocation register* that is itself stored in the control block. To allow initial access to the relocation register, the control block starting address after processor reset is set to address 0xFF00 in the I/O address space. The relocation register is at offset 0xFE of the control block; that is, its address at startup is I/O port 0xFFFE. For more details on the relocation register, and on how to program the 80186's integrated peripherals, see [Intel, 1986].

Exception handling on the 80186 is extended as follows:

- interrupt vector 5 is used to signal BOUND faults. This is generated by the BOUND instruction.

- an attempt to execute certain invalid opcodes signals an INVALID_INSTR exception. The invalid ones are opcodes 0x0F and 0xF1, opcodes 0x63 through 0x67 inclusive, group opcode 0xFE with extension 7, and group opcode 0xFF with extension 7. The machine state resulting from executing any other unused opcode is *undefined*.

In comparison to the 8086, the design of the 80186's core CPU has been improved in many areas. The main improvements are as follows:

- OFFSET computations are done with a specialized adder that is separate from the adder in the ALU. This is unlike the 8086, where both arithmetic and OFFSET computations are done using a central ALU. The dedicated OFFSET adder substantially improved address computation times.

- Both the multiply and divide instructions execute substantially faster than on the 8086.

- A string move instruction takes eight cycles per element moved. This is as fast as the 80186's memory bus will allow.

2.19.3 The 80286

The 80286, introduced shortly after the 80186, is the first 80*x*86 family member to feature memory protection. It is also a 16-bit processor; that is, OFFSETs can only be 16-bit quantities. The programmer visible registers are the 16-bit general registers, the segment registers, the FLAG register, and the machine status word MSW. The MSW, new to the 80286, holds assorted control information.

Both REAL and PROTECTED modes are supported in this processor. The processor resets to REAL mode; PROTECTED mode is entered by setting the PE flag (found in the MSW). Unlike the 80386 and i486, the 80286 cannot exit PROTECTED mode once it enters it.[30] Only the 16-bit variants of descriptors are supported by the 80286; the high-order WORD of all descriptors must be set to zero. Both the granularity and DefaultAttr flags are stored in this WORD, as are the high 8 bits of a descriptor's Base, and the 4 most significant Limit bits. As a consequence, a segment's base address is can only be a 24-bit quantity and its limit (i.e., largest OFFSET value) cannot exceed 0xFFFF.

The 80286 does a far more complete job of trapping undefined instruction opcodes than the 80186. It also fixes a bug in the 8086 which made it possible to single-step into an external interrupt handler. Unlike the 8086, the 80286 does not permit arbitrarily long instructions. (Such instructions can be generated by using an arbitrary number of redundant prefixes.) Attempting to execute an instruction longer than 11 bytes generates a GP fault. If an exception occurs on any instruction that uses prefixes, the 80286 enters the exception handler pointing at the first instruction prefix. This (desirable) behavior is new to the 80286. The 80186 only keeps track of at most one prefix when entering an exception handler. The 80286 services NMIs using standard 80x86 semantics: that is, NMIs are inhibited when executing an NMI handler. This feature, useful for preventing infinite NMI loops, is not found on the 8086.

The exception handling interface between the 80286 and the 80287 processor extension is subtantially different from the interface between the the 8086 and the 8087. The 8087 uses an interrupt line INT to signal exceptions. The intent is that this line be connected to a harware interrupt line on the 8086. For example, on the PC/XT, INT is connected to the NMI pin of the 8088. On the 80286, however, 80x87 exceptions are reported via the ERROR pin. Activating this pin on the 80286 signals the PE_ERROR exception, which is serviced via interrupt vector entry 16.[31]

The 80286 synchronizes with the 80287 in a somewhat different manner also. The 8086 requires the use of a WAIT instruction to ensure that the 8087 is ready to accept a command. The WAIT is built into most 80286 processor extension instructions. This does not affect the compatibility of existing, well-formed 8086/8087 code, since the WAIT instruction simply performs a superfluous action

---

[30] 80286-based PC/AT systems can seem to switch between REAL and PROTECTED modes; for example, when using the compatibility box of MS-OS/2. Transitions to REAL mode are done by a BIOS call that resets the 80286 microprocessor.

[31] The PC/AT attempts to simulate the PC/XT 80x87 interface by connecting the 80287 ERROR output to an interrupt line; see §3.9 for more details.

on the 80286/80287. Finally, note that the 80*x*87 exception address registers store the address of the last ESC instruction, including its prefixes. On the 8086, the exception address points at the ESC byte itself; the prefix bytes are skipped.

The 80286 also has a unique instruction: LOADALL286. This instruction allows a program operating in either REAL or PROTECTED mode to initialize all the segment descriptor registers. This is useful, for it allows a REAL mode program to set up descriptor registers so that access beyond one megabyte is possible. Although LOADALL286 is useful conceptually, its long running time (about 200 clocks) limits its use in practice. See page 478 for more information on this instruction.

2.19.4 The 80386 and 80386SX

The 80386 is the first 32-bit implementation of the 80*x*86 family. But for BSWAP it supports all 80*x*86 application instructions in all their formats. The system-level features missing from the 80386 (but available on the i486) are as follows:

1.   The alignment check feature (AC and AM flags) is unavailable.

2.   The ability to write-protect supervisor pages (via the WP flag) is unavailable.

3.   There is no on-chip cache.

4.   Multiprocessor support features (e.g. pseudo lock) is unavailable.

With respect to the 80286, the 80386 can be viewed as a 80286 with a complete set of 32-bit extensions and demand-paged memory management. The introduction of debug registers provides hardware-assisted instruction and data breakpoints, whereas the test registers give low-level access to the paging TLB. Invalid instruction detection is also improved. In particular, the use of REP*x* and LOCK prefixes in front of instructions that cannot be repeated or locked signals an INVALID_INSTR exception. Finally, locking of REPeated string operations is unconditionally disallowed. (The 8086 always allows repeated string operations to be locked. On the 80286, the operation is IOPL-sensitive.)

The performance of the 80386 (in clock cycles) is similar to that of the 80286. For example, a register-to-register add occurs in 2 clock cycles on both implementations. However, the fact that the 80386 performs 32-bit adds and fetches instructions and data in 32-bit chunks effectively gives it added performance in many applications. Another reason that 80386 systems can be faster than 80286 systems is that high-end 80386's run at higher clock rates than the 80286. Minor design improvements also contribute to greater performance. For example, the multiply instructions' product accumulation loop skips over leading zeros (or ones) in a multiplier.

The 80386SX is identical to the 80386 in structure, except for its instruction and memory data interface. The 80386 bus size is 32 bits whereas the 80386SX bus size is 16 bits. Also, the 80386 has 32 physical address lines, whereas the 80386SX only has 24 physical address lines.

2.19.5 The 80376

The 80376 is a defeatured 80386 that is positioned as a 32-bit microcontroller. REAL and VM86 modes have been removed, so as to prevent its use in MS-DOS applications. The only execution environment available to the 80376 is 32-bit PROTECTED mode without paging. Sixteen-bit instructions can be executed, but only with address size and/or operand size override prefixes. The prefix requirement makes the encoding of 16-bit 80376 operations incompatible with the 80286. All descriptors are restricted to their 32-bit forms. For example, CALLGATE32 is supported, but CALLGATE16 is not. Using an unsupported descriptor format signals a GP fault.

For the instructions that are supported, the performance (in clock cycles) of the 80376 is the same as that of the 80386SX. In general, the 80376 can be thought of as being "sideways-compatible" with the 80386.

2.19.6 The i486

The i486 is the most complete implementation of the 80*x*86 architecture. Its features beyond those available in the 80386 are mentioned in subsection above that discusses the 80386. The new instructions in it are:

- BSWAP : Reverses byte order in a 32-bit general register.
- INVD, WBINVD : Invalidates on-chip cache.
- INVLPG : Selectively invalidates paging TLB entries.
- CMPXCHG : Transfers operand based on comparison result.
- XADD : Exchanges two operands, and increments one of them.

Apart form these features, the i486 has a substantially improved internal design. Assuming hits in its internal cache, the i486 is able to perform a register-to-register add in 1 clock cycle (vs. 2 clocks for the 80386). It can read data from the cache in 1 clock cycle (vs. 4 clocks for the 80386), and execute a branch in 3 clock cycles (vs. 9 clocks for the 80386).

Chapter 3

The 80x87 Processor Extension

The 80x87 is an extension of the core 80x86 architecture that provides support for scalar, floating point operations. It is possible to implement floating point support akin to that provided by the 80x87 entirely using 80x86 software routines. However, Intel provides single-chip VLSI implementations of the 80x87 architecture that usually execute floating point operations faster than their software-only counterparts. Each major implementation of the 80x86 family has a corresponding 80x87 implementation. The 8086, 8088, 80186, and 80188 interface to the 8087, the 80286 interfaces with the 80287, and the 80386 interfaces with the 80387. The 80386SX and the 80376 (which are 16-bit memory bus variants of the 80386) interface to the 80387SX. The i486 is special in that it integrates 80x86 and 80x87 functions onto a single chip.

3.1 The IEEE floating point standard and the 80x87

Two's complement representation of integers in digital computers is both universally accepted and straightforward to implement. However, the added structure inherent in real values makes their representation more of a problem. There is general agreement that exponential notation should be used. Exponential notation is a floating point notation of the form

$$n.f \times R^e$$

where n, and e are integer values occupying fixed numbers of bits, R is a constant floating point radix (usually either 2 or 16), and f is a binary string occupying a fixed number of bits that is interpreted as a radix-R fractional value. There is sufficient generality in the exponential notation described that numerous incompatible representation schemes can be (and have been) devised. The IEEE floating point standard (described in [IEEE, 1985], and hereafter referred to as

"IEEE Std. 754", or "the Standard") resolves this issue by specifying R (as 2), and defining acceptable ranges for *n*, *f*, and *e*. The Standard also specifies the relative bit order in which the values should be stored in memory.

Most floating point values that can be stored in computer memory are only approximations of the intended real values. This happens for two reasons:

1. But for nonrecurring fractions, a real number cannot be represented as a finite number of digits in floating point notation.

2. Even for nonrecurring fractions, it may be that the number of digits needed for exact representation exceeds the number available to the floating point representation.

The approximate nature of floating point values, along with the fact that real-valued functions are often operations on a long series of real-valued subexpressions, makes floating point computations susceptible to errors. The IEEE Std. 754 helps in this regard as follows:

1. A minimum acceptable precision for floating point values (called *single precision*) is defined.

2. Implementation of floating point representation formats that are more precise than single precision are recommended (though not required).

3. The result stored from a floating point operations defined by the Standard is required to be the same as the infinitely precise result of the operation, rounded to the precision of the result register. This ensures that a floating point unit that conforms to the Standard computes values that are accurate to the least significant bit of the destination.[32] (Of course, errors can still accumulate when evaluating an expression consisting of many operations.)

4. A mechanism is defined for propagating an exceptional event (e.g. an underflow or overflow) in a chain of computations all the way to the top of the expression.

The initial implementation of the 80x87, the 8087, is one of the earliest (if not the first) hardware implementation of the IEEE floating point standard. Because the 8087 was introduced when the floating point standard was still a proposal, some of its aspects do not conform to IEEE Std. 754. This is true of the 80287 also.

---

[32] In fact, the result has to be computed more accurately than the destination's accuracy to allow rounding to be performed correctly.

Since the 80387, the 80387SX, and the i486 were all introduced after the
publication of IEEE Std. 754, they have been modified to conform to the
Standard. An exception to conformance is in the area of BCD data; none of the
80x87 implementations supports BCD conversions as specified by the Standard.
This matter is discussed further in §3.3.3.

In addition to implementing IEEE Std. 754, the 80x87 provides numerous
facilities that are outside the Standard specification; examples are transcendental
functions such as sin and cos. The differences between the proposed standard
and the finalized standard, as well as the streamlining of features outside the
Standard, has resulted in some operational differences between the two groups of
80x87 implementations. The descriptions that follow apply to *all* versions of the
80x87. Features of the 8087 and the 80287 that vary from the Standard are
pointed out explicitly.

3.2 Organization of this chapter

IEEE Std. 754 only specifies floating point data representation rules and a set of
operations on the data. The Standard encourages extensions to this basic set of
operations. Furthermore, the programming model (number of registers,
addressing modes, etc.) is left unspecified. This chapter provides both an
overview of the Standard, and details of the programming model employed by
the 80x87. The chapter ends with a list of instructions supported by the 80x87.
Detailed descriptions of the instructions are deferred to Chapter 4, where all
instructions (including those of the 80x86) are described.

Concepts related to the Standard occupy the next two subsections: §3.3 discusses
80x87 data formats, and §3.4 (starting on page 225) provides an overview of the
IEEE floating point arithmetic concepts. The remainder of the chapter discusses
details specific to the 80x87 architecture.

3.3 80x87 data representation

In addition to providing extensive floating point support, the 80x87 supports
conversion between 16-bit, 32-bit, and 64-bit integers and floating point values.
It also supports conversion between packed BCD string and floating point values.
These conversion operations are required by the Standard and provide indirect

support for operations on high-precision integers and packed BCD data. (There are no 80*x*87 instructions that perform arithmetic directly on integers or BCD quantities. These quantities must be converted to floating point, operated on, then converted back.)

3.3.1 Floating point data

A floating point data type has two components: a **significand** and an **exponent**. In the IEEE Std. 754, the value represented by these two components is computed as

significand $\times 2^{\text{exponent}}$

The Standard specifies the exponent using a *biased notation*, as follows. For a floating point format that supports exponents in the range E_{min} to E_{max} inclusive, the exponent's bias value EBIAS is set to

$$\text{EBIAS} = \text{-}E_{min} + 1$$

In this scheme an exponent value *e* is represented as

$$be = e + \text{EBIAS}$$

where *be* denotes the **biased exponent**. Since the biased exponent representation of the least exponent (E_{min}) is 1, this notation has the property that all exponents appear as positive values. In general, if *n* bits are used to represent the exponent E_{min} and E_{max} are set as follows

$$E_{min} = \text{-}2^{n-1} - 2$$
$$E_{max} = +2^{n-1} - 1$$

Since EBIAS is $-2^{n-1} - 1$, it is easily verified that the biased exponent values 0 and 2^n-1 are not used. These values denote special entities (e.g., infinity); their definitions are discussed later. The significand portion of the floating point value can either be of the form 0.*f* or 1.*f*, where *f* is the fractional component of the significand. The applicable form is determined by whether or not the exponent denotes a special value, and the floating point format used.

IEEE Std. 754 allows for four floating point representation formats: *single precision, extended single precision, double precision,* and *extended double precision.* The primary difference between these formats is the number of bits available for storing a floating point value. For the purposes of writing code that is portable among different architectures, note that the Standard requires implementation of only the single precision format. Most machines (including the 80x87), however, implement both the the single precision and double precision formats. Additionally, the 80x87 defines an extended double precision format. The layout of the extended double format is not specified by the Standard, although minimum precision capabilities are outlined. In fact, many implementations of the IEEE Std. 754 do not support this extended format. Hence, floating point data meant for export to foreign machines should not be represented in the extended format.

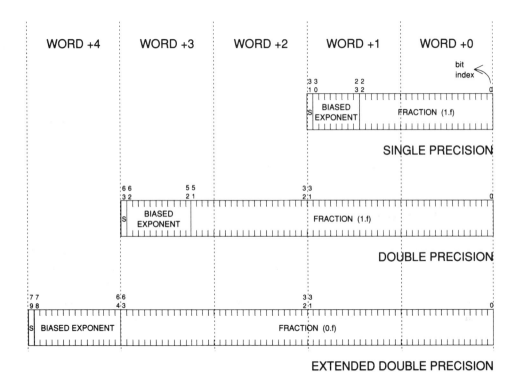

Figure 3.1: 80x87 floating point data representation

The representations of floating point data used by the 80x87 are depicted in Figure 3.1. The figure shows that there are three components to a floating point value: a sign *s*, a biased exponent *be*, and a fraction *f*. The significand is determined by the sign and the fraction fields, whereas the true exponent is determined by subtracting EBIAS from the biased exponent value. For the SINGLE and DOUBLE formats, the general interpretation of the fields is as follows

$$v = (-1)^s \times 2^{(be-EBIAS)} \times 1.f$$

where *v* is the floating point value denoted. The expression implies that if the sign field *s* is set to 1, the value is negative, and if it is set to 0, the value is positive or zero. The exponent bias value, EBIAS, for each of the formats is tabulated in Figure 3.2. It is dependant on the number of bits available for encoding the exponent, as described earlier. To maximize representational accuracy, the significand's magnitude is represented as 1.f; the integer component (i.e., 1) is implied, only the fractional component is stored. A floating point value stored in this method is termed **normalized**.

The EXTENDED format is interpreted like the SINGLE and DOUBLE formats, except that the fraction component *f* is interpreted as 0.f instead of 1.f; that is,

$$v = (-1)^s \times 2^{(be-EBIAS)} \times 0.f$$

3.3.1.1 Unnormalized values

The Standard requires floating point values to be stored in normalized form whenever possible. This rule is easily enforced for SINGLE and DOUBLE values because any possible bit pattern (with the biased exponent is in the range E_{min} to E_{max}) denotes a unique floating point value. This is not true of EXTENDED values. For example, the (decimal) value 0.5 is representable as

0.1×2^0 (0.1 is a binary fraction)

or

0.001×2^2 (0.001 is a binary fraction)

The form where the fraction has leading zeros is termed **unnormalized**. The 8087 and 80287 allow operations on unnormalized values. The 80387 and i486, however, generate an exception if such an operation is attempted. This difference does not affect conformance with IEEE Std. 754 since the Standard does not specify how unnormalized values should be handled. It is worthwhile

Attribute	Single precision	Double precision	Extended precision
Largest magnitude	$3.4*10^{38}$	$1.8*10^{308}$	$5.9*10^{4931}$
Smallest magnitude (denormalized)	$1.4*10^{-45}$	$4.9*10^{-324}$	$1.6*10^{-4950}$
Precision (in decimal digits)	6	15	18
Exponent bias (EBIAS)	127	1023	16383
Emax	+127	+1023	+16383
Emin	−126	−1022	−16382
Number of bits in biased exponent field	8	11	15
Number of bits in fraction (including implied 1., if used)	24	53	64
Total number of bits in format (incl. sign bit, but excluding implied 1., if used)	32	64	80

Figure 3.2: Attributes of 80*x*87 floating point formats

emphasizing that unnormalized values can only appear in the context of EXTENDED precision values.

3.3.1.2 Denormalized values

Consider the smallest, normalized value in a given format, that is,

$\pm 1.0 \times 2^{E_{min}}$

This value, call it FMIN, has the problem that the closest representable normalized value less than it is zero. To dramatize the problem here, consider the function

$y = 0.4^* x * 2^{100}$

If x is FMIN, $0.4^* x$ will evaluate to 0.0; hence, y will evaluate to 0.0 also. If, on the other hand, $0.4^* x$ were representable with a few digits of accuracy, the result would be close to $0.4 \times 2^{100-E_{min}}$ (the correct answer).

Loss of precision is unavoidable in the context of IEEE Standard arithmetic. However, the Standard delays eventual truncation to 0 by allowing values smaller than the smallest normalized value to be represented in unnormalized form. Such special cases of unnormalized values are known as **denormals**; the true value that they are meant to approximate are called **tiny numbers**. Representation of tiny number using denormals is done as follows. Recall that the biased exponent (*be*) value 0 is reserved. This value is used to signify denormalized values. Floating point format interpretation for denormalized values is as follows

$v = (-1)^s \times 2^{E_{min}} \times 0.f$

where s is the sign bit, f is the fraction, and v is the resulting floating point value. Note that the fraction now has a leading 0, much like the extended precision format. By placing leading zeros in the fraction component, exponents less than E_{min} can be represented. Of course, doing so reduces the number of significant bits in the fraction. The ability of the Standard to accommodate operations on denormals is called **gradual underflow**. Figure 3.3 shows the denormal data formats.

3.3.1.3 Zero and pseudozero representation

If a denormal's fraction component f is set to 0, the resulting value is

$v = (-1)^s \times 2^{E_{min}} \times 0.0$

that is, v is 0. The sign bit s determines the zero's "sign"; that is, +0 and −0 are distinct, representable values. Retaining the sign is useful in cases where the zero is generated because of a loss of precision: at the very least the result of

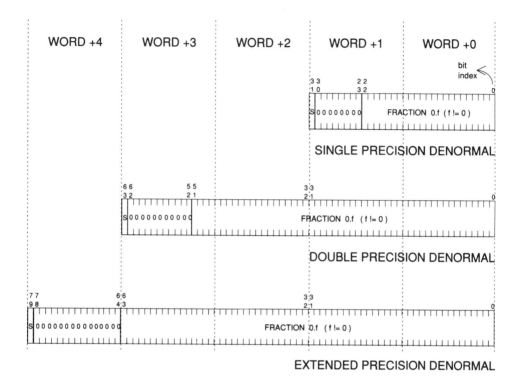

Figure 3.3: 80x87 denormal data representation

operations like multiplication and division on such numbers retains the correct sign.

IEEE Std. 754 rules only allow zeros to be represented in the form shown above (that is, as a denormal whose significand is 0). However, what is the interpretation of a number of the form

$$v = (-1)^s \times 2^{be\text{-}EBIAS} \times 0.0$$

where the biased exponent *be* is greater than 0 and less than or equal to EBIAS? The Standard does not define such a number format, and the 80387 and i486 conform to the Standard by rejecting operands of this form. However, to the 8087 and 80287, such numbers are simply unnormal values whose significand is 0. Since the value of such unnormals is zero, they are given the special term **"pseudozero"**. The 8087 and 80287 generate a pseudozero result only in the case where two unnormals that have a total of more than 64 leading zero bits are multiplied together. Keep in mind that, like an unnormal, a pseudozero can be

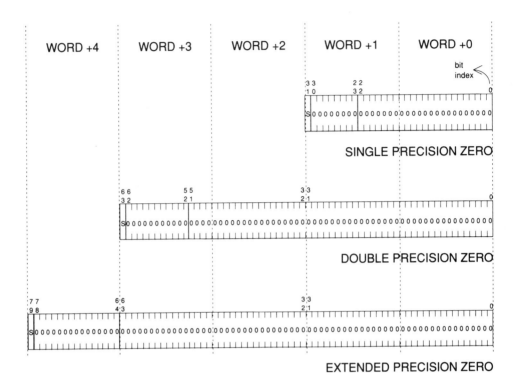

Figure 3.4: 80*x*87 zero representation

represented only as an **EXTENDED** precision value. Figure 3.4 shows the representation of zero in the various formats.

3.3.1.4 Infinity representation

IEEE Std. 754 defines two infinite values $-\infty$ (negative infinity), a value lesser than the least value representable in a given floating point format, and $+\infty$ (positive infinity), a value greater than the greatest value representable in a given floating point format. The 80*x*87 generates $-\infty$ from two finite values if numerical underflow occurs during an operation and processing of underflow exceptions is masked, or if a number *x* is divided by zero, and the sign of *x* is the opposite of the zero's sign. (Recall from the previous subsection that zeros are always signed.) Similarly, $+\infty$ is generated from two finite values if numerical overflow occurs during an operation, and processing of overflow exceptions is masked. An infinity is sometimes generated when one of the inputs to an operation is itself an infinity. The cases when this happens are outlined in the description of the individual instructions.

The scheme with two infinity values, $-\infty$ and $+\infty$, to denote unrepresentably large quantities is known as the **affine model of infinity**. An alternate infinity representation, supported only by the 8087 and the 80287, is the **projective model of infinity**. In this model, no distinction is made between $-\infty$ and $+\infty$. The model of infinity active for a particular operation is determined by the "infinity control" (IC) mode flag in the 80x87 control word FCW. (See §3.6.2 on page 234 for a description of the FCW register.) The difference between the projective and affine infinity models is in the manner in which infinity operands are treated. Usually, it is possible to perform more operations using the affine infinity model than with the projective model. See the descriptions of the individual instructions for details. Keep in mind that IEEE Std. 754 only requires the affine model of infinity. It is for this reason that the projective infinity model is not supported by the 80387 and i486.

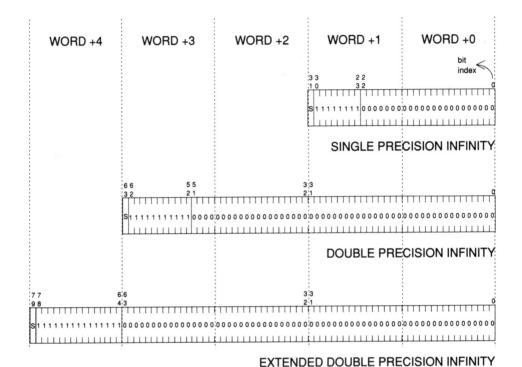

Figure 3.5: 80*x*87 representation of infinity

Infinity is encoded as shown in Figure 3.5. The biased exponent field *be* is set to its greatest value, and the fraction component *f* is set to zero. The sign bit *s* determines the infinity's sign: *s* is set to 1 for –∞; it is set to 0 for +∞.

3.3.1.5 NaN representation

In addition to infinity, the Standard defines the notion of "not-a-number," or **NaN**. There are two types of NaNs: **quiet** NaNs (or **QNaNs**), and **signaling** NaNs (or **SNaNs**). A QNaN is generated by an 80*x*87 operation on non-NaN inputs if the operation is invalid (e.g., because the input values are outside the operation's domain) and the processing of invalid operations is disabled. This allows expression evaluation to continue, even though an intermediate term's

evaluation may have resulted in an invalid operation.   Since operations on
QNaNs invariably yield QNaNs, the invalid operation marker (i.e., the QNaN)
propagates to the top level of the expression.   Here the overall validity of the
expression can be verified by making sure it is not a QNaN.

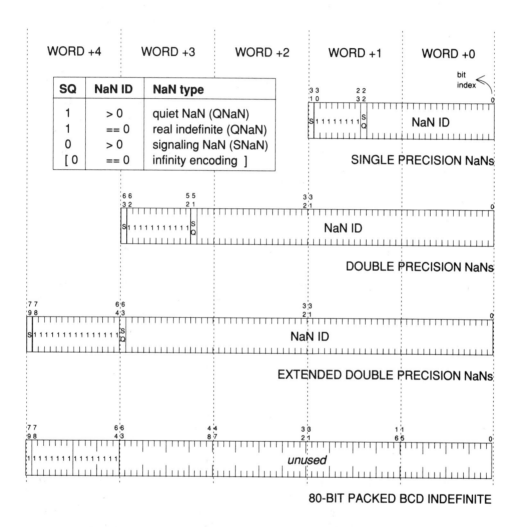

Figure 3.6: Representing NaNs in the 80x87

The encoding of both SNaNs and QNaNs is shown in Figure 3.6.   Note that all
NaNs have a NaN ID field.   This field's purpose is to allow the programmer to

encode exception information. If a NaN appears as an input to an operation, the result invariably is the NaN with the NaN ID field preserved. If two NaNs appear as inputs to an operation, the result is the NaN whose NaN ID field has the numerically greater value. (NaN IDs are interpreted as unsigned quantities stored in Little Endian notation.) If a QNaN is generated by the 80x87 from non-NaN inputs, the NaN ID field is always set to 0. This QNaN is called the **real indefinite**. The sign bit of the real indefinite is set to 1.

The 80x87 never generates a signaling NaN (i.e., SNaN). However, SNaNs (as well as QNaNs) can be specified by the 80x87 as operands. Except for 80x87 register[33] load instructions, and the FXCH, FCHS, and FABS operations, an operation executed with an SNaN as an operand always signals the invalid operation exception. If the processing of invalid operations is masked, the operation yields the QNaN corresponding to the SNaN as the result. An SNaN is converted to a QNaN by copying the sign (s) and NaN ID fields of the SNaN to a QNaN of the type specified by the operation's destination.

3.3.2 Integer data representation

IEEE Std. 754 does not require operations on integers; however, it requires that conversion operators between all supported floating point and integer formats be supplied. The 80x87 architecture interprets this requirement by supporting conversion to and from WORD (16-bit), DWORD (32-bit), and QWORD (64-bit) integers. Furthermore, it goes beyond the Standard's requirements by supporting addition, subtraction, multiplication, division, and comparison between EXTENDED format floating point values and an integer in either the WORD or DWORD formats. As shown in Figure 3.7, the encoding used by the 80x87 for integers matches that used by the 80x86.

By converting integers to floating point, expressions containing both integers and floating point values can be evaluated. It is possible to perform integer-only arithmetic also by converting the integer operands to floating point, operating on the floating point values, then converting the result back to an integer. However, for simple operations this approach takes longer than if the integer operation (even if it is 64 bits wide) were performed on the 80x86 using a sequence of instructions. This is because of the added time required to do the conversions, communicate with the 80x87, and perform calculations in floating point format.

All supported integer formats are convertible to floating point formats. However, when converting a floating point value to a integer, it is possible that the

---

[33] The 80x87 register set is described in §3.6.

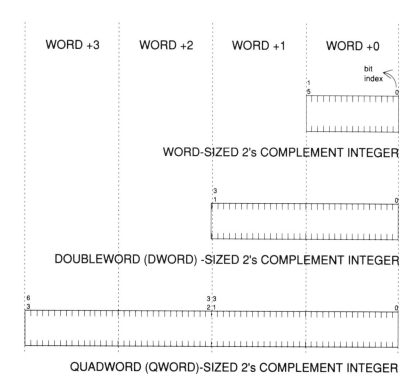

Figure 3.7: 80x87 integer data representation

operation may not succeed, either because the value is out of range of the integer or because the value is a NaN. In such cases, an invalid operation is signaled. If processing of invalid operations is masked, the value stored in the integer is the least negative number representable by the format (i.e., 2^{n-1} for an integer format occupying n bits).

3.3.3 Packed BCD data representation

The 80x87 deviates from IEEE Std. 754 in its handling of BCD data. The Standard requires that all its implementations be able to convert data represented in decimal notation that is in the range $\pm 10^{108}$ to an equivalent floating point value. Furthermore, the Standard requires that floating point data that is in the range $\pm 10^{62}$ should be convertible to decimal notation. The Standard also specifies a minimum number of acceptable digits of precision and a range of values over which the conversions have to be rounded correctly.

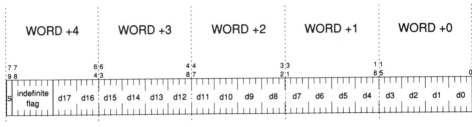

80-BIT PACKED BCD

Figure 3.8: 80*x*87 packed BCD data representation

The 80*x*87 has a substantially restricted notion of BCD data than that specified by IEEE Std. 754. As shown in Figure 3.8 only one packed BCD storage format is defined. This format can store an 18-decimal-digit integer value; there is no way to store fractional data or an exponent. Packed BCD operands of the type shown in the figure can be converted to floating point format. Similarly floating point values can be converted into packed BCD data. When converting floating point data to packed BCD format, the fractional component of the floating point value is rounded off. See §3.4.1 for a discussion of rounding methods. The formal type name for the packed BCD quantity supported by the 80*x*87 is PACKED_BCD.

Any PACKED_BCD is convertible to floating point formats (via the FBLD instruction). However, when converting a floating point value to PACKED_BCD, it is possible that the operation may not succeed, either because the value is out of the PACKED_BCD range or because the value is a NaN. In such cases, an invalid operation is signaled. If processing of invalid operations is masked, the value stored in the packed BCD is the **packed BCD indefinite**. The encoding for this indefinite is shown in Figure 3.6 on page 221. Since the only way to convert a floating point value to PACKED_BCD is via the FBSTP instruction, only this instruction generates the packed BCD indefinite. Also note that executing FBLD (the packed BCD load instruction) with the packed BCD indefinite as the operand value is not allowed. Doing so loads an *undefined* value into the destination.

3.4 IEEE floating point arithmetic principles

We have already observed that floating point is simply an approximate representation of the real numbers. This is graphically illustrated in Figure 3.9: the line is composed of an uncountable infinity of points that represent real numbers. However, the only reals that are exactly representable are those shown by the enlarged dots. Furthermore, only a finite range of real values is representable in any given floating point format. Floating point representation treats reals outside this range as either $-\infty$ (if the real is less than the least representable value) or $+\infty$ (if the real is greater than the greatest representable value).

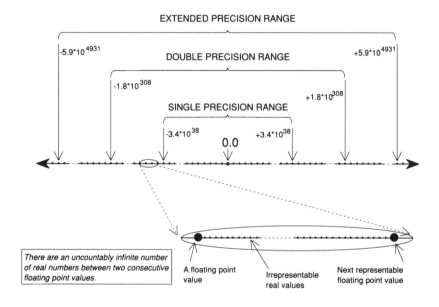

Figure 3.9: The relation between real numbers and floating point

Approximating real values with floating point values raises the issues of how to round results, and how to handle operations when one of the operands is infinity. The IEEE Std. 754 rules for handling rounding is outlined below. Infinity arithemetic is discussed in §3.3.1.4 on page 218. Also discussed below is the way in which the Standard handles comparison of numbers, and the treatment of exceptional conditions.

3.4.1 Rounding

Any floating point operation can cause a situation where the number of result bits exceed the number of bits available in the destination storage location. This can happen either because the result requires an infinite number of bits (e.g., as in the case of a recurring fraction), or because a finite sized-result simply occupies more bits than the destination has available. In either case, the infinitely precise result is rounded so as to fit in the (finite-sized) destination register or memory location.

Rounding can be done in one of four ways: *round to nearest, round down, round up*, and *round toward zero* (i.e., *chop*). **Round to nearest** takes the infinitely precise result *r* and chooses the floating point value that is closest to it. If *r* is exactly at the midpoint of two consecutive floating point values, the value chosen is the one whose least significant fraction bit is 0; that is, the even fraction is preferred over the odd fraction.

Round down rounding chooses the largest floating point value that is no greater than the infinitely precise real *r*, that is, the first floating point value in the $-\infty$ direction is chosen. Correspondingly, **round up** rounding chooses the least floating point value that is no less than the infinitely precise real *r*, that is, the first floating point value in the $+\infty$ direction is chosen.

Finally, **round toward zero**, or **chop**, simply discards all significant bits of the infinitely precise result *r* that do not fit in the destination. This is equivalent to a rounding mode which rounds down if *r* is positive, and rounds up if *r* is negative. The 80*x*87 uses the RC (rounding control) bits to select the active rounding mode. RC is a user-programmable field stored within the 80*x*87 control register FCW. See §3.6.2 on page 234 for a description of FCW.

3.4.1.1 Round to integer

The four rounding modes discussed above have special application in the context of floating point to integer conversion. IEEE Std. 754 requires that all four rounding modes be supported when converting a floating point value to an integer. The conversion operations can be declared as follows

- int round_nearest(EXTENDED r) : the EXTENDED precision value *r* is rounded to the nearest integer value. If *r*'s value is exactly *i*.5, where *i* is some integer, then the round_nearest yields the nearest integer value that is even.

- int round_down(EXTENDED r) : the EXTENDED precision value *r* is rounded down to its integer value; that is, the largest integer that is no greater than *r* is used.

- int round_up(EXTENDED r) : the EXTENDED precision value *r* is rounded up to its integer value; that is, the least integer that is no less than *r* is used.

- int chop(EXTENDED r) : all fraction digits of the EXTENDED precision value *r* are discarded.

The 80*x*87 instruction FRNDINT performs integer rounding; that is, conversion from floating point to integer. The description of this instruction (see page 398) uses the integer rounding functions described above.

3.4.2 Floating point comparison

In normal arithmetic comparison the comparison of two values *a* and *b* yields one of the following three results

1. $a < b$
2. $a == b$
3. $a > b$

This comparison method is incomplete if either of *a* or *b* is a QNaN. Since a QNaN is not a valid numeric entity, comparing any value (including another QNaN) with a QNaN yields the special relation "unordered." The ability to check for an unordered result allows a QNaN to be propagated through a complex calculation, and then checked for at the expression's top level. Unordered comparison works well with the affine model of infinity: $+\infty$ equals $+\infty$ and is greater than any other (non-NaN) value, and $-\infty$ equals $-\infty$ and is less than any other (non-NaN) value. As with most operations, if *a* or *b* or both *a* and *b* are SNaNs, an invalid operation (INVALID_FOP) exception is signaled.

In addition to reporting the "unordered" relation, the user may sometimes want to flag all NaN operands, including QNaNs, as an error. Such a comparison (called an "ordered compare") yields only one of "less than", "equal to", or "greater than" as a result. If one or both of the operands is a NaN, an invalid operation exception (INVALID_FOP) is signaled. Infinity operands in ordered comparison behave as described for unordered compare under the affine infinity model. In the projective infinity model, *a* equals *b* if both *a* and *b* are ∞. If only one operand is ∞, an invalid operation is signaled.

Support for both ordered and unordered comparisons is required by IEEE Std. 754. However, the early 80x87 implementations, the 8087 and 80287, only provide for ordered comparison. The ordered compare instructions are FCOM, FCOMP, FCOMPP, FICOM, and FICOMP. All these instructions are available on the 80387 and i486. In addition, the unordered compare instructions FUCOM, FUCOMP, and FUCOMPP are also supported on these later implementations.

For both ordered and unordered comparison an invalid operation (INVALID_FOP) exception always sets the condition code to "unordered." Therefore the behavior of FCOMx and FUCOMx are the same when INVALID_FOP handling is masked.

3.4.3 Floating point exceptions

IEEE Std. 754 requires that all conforming implementations detect the following five exceptional conditions: invalid operation, division by zero, overflow, underflow, and precision loss. Furthermore, the Standard requires that the programmer should be able to disable detection of any of these exceptions. The 80x87 conforms to these requirements, and as well, adds the ability to detect denormalized operands. A brief discussion of each exception type follows. See §3.9 for a discussion of how these exceptions are serviced by the 80x87.

3.4.3.1 Invalid operation

An invalid operation is signaled if an operand is invalid for the type of operation being performed; for example, if evaluation of the square root of a negative number is attempted. If trapping of this exception is masked, the operation stores the real indefinite, or for BCD operations, the packed BCD indefinite. If an invalid comparison operation is disabled, the comparison result is "unordered". An invalid operation is denoted in the book as INVALID_FOP.

3.4.3.2 Division by zero

Division by zero is signaled if the divisor is zero and the dividend is a finite, nonzero value. If trapping of this exception is masked, the result generated is a correctly signed ∞. Division by zero is denoted in the book as ZERO_FOP.

3.4.3.3 Overflow

Overflow is signaled whenever the magnitude of the result of an operation exceeds the largest magnitude (be it positive or negative in value) that can be stored in the destination, after rounding is performed. If trapping of this exception is masked, the result stored depends on the current rounding mode and the sign of the (infinitely precise) result, as follows:

- With round to nearest, a negative result generates $-\infty$ and a positive true result generates $+\infty$.
- With round toward $-\infty$, a negative true result generates $-\infty$ and a positive true result generates the most positive finite number storable in the destination.
- With round toward +INFINITY, a negative true result generates the most negative finite number storable in the destination and a positive true result generates $+\infty$.
- With round toward zero (chop), the result generated is greatest finite magnitude storable in the destination. The sign stored matches the sign of the true result.

Overflow is denoted in this book as F_OVERFLOW.

3.4.3.4 Underflow

Underflow is signaled based on whether or not the underflow exception is masked. If it is not masked, the exception is signaled whenever a tiny number is generated as the result of an operation. (Recall that tiny number is a true result that lies strictly between $\pm 2^{E_{min}}$.) If the exception is masked, overflow occurs if a tiny number is created and if the tiny number is not representable exactly as a denormal in the destination's format. Underflow is denoted in this book as F_UNDERFLOW.

If F_UNDERFLOW is masked, the result generated is either a denormal (if the tiny number is representable as such), or zero (it it is not representable as a denormal). If the exception is unmasked, however, result generated depends on whether the destination is the 80x87 stack, or a location in memory. If the destination is the 80x87 stack, the true result is multiplied by $2^{24,576}$. This scaled value is rounded using normal rounding rules, and the resulting value is stored onto the stack. If the destination is a memory location, no value is stored into memory, and the value on the stack is left intact. The intent is that the F_UNDERFLOW exception handler should look at the offending value and do something meaningful with it. Note that underflow with a memory destination can only occur with store instructions.

3.4.3.5 Loss of precision

The loss-of-precision exception (also called the inexact result exception) is raised whenever the result of an operation cannot be stored exactly in the result's destination location. This exception can occur either because the true result is recurring fraction, or because the true result has a finite number of bits in it, but the precision exceed the destination's precision. Loss-of-precision is denoted in this book as the PRECISION exception.

The PRECISION exception can occur very easily; for example, 1/10 is not representable exactly using binary floating point notation. Note also transcendental functions almost always yield inexact results. On the 80387 and the i486, the C1 condition code indicates the rounding direction whenever the PRECISION exception occurs. C1 is set to 1 if the result is rounded up and is set to 0 if the result is rounded down.

3.4.3.6 Denormal operand

A denormal-operand exception is signaled whenever an attempt is made to operate on a denormal.[34] If this exception is masked, execution proceeds using the denormal value. The FDE flag is set regardless, to indicate that a denormal was encountered. Note that on a 8087 and 80287, loading a SINGLE or DOUBLE denormal causes an unnormalized value to be loaded. On the 80387 and i486, however, the value is always normalized. Normalization is always guaranteed, since the 80x87 stack has EXTENDED precision entries. The denormal-operand exception is denoted in this book by DENORMAL.

3.5 Overview of the 80x87

The 80x87 is an architectural extension of the 80x86. In particular, the 80x87 is defined in a way that allows it to be implemented as a subsystem that is outside the 80x86 CPU. The 80x87 has a private register set that is distinct from the

---

[34] Note that on the 80387 and i486, no denormal exception is signaled when an EXTENDED format value is loaded using the FLD instruction.

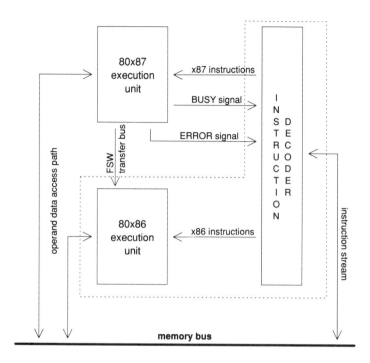

Figure 3.10: The relationship between an 80x86 and an 80x87

register set of the 80x86. Virtually all operand data communication between the 80x86 and 80x87 is via shared memory.[35]

The conceptual relationship between an 80x86 and 80x87 is shown in Figure 3.10. Instructions are transmitted to either the 80x86 or 80x87 execution units, depending on the opcode. The BUSY signal from the 80x87 execution unit can hold up the instruction dispatcher if it still processing a prior instruction. If BUSY is active long enough that an external interrupt comes along, the instruction decoder may service the interrupt first. (A similar synchronization signal, not shown in the figure, exists between the 80x86 execution unit and the instruction decoder.) While an 80x87 operation is in progress, the instruction decoder is free to dispatch an arbitrary number of 80x86 operations. Therefore, much of the 80x87 execution time can, in principle, be overlapped with 80x86 instruction execution. Of course, all instructions are executed in sequence; that is, an 80x87 instruction is never skipped because the 80x87 execution unit is busy.

---

[35] The only exception is the special instruction FSTSW AX that directly copies the 80x87 status word FSW into the 80x86 FLAGS register. This allows condition codes set by the 80x87 to be quickly checked via 80x86 conditional jump instructions. Note that FSTSW AX is not supported by the 8087.

If an 80x87 operation generates an unmasked exception, it activates the ERROR signal. The instruction decoder responds by generating an 80x86 interrupt. The type of interrupt generated depends on a variety of factors; their discussion is deferred to §3.9 on page 251.

Because the 80x87 architecture exposes the 80x86 — 80x87 interaction to the user, 80x87 instructions can be classified broadly into two groups: **nonadministrative**, and **administrative**. Nonadministrative instructions are those used to perform floating point operations; for example, FADD, the floating point addition instruction, is nonadministrative. Administrative instructions are overhead instructions: for example, FSAVE, the instruction that dumps the state of 80x87 registers to memory, is an administrative instruction.

3.6 80x87 registers

The primary registers of the 80x87 are eight floating point registers (FSTK[0] through FSTK[7]), eight associated tag fields (FTAG[0] through FTAG[7]) that classify the contents of each floating point register, a status register FSW, and a control register FCW. As shown in Figure 3.11, the floating point registers are organized as a push-down stack of eight elements. The current stack-top (denoted as ST(0), or simply ST) is simply the register in the FSTK vector indexed by the TOP field in the status register **FSW**; that is, ST is FSTK[TOP]. In C notation, stack-top-relative addresses can be defined as

```
#define ST(i)  FSTK[(TOP + i) & 7]      /* Wrap to 0 after address 7 */
```

Stack operations are discussed in §3.7. The status register FSW, and the 80x87 control register FCW (shown in Figure 3.12) are discussed in §3.6.2.

3.6.1 The FTAG register

The FTAG register, shown in Figure 3.11, can be viewed as an extension of the FSTK register file. Each FSTK[i] has an associated tag FTAG[i]. Tag FTAG[i] identifies whether or not the corresponding floating point register (FSTK[i]) has been initialized (i.e., used), and if so, whether its contents are zero, a special value (e.g., a NaN), or a normal value. The encodings for these values, shown in Figure 3.11, are reiterated in C notation below.

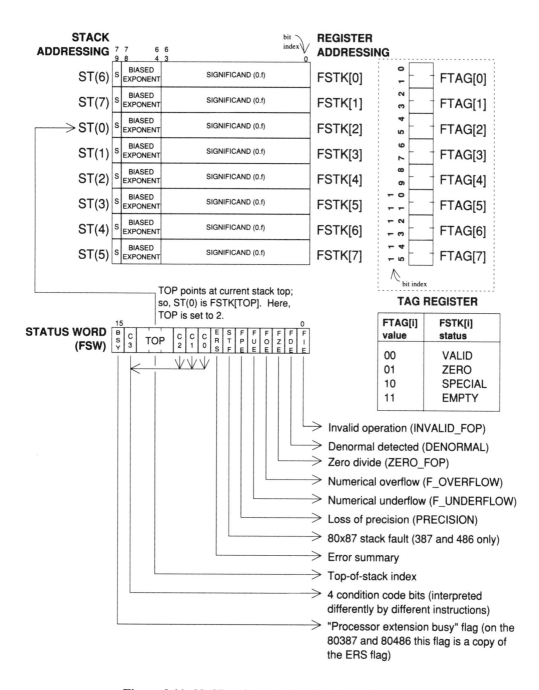

Figure 3.11: 80x87 register stack and status register

```
#define  VALID    0        /* Normal value in register */
#define  ZERO     1        /* Value in register is a zero */
#define  SPECIAL  2        /* Special value (e.g., INFINITY) */
#define  EMPTY    3        /* Register has no value (i.e., unused) */
```

The only interest that the user should have in the FTAG register is when switching contexts; this register should be saved or restored whenever the floating point register stack is saved or restored. Otherwise, the 80x87 automatically manages the contents of the individual FTAG fields. In fact, the 8087 and 80287 manage the FTAG register differently from the 80387 and the i486. In the 8087 and 80287, FTAG[i] is always consulted first whenever an operation using FSTK[i] occurs. If, for example, FTAG[i] is ZERO, FSTK[i] is assumed to contain a zero, regardless of the value actually stored in it. Since all arithmetic operations and register loads that update FSTK[i] automatically update FTAG[i], there is no problem with this strategy. However, when restoring context (via the FLDENV or FRSTOR instructions), the FTAG register is loaded independently of the FSTK registers. Hence, it is possible for a user to load an 80x87 environment where the state of FTAG[i] does not correspond to the value in FSTK[i]. In such cases, the state of FTAG[i] takes priority over the actual value in FSTK[i]. In the 80387 and i486, however, FTAG[i] is used only to indicate whether or not FSTK[i] is EMPTY. In all arithmetic operations and register loads that update FSTK[i], the 80387 and i486 only sets FTAG[i] to indicate that it has a VALID value. The determination of whether or not FSTK[i] contains a ZERO or SPECIAL value is made by actually inspecting FSTK[i] whenever it is used. Thus, on the 80387 and i486, it is not possible for the programmer to create a discrepancy between the state of FTAG[i] and FSTK[i]. To retain data structure compatibility, the 80387 and i486 FSTENV and FSAVE instructions inspect the contents of FSTK[i] and store a FTAG register image that is compatible with that of the 8087 and 80287.

3.6.2 The status and control registers

The 80x87 control word, FCW, is a programmable register that selects a variety of 80x87 operating modes. The 80x87 status word, FSW, stores all the 80x87 exception flags and condition code bits. It also stores the 80x87 stack-top pointer, TOP. Both FSW and FCW can be loaded and stored under program control. The applicable instructions are FLDCW, FSTCW, FSTSW, FLDENV, FRESTOR, FSTENV, and FSAVE. Let us look at these two registers in detail, starting with the control word.

The FCW, shown in Figure 3.12, has four types of control data

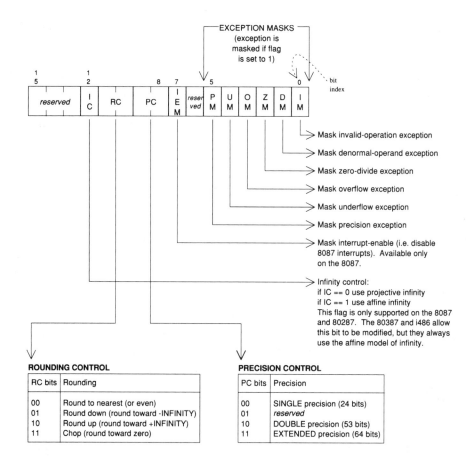

Figure 3.12: The 80x87 control register (FCW)

1. exception masks

2. rounding control bits

3. precision control bits

4. infinity control flag

There are six basic exception masks PM, UM, OM, ZM, DM, and IM, for each of the six exception types processed by the 80x87. If any of these flags is set to 1, the corresponding exception is masked. The 80x87 (and only the 80x87) also defines a global interrupt inhibit flag, IEM. This flag, if set to 1, inhibits the interrupt signal from the 8087 to the 8086. See §3.9 for more information on this flag.

The rounding control field RC controls the rounding method used when storing a result in a destination register. The four rounding methods, round to nearest, round down, round up, and chop, were discussed in §3.4.1. The precision control field determines the precision with which calculations are performed. Although 80x87 implementations are designed to compute results using EXTENDED precision, a lesser precision is allowed so that arithmetic on IEEE Std. 754-conforming floating point units that do not support EXTENDED precision can be simulated. This (rather arcane) feature is a requirement of IEEE Std. 754.

The infinity control flag, IC, selects between the projective model of infinity (IC == 0), and the affine model of infinity (IC == 1). (See §3.3.1.4 on page 218 for a discussion of infinity concepts.) Since only the 8087 and 80287 support the projective model of infinity, the IC flag is meaningful only on these 80x87 implementations. The 80387 and 80386 allow the programmer to modify this flag; however, infinity is always treated in the affine sense.

The 80x87 status register FSW is shown in Figure 3.11 on page 233. It also has four types of information packed into it

1. exception condition flags

2. condition codes

3. the 80x87 top-of-stack pointer

4. a "80x87 busy" indicator

There are six basic exception condition flags FPE, FUE, FOE, FZE, FDE, and FIE. The conditions that causes each of these flags to get set is tabulated in Figure 3.11. A separate flag, ERS, is set whenever any one of the exception condition flags is set and its corresponding mask flag in FCW is set to 0. Therefore, setting ERS activates the 80x87 ERROR signal.

The four condition code flags C0, C1, C2, and C3 are general purpose flags that are set as follows

1. the comparison instructions FCOMx, FUCOMx, and FTST set flags C0, C2, and C3 based on the result of the comparison.

2. the FXAM instruction uses C0, C2, and C3 to encode the operand class. Condition code C1 reflects the sign of FXAM's operand.

3. the remainder instructions FPREM and FPREM1 store the three least significant bits of the quotient in C0, C3, and C1. Condition code C2 is set to 1 if the remainder operation is incomplete; if it completes it is set to 0.

4. the transcendentals FPTAN, FSIN, FCOS, and FSINCOS set C2 to 1 if the input value is out of range. This is only done on the 80387 and i486, however. On the 8087 and 80287, C2 is *undefined* after the transcendental function is computed.

Whenever a 80x87 stack overflow or stack underflow occurs, an INVALID_FOP exception is signaled. The INVALID_FOP exception sets the FIE flag to 1. On the 80387 and i486, it also sets the STF flag to 1 (to indicate stack fault rather than an invalid operand value). Also set is condition code C1 to distinguish between overflow and overflow. C1 set to 1 indicates overflow, and C1 set to 0 indicates underflow. On the 8087 and 80287 FSW⟨6⟩, the bit position occupied by the STF flag, is *reserved*.

The stack-top pointer FTOP is a three bit field that indexes into the floating point register array FSTK. FTOP always points at the register that is the current stack-top. To push a value onto the stack, FTOP is decremented and register FSTK[FTOP] is written. To pop a value from the stack, FSTK[FTOP] is read and FTOP is incremented. Stack operations are discussed in detail in §3.7 below.

3.6.3 Exception address registers

Recall from §3.5 that 80x87 instructions are dispatched by the instruction decoder, and can execute in parallel with 80x86 instructions. Now consider what happens if an 80x87 exception occurs. The exception signals an interrupt, which in turn activates an interrupt handler. The problem is that, typically, the interrupt handler's return address is not the address of the floating point instruction. Instead, it is the address of the 80x86 instruction that was executing (or the 80x87 instruction waiting to be dispatched) when the error was detected. This problem is solved by recording the instruction address (CS:EIP), and memory operand address, if any, in dedicated registers. The 80x87 opcode is also saved. Their definitions are as follows.

```
SELECTOR X87CS;          /* CS of previous floating point op */
DWORD X87EIP;            /* EIP of previous floating point op */
```

```
SELECTOR X87DSEL;              /* SELECTOR of floating point mem. op. (if any) */
DWORD X87DOFF;                 /* OFFSET of floating point mem. op. (if any) */

WORD X87OPER;                  /* Opcode (see text) */
```

The 80x87 exception handler can examine the contents of these registers to get at the faulty instruction. The registers can be saved and restored using FSTENV and FLDENV, or via FSAVE and FRESTOR. The registers are only loaded for nonadministrative floating point instructions. This makes sense, since otherwise, an instruction like FLDENV would always initialize the exception registers to point at the FLDENV.

The format in which the registers are saved and restored depends on the current execution mode, and the operand size attribute, as described below.

3.6.4 Saving and restoring 80x87 state

We have seen that 80x87 state consists of the following items

1. the control word register FCW

2. the status word register FSW

3. the tag word register FTAG

4. the exception address registers X87CS, X87EIP, X87DOFF, X87DSEL, and X87OPER

5. the eight 80-bit floating point registers FSTK[0] through FSTK[7]

The first four items (i.e., all registers except for the floating point stack registers) are collectively called the **80x87 environment**. The complete set of 80x87 registers (including FSTK) is called the **80x87 state**.

The instruction FSTENV stores the 80x87 environment into memory, and the instruction FLDENV loads the registers image from memory to the 80x87. The corresponding instructions FSAVE and FRSTOR store and load the entire 80x87 state. The load/store of the environment component of these instructions occurs in one of four different formats, depending on the combination of the execution mode and the operand size active when the load/store is performed. The formats supported are shown in Figure 3.13 and Figure 3.14.

Why four separate formats? The reasons are primarily historical. The original implemenatation of the 80x87, the 8087, works only with the 8086. Since the

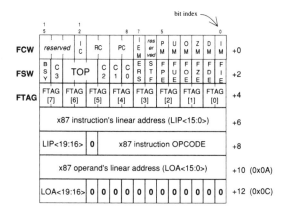

(a) REAL/VM86 mode, 16-bit environment format.

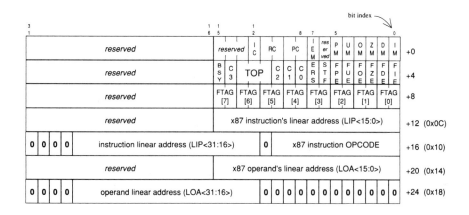

(b) REAL/VM86 mode, 32-bit environment format.

Figure 3.13: REAL and VM86 mode environment formats

8086 is a 16-bit, REAL-mode only part, only the 16-bit, REAL mode format shown in Figure 3.13 (a) is supported by it. The instruction and operand addresses are stored as linear addresses; that is, the value of the instruction linear address field LIP is X87CS * 16 + X87EIP, and the value of the operand linear address field LOA is X87DSEL * 16 + X87DOFF.

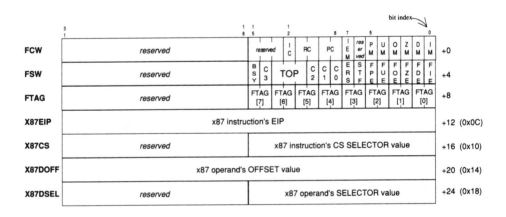

(a) PROTECTED mode, 16-bit environment format.

(b) PROTECTED mode, 32-bit environment format.

Figure 3.14: PROTECTED mode environment formats

The introduction of the 80286 and 80287 made the linear address storage scheme infeasible. This is because linear addresses in the 80286 occupy 24 bits. To encode the additional bits would have been clumsy, and also not readily capture the notion of PROTECTED mode SELECTORs. To address this problem, the format shown in Figure 3.14 (a) was devised. This format stores instruction and operand addresses as SELECTOR:OFFSET pairs, rather than as linear addresses. The OPCODE field is removed to make room for the added space requirements;

	_BYTE OFFSET	
	16-bit format	32-bit format
ST(0) (FSTK[TOP])	14 (0xE)	28 (0x1C)
ST(1)	24 (0x18)	38 (0x26)
ST(2)	34 (0x22)	48 (0x30)
ST(3)	44 (0x2C)	58 (0x3A)
ST(4)	54 (0x36)	68 (0x44)
ST(5)	64 (0x40)	78 (0x4E)
ST(6)	74 (0x4A)	88 (0x58)
ST(7)	84 (0x54)	98 (0x62)

Figure 3.15: Memory image of stack used by 80x87 state

the opcode can still be inferred by examining memory at the instruction address. Note that the OFFSET fields are (16 bits) wide. This suffices for the 80286, which only supports WORD-sized effective addresses. For compatibility with the 8086/8087, the 80286/80287 uses the 16 bit, REAL mode environment format when executing in REAL mode.

The 80386's ability to process 32-bit effective addresses presented yet another capacity problem. Since there was no way to squeeze in a 32-bit OFFSET into the existing 16-bit data structures, the decision was made to double the size of the environment, for both REAL and PROTECTED modes. The expanded formats are shown in Figure 3.13 (b) and Figure 3.14 (b), respectively. Environment access in VM86 mode uses the REAL mode format. For compatibility, a 80386/80387 system support both 16-bit formats, as well as 32-bit formats. If the operand size attribute of the instruction loading or storing the environment is 16, the 16-bit formats are used; if the attribute is 32, the 32-bit formats apply.

The i486 has added no new concepts with regard to the 80x87 environment. Hence the i486 is compatible with the 80386 in its treatment of 80x87 environment formats. Note, however, that the 80376 only operates in PROTECTED mode. Therefore, it only uses the 16-bit and 32-bit PROTECTED mode environment formats.

When loading and storing the 80x87 registers (via FSAVE and FRSTOR) the stack image always appear just after the environment area. Since there are two environment sizes, the starting offset of stack image depends on whether the 16-bit or the 32-bit format is used for the 80x87 state. The overall appearance of the stack image is shown in Figure 3.15. Since 80x87 stack entries are EXTENDED quantities, each stack element occupies 10 bytes of memory storage. Note that the first element in the stack image is the 80x87 stack-top ST(0), rather than FSTK[0].

The descriptions of the FLDENV and FRESTOR instructions reference the routines load_env_16 and load_env_32 to initialize the 80x87 with 16-bit and 32-bit environments, respectively. The definitions of the these routines are as follows.

```
load_env_16(env)
WORD *env;
{
    /* == Load FCW, FSW, and FTAG without regard to execution mode. == */
    FCW = env[0];
    FSW = env[1];
    FTAG = env[2];

    /* == Load exception pointers based on execution mode. == */
    if ( mode == PROTECTED )
    {   X87EIP = env[3];
        X87CS = env[4];
        X87DOFF = env[5];
        X87DSEL = env[6];
        X87OPER = undefined;
    }

    else  /* mode is either REAL or VM86 */
    {
        /* Initialize X87EIP, X87CS, X87DOFF, and X87DSEL based on the instruction and
           operand linear addresses.  Note that the architecture only guarantees that a
           subsequent store done in REAL or VM86 mode will store the pointers that were
           loaded.  If the store is done in PROTECTED mode, the pointer values stored are
           undefined.  */
        X87EIP⟨15:0⟩ = env[3];
        X87EIP⟨19:16⟩ = env[4]⟨15:12⟩;
        X87EIP⟨31:20⟩ = 0;
        X87CS = 0;

        X87DOFF⟨15:0⟩ = env[5];
        X87DOFF⟨19:16⟩ = env[6]⟨15:12⟩;
        X87DOFF⟨31:20⟩ = 0;
        X87DSEL = 0;
```

```
    /* Set opcode register */
    X87OPER = env[4]⟨10:0⟩;
  }
}


load_env_32(env)
DWORD *env;
{

  /* == Load FCW, FSW, and FTAG without regard to execution mode. == */
    FCW = env[0]⟨15:0⟩;
    FSW = env[1]⟨15:0⟩;
    FTAG = env[2]⟨15:0⟩;

  /* == Load exception pointers based on execution mode. == */
  if ( mode == PROTECTED )
  {  X87EIP = env[3];
     X87CS = env[4]⟨15:0⟩;
     X87DOFF = env[5];
     X87DSEL = env[6]⟨15:0⟩;
     X87OPER = undefined;
  }

  else  /* mode is either REAL or VM86 */
    {
    /* Initialize X87EIP, X87CS, X87DOFF, and X87DSEL based on the instruction and
       operand linear addresses. Note that the architecture only guarantees that a
       subsequent store done in REAL or VM86 mode will store the pointers that were
       loaded. If the store is done in PROTECTED mode, the pointer values stored are
       undefined. */
    X87EIP⟨15:0⟩ = env[3];
    X87EIP⟨31:16⟩ = env[4]⟨27:12⟩;
    X87CS = 0;

    X87DOFF⟨15:0⟩ = env[5];
    X87DOFF⟨31:16⟩ = env[6]⟨27:12⟩;
    X87DSEL = 0;

    /* Set opcode register */
    X87OPER = env[4]⟨10:0⟩;
  }
}
```

The instructions FSTENV and FSAVE reference the store_env_16 and store_env_32 routines to store the environment in memory. These routines' definitions are as follows:

```
store_env_16(env)
WORD *env;
{
   if ( mode == PROTECTED )
   {  env[0] = FCW;
      env[1] = FSW;
      env[2] = FTAG;
      env[3] = X87EIP⟨15:0⟩;
      env[4] = X87CS;
      env[5] = X87DOFF⟨15:0⟩;
      env[6] = X87DSEL;
   }

   else  /* mode is either REAL or VM86 */
   {  DWORD LIP = X87CS * 16 + X87EIP;
      DWORD LOA = X87DSEL * 16 + X87DOFF;

      env[0] = FCW;
      env[1] = FSW;
      env[2] = FTAG;
      env[3] = LIP⟨15:0⟩;
      env[4]⟨15:12⟩ = LIP⟨19:16⟩;
      env[4]⟨11⟩ = 0;
      env[4]⟨10:0⟩ = X87OPER;
      env[5] = LOA⟨15:0⟩;
      env[6]⟨15:12⟩ = LOA⟨19:16⟩;
      env[6]⟨11:0⟩ = 0;
   }
}

store_env_32(env)
DWORD *env;
{
   if ( mode == PROTECTED )
   {  env[0] = FCW;
      env[1] = FSW;
      env[2] = FTAG;
      env[3] = X87EIP;
      env[4] = X87CS;
      env[5] = X87DOFF;
      env[6] = X87DSEL;
   }

   else  /* mode is either REAL or VM86 */
   {  DWORD LIP = X87CS * 16 + X87EIP;
      DWORD LOA = X87DSEL * 16 + X87DOFF;
```

```
      env[0] = FCW;
      env[1] = FSW;
      env[2] = FTAG;
      env[3] = LIP⟨15:0⟩;
      env[4]⟨15:12⟩ = LIP⟨19:16⟩;
      env[4]⟨11⟩ = 0;
      env[4]⟨10:0⟩ = X87OPER;
      env[5] = LOA⟨15:0⟩;
      env[6]⟨15:12⟩ = LOA⟨19:16⟩;
      env[6]⟨11:0⟩ = 0;
  }
}
```

The definition of store_env_32, used to store the 80x87 environment in its 32-bit format, is very similar to that of store_env_16. The principal difference is that the environment consists of DWORD entries, rather than WORD entries. The settings of bits that are unused (and marked *reserved*) in this expanded environment are *undefined*.

Before leaving the topic of 80x87 environment formats, note the somewhat strange packing of the linear addresses in REAL/VM86 modes: for example, the least significant 16 bits of LIP is stored at BYTE offsets +6 and +7, but the remaining four bits are stored in the most significant bits of the BYTE at offset +9. Also note that the OPCODE field only has 11 bits. The three most significant bits of this field store the three least significant bits of the first opcode byte. The remaining 8 bits store the second opcode byte in it entirety. This is unusual in that the second opcode byte appears in the first byte of the OPCODE field. See §3.12 for more on the encoding of 80x87 instructions.

3.6.4.1 Mixing environment formats

What happens when an environment is saved in one format, but restored in a different format, or vice versa? If an environment is saved in a particular execution mode, it must be restored in the same execution mode. This is because there is no way for the 80x86/80x87 to know the mode in which a particular environment was saved. The same applies for operand size changes, since the operand size effects the size of the environment image in memory.

What if an environment is loaded in a particular format, and stored in a different format? The following rules apply

1. if an environment is loaded in REAL or VM86 modes, the instruction and operand linear addresses are converted to equivalent SELECTOR:OFFSET pairs and stored in X87CS:X87EIP and X87DSEL:X87DOFF, respectively.

However, if an environment loaded in this manner is stored back in PROTECTED mode, the pointer values stored are *undefined*.

2. if an environment is loaded in PROTECTED mode, the X87OPER register is set to an *undefined* value. X87OPER is always initialized when instruction information is being saved.

3. on 80376-, 80386-, and i486-based systems, storing environments using 16-bit formats only stores 20-bit linear addresses (in the case of REAL/VM86 formats), and 16-bit OFFSETs (in the case of PROTECTED mode formats). If additional address bits are present in the exception address registers, they are lost without warning.

Rule 1 implies that an environment loaded in REAL or VM86 mode must be stored back in REAL (or VM86) mode. It is acceptable to mix the two modes; for example, to load in REAL mode and store back in VM86 mode. Rule 2 implies that if an environment is loaded in PROTECTED mode, and then stored in REAL/VM86 mode without any intervening nonadministrative 80x87 instructions, the value stored in the OPCODE field is *undefined*. However, if a nonadministrative 80x87 instruction is executed in PROTECTED mode and the 80x87 environment is then stored in REAL/VM86 modes, the OPCODE field is initialized correctly.

3.7 80x87 stack operations

The 80x87 floating point register file FSTK (see Figure 3.11) is managed as a stack, where the stack pointer TOP is a 3-bit-wide field stored in the 80x87 status register FSW. TOP points at the current stack-top within FSTK; for example, if TOP is set to 2, the current stack-top is FSTK[2]. Following 80x86 conventions, a push operation pre-decrements TOP, and a pop operation returns the value at FSTK[TOP] and then increments TOP. All increment, decrement, and offset calculations involving TOP are done using unsigned, modulo-8 arithmetic. Thus, if TOP's value is 0, its new value after a push operation is 7. Similarly, if TOP's value is 7, its new value after a pop operation is 0.

Stack wraparound resulting from modulo-8 arithmetic on TOP can inadvertently destroy the contents of a register that is already in use. To prevent this, the tag corresponding to a floating point register is always checked before a value is pushed into it. If the tag value is not EMPTY, an INVALID_FOP exception is signaled. If INVALID_FOP processing is masked, however, the real indefinite value overwrites the register contents. A similar check is made when popping an element off FSTK. If the tag corresponding to the register referenced is marked EMPTY, an INVALID_FOP exception is signaled. If INVALID_FOP processing is masked, however, the pop operation returns the real indefinite or, in the case of the BCD pop instruction FBSTP, the BCD indefinite.

The push and pop operations are described as C language functions below.

```
push_FSTK(fv)
EXTENDED fv;
{   int new_top = ( (TOP == 0) ? 7 : TOP-1 );

    if ( FTAG[new_top] != EMPTY )
    {   /* == If INVALID_FOP is masked, push a real indefinite. == */
        if ( signal_87(INVALID_FOP) )              /* see page 255 */
            fv = REAL_INDEFINITE;
        else
            goto NEXT_INSTR;                   /* skip rest of current instruction */
    }

    FSTK[new_top] = fv;
    TOP = new_top;
}


EXTENDED pop_FSTK()
{   int new_top = ( (TOP == 7) ? 0 : TOP+1 );
    EXTENDED pop_value;

    if ( FTAG[new_top] == EMPTY )
    {   /* == If INVALID_FOP is masked, push a real indefinite. == */
        if ( signal_87(INVALID_FOP) )              /* see page 255 */
            goto NEXT_INSTR;                   /* skip rest of current instruction */
        else
            pop_val = REAL_INDEFINITE;
    }

    else
        pop_val = FSTK[TOP];

    /* == Set up TOP to reflect pop, clear the popped register, and return popped value ==
        */
    {   TOP = new_top;
        FTAG[TOP] = EMPTY;
        return( pop_val );
    }
}
```

The 80x87 instruction descriptions shown in Chapter 4 use the function call push_FSTK to push a value onto the stack, and the function call pop_FSTK to pop a value off it.

3.8 Coordinating an 80x86 with an 80x87

The 80x87 overview of §3.5 stated that the 80x87 synchronizes with the 80x86 using the BUSY signal. This is done for most, but not all, 80x87 instructions.[36] In the instruction descriptions in Chapter 4 this check is denoted as a call to the check_BUSY function. Its definition is as follows.

```
check_BUSY()
{
   while ( « BUSY pin active » )
   {  if ( external_interrupt() )        /* see page 166 */
      {  EIP = prev_EIP;
         goto NEXT_INSTR;                /* try instruction again after interrupt service */
      }
   }
}
```

While waiting for BUSY to deactivate check_BUSY looks for any external interrupts that are enabled. If so, the BUSY-wait loop is exit, and the interrupt is serviced. The interrupt routine is entered with the return address pointing at the 80x87 instruction that called check_BUSY. Therefore, after interrupt service is complete, the 80x87 instruction is retried. Since the instruction pointer normally points at the next instruction, it has to be restored. This is done by copying prev_EIP to EIP.

80x87 instructions are dispatched only if both the emulate-math flag EM, and the task-switched flag TS are both set to 0. The EM flag is further discussed in §3.10, and there is more on the TS flag in §3.8.2. For the moment, note that if either EM or TS is set, a PE_UNAVAILABLE exception is signaled. The function check_TS_EM performs these checks, as follows.

```
check_TS_EM()
{
   if ( EM || TS )                       /* check CR0⟨2⟩ and CR0⟨3⟩, respectively */
      signal_fault(PE_UNAVAILABLE);
}
```

---

[36] The exceptions are FNCLEX, FNDISI, FNENI, FNINIT, and FNSETPM.

Assuming that flags TS and EM are both set to 0, and that the 80*x*87 execution unit is available (i.e., BUSY is inactive), a final check before an 80*x*87 instruction's execution begins makes sure that there are no pending 80*x*87 errors. This is done by interrogating the ERROR line, as follows.

```
check_ERROR()
{
    if ( « ERROR pin active » )
        signal_imprecise(PE_ERROR);
}
```

It is worthwhile noting that the treatment of an error condition on a 8086/8087 system differs from the way it is treated on other 80*x*86/80*x*87 systems. See §3.8.1 and §3.9 for more information.

If the TS, EM, and error condition checks pass, the instruction unit dispatches the 80*x*87 instruction to the 80*x*87 execution unit. The first action taken in this case is to save the address of the instruction, the address of the memory operand (if any), and the opcode. This is done by the save_x87_instr_ptr routine, as follows:

```
save_x87_instr_ptr()
{
    /* Save pointer to current instruction. */
    X87SEL = CS;
    X87EIP = prev_EIP;

    /* Save current memory operand address. If there is no memory operand, these
       registers are set to undefined values. */
    X87DSEL = « SELECTOR of memory operand, if any »;
    X87DOFF = « OFFSET of memory operand, if any »;

    /* Save opcode bytes, reversing byte order to match 80x87 environment format. Note
       that the architecture does not require a memory access here. In particular, the
       opcode might be saved during instruction fetch. */
    X87OPER = (read1(CS_desc, prev_EIP+1) << 8) | read1(CS_desc, prev_EIP);
}
```

3.8.1 8086 coordination with an 8087

The TS and EM flag checks done before executing an 80*x*87 instruction are done by all 80*x*86/80*x*87 systems, except those based on the 80*x*86 and 80186. These implementations do not have any hardware task-switch capabilities, and so, the TS flag is not meaningful on them. Math emulation capability afforded by the EM flag is also not supported on the 8086. The 80186 does allow traps on 80*x*87 instruction access, but the flag checked is called the "ESC trap", or ET flag.[37] See [Intel, 1986] for further details on the 80186 ET flag.

In addition to not checking for TS and EM, 8086- and 80186-based systems also do not automatically verify that the 80x87 is idle (i.e. BUSY is inactive) before sending an instruction to it. Software must always check for BUSY deactivation explicitly before issuing an 80x87 operation. This is done by issuing the WAIT instruction. If the assembly is for a 8087, most 80x86/80x87 assemblers automatically insert a WAIT in front of all nonadministrative 80x87 instructions. The programmer informs the assembler that a 80287 or 80387 is being used by placing one of the following directives at the start of the assembly language module:

- .287: disables automatic WAIT insertion, and enables generation of the 80287-specific instruction FSETPM.

- .387: disables automatic WAIT insertion, and enables generation of the 80387- and i486-specific floating point instructions.

3.8.2 Saving processor extension state on a task switch

The 80x86 implementations that have built-in task switching features, namely, the 80286 and its successors, only save 80x86-specific state; see §2.11 for a discussion of task switching. In particular, 80x87 state is not saved. Rather, what is provided is a "hook" to allow tasks that use the 80x87 to save state when needed.

How can this hook, called the "task switched" flag, or TS be used by an operating system? Assume that the O.S. has a pointer *ps_87* that points at that the process state of the last process that used the 80x87. *Ps_87* is initialized to *null*. Also assume that the TS flag is initially set to 0. The following steps allow for 80x87 state saves on an as-needed basis:

1. Whenever a task switch occurs via the built-in task switch features of the 80x86, the TS flag is set to 1. A system that does not use the built-in task switch features can set the TS flag, stored in the EFLAGS register, explicitly.

---

[37] Do not confuse this flag with the ET flag found on early versions of the 80386.

2. Whenever an 80*x*87 instruction's execution is attempted, the TS flag is checked automatically by the 80*x*86. If it is set the instruction is not executed; instead, a PE_UNAVAILABLE exception is signaled.

3. The PE_UNAVAILABLE exception handler uses the CLTS instruction to clear the TS flag. Then it saves the 80*x*87 state in the (software-defined) area allocated in the process state pointed at by *ps_87*. This is done only if *ps_87* is not *null*. After the state save, *ps_87* is made to point at the current process state area.

The *ps_87* pointer, along with the TS flag implement a mechanism whereby 80*x*87 state is saved only when a new task requests use of the 80*x*87. Of course, the process state pointed at by *ps_87* may not be accessible readily; for example, the state might belong to a process that is defunct or one that is swapped out. In such systems the TS flag can be used simply to detect whether or not a process is using the 80*x*87. Whenever such a process is swapped out, 80*x*87 state can be saved unconditionally.

3.9 80*x*87 exception reporting

Exceptions processed by the 80*x*87 were described in §3.4.3 on page 228. Here we see how the 80*x*87 responds to an unmasked exception. 80*x*87 exception processing is somewhat complicated by the fact that the Intel-specified 8086/8087 interface differs from the interface used on the 80286/80287 and its successors. As shown in Figure 3.16, the 8087 signals an exception via the INT output pin. INT can be connected to any interrupt generation source; for example, it might be connected as an input to an 8259 interrupt controller. The PC/XT chooses to connect it to the 8086s NMI pin. Since an 8087 exception appears as a hardware interrupt to the 8086, it is reported at the first instruction boundary following INT activation.

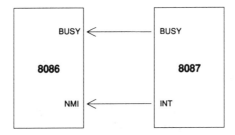

(a) Intel-recommended, PC/XT processor extension interface.

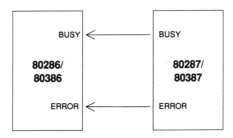

(b) Intel-recommended interface for 80287 and 80387.

Figure 3.16: The Intel-recommended processor extension interface

The Intel-recommended interface for the 80286 and 80386, however, utilizes a dedicated ERROR output pin from the 80287 and 80387 that is connected to a dedicated ERROR input pin on the 80286 and 80386. The ERROR pin is not checked on every instruction boundary; the only times it is interrogated is at the start of nonadministrative floating point operations, and at the end of the WAIT instruction. This results in the following incompatibilities:

1. 80x87 exception reporting is delayed, since the error is sensed by the 80x86 only when the next floating point instruction or WAIT is executed.

2. If an exception occurs in the very last floating point instruction in a
   program, it will not be reported unless it is followed by a WAIT.

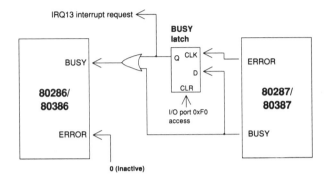

Figure 3.17: The PC/AT processor extension interface

The PC/AT handles these incompatibilities by connecting the 80x87 to the 80x86
in a nonstandard manner.[38] This nonstandard interface is shown
diagrammatically in Figure 3.17. Here, the ERROR input to the 80286/80386 is
tied inactive permanently. However, the BUSY input is activated if the
80287/80387 BUSY is active, or if an ERROR is detected. (The BUSY latch
serves to delay BUSY deactivation whenever an ERROR occurs.)

The BUSY latch output is connected interrupt input IRQ13 on an 8259 interrupt
controller. Since BUSY is active, further processing of 80x87 instructions by the
80286/80386 is inhibited. Furthermore, since IRQ13 is active, activation of the
IRQ13 interrupt service routine is imminent. When the IRQ13 handler is entered,
it resets the BUSY latch and then transfers control to the NMI handler. This
scheme approximates PC/XT behavior.

The fact that the i486 has an integrated 80x87 functional unit presents yet another
set of issues! Since the BUSY and ERROR pins are no longer exposed to the
system, there has to be a way to configure the i486 to report exceptions either in
the Intel-specified manner, or in the PC/AT manner. This is done using the
i486-specific flag NE. NE is stored in CR0. If NE is 1, the Intel-specified
exception interface is used. However, if it is 0, the ERROR line internal to the
i486 is deactivated. Instead the internal BUSY line is activated whenever BUSY

---

[38] The PC/AT approach is used on PS/2 systems also.

or ERROR is active, *and* the dedicated input pin IGNNE is inactive. When active, IGNNE says "ignore numerics exception when using the PC/AT exception interface." Therefore, if there is an ERROR and IGNNE is inactive and NE is clear, the 80x87 instructions that check for BUSY deactivation are made to wait. In a i486 system using PC/AT-style exception reporting, the wait ends when the IRQ13 handler is entered. If the BUSY latch output (external to the i486) is tied to IGNNE, the actions taken by the IRQ13 handler discussed above can activate IGNNE, therefore reallowing 80x87 instruction execution. Of course, the BUSY latch needs an input to tell it that an error has occurred. This is done via the FERR pin. This pin is the functional equivalent of the ERROR pin of other 80x87 implementations.

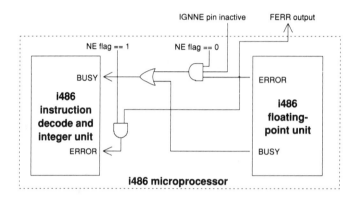

Figure 3.18: The i486 processor extension interface

Now let us see what happens when one of the six 80x87 exceptions (discussed in §3.4.3) occur. The 80x87 processes the exception by setting the corresponding flag in the status word FSW. If the exception is unmasked, the ERROR pin (or FERR pin on the i486) is activated as described above. These actions are better formalized in the C language routine signal_87 described below. This function returns TRUE if the exception that was signaled is masked. This allows the caller to perform masked exception processing, as appropriate.

```
BOOLEAN signal_87( xcp )
int xcp;
{
    /* == Process exception == */
    switch ( xcp )
    {   case INVALID_FOP:
            FIE = 1;
            if ( IM )
            {   « perform masked exception processing; see §3.4.3 »
                return( TRUE );
            }
            break;

        case DENORMAL:
            FDE = 1;
            if ( DM )
            {   « perform masked exception processing; see §3.4.3 »
                return( TRUE );
            }
            break;

        case ZERO_FOP:
            FZE = 1;
            if ( ZM )
            {   « perform masked exception processing; see §3.4.3 »
                return( TRUE );
            }
            break;

        case F_OVERFLOW:
            FOE = 1;
            if ( OM )
            {   « perform masked exception processing; see §3.4.3 »
                return( TRUE );
            }
            break;

        case F_UNDERFLOW:
            FUE = 1;
            if ( UM )
            {   « perform masked exception processing; see §3.4.3 »
                return( TRUE );
            }
            break;
```

```
      case PRECISION:
        FPE = 1;
        if ( PM )
        {  « perform masked exception processing; see §3.4.3 »
           return( TRUE );
        }
        break;
  }

  /* == Set global error indicator flag ERS, and activate ERROR signals, as appropriate
        == */
  ERS = 1;
  if ( « CPU is 8086 » && ! IEM )
     « activate INT pin »;
  else
     « activate ERROR pin »;

  /* == Return FALSE if exception is not masked == */
  return( FALSE );
}
```

3.9.1 The PE_OVERRUN exception

The size of many 80x87 operands is such that multiple memory references are often required to transfer data between the 80x87 and memory; for example, the 32-bit 80x87 environment occupies seven contiguous DWORDs. What happens if a memory access fault occurs in the middle of such a long operand? On the 80286, a PE_OVERRUN exception is signaled. Since the 80286 only has segment-based protection, this indicates that a long operand was encountered that spanned the segment's limit.

On the 80376, 80386, and i486, the first and last BYTEs of long 80x87 operands are checked for validity before data transfer begins. If a fault is detected a normal GP or PAGE fault is reported, as appropriate. If the checks pass, the transfer is initiated. Since both ends of the operand are looked at, the transfer is guaranteed to succeed as long as the operand spans no more than two pages. Since the longest 80x87 operand is 108 bytes (the 32-bit 80x87 state structure), the two-page rule is almost always met. However, it is possible to contrive an 80x87 operand that spans three pages! This can be done by setting the base of a segment within a few bytes of the end of a page, and setting the long operand's address to with a few bytes of the end of the segment. Operand access starts near the end of the segment, wraps around to the start of the segment (which is mapped onto an area near the end of a page) and continues on to the next page. Since only the first and last bytes of the operand are checked, a faulty middle page can result in an unexpected fault in the middle of an operand transfer. (A similar condition can occur if the segment is an expand-down segment whose limit is very close to 0.) On the 80376 and 80386, this (rather obscure) condition is handled by signaling a PE_OVERRUN. On the i486, a GP fault is signaled. Note that both PE_OVERRUN and GP faults are 80x86 exceptions.

In the 80x86 implementations that result in a PE_OVERRUN exception, it may be the case that the 80x87 is still in a state where it is expecting further data from the 80x86 after the PE_OVERRUN occurs. Therefore, it is necessary for a PE_OVERRUN handler to first clear the 80x87 (via an FNINIT). This makes it safe to issue further 80x87 operations. Note that the 8086 does not have any memory protection features; therefore, PE_OVERRUN can never occur on it.

3.10 Emulating the numerics processor extension

All 80x86 systems except for those based on the 8086 allow automatic trapping of 80x87 instructions. The 80286 and its successors do this via the "emulate math" flag EM. The 80186 uses the "ESC trap" flag ET stored in the I/O relocation register.[39] See [Intel, 1986] for a discussion of the I/O relocation register. In either case, the EM (or ET) flag is checked before an 80x87 instruction is attempted. If set, the PE_UNAVAILABLE exception is raised. Recall that this exception is also raised if the TS flag is set. It is up to the PE_UNAVAILABLE exception handler to interrogate both flags to determine its cause. If the EM flag is found set, the return address of the interrupt handler (which points at the 80x87 instruction) can be used to decode and emulate the floating point operation.

3.11 80x87 initial state

The 80x87 processor extension must be initialized prior to use. This is done using the FNINIT instruction. This instruction initializes a minimum number of fields in the control word (FCW), status word (FSW), and tag word (FTAG). The initialization performed is shown in the definition of function reset_x87 below.

---

[39] Do not confuse this flag with the ET flag found in early revisions of the 80386.

```
reset_x87()
{
    /* == Initialize control word FCW == */
    FCW⟨15:13⟩ = undefined;     /* reserved bits */
    IC = 0;                     /* FCW⟨12⟩ (infinity control set to projective: only used on
                                    8087/80287) */
    RC = 0;                     /* FCW⟨11:10⟩ (rounding control set to round-to-nearest) */
    PC = 3                      /* FCW⟨9:8⟩ (precision control set to EXTENDED-precision) */
    if ( « processor extension is 8087 » )
        IEM = 1;                /* disable 8087 interrupt generation */
    else
        IEM = 0;                /* IEM is not defined on 80287 and follow-ons */
    /* Disable all exception classes after initialization */
    PM = UM = OM = ZM = DM = IM = 1;

    /* == Initialize status word FSW == */
    BSY = 0;                    /* FSW⟨15⟩ (clear "busy" flag) */
    C3 = undefined;             /* FSW⟨14⟩ (condition code C3) */
    TOP = 0;                    /* FSW⟨13:11⟩ (80x87 stack-top pointer) */
    C2 = undefined;             /* FSW⟨14⟩ (condition code C2) */
    C1 = undefined;             /* FSW⟨14⟩ (condition code C1) */
    C0 = undefined;             /* FSW⟨14⟩ (condition code C0) */
    /* All exception condition bits are cleared */
    ERS = STF = FPE = FUE = FOE = FZE = FDE = FIE = 0;

    /* == Initialize all tags to EMPTY (i.e., FTAG = 0xFFFF) == */
    FTAG[0] = FTAG[1] = FTAG[2] = FTAG[3] = FTAG[4] = FTAG[5] = FTAG[6] =
    FTAG[7] = EMPTY;

    /* == Opcode, instruction pointer, and data pointer registers have underlined{undefined} values in
        them. == */
    X87OPER = undefined;
    X87CS = undefined;
    X87EIP = undefined;
    X87DSEL = undefined;
    X87DOFF = undefined;
}
```

Note that the precision control field PC is set to 3, indicating that all computation should be done in EXTENDED precision. Also note that all exception classes are disabled after initialization. In addition to FNINIT, reset_x87 actions are also done after an FNSAVE state save. Both FNINIT and FNSAVE are described in Chapter 4.

3.12 80*x*87 instruction encoding

Although some 80*x*87 instruction fields are interpreted differently, the "look and feel" of their encoding matches that of 80*x*86 instructions. This is expected, since 80*x*87 implementations typically rely on the 80*x*86 instruction decoder for instruction dispatch. The general format of 80*x*87 instructions is shown in Figure 3.19.

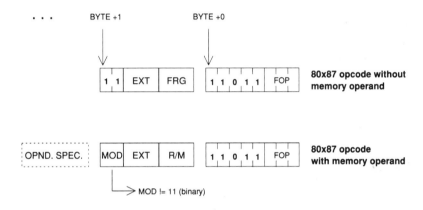

Figure 3.19: Encoding of 80*x*87 instructions

The instructions use primary opcode bytes 0xD8 through 0xDF, inclusive; all these instructions have a MOD/RM byte following. If the MOD value is 3 (i.e. 11_2) the instruction does not make any memory references. In this case, the FOP, EXT, and FRG fields encode the operation to be performed. In cases where an 80*x*87 stack address is involved, the three-bit FRG field encodes the stack-top relative register address. If the MOD value is 0, 1, or 2 a memory operand the instruction has a memory operand. In this case, the operation is encoded in the FOP and EXT fields. See §2.18.3 on page 191 for a description of how the MOD/RM byte is used to encode memory addresses.

3.13 80x87 detection method

Most 80x86 systems give the user the option of using a 80x87. However, not all such systems actually have an 80x87 plugged in. Therefore, a mechanism is needed whereby software can detect whether or not a 80x87 is present. Furthermore, if an 80x87 is present, it is useful to distinguish between an 8087/80287 versus an 80387/i486. This is because, as described throughout this chapter, the 80387 and i486 handles special various numeric conditions differently from the 8087 and 80287.

The Intel-recommended sequence for detecting an 80x87 relies on the FSW register value returned by an initialized 80x87. The method used to detect a 80387/i486 relies on the fact that they only support the affine model of infinity, whereas the 8087/80287 support both the affine and projective models. A possible code sequence is as follows:

```
; DATA AREA
FSW      DW ?                     ; Save area for status word


; CODE AREA
FNINIT
FSTSW    FSW                      ; get FSW right after initialization
CMP      BYTE PTR FSW, 0          ; FSW⟨7:0⟩ all zeros?
JNE      no_x87                   ; no 80x87 present

; Have an 80x87: is it a 80387 or i486?
FLD1                              ; generate a +∞
FLDZ
FDIV

FLD      ST                       ; generate a −∞
FCHS

FCOMPP                            ; compare −∞ with +∞
FSTSW    FSW
MOV      AX, FSW
SAHF
JNZ      using_387_486            ; −∞ != +∞ on 80387 and i486

; Reaches here if 8087 or 80287 is in use
using_87_287:
```

Chapter 4

The Instruction Set

This chapter defines the entire 80*x*86 and 80*x*87 instruction set in alphabetic order. In particular, it provides a definition of the execute function invoked in the main instruction interpretation loop (see page 11). Not all instructions are available on all implementations. Whenever an instruction's availability is restricted, it is denoted in the heading line introducing the instruction. For some instructions, availability restrictions only apply to certain aspects of the instructions' operation. The descriptions of such an instruction delineates these restrictions.

For ease of reference, the following section lists all 80*x*86 and 80*x*87 instruction mnemonics by function. Only a terse description of each instruction is in this section. The reader should refer to the alphabetic list of instructions starting on page 272 for the detailed definition of the instruction. Before making use of the alphabetic reference, review §4.2 for information on the notation used in the instruction descriptions.

4.1 Instruction mnemonics by function

DATA TRANSFER:

BSWAP	Swap byte order of DWORD general register
CBW/CWDE	Sign-extend AL to AX, or AX to EAX
CMPXCHG	Transfer source operand to destination if destination equals AL/AX/EAX; otherwise, copy destination to AL/AX/EAX
CWD/CDQ	Sign-extend AX to DX:AX, or EAX to EDX:EAX
MOV	Transfer data between a general register or memory, between two general registers, between a segment register an memory, or between a general register and any of a segment register, control register, debug register, or test register
MOVSX	Sign-extend a BYTE to a WORD or DWORD, or sign-extend a WORD to a DWORD
MOVZX	Zero-extend a BYTE to a WORD or DWORD, or zero-extend a WORD to a DWORD
POP	Pop 80x86 stack into a general register, segment register, or memory location
POPA[D]	Pop 80x86 stack into all general registers (WORD or DWORD sized)
PUSH	Push a general register, segment register, or memory location onto 80x86 stack
PUSHA[D]	Push all general registers (WORD or DWORD sized) onto 80x86 stack
XADD	Exchange and add
XCHG	Exchange contents of two general registers, or contents of a general register and a memory location

ARITHMETIC OPERATIONS (also see 80x87 OPERATIONS):

AAA	ASCII adjust after add (used for unpacked BCD add)
AAD	ASCII adjust before divide (used for unpacked BCD divide)
AAM	ASCII adjust after multiply (used for unpacked BCD multiply)
AAS	ASCII adjust after subtract (used for unpacked BCD subtract)
ADC	Add source operand and CF to destination
ADD	Add source operand to destination
CMP	Compare two operands, and set flags
DAA	Decimal adjust after add (used for packed BCD addition)
DAS	Decimal adjust after subtract (used for packed BCD subtraction)
DEC	Decrement destination operand by 1
DIV	Unsigned divide
IDIV	Signed divide
IMUL	Signed multiply
INC	Increment destination operand by 1
MUL	Unsigned multiply
NEG	Compute two's complement of destination
SBB	Subtract source operand and CF from destination
SUB	Subtract source operand from destination

LOGICAL OPERATIONS:

AND	Bitwise-AND source operand into destination
NOT	Bitwise-negate destination
OR	Bitwise-OR source operand into destination
TEST	Bitwise-AND two source operands, and set flags
XOR	Bitwise-XOR source operand into destination

SHIFT/ROTATE OPERATIONS:

RCL	Rotate left through carry flag CF
RCR	Rotate right through carry flag CF
ROL	Rotate left
ROR	Rotate right
SAL/SHL	Shift left arithmetic
SAR	Shift right arithemtic
SHLD	Shift left logical double (funnel shift)
SHR	Shift right logical
SHRD	Shift right logical double (funnel shift)

CONTROL TRANSFER:

CALL	Subroutine call or nested task switch
J*cond*	Conditional jump (e.g. JZ jumps if ZF set)
J[E]CXZ	Jump on [E]CX zero
JMP	Unconditional jump or nonnested task switch
LOOP	Loop [E]CX times
LOOPNZ	Loop [E]CX times or till ZF clear
LOOPZ	Loop [E]CX times or till ZF set
RET	Return from subroutine call
SET*cond*	Set byte on condition (e.g. SETZ set byte to 1 if ZF set)

POINTER MANIPULATION:

L*x*S	Load a far pointer into a segment register and a general register (e.g. LES loads ES and a general register)
LEA	Load effective address into general register

BIT MANIPULATION:

BSF	Bit scan forward
BSR	Bit scan reverse
BT	Bit test
BTC	Bit test and complement
BTR	Bit test and reset
BTS	Bit test and set

STRING MANIPULATION (usable with REP prefixes):

CMPS*x*	Compare string element
LODS*x*	Load BYTE/WORD/DWORD string element into AL/AX/EAX
MOVS*x*	Move string element from source to destination
SCAS*x*	Scan string element for match against AL/AX/EAX
STOS*x*	Store AL/AX/EAX into string element
XLATB	Lookup AL in translate table

[E]FLAG CONTROL:

CLC	Clear carry flag CF
STC	Set carry flag CF
CMC	Complement carry flag CF
CLD	Clear direction flag DF
CLI	Clear interrupt flag IF
LAHF	Load AH into FLAGS
POPF[D]	Pop into FLAGS/EFLAGS
PUSHF[D]	Push FLAGS/EFLAGS onto stack
SAHF	Store FLAGS into AH
STD	Set direction flag DF
STI	Set interrupt flag IF

PROTECTION CONTROL:

ARPL	Adjust RPL
LAR	Load access rights
LGDT	Initialize global descriptor table's descriptor register
LIDT	Initialize interrupt descriptor table's descriptor register
LLDT	Initialize local descriptor table's descriptor register
LMSW	Load machine status word (see also, MOV instruction)
LSL	Load segment limit
LTR	Load TSS SELECTOR register and TSS descriptor register
SGDT	Store global descriptor table's descriptor register
SIDT	Store interrupt descriptor table's descriptor register
SLDT	Store local descriptor table's SELECTOR
SMSW	Store machine status word (see also, MOV instruction)
STR	Store TSS SELECTOR
VERR	Verify SELECTOR for read access
VERW	Verify SELECTOR for write access

MISCELLANEOUS:

BOUND	Verify that value is in specified range
CLTS	Clear task-switched flag TS
ENTER	Enter nested procedure
HLT	Cease execution until interrupt detected
INT	Generate software interrupt
INTO	Generate INT 4 software interrupt if OF set
INVD	Invalidate i486 cache
INVLPG	Invalidate TLB entry
IRET[D]	Return from interrupt handler or nested task
LEAVE	Leave nested procedure
NOP	No operation (actually an XCHG operation)
WAIT	Wait for BUSY to deactivate
WBINVD	Invalidate i486 cache

ADMINISTRATIVE 80*x*87 OPERATIONS:

F[N]CLEX	Clear all pending 80*x*87 exceptions
F[N]DISI	Disable 8087 interrupts (8087 only)
F[N]ENI	Enable 8087 interrupts (8087 only)
F[N]INIT	Initialize 80*x*87
FLDCW	Load 80*x*87 control word FCW
FLDENV	Load 80*x*87 environment
FRSTOR	Load all 80*x*87 state
FSAVE	Store all 80*x*87 state
FSTENV	Store 80*x*87 environment
FSTCW	Store 80*x*87 control word FCW
FSTENV	Store 80*x*87 environment
FSTSW	Store 80*x*87 status word FSW

NONADMINISTRATIVE 80*x*87 OPERATIONS:

F2XM1	Compute 2^x-1
FABS	Compute absolute value
FADD[P]	Add floating point [and pop]
FBLD	Load packed BCD value
FBSTP	Store packed BCD value and pop
FCHS	Change sign
FCOM[P][P]	Compare ordered [and pop] [and pop again]
FCOS	Compute cosine
FDECSTP	Decrement stack pointer
FDIV[R][P]	Divide [reversed] [and pop]
FFREE	Mark 80*x*87 stack entry as "unused"
FIADD	Add integer
FICOM[P]	Compare integer [and pop]
FIDIV[R]	Divide by integer [reversed]
FILD	Load integer
FIMUL	Multiply by integer
FINCSTP	Increment stack pointer
FIST[P]	Store integer [and pop]
FISUB[R]	Subtract integer [reversed]
FLD	Load floating point value
FLD1	Load constant 1.0
FLDL2E	Load constant $\log_2 e$
FLDL2T	Load constant $\log_2 10$
FLDLG2	Load constant $\log_{10} 2$
FLDLN2	Load constant $\log_e 2$
FLDPI	Load constant π
FLDZ	Load constant +0.0
FMUL[P]	Multiply [and pop]
FNOP	80*x*87 no operation
FPATAN	Compute partial arctangent
FPREM	Compute partial remainder

FPREM1	Compute IEEE-compatible partial remainder
FPTAN	Compute tangent
FRNDINT	Round to integer
FSCALE	Scale by a power of 2
FSIN	Compute sine
FSINCOS	Compute sine and cosine
FSQRT	Compute square root
FST[P]	Store as floating point value [and pop]
FSUB[R][P]	Subtract [reversed] [and pop]
FTST	Compare with 0.0
FUCOM[P][P]	Compare unordered [and pop] [and pop again]
FXAM	Classify operand
FXCHG	Exchange register contents
FXTRACT	Extract exponent
FYL2X	Compute y * $\log_2$ x
FYL2XP1	Compute y * $\log_2$ (x+1)

4.2 Notation

The definition of a $80x86/80x87$ mnemonic in §4.3 begins with a list of all possible instruction formats that use the mnemonic, followed by a summary of the instruction's behavior in prose. The summary is followed by a formal description of the instruction's operation using C language notation. This in turn is followed by one or two simple examples demonstrating the mnemonic's use. The examples are followed by a section that notes any special features or restrictions that apply to the mnemonic. Finally, a section lists any notes that apply to commonly used assembly language notation; for example, alternate mnemonics recognized by the assembler, and the like. It is worthwhile noting that the instruction mnemonics used here match those originated by Intel. These names are used by commonly available assemblers like Microsoft MASM and Borland TASM. However, some assemblers might support alternate mnemonics; for example, some UNIX assemblers for the $80x86$ use UNIX-style mnemonics.

Unlike the assembly language used by many other architectures, $80x86/80x87$ assembly language mnemonics are typed. In particular, an $80x86$ mnemonic identifies a function, rather than the operand's storage class, its size, and the like. For example, all three assembler instructions

```
ADD    AX, 2                ; increment WORD register AX by 2
ADD    BYTE PTR [ESI], DL   ; Add DL to BYTE in memory
ADD    ESP, ECX             ; Add DWORD register ECX to ESP
```

perform additions, but on objects of different sizes and storage classes. In fact, the opcode used by each instruction is different; the assembler automatically makes the correct choice based on the operand type. In many cases there are multiple ways to encode the same mnemonic. When this happens, the assembler invariably uses the most compact encoding. (Within encodings of the same density, the choice made is up to the particular assembler.)

The following strategy is used to describe the many possible instruction opcodes associated with a mnemonic. The instruction formats list enumerates all valid operand types for a given mnemonic. The operand types have predefined names; for example, the *r/m8* operand type specifies an operand that is either a BYTE in memory or a BYTE-sized general register. The name also specifies how the operand is encoded. In some cases, a name can denote either an operand of multiple sizes. For example, *imm* denotes an immediate field that is either is either a WORD or a DWORD. In this case, the choice is made based on the operand size attribute of the instruction.

Next to each format is a field that assigns operand names to (arbitrary) parameter names. These parameter names are used in the formal C language definition of the mnemonic. Next to the parameters list is the base opcode structure for the format. The placement of opcodes and operands in a instruction's encoding is discussed in detail in §2.18 (starting on page 185). For 80*x*87 instructions, also see §3.12.

Now let us look at a list of all the predefined operand type names.

AL   an implicit reference to the AL register; that is, no bits are used to encode it

eAX   an implicit reference to either AX (if *os* is 16), or to EAX (if *os* is 32)

CL   shift/rotate count register (implied by instruction opcode)

cr   a control register encoded in REG field

dr   a debug register encoded in REG field

ecode   a six-bit field used by ESC (floating point) instructions

frsz   a special WORD-sized immediate field used only by the ENTER instruction that appears immediately after the opcode byte. (See also, the *lev* field.)

imm   a WORD-sized or DWORD-sized immediate value encoded as the last field in an instruction. The size of the field always matches the instruction's operand size attribute.

imm8   a BYTE-sized immediate value encoded as the last field in an instruction. The BYTE value might be sign-extended to fit the operand size. The definition of an instruction that uses an *imm8* type operand specifies whether or not sign extension is done.

imm16   a WORD-sized unsigned immediate used by RET instructions

lev   a special BYTE-sized immediate field used only by the ENTER instruction that appears immediately after the *frsz* field. (See the definition of the *frsz* field.)

m   a memory location encoded in *r/m* field of the MOD/RM byte. There is considerable variability as to the operand's size. For example, BT*x* instructions, *m* is a bit string, whereas for indirect far JMP *m* stores a far pointer.

m16   a WORD sized quantity encoded in the R/M field of MOD/RM byte. The WORD is usually interpreted as an integer, but might be a SELECTOR, etc.

m32   a DWORD sized quantity encoded in the R/M field of MOD/RM byte. The DWORD is usually interpreted as an integer, or as a SINGLE precision floating point value. The latter only occurs for floating point instructions.

m64   a QWORD (64 bit) sized quantity encoded in the R/M field of MOD/RM byte. The QWORD is interpreted as a DOUBLE precision floating point value, or as a 64-bit integer. *m64* operands only appear in floating point instructions.

m80   a ten-BYTE quantity encoded in the R/M field of MOD/RM byte. The fields is interpreted as an EXTENDED-precision floating point value and is used only in the context of floating point instructions.

moff   a WORD/DWORD value similar to a *rel*-type operand. However, *moff* is an OFFSET specification for a data item (rather than an [E]IP-relative branch value, as in the case of *rel* operands). The *moff* field immediately follows the opcode byte.

r   a WORD/DWORD general register encoded using the REG field; the operand size attribute *os* determines choice of WORD versus DWORD

r8   a BYTE general register encoded using the REG field

r16   a WORD general register encoded using the REG field

r32   a DWORD general register. *The register is encoded in r/m field of the MOD/RM byte, rather than in the REG field, as is the case with r8 and r16 operands.* The control, debug, and test register MOV instructions use this format.

reg   WORD/DWORD general register encoded in three least significant bits of the opcode byte. The base opcode's three least significant bits are always 0 in this case. The operand size attribute *os* determines choice of WORD/DWORD register.

rel   a WORD/DWORD field that is added to IP or EIP. The sum is the effective address of the operand. IP and a WORD are used if the operand size attribute *os* is 16; otherwise, EIP and a DWORD are used.

rel8   a BYTE field that is sign-extended and then added to IP or EIP. The sum is the effective address of the operand. IP is used if the operand size attribute *os* is 16; otherwise, EIP is used.

r/m   BYTE/WORD/DWORD general register or memory location encoded in R/M field of MOD/RM byte. BYTE encoding is differentaited from the WORD/DWORD encoding based on choice shown in the OPCODE column of the instruction's definition. In the WORD/DWORD case, resolving whether a WORD or DWORD is applicable is determined by the operand size (*os*) attribute.

r/m8   a BYTE general register or memory location encoded in the R/M field of MOD/RM byte

r/m16   a WORD general register or memory location encoded in the R/M field of MOD/RM byte

r/m32   a DWORD general register or memory location encoded in the R/M field of MOD/RM byte

sr   a segment register encoded in the REG field of a MOD/RM byte

ST   the 80*x*87 stack-top register, *ST(0)*. This register reference is implied by the instruction; that is, no bits are used to encode it.

ST(*n*)   the *n*th element from the top of the 80*x*87 floating point stack. *n* is a value between 0 and 7 inclusive that is encoded in the FRG field of the MOD/RM byte; see §3.12 for information on 80*x*87 instruction encoding. Note that MOD is always set to 11 when *ST(n)* is selected.

tr   a test register encoded in REG field

There are two functions, evenParity and signex, that are used commonly throughout the instruction definitions. The signex function sign-extends its parameter to fit the destination size. The evenParity function computes the even parity of the bits in the least significant BYTE of its parameter. This is defined as follows:

```
BOOLEAN evenParity( v )
BYTE v;
{
    /* "^" is the exclusive-OR operator */
    return( (v⟨7⟩ ^ v⟨6⟩ ^ v⟨5⟩ ^ v⟨4⟩ ^ v⟨3⟩ ^ v⟨2⟩ ^ v⟨1⟩ ^ v⟨0⟩) == 0 );
}
```

Another notational device used is the "&" operator. This operator is used to evaluate the address of a memory operand. For example,

```
WORD *bVec = & src2;
```

creates a far pointer *bVec* that points at the *src2* operand; that is a far pointer whose OFFSET component is the effective address of the *src2* operand, and whose SELECTOR component is the SELECTOR stored in the applicable segment register, including the effect of segment override prefixes.

Let us complete the discussion of instruction description notation with an example. The ADD mnemonic, defined on page 278, supports the following operand formats:

Add: Signed and unsigned integer add

INSTRUCTION	PARAMETERS	OPCODE
ADD r, r/m	dst ≡ r, src = r/m, os ∈ {8,16,32}	02 {8}, 03 {16,32}
ADD r/m, r	dst ≡ r/m, src = r, os ∈ {8,16,32}	00 {8}, 01 {16,32}
ADD r/m, imm	dst ≡ r/m, src = imm, os ∈ {8,16,32}	80 /0 {8}, 81 /0 {16,32}
ADD r/m, imm8	dst ≡ r/m, src = signex(imm8), os ∈ {16,32}	83 /0 {16,32}
ADD AL, imm8	dst ≡ AL, src = imm8, os = 8	04
ADD eAX, imm	dst ≡ eAX, src = imm, os ∈ {16,32}	05 {16,32}

The first instruction format accepts a general register r for the adds destination, and either a general register or a memory location r/m for the increment value. As long as the size of both operands is the same (a constraint of most 80x86 arithmetic and logical operations) they can either be a BYTE, 2 WORD, or a DWORD. (Keep in mind that DWORD operations are only available on the 80376, 80386, and i486.) The opcode for the BYTE operation is 0x02, whereas the opcode for the WORD/DWORD operation is 0x03. Whether or not a WORD or DWORD is used depends on the operand size attribute of the instruction. How the operand size attribute is determined is discussed in §2.18. The parameters description shows that the register operand r is bound to the *dst* parameter, and the register/memory operand r/m is assigned to the *src* parameter. The names *dst* and *src* are arbitrary, but they give us an idea of what the source and destination operands are. (Of course, *dst* is also one of the source operands.)

The second instruction format is very similar to the first, except that the order of the *src* and *dst* operands is reversed. Note the convention of having the first operand be the destination. This rule is almost always followed in 80x86 assembly language. The third instruction format accepts an immediate value as the *src*, and a general register or memory location as the destination. The size of the immediate must match the size of the destination. The fourth instruction format is similar to the third, except that the immediate value is always BYTE-sized. The value encoded is sign extended to natch the destination's size. The reason for providing the alternate format is encoding efficiency.

The last two formats use a fixed destination: either the AL, AX, or EAX registers. These formats are subsets of the **ADD r/m, imm** format seen above, and are provided for encoding efficiency.

The instructions list specifies the ADD mnemonic in terms of three parameters: the source *src*, the destination *dst*, and the operand size attribute *os*. Assigning specific operands to generalized parameters simplifies the formal description of operations. For example, the addition is specified as

result = src + dst
dst = *result*

To understand the operation of a particular instruction format, simply substitute the actual operand for the parameter. For example, the addition component of the instruction format

ADD   r/m, imm

becomes

result = r/m + imm
r/m = *result*

As noted early in §1, the *result* variable is special in that it can hold infinitely precise value. Doing so simplifies the specification of certain flag settings, for example, the overflow flag.

What does it mean to use an operand type in an expression? For non-memory operands, the answer is straightforward. For example, the instruction

ADD   CX, 5

is an instance of the instruction format we just saw, since CX fits into the *r/m* category and 5 is a valid *imm*. The addition performed by it is done as follows

result = AX + 5
AX = *result*

For memory operands, we have to be aware of the fact that program-generated 80x86 memory references always have two components: a SELECTOR and an OFFSET. Therefore, an abstract expression like

result = r/m + imm

actually expands to

result = read$n$(desc, offset) + imm

when *r/m* is a reference to a memory operand. Here, n is the number of BYTEs in the memory operand, *desc* is the name of the descriptor register corresponding to the segment register used to store the SELECTOR, and *off* is the OFFSET. Similarly, an assignment like

r/m = *result*

expands to

writen(desc, offset, *result*)

The OFFSET of a memory reference is simply its effective address. A memory references SELECTOR is usually the SELECTOR stored in the default segment register for the type of effective address employed; see §2.18 for details. However, the default segment register can be changed via a segment override prefix. Memory access, and the details of the definitions of *readx* and *writex* are discussed in §2.7.

4.3 Instructions sorted by mnemonic

AAA: ASCII Adjust AL after Add

INSTRUCTION	PARAMETERS	OPCODE
AAA		37

SUMMARY

AAA simulates the addition of two unpacked BCD (i.e., ASCII) digits by correcting the result of a binary addition into the AL register. Hence, AAA is useful only after an ADD or ADC instruction. AAA operates by checking whether the value in AL is greater than 9. If so, the true decimal value is obtained by adding 6. The carry into the next decimal digit is signaled by incrementing AH and setting the AF and CF flags.

OPERATION

```
if (AL⟨3:0⟩ > 9 || AF == 1)
{   AL = (AL + 6) & 0xF;
    AH = AH + 1;
    AF = 1;
}
else
    AF = 0;

CF = AF;
OF = undefined
PF = undefined
SF = undefined
ZF = undefined
PF = undefined
```

EXAMPLE

```
; Add the two unpacked digits in AX and BX. Store in CX.
ADD    AL, BL      ; Add low-order digits
AAA                ; Make result digit a decimal; increment AH on carry
MOV    CL, AL      ; Store low-order digit in CL
SHR    AX, 8       ; AL = AH;  AH = 0 (Get high-order addend)
ADD    AL, BH      ; Add high-order digit
AAA                ; Fixup high-order digit; AH set to 1 on overflow
MOV    CH, AL      ; Store high-order digit in CH
```

AAD: ASCII Adjust AX before Divide

INSTRUCTION	PARAMETERS	OPCODE
AAD		D5 0A

SUMMARY

AAD assumes that AX stores two digits of an unpacked BCD divisor, with AH containing the high-order digit. The instruction converts the two decimal digits to their binary equivalent and stores the result back into AX. Although termed "ASCII," the high order nibbles of the bytes storing the decimal digits must be zero.

OPERATION

AL = AH * 10 + AL;
AH = 0;
/* Set arithmetic flags */
OF = *undefined*
SF = AL$\langle 7 \rangle$
ZF = (AL == 0)
AF = *undefined*
PF = evenParity(AL)
CF = *undefined*

EXAMPLE

```
; Divide the two unpacked BCD digits in AX by BL.
AAD                                 ; AX = AH*10 + AL
DIV      BL                         ; tmp = AX / BL;  AH = AX % BL;  AL = tmp
```

AAM: ASCII Adjust AX after Multiply

INSTRUCTION	PARAMETERS	OPCODE
AAM		D4 0A

SUMMARY
AAM converts the binary value in AL into two unpacked BCD (i.e., ASCII) decimal digits. The high-order digit is stored in AH, and the low-order digit is stored in AL. This allows its use in converting the product of two packed BCD digits generated using the MUL instruction back into packed BCD format. The initial value in AL should be no greater than 100. But for the flag settings, AAM is a generalization of AAA.

OPERATION
AH = AL $/_u$ 10;
AL = AL $\%_u$ 10;
/* Set arithmetic flags */
OF = *undefined*
SF = AL$\langle 7 \rangle$
ZF = (AL == 0)
AF = *undefined*
PF = evenParity(AL)
CF = *undefined*

EXAMPLE
```
; Multiply unpacked digits AL and BL.  Store result in AX.
MUL      BL                    ; AX = AL * BL
AAM                            ; AH = high-order digit;  AL = low-order digit
```

AAS: ASCII Adjust AL after Subtract

INSTRUCTION	PARAMETERS	OPCODE
AAS		3F

SUMMARY
AAS simulates the subtraction of two unpacked BCD (i.e., ASCII) digits by correcting the result of a binary subtraction from the AL register. Hence, AAS is useful only after an SUB, SBB, or NEG instruction. AAS operates by checking whether the value in AL is greater than 9. If so, the true decimal value is obtained by subtracting 6. The borrow from the next decimal digit is signaled by decrementing AH and setting the AF and CF flags.

OPERATION
if (AL⟨3:0⟩ > 9 || AF == 1)
{   AL = AL⟨3:0⟩ - 6;
    AH = AH - 1;
    AF = 1;
}
else
    AF = 0;

CF = AF;
OF = *undefined*
PF = *undefined*
SF = *undefined*
ZF = *undefined*
PF = *undefined*

EXAMPLE
; Subtract the two unpacked BCD digits in BX from AX. Store in CX.

SUB	AL, BL	; Subtract low-order digits
AAS		; Make result digit a decimal; increment AH on carry
MOV	CL, AL	; Store low-order digit in CL
SHR	AX, 8	; AL = AH; AH = 0 (Get high-order addend)
SUB	AL, BH	; Subtract high-order digit
AAS		; Fixup high-order digit; AH set to -1 on borrow
MOV	CH, AL	; Store high-order digit in CH

ADC: Signed and unsigned integer add with carry

INSTRUCTION	PARAMETERS	OPCODE
ADC r, r/m	dst ≡ r, src = r/m, os ∈ *{8,16,32}*	12 *{8}*, 13 *{16,32}*
ADC r/m, r	dst ≡ r/m, src = r, os ∈ *{8,16,32}*	10 *{8}*, 11 *{16,32}*
ADC r/m, imm	dst ≡ r/m, src = imm, os ∈ *{8,16,32}*	80 /2 *{8}*, 81 /2 *{16,32}*
ADC r/m, imm8	dst ≡ r/m, src = signex(imm8), os ∈ *{16,32}*	83 /2 *{16,32}*
ADC AL, imm8	dst ≡ AL, src = imm8, os = *8*	14
ADC *e*AX, imm	dst ≡ *e*AX, src = imm, os ∈ *{16,32}*	15 *{16,32}*

SUMMARY

ADC adds the values of the source and destination operands and the carry flag (CF), and stores the result in the destination. All arithmetic flags are set. The remaining flags are left unmodified. An ADC instruction with a memory operand is LOCKable.

OPERATION

```
/* Compute result */
result = dst + src + CF
dst = result
/* Set arithmetic flags */
```
$OF = result < -2^{os-1} \;||\; result > 2^{os-1}-1$
$SF = dst\langle os-1 \rangle$
$ZF = (dst == 0)$
$AF = dst\langle 3{:}0 \rangle + src\langle 3{:}0 \rangle + CF >_u 15$
$PF = evenParity(dst)$
$CF = result >_u 2^{os}-1$

EXAMPLES

```
ADC     EAX, 4               ; EAX = EAX + 4 + CF
ADC     AH, BYTE PTR [ESI]   ; AH = AH + *( (BYTE *) ESI ) + CF
```

ADD: Signed and unsigned integer add

INSTRUCTION	PARAMETERS	OPCODE
ADD r, r/m	dst ≡ r, src = r/m, os ∈ {8,16,32}	02 {8}, 03 {16,32}
ADD r/m, r	dst ≡ r/m, src = r, os ∈ {8,16,32}	00 {8}, 01 {16,32}
ADD r/m, imm	dst ≡ r/m, src = imm, os ∈ {8,16,32}	80 /0 {8}, 81 /0 {16,32}
ADD r/m, imm8	dst ≡ r/m, src = signex(imm8), os ∈ {16,32}	83 /0 {16,32}
ADD AL, imm8	dst ≡ AL, src = imm8, os = 8	04
ADD eAX, imm	dst ≡ eAX, src = imm, os ∈ {16,32}	05 {16,32}

SUMMARY
ADD adds the values of the source and destination operands and stores the result in the destination. All arithmetic flags are set. The remaining flags are left unmodified. An ADD instruction with a memory operand is LOCKable.

OPERATION
/* Compute result */
result = dst + src
dst = *result*
/* Set arithmetic flags */
OF = *result* < -2^{os-1} || *result* > 2^{os-1}-1
SF = dst⟨os-1⟩
ZF = (dst == 0)
AF = dst⟨3:0⟩ + src⟨3:0⟩ >$_u$ 15
PF = evenParity(dst)
CF = *result* >$_u$ 2os-1

EXAMPLES
```
ADD      EAX, EBX              ; EAX = EAX + EBX
ADD      AH, BYTE PTR [ESI]    ; AH = AH + *( (BYTE *) ESI )
```

address size override (prefix): Toggle address size attribute of following instruction (376, 386, 486 only)

INSTRUCTION	PARAMETERS	OPCODE
see *ASM USAGE NOTES* below		
		67

SUMMARY

The 80376, 80386, and i486 support both 16-bit and 32-bit segment offsets (although the 80376 does so in a very limited fashion). Sixteen-bit offsets retain compatibility with the 80286 and its predecessors. Normally, the number of bits in the offset of an instruction, also called its *address size attribute*, is determined by the default address size attribute of the code segment in which the instruction appears. However, the default value can be changed for any particular instruction by placing the "address override" prefix in front of it. If the default address size is 32, use of the prefix makes it 16. Conversely, if it is 16, use of the prefix makes it 32. See §2.18.3.3 on page 195 for more details.

NOTE

1. On a 80376, 80386, and i486, the address override prefix is ignored if placed in front of an instruction that does not access memory. On an 80186 and 80286, use of this prefix generates an INVALID_INSTR fault. Its effect on the 8086 is undefined. The address size is restricted to be 16 on the 80286, 80186, and 8086.

ASSEMBLER USAGE NOTE

1. An address size override prefix is automatically generated by an assembler whenever the offset size implied by the instruction does not match the default offset size (i.e., address size) for the segment in which the instruction appears. Hence, no explicit "address size override" mnemonic is required. The assembly language segment attribute USE16 specifies a default address size of 16; the attribute USE32 specifies a default address size of 32.

AND: Bitwise logical AND

INSTRUCTION	PARAMETERS	OPCODE
AND r, r/m	dst ≡ r, src = r/m, os ∈ {8,16,32}	22 {8}, 23 {16,32}
AND r/m, r	dst ≡ r/m, src = r, os ∈ {8,16,32}	20 {8}, 21 {16,32}
AND r/m, imm	dst ≡ r/m, src = imm, os ∈ {8,16,32}	80 /4 {8}, 81 /4 {16,32}
AND r/m, imm8	dst ≡ r/m, src = signex(imm8), os ∈ {16,32}	83 /4 {16,32}
AND AL, imm8	dst ≡ AL, src = imm8, os = 8	24
AND eAX, imm	dst ≡ eAX, src = imm, os ∈ {16,32}	25 {16,32}

SUMMARY

AND performs a bitwise ANDing of the source and destination operands and stores the result in the destination. All arithmetic flags except **AF** are set. AF's value is undefined; the nonarithmetic flags are left unmodified. Since this is a logical operation, there can never be a carry or overflow. Hence, the instruction always clears **CF** and **OF**. An AND instruction with a memory operand is LOCKable.

OPERATION

```
/* Compute result */
result = dst & src
dst = result
/* Set arithmetic flags */
OF = 0
SF = dst⟨os-1⟩
ZF = (dst == 0)
AF = undefined
PF = evenParity(dst)
CF = 0
```

EXAMPLES

```
AND     WORD PTR [EAX], BX      ; *( (WORD *) EAX ) &= BX
AND     AL, 15                  ; AL = AL & 0x0F
```

ARPL: Adjust RPL field of selector (286, 376, 386, 486 only)

INSTRUCTION	PARAMETERS	OPCODE
ARPL r/m16, r16	dst ≡ r/m16, src ≡ r16	63

SUMMARY

ARPL compares the RPL (requestor's privilege level) field of the two selectors specified by the source and destination operands. If the destination's RPL specifies a greater privilege than that of the source (i.e., if the destination's RPL is numerically less than that of the source), its value is updated to the source's RPL.

ARPL can be used to force the RPL field of a SELECTOR passed to a routine via an interlevel call to be no more privileged than the CPL of the caller. To do so, load the source operand register (src) with the caller's CS. (The caller's CS is stored on the stack. Its RPL field RPL field contains the caller's CPL.) Use the SELECTOR to be modified as the destination operand, dst. If the destination operand's RPL is less than (i.e., more privileged than) the caller's CPL, the caller's CPL value is copied into the destination's RPL.

OPERATION

```
/* ARPL is only available in PROTECTED mode */
if ( mode == REAL || mode == VM86 )
   signal_fault(INVALID_INSTR);

/* dst.RPL = max( dst.RPL, src.RPL ) */
if ( src⟨1:0⟩ > dst⟨1:0⟩ ) /* src.RPL > dst.RPL? */
{  dst⟨1:0⟩ = src⟨1:0⟩;
   ZF = 1;
}
else
   ZF = 0;
```

EXAMPLES

```
; Ensure that the RPL passed via an inter-level CALL is OK.
MOV     DX, WORD [ESP+4]      ; DX = caller's CS
ARPL    WORD [ESP+8], DX      ; WORD at [ESP+8] contains selector
```

BOUND: Check array index against bounds (unavailable on the 8086)

INSTRUCTION	PARAMETERS	OPCODE
BOUND r, m	src1 = r, src2 = m, os ∈ *{16,32}*	62

SUMMARY
BOUND verifies that the value of the register operand specified by src1 is within the bounds low and high, where low is the memory location referenced by src2 and high is the memory location following src2. If WORD-sized operands are used (i.e., if the operand size attribute *os* is 16), high is located a WORD away from low; otherwise, high is located a DWORD away from low. Note that src2 must be memory based.

OPERATION
```
/* Use WORD-sized bounds if os == 16; DWORD-sized if os == 32 */
if ( os == 16 )
{   WORD *bVec2 = &src2;
    if ( src1 < bVec2[0] || src1 > bVec2[1] )
       signal_fault(BOUND);
}
else /* os == 32 */
{   DWORD *bVec4 = &src2;
    if ( src1 < bVec4[0] || src1 > bVec4[1] )
       signal_fault(BOUND);
}
```

EXAMPLE
```
BOUND    EAX, dBnd              ; Ensure dBnd[0] <= EAX <= dBnd[1]
```

NOTE
1. The INVALID_INSTR fault is signaled if src2 is a register operand.

BSF: Bit scan forward (376, 386, 486 only)

INSTRUCTION	PARAMETERS	OPCODE
BSF r, r/m	dst ≡ r, src = r/m, os ∈ *{16,32}*	0F BC

SUMMARY
Starting from bit index 0, BSF scans the source operand for the first bit set to 1.
If such a bit is located, the bit index is returned in the destination register, and the
ZF flag is cleared. If the source operand's value is 0, the destination register is
assigned an *undefined* value and the ZF flag is set to 1.

OPERATION
```
for ( i = 0;  i < os;  i++ )
   if ( src⟨i⟩ == 1 )
      break;

if ( i == os )  /* bit set to 1 not found */
{   dst = undefined;
    ZF = 1;
}
else  /* 1 bit found: report its position */
{   dst = i;
    ZF = 0;
}
```

EXAMPLE
```
; Find the first bit set to a zero in EBX.  Store index in EAX.
NOT      EBX                    ; Convert 1's to 0's and vice versa
BSF      EAX, EBX               ; Scan for a 1: finds a 0
```

NOTE
1. Since bit 0 is the least significant bit of a number, a BSF operation can be
   thought of as a "backward" scan (i.e., from the least significant to the most
   significant bit) if the source operand is a numeric value.

BSR: Bit scan reverse (376, 386, 486 only)

INSTRUCTION	PARAMETERS	OPCODE
BSR r, r/m	dst ≡ r, src = r/m, os ∈ {16,32}	0F BD

SUMMARY
Starting from the most significant bit (i.e., bit index *os*-1), BSR scans the source operand for the first bit set to 1. If such a bit is located, the bit index is returned in the destination register, and the ZF flag is cleared. If the source operand's value is 0, the destination register is assigned an *undefined* value and the ZF flag is set to 1.

OPERATION
```
for ( i = os-1;  i < 0;  i-- )
   if ( src⟨i⟩ == 1 )
      break;

if ( i < 0 )  /* no bit is set to 1 */
{   dst = undefined;
    ZF = 1;
}
else  /* 1 bit found: report its position */
{   dst = i;
    ZF = 0;
}
```

EXAMPLE
```
; Find first 1 bit in CX, starting with bit 15.  Store the bit index in SI.  Note that the upper
  half of the ESI register is not modified.
BSR      SI, CX
```

NOTE
1. Since bit 0 is the least significant bit of a number, a BSR operation can be thought of as a "forward" scan (i.e., from the most significant to the least significant bit) if the source operand is a numeric value.

BSWAP: Byte-order swap (486 only)

INSTRUCTION	PARAMETERS	OPCODE
BSWAP reg	dst ≡ reg, src = reg, os = *32*	0F C8+*reg*

SUMMARY
BSWAP (available only on the i486) reverses the byte ordering of the DWORD register named by reg. This is used to convert data stored in Big Endian format into Little Endian format and Little Endian data to Big Endian format. No flags are afftected by this instruction.

OPERATION
temp = src;
dst⟨31:24⟩ = temp⟨7:0⟩;
dst⟨23:16⟩ = temp⟨15:8⟩;
dst⟨15:8⟩ = temp⟨23:16⟩;
dst⟨7:0⟩ = temp⟨31:24⟩;

EXAMPLE
BSWAP   EAX

NOTES
1. A use of BSWAP apart from converting Big Endian numeric data is in reversing four byte groups within a string. This can be done to speed up string comparison and to perform decimal arithmetic on decimal strings stored in Big Endian format.

2. The BSWAP instruction is only available on the i486 processor. To swap a DWORD quantity (e.g., in EBX) on the 80386, use the following instruction sequence:
   ```
   ror      bx, 8
   ror      ebx, 16
   ror      bx, 8
   ```
   The primary advantage of BSWAP is speed: it executes in one clock cycle, whereas the ROR sequence requires a minimum of 6 clock cycles.

3. The ROR instruction can be used to swap the byte order of a 16-bit register. For example, to swap the bytes in register SI, use the instruction

   ```
   ror  si, 8
   ```

BT: Bit test (376, 386, 486 only)

INSTRUCTION	PARAMETERS	OPCODE
BT r_1, r_2	src ≡ r_1, ind = r_2 % os, os ∈ {16,32}	0F A3
BT m, r	src ≡ m, ind = signex(r), os ∈ {16,32}	0F A3
BT r/m, imm8	src ≡ r/m, ind = imm8 % os, os ∈ {16,32}	0F BA /4

SUMMARY
BT reads bit position ind of operand src. If clear, CF is cleared; if set, CF is set to 1. Thus, BT copies to CF the value of the bit read. No flags other than CF are modified.

If *ind* is a register, its size must match the operand size *os*; for example, if *os* is 16, *ind* must be a WORD-sized register. If *ind* is an immediate, it is always BYTE-sized. If *ind* is a register and *src* is a memory address, *ind* is treated as a signed bit index into *src*. In all other cases only the least significant four bits (allowing bit indexes from 0 .. 15), or the least significant five bits (allowing bit indexes from 0 .. 31) of ind form the bit index. Four bits are chosen if the operand size is 16; otherwise, 5 bits are chosen.

OPERATION
CF = src⟨ind⟩

EXAMPLES
BT	SI, DI	; CF = SI⟨DI & 0x0F⟩ [bottom 4 bits of DI used]
BT	ESI, EDI	; CF = ESI⟨EDI & 0x1F⟩ [bottom 5 bits of EDI used]
BT	mem, AX	; CF = mem⟨AX⟩ [AX is a signed WORD quantity]

NOTES
1. The instruction form BT *m, r* uses the entire register contents as a signed bit index. Thus, *m* can be viewed as a bit string of 2os bits whose center is byte *m*.

2. If *ea* is the effective address of a memory based BT operand, the 80x86 is free to access the DWORD starting at

   ea + ((ind / 32) * 4)

   in the course of executing the instruction. If this is a problem (e.g., because the bit accessed is near a segment boundary, or because it is a memory-mapped I/O location), the memory value should be read into a register using MOV and the BT applied to the register.

BTC: Bit test and complement (376, 386, 486 only)

INSTRUCTION	PARAMETERS	OPCODE
BTC r_1, r_2	src ≡ r_1, ind = r_2 % os, os ∈ {16,32}	OF BB
BTC m, r	src ≡ m, ind = signex(r), os ∈ {16,32}	OF BB
BTC r/m, imm8	src ≡ r/m, ind = imm8 % os, os ∈ {16,32}	OF BA /7

SUMMARY
BTC copies the value of bit index *ind* of operand *src* to the flag CF. Then it writes back the complement of the bit value into the bit position just read. No flags other than CF are modified.

If *ind* is a register, its size must match the operand size *os*; for example, if *os* is 16, *ind* must be a WORD-sized register. If *ind* is an immediate, it is always BYTE-sized. If *ind* is a register and *src* is a memory address, *ind* is treated as a signed bit index into *src*. In all other cases only the least significant four bits (allowing bit indexes from 0 .. 15), or the least significant five bits (allowing bit indexes from 0 .. 31) of *ind* form the bit index. Four bits are chosen if the operand size is 16; otherwise, 5 bits are chosen. A BTC instruction with a memory operand is LOCKable.

OPERATION
CF = src⟨ind⟩;
src⟨ind⟩ = ~CF;

EXAMPLES

BTC	SI, DI	; CF = SI⟨DI & 0x0F⟩ [bottom 4 bits of DI used] ; SI⟨DI & 0x0F⟩ = ~CF
BTC	ESI, 0x34	; CF = ESI⟨0x14⟩ [bottom 5 bits of 0x34 used] ; ESI⟨0x14⟩ = ~CF
BTC	mem, AX	; CF = mem⟨AX⟩ [AX is a signed WORD quantity] ; mem⟨AX⟩ = ~CF

NOTES
1. The instruction form BTC *m, r* uses the entire register contents as a signed bit index. Thus, *m* can be viewed as a bit string of 2os bits whose center is byte *m*.

2. If *ea* is the effective address of a memory based BTC operand, the 80x86 is free to access the entire DWORD starting at

$$ea + (\, (\text{ind} \, / \, 32) * 4 \,)$$

in the course of executing the instruction. If this is a problem (e.g., because the bit accessed is near a segment boundary, or because it is a memory-mapped I/O location), the memory value should be read into a register using MOV and the BTC applied to the register. The register value can then be written back to memory using another MOV.

BTR: Bit test and reset (376, 386, 486 only)

INSTRUCTION	PARAMETERS	OPCODE
BTR r$_1$, r$_2$	src $\equiv$ r$_1$, ind = r$_2$ % os, os $\in$ {16,32}	0F B3
BTR m, r	src $\equiv$ m, ind = signex(r), os $\in$ {16,32}	0F B3
BTR r/m, imm8	src $\equiv$ r/m, ind = imm8 % os, os $\in$ {16,32}	0F BA /6

SUMMARY
BTR copies the value of bit index *ind* of operand *src* to the flag CF. Then it writes a zero into the bit position just read. No flags other than CF are modified.

If *ind* is a register, its size must match the operand size *os*; for example, if *os* is 16, *ind* must be a WORD-sized register. If *ind* is an immediate, it is always BYTE-sized. If *ind* is a register and *src* is a memory address, *ind* is treated as a signed bit index into *src*. In all other cases only the least significant four bits (allowing bit indexes from 0 .. 15), or the least significant five bits (allowing bit indexes from 0 .. 31) of *ind* form the bit index. Four bits are chosen if the operand size is 16; otherwise, 5 bits are chosen. A BTR instruction with a memory operand is LOCKable.

OPERATION
CF = src⟨ind⟩;
src⟨ind⟩ = 0;

EXAMPLES
BTR	SI, DI	; CF = SI⟨DI & 0x0F⟩ [bottom 4 bits of DI used]
		; SI⟨DI & 0x0F⟩ = 0
BTR	ESI, 0x34	; CF = ESI⟨0x14⟩ [bottom 5 bits of 0x34 used]
		; ESI⟨0x14⟩ = 0
BTR	mem, AX	; CF = mem⟨AX⟩ [AX is a signed WORD quantity]
		; mem⟨AX⟩ = 0

NOTES
1. The instruction form BTR *m, r* uses the entire register contents as a signed bit index. Thus, *m* can be viewed as a bit string of 2os bits whose center is byte *m*.

2. If *ea* is the effective address of a memory based BTR operand, the 80*x*86 is free to access the entire DWORD starting at

   ea + ((ind / 32) * 4)

in the course of executing the instruction. If this is a problem (e.g., because
the bit accessed is near a segment boundary, or because it is a memory-
mapped I/O location), the memory value should be read into a register using
MOV and the BTR applied to the register. The register value can then be
written back to memory using another MOV.

BTS: Bit test and set (376, 386, 486 only)

INSTRUCTION	PARAMETERS	OPCODE
BTS r₁, r₂	src ≡ r₁, ind = r₂ % os, os ∈ {16,32}	0F AB
BTS m, r	src ≡ m, ind = signex(r), os ∈ {16,32}	0F AB
BTS r/m, imm8	src ≡ r/m, ind = imm8 % os, os ∈ {16,32}	0F BA /5

SUMMARY
BTS copies the value of bit index *ind* of operand *src* to the flag CF. Then it writes a one into the bit position just read. No flags other than CF are modified.

If *ind* is a register, its size must match the operand size *os*; for example, if *os* is 16, *ind* must be a WORD-sized register. If *ind* is an immediate, it is always BYTE-sized. If *ind* is a register and *src* is a memory address, *ind* is treated as a signed bit index into *src*. In all other cases only the least significant four bits (allowing bit indexes from 0 .. 15), or the least significant five bits (allowing bit indexes from 0 .. 31) of *ind* form the bit index. Four bits are chosen if the operand size is 16; otherwise, 5 bits are chosen. A BTS instruction with a memory operand is LOCKable.

OPERATION
CF = src⟨ind⟩;
src⟨ind⟩ = 1;

EXAMPLES
BTS	SI, DI	; CF = SI⟨DI & 0x0F⟩ [bottom 4 bits of DI used] ; SI⟨DI & 0x0F⟩ = 1
BTS	ESI, 0x34	; CF = ESI⟨0x14⟩ [bottom 5 bits of 0x34 used] ; ESI⟨0x14⟩ = 1
BTS	mem, AX	; CF = mem⟨AX⟩ [AX is a signed WORD quantity] ; mem⟨AX⟩ = 1

NOTES
1. The instruction form BTS *m, r* uses the entire register contents as a signed bit index. Thus, *m* can be viewed as a bit string of 2os bits whose center is byte *m*.

2. If *ea* is the effective address of a memory based BTS operand, the 80x86 is free to access the entire DWORD starting at

ea + ((ind / 32) * 4)

in the course of executing the instruction. If this is a problem (e.g., because the bit accessed is near a segment boundary, or because it is a memory-mapped I/O location), the memory value should be read into a register using MOV and the BTS applied to the register. The register value can then be written back to memory using another MOV.

CALL (near): Call subroutine in same segment

INSTRUCTION	PARAMETERS	OPCODE
CALL rel	addr = EIP + signex(rel), os ∈ *{16,32}*	E8
CALL r/m	addr = r/m, os ∈ *{16,32}*	FF /2

SUMMARY
The "near" CALL instruction invokes a subroutine by pushing the EIP (if operand size is 32) or IP (if operand size is 16) onto the stack, and then branching to *addr*. The near CALL is used for branching within the same segment only. Use the far CALL or task CALL instructions (described next) to invoke a subroutine in a different segment, or to link to a new task.

OPERATION
```
push OS(EIP);                        /* see page 118 */
if ( os == 32 )  /* Execute next instruction at addr */
    EIP = addr;
else  /* os == 16: use low 16 bits only */
    EIP = addr⟨15:0⟩;
```

EXAMPLES
CALL	DWORD PTR [123]	; Call routine whose offset is stored in ; offset 123 of the data segment. (Indirect CALL)
CALL	EAX	; Call routine at offset EAX of current ; CS segment. (Indirect CALL)
CALL	proc	; Call routine labelled *proc*. Assumes *proc*'s address ; is encoded as a *rel* type operand (i.e., as an ; EIP-relative displacement.)

NOTES
1. Unlike many instructions, the operand size (os) attribute a *direct* near CALL assembly language instruction cannot be determined by its operand. Direct near CALLs always inherits the os attribute of the code segment containing it. Thus, in a USE16 code segment a direct near CALL has an os attribute of 16, but in a USE32 code segment it has an os attribute of 32.

2. When the operand size is 16, the upper 16 bits of the new EIP are forced to zeros. This allows proper handling of a 16-bit CALL followed by a 32-bit CALL.

CALL (far): Call subroutine in any segment

INSTRUCTION	PARAMETERS	OPCODE
CALL sel:off	os ∈ {16,32}	9A
CALL m	os ∈ {16,32}	FF /3

SUMMARY

In its simplest form, the "far" CALL instruction (alternate mnemonic CALLF) pushes the current CS:[E]IP value onto the stack and transfers control to the far pointer specified by the instruction operand. Since instructions are always fetched from CS:[E]IP the transfer of control entails loading CS with the SELECTOR of the far pointer, and EIP or IP with its offset component.

The far pointer may be specified in two ways: either directly in the instruction, or via a pointer to an area in memory that itself stores the far pointer. The latter form (shown as the format "CALL m" above) is termed an "indirect call." In an indirect CALL the offset *off* is fetched from location *m* in memory; its size matches the CALL's operand size atibute. *sel* is fetched from location *m* + 4 (if the operand size is 32) or from *m* + 2 (if the operand size is 16).

The details of how the instruction operates varies, depending on the current execution mode, as follows:

In REAL *or* VM86 *modes:* CS and IP (if *os* == 16) or CS and EIP (if *os* == 32) are pushed onto the stack. Then the SELECTOR *sel* is loaded into CS, and the Base of the CS descriptor register is set to *sel* * 16. (This is in accordance with normal REAL/VM86 mode segment access rules.) Then, a branch to offset *off* is executed.

In PROTECTED *mode: sel* is used to index into a descriptor table; see the description of the read_descr routine (on page 63) for details. If the descriptor that is read is for a code segment, and the rules for code segment access pass, control is transferred to offset *off* of the code segment. The access rules applied are detailed in the description of the load_CS routine; see page 69. Note for the moment though that far CALLs via code segments descriptors are only allowed if the target descriptor's privilege level (i.e., DPL) matches CPL.

If in PROTECTED mode and the descriptor selected by *sel* is not a code segment, the "CALL" can be processed in a number of different ways, as follows:

1. *descriptor is for a* TASKGATE *or a TSS:* A task switch is performed; see the description of the CALL (task) instruction on page 301 for details.

2. *descriptor is for a CALL gate, and the DPL of the descriptor pointed at by the CALL gate equals the CPL:* The SELECTOR and offset specified in the CALL gate (call them *gSel* and *gOff*, respectively) are used as the target of the far CALL. The offset value specified by the instruction operand is ignored.

3. *descriptor is for a CALL gate, and the DPL of the descriptor pointed at by the CALL gate is less than the CPL:* The SELECTOR and offset specified in the CALL gate (call them *gSel* and *gOff*, respectively) are used as the target of an *inter-level* far CALL; that is, the CPL value changes. The offset value specified by the instruction operand is ignored.

OPERATION
```
WORD mem16[ ] = memVec;        /* Memory accessed as WORDs */
DWORD mem32[ ] = memVec;       /* Memory accessed as DWORDs */

/* == Get tentative selector and offset values == */
if ( « CALL sel:off » )  /* [direct jump] */
{   offset = off;
    selector = sel;
}
else /* « CALL m » [indirect jump] */
{   if ( os == 32 )  /* DWORD offset; WORD selector */
    {   mem32 = &m;
        offset = mem32[0];
        selector = mem32[1];
    }
    else  /* WORD offset; WORD selector */
    {   mem16 = &m;
        offset = mem16[0];
        selector = mem16[1];
    }
}

/* == Place new SELECTOR value in CS == */
CS = selector;

/* == If in REAL/VM86 mode, all that needs doing is to set the base address of CS_desc.
      == */
if ( mode == REAL || mode == VM86 )
    CS_desc.Base = CS * 16;  /* REAL-mode style segment base */
```

```
/* == mode == PROTECTED: access LDT/GDT and act based on value read == */
else
{
   CS_desc = load_CS(CS, FALSE);  /* see page 69 */

   /* == Check if segment is executable; if so, the  load_CS  routine has already
         performed all necessary protection checks: update CS.RPL and EIP. == */
   if ( CS_desc.Executable )
   {  CS.RPL = CPL;

      /* == Execute next instruction at offset == */
      if ( os == 32 )
         EIP = offset;
      else  /* os == 16: use low 16 bits only */
         EIP = offset⟨15:0⟩;
   }

   /* == If not a code segment descriptor, check if CALL gate, TASKGATE, or TSS
         descriptor == */
   if ( !CS_desc.CDSeg )
   {  if ( CS_desc.Type == CALLGATE16 ||
           CS_desc.Type == CALLGATE32 )  /* gated CALL */
      {  if ( CPL > CS_desc.DPL || CPL > selector.RPL )  /* insufficient privilege */
            signal_fault(GP, CS & 0xFFFC);

         /* == Signal error if "Present" flag of gate descriptor is FALSE == */
         if ( !CS_desc.Valid )
            signal_fault(NP, CS & 0xFFFC);

         /* == Process gated CALL (load_gate_CS routine is defined below)  == */
         load_gate_CS(CS_desc);
      }

      else if ( CS_desc.Type == TASKGATE  || CS_desc.Type == NOTBUSY_TSS16 ||
                CS_desc.Type == NOTBUSY_TSS32 )  /* task switch */
         « see CALL (task) definition on page 301 »

      else  /* not a CALL gate, TASK gate, or TSS: report error */
         signal_fault(GP, CS & 0xFFFC);
   }
}
```

```
/* == This routine expects gate_desc to be a CALLGATE16 or CALLGATE32 descriptor.
      The SELECTOR stored in the descriptor is used to fetch the code segment
      descriptor. If the DPL of this descriptor equals CPL, a same-level call is performed
      (i.e., only CS:[E]IP is pushed); if the DPL is less than the CPL, an interlevel call is
      performed (i.e., the CPL is updated to be the DPL, the current SS:[E]SP and
      CS:[E]IP are pushed onto the stack corresponding to the new CPL, and a number of
      parameters (specified by gate_desc.ParamCount) are copied from the old CPL's
      stack to the new stack). == */
load_gate_CS(gate_desc)
DESCR gate_desc;
{  DESCR desc;

   /* == Signal error if SELECTOR named by CALL gate is null == */
   if ( nullSel(gate_desc.Selector) )
      signal_fault(GP, 0)

   /* == Setup SELECTOR named by CALL gate == */
   CS = gate_desc.Selector;

   /* == Prevent other system agents from accessing descriptor table. See ı2.7.11
         (page 111) == */
   lock(DESCR_TABLE);

   /* == Read raw descriptor and verify that it is a code segment. If so, perform same level
         CALL (CPL == DPL) or inter-level CALL (CPL > DPL)  == */
   desc = read_descr(CS, FALSE);
   if
   ( desc.Executable  &&  ( ( desc.Conforming && CPL >= desc.DPL )  ||
                            ( !desc.Conforming && CPL == desc.DPL ) ) )
   {  if ( ! desc.Valid )
         signal_fault(NP, (CS & 0xFFFC));

      /* == Perform same-level call == */
      if ( gate_desc.Type == CALLGATE16 )
      {  push2(CS);                  /* see page 116 */
         push2(EIP);
      }
      else /* gate_desc.Type == CALLGATE32 */
      {  push4(CS);                  /* see page 116 */
         push4(EIP);
      }
   }

   else  /* == Check for interlevel CALL == */
   if ( desc.Executable  &&  ( !desc.Conforming && CPL > desc.DPL ) )
   {  if ( ! desc.Valid )
         signal_fault(NP, (CS & 0xFFFC));
```

```
        /* == Perform interlevel call (see page 124 for a description of how this is done) == */
        if ( gate_desc.Type == CALLGATE16 ) /* use 16 bit transfers */
            priv_lev_switch_CALL(16, desc, gate_desc.ParamCount);
        else /* gate_desc.Type == CALLGATE32: use 32 bit transfers */
            priv_lev_switch_CALL(32, desc, gate_desc.ParamCount);
    }

    else  /* == CPL < DPL  or  descriptor is not a code segment: report error == */
        signal_fault(GP, (CS & 0xFFFC));

    /* == Mark the new CS descriptor "accessed" and reallow other agents to access
            descriptor tables == */
    mark_accessed(sel);
    unlock(DESCR_TABLE);

    /* == Set RPL of new CS to CPL.  Note that for the interlevel CALL case, the CPL value
            itself may have changed === */
    CS.RPL = CPL;

    /* == Execute next instruction at offset specified by gate. == */
    if ( gate_desc.Type == CALLGATE32 )
        EIP = gate_desc.Offset;
    else  /* gate_desc.Type == CALLGATE32: use low 16 bits only */
        EIP = gate_desc.Offset⟨15:0⟩;
}
```

EXAMPLES
```
; Call procedure whose WORD offset is stored at offset 123 and whose
; SELECTOR is stored at offset 125 of the data segment. [Indirect call]
CALLF     WORD PTR [123]

; Call procedure at label far_lab
CALLF     far_lab
```

NOTES

1. Since CS:[E]IP always points at the next instruction to be executed, pushing it onto the stack allows the RETF instruction (see page 543) to recover its value from the stack and transfer control back to the instruction following the CALL. This mechanism is used to handle procedure calls.

2. If it is known that the CALL's target is in the same segment the more efficient, "near" CALL instruction can be used.

3. Unlike many instructions, the operand size (os) attribute a *direct* far CALL assembly language instruction cannot be determined by its operand. Direct far CALLs always inherit the os attribute of the code segment referenced by the operand. Thus, if in the instruction

CALL proc

proc is a label in a USE16 code segment the *os* attribute is 16; it has an os attribute of 32 if *proc* appears in a USE32 code segment.

4. When the operand size is 16, the upper 16 bits of the new EIP are forced to zeros. This allows proper handling of a 16-bit CALL followed by a 32-bit CALL.

5. The indirect far CALL instruction ("CALL m") can only be used with a memory operand. If a register operand is specified, an INVALID_INSTR fault is signaled.

CALL (task): Invoke a new task (nested) (286, 376, 386, 486 only)

INSTRUCTION	PARAMETERS	OPCODE
CALL sel:off	os ∈ {16,32}	9A
CALL m	os ∈ {16,32}	FF /3

SUMMARY
The "task" CALL instruction is available only in PROTECTED mode. Its instruction encoding is the same as for a far CALL. If the SELECTOR specified in the instruction selects a task gate, a TSS16, or a TSS32 descriptor it is assumed to be a task CALL. (Since SELECTORs access descriptor tables only in PROTECTED mode, an 80x86 operating in REAL or VM86 modes can never execute a task CALL. In particular, the 8086 and 80186 do not support this instruction form.)

If the SELECTOR points to a TSS16 or a TSS32 and the TSS descriptor is marked "not busy," the current task state is saved in the existing TSS and the task state named by the TSS16 or TSS32 is loaded. If the SELECTOR points to a task gate, the TSS16 or TSS32 referenced by the task gate is used in the operation just described. In either case, the SELECTOR of the new task's TSS is saved in the BackLink field of the old TSS, and the "nested task" (NT) flag is set to 1 in the new task's flags. The task switch operation is specified in detail in §2.11 on page 128.

OPERATION
```
WORD mem16[ ] = memVec;      /* Memory accessed as WORDs */
DWORD mem32[ ] = memVec;     /* Memory accessed as DWORDs */
DESCR desc;                  /* Holding tank for gate descriptor */

if ( mode == REAL || mode == VM86 )
   « see far CALL instruction on page 297 »
```

```
/* == Get SELECTOR and offset values == */
if ( « CALL sel:off » )  /* [direct call] */
{  offset = off;
   selector = sel;
}
else /* « CALL m » [indirect jump] */
{  if ( os == 32 )  /* DWORD offset; WORD selector */
   {  mem32 = &m;
      offset = mem32[0];
      selector = mem32[1];
   }
   else  /* WORD offset; WORD selector */
   {  mem16 = &m;
      offset = mem16[0];
      selector = mem16[1];
   }
}

/* == Read CS descriptor, and select CALL type == */
desc = load_CS(selector, FALSE);  /* see page 69 */
if ( desc.CDSeg )  /* not a control descriptor */
   « see CALL (far) definition on page 297 »

else /* desc.CDSeg == 0: check control descriptor type */
{  if ( desc.Type == CALLGATE16 || desc.Type == CALLGATE32 )
      « see CALL (far) definition on page 297 »

   else if ( desc.Type == TASKGATE || desc.Type == NOTBUSY_TSS16 || desc.Type ==
   NOTBUSY_TSS32 )  /* task switch */
   {  if ( CPL > descr.DPL || CPL > selector.RPL )  /* insufficient privilege */
         signal_fault(GP, (selector & 0xFFFC));

      if ( !desc.Valid )
         signal_fault(NP, (selector & 0xFFFC));

      if ( desc.Type == TASKGATE )
      {  selector = desc.Selector;  /* Read SELECTOR named by gate */
         /* Ensure selector named in task gate is not NULL, or in the LDT */
         if ( nullSel(selector) || selector.TI == 1 )
            signal_fault(GP, (selector & 0xFFFC));
         /* Ensure task gate selector names a not-busy TSS16 or TSS32 */
         desc = readDescr(selector);
         if ( desc.Type != NOTBUSY_TSS16 && desc.Type != NOTBUSY_TSS32 )
            signal_fault(GP, (selector & 0xFFFC));

         if ( !desc.Valid )
            signal_fault(NP, (selector, 0xFFFC));
      }
```

```
        /* == Do the task switch as a nested switch ("TRUE" parameter), and do not report
                an error code ("FALSE" parameter.)  See page 134 for details == */
        enter_new_task(selector, desc, TRUE, FALSE);
    }
    else signal_fault(GP, (selector & 0xFFFC));
}
```

CBW: Convert byte to word

INSTRUCTION	PARAMETERS	OPCODE
CBW		98

SUMMARY
CBW sign-extends the contents of AL and assigns it to AX.

OPERATION
AX = signex(AL);

EXAMPLE
CBW

NOTES
1. CBW is the 16-bit operand size variant of the CWDE (convert word to doubleword extended) instruction.

2. CBW is a special case of the MOVSX instruction. It is provided solely for compatibility with the 80386's predecessors (the 8086, 80186, and 80286.)

CDQ: Convert doubleword to quadword (376, 386, 486 only)

INSTRUCTION	PARAMETERS	OPCODE
CDQ		99

SUMMARY
CDQ sign-extends the contents of EAX and assigns the sign-extension value (i.e., 0 or −1) to EDX. Thus, CDQ assigns to the register pair EDX:EAX the sign-extension of EAX.

OPERATION
```
if ( EAX < 0 )
   EDX = 0xFFFFFFFF;
else
   EDX = 0;
```

EXAMPLE
```
CDQ
```

NOTE
1. CDQ is the 32 bit operand size variant of the CWD (convert word to doubleword) instruction. Note that CWD and CWDE are distinct instructions.

CLC: Clear carry flag

INSTRUCTION	PARAMETERS	OPCODE
CLC		F8

SUMMARY
CLC clears CF, the carry flag. No other flags are modified.

OPERATION
CF = 0

EXAMPLE
CLC

CLD: Clear direction flag

INSTRUCTION	PARAMETERS	OPCODE
CLD		FC

SUMMARY
CLD clears DF, the direction flag. No other flags are modified.

OPERATION
DF = 0

EXAMPLE
CLD

CLI: Clear interrupt flag

INSTRUCTION	PARAMETERS	OPCODE
CLI		FA

SUMMARY
CLI clears IF, the interrupt flag. The instruction can only be executed if the task has I/O privilege (i.e., CPL <= IOPL.) If not, a general protection fault is signaled. No flags other than IF are modified.

OPERATION
```
if ( CPL <= IOPL )
   IF = 0;
else
   signal_fault(GP, 0);
```

EXAMPLE
CLI

NOTES
1. CLI is always executable in REAL mode, since REAL mode code can be viewed as executing with a CPL of 0.

2. CLI is executable in VM86 mode only if IOPL is set to 3.

CLTS: Clear task-switched flag in CR0 (286, 376, 386, 486 only)

INSTRUCTION	PARAMETERS	OPCODE
CLTS		0F 06

SUMMARY
CLTS clears TS, the task-switched flag. The instruction can only be executed when CPL is zero. At any other level a general protection fault is signaled. No flags other than TS are modified.

OPERATION
```
if ( CPL == 0 )
   TS = 0;  /* TS is bit CR0⟨3⟩ */
else
   signal_fault(GP, 0);
```

EXAMPLE
CLTS

NOTES
1. CLTS is always executable in REAL mode, since REAL mode code can be viewed as executing with a CPL of 0.

2. CLTS will always signal a GP fault in VM86 mode. (Recall that VM86 mode executes with CPL set to 3.)

CMC: Complement carry flag

INSTRUCTION	PARAMETERS	OPCODE
CMC		F5

SUMMARY
CMC complements the value of CF, the carry flag. No other flags are modified.

OPERATION
CF = ~CF

EXAMPLE
CMC

CMP: Compare scalar operands

INSTRUCTION	PARAMETERS	OPCODE
CMP r, r/m	src_1 = r, src_2 = r/m, os ∈ {8,16,32}	3A {8}, 3B {16,32}
CMP r/m, r	src_1 = r/m, src_2 = r, os ∈ {8,16,32}	38 {8}, 39 {16,32}
CMP r/m, imm	src_1 = r/m, src_2 = imm, os ∈ {8,16,32}	80 /7 {8}, 81 /7 {16,32}
CMP r/m, imm8	src_1 = r/m, src_2 = signex(imm8), os ∈ {8,16,32}	83 /7 {16,32}
CMP AL, imm8	src_1 = AL, src_2 = imm8, os = 8	3C
CMP eAX, imm	src_1 = AX/EAX, src_2 = imm, os ∈ {8,16,32}	3D {16,32}

SUMMARY

CMP compares the first source operand against the second source operand by subtracting the value of the second from the first. The arithmetic flags set in the process are interrogated by a subsequent J*cond*, SET*cond*, or similar instruction. The result of the subtraction is discarded. Nonarithmetic flags are left unmodified.

OPERATION

$result$ = src_1 - src_2
/* Set arithmetic flags */
OF = $result < -2^{os-1}$ || $result > 2^{os-1}-1$
SF = $result\langle os-1\rangle$
ZF = (src_1 == src_2)
AF = $src_1\langle 3:0\rangle <_u src_2\langle 3:0\rangle$
PF = evenParity($result$)
CF = $src_1 <_u src_2$

EXAMPLES

```
CMP     EAX, 4                  ; Compare EAX vs. 4
CMP     AH, BYTE PTR [ESI]      ; Compare AH vs. *( (BYTE *) ESI )
```

CMPSB/CMPSD/CMPSW: Compare string operands

INSTRUCTION	PARAMETERS	OPCODE
CMPSB	os = *8*, as ∈ {16,32}	A6
CMPSW	os = *16*, as ∈ {16,32}	A7
CMPSD	os = *32*, as ∈ {16,32}	A7

SUMMARY
CMPS*x* compares the two BYTEs (*os*==8), WORDs (*os*==16), or DWORDs (*os*==32) in memory pointed at by [E]SI and [E]DI. This is done by subtracting the value of the [E]DI operand from the [E]SI operand. ESI and EDI are used if the address size attribute is 32; if it is 16, SI and DI participate. After the comparison both [E]SI and [E]DI are incremented by 2 or 4, depending on the operand size. The result of the subtraction is discarded. Non-arithmetic flags are left unmodified. The arithmetic flags set by the subtraction can be interrogated by a subsequent J*cond*, SET*cond*, or similar instruction.

Offset [E]SI is relative to the segment referenced by the DS segment register, unless it is overridden by the segment override prefix. Offset [E]DI is always relative to the segment referenced by the ES segment register; it cannot be overriden.

OPERATION
```
src1 = ( (as == 16) ? SI : ESI );
src2 = ( (as == 16) ? DI : EDI );

/* Compare src1 against src2 */
switch (os)
{   case 8:    result = *( (char *) src1 ) - *( (char *) src2 );
               break;
    case 16:   result = *( (short *) src1 ) - *( (short *) src2 );
               break;
    case 32:   result = *( (int *) src1 ) - *( (int *) src2 );
               break;
}
```

```
/* Increment operand pointers */
src₁ += (DF ? -os/8 : os/8);
src₂ += (DF ? -os/8 : os/8);
if ( as == 32 )  /* 32-bit addressing */
{   ESI = src₁;
    EDI = src₂;
}
else /* as == 16 : 16-bit addressing */
{   SI = src₁;
    DI = src₂;
}
```

/* Set arithmetic flags */
$OF = result < -2^{os-1} \ || \ result > 2^{os-1}-1$
$SF = result\langle os-1\rangle$
$ZF = (result\langle os-1 : 0\rangle == 0)$
$AF = src_1\langle 3:0\rangle <_u src_2\langle 3:0\rangle$
$PF = evenParity(result)$
$CF = src_1 <_u src_2$

EXAMPLES
; Compare BYTE strings at DS:[ESI] and ES:[EDI], or DS:[SI] and ES:[DI].
; The registers chosen matches the default address size attribute
CMPSB

; Compare BYTE strings, making sure that they are addressed via DS:[ESI] and DS:[EDI].
; An address size override is generated if the default address size is 16.
CMPS   BYTE PTR [ESI], BYTE PTR [EDI]

NOTE
1. The CMPSx instructions are restricted forms of the REPx CMPSx instructions. The REPx form of the instructions repeatedly execute the specified CMPSx operation until one of a variety of flags is set. This provides a single instruction implementation of string compare.

ASSEMBLER USAGE NOTE
1. Address register selection (i.e., SI and DI vs. ESI and EDI) depends on the address size attribute. To ensure that an address size override prefix is generated (if needed), use the assembler notation where explicit operands to CMPSx are provided. For example, a repeated CMPSW between ES:ESI and ES:EDI should be written as follows
REP CMPS ES:WORD PTR [ESI], ES:WORD PTR [EDI]
This also provides a convenient way to specify segment overrides.

CMPXCHG: Compare and exchange (486 only)

INSTRUCTION	PARAMETERS	OPCODE
CMPXCHG r/m8, r8	$op_1 \equiv$ r/m8, $op_2 =$ r8, acc $\equiv$ AL, os = 8	0F A6
CMPXCHG r/m, r	$op_1 \equiv$ r/m, $op_2 =$ r, acc $\equiv$ AX/EAX, os $\in$ {16,32}	0F A7 {16,32}

SUMMARY
CMPXCHG, available only on the i486, compares the the value of op_1 with *acc*. If the values are equal, op_1 is assigned the value of op_2, and ZF is set to 1. If the values are unequal, *acc* is assigned the value of op_1 and ZF is set to 0. The arithmetic flags are set as if op_1 were compared against *acc*. No other flags are modified.

The CMPXCHG instruction with a memory operand is LOCKable.

OPERATION
result = op_1 - acc

```
/* Exchange operands if unequal */
if ( op₁ == acc )
    op₁ = op₂;
else
    acc = op₁;
```

/* Set arithmetic flags */
OF = *result* $< -2^{os-1}$ || *result* $> 2^{os-1}$-1
SF = *result*$\langle os-1\rangle$
ZF = (op_1 == acc)
AF = $op_1\langle 3:0\rangle <_u$ acc$\langle 3:0\rangle$
PF = evenParity(*result*)
CF = $op_1 <_u$ acc

EXAMPLE
LOCK CMPXCHG sema, BX

NOTE
1. The i486 always writes to op_1, regardless of whether op_1 equals *acc*. In the case where the two values are unequal op_1's original value is written back.

CS: (prefix): Use CS for memory access

INSTRUCTION	PARAMETERS	OPCODE
CS:		2E

SUMMARY

An instruction making a memory reference always uses an implied segment register. The segment register implied depends on the way the memory offset is generated (see §2.18 on page 185 for more on this). Specifying the CS: override prefix changes the segment register used to CS (and the segment descriptor register to CS_desc). This change is effective *only* for the instruction immediately following the CS: prefix.

Some string operations (e.g., MOVS*x*) have two memory operands. The override prefix only changes the DS in the source operand; that is, the source operand becomes CS:[E]SI. The implied use of ES for the destination operand is not changeable.

EXAMPLE
; Use CS instead of DS (the default) in the following ADD.
ADD   AX, CS:[104]   ; AX = AX + « WORD at CS:104 »

NOTES

1. Segment override prefixes apply only to memory data references; instruction fetches are always done with respect to CS. Furthermore, the stack manipulation instructions (i.e., PUSH, PUSHA, POP, POPA, PUSHF, POPF, CALL, RET, INT, and IRET) always reference the stack via SS. (The segment used by a PUSH or POP whose *operand* is a memory variable can be overridden, as can the pointer operand in an *indirect* CALL or JMP.) Segment override prefix use in front of instructions where it is not meaningful is ignored without warning.

2. Segment override prefixes for each of the other segment registers (DS, ES, FS, GS, and SS) are also supported. Apart from these prefixes the 80*x*86 has prefixes that implement string instructions (REP*x*) and perform atomic read-modify-write of memory locations (LOCK). Two additional prefixes, the "address size prefix" and "operand size prefix," are also used on the 80376, 80386, and i486 to encode these later processors' 32-bit instruction extensions.

CWD: Convert word to doubleword

INSTRUCTION	PARAMETERS	OPCODE
CWD		99

SUMMARY
CWQ sign-extends the contents of AX and assigns the sign-extension value (i.e., 0 or −1) to DX. Thus, CWD assigns to the register pair DX:AX the sign-extension of AX.

OPERATION
```
if ( AX < 0 )
   DX = 0xFFFF;
else
   DX = 0;
```

EXAMPLE
```
CWD
```

NOTES
1. CWD is the 16 bit operand size variant of the CDQ (convert doubleword in EAX to quadword in EDX:EAX) instruction.

2. Also see CWDE, which sign-extends AX to EAX.

CWDE: Convert word to doubleword extended (376, 386, 486 only)

INSTRUCTION	PARAMETERS	OPCODE
CWDE		98

SUMMARY
CWDE sign-extends the contents of AX and assigns it to EAX.

OPERATION
EAX = signex(AX);

EXAMPLE
CWDE

NOTES
1. CWDE is the 32-bit operand size variant of the CBW (convert byte to word) instruction.

2. CWDE is a special case of the MOVSX instruction. It is provided solely for compatibility with the 80386's predecessors (the 8086, 80186, and 80286.) Note that CWDE and CWD are distinct instructions.

DAA: Decimal Adjust AL after Add

INSTRUCTION	PARAMETERS	OPCODE
DAA		27

SUMMARY
DAA simulates the addition of two packed BCD (i.e., decimal) digits by correcting the result of a binary addition into the AL register. Hence, DAA is useful only after an ADD or ADC instruction. DAA operates by checking whether the previous addition left a value greater than 9 in AL's low-order nibble. If so, the true decimal value is obtained by adding 6, and AF is set to 1 to signal that the correction occurred. If the high-order nibble exceeds 9 it too is incremented by 6 and CF is set.

OPERATION
```
if (AL⟨3:0⟩ > 9 || AF == 1)
{   AL = AL + 6;
    AF = 1;
}
else
    AF = 0;

if (AL⟨7:4⟩ > 9 || CF == 1)
{   AL⟨7:4⟩ = AL⟨7:4⟩ + 6;
    CF = 1;
}
else
    CF = 0;

OF = undefined;
SF = AL⟨7⟩;
ZF = AL == 0;
PF = evenParity(AL);
```

EXAMPLE
```
; Add the four packed digits in AX and BX. Store in CX.
ADD     AL, BL              ; Add low-order digits
DAA                         ; Make result digit a decimal
MOV     CL, AL              ; Store low-order digit in CL
MOV     AL, AH              ; Get high-order addend
ADC     AL, BH              ; Add high-order digits, factoring previous carry
DAA                         ; Fixup high-order digit; CF set to 1 on overflow
MOV     CH, AL              ; Store high-order digit in CH
```

DAS: Decimal Adjust AL after Subtract

INSTRUCTION	PARAMETERS	OPCODE
DAS		2F

SUMMARY

DAS simulates the subtraction of two packed BCD (i.e., decimal) digits by correcting the result of a binary subtraction from the AL register. Hence, DAS is useful only after an SUB or SBB instruction. DAS operates by checking whether the previous addition left a value less than 0 in AL's low-order nibble. If so, the true decimal value is obtained by subtracting 6, and AF is set to 1 to signal that the correction occurred. If the high-order nibble is less than zero it too is decremented by 6 and CF is set.

OPERATION

```
if (AL⟨3:0⟩ > 9 || AF == 1)
{   AL = AL - 6;
    AF = 1;
}
else
    AF = 0;

if (AL⟨7:4⟩ > 9 || CF == 1)
{   AL⟨7:4⟩ = AL⟨7:4⟩ - 6;
    CF = 1;
}
else
    CF = 0;

OF = undefined;
SF = AL⟨7⟩;
ZF = AL == 0;
PF = evenParity(AL);
```

EXAMPLE

```
; Subtract the four packed digits in BX from AX. Store in CX. [18 clocks]
SUB     AL, BL        ; Subtract low-order digits
DAS                   ; Make result digit a decimal
MOV     CL, AL        ; Store low-order digit in CL
MOV     AL, AH        ; Get high-order subtrahend
SBB     AL, BH        ; Subtract high-order digits, factoring previous
                        borrow
DAS                   ; Fixup high-order digit; CF set to 1 on overflow
MOV     CH, AL        ; Store high-order digit in CH
```

DEC: Decrement by one

INSTRUCTION	PARAMETERS	OPCODE
DEC r/m	dst ≡ r/m, os ∈ *{8,16,32}*	FE /1 *{8}*, FF /1 *{16,32}*
DEC reg	dst ≡ reg, os ∈ *{16,32}*	48+*reg {16,32}*

SUMMARY
DEC decrements the dst operand by 1. All arithmetic flags except CF are modified; CF is left unchanged. Nonarithmetic flags are not affected. A DEC instruction with a memory operand is LOCKable.

OPERATION
```
/* Compute result */
result = dst - 1
dst = result
/* Set arithmetic flags (except CF) */
```
$OF = result < -2^{os-1} \,||\, result > 2^{os-1}-1$
$SF = dst\langle os\text{-}1\rangle$
$ZF = (dst == 0)$
$AF = dst\langle 3{:}0\rangle == 0$
$PF = evenParity(dst)$

EXAMPLES
```
DEC     EAX                  ; EAX -= 1
DEC     BYTE PTR [ESI]       ; *( (BYTE *) ESI ) -= 1
```

DIV: Unsigned divide

INSTRUCTION	PARAMETERS	OPCODE
DIV r/m8	quo ≡ AL, rem ≡ AH, dvd = AX, dvr = r/m8, os = 8	F6 /6
DIV r/m16	quo ≡ AX, rem ≡ DX, dvd = DX:AX, dvr = r/m16, os = 16	F7 /6
DIV r/m32	quo ≡ EAX, rem ≡ EDX, dvd = EDX:EAX, dvr = r/m32, os = 32	F7 /6

SUMMARY

DIV divides the unsigned dividend *dvd* by the unsigned divisor *dvr* and stores the quotient in *quo* and the remainder in *rem*.

Except for the divisor, all operands are stored in fixed registers, as follows. For BYTE division, the dividend is fetched from AX, and the resulting quotient and remainder are stored in AL and AH, respectively. For WORD and DWORD division, the dividend is fetched from the register pair DX:AX or EDX:EAX, with DX and EDX storing the most significant bits. The quotient and remainder generated by the division are stored in AX/EAX and DX/EDX, respectively.

OPERATION

```
/* All arithmetic flags are undefined after a DIV */
OF = undefined
SF = undefined
ZF = undefined
AF = undefined
PF = undefined
CF = undefined

/* Compute quotient and remainder, checking for overflow and zero divide */
if ( dvr == 0 )
    signal_fault(DIVIDE);
result = dvd /u dvr;
if ( result >u 2os-1 )
    signal_fault(DIVIDE);

/* Store result */
quo = result
rem = dvd %u dvr
```

EXAMPLES

```
DIV      EAX              ; EAX = EDX:EAX /u EAX
                          ; EDX = EDX:EAX %u EAX
DIV      BYTE PTR [ESI]   ; AL = AL /u *( (BYTE *) ESI )
                          ; AH = AH %u *( (BYTE *) ESI )
```

NOTE
1. On a 8086, the DIVIDE exception is a *trap*: on entry to the exception handler, the return address points at the instruction following the DIV. (On all other 80*x*86 implementations the return address points at the DIV.)

DS: (prefix): Use DS for memory access

INSTRUCTION	PARAMETERS	OPCODE
DS:		3E

SUMMARY

An instruction making a memory reference always uses an implied segment register. The segment register implied depends on the way the memory offset is generated (see §2.18 on page 185 for more on this). Specifying the DS: override prefix changes the segment register used to DS (and the segment descriptor register to DS_desc). This change is effective *only* for the instruction immediately following the DS: prefix.

Some string operations (e.g., MOVS*x*) have two memory operands. The override prefix only changes the DS in the source operand; the implied use of ES for the destination operand is not changeable. (Since the source operand's segment is already DS, it is redundant to place a DS: prefix in front of a string operation.)

EXAMPLE
; Use DS instead of SS (the default) in the following ADD.
OR   AX, DS:[BP+10]   ; AX = AX | « WORD at DS:(BP+10) »

NOTES
1. Segment override prefixes apply only to memory data references; instruction fetches are always done with respect to CS. Furthermore, the stack manipulation instructions (i.e., PUSH, PUSHA, POP, POPA, PUSHF, POPF, CALL, RET, INT, and IRET) always reference the stack via SS. (The segment used by a PUSH or POP whose *operand* is a memory variable can be overridden, as can the pointer operand in an *indirect* CALL or JMP.) Segment override prefix use in front of instructions where it is not meaningful is ignored without warning.

2. Segment override prefixes for each of the other segment registers (CS, ES, SS, FS and GS) are also supported. Apart from these prefixes the 80*x*86 has prefixes that implement string instructions (REP*x*) and perform atomic read-modify-write of memory locations (LOCK). Two additional prefixes, the "address size prefix" and "operand size prefix," are also used on the 80376, 80386, and i486 to encode these later processors' 32-bit instruction extensions.

ENTER: Enter nested procedure (unavailable on the 8086)

INSTRUCTION	PARAMETERS	OPCODE
ENTER frsz, lev	os ∈ {16,32}	C8 {16,32}

SUMMARY
When executed on entry to a subroutine, ENTER performs the actions necessary to implement the standard procedure calling sequence recommended by the $80x86$ architecture. It also optionally creates the display needed to access global variables in high-level languages that support recursively callable nested procedures.

The standard calling sequence entails pushing [E]BP (the caller's frame pointer) and then updating [E]BP to point at the new stack frame. Display creation is done by pushing onto the new frame *lev*-2 [D]WORDs from the caller's display, and then pushing the current frame pointer ([E]BP) onto the stack also. Finally, [E]SP is decremented by the requested frame size (*frsz*) to allocate space for local variables. Registers SP and BP are used if the operand size attribute, *os*, is 16; otherwise, ESP and EBP are used.

OPERATION
```
pushOS(EBP);
level = lev %u 32;  /* 0 <= level <= 31 */
framePtr = ESP;

if ( i > 0 )
{  for ( i = 1 ;  i <= level-1 ;  i++ )
   {  if ( os == 32 )
      {  EBP = EBP - 4;
         push4( *( (DWORD *) EBP ) );
      }
      else  /* os == 16 */
      {  BP = BP - 2;
         push2( *( (WORD *) BP ) );
      }
   }
   pushOS(framePtr);
}
```

```
if ( os == 32 )
   EBP = framePtr;
else  /* os == 16 */
   BP = framePtr;
if ( SS_desc.Default ) /* "Big" (4 gigabyte) stack */
   ESP = ESP - frsz;
else /* Small (64 kilobyte) stack */
   SP = SP - frsz;
```

EXAMPLES

ENTER	32, 0	; Preface to routine at lex level 0
		; with a 32 byte local stack frame.
ENTER	10, 9	; Preface to a routine at lexical level 9
		; with a ten byte local stack frame.

NOTES

1. Use the LEAVE instruction to undo the effect of ENTER.

2. When the *lev* operand is 0, ENTER degenerates to the sequence
   ```
   PUSH    [E]BP
   MOV     [E]BP, [E]SP
   SUB     [E]SP, frsz
   ```
   This sequence is faster than "ENTER frsz, 0" in all cases except when very slow memory is used to store the instructions.

3. On entry to a routine at lexical level *l* that needs *sz* bytes of local storage, the instruction
   ```
   enter    sz, l
   ```
   should be executed. Just prior to the RET for the routine, a LEAVE instruction should be issued to delete the display.

ES (prefix): Use ES for memory access

INSTRUCTION	PARAMETERS	OPCODE
ES:		26

SUMMARY

An instruction making a memory reference always uses an implied segment register. The segment register implied depends on the way the memory offset is generated (see §2.18 on page 185 for more on this). Specifying the ES: override prefix changes the segment register used to ES (and the segment descriptor register to ES_desc). This change is effective *only* for the instruction immediately following the ES: prefix.

Some string operations (e.g., MOVS*x*) have two memory operands. The override prefix only changes the DS in the source operand; that is, the source operand becomes ES:[E]SI. The implied use of ES for the destination operand is not changeable.

EXAMPLE

```
; Use ES instead of DS (the default) when reading the WORD at offset [EBX+10]
; Note that the stack write (i.e., PUSH) is still done at SS:[E]SP.
PUSH     WORD PTR ES:[EBX+10]     ; push the WORD at ES:(EBX+10)
```

NOTES

1. Segment override prefixes apply only to memory data references; instruction fetches are always done with respect to CS. Furthermore, the stack manipulation instructions (i.e., PUSH, PUSHA, POP, POPA, PUSHF, POPF, CALL, RET, INT, and IRET) always reference the stack via SS. (The segment used by a PUSH or POP whose *operand* is a memory variable can be overridden, as can the pointer operand in an *indirect* CALL or JMP.) Segment override prefix use in front of instructions where it is not meaningful is ignored without warning.

2. Segment override prefixes for each of the other segment registers (CS, DS, FS, GS and SS) are also supported. Apart from these prefixes the 80*x*86 has prefixes that implement string instructions (REP*x*) and perform atomic read-modify-write of memory locations (LOCK). Two additional prefixes, the "address size prefix" and "operand size prefix," are also used on the 80376, 80386, and i486 to encode these later processors' 32-bit instruction extensions.

ESC: Escape to processor extension (*x87* needed)

INSTRUCTION	PARAMETERS	OPCODE
ESC ecode, r	fop = ecode⟨5:3⟩, ext = ecode⟨2:0⟩	D8+*fop* /*ext*
ESC ecode, m	fop = ecode⟨5:3⟩, ext = ecode⟨2:0⟩	D8+*fop* /*ext*

SUMMARY

The ESC "instruction" is an assembly language mnemonic that provides an alternate way to encode floating point instructions. Recall from §3.12 on page 258 that the primary floating point opcode is a 6-bit value. The most significant three bits of this opcode (*fop*) is encoded in bit positions 2 through 0 of the 80*x*86 instruction opcode 0xC8. The least significant 3 bits are stored as the opcode extension (*ext*) in the MOD/RM byte that follows.

EXAMPLE

ESC   2, BX

F2XM1: Compute 2^x-1 (*x87 needed*)

INSTRUCTION	PARAMETERS	OPCODE
F2XM1		D9 F0

SUMMARY
F2XM1 replaces the value at the top of the floating point stack (ST) with $2^{ST} - 1$. The $80x87$ flags C0, C2, and C3 are set to an *undefined* state after F2XM1 executes. If the operation results in a PRECISION exception (i.e., the FPE flag is set), condition code C1 is set to 1 if the rounding is upward; if it is downward, it is set to 0.

OPERATION
```
check_TS_EM();          /* see page 248 */
check_BUSY();           /* see page 248 */
check_ERROR();          /* see page 249 */
save_x87_instr_ptr();   /* see page 249 */

ST(0) = 2^ST(0) - 1;
```

EXAMPLE
F2XM1

NOTE
1. F2XM1 computes 2^x-1 rather than 2^x so that a maximum number of significant digits are retained when 2^x is close to 1 (i.e., x is close to zero). Of course, if 2^x is close to 2, 2^x-1 will be close to 1 and so significant digits may be lost (e.g., if the result is a number like 1.00000000625). However, in such cases, loss of significant digits would occur even if 2^x were computed.

FABS: Compute absolute value (*x*87 needed)

INSTRUCTION	PARAMETERS	OPCODE
FNABS		D9 E1

SUMMARY
FABS replaces the value at the top of the floating point stack with its absolute value. The 80*x*87 flags C0, C2, and C3 are set to an *undefined* state after FABS executes. If the operation results in a PRECISION exception (i.e., the FPE flag is set), condition code C1 is set to 1 if the rounding is upward; if it is downward, it is set to 0.

OPERATION
```
check_TS_EM();              /* see page 248 */
check_BUSY();               /* see page 248 */
check_ERROR();              /* see page 249 */
save_x87_instr_ptr();       /* see page 249 */

ST(0) = abs( ST(0) );
```

EXAMPLE
FABS

FADD: Add real and 80x87 stack-top (x87 needed)

INSTRUCTION	PARAMETERS	OPCODE
FADD m32	dst ≡ ST(0), src = m32	D8 /0
FADD m64	dst ≡ ST(0), src = m64	DC /0
FADD ST,ST(n)	dst ≡ ST(0), src = ST(n)	D8 C0+n
FADD ST(n),ST	dst ≡ ST(n), src = ST(0)	DC C0+n

SUMMARY
FADD adds the floating point values *src* and *dst* and stores the result back into the dst operand. Note that the destination (*dst*) is limited to either the 80x87 stack-top, or one of the registers in the 80x87 stack.

If the *src* operand is either SINGLE or DOUBLE, it is automatically converted to EXTENDED before being operated on. As always, the number of significant bits in the stored result depends on the effective precision specified by the PC control bits. Result rounding is done using the current RC setting.

The 80x87 flags C0, C2, and C3 are set to an *undefined* state after FADD executes. If the operation results in a PRECISION exception (i.e., the FPE flag is set), condition code C1 is set to 1 if the rounding is upward; if it is downward, it is set to 0.

OPERATION
```
check_TS_EM();              /* see page 248 */
check_BUSY();               /* see page 248 */
check_ERROR();              /* see page 249 */
save_x87_instr_ptr();       /* see page 249 */

dst = (EXTENDED) dst + (EXTENDED) src
```

EXAMPLE
```
FADD    ST, ST(0)                ; ST(0) = ST(0)*2.0
```

ASSEMBLER USAGE NOTE
1. Assemblers like Microsoft MASM and Borland TASM allow the mnemonic
   FADD
   without any arguments. The purpose is to simulate a classical stack add; that is, pop the top two stack elements, add them, and push the result. See the

Assembler Usage Notes of the FADDP instruction (following) for a description of FADD.

FADDP: Add 80x87 stack-top to destination and pop (x87 needed)

INSTRUCTION	PARAMETERS	OPCODE
FADDP ST(n),ST		DE C0+n

SUMMARY

FADDP adds the floating point value at the 80x87 stack-top to the nth register relative to the stack-top. After the addition, the stack is popped. Unlike ADD, the 80x86 integer counterpart of this instruction, FADDP does not affect the floating point flags.

The 80x87 flags C0, C2, and C3 are set to an *undefined* state after FADDP executes. If the FIE and STF flags are set (indicating a stack fault), flag C1 is set to 0 to indicate a stack underflow. If the operation results in a PRECISION exception (i.e., the FPE flag is set), condition code C1 is set to 1 if the rounding is upward; if it is downward, it is set to 0.

OPERATION

```
check_TS_EM();          /* see page 248 */
check_BUSY();           /* see page 248 */
check_ERROR();          /* see page 249 */
save_x87_instr_ptr();   /* see page 249 */

ST(n) = ST(n) + ST(0);
pop_FSTK(); /* Discard addend */
```

EXAMPLE

```
; Pop top two stack elements, add them, and push result
FADDP    ST(1), ST
```

ASSEMBLER USAGE NOTE

1. Assemblers like Microsoft MASM and Borland TASM allow the mnemonic
   FADD
   without any arguments. This is equivalent to
   FADDP ST(1), ST
   that is, the top two elements are added and the result is placed in the element below the stack-top. Then the stack is popped, thus making the register storing the sum the new stack-top. This simulates a classical stack add.

FBLD: Push packed BCD data onto 80*x*87 stack (*x*87 needed)

INSTRUCTION	PARAMETERS	OPCODE
FBLD m80	src = m80	DF /4

SUMMARY

FBLD converts its PACKED_BCD memory-based operand into an EXTENDED floating point value; the EXTENDED value is then pushed onto the floating point stack. Conversions are only defined for valid packed BCD values; an attempt to load any other value (including the packed BCD indefinite) will push an *undefined* value onto the stack.

If the stack is full (i.e., FTAG[(TOP-1) & 7] is not marked EMPTY) the INVALID_FOP exception is signaled. On the 80387 and i486 the STF flag is also set. If INVALID_FOP processing is masked, the real indefinite value is pushed, overwriting a nonempty register location.

The 80*x*87 flags C0, C2, and C3 are set to an *undefined* state after FBLD executes. If the FIE and STF flags are set (indicating a stack fault), flag C1 is also set to 1 to indicate a stack overflow.

Instructions that push SINGLE, DOUBLE, and EXTENDED values onto the stack are also available; see FLD on page 365 for details. Similarly, the FILD instructions (see page 357) convert integer quantities to EXTENDED format and push the result onto the top of stack.

OPERATION

```
check_TS_EM();              /* see page 248 */
check_BUSY();               /* see page 248 */
check_ERROR();              /* see page 249 */
save_x87_instr_ptr();       /* see page 249 */

push_FSTK( (EXTENDED) src );   /* see page 247 */
```

EXAMPLES

```
FBLD    bdata           ; ST(-1) = (EXTENDED) bdata
                        ; TOP = TOP - 1
```

FBSTP: Pop 80*x*87 stack to packed BCD storage (*x*87 needed)

INSTRUCTION	PARAMETERS	OPCODE
FBSTP m80	dst ≡ m80	DF /6

SUMMARY

FBSTP pops the floating point value in the top element of the 80*x*87 stack, converts it to PACKED_BCD format, and stores the converted value into a 10-byte storage area in memory. The fractional component of the floating point value is rounded off using the rounding mode specified by RC.

If the stack is empty (i.e., FTAG[TOP] is marked EMPTY) the INVALID_FOP exception is signaled. On the 80387 and i486 the STF flag is also set. This flag lets the INVALID_FOP handler distinguish the cause of the invalid operation. If INVALID_FOP processing is masked, or if the floating point value is not representable as a PACKED_BCD (either because of overflow, or because it is a NaN), the destination is initialized to the packed BCD indefinite. The encoding for the packed BCD indefinite is shown in Figure 3.4 on page 221.

The 80*x*87 flags C0, C2, and C3 are set to an *undefined* state after FBSTP executes. If the FIE and STF flags are set (indicating a stack fault), flag C1 is also set to 0 to indicate a stack underflow. If the operation results in a PRECISION exception (i.e., the FPE flag is set), condition code C1 is set to 1 if the rounding is upward; if it is downward, it is set to 0.

OPERATION

```
check_TS_EM();              /* see page 248 */
check_BUSY();               /* see page 248 */
check_ERROR();              /* see page 249 */
save_x87_instr_ptr();       /* see page 249 */

dst = (PACKED_BCD) pop_FSTK()
```

EXAMPLES

```
FSTP    var                 ; var = (PACKED_BCD) ST(0)
                            ; TOP = TOP+1
```

NOTES

1. If the stack-top contains the denormal, the 8087 and 80287 signal an INVALID_FOP exception. The 80387 and i486, however, perform the operation. The change was made to reflect IEEE Std. 754 requirements.

FCHS: Change sign (*x*87 needed)

INSTRUCTION	PARAMETERS	OPCODE
FCHS		D9 E0

SUMMARY
FCHS changes the sign of the value of the 80*x*87 stack-top. (The result replaces the stack-top.) The sign is changed for all values, including zero, infinites, and NaNs. The INVALID_FOP exception is never signaled (even if the operand is a signaling NaN).

The 80*x*87 flags C0, C2, and C3 are set to an *undefined* state after FCHS executes. If the operation results in a PRECISION exception (i.e., the FPE flag is set), condition code C1 is set to 1 if the rounding is upward; if it is downward, it is set to 0.

OPERATION
```
check_TS_EM();          /* see page 248 */
check_BUSY();           /* see page 248 */
check_ERROR();          /* see page 249 */
save_x87_instr_ptr();   /* see page 249 */

ST(0) = -ST(0)
```

EXAMPLES
FCHS

FCLEX: Clear all 80*x*87 exceptions (*x*87 needed)

INSTRUCTION	PARAMETERS	OPCODE
FCLEX		9B DB E2

SUMMARY

FCLEX is a mnemonic that is expanded by most 80*x*86 assemblers to

FWAIT
FNCLEX

See the description of the FNCLEX instruction for more information.

EXAMPLES
FCLEX

FCOM: Compare 80x87 stack-top with real value (x87 needed)

INSTRUCTION	PARAMETERS	OPCODE
FCOM m32	src = m32	D8 /2
FCOM m64	src = m64	DC /2
FCOM ST(n)	src = ST(n)	D8 D0+n

SUMMARY

FCOM compares the 80x87 stack-top with the *src* operand. The result of the comparison sets the 80x87 flags C0, C2, and C3. If either operand is a SNaN, a QNaN, or if the 80x87 stack is empty (i.e., FTAG[TOP] is marked EMPTY), an INVALID_FOP is signaled and the comparison result flags are set to "unordered." On the 80387 and i486, an undefined-format operand (e.g., a pseudo zero or an unnormal) also causes the exception condition just described. These later implementations also define the STF flag to distinguish between a stack fault and an invalid operand: in the case of a stack fault, STF is set to 1, otherwise it is cleared. Furthermore, the C1 flag is set to 0 (indicating a stack underflow).

OPERATION

```
check_TS_EM();                /* see page 248 */
check_BUSY();                 /* see page 248 */
check_ERROR();                /* see page 249 */
save_x87_instr_ptr();         /* see page 249 */
if ( ST(0) > (EXTENDED) src )
{   C3 = 0;  C2 = 0;  C0 = 0;
}
else if ( ST(0) < (EXTENDED) src )
{   C3 = 0;  C2 = 0;  C0 = 1;
}
else if ( ST(0) == (EXTENDED) src )
{   C3 = 1;  C2 = 0;  C0 = 0;
}
else /* ST(0) and src are not comparable */
{   C3 = 1;  C2 = 1;  C0 = 1;
    signal_87(INVALID_FOP);        /* see page 255 */
}
```

EXAMPLE

```
FCOM    ST(2)                 ; Compare ST against ST(2)
```

NOTES
1. FCOM always signals an INVALID_FOP if either operand is a NaN. The
   IEEE Std. 754, however, requires support for comparisons that do not signal
   an exception when comparing NaNs. The 80387 and i486 remedy this
   problem by introducing the FUCOM instruction. This instruction does not
   signal a fault when one of the operands is a NaN.

2. The bit positions occupied by C3, C2, and C0 in the status register FSW are
   such that the instruction sequence
   FSTSW AX
   SAHF
   copies C3 to ZF, C2 to PF, and C0 to CF, where ZF, PF, and CF are $80x86$
   arithmetic flags. This allows the use of normal conditional branch
   instructions to check the result of floating point comparisions. For example,
   ; jump to *lab* if ST(0) > *src* operand
   JA lab   ; check that CF and ZF are 0

   ; jump to *lab* if ST(0) < *src* operand
   JB lab   ; check that CF is 1

   ; jump to *lab* if ST(0) == *src* operand
   JE lab   ; check that ZF is 1

   ; jump to *lab* if ST(0) and *src* are not comparable
   JP lab   ; check that PF is 1

ASSEMBLER USAGE NOTE
1. Assemblers like Microsoft MASM and Borland TASM allow the mnemonic
   FCOM
   without any arguments. This is equivalent to
   FCOM ST(1)

FCOMP[P]: Compare 80*x*87 stack-top with real value, and pop (*x*87 needed)

INSTRUCTION	PARAMETERS	OPCODE
FCOMP m32	src = m32	D8 /3
FCOMP m64	src = m64	DC /3
FCOMP ST(*n*)	src = ST(*n*)	D8 D8+*n*
FCOMPP	src = ST(1)	DE D9

SUMMARY

Both FCOMP and FCOMPP compare the 80*x*87 stack-top with the *src* operand. The result of the comparison sets the 80*x*87 flags C0, C2, and C3. FCOMP pops the 80*x*87 stack after the comparison; FCOMPP pops the top two stack elements. Note that FCOMPP restricts the *src* operand to ST(1); that is, this instruction compares the top two stack elements, then discards the operands.

If either operand is a SNaN, a QNaN, or if the 80*x*87 stack is empty (i.e., FTAG[TOP] is marked EMPTY), an INVALID_FOP is signaled and the comparison result flags are set to "unordered." On the 80387 and i486, an undefined-format operand (e.g., a pseudo zero or an unnormal) also causes the exception condition just described. These later implementations also define the STF flag to distinguish between a stack fault and an invalid operand: in the case of a stack fault, STF is set to 1, otherwise it is cleared. Furthermore, the C1 flag is set to 0 (indicating a stack underflow).

OPERATION
FCOMP:
check_TS_EM();   /* see page 248 */
check_BUSY();   /* see page 248 */
check_ERROR();   /* see page 249 */
save_x87_instr_ptr();   /* see page 249 */

if (ST(0) > (EXTENDED) src)
{   C3 = 0;   C2 = 0;   C0 = 0;
}
else if (ST(0) < (EXTENDED) src)
{   C3 = 0;   C2 = 0;   C0 = 1;
}
else if (ST(0) == (EXTENDED) src)
{   C3 = 1;   C2 = 0;   C0 = 0;
}
else /* ST(0) and src are not comparable */
{   C3 = 1;   C2 = 1;   C0 = 1;
    signal_87(INVALID_FOP);   /* see page 255 */
}
/* Discard stack top */
pop_FSTK();   /* see page 247 */

FCOMPP:
check_TS_EM();   /* see page 248 */
check_BUSY();   /* see page 248 */
check_ERROR();   /* see page 249 */
save_x87_instr_ptr();   /* see page 249 */

if (ST(0) > ST(1))
{   C3 = 0;   C2 = 0;   C0 = 0;
}
else if (ST(0) < ST(1))
{   C3 = 0;   C2 = 0;   C0 = 1;
}
else if (ST(0) == ST(1))
{   C3 = 1;   C2 = 0;   C0 = 0;
}
else /* ST(0) and ST(1) are not comparable */
{   C3 = 1;   C2 = 1;   C0 = 1;
}
/* Discard top two stack elements */
pop_FSTK();   /* see page 247 */
pop_FSTK();

EXAMPLES
FCOMP   ST(2)   ; Compare ST against ST(2), then pop stack
FCOMPP   ; Compare ST against ST(1), then discard ST and
                                  ST(1)

NOTES

1. FCOMP[P] always signals an INVALID_FOP if either operand is a NaN. This is incompatible with IEEE Std. 754, which requires support for comparisons that do not signal an exception when comparing NaNs. The 80387 and i486 remedy this problem by introducing the FUCOMP[P] instructions. These instruction do not signal a fault when one of the operands is a NaN.

2. The bit positions occupied by C3, C2, and C0 in the status register FSW are such that the instruction sequence
   FSTSW AX
   SAHF
   copies C3 to ZF, C2 to PF, and C0 to CF, where ZF, PF, and CF are 80x86 arithmetic flags. See the description of the FCOM instruction above to see how comparison results can be checked using these flags.

ASSEMBLER USAGE NOTE

1. Assemblers like Microsoft MASM and Borland TASM allow the mnemonic
   FCOMP
   without any arguments. This is equivalent to
   FCOMP ST(1)

FCOS: Compute cosine (80387 and i486 only)

INSTRUCTION	PARAMETERS	OPCODE
FCOS		D9 FF

SUMMARY
FCOS, available only on the 80387 and i486, replaces the contents of the 80x87 stack-top (ST) with its cosine value. ST is assumed to be in radians, and must be in the range $-2^{63} < ST < 2^{63}$. If the operation completes, flag C2 is set to 0. However, if ST is out of range, C2 is set to 1 and ST is left unmodified. Flags C0 and C3 are left in an *undefined* state after the operation.

If the 80x87 stack is empty, an INVALID_FOP is signaled. An undefined-format operand (e.g., a pseudo zero or an unnormal) also causes an INVALID_FOP. The 80387 and i486 also set the STF flag to 1 in case of a stack fault, and set the C1 flag to 0 (indicating a stack underflow).

OPERATION
```
check_TS_EM();          /* see page 248 */
check_BUSY();           /* see page 248 */
check_ERROR();          /* see page 249 */
save_x87_instr_ptr();   /* see page 249 */

if ( -2^63 < ST(0)  &&  ST(0) > 2^63 )
{   ST(0) = cos( ST(0) );
    C2 = 0;
}
else
    C2 = 1;
```

EXAMPLE
```
FCOS
```

FDECSTP: Decrement 80*x*87 stack pointer (*x*87 needed)

INSTRUCTION	PARAMETERS	OPCODE
FDECSTP		D9 F6

SUMMARY
FDECSTP decrements the 80*x*87 stack pointer TOP. If TOP's value is 0, it wraps around to 7. The contents of other 80*x*87 registers (e.g., the FTAG bits) are left unmodified. Flags C0, C2, and C3 are set to *undefined* values after FDECSTP; flag C1 is set to 0.

OPERATION
```
check_TS_EM();              /* see page 248 */
check_BUSY();               /* see page 248 */
check_ERROR();              /* see page 249 */
save_x87_instr_ptr();       /* see page 249 */

TOP = ( (TOP == 0)  ?  7 : (TOP - 1) );
```

EXAMPLE
FDECSTP

FDISI: Disable float interrupts (8087 only)

INSTRUCTION	PARAMETERS	OPCODE
FDISI		9B DB E1

SUMMARY

FDISI is a mnemonic that is expanded by most 80x86 assemblers to

        FWAIT
        FNDISI

See the description of the FNDISI instruction for more information.

EXAMPLE

FDISI

FDIV[R]: Divide real and 80*x*87 stack-top (*x*87 needed)

INSTRUCTION	PARAMETERS	OPCODE
FDIV m32	dst ≡ ST(0), src = m32	D8 /6
FDIV m64	dst ≡ ST(0), src = m64	DC /6
FDIV ST,ST(*n*)	dst ≡ ST(0), src = ST(*n*)	D8 F0+*n*
FDIV ST(*n*),ST	dst ≡ ST(*n*), src = ST(0)	DC F8+*n*
FDIVR m32	dst ≡ ST(0), src = m32	D8 /7
FDIVR m64	dst ≡ ST(0), src = m64	DC /7
FDIVR ST,ST(*n*)	dst ≡ ST(0), src = ST(*n*)	D8 F8+*n*
FDIVR ST(*n*),ST	dst ≡ ST(*n*), src = ST(0)	DC F0+*n*

SUMMARY

FDIV divides dst by src; FDIVR (divide reversed) divides src by dst. In both cases the result is stored back in the destination operand (dst). Note that the destination is limited to either the 80*x*87 stack-top, or one of the registers in the 80*x*87 stack.

If the src operand is either SINGLE or DOUBLE, it is automatically converted to EXTENDED before being operated on. As always, the number of significant bits in the stored result depends on the effective precision specified by the PC control bits. Result rounding is done using the current RC setting.

The 80*x*87 flags C0, C2, and C3 are set to an *undefined* state after FDIV[R] executes. If the operation results in a PRECISION exception (i.e., the FPE flag is set), condition code C1 is set to 1 if the rounding is upward; if it is downward, it is set to 0.

OPERATION

FDIV :

```
check_TS_EM();          /* see page 248 */
check_BUSY();           /* see page 248 */
check_ERROR();          /* see page 249 */
save_x87_instr_ptr();   /* see page 249 */

dst = dst / (EXTENDED) src
```

FDIVR :

```
check_TS_EM();          /* see page 248 */
check_BUSY();           /* see page 248 */
check_ERROR();          /* see page 249 */
save_x87_instr_ptr();   /* see page 249 */
```

dst = (EXTENDED) src / dst

EXAMPLE
FDIV   ST, ST(4)   ; ST(0) = ST(0) / ST(4)

NOTE
1. If one of the operands is a denormal, the 8087 and 80287 signal an INVALID_FOP exception. The 80387 and i486, however, perform the operation. The change was made to reflect IEEE Std. 754 requirements.

ASSEMBLER USAGE NOTE
1. Assemblers like Microsoft MASM and Borland TASM allow the mnemonics
FDIV
FDIVR
without any arguments. The purpose is to simulate a classical stack divide; that is, pop the top two stack elements, compute their quotient, and push the result. See the *Assembler Usage Notes* of the FDIVP instruction (following) for a description of how this is achieved.

FDIV[R]P: Divide real and 80x87 stack-top, and pop (x87 needed)

INSTRUCTION	PARAMETERS	OPCODE
FDIVP ST(n),ST		DE F8+n
FDIVRP ST(n),ST		DE F0+n

SUMMARY

FDIVP (divide and pop) divides the nth register relative to the stack-top (i.e., ST(n)) by the stack-top value; FDIVRP (divide reversed and pop) divides the stack-top by the nth register from the stack-top. In both cases the result is stored back in ST(n). The stack is popped after the quotient is stored.

The 80x87 flags C0, C2, and C3 are set to an *undefined* state after FDIV[R]P executes. If the FIE and STF flags are set (indicating a stack fault), flag C1 is set to 0 to indicate a stack underflow. If the operation results in a PRECISION exception (i.e., the FPE flag is set), condition code C1 is set to 1 if the rounding is upward; if it is downward, it is set to 0.

OPERATION
FDIVP :
```
check_TS_EM();              /* see page 248 */
check_BUSY();               /* see page 248 */
check_ERROR();              /* see page 249 */
save_x87_instr_ptr();       /* see page 249 */

ST(n) = ST(n) / ST(0);
pop_FSTK(); /* Discard divisor */
```

FDIVRP :
```
check_TS_EM();              /* see page 248 */
check_BUSY();               /* see page 248 */
check_ERROR();              /* see page 249 */
save_x87_instr_ptr();       /* see page 249 */

ST(n) =  ST(0) / ST(n);
pop_FSTK(); /* Discard dividend */
```

EXAMPLE
```
; Pop top two stack elements, divide top from next element, and push result
FDIVP     ST(1), ST
```

ASSEMBLER USAGE NOTE

1. Assemblers like Microsoft MASM and Borland TASM allow the mnemonics
   FDIV
   FDIVR
   without any arguments. These are equivalent to
   FDIVP ST(1), ST
   FDIVRP ST, ST(1)
   that is, the result of dividing the next from top by the stack-top (or the stack-top by the next element, for FDIVR), is placed in the next-from-top element. Then the stack is popped, thus making the stack element storing the quotient the new stack-top. This simulates a classical stack divide.

FENI: Enable float interrupts (8087 only)

INSTRUCTION	PARAMETERS	OPCODE
FENI		9B DB E0

SUMMARY

FENI is a mnemonic that is expanded by most 80x86 assemblers to
>   FWAIT
>   FNENI

See the description of the FNENI instruction for more information.

EXAMPLE

FENI

FFREE: Free 80*x*87 register (*x*87 needed)

INSTRUCTION	PARAMETERS	OPCODE
FFREE ST(*n*)		DD C0+*n*

SUMMARY
FFREE frees the 80*x*87 register ST(*n*) by marking FTAG[TOP+*n*] EMPTY. Only the FTAG field of the selected register is modified. The actual data in the 80*x*87 stack is not updated.

OPERATION
```
check_TS_EM();          /* see page 248 */
check_BUSY();           /* see page 248 */
check_ERROR();          /* see page 249 */
save_x87_instr_ptr();   /* see page 249 */

FTAG[TOP+n] = EMPTY;    /* tag bits set to 3 */
```

EXAMPLE
FFREE ST(6)

FIADD: Add integer to 80x87 stack-top (x87 needed)

INSTRUCTION	PARAMETERS	OPCODE
FIADD m16	src = m16	DE /0
FIADD m32	src = m32	DA /0

SUMMARY

FIADD converts the WORD or DWORD integer specified by the src operand to EXTENDED format, and adds it to the contents of the 80x87 stack-top. As always, the number of significant bits in the result stored depends on the effective precision specified by the PC control bits. Result rounding is done using the current RC setting.

The 80x87 flags C0, C2, and C3 are set to an *undefined* state after FIADD executes. If the operation results in a PRECISION exception (i.e., the FPE flag is set), condition code C1 is set to 1 if the rounding is upward; if it is downward, it is set to 0.

OPERATION

```
check_TS_EM();              /* see page 248 */
check_BUSY();               /* see page 248 */
check_ERROR();              /* see page 249 */
save_x87_instr_ptr();       /* see page 249 */

ST(0) = ST(0) + (EXTENDED) src
```

EXAMPLE

```
FIADD     WORDvar              ; ST(0) = ST(0) + (EXTENDED) WORDvar
```

FICOM: Compare 80x87 stack-top with integer (*x87* needed)

INSTRUCTION	PARAMETERS	OPCODE
FICOM m16	src = m16	DE /2
FICOM m32	src = m32	DA /2

SUMMARY

FICOM compares the $80x87$ stack-top with the integer WORD or DWORD specified by the *src* operand. *src* is automatically converted to EXTENDED precision prior to the comparison. The result of the comparison sets the $80x87$ flags C0, C2, and C3.

If either operand is a SNaN, a QNaN, or if the $80x87$ stack is empty (i.e., FTAG[TOP] is marked EMPTY), an INVALID_FOP is signaled and the comparison result flags are set to "unordered." On the 80387 and i486, an undefined-format operand (e.g., a pseudo zero or an unnormal) also causes an INVALID_FOP. These later implementations also define the STF flag to distinguish between a stack fault and an invalid operand: in the case of a stack fault, STF is set to 1, otherwise it is cleared. Furthermore, the C1 flag is set to 0 (indicating a stack underflow).

OPERATION

```
check_TS_EM();              /* see page 248 */
check_BUSY();               /* see page 248 */
check_ERROR();              /* see page 249 */
save_x87_instr_ptr();       /* see page 249 */

if ( ST(0) > (EXTENDED) src )
{   C3 = 0;   C2 = 0;   C0 = 0;
}
else if ( ST(0) < (EXTENDED) src )
{   C3 = 0;   C2 = 0;   C0 = 1;
}
else if ( ST(0) == (EXTENDED) src )
{   C3 = 1;   C2 = 0;   C0 = 0;
}
else /* ST(0) and src are not comparable */
{   C3 = 1;   C2 = 1;   C0 = 1;
}
```

EXAMPLE

```
FICOM     DWORD PTR ivar          ; Compare ST against the 32-bit integer ivar
```

NOTES

1. FICOM always signals an INVALID_FOP if either operand is a NaN. This IEEE Std. 754, however, requires support for comparisons that do not signal an exception when comparing NaNs. On the 80387 and i486, unordered comparisons between an integer (call it *ivar*) and a floating point value on the 80*x*87 stack-top can be done as follows
   ```
   FLD ivar
   FUCOMP
   ```
   Note that the integer is converted to EXTENDED format prior to the comaprison: there is no instruction that does an unordered compare of an integer value and a floating point register.

2. The bit positions occupied by C3, C2, and C0 in the status register FSW are such that the instruction sequence
   ```
   FSTSW AX
   SAHF
   ```
   copies C3 to ZF, C2 to PF, and C0 to CF, where ZF, PF, and CF are 80*x*86 arithmetic flags. This allows the use of normal conditional branch instructions to check the result of floating point comparisons. For example,
   ```
   ; jump to lab if ST(0) > src operand
   JA  lab                 ; check that CF and ZF are 0

   ; jump to lab if ST(0) < src operand
   JB  lab                 ; check that CF is 1

   ; jump to lab if ST(0) == src operand
   JE  lab                 ; check that ZF is 1

   ; jump to lab if ST(0) and src are not comparable
   JP  lab                 ; check that PF is 1
   ```

FICOMP: Compare 80x87 stack-top with integer, then pop (x87 needed)

INSTRUCTION	PARAMETERS	OPCODE
FICOMP m16	src = m16	DE /3
FICOMP m32	src = m32	DA /3

SUMMARY
FICOMP behaves like FICOM except that it pops the stack after the comparison. That is, it compares the 80x87 stack-top with the integer WORD or DWORD specified by the *src* operand, then discards the stack-top.

OPERATION
```
check_TS_EM();              /* see page 248 */
check_BUSY();               /* see page 248 */
check_ERROR();              /* see page 249 */
save_x87_instr_ptr();       /* see page 249 */

if ( ST(0) > (EXTENDED) src )
{   C3 = 0;   C2 = 0;   C0 = 0;
}
else if ( ST(0) < (EXTENDED) src )
{   C3 = 0;   C2 = 0;   C0 = 1;
}
else if ( ST(0) == (EXTENDED) src )
{   C3 = 1;   C2 = 0;   C0 = 0;
}
else /* ST(0) and src are not comparable */
{   C3 = 1;   C2 = 1;   C0 = 1;
}
pop_FSTK();
```

EXAMPLE
```
FICOMP   WORD PTR ivar        ; Compare ST against the 16-bit integer ivar,
                              ; then pop stack
```

NOTE
1. FICOMP always signals an INVALID_FOP if either operand is a NaN. This is incompatible with IEEE Std. 754, which requires support for comparisons that do not signal an exception when comparing NaNs. See the *Notes* in the description of FICOM for information on how to perform an unordered compare between an integer and a floating point value.

FIDIV[R]: Divide integer and 80*x*87 stack-top (*x*87 needed)

INSTRUCTION	PARAMETERS	OPCODE
FIDIV m16	src = m16	DE /6
FIDIV m32	src = m32	DA /6
FIDIVR m16	src = m16	DE /7
FIDIVR m32	src = m32	DA /7

SUMMARY

FIDIV divides the stack-top by the WORD or DWORD integer specified by *src*;
FIDIVR divides the WORD or DWORD integer by the stack-top. The stack-top is
updated with the result in either case. The WORD (or DWORD) is implicitly
converted to EXTENDED format prior to the divide. As always, the number of
significant bits in the stored result depends on the effective precision specified by
the PC control bits. Result rounding is done using the current RC setting.

The 80*x*87 flags C0, C2, and C3 are set to an *undefined* state after FIDIV[R]
executes. If the operation results in a PRECISION exception (i.e., the FPE flag is
set), condition code C1 is set to 1 if the rounding is upward; if it is downward, it
is set to 0.

OPERATION
FIDIV :
```
check_TS_EM();                    /* see page 248 */
check_BUSY();                     /* see page 248 */
check_ERROR();                    /* see page 249 */
save_x87_instr_ptr();             /* see page 249 */

ST(0) = ST(0) / (EXTENDED) src
```

FIDIVR :
```
check_TS_EM();                    /* see page 248 */
check_BUSY();                     /* see page 248 */
check_ERROR();                    /* see page 249 */
save_x87_instr_ptr();             /* see page 249 */

ST(0) = (EXTENDED) src / ST(0)
```

EXAMPLES
```
FIDIV     WORDvar              ; ST(0) = ST(0) - (EXTENDED) WORDvar
```

FILD: Push integer data onto 80x87 stack (x87 needed)

INSTRUCTION	PARAMETERS	OPCODE
FILD m16	src = m16	DF /0
FILD m32	src = m32	DB /0
FILD m64	src = m64	DF /5

SUMMARY

FILD converts its WORD, DWORD, or QWORD (64-bit) memory-based integer operand into an extended precision floating point value and pushes it onto the floating point stack. The tag word corresponding to the top-of-stack is set to "VALID," to reflect its contents.

If the stack is full (i.e., FTAG[(TOP-1) & 7] is not marked EMPTY) the INVALID_FOP exception is signaled. On the 80387 and i486 the STF flag is also set. If INVALID_FOP processing is masked, the real indefinite value is pushed, overwriting a nonempty register location.

The 80x87 flags C0, C2, and C3 are set to an *undefined* state after FILD executes. If the FIE and STF flags are set (indicating a stack fault), flag C1 is also set to 1 to indicate a stack overflow.

Instructions that push SINGLE, DOUBLE, and EXTENDED values onto the stack are also available; see FLD on page 365 for details. Similarly, the FBLD instruction converts a packed BCD quantity into extended precision format and pushes the result onto the top of stack.

OPERATION

```
check_TS_EM();              /* see page 248 */
check_BUSY();               /* see page 248 */
check_ERROR();              /* see page 249 */
save_x87_instr_ptr();       /* see page 249 */

push_FSTK( (EXTENDED) src );   /* see page 247 */
```

EXAMPLES

```
FILD    var          ; ST(-1) = (EXTENDED) var
                     ; TOP = TOP-1
```

FIMUL: Multiply 80x87 stack-top by an integer (x87 needed)

INSTRUCTION	PARAMETERS	OPCODE
FIMUL m16	src = m16	DE /1
FIMUL m32	src = m32	DA /1

SUMMARY

FIMUL multiplies the contents of the 80x87 stack-top by the WORD or DWORD integer specified by the *src* operand. The stack-top is updated with the result. The WORD or DWORD multiplier are implicitly converted to EXTENDED format prior to the multiply. As always, the number of significant bits in the stored result depends on the effective precision specified by the PC control bits. Result rounding is done using the current RC setting.

The 80x87 flags C0, C2, and C3 are set to an *undefined* state after FIMUL executes. If the operation results in a PRECISION exception (i.e., the FPE flag is set), condition code C1 is set to 1 if the rounding is upward; if it is downward, it is set to 0.

OPERATION

```
check_TS_EM();              /* see page 248 */
check_BUSY();               /* see page 248 */
check_ERROR();              /* see page 249 */
save_x87_instr_ptr();       /* see page 249 */

ST(0) = ST(0) * (EXTENDED) src
```

EXAMPLES

```
FIMUL    WORDvar            ; ST(0) = ST(0) * (EXTENDED) WORDvar
```

FINCSTP: Increment 80x87 stack pointer (x87 needed)

INSTRUCTION	PARAMETERS	OPCODE
FINCSTP		D9 F7

SUMMARY
FINCSTP increments the 80x87 stack pointer TOP. If TOP's value is 7, it wraps around to 0. The contents of other 80x87 registers (e.g., the FTAG bits) are left unmodified. Flags C0, C2, and C3 are set to *undefined* values after FINCSTP; flag C1 is set to 0.

OPERATION
```
check_TS_EM();              /* see page 248 */
check_BUSY();               /* see page 248 */
check_ERROR();              /* see page 249 */
save_x87_instr_ptr();       /* see page 249 */

TOP = ( (TOP == 7)  ?  0 : (TOP + 1) );
```

EXAMPLES
FINCSTP

FINIT: Initialize processor extension (*x*87 needed)

INSTRUCTION	PARAMETERS	OPCODE
FINIT		9B DB E3

SUMMARY
FINIT is a mnemonic that is expanded by most 80*x*86 assemblers to
> FWAIT
> FNINIT

Its effect is to wait for the processor extension to become idle before initializing it. The raw FNINIT instruction, described on page 382, unconditionally resets the 80*x*87, without waiting.

EXAMPLES
FINIT

FIST: Store 80x87 stack-top as integer (x87 needed)

INSTRUCTION	PARAMETERS	OPCODE
FIST m16	dst ≡ m16	DF /2
FIST m32	dst ≡ m32	DB /2

SUMMARY

FIST stores the floating point value in the top element of the 80x87 stack into a WORD, or DWORD storage area in memory. The floating point value is converted into an integer of the width specified by the destination. The fractional component of the floating point value is rounded off using the rounding mode specified by RC.

If the stack is empty (i.e., FTAG[TOP] is marked EMPTY) the INVALID_FOP exception is signaled. On the 80387 and i486 the STF flag is also set. This flag lets the INVALID_FOP handler distinguish the cause of the invalid operation. If INVALID_FOP processing is masked, or if the floating point value is not representable as an integer (either because of overflow, or because it is a NaN), the destination is initialized to -2^{n-1}, where n is the number of bits in the integer destination.

The 80x87 flags C0, C2, and C3 are set to an *undefined* state after FIST executes. Flag C1 is set to 0. If the operation results in a PRECISION exception (i.e., the FPE flag is set), condition code C1 is set to 1 if the rounding is upward; if it is downward, it is set to 0.

OPERATION

```
check_TS_EM();          /* see page 248 */
check_BUSY();           /* see page 248 */
check_ERROR();          /* see page 249 */
save_x87_instr_ptr();   /* see page 249 */

dst = ST(0)
```

EXAMPLE

```
FIST     DWORDvar          ; DWORDvar = (DWORD) ST(0)
```

NOTE

1. If the stack-top contains a denormal, the 8087 and 80287 signal an INVALID_FOP exception. The 80387 and i486, however, perform the operation. The change was made to reflect IEEE Std. 754 requirements.

FISTP: Pop 80*x*87 stack to integer storage (*x*87 needed)

INSTRUCTION	PARAMETERS	OPCODE
FISTP m16	dst ≡ m16	DF /3
FISTP m32	dst ≡ m32	DB /3
FISTP m64	dst ≡ m64	DF /7

SUMMARY
FISTP pops the floating point value in the top element of the 80*x*87 stack into a WORD, DWORD, or QWORD (64-bit) storage area in memory. The floating point value is converted into an integer of the width specified by the destination. The fractional component of the floating point value is rounded off using the rounding mode specified by RC.

If the stack is empty (i.e., FTAG[TOP] is marked EMPTY) the INVALID_FOP exception is signaled. On the 80387 and i486 the STF flag is also set. This flag lets the INVALID_FOP handler distinguish the cause of the invalid operation. If INVALID_FOP processing is masked, or if the floating point value is not representable as an integer (either because of overflow, or because it is a NaN), the destination is initialized to -2^{n-1}, where *n* is the number of bits in the integer destination.

The 80*x*87 flags C0, C2, and C3 are set to an *undefined* state after FISTP executes. If the FIE and STF flags are set (indicating a stack fault), flag C1 is set to 0 to indicate a stack underflow. If the operation results in a PRECISION exception (i.e., the FPE flag is set), condition code C1 is set to 1 if the rounding is upward; if it is downward, it is set to 0.

OPERATION
```
check_TS_EM();          /* see page 248 */
check_BUSY();           /* see page 248 */
check_ERROR();          /* see page 249 */
save_x87_instr_ptr();   /* see page 249 */

dst = pop_FSTK()
```

EXAMPLE
```
FISTP     DWORDvar          ; DWORDvar = (DWORD) ST(0)
                            ; TOP = TOP+1
```

NOTE
1. If the stack-top contains a denormal, the 8087 and 80287 signal an INVALID_FOP exception. The 80387 and i486, however, perform the operation. The change was made to reflect IEEE Std. 754 requirements.

FISUB[R]: Subtract integer and 80x87 stack-top (x87 needed)

INSTRUCTION	PARAMETERS	OPCODE
FISUB m16	src = m16	DE /4
FISUB m32	src = m32	DA /4
FISUBR m16	src = m16	DE /5
FISUBR m32	src = m32	DA /5

SUMMARY

FISUB subtracts the WORD or DWORD integer specified by *src* from the stack-top; FISUBR subtracts the stack-top value from the WORD or DWORD integer. In either case the stack-top is updated with the result. The WORD (or DWORD) is implicitly converted to EXTENDED format prior to the subtract. As always, the number of significant bits in the stored result depends on the effective precision specified by the PC control bits. Result rounding is done using the current RC setting.

The 80x87 flags C0, C2, and C3 are set to an *undefined* state after FISUB[R] executes. If the operation results in a PRECISION exception (i.e., the FPE flag is set), condition code C1 is set to 1 if the rounding is upward; if it is downward, it is set to 0.

OPERATION
FISUB :
check_TS_EM();   /* see page 248 */
check_BUSY();   /* see page 248 */
check_ERROR();   /* see page 249 */
save_x87_instr_ptr();   /* see page 249 */

ST(0) = ST(0) - (EXTENDED) src

FISUBR :
check_TS_EM();   /* see page 248 */
check_BUSY();   /* see page 248 */
check_ERROR();   /* see page 249 */
save_x87_instr_ptr();   /* see page 249 */

ST(0) = (EXTENDED) src - ST(0)

EXAMPLE
FISUB   WORDvar   ; ST(0) = ST(0) - (EXTENDED) WORDvar

FLD: Push real data onto 80*x*87 stack (*x*87 needed)

INSTRUCTION	PARAMETERS	OPCODE
FLD m32	src = m32	D9 /0
FLD m64	src = m64	DD /0
FLD m80	src = m80	DB /5
FLD ST(*n*)	src = ST(*n*)	D9 C0+*n*

SUMMARY

FLD pushes its SINGLE, DOUBLE, or EXTENDED type memory-based floating point operand onto the floating point stack. If the operand is of the form ST(*n*), the nth register from the top of the floating point stack is pushed. Since the top-of-stack pointer (TOP) decrements as a result of the push, note that TOP + *n* is computed *prior* to the decrement operation. In all cases, the tag word corresponding to the top-of-stack is set to reflect its contents.

SINGLE and DOUBLE operands are automatically converted to EXTENDED (recall that the floating point registers are EXTENDED type). If the stack is full (i.e., FTAG[(TOP-1) & 7] is not marked EMPTY) the INVALID_FOP exception is signaled. On the 80387 and i486 the STF flag is also set. If INVALID_FOP processing is masked, the real indefinite value is pushed, overwriting a nonempty register location.

The 80*x*87 flags C0, C2, and C3 are set to an *undefined* state after FLD executes. If the FIE and STF flags are set (indicating a stack fault), flag C1 is also set to 1 to indicate a stack overflow.

Instructions that convert integers to EXTENDED precision format and push the result are available; see FILD on page 359 for details. Similarly, the FBLD instruction converts a packed BCD quantity into extended precision format and pushes the result onto the top of stack.

OPERATION

```
check_TS_EM();          /* see page 248 */
check_BUSY();           /* see page 248 */
check_ERROR();          /* see page 249 */
save_x87_instr_ptr();   /* see page 249 */
```

push_FSTK((EXTENDED) src);   /* see page 247 */

EXAMPLE
FLD   ST(0)   ; ST(-1) = ST(0) (duplicate stack-top)
                                              ; TOP = TOP - 1

FLD1: Push 1.0 onto 80*x*87 stack (*x*87 needed)

INSTRUCTION	PARAMETERS	OPCODE
FLD1		D9 E8

SUMMARY

FLD1 pushes the constant +1.0 onto the 80*x*87 stack. If the stack is full (i.e., FTAG[(TOP-1) & 7] is not marked EMPTY) the INVALID_FOP exception is signaled. On the 80387 and i486 the STF and C1 flags are also set. (The STF flag indicates a stack fault, whereas the C1 flag indicates a stack overflow.) If INVALID_FOP processing is masked, the real indefinite value is pushed, overwriting a nonempty register location. The 80*x*87 flags C0, C2, and C3 are set to an *undefined* state after FLD1 executes.

OPERATION

```
check_TS_EM();          /* see page 248 */
check_BUSY();           /* see page 248 */
check_ERROR();          /* see page 249 */
save_x87_instr_ptr();   /* see page 249 */

push_FSTK( (EXTENDED) 1.0 );      /* see page 247 */
```

EXAMPLE

FLD1

FLDCW: Load control word (*x*87 needed)

INSTRUCTION	PARAMETERS	OPCODE
FLDCW m16		D9 /5

SUMMARY
FLDCW loads the 80*x*87 control word FCW with the contents of *m16*. The condition codes C0, C1, C2, and C3 are set to *undefined* values after the instruction completes.

FLDCW does not ever signal an exception. However, the new exception mask settings may unmask a pending exception.

OPERATION
```
check_TS_EM();          /* see page 248 */
check_BUSY();           /* see page 248 */
check_ERROR();          /* see page 249 */

FCW = m16;
```

EXAMPLE
```
FLDCW new_FCW
```

FLDENV: Load 80x87 environment registers (x87 needed)

INSTRUCTION	PARAMETERS	OPCODE
FLDENV m	os ∈ {16,32}	D9 /4

SUMMARY

FLDENV initializes the 80x87 environment registers from an image stored in memory. The environment is composed of seven registers. The format of the memory image depends on two factors

1. the operand size attribute *os*: if *os* is 16, the seven registers are loaded from seven consecutive WORDs; if *os* is 32, the registers are loaded from seven consecutive DWORDs.

2. the execution mode: the interpretation of the 80x87 instruction and operand pointers depends on whether or not FLDENV is executed in PROTECTED mode.

See §3.6.4 on page 238 for more details on saving and restoring 80x87 state.

OPERATION

```
check_TS_EM();          /* see page 248 */
check_BUSY();           /* see page 248 */
check_ERROR();          /* see page 249 */

if ( os == 16 )  /* use 14 byte image (7 WORD locations) */
    load_env_16( (WORD *) &m );
else  /* os == 32 :  use 28 byte image (7 DWORD locations) */
    load_env_32( (DWORD *) &m );
```

EXAMPLE

```
FLDENV env_data
```

FLDL2E: Push $\log_2 e$ onto 80x87 stack (*x87 needed*)

INSTRUCTION	PARAMETERS	OPCODE
FLDL2E		D9 EA

SUMMARY

FLDL2E pushes the constant $\log_2 e$ onto the 80x87 stack. The value loaded is rounded to match the effective precision specified by the precision control (PC) field. The PRECISION exception is *not* signaled, however.

If the stack is full (i.e., FTAG[(TOP-1) & 7] is not marked EMPTY) the INVALID_FOP exception is signaled. On the 80387 and i486 the STF and C1 flags are also set. (The STF flag indicates a stack fault, whereas the C1 flag indicates a stack overflow.) If INVALID_FOP processing is masked, the real indefinite value is pushed, overwriting a nonempty register location. The 80x87 flags C0, C2, and C3 are set to an *undefined* state after FLD1 executes.

OPERATION

```
check_TS_EM();              /* see page 248 */
check_BUSY();               /* see page 248 */
check_ERROR();              /* see page 249 */
save_x87_instr_ptr();       /* see page 249 */

push_FSTK( (EXTENDED) (log₂ e) );      /* see page 247 */
```

EXAMPLE
FLDL2E

NOTE

1. On the 8087 and 80287 the value of $\log_2 e$ loaded is accurate to EXTENDED precision; i.e., the significand has 64 bits of accuracy, with rounding done using round-to-nearest mode. On the 80387 and i486, however, the constant is stored internally with greater than 64 bits of significand accuracy. Rounding is performed using the current rounding mode (as specified by the RC field in the control word FCW). To get the same constant that the 8087 and 80287 generate, set RC to round-to-nearest.

FLDL2T: Push log$_2$ 10 onto 80x87 stack (x87 needed)

INSTRUCTION	PARAMETERS	OPCODE
FLDL2T		D9 E9

SUMMARY

FLDL2T pushes the constant log$_2$ 10 onto the 80x87 stack. The value loaded is rounded to match the effective precision specified by the precision control (PC) field. The PRECISION exception is *not* signaled, however.

If the stack is full (i.e., FTAG[(TOP-1) & 7] is not marked EMPTY) the INVALID_FOP exception is signaled. On the 80387 and i486 the STF and C1 flags are also set. (The STF flag indicates a stack fault, whereas the C1 flag indicates a stack overflow.) If INVALID_FOP processing is masked, the real indefinite value is pushed, overwriting a nonempty register location. The 80x87 flags C0, C2, and C3 are set to an *undefined* state after FLD1 executes.

OPERATION

```
check_TS_EM();               /* see page 248 */
check_BUSY();                /* see page 248 */
check_ERROR();               /* see page 249 */
save_x87_instr_ptr();        /* see page 249 */

push_FSTK( (EXTENDED) (log₂ 10) );      /* see page 247 */
```

EXAMPLE
FLDL2T

NOTE

1. On the 8087 and 80287 the value of log$_2$ 10 loaded is accurate to EXTENDED precision; i.e., the significand has 64 bits of accuracy, with rounding done using round-to-nearest mode. On the 80387 and i486, however, the constant is stored internally with greater than 64 bits of significand accuracy. Rounding is performed using the current rounding mode (as specified by the RC field in the control word FCW). To get the same constant that the 8087 and 80287 generate, set RC to round-to-nearest.

FLDLG2: Push log$_{10}$ 2 onto 80x87 stack (x87 needed)

INSTRUCTION	PARAMETERS	OPCODE
FLDLG2		D9 EC

SUMMARY

FLDLG2 pushes the constant log$_{10}$ 2 onto the 80x87 stack. The value loaded is rounded to match the effective precision specified by the precision control (PC) field. The PRECISION exception is *not* signaled, however.

If the stack is full (i.e., FTAG[(TOP-1) & 7] is not marked EMPTY) the INVALID_FOP exception is signaled. On the 80387 and i486 the STF and C1 flags are also set. (The STF flag indicates a stack fault, whereas the C1 flag indicates a stack overflow.) If INVALID_FOP processing is masked, the real indefinite value is pushed, overwriting a nonempty register location. The 80x87 flags C0, C2, and C3 are set to an *undefined* state after FLD1 executes.

OPERATION

```
check_TS_EM();              /* see page 248 */
check_BUSY();               /* see page 248 */
check_ERROR();              /* see page 249 */
save_x87_instr_ptr();       /* see page 249 */

push_FSTK( (EXTENDED) (log₁₀ 2) );      /* see page 247 */
```

EXAMPLE
FLDLG2

NOTE

1. On the 8087 and 80287 the value of log$_{10}$ 2 loaded is accurate to EXTENDED precision; that is, the significand has 64 bits of accuracy, with rounding done using round-to-nearest mode. On the 80387 and i486, however, the constant is stored internally with greater than 64 bits of significand accuracy. Rounding is performed using the current rounding mode (as specified by the RC field in the control word FCW). To get the same constant that the 8087 and 80287 generate, set RC to round-to-nearest.

FLDLN2: Push ln 2 onto 80*x*87 stack (*x*87 needed)

INSTRUCTION	PARAMETERS	OPCODE
FLDLN2		D9 EC

SUMMARY

FLDLN2 pushes the constant ln 2 onto the 80*x*87 stack. The value loaded is rounded to match the effective precision specified by the precision control (PC) field. The PRECISION exception is *not* signaled, however.

If the stack is full (i.e., FTAG[(TOP-1) & 7] is not marked EMPTY) the INVALID_FOP exception is signaled. On the 80387 and i486 the STF and C1 flags are also set. (The STF flag indicates a stack fault, whereas the C1 flag indicates a stack overflow.) If INVALID_FOP processing is masked, the real indefinite value is pushed, overwriting a nonempty register location. The 80*x*87 flags C0, C2, and C3 are set to an *undefined* state after FLD1 executes.

OPERATION

```
check_TS_EM();            /* see page 248 */
check_BUSY();             /* see page 248 */
check_ERROR();            /* see page 249 */
save_x87_instr_ptr();     /* see page 249 */

push_FSTK( (EXTENDED) (ln 2) );        /* see page 247 */
```

EXAMPLE
FLDLN2

NOTE

1. On the 8087 and 80287 the value of ln 2 loaded is accurate to EXTENDED precision; that is, the significand has 64 bits of accuracy, with rounding done using round-to-nearest mode. On the 80387 and i486, however, the constant is stored internally with greater than 64 bits of significand accuracy. Rounding is performed using the current rounding mode (as specified by the RC field in the control word FCW). To get the same constant that the 8087 and 80287 generate, set RC to round-to-nearest.

FLDPI: Push π onto 80x87 stack (x87 needed)

INSTRUCTION	PARAMETERS	OPCODE
FLDPI		D9 E8

SUMMARY
FLDPI pushes the constant π onto the 80x87 stack. The value loaded is rounded to match the effective precision specified by the precision control (PC) field. The PRECISION exception is *not* signaled, however.

If the stack is full (i.e., FTAG[(TOP-1) & 7] is not marked EMPTY) the INVALID_FOP exception is signaled. On the 80387 and i486 the STF and C1 flags are also set. (The STF flag indicates a stack fault, whereas the C1 flag indicates a stack overflow.) If INVALID_FOP processing is masked, the real indefinite value is pushed, overwriting a nonempty register location. The 80x87 flags C0, C2, and C3 are set to an *undefined* state after FLD1 executes.

OPERATION
```
check_TS_EM();              /* see page 248 */
check_BUSY();               /* see page 248 */
check_ERROR();              /* see page 249 */
save_x87_instr_ptr();       /* see page 249 */

push_FSTK( (EXTENDED) π );          /* see page 247 */
```

EXAMPLE
FLDPI

NOTE
1. On the 8087 and 80287 the value of π loaded is accurate to EXTENDED precision; that is, the significand has 64 bits of accuracy, with rounding done using round-to-nearest mode. On the 80387 and i486, however, the constant is stored internally with greater than 64 bits of significand accuracy. Rounding is performed using the current rounding mode (as specified by the RC field in the control word FCW). To get the same constant that the 8087 and 80287 generate, set RC to round-to-nearest.

FLDZ: Push 0.0 onto 80*x*87 stack (*x*87 needed)

INSTRUCTION	PARAMETERS	OPCODE
FLDZ		D9 EE

SUMMARY
FLDZ pushes the constant 0.0 onto the 80*x*87 stack. If the stack is full (i.e., FTAG[(TOP-1) & 7] is not marked EMPTY) the INVALID_FOP exception is signaled. On the 80387 and i486 the STF flag is also set. If INVALID_FOP processing is masked, the real indefinite value is pushed, overwriting a nonempty register location.

If the stack is full (i.e., FTAG[(TOP-1) & 7] is not marked EMPTY) the INVALID_FOP exception is signaled. On the 80387 and i486 the STF and C1 flags are also set. (The STF flag indicates a stack fault, whereas the C1 flag indicates a stack overflow.) If INVALID_FOP processing is masked, the real indefinite value is pushed, overwriting a nonempty register location. The 80*x*87 flags C0, C2, and C3 are set to an *undefined* state after FLD1 executes.

OPERATION
```
check_TS_EM();              /* see page 248 */
check_BUSY();               /* see page 248 */
check_ERROR();              /* see page 249 */
save_x87_instr_ptr();       /* see page 249 */

push_FSTK( (EXTENDED) 0.0 );        /* see page 247 */
```

EXAMPLE
FLDZ

FMUL: Multiply real and 80*x*87 stack-top (*x*87 needed)

INSTRUCTION	PARAMETERS	OPCODE
FMUL m32	dst ≡ ST(0), src = m32	D8 /1
FMUL m64	dst ≡ ST(0), src = m64	DC /1
FMUL ST,ST(*n*)	dst ≡ ST(0), src = ST(*n*)	D8 C8+*n*
FMUL ST(*n*),ST	dst ≡ ST(*n*), src = ST(0)	DC C8+*n*

SUMMARY

FMUL multiplies the floating point values src and dst, and stores the result back into the dst operand. Note that the destination (dst) is limited to either the 80*x*87 stack-top, or one of the registers in the 80*x*87 stack.

If the src operand is either SINGLE or DOUBLE, it is automatically converted to EXTENDED before being operated on. As always, the number of significant bits in the stored result depends on the effective precision specified by the PC control bits. Result rounding is done using the current RC setting.

The 80*x*87 flags C0, C2, and C3 are set to an *undefined* state after FMUL executes. If the operation results in a PRECISION exception (i.e., the FPE flag is set), condition code C1 is set to 1 if the rounding is upward; if it is downward, it is set to 0.

OPERATION

```
check_TS_EM();          /* see page 248 */
check_BUSY();           /* see page 248 */
check_ERROR();          /* see page 249 */
save_x87_instr_ptr();   /* see page 249 */

dst = (EXTENDED) dst * (EXTENDED) src
```

EXAMPLE

```
FMUL     ST, ST(4)              ; ST(0) = ST(0) * ST(4)
```

ASSEMBLER USAGE NOTE

1. Assemblers like Microsoft MASM and Borland TASM allow the mnemonic
   FMUL
   without any arguments. The purpose is to simulate a classical stack multiply; that is, pop the top two stack elements, multiply them, and push the result.

See the *Assembler Usage Notes* of the FMULP instruction (following) for a description of how this is achieved.

FMULP: Multiply real by 80x87 stack-top, and pop (x87 needed)

INSTRUCTION	PARAMETERS	OPCODE
FMULP ST(n),ST		DE C8+n

SUMMARY

FMULP multiplies the nth register relative to the stack-top by the floating point value at the 80x87 stack-top. The stack is popped after the multiplication.

If the stack-top is marked EMPTY the INVALID_FOP exception is signaled. On the 80387 and i486 the STF flag is set to 1, and the C1 flag is cleared. (STF flag set to 1 indicates a stack fault, and the C1 flag set to 0 indicates a stack underflow.) The 80x87 flags C0, C2, and C3 are set to an *undefined* state after FMULP executes. If the operation results in a PRECISION exception (i.e., the FPE flag is set), condition code C1 is set to 1 if the rounding is upward; if it is downward, it is set to 0.

OPERATION

```
check_TS_EM();          /* see page 248 */
check_BUSY();           /* see page 248 */
check_ERROR();          /* see page 249 */
save_x87_instr_ptr();   /* see page 249 */

ST(n) = ST(n) * ST(0);
pop_FSTK(); /* Discard multiplier */
```

EXAMPLE

```
; Pop top two stack elements, multiply them, and push result
FMULP    ST(1), ST
```

ASSEMBLER USAGE NOTE

1. Assemblers like Microsoft MASM and Borland TASM allow the mnemonic
   FMUL
   without any arguments. This is equivalent to
   FMULP ST(1), ST
   that is, the top two elements are multiplied and the result is placed in the element below the stack-top. Then the stack is popped, thus making the register storing the product the new stack-top. This simulates a classical stack multiply.

FNCLEX: Clear all 80x87 exceptions (x87 needed)

INSTRUCTION	PARAMETERS	OPCODE
FNCLEX		DB E2

SUMMARY
FNCLEX removes all pending 80x87 exceptions by clearing all exception flags in the 80x87 status register FSW. The only field in the FSW that is not updated is TOP, the top-of-stack register. Note that FNCLEX only checks the TS and EM flags in CR0; the instruction does not wait for BUSY to deactivate, nor does it signal PE_ERROR if an 80x87 error has occurred.

Use the mnemonic FCLEX if you want to ensure that no 80x87 operation is pending. 80x86 assemblers translate FCLEX as

```
            FWAIT
            FNCLEX
```

Since FWAIT checks for errors, as well as BUSY deactivation, FCLEX will signal PE_ERROR if an error is pending.

OPERATION
```
check_TS_EM();                    /* see page 248 */
/* All flags below are from the status register */
BSY = 0;
C3 = undefined;
C2 = undefined;
C1 = undefined;
C0 = undefined;
ERS = 0;
STF = 0;
FPE = 0;
FUE = 0;
FOE = 0;
FZE = 0;
FDE = 0;
FIE = 0;
```

EXAMPLE
```
FNCLEX
```

FNDISI: Disable float interrupts (8087 only)

INSTRUCTION	PARAMETERS	OPCODE
FNDISI		DB E1

SUMMARY
FNDISI sets the interrupt enable mask flag (IEM) in the floating point control word. This disables exception generation by the 8087. The 80287, 80387, and the floating point unit of the i486 are not designed to use interrupts to signal exceptions. Therefore, FNDISI performs an action only on the 8087. If executed on the later implementations of the 80x87, the instruction is ignored. (See §3.9 (starting on page 251), however, for notes on the nonstandard way in which the IBM PC/AT system architecture reports processor extension exceptions.)

As with all 8087 instructions, FNDISI does not wait for BUSY to deactivate (the "N" in FNDISI denotes "no wait"). Use the mnemonic FDISI if you are not certain that BUSY is inactive. 80x86 assemblers translate FDISI as
            WAIT
            FNDISI
Since FWAIT checks for errors, as well as BUSY deactivation, FDISI will signal PE_ERROR if an error is pending.

OPERATION
check_TS_EM();   /* see page 248 */
IEM = 1;

EXAMPLE
FNDISI

NOTE
1. Code that uses the FNDISI instruction (presumably written with the 8087 in mind) should be carefully examined to see why the instruction was used. Although FNDISI is ignored by the 8087's successors, it is unlikely that code containing the instruction will port without change to the 80287-, 80387-, or i486-based systems.

FNENI: Enable float interrupts (8087 only)

INSTRUCTION	PARAMETERS	OPCODE
FNENI		DB E0

SUMMARY
FNENI clears the interrupt enable mask flag (IEM) in the floating point control word. This enables exception generation by the 8087. The 80287, 80387 and the floating point unit of the i486 are not designed to use interrupts to signal exceptions. Therefore, FNENI performs an action only on the 8087. If executed on the later implementations of the 80x87, the instruction is ignored. (See §3.9 (starting on page 251), however, for notes on the nonstandard way in which the IBM PC/AT system architecture reports processor extension exceptions.)

As with all 8087 instructions, FNENI does not wait for BUSY to deactivate (the "N" in FNENI denotes "no wait"). Use the mnemonic FENI if you are not certain that BUSY is inactive. 80x86 assemblers translate FENI as
```
        WAIT
        FNENI
```
Since FWAIT checks for errors, as well as BUSY deactivation, FENI will signal PE_ERROR if an error is pending.

OPERATION
```
check_TS_EM();              /* see page 248 */
IEM = 0;
```

EXAMPLE
```
FNENI
```

NOTE
1. Code that uses the FNENI instruction (presumably written with the 8087 in mind) should be carefully examined to see why the instruction was used. Although FNENI is ignored by the 8087's successors, it is unlikely that code containing the instruction will port without change to the 80287-, 80387-, or i486-based systems.

FNINIT: Initialize processor extension (*x*87 needed)

INSTRUCTION	PARAMETERS	OPCODE
FNINIT		DB E3

SUMMARY
FNINIT resets the 80*x*87 processor extension by initializing the control word FCW, the status word FSW, and the tag word FTAG. It does so without waiting for the 80*x*87 to become not busy. Nor does it check for pending processor extension errors. If an operation is executing in the 80*x*87 when FNINIT is executed, it is unconditionally aborted.

OPERATION
reset_x87();   /* see page 257 */

EXAMPLE
FNINIT

ASSEMBLER USAGE NOTES
1. Use the FINIT assembler instruction to wait for BUSY to deactivate before initialization. Assemblers expand this mnemonic into
   WAIT
   FNINIT
   Note that the WAIT reports any pending processor extension errors also.

2. A PE_OVERRUN exception can leave an 80*x*87 in a state where it is expecting further data from the 80*x*86. Therefore, in general, a PE_OVERRUN exception handler must issue an FNINIT before any other 80*x*87 operations are attempted.

FNOP: 80*x*87 no operation (*x*87 needed)

INSTRUCTION	PARAMETERS	OPCODE
FNOP		D9 D0

SUMMARY
FNOP is the 80*x*87 "no operation" instruction. It performs no floating point operation. However, on the 80287, 80387, and i486, it waits for the 80*x*87 to become not busy, and reports any pending 80*x*87 exceptions.

OPERATION
check_TS_EM();   /* see page 248 */
check_BUSY();   /* see page 248 */
check_ERROR();   /* see page 249 */
save_x87_instr_ptr();   /* see page 249 */

EXAMPLE
FNOP

NOTE
1. On 80*x*87 implementations other than the 8087, FNOP's operation is very similar to that of WAIT. However, executing FNOP causes the exception address registers X87OPER, X87CS, and X87EIP to be loaded. Executing WAIT does not affect these registers.

FNSAVE: Save 80x87 state (x87 needed)

INSTRUCTION	PARAMETERS	OPCODE
FNSAVE m	os ∈ *{16,32}*	DD /6

SUMMARY

FNSAVE dumps the contents of the environment registers and the 80x87 stack to the memory area *m*. Then it initializes the 80x87. The initialization performed is equivalent to executing an FNINIT. The environment is composed of seven registers and the 80x87 stack consists of eight EXTENDED format (10-byte) registers. The format of the 80x87 stack is fixed. However, the format of the environment image depends on the operand size attribute and the current execution mode. See the description of the FRSTOR instruction and §3.6.4 on page 238 for more details on saving and restoring 80x87 state.

Note that the FNSAVE instruction waits for BUSY to deactivate, but does not check for errors. If an error check is desired, use the assembler mnemonic FSAVE.

OPERATION

```
WORD *word_vec;
EXTENDED *stack_img;

check_TS_EM();                /* see page 248 */
check_BUSY();                 /* see page 248 */

/* Store environment */
if ( os == 16 )  /* use 14 byte image (7 WORD locations) */
    store_env_16( (WORD *) &m );          /* see page 244 */
else  /* os == 32 : use 28 byte image (7 DWORD locations) */
    store_env_32( (DWORD *) &m );         /* see page 244 */

/* Store 80x87 registers, starting with ST(0) */
word_vec = &m;
if ( os == 16 )
    stack_img = &word_vec[7];
else  /* os == 32 */
    stack_img = &word_vec[14];
for ( i = 0;  i <= 7;  i++ )
    stack_img[i] = FSTK[(TOP + i) & 7];
```

```
/* Initialize 80x87 */
reset_x87()                              /* see page 257 */
```

EXAMPLE
```
FNSAVE x87_state
```

FNSETPM: Set 80x87 to PROTECTED mode (80287 only)

INSTRUCTION	PARAMETERS	OPCODE
FNSETPM		DB E4

SUMMARY

FNSETPM is used to inform an 80287 that the 80286 has entered PROTECTED mode. The 80287 needs to know this so that it can load and store the 80x87 environment structure using the PROTECTED mode format. Note that it is the programmer's responsibility to issue FNSETPM whenever PROTECTED mode is entered on the 80286.

Since there is no PROTECTED mode on the 8086 and 80186, FNSETPM is not defined on these implementations; i.e. the opcode is *reserved*. The 80386 and i486 handles all exception address information internally, so there is no need to communicate execution mode switches on these implementations. Executing FNSETPM on these implementations has no effect; the instruction is treated as a no-op.

FNSETPM executes without waiting for BUSY to dcactivate. Nor does it check for pending exceptions. If these checks are desired, use the assembler mnemonic FSETPM. This mnemonic inserts a WAIT in front of the FNSETPM.

OPERATION
check_TS_EM();   /* see page 248 */

« set 80287 **mode** to PROTECTED »

EXAMPLE
FNSETPM

FNSTCW: Store 80*x*87 control word (*x*87 needed)

INSTRUCTION	PARAMETERS	OPCODE
FNSTCW m16		D9 /7

SUMMARY

FNSTCW stores the 80*x*87 control word FCW into *m16*.

Note that on all 80*x*87s other than the 8087, the FNSTCW instruction waits for BUSY to deactivate before storing FCW, but does not check for errors. If an error check is desired, use the assembler mnemonic FSTCW.

OPERATION

```
check_TS_EM();          /* see page 248 */
check_BUSY();           /* see page 248 */

dst = FCW;
```

EXAMPLE

FNSTCW ctl

FNSTENV: Store 80x87 environment (x87 needed)

INSTRUCTION	PARAMETERS	OPCODE
FNSTENV m	os ∈ {16,32}	D9 /6

SUMMARY
FNSTENV dumps the contents of the environment registers to the memory area *m*. Then it disables all 80x87 exceptions by setting all the exception masks. The environment is composed of seven registers. Their format in memory depends on the operand size attribute and the current execution mode. See the description of the FRSTOR instruction and §3.6.4 on page 238 for more details on saving and restoring 80x87 state.

Note that the FNSTENV instruction waits for BUSY to deactivate, but does not check for errors. If an error check is desired, use the assembler mnemonic FSTENV.

OPERATION
```
check_TS_EM();              /* see page 248 */
check_BUSY();               /* see page 248 */

/* Store environment */
if ( os == 16 )  /* use 14 byte image (7 WORD locations) */
    store_env_16( (WORD *) &m );          /* see page 244 */
else  /* os == 32 : use 28 byte image (7 DWORD locations) */
    store_env_32( (DWORD *) &m );         /* see page 244 */

/* Set exception masks */
PM = UM = OM = ZM = DM = IM = 1;
```

EXAMPLE
FNSTENV x87_env

FNSTSW: Store 80*x*87 status word (*x*87 needed)

INSTRUCTION	PARAMETERS	OPCODE
FNSTSW m16	dst ≡ m16	DD /7
FNSTSW AX	dst ≡ AX	DF E0

SUMMARY

FNSTSW stores the 80*x*87 status word FSW into *dst*. *Dst* can either be a WORD in memory or the AX register. However, the AX form is unavailable on the 8087.

Note that on all 80*x*87s other than the 8087, the FNSTSW instruction waits for BUSY to deactivate, but does not check for errors. If an error check is desired, use the assembler mnemonic FSTSW.

OPERATION
```
check_TS_EM();          /* see page 248 */
check_BUSY();           /* see page 248 */

dst = FSW;
```

EXAMPLE
FNSTSW status

FPATAN: Compute (partial) arctangent (*x*87 needed)

INSTRUCTION	PARAMETERS	OPCODE
FPATAN		D9 F3

SUMMARY
FPATAN computes the arctangent of the ratio between ST(1) and ST(0). Both stack elements are popped, and the resulting arctangent, expressed in radians, is pushed onto the 80*x*87 stack.

On the 8087 and 80287, the inputs ST(0) and ST(1) are restricted to

$$0 \le ST(1) < ST(0) < +\infty$$

This restriction results in the instruction name "*partial arctan*gent." The 80387 and the i486 remove these restrictions. However, for the sake of compatibility, the mnemonic FPATAN is retained.

If the 80*x*87 stack is empty, an INVALID_FOP is signaled. An undefined-format operand (e.g., a pseudo zero or an unnormal) also causes an INVALID_FOP. The 80387 and i486 also set the STF flag to 1 in case of a stack fault, and set the C1 flag to 0 (indicating a stack underflow).

OPERATION
```
check_TS_EM();          /* see page 248 */
check_BUSY();           /* see page 248 */
check_ERROR();          /* see page 249 */
save_x87_instr_ptr();   /* see page 249 */

x = pop_FSTK();         /* ST(0) */
y = pop_FSTK();         /* ST(1) */
push_FSTK( y / x );
```

EXAMPLE
```
FPATAN
```

FPREM: Compute partial remainder (*x87* needed)

INSTRUCTION	PARAMETERS	OPCODE
FPREM		D9 F8

SUMMARY

FPREM computes a partial remainder from dividing the stack-top (ST(0)) with the element next to the stack top (ST(1)). The result replaces the stack-top's contents. (The remainder computed by FPREM is not compatible with IEEE Std. 754; use FPREM1 to compute the remainder specified by the Standard.)

To understand the definition of "partial remainder," observe that the (complete) remainder *r* is defined as

r = ST(0) - ST(1) * chop(ST(0) / ST(1))

where the chop function (defined on page 227) simply truncates the fractional component of the floating point quotient. 80*x*87 implementations attempt to compute the remainder via an iterative reduction algorithm whose running time is proportional to the *difference in order of magnitude* of the dividend and the divisor. If this difference is very large (e.g., ST(0) is of order 2^{500} and ST(1) is of order 2^{-200}) the running time of the remainder computation becomes correspondingly large. (It takes current 80*x*87 implementations between 138 and 190 clock periods to reduce a dividend 63 binary orders of magnitude.) To keep the running time manageable, the FPREM instruction reduces the dividend by a maximum of (but not including) 2^{64}. Thus the partial remainder *pr* generated by FPREM is defined as

pr = ST(0) - m * chop(ST(0) / ST(1))

where *m* is the integer with the largest magnitude that satisfies the relation

abs(m * chop(ST(0) / ST(1))) < 2^{64}

If the reduction is incomplete, the floating point condition code C2 is set to 1; if it is complete (i.e., *pr* contains the true remainder), C2 is set to 0. In the latter case, the 3-bit number constructed from the FSW flags C0:C3:C1 denotes the three least significant bits of the chopped quotient. (Here, C0 is the most significant bit, and C1 the least significant bit.)

OPERATION

```
check_TS_EM();                      /* see page 248 */
check_BUSY();                       /* see page 248 */
check_ERROR();                      /* see page 249 */
save_x87_instr_ptr();               /* see page 249 */
```

ST(0) = ST(0) - m * chop(ST(0) / ST(1)); /* m is defined above; chop is defined on
                                                            page 227 */

EXAMPLE
FPREM

NOTES

1. If $\log_2$ ST(0) $-$ $\log_2$ ST(1) $\geq$ 64 the FPREM instruction will only compute a partial remainder. Under such circumstances a software loop has to complete the reduction; for example,

```
; Compute (complete) remainder from ST(0) / ST(1)
lp:
FPREM
FSTSW     AX          ; Transfer 80x87 flags to AX
SAHF                  ; Transfer 80x87 flags to 80x86 flags
JP        lp          ; If PF set reduction is not complete
                      ; (Note that FSTSW/SAHF copies 80x87's C2 to
                      ;  80x86's PF)
```

2. If the stack-top contains a denormal, the 8087 and 80287 signal an INVALID_FOP exception. The 80387 and i486, however, perform the operation. The change was made to reflect IEEE Std. 754 requirements.

3. If the dividend is of the form 64^n+1 or 64^n+2, where n is a positive integer, both the 8087 and the 80287 produce incorrect quotient bits in C0, C3, and C1 of FSW. This bug has been corrected in the 80387 and the i486.

4. FPREM is the remainder instruction provided by the 8087 and 80287. It differs from FPREM1 (compatible with IEEE Std. 754, but available only on the 80387 and the i486) in the way in which the integer quotient is computed. FPREM chops the real quotient to obtain the integer, whereas FPREM1 uses round-to-nearest rounding.

FPREM1: Compute partial remainder (IEEE compatible) (80387 and i486 only)

INSTRUCTION	PARAMETERS	OPCODE
FPREM1		D9 F5

SUMMARY

FPREM1 computes an IEEE-compatible partial remainder from dividing the stack-top (ST(0)) with the element next to the stack top (ST(1)). The result replaces the stack-top's contents. Note that this instruction is only available on the 80387 and the i486.

To understand the definition of "partial remainder," observe that the (complete) remainder r is defined as

$$r = ST(0) - ST(1) * \text{round\_nearest}(ST(0) / ST(1))$$

where the round_nearest function (defined on page 226) rounds the floating point quotient to its *nearest* integer. 80x87 implementations attempt to compute the remainder via an iterative reduction algorithm whose running time is proportional to the *difference in order of magnitude* of the dividend and the divisor. If this difference is very large (e.g., ST(0) is of order 2^{500} and ST(1) is of order 2^{-200}) the running time of the remainder computation becomes correspondingly large. (It takes the 80387 and i486 betwen 170 and 185 clock periods to reduce a dividend 63 binary orders of magnitude.) To keep the running time manageable, FPREM1 reduces the dividend by a maximum of (but not including) 2^{64}. Thus the partial remainder pr generated by FPREM is defined as

$$pr = ST(0) - m * \text{round\_nearest}(ST(0) / ST(1))$$

where m is the integer with the largest magnitude that satisfies the relation

$$\text{abs}(m * \text{round\_nearest}(ST(0) / ST(1))) < 2^{64}$$

If the reduction is incomplete, the floating point condition code C2 is set to 1; if it is complete (i.e., *pr* contains the true remainder), C2 is set to 0. In the latter case, the three bit number constructed from the FSW flags C0:C3:C1 denotes the three least significant bits of the rounded quotient. (Here, C0 is the most significant bit, and C1 the least significant bit.)

OPERATION
```
check_TS_EM();                    /* see page 248 */
check_BUSY();                     /* see page 248 */
check_ERROR();                    /* see page 249 */
save_x87_instr_ptr();             /* see page 249 */
```

ST(0) = ST(0) − m * round_nearest(ST(0) / ST(1)); /* m is defined above; round_nearest
                                                        is defined on page 226 */

EXAMPLE
FPREM1

NOTE

1. If $\log_2 ST(0) - \log_2 ST(1) \geq 64$ the FPREM1 instruction will only compute
   a partial remainder. Under such circumstances a software loop has to
   complete the reduction; for example,
```
; Compute (complete) remainder from ST(0) / ST(1)
lp:
FPREM1
FSTSW     AX        ; Transfer 80x87 flags to AX
SAHF                ; Transfer 80x87 flags to 80x86 flags
JP        lp        ; If PF set reduction is not complete
                    ; (Note that FSTSW/SAHF copies 80x87's C2 to 80x86's PF)
```

FPTAN: Compute partial tangent (*x*87 needed)

INSTRUCTION	PARAMETERS	OPCODE
FPTAN		D9 F2

SUMMARY

FPTAN replaces the contents of the 80*x*87 stack-top (ST) with its tangent value. Then, it pushes the constant 1.0 onto the stack. The input value, ST, is assumed to be in radians. For the 8087 and 80287 the value must be in the range $0 \le ST \le \pi / 4$. For the 80387 and i486, the range restriction is relaxed to $-2^{63} < ST < 2^{63}$. An out-of-range operand on the 8087 and 80287 produces an *undefined* result. On the 80387 and i486, an out-of-range condition is specified by setting flag C2 to 1. ST is left unmodified in this case. If the operand is in range, flag C2 is set to 0. Flags C0 and C3 are left in an *undefined* state after the operation.

If the 80*x*87 stack is empty, an INVALID_FOP is signaled. An undefined-format operand (e.g., a pseudo zero or an unnormal) also causes an INVALID_FOP. The 80387 and i486 also set the STF flag to 1 in case of a stack fault, and set the C1 flag to 0 (indicating a stack underflow).

OPERATION

```
check_TS_EM();              /* see page 248 */
check_BUSY();               /* see page 248 */
check_ERROR();              /* see page 249 */
save_x87_instr_ptr();       /* see page 249 */

if ( -2^63 < ST(0)  &&  ST(0) > 2^63 )  /* see SUMMARY above for 8087/80287 restrictions */
{   ST(0) = tan( ST(0) );
    C2 = 0;
    push_FSTK(1.0);         /* see page 247 */
}
else
    C2 = 1;
```

EXAMPLE

```
FPTAN
```

FRNDINT: Round to integer (*x*87 needed)

INSTRUCTION	PARAMETERS	OPCODE
FRNDINT		D9 FC

SUMMARY

FRNDINT rounds the stack-top value to an integer, and stores the rounded result back to the stack-top. (The integer is represented, of course, as an EXTENDED value.) Rounding is done according to the current RC setting.

If the 80*x*87 stack is empty, an INVALID_FOP is signaled. An undefined-format operand (e.g., a pseudo zero or an unnormal) also causes an INVALID_FOP. The 80387 and i486 also set the STF flag to 1 in case of a stack fault, and set the C1 flag to 0 (indicating a stack underflow). The 80*x*87 flags C0, C2, and C3 are set to an *undefined* state after FRNDINT executes. If the operation results in a PRECISION exception (i.e., the FPE flag is set), condition code C1 is set to 1 if the rounding is upward; if it is downward, it is set to 0.

OPERATION

```
check_TS_EM();              /* see page 248 */
check_BUSY();               /* see page 248 */
check_ERROR();              /* see page 249 */
save_x87_instr_ptr();       /* see page 249 */

if ( RC == ROUND_NEAREST )
   ST(0) = round_nearest( ST(0) );  /* see page 226 */
else if ( RC == ROUND_DOWN )
   ST(0) = round_down( ST(0) );     /* see page 227 */
else if ( RC == ROUND_UP )
   ST(0) = round_up( ST(0) );       /* see page 227 */
else /* RC == CHOP */
   ST(0) = chop( ST(0) );           /* see page 227 */
```

EXAMPLE

FRNDINT

FRSTOR: Load 80x87 state (x87 needed)

INSTRUCTION	PARAMETERS	OPCODE
FRSTOR m	os ∈ {16,32}	DB /4

SUMMARY

FRSTOR initializes the 80x87 environment registers and the 80x87 floating point stack from an image stored in memory. The environment is composed of seven registers and the 80x87 stack consists of eight EXTENDED format (10-byte) registers. The format of the 80x87 stack is fixed. However, the format of the environment image depends on two factors

1. the operand size attribute *os*: if *os* is 16, the seven registers are loaded from seven consecutive WORDs; if *os* is 32, the registers are loaded from seven consecutive DWORDs.

2. the execution mode: the interpretation of the 80x87 instruction and operand pointers depends on whether or not FLDENV is executed in PROTECTED mode.

If *os* is 16, the environment occupies 14 bytes; otherwise, the environment occupies 28 bytes. This determines the relative offset of the stack image. Keep in mind that the first element of the stack image is the stack top FSTK[TOP], rather than the first physical register FSTK[0]. See §3.6.4 on page 238 for more details on saving and restoring 80x87 state.

OPERATION

```
WORD *word_vec;
EXTENDED *stack_img;

check_TS_EM();          /* see page 248 */
check_BUSY();           /* see page 248 */
check_ERROR();          /* see page 249 */

/* Load environment */
if ( os == 16 )  /* use 14 byte image (7 WORD locations) */
   load_env_16( (WORD *) &m );
else  /* os == 32 :  use 28 byte image (7 DWORD locations) */
   load_env_32( (DWORD *) &m );
```

```
/* Load 80x87 registers, starting with ST(0) */
word_vec = &m;
if ( os == 16 )
   stack_img = &word_vec[7];
else  /* os == 32 */
   stack_img = &word_vec[14];
for ( i = 0;  i <= 7;  i++ )
   FSTK[(TOP + i) & 7] = stack_img[i];
```

EXAMPLE
FRSTOR x87_state

FS (prefix): Use FS for memory access (376, 386, 486 only)

INSTRUCTION	PARAMETERS	OPCODE
FS:		64

SUMMARY

An instruction making a memory reference always uses an implied segment register. The segment register implied depends on the way the memory offset is generated (see §2.18 on page 185 for more on this). Specifying the FS: override prefix changes the segment register used to FS (and the segment descriptor register to FS_desc). This change is effective *only* for the instruction immediately following the FS: prefix.

Some string operations (e.g., MOVS*x*) have two memory operands. The override prefix only changes the DS in the source operand; that is, the source operand becomes FS:[E]SI. The implied use of ES for the destination operand is not changeable.

The FS segment register, and so the FS: prefix, is only supported on the 80376, 80386, and i486.

EXAMPLE
; Use FS instead of DS (the default) in the following BYTE string MOV.
; Note that the destination segment cannot be overridden; it must be ES.
REP MOVS ES:[EDI], FS:[ESI]

NOTES
1. Segment override prefixes apply only to memory data references; instruction fetches are always done with respect to CS. Furthermore, the stack manipulation instructions (i.e., PUSH, PUSHA, POP, POPA, PUSHF, POPF, CALL, RET, INT, and IRET) always reference the stack via SS. (The segment used by a PUSH or POP whose *operand* is a memory variable can be overridden, as can the pointer operand in an *indirect* CALL or JMP.) Segment override prefix use in front of instructions where it is not meaningful is unconditionally ignored.

2. FS: is actually an instruction prefix, rather than an instruction. Segment override prefixes for each of the other segment registers (CS, DS, ES, GS, and SS) are also supported. Apart from these prefixes the 80*x*86 has prefixes that implement string instructions (REP*x*) and perform atomic read-modify-

write of memory locations (LOCK). Two additional prefixes, the "address size prefix" and "operand size prefix," are also used on the 80376, 80386, and i486 to encode these later processors' 32-bit instruction extensions.

FSAVE: Save 80*x*87 state (*x*87 needed)

INSTRUCTION	PARAMETERS	OPCODE
FSAVE		9B DD /6

SUMMARY

FSAVE is a mnemonic that is expanded by most 80*x*86 assemblers to

    FWAIT
    FNSAVE

FNSAVE on the 80287, 80387, and i486 normally waits for the processor extension to become idle before saving state. However, it does not check for 80*x*87 exceptions. Using FSAVE causes the implicit FWAIT to report any pending 80*x*87 exceptions. See the description of FNSAVE for further details.

EXAMPLES

FSAVE

FSCALE: Scale by an integer power of 2 (*x*87 needed)

INSTRUCTION	PARAMETERS	OPCODE
FSCALE		D9 FD

SUMMARY
FSCALE multiplies the stack-top value by 2^s, where s is the integer component of the element next to the stack-top (i.e., ST(1)). s is computed by unconditionally chopping the fraction part of ST(1). The scaled result is rounded according to the current RC setting, and stored back into the stack-top.

The 80*x*87 flags C0, C2, and C3 are set to an *undefined* state after FSCALE executes. If the operation results in a PRECISION exception (i.e., the FPE flag is set), condition code C1 is set to 1 if the rounding is upward; if it is downward, it is set to 0.

OPERATION
```
check_TS_EM();          /* see page 248 */
check_BUSY();           /* see page 248 */
check_ERROR();          /* see page 249 */
save_x87_instr_ptr();   /* see page 249 */
```

$ST(0) = ST(0) * 2^{chop(ST(1))}$

EXAMPLE
FSCALE

NOTE
1. If the scale factor evaluates to 0 (after chopping) the 8087 and 80287 generate an undefined result; no exception is signaled. On the 80387 and i486, however, the function is performed correctly (i.e., the stack-top value is left unchanged).

FSETPM: Set 80*x*87 to PROTECTED mode (80287 only)

INSTRUCTION	PARAMETERS	OPCODE
FSETPM		9B DB E4

SUMMARY

FSETPM is a mnemonic that is expanded by most 80*x*86 assemblers to
>   FWAIT
>   FNSETPM

See the description of the FNSETPM instruction for more information.

EXAMPLE

FSETPM

FSIN: Compute sine (80387 and i486 only)

INSTRUCTION	PARAMETERS	OPCODE
FSIN		D9 FE

SUMMARY

FSIN, available only on the 80387 and i486, replaces the contents of the 80x87 stack-top (ST) with its sine value. ST is assumed to be in radians, and must be in the range $-2^{63} <$ ST $< 2^{63}$. If the operation completes, flag C2 is set to 0. However, if ST is out of range, C2 is set to 1 and ST is left unmodified. Flags C0 and C3 are left in an *undefined* state after the operation.

If the 80x87 stack is empty, an INVALID_FOP is signaled. An undefined-format operand (e.g., a pseudo zero or an unnormal) also causes an INVALID_FOP. The 80387 and i486 also set the STF flag to 1 in case of a stack fault, and set the C1 flag to 0 (indicating a stack underflow).

OPERATION

```
check_TS_EM();              /* see page 248 */
check_BUSY();               /* see page 248 */
check_ERROR();              /* see page 249 */
save_x87_instr_ptr();       /* see page 249 */

if ( -2^63 < ST(0)  &&  ST(0) > 2^63 )
{   ST(0) = sin( ST(0) );
    C2 = 0;
}
else
    C2 = 1;
```

EXAMPLE

```
FSIN
```

FSINCOS: Compute sine and cosine (80387 and i486 only)

INSTRUCTION	PARAMETERS	OPCODE
FSINCOS		D9 FB

SUMMARY

FSINCOS, available only on the 80387 and i486, pops the $80x87$ stack-top (ST) and pushes back the popped value's sine and cosine. ST is assumed to be in radians, and must be in the range $-2^{63} < \text{ST} < 2^{63}$. If the operation completes, flag C2 is set to 0. However, if ST is out of range, C2 is set to 1 and ST is left unmodified. Flags C0 and C3 are left in an *undefined* state after the operation.

If the $80x87$ stack is empty, or if stack overflow occurs during the second push, an INVALID_FOP is signaled. An undefined-format operand (e.g., a pseudozero or an unnormal) also causes an INVALID_FOP. The 80387 and i486 also set the STF flag to 1 in case of a stack fault, and set the C1 flag to 0 if there was a stack underflow, or 1 if there was a stack overflow.

OPERATION

```
check_TS_EM();                  /* see page 248 */
check_BUSY();                   /* see page 248 */
check_ERROR();                  /* see page 249 */
save_x87_instr_ptr();           /* see page 249 */

if ( -2^63 < ST(0)  &&  ST(0) > 2^63 )
{   EXTENDED v = pop_FSTK();         /* see page 247 */
    push_FSTK( sin( v ) );           /* see page 247 */
    push_FSTK( cos( v ) );
    C2 = 0;
}
else
    C2 = 1;
```

EXAMPLE
FSINCOS

NOTE

1. Executing the FSIN and FCOS instructions separately to compute the sine and cosine of a value is substantially slower than using FSINCOS.

FSQRT: Compute square root (*x*87 needed)

INSTRUCTION	PARAMETERS	OPCODE
FSQRT		D9 FA

SUMMARY
FSQRT replaces the 80*x*87 stack-top's value with its square root. Since zero is always signed in the 80*x*87, note that the square root of −0 is defined as −0. If computing the square root of a negative value is attempted, INVALID_FOP is signaled.

The 80*x*87 flags C0, C2, and C3 are set to an *undefined* state after FSQRT executes. If the operation results in a PRECISION exception (i.e., the FPE flag is set), condition code C1 is set to 1 if the rounding is upward; if it is downward, it is set to 0.

OPERATION
```
check_TS_EM();              /* see page 248 */
check_BUSY();               /* see page 248 */
check_ERROR();              /* see page 249 */
save_x87_instr_ptr();       /* see page 249 */

ST(0) = sqrt( ST(0) );
```

EXAMPLE
FSQRT

NOTE
1. If the stack-top contains the denormal, the 8087 and 80287 signal an INVALID_FOP exception. The 80387 and i486, however, perform the operation. The change was made to reflect IEEE Std. 754 requirements.

FST: Store 80*x*87 stack-top as real data (*x*87 needed)

INSTRUCTION	PARAMETERS	OPCODE
FST m32	dst ≡ m32	D9 /2
FST m64	dst ≡ m64	DD /2
FST ST(*n*)	dst ≡ ST(*n*)	DD D0+*n*

SUMMARY
FST stores the floating point value in the top element of the 80*x*87 stack into a SINGLE or DOUBLE storage area in memory. If the operand is of the form ST(*n*), the top element is copied to the nth register from the top of the 80*x*87 stack. Note that the stack is not popped after the store. To pop the stack, use the FSTP instruction. FSTP also allows data to be stored in an EXTENDED operand in memory, whereas FST only supports SINGLE and DOUBLE operands.

The 80*x*87 flags C0, C2, and C3 are set to an *undefined* state after FST executes. If the operation results in a PRECISION exception (i.e., the FPE flag is set), condition code C1 is set to 1 if the rounding is upward; if it is downward, it is set to 0.

OPERATION
```
check_TS_EM();              /* see page 248 */
check_BUSY();               /* see page 248 */
check_ERROR();              /* see page 249 */
save_x87_instr_ptr();       /* see page 249 */

dst = ST(0)
```

EXAMPLES
```
FST      ST(2)              ; ST(2) = ST(0)
FST      var                ; var = ST(0)
```

FSTCW: Store 80*x*87 control word (*x*87 needed)

INSTRUCTION	PARAMETERS	OPCODE
FSTCW		9B D9 /7

SUMMARY

FSTCW is a mnemonic that is expanded by most 80*x*86 assemblers to

     FWAIT
     FNSTCW

FNSTCW on the 80287, 80387, and i486 normally waits for the processor extension to become idle before storing the FCW register. However, it does not check for 80*x*87 exceptions. Using FSTCW causes the implicit FWAIT to report any pending 80*x*87 exceptions. See the description of FNSTCW for further details.

EXAMPLES

FSTCW   ctl

FSTENV: Store 80*x*87 environment (*x*87 needed)

INSTRUCTION	PARAMETERS	OPCODE
FSTENV		9B D9 /6

SUMMARY

FSTENV is a mnemonic that is expanded by most 80*x*86 assemblers to

        FWAIT
        FNSTENV

FNSTENV on the 80287, 80387, and i486 normally waits for the processor extension to become idle before saving the environment. However, it does not check for 80*x*87 exceptions. Using FSTENV causes the implicit FWAIT to report any pending 80*x*87 exceptions. See the description of FNSTENV for further details.

EXAMPLES

FSTENV save_env

FSTSW: Store 80*x*87 status word (*x*87 needed)

INSTRUCTION	PARAMETERS	OPCODE
FSTSW m16		9B DD /7
FSTSW AX		9B DF E0

SUMMARY
FSTSW is a mnemonic that is expanded by most 80*x*86 assemblers to

> FWAIT
> FNSTSW

On the 80287, 80387, and i486, FNSTSW normally waits for the processor extension to become idle before storing the FSW register. However, it does not check for 80*x*87 exceptions. Using FSTSW causes the implicit FWAIT to report any pending 80*x*87 exceptions. See the description of FNSTSW for further details.

EXAMPLES
```
FSTSW    AX              ; Special form (unavailable on the 8087)
FSTSW    stat            ; Available in all implementations
```

FSTP: Pop 80x87 stack to real storage (*x87* needed)

INSTRUCTION	PARAMETERS	OPCODE
FSTP m32	dst ≡ m32	D9 /3
FSTP m64	dst ≡ m64	DD /3
FSTP m80	dst ≡ m80	DB /7
FSTP ST(n)	dst ≡ ST(n)	DD D8+n

SUMMARY

FSTP pops the floating point value in the top element of the 80x87 stack into a SINGLE, DOUBLE, or EXTENDED storage area in memory. If the operand is of the form ST(n), the top element is copied to the nth register from the top of the 80x87 stack. Since the top-of-stack pointer (TOP) is incremented as a result of the pop, note that TOP + n is computed *prior* to the increment.

If the stack is empty (i.e., FTAG[TOP] is marked EMPTY) the INVALID_FOP exception is signaled. On the 80387 and i486 the STF flag is also set. This flag lets the INVALID_FOP handler distinguish the cause of the invalid operation. If INVALID_FOP processing is masked, the destination is initialized to the real indefinite.

The 80x87 flags C0, C2, and C3 are set to an *undefined* state after FSTP executes. If the FIE and STF flags are set (indicating a stack fault), flag C1 is set to 0 to indicate a stack underflow. If the operation results in a PRECISION exception (i.e., the FPE flag is set), condition code C1 is set to 1 if the rounding is upward; if it is downward, it is set to 0.

OPERATION

```
check_TS_EM();            /* see page 248 */
check_BUSY();             /* see page 248 */
check_ERROR();            /* see page 249 */
save_x87_instr_ptr();     /* see page 249 */

dst = pop_FSTK()
```

EXAMPLES

```
FSTP      ST(2)           ; ST(2) = ST(0)
                          ; TOP = TOP+1
FST       var             ; var = ST(0)
                          ; TOP = TOP+1
```

FSUB[R]: Subtract real and 80x87 stack-top (x87 needed)

INSTRUCTION	PARAMETERS	OPCODE
FSUB m32	dst ≡ ST(0), src = m32	D8 /4
FSUB m64	dst ≡ ST(0), src = m64	DC /4
FSUB ST,ST(*n*)	dst ≡ ST(0), src = ST(*n*)	D8 E0+*n*
FSUB ST(*n*),ST	dst ≡ ST(*n*), src = ST(0)	DC E8+*n*
FSUBR m32	dst ≡ ST(0), src = m32	D8 /5
FSUBR m64	dst ≡ ST(0), src = m64	DC /5
FSUBR ST,ST(*n*)	dst ≡ ST(0), src = ST(*n*)	D8 E8+*n*
FSUBR ST(*n*),ST	dst ≡ ST(*n*), src = ST(0)	DC E0+*n*

SUMMARY

FSUB subtracts src from dst; FSUBR (subtract reversed) subtracts dst from src. In both cases the result is stored back in the destination operand (dst). Note that the destination is limited to either the 80x87 stack-top, or one of the registers in the 80x87 stack.

If the src operand is either SINGLE or DOUBLE, it is automatically converted to EXTENDED before being operated on. As always, the number of significant bits in the stored result depends on the effective precision specified by the PC control bits. Result rounding is done using the current RC setting.

The 80x87 flags C0, C2, and C3 are set to an *undefined* state after FSUB[R] executes. If the FIE and STF flags are set (indicating a stack fault), flag C1 is set to 0 to indicate a stack underflow. If the operation results in a PRECISION exception (i.e., the FPE flag is set), condition code C1 is set to 1 if the rounding is upward; if it is downward, it is set to 0.

OPERATION
FSUB :
```
check_TS_EM();              /* see page 248 */
check_BUSY();               /* see page 248 */
check_ERROR();              /* see page 249 */
save_x87_instr_ptr();       /* see page 249 */

dst = dst - (EXTENDED) src
```

FSUBR :
```
check_TS_EM();              /* see page 248 */
check_BUSY();               /* see page 248 */
check_ERROR();              /* see page 249 */
save_x87_instr_ptr();       /* see page 249 */
```

dst = (EXTENDED) src - dst

EXAMPLE
FSUB   ST, ST(4)   ; ST(0) = ST(0) - ST(4)

ASSEMBLER USAGE NOTE
1. Assemblers like Microsoft MASM and Borland TASM allow the mnemonic
   FSUB
   without any arguments. The purpose is to simulate a classical stack subtract;
   that is, pop the top two stack elements, compute their difference, and push
   the result. See the *Assembler Usage Notes* of the FSUBP instruction
   (following) for a description of how this is achieved.

FSUB[R]P: Subtract real and 80x87 stack-top and pop (x87 needed)

INSTRUCTION	PARAMETERS	OPCODE
FSUBP ST(n),ST		DE E8+n
FSUBRP ST(n),ST		DE E0+n

SUMMARY

FSUBP (subtract and pop) subtracts the stack-top value from the nth register relative to the stack-top (i.e., ST(n)); FSUBRP (subtract reversed and pop) subtracts the nth register from the stack-top. In both cases the result is stored back in ST(n). The stack is popped after the subtraction result is stored.

The 80x87 flags C0, C2, and C3 are set to an *undefined* state after FSUB[R]P executes. If the FIE and STF flags are set (indicating a stack fault), flag C1 is set to 0 to indicate a stack underflow. If the operation results in a PRECISION exception (i.e., the FPE flag is set), condition code C1 is set to 1 if the rounding is upward; if it is downward, it is set to 0.

OPERATION
FSUBP :
```
check_TS_EM();              /* see page 248 */
check_BUSY();              /* see page 248 */
check_ERROR();             /* see page 249 */
save_x87_instr_ptr();      /* see page 249 */

ST(n) = ST(n) - ST(0);
pop_FSTK();  /* Discard subtrahend */
```

FSUBRP :
```
check_TS_EM();              /* see page 248 */
check_BUSY();              /* see page 248 */
check_ERROR();             /* see page 249 */
save_x87_instr_ptr();      /* see page 249 */

ST(n) = ST(0) - ST(n);
pop_FSTK();  /* Discard minuend */
```

EXAMPLE
```
; Pop top two stack elements, subtract top from next element, and push result
FSUBP    ST(1), ST
```

ASSEMBLER USAGE NOTE

1. Assemblers like Microsoft MASM and Borland TASM allow the mnemonic
   FSUB
   without any arguments. This is equivalent to
   FSUBP ST(1), ST
   that is, the result of subtracting the stack-top from the next element is placed
   in the next element. Then the stack is popped, thus making the register
   storing the difference the new stack-top. This simulates a classical stack
   subtract.

FTST: Compare 80*x*87 stack-top with 0.0 (*x*87 needed)

INSTRUCTION	PARAMETERS	OPCODE
FTST		D9 E4

SUMMARY
FTST performs an ordered compare of the 80*x*87 stack-top with the constant 0.0. The result of the comparison sets the 80*x*87 flags C0, C2, and C3. If either operand is a SNaN, a QNaN, or if the 80*x*87 stack is empty (i.e., FTAG[TOP] is marked EMPTY), an INVALID_FOP is signaled and the comparison result flags are set to "unordered." On the 80387 and i486, an undefined-format operand (e.g., a pseudozero or an unnormal) also causes the exception condition just described. These later implementations also define the STF flag to distinguish between a stack fault and an invalid operand: in the case of a stack fault, STF is set to 1, otherwise it is cleared. Furthermore, the C1 flag is set to 0 (indicating a stack underflow).

OPERATION
```
check_TS_EM();              /* see page 248 */
check_BUSY();               /* see page 248 */
check_ERROR();              /* see page 249 */
save_x87_instr_ptr();       /* see page 249 */

if ( ST(0) > 0.0 )
{   C3 = 0;   C2 = 0;   C0 = 0;
}
else if ( ST(0) < 0.0 )
{   C3 = 0;   C2 = 0;   C0 = 1;
}
else if ( ST(0) == 0.0 )
{   C3 = 1;   C2 = 0;   C0 = 0;
}
else /* ST(0) in not numeric */
{   C3 = 1;   C2 = 1;   C0 = 1;
    signal_87(INVALID_FOP);     /* see page 255 */
}
```

EXAMPLE
FTST

NOTES

1. FTST always signals an INVALID_FOP if either operand is a NaN. The IEEE Std. 754, however, requires support for comparisons that do not signal an exception when comparing NaNs. For general unordered compare, use the FUCOM instruction. This instruction does not signal a fault when one of the operands is a quiet NaN.

2. FTST is special case of the FCOM instruction. See this instruction's definition for a description of how to branch based on the result of the FTST.

FUCOM: Compare unordered 80x87 stack-top with register (80387 and i486 only)

INSTRUCTION	PARAMETERS	OPCODE
FUCOM ST(*n*)		DD E0+*n*

SUMMARY

FUCOM performs an unordered compare of the 80x87 stack-top with ST(*n*). The result of the comparison sets the 80x87 flags C0, C2, and C3. If either operand is a SNaN, or if the 80x87 stack is empty (i.e., FTAG[TOP] is marked EMPTY), an INVALID_FOP is signaled and the comparison result flags are set to "unordered." On the 80387 and i486, an undefined-format operand (e.g., a pseudozero or an unnormal) also causes the exception condition just described. These later implementations also define the STF flag to distinguish between a stack fault and an invalid operand: in the case of a stack fault, STF is set to 1, otherwise it is cleared. Furthermore, the C1 flag is set to 0 (indicating a stack underflow).

OPERATION

```
check_TS_EM();              /* see page 248 */
check_BUSY();               /* see page 248 */
check_ERROR();              /* see page 249 */
save_x87_instr_ptr();       /* see page 249 */

if ( ST(0) > (EXTENDED) ST(n) )
{   C3 = 0;   C2 = 0;   C0 = 0;
}
else if ( ST(0) < (EXTENDED) ST(n) )
{   C3 = 0;   C2 = 0;   C0 = 1;
}
else if ( ST(0) == (EXTENDED) ST(n) )
{   C3 = 1;   C2 = 0;   C0 = 0;
}
else /* ST(0) and src are not comparable */
{   C3 = 1;   C2 = 1;   C0 = 1;
    if ( «ST(0) is an SNaN» || «ST(n) is an SNaN» )
       signal_87(INVALID_FOP);     /* see page 255 */
}
```

EXAMPLE

```
FUCOM   ST(2)                    ; Compare ST against ST(2)
```

NOTES

1. FUCOM only signals an INVALID_FOP if either operand is an SNaN. The FCOM instruction traps on both QNaNs and SNaNs.

2. The bit positions occupied by C3, C2, and C0 in the status register FSW are such that the instruction sequence
   FSTSW AX
   SAHF
   copies C3 to ZF, C2 to PF, and C0 to CF, where ZF, PF, and CF are $80x86$ arithmetic flags. This allows the use of normal conditional branch instructions to check the result of floating point comparisions. For example,
   ; jump to *lab* if ST(0) > *src* operand
   JA lab   ; check that CF and ZF are 0

   ; jump to *lab* if ST(0) < *src* operand
   JB lab   ; check that CF is 1

   ; jump to *lab* if ST(0) == *src* operand
   JE lab   ; check that ZF is 1

   ; jump to *lab* if ST(0) and *src* are not comparable
   JP lab   ; check that PF is 1

ASSEMBLER USAGE NOTE

1. Most $80x86$ assemblers allow the mnemonic
   FUCOM
   without any arguments. This is equivalent to
   FUCOM ST(1)

FUCOMP[P]: Compare unordered 80x87 stack-top with register, and pop (80387 and i486 only)

INSTRUCTION	PARAMETERS	OPCODE
FUCOMP ST(*n*)		DD E8+*n*
FUCOMPP		DA E9

SUMMARY

Both FUCOMP and FUCOMPP perform an unordered compare of the 80x87 stack-top with ST(*n*). The result of the comparison sets the 80x87 flags C0, C2, and C3. FUCOMP pops the 80x87 stack after the comparison; FCOMPP pops the top two stack elements. Note that FUCOMPP compares ST with ST(*n*).

If either operand is an SNaN, or if the 80x87 stack is empty (i.e., FTAG[TOP] is marked EMPTY), an INVALID_FOP is signaled and the comparison result flags are set to "unordered." On the 80387 and i486, an undefined-format operand (e.g., a pseudozero or an unnormal) also causes the exception condition just described. These later implementations also define the STF flag to distinguish between a stack fault and an invalid operand: in the case of a stack fault, STF is set to 1, otherwise it is cleared. Furthermore, the C1 flag is set to 0 (indicating a stack underflow).

OPERATION
FUCOMP:
```
check_TS_EM();            /* see page 248 */
check_BUSY();             /* see page 248 */
check_ERROR();            /* see page 249 */
save_x87_instr_ptr();     /* see page 249 */
```

```
if ( ST(0) > (EXTENDED) src )
{   C3 = 0;   C2 = 0;   C0 = 0;
}
else if ( ST(0) < (EXTENDED) src )
{   C3 = 0;   C2 = 0;   C0 = 1;
}
else if ( ST(0) == (EXTENDED) src )
{   C3 = 1;   C2 = 0;   C0 = 0;
}
else /* ST(0) and src are not comparable */
{   C3 = 1;   C2 = 1;   C0 = 1;
    if ( «ST(0) is an SNaN» || «ST(n) is an SNaN» )
        signal_87(INVALID_FOP);      /* see page 255 */
}
/* Discard stack top */
pop_FSTK();                          /* see page 247 */
```

FUCOMPP:
```
check_TS_EM();                       /* see page 248 */
check_BUSY();                        /* see page 248 */
check_ERROR();                       /* see page 249 */
save_x87_instr_ptr();                /* see page 249 */

if ( ST(0) > ST(1) )
{   C3 = 0;   C2 = 0;   C0 = 0;
}
else if ( ST(0) < ST(1) )
{   C3 = 0;   C2 = 0;   C0 = 1;
}
else if ( ST(0) == ST(1) )
{   C3 = 1;   C2 = 0;   C0 = 0;
}
else /* ST(0) and ST(1) are not comparable */
{   C3 = 1;   C2 = 1;   C0 = 1;
    if ( «ST(0) is an SNaN» || «ST(n) is an SNaN» )
        signal_87(INVALID_FOP);      /* see page 255 */
}
/* Discard top two stack elements */
pop_FSTK();                          /* see page 247 */
pop_FSTK();
```

EXAMPLES

```
FUCOMP  ST(2)          ; Compare ST against ST(2), then pop stack
FUCOMPP                ; Compare ST against ST(1), then discard ST and
                         ST(1)
```

NOTES

1. FUCOMP[P] only signals an INVALID_FOP if either operand is an SNaN. The FCOMP[P] instruction traps on both QNaNs and SNaNs.

2. The bit positions occupied by C3, C2, and C0 in the status register FSW are such that the instruction sequence
FSTSW AX
SAHF
copies C3 to ZF, C2 to PF, and C0 to CF, where ZF, PF, and CF are $80x86$ arithmetic flags. See the description of the FUCOM instruction above to see how comparison results can be checked using these flags.

ASSEMBLER USAGE NOTE
 1. Most assemblers allow the mnemonic
FUCOMP
without any arguments. This is equivalent to
FUCOMP ST(1)

FWAIT: Wait until BUSY pin inactive

INSTRUCTION	PARAMETERS	OPCODE
FWAIT		9B

SUMMARY

FWAIT is an assembler mnemonic equivalent to the WAIT instruction. See the description of the WAIT instruction (page 579) for details.

FXAM: Examine 80x87 stack top (x87 needed)

INSTRUCTION	PARAMETERS	OPCODE
FXAM		D9 E5

SUMMARY
FXAM examines the contents of the 80x87 stack-top, and sets conditions codes
C3, C2, and C0 according to the mapping shown in the table below.

Object type	Flag settings		
	C3	C2	C0
Unsupported	0	0	0
NaN	0	0	1
Valid value	0	1	0
Infinity	0	1	1
Zero	1	0	0
Empty	1	0	1
Denormal	1	1	0

The sign bit of ST is copied to condition code C1.

OPERATION
```
check_TS_EM();          /* see page 248 */
check_BUSY();           /* see page 248 */
check_ERROR();          /* see page 249 */
save_x87_instr_ptr();   /* see page 249 */
```

« set condition codes according to table above »

EXAMPLE
FXAM

FXCH: Exchange 80*x*87 register with 80*x*87 stack top (*x*87 needed)

INSTRUCTION	PARAMETERS	OPCODE
FXCH ST(*n*)		D9 C8+*n*

SUMMARY
FXCH exchanges the contents of the 80*x*87 stack-top with the nth register relative to the stack-top (i.e., ST(*n*)).

OPERATION
```
check_TS_EM();            /* see page 248 */
check_BUSY();             /* see page 248 */
check_ERROR();            /* see page 249 */
save_x87_instr_ptr();     /* see page 249 */

tmp = ST(0);
tmp_tag = FTAG[TOP];

ST(0) = ST(n);
FTAG[TOP] = FTAG[(TOP+n) & 7];

ST(n) = tmp;
FTAG[(TOP+n) & 7] = tmp_tag;
```

EXAMPLES
```
FXCH      ST(7)                    ; ST(0) ↔ ST(7)
FXCH                               ; ST(0) ↔ ST(1)
```

ASSEMBLER USAGE NOTE
1. For notational convenience assemblers like Microsoft MASM and Borland TASM allow the user to specify FXCH without an operand. This instruction simply swaps the top two stack elements; that is,

   ```
   FXCH ST(1)
   ```

FXTRACT: Extract exponent and significand (*x*87 needed)

INSTRUCTION	PARAMETERS	OPCODE
FXTRACT		D9 F4

SUMMARY

FXTRACT pops the 80*x*87 stack breaks the popped value into two values: its true exponent and its significand. The true exponent (rather than the biased exponent) is pushed onto the stack as an integer (represented in EXTENDED format). This is followed by a push of the significand component. The significand (including the sign bit) is a bitwise copy of the original significand. In particular, the significand's true exponent is always 0, even if can be normalized (because the original number was a denormal or unnormal).

It is possible for the 80*x*87 stack to overflow when the significand is pushed. If this happens the INVALID_FOP exception is signaled. On the 80387 and i486 the STF flag is also set. If INVALID_FOP processing is masked, the real indefinite value is pushed, overwriting a nonempty register location.

FXTRACTs treatment of zero, infinities, and NaNs different in the 8087 and 80287 from that of the 80387 and i486. The 80387/i486 behavior conforms with that of the IEEE Std. 754-recommended function logb. The purpose of this function is to report the true (unbiased) exponent of its argument. FXTRACT implements a superset of this function in that it reports the exponent and the significand.

Zero arithmetic: If the value being converted is ±0.0, the 8087 and 80287 stores a zero for the exponent (in ST(1)). The 80387 and i486, however, signal the ZERO_FOP exception. If processing of ZERO_FOP exceptions is masked, $-\infty$ is stored in ST(1).

Infinity arithmetic: If the value being converted is ±∞, the 8087 and 80287 signal the INVALID_FOP exception. The 80387 and i486 store +∞ in ST(1).

NaN *arithmetic:* If the value being converted is a NaN the 8087 and 80287 signal the INVALID_FOP exception. The 80387 and i486 store the real indefinite in ST(1).

OPERATION
```
check_TS_EM();                    /* see page 248 */
check_BUSY();                     /* see page 248 */
check_ERROR();                    /* see page 249 */
save_x87_instr_ptr();             /* see page 249 */

v = pop_FSTK();
push_FSTK( «true exponent of v» );
push_FSTK( «significand of v» );
```

EXAMPLE
FXTRACT

FYL2X: Compute y*log₂ x (*x87* needed)

INSTRUCTION	PARAMETERS	OPCODE
FYL2X		D9 F1

SUMMARY
FYL2X pops ST and ST(1) and pushes the value ST(1) * $\log_2$ ST, where ST and ST(1) represent the values of the popped elements. The $80x87$ flags C0, C2, and C3 are set to an *undefined* state after F2XM1 executes. If the operation results in a PRECISION exception (i.e., the FPE flag is set), condition code C1 is set to 1 if the rounding is upward; if it is downward, it is set to 0.

If ST is less than zero in value, INVALID_FOP is signaled.

OPERATION
```
check_TS_EM();              /* see page 248 */
check_BUSY();               /* see page 248 */
check_ERROR();              /* see page 249 */
save_x87_instr_ptr();       /* see page 249 */

x = pop_FSTK();             /* see page 247 */
y = pop_FSTK();
push_FSTK( y * log₂ x )
```

EXAMPLE
```
FYL2X
```

FYL2XP1: Compute y*log$_2$ x (*x87* needed)

INSTRUCTION	PARAMETERS	OPCODE
FYL2XP1		D9 F9

SUMMARY

FYL2XP1 pops ST and ST(1) and pushes the value ST(1) * log$_2$ (ST + 1), where ST and ST(1) represent the values of the popped elements. The 80*x*87 flags C0, C2, and C3 are set to an *undefined* state after F2XM1 executes. If the operation results in a PRECISION exception (i.e., the FPE flag is set), condition code C1 is set to 1 if the rounding is upward; if it is downward, it is set to 0.

If the absolute value of ST is not less than $1 - \text{sqrt}(2)/2$, INVALID_FOP is signaled. The principal use of FYL2XP1 is in computing the logarithm of a number that is very close to 1 with better accuracy than FYL2X.

OPERATION

```
check_TS_EM();              /* see page 248 */
check_BUSY();               /* see page 248 */
check_ERROR();              /* see page 249 */
save_x87_instr_ptr();       /* see page 249 */

x = pop_FSTK();             /* see page 247 */
y = pop_FSTK();
push_FSTK( y * log₂ (x+1) )
```

EXAMPLE

```
FYL2XP1
```

GS: (prefix): Use GS for memory access (376, 386, 486 only)

INSTRUCTION	PARAMETERS	OPCODE
GS:		65

SUMMARY

An instruction making a memory reference always uses an implied segment register. The segment register implied depends on the way the memory offset is generated (see §2.18 on page 185 for more on this). Specifying the GS: override prefix changes the segment register used to GS (and the segment descriptor register to GS_desc.) This change is effective *only* for the instruction immediately following the GS: prefix.

Some string operations (e.g., MOVS*x*) have two memory operands. The override prefix only changes the DS in the source operand; that is, the source operand becomes GS:[E]SI. The implied use of ES for the destination operand is not changeable.

The GS segment register, and so the GS: prefix, is only supported on the 80376, 80386, and i486.

EXAMPLE
; Use GS instead of SS (the default) to fetch the address of the branch target.
; Note that the branch itself is always via CS.
JMP WORD PTR GS:[ESP]

NOTES
1. Segment override prefixes apply only to memory data references; instruction fetches are always done with respect to CS. Furthermore, the stack manipulation instructions (i.e., PUSH, PUSHA, POP, POPA, PUSHF, POPF, CALL, RET, INT, and IRET) always reference the stack via SS. (The segment used by a PUSH or POP whose *operand* is a memory variable can be overridden, as can the pointer operand in an *indirect* CALL or JMP.) Segment override prefix use in front of instructions where it is not meaningful is unconditionally ignored.

2. Segment override prefixes for each of the other segment registers (CS, DS, ES, FS, and SS) are also supported. Apart from these prefixes the 80*x*86 has prefixes that implement string instructions (REP*x*) and perform atomic read-modify-write of memory locations (LOCK). Two additional prefixes, the

"address size prefix" and "operand size prefix," are also used on the 80376, 80386, and i486 to encode these later processors' 32-bit instruction extensions.

HLT: Halt processor

INSTRUCTION	PARAMETERS	OPCODE
HLT		F4

SUMMARY

HLT stops all processor execution until an unmasked interrupt or NMI condition is detected. When detected, the appropriate interrupt handler is invoked, with the return address pointing at the instruction immediately following the HLT. Thus, HLT may be viewed as a "pause for interrupt" instruction. HLT is a privileged instruction.

OPERATION

```
if ( CPL != 0 )
   signal_fault(GP, 0);

/* Wait for external interrupt (NMI or normal INTR). */
while ( ! external_interrupt() )        /* see page 166 */
   continue;
```

EXAMPLE

```
HLT
```

NOTES

1. HLT is always executable in REAL mode, since REAL mode code can be viewed as executing with CPL set to 0.

2. HLT will always signal a GP fault in VM86 mode. (Recall that VM86 mode executes with CPL set to 3.)

IDIV: Signed divide

INSTRUCTION	PARAMETERS	OPCODE
IDIV r/m8	quo ≡ AL, rem ≡ AH, dvd = AX, dvr = r/m8, os = *8*	F6 /7
IDIV r/m16	quo ≡ AX, rem ≡ DX, dvd = DX:AX, dvr = r/m16, os = *16*	F7 /7
IDIV r/m32	quo ≡ EAX, rem ≡ EDX, dvd = EDX:EAX, dvr = r/m32, os = *32*	F7 /7

SUMMARY

IDIV divides the signed dividend dvd by the signed divisor dvr and stores the quotient in quo and the remainder in rem. Note that, except for the divisor, all operands are stored in fixed registers. For WORD and DWORD division, the dividend is stored in the register pair DX:AX or EDX:EAX, with DX and EDX storing the most significant bits.

OPERATION

```
/* All arithmetic flags are undefined after an IDIV */
OF = undefined
SF = undefined
ZF = undefined
AF = undefined
PF = undefined
CF = undefined

/* Compute quotient and remainder, checking for overflow and zero divide */
if ( dvr == 0 )
   signal_fault(DIVIDE);
result = dvd / dvr;
if ( result < 2^{os-1} || result > 2^{os-1}-1 )
   signal_fault(DIVIDE);

/* Store result */
quo = result
rem = dvd % dvr
```

EXAMPLES

```
IDIV    EAX              ; EAX = EDX:EAX / EAX
IDIV    BYTE PTR [ESI]   ; AL = AL / *( (BYTE *) ESI )
```

NOTES

1. The remainder always has the same sign as the dividend, and the absolute value of the remainder is always less than the absolute value of the divisor.

2. On an 8086, the DIVIDE exception is a *trap*: on entry to the exception
   handler, the return address points at the instruction following the IDIV. (On
   all other 80*x*86 implementations the return address points at the IDIV.)

3. On an 8086, an IDIV where the quotient is the smallest negative number (i.e.,
   0x80 for BYTE IDIV or 0x8000 for WORD IDIV) generates a DIVIDE
   exception. On other 80*x*86 implementations, the correct quotient is produced
   (and no exception is generated).

IMUL: Signed multiply

INSTRUCTION	PARAMETERS	OPCODE
IMUL r/m8	prd ≡ AX, mnd = AL, mpr = r/m8, os = *8*	F6 /5
IMUL r/m16	prd ≡ DX:AX, mnd = AX, mpr = r/m16, os = *16*	F7 /5
IMUL r/m32	prd ≡ EDX:EAX, mnd = EAX, mpr = r/m32, os = *32*	F7 /5
IMUL r, r/m, imm	prd ≡ r, mnd = r/m, mpr = imm, os ∈ *{16,32}*	69 *{16,32}*
IMUL r, r/m, imm8	prd ≡ r, mnd = r/m, mpr = signex(imm8), os ∈ *{16,32}*	6B *{16,32}*
IMUL r, r/m	prd ≡ r, mnd = r, mpr = r/m, os ∈ *{16,32}*	0F AF *{16,32}*

SUMMARY

IMUL generates the product of a signed multiplicand (mnd) and a signed multiplier (mpr) and stores the result in the product prd. prd must always be a register or register pair.

OPERATION

result = mnd × mpr;
if (*result* < -2^{os-1} || *result* > $2^{os-1}-1$)
{   CF = 1;
    OF = 1;
}
else
{   CF = 0;
    OF = 0;
}

/* Set remaining flags */
SF = *undefined*
ZF = *undefined*
AF = *undefined*
PF = *undefined*
/* Store result */
prd = *result*;

EXAMPLES

IMUL   EAX   ; EDX:EAX = EAX * EAX
IMUL   BYTE PTR [ESI] ; AX = AL * *((BYTE *) ESI)

IN: Input from I/O port

INSTRUCTION	PARAMETERS	OPCODE
IN AL, imm8	dst ≡ AL, port = imm8, os = *8*	E4
IN AX/EAX, imm8	dst ≡ AX/EAX, port = imm8, os ∈ *{16,32}*	E5
IN AL, DX	dst ≡ AL, port = DX, os = *8*	EC
IN AX/EAX, DX	dst ≡ AX/EAX, port = DX, os ∈ *{16,32}*	ED

SUMMARY
IN reads a BYTE, WORD or DWORD (depending on **os**) from the I/O port addressed by port, and stores the result in AL, AX or EAX, respectively.

IN is an IOPL-sensitive instruction; that is, in PROTECTED or VM86 modes the I/O port read is done only if CPL <= IOPL. If CPL > IOPL a general protection fault is signaled if the active TSS is a TSS16. If the active TSS is a TSS32 (and CPL > IOPL), the I/O permission map entry for the I/O port named by DX determines whether the I/O port read is allowed. See §2.9 (page 118) for a description of the I/O permission map check algorithm.

OPERATION
```
/* Check if instruction execution is permitted. */
if ( CPL > IOPL  &&  mode != REAL )
{   if ( !IOPermission(port, os) )
       signal_fault(GP, 0);
}
switch (os)
{   case 8:        AL = *( (BYTEPORT *) port );
               break;
    case 16:       AX = *( (WORDPORT *) port);
               break;
    case 32:       EAX = *( (DWORDPORT *) port);
               break;
}
```

EXAMPLES
```
IN      EAX, DX          ; EAX = *( (DWORDPORT *) DX )
IN      AL, 200          ; AL = *( (BYTEPORT *) 200 )
```

INC: Increment by one

INSTRUCTION	PARAMETERS	OPCODE
INC r/m	dst ≡ r/m, os ∈ {8,16,32}	FE /0 {8}, FF /0 {16,32}
INC reg	dst ≡ reg, os ∈ {16,32}	40+reg {16,32}

SUMMARY

INC increments the dst operand by one. All arithmetic flags except CF are modified; CF is left unchanged. Nonarithmetic flags are not affected. An INC instruction with a memory operand is LOCKable.

OPERATION

result = dst + 1
/* Set arithmetic flags (except CF) */
$OF = result < -2^{os-1} \,||\, result > 2^{os-1}-1$
SF = dst⟨os-1⟩
ZF = result == 0
AF = dst⟨3:0⟩ $>_u$ 14
PF = evenParity(result)
/* Store result */
dst = result

EXAMPLES

```
INC      AX                      ; AX = AX + 1
INC      BYTE PTR [ESI]          ; *( (BYTE *) ESI )  += 1
```

INSB/INSD/INSW: Input from I/O port to string element (unavailable on the 8086)

INSTRUCTION	PARAMETERS	OPCODE
INSB	os = 8, as ∈ {16,32}	6C
INSW	os = 16, as ∈ {16,32}	6D
INSD	os = 32, as ∈ {16,32}	6D

SUMMARY

INS*x* reads a BYTE, WORD, or DWORD from the port pointed at by the DX register and stores it in the BYTE, WORD, or DWORD at offset EDI or offset DI of the segment named by the ES register. The operand size (*os*) attribute selects whether a BYTE, WORD, or DWORD participates, and the address size (*as*) attribute selects whether DI (*as* set to 16) or EDI (*as* set to 32) is used. After the store, EDI is incremented 2 or 4, depending on the operand size. Thus, repeated use of an INS*x* instruction copies data from an I/O port to a string in memory.

The INS*x* instructions are IOPL-sensitive; that is, in PROTECTED or VM86 modes the I/O port read is done only if CPL <= IOPL. If CPL > IOPL a general protection fault is signaled if the active TSS is a TSS16. If the active TSS is a TSS32 (and CPL > IOPL), the I/O permission map entry for the I/O port named by DX determines whether the I/O port read is allowed. See §2.9 (page 118) for a description of the I/O permission map check algorithm.

OPERATION

```
/* Check if instruction execution is permitted. */
if ( CPL > IOPL  &&  mode != REAL )
{   if ( !IOPermission(port, os) )
      signal_fault(GP, 0);
}

/* Checks passed: read I/O port */
dst = ( (as == 16) ? DI : EDI );
/* Read from port address into dst */
switch (os)
{   case 8:        *( (BYTE *) dst )  =  *( (BYTEPORT *) port );
                   break;
    case 16:       *( (WORD *) dst )  =  *( (WORDPORT *) port );
                   break;
    case 32:       *( (DWORD *) dst )  =  *( (DWORDPORT *) port );
                   break;
}
```

```
if ( as == 32 )  /* 32-bit addressing */
    EDI = dst + (DF ? -os/8 : os/8);
else /* as == 16 : 16-bit addressing */
    DI = dst + (DF ? -os/8 : os/8);
```

EXAMPLES
INSB
INSD

NOTES

1. The execution time of INS*x* depends on the current mode of the 80386, as follows. REAL mode: 15 clocks; VM86 mode: 29 clocks; PROTECTED mode: 9 clocks if CPL ≤ IOPL, 29 clocks if CPL > IOPL.

2. The INS*x* instructions are restricted forms of the REP INS*x* instructions. The REP form of the instructions repeatedly execute the specified INS*x* operation until ECX's value becomes zero. See the discussion of the REP prefix for more details.

ASSEMBLER USAGE NOTE

1. A segment override prefix, if applied to an INS*x* type instruction, is unconditionally ignored. The destination address must always be relative to the segment referenced by the ES segment register.

2. Address register selection (i.e., DI versus EDI) depends on the address size attribute. To ensure that an address size override prefix is generated (if needed), the assembler notation where explicit operands to INS*x* are provided is recommended. For example, a repeated INSD to ES:EDI should be encoded as follows
REP INS DWORD PTR [EDI]

INT: Generate software interrupt

INSTRUCTION	PARAMETERS	OPCODE
INT imm8	intnum = imm8	CD

SUMMARY

The INT instruction is used by software to signal any of the 256 interrupts supported by the 80x86 architecture. The number of the interrupt vector entry used to service the interrupt is encoded in the byte following the INT opcode.

As with all interrupts, an interrupt occurring while in VM86 mode is fielded using the PROTECTED mode interrupt vector. To allow for flags virtualization, the INT instruction is also IOPL-sensitive when executed in VM86 mode.

OPERATION

```
if ( mode == VM86  &&  CPL > IOPL )
   signal_fault(GP, 0);

software_interrupt(intnum);  /* see page 151 */
```

EXAMPLE

```
INT      22                          ; signal interrupt 22
```

ASSEMBLER USAGE NOTES

1. If the instruction

   ```
   INT      3
   ```

   is specified, an assembler will automatically encode it using the special one-byte INT 3 instruction opcode. The INT 3 instruction is described next.

INT 3: Signal code breakpoint

INSTRUCTION	PARAMETERS	OPCODE
INT 3		CC

SUMMARY
INT 3 is a single-byte opcode that generates an interrupt via vector entry 3. Unlike the two-byte INT *n* instruction described previously, INT 3 is not IOPL-sensitive in VM86 mode. As with all interrupts, an interrupt occurring while in VM86 mode is fielded using the PROTECTED-mode interrupt vector.

OPERATION
software_interrupt(3); /* see page 151 */

EXAMPLE
INT 3

NOTES
1. The main purpose of INT 3 is to set instruction breakpoints. This is done by replacing the first byte of the instruction to be breakpointed with INT 3. Should the instruction be executed, the INT 3 is signaled. All this assumes, of course, that a instruction breakpoint handler is available at vector entry 3.

2. On the 80386 and i486 the debug registers can be used as an alternate means of setting instruction breakpoints. This has the advantage that no code needs to be modified, thus making possible instruction breakpoints in ROM-based programs and simplifying such breakpoints in shared code. The disadvantage is that there are only a fixed number of breakpoint registers; using the INT 3 approach allows an indefinite number of instruction breakpoints.

INTO: Generate INT 4 on overflow

INSTRUCTION	PARAMETERS	OPCODE
INTO		CE

SUMMARY
INTO generates an interrupt via interrupt vector entry 4 if the overflow flag OF is set. If OF is clear, INTO does nothing. As with all interrupts, an INTO occurring while in VM86 mode is fielded using the PROTECTED mode interrupt vector.

OPERATION
```
if ( OF )
   software_interrupt(4);  /* see page 151 */
```

EXAMPLE
```
INTO
```

INVD: Invalidate instruction/data cache (486 only)

INSTRUCTION	PARAMETERS	OPCODE
INVD		0F 08

SUMMARY

INVD, defined only on the i486, unconditionally invalidates the entire on-chip cache. The i486 also signals the external memory system to flush external caches (if any). See also the definition of the WBINVD instruction on page 581. INVD is a privileged instruction.

OPERATION

```
if ( CPL != 0 )
   signal_fault(GP, 0);

/* == Clear all valid bits in the i486 cache.  The i486 cache is described on page 103. == */
for ( set_sel = 0;  set_sel <= 127;  set_sel++ )
   for ( set_elem = 0;  set_elem <= 3;  set_elem++ )
      cache_486[set_sel][set_elem].Valid = 0;
```

EXAMPLE

```
INVD
```

INVLPG: Invalidate TLB entry (486 only)

INSTRUCTION	PARAMETERS	OPCODE
INVLPG m	src = m	0F 01 /7

SUMMARY
INVLPG, defined only on the i486, looks up the paging TLB using the memory address (*src*) specified as the instruction operand. If there is no TLB entry to map the operand's linear address, no action is taken. However, if a mapping entry is in the TLB, it is invalidated. INVLPG is a privileged instruction.

OPERATION
```
if ( CPL != 0 )
   signal_fault(GP, 0);

lin_addr = « linear address of m » ;

/* == Check the TLB for a linear address match.  The TLB data structure is defined on
      page 510. == */
set_sel = lin_addr⟨14:12⟩;
for ( set_elem = 0;  set_elem <= 3;  set_elem++ )
   if ( TLB_x86[set_sel][set_elem].LinAddr == lin_addr⟨31:15⟩ )
      TLB_x86[set_sel][set_elem].V = 0;
```

EXAMPLE
INVLPG region

NOTE
1. The memory operand *m* to INVLPG is encoded using normal MOD/RM encoding. This allows a general register to be specified as the operand. If an attempt is made to execute an INVLPG with a register operand, an INVALID_INSTR exception is signaled.

IRET/IRETD (protected): Return from interrupt handler or task

INSTRUCTION	PARAMETERS	OPCODE
IRET	os = *16*, as ∈ {16,32}	CF
IRETD	os = *32*, as ∈ {16,32}	CF

SUMMARY

In PROTECTED mode IRET or IRETD can be used to either return from an interrupt handler or to return from a task switch. A task switch return is signified if the NT flag is set when IRET (or IRETD) is executed. For a description of these instructions when executed in REAL or VM86 modes, see the following instruction description.

When used to return from interrupt, IRET pops WORD-sized quantities from the stack, whereas IRETD pops DWORD-sized quantities. Since the stack is not used in when performing a task return, IRET and IRETD perform the same actions when executed with NT == 1.

OPERATION

```
if ( mode == REAL || mode == VM86 )
    « see IRET/IRETD (REAL/VM86) instruction description below »

/* PROTECTED mode IRET definition */
/* == Reallow NMI interrupts, in case this is an exit from NMI handler. == */
NMI_handler_active = FALSE;

if ( NT )  /* nested task flag (EFLAGS⟨14⟩) set: task return */
    exit_task();  /* see page 142 */

else  /* NT == 0 : return from interrupt procedure */
{  /* == Pop CS:(E)IP off stack == */
    if ( os == 32 )       /* Execute next instruction at offset */
        EIP = popOS();
    else  /* os == 16: use low 16 bits only */
        EIP = popOS() & 0xFFFF;
    CS = popOS();

    /* == Pop flags image into a temporary register. == */
    flg = popOS();
```

```
/* == Store flags bits based on EFLAGS update rules. == */
if ( os == 32 )              /* Update VM and RF if IRETD instruction */
{   VM = flg⟨17⟩;
    RF = flg⟨16⟩;
}
EFLAGS⟨15⟩ = 0;         /* Bit 15 of EFLAGS is always 0 */
NT = flg<14>;
if ( CPL == 0 )            /* IOPL update is privileged */
    IOPL = flg⟨13:12⟩;
OF = flg⟨11⟩;
DF = flg⟨10⟩;
IF = flg⟨9⟩;
TF = flg⟨8⟩;
SF = flg⟨7⟩;
ZF = flg⟨6⟩;
EFLAGS⟨5⟩ = 0;          /* Bit 5 of EFLAGS is always 0 */
AF = flg⟨4⟩;
EFLAGS⟨3⟩ = 0;          /* Bit 3 of EFLAGS is always 0 */
PF = flg⟨2⟩;
EFLAGS⟨1⟩ = 1;          /* Bit 1 of EFLAGS is always 1 */
CF = flg⟨0⟩;

/* ==If caller's EFLAGS indicates it was a VM86 task, pop segment selectors and load
       using VM86 semantics. == */
if ( VM )
{   tmpESP = pop4();   /* Pop ESP into a temp, to allow following pops */
    SS = (WORD) pop4(); /* Use low WORD as SELECTOR, discard high WORD */
    ES = (WORD) pop4(); /* Use low WORD as SELECTOR, discard high WORD */
    DS = (WORD) pop4(); /* Use low WORD as SELECTOR, discard high WORD */
    FS = (WORD) pop4(); /* Use low WORD as SELECTOR, discard high WORD */
    GS = (WORD) pop4(); /* Use low WORD as SELECTOR, discard high WORD */
    ESP = tmpESP;

    CPL = 3; /* VM-86 tasks always execute with CPL set to 3 */

    /* == Initialize descriptors corresponding to segment registers using VM-86 rules. ==
         */
    init_VM_desc(); /* see page 139 */
}

/* == If caller's VM bit is clear, treat popped CS:[E]IP as branch target of a
       PROTECTED mode intersegment (far) RETurn. == */
else /* mode == PROTECTED */
{   /* == Check if caller's SELECTOR is null or has bad CPL. == */
    if ( nullSel(CS) || CPL > CS.RPL )
        signal_fault(GP, CS & 0xFFFC);

    if ( CS⟨1:0⟩ == CPL ) /* IRET to caller at same privilege level */
        CS_desc = load_CS(CS, FALSE);
    else  /* interlevel IRET */
    { DWORD callerESP;
```

```
/* == Setup caller's CPL, then check caller's CS's validity == */
CPL = CS.RPL;
CS_desc = load_CS(CS, FALSE);

/* == Read caller's SS:(E)SP off current stack, and check it == */
callerESP = popOS();  /* save in temp so that SS can be popped */
SS = popOS()
SS_desc = load_SS(SS, FALSE);

/* == Setup caller's ESP, taking into account the "B" bit == */
if ( SS_desc.DefaultAttr )  /* 32 bit addressing */
   ESP = callerESP;
else
   SP = (WORD) callerESP;

/* == Invalidate ES, DS, FS, GS if they are too privileged for caller's environment
      == */
if ( ES_desc.DPL < CPL )
   ES_desc.Valid = FALSE;
if ( DS_desc.DPL < CPL )
   DS_desc.Valid = FALSE;
if ( FS_desc.DPL < CPL )
   FS_desc.Valid = FALSE;
if ( GS_desc.DPL < CPL )
   GS_desc.Valid = FALSE;
   }
 }
}
```

EXAMPLES
IRETD
IRET

NOTES

1. Since the restart flag RF is in the high-order WORD of EFLAGS, an IRET can never set it. Therefore, a debug fault handler that makes use of RF should always use IRETD.

2. When a nonmaskable interrupt (NMI) handler is entered, further NMIs are disabled until the handler exits via an IRET or IRETD.

IRET/IRETD (REAL/VM86): Return from interrupt handler

INSTRUCTION	PARAMETERS	OPCODE
IRET	os = *16*, as ∈ {16,32}	CF
IRETD	os = *32*, as ∈ {16,32}	CF

SUMMARY
In REAL and VM86 modes IRET or IRETD is used to return from an interrupt handler. For a description of these instructions when executed in PROTECTED mode, see the previous instruction description.

To support flags virtualization, IRET and IRETD are both IOPL-sensitive when executed in VM86 mode. The instruction is always executable in REAL mode.

When used to return from interrupt, IRET pops WORD-sized quantities from the stack, whereas IRETD pops DWORD-sized quantities.

OPERATION
```
if ( mode == PROTECTED )
    « see IRET/IRETD (protected) instruction description above »

/* REAL/VM86 mode IRET definition */
if ( mode == VM86  &&  CPL > IOPL )
    signal_fault(GP, 0);

/* == Reallow NMI interrupts, in case this is an exit from NMI handler. == */
NMI_handler_active = FALSE;

/* == Pop CS:(E)IP off stack == */
if ( os == 32 )          /* Execute next instruction at offset */
    EIP = popOS();
else  /* os == 16: use low 16 bits only */
    EIP = popOS() & 0xFFFF;
CS = popOS();

/* == Pop flags image into a temporary register. == */
flg = popOS();

/* == Store flags bits based on flag update rules. == */
if ( os == 32 )  /* Update RF if IRETD instruction (leave VM unmodified) */
    RF = flg⟨16⟩;
```

```
EFLAGS⟨15⟩ = 0;              /* Bit 15 of EFLAGS is always 0 */
NT = flg⟨14⟩;
if ( CPL == 0 )             /* IOPL update is privileged */
   IOPL = flg⟨13:12⟩;
OF = flg⟨11⟩;
DF = flg⟨10⟩;
IF = flg⟨9⟩;
TF = flg⟨8⟩;
SF = flg⟨7⟩;
ZF = flg⟨6⟩;
EFLAGS⟨5⟩ = 0;   /* Bit 5 of EFLAGS is always 0 */
AF = flg⟨4⟩;
EFLAGS⟨3⟩ = 0;   /* Bit 3 of EFLAGS is always 0 */
PF = flg⟨2⟩;
EFLAGS⟨1⟩ = 1;   /* Bit 1 of EFLAGS is always 1 */
CF = flg⟨0⟩;
```

EXAMPLES
IRETD
IRET

NOTES

1. IRET[D] in REAL and VM86 modes is very similar to the corresponding far RET instruction; the main difference is that it pops a flags image in addition to the CS and EIP values.

2. Since the restart flag RF is in the high-order WORD of EFLAGS, an IRET can never set it. Therefore, a debug fault handler that makes use of RF should always use IRETD.

3. When a nonmaskable interrupt (NMI) handler is entered, further NMIs are disabled until the handler exits via an IRET or IRETD.

Jcond: Jump if condition is met

INSTRUC-TION	RELA-TION	PARAMETERS	OP-CODE
JE/JZ rel	==	broff = EIP + rel, cnd = (ZF==1), os ∈ {16,32}	0F 84
JE/JZ rel8	==	broff = EIP + signex(rel8), cnd = (ZF==1), os ∈ {16,32}	74
JNE/JNZ rel	!=	broff = EIP + rel, cnd = (ZF==0), os ∈ {16,32}	0F 85
JNE/JNZ rel8	!=	broff = EIP + signex(rel8), cnd = (ZF==0), os ∈ {16,32}	75
JA/JNBE rel	$>_u$	broff = EIP + rel, cnd = (CF==0 & ZF==0), os ∈ {16,32}	0F 87
JA/JNBE rel8	$>_u$	broff = EIP + signex(rel8), cnd = (CF==0 & ZF==0), os ∈ {16,32}	77
JBE/JNA rel	$<=_u$	broff = EIP + rel, cnd = (CF==1 | ZF==1), os ∈ {16,32}	0F 86
JBE/JNA rel8	$<=_u$	broff = EIP + signex(rel8), cnd = (CF==1 | ZF==1), os ∈ {16,32}	76
JB/JNAE rel	$<_u$	broff = EIP + rel, cnd = (CF==1), os ∈ {16,32}	0F 82
JB/JNAE rel8	$<_u$	broff = EIP + signex(rel8), cnd = (CF==1), os ∈ {16,32}	72
JAE/JNB rel	$>=_u$	broff = EIP + rel, cnd = (CF==0), os ∈ {16,32}	0F 83
JAE/JNB rel8	$>=_u$	broff = EIP + signex(rel8), cnd = (CF==0), os ∈ {16,32}	73
JG/JNLE rel	>	broff = EIP + rel, cnd = (SF==OF & ZF==0), os ∈ {16,32}	0F 8F
JG/JNLE rel8	>	broff = EIP + signex(rel8), cnd = (SF==OF & ZF==0), os∈ {16,32}	7F
JGE/JNL rel	>=	broff = EIP + rel, cnd = (SF==OF), os ∈ {16,32}	0F 8D
JGE/JNL rel8	>=	broff = EIP + signex(rel8), cnd = (SF==OF), os ∈ {16,32}	7D
JL/JNGE rel	<	broff = EIP + rel, cnd = (SF!=OF), os ∈ {16,32}	0F 8C
JL/JNGE rel8	<	broff = EIP + signex(rel8), cnd = (SF!=OF), os ∈ {16,32}	7C
JLE/JNG rel	<=	broff = EIP + rel, cnd = (SF!=OF | ZF==1), os ∈ {16,32}	0F 8E
JLE/JNG rel8	<=	broff = EIP + signex(rel8), cnd = (SF!=OF | ZF==1), os ∈ {16,32}	7E
JS rel	SF==1	broff = EIP + rel, cnd = (SF==1), os ∈ {16,32}	0F 88
JS rel8	SF==1	broff = EIP + signex(rel8), cnd = (SF==1), os ∈ {16,32}	78
JNS rel	SF==0	broff = EIP + rel, cnd = (SF==0), os ∈ {16,32}	0F 89
JNS rel8	SF==0	broff = EIP + signex(rel8), cnd = (SF==0), os ∈ {16,32}	79
JO rel	OF==1	broff = EIP + rel, cnd = (OF==1), os ∈ {16,32}	0F 80
JO rel8	OF==1	broff = EIP + signex(rel8), cnd = (OF==1), os ∈ {16,32}	70
JNO rel	OF==0	broff = EIP + rel, cnd = (OF==0), os ∈ {16,32}	0F 81
JNO rel8	OF==0	broff = EIP + signex(rel8), cnd = (OF==0), os ∈ {16,32}	71
JP rel	PF==1	broff = EIP + rel, cnd = (PF==1), os ∈ {16,32}	0F 8A
JP rel8	PF==1	broff = EIP + signex(rel8), cnd = (PF==1), os ∈ {16,32}	7A
JNP rel	PF==0	broff = EIP + rel, cnd = (PF==0), os ∈ {16,32}	0F 8B
JNP rel8	PF==0	broff = EIP + signex(rel8), cnd = (PF==0), os ∈ {16,32}	7B

SUMMARY

The *Jcond* class of instructions branches to offset *broff* in the current code segment if the specified condition *cnd* is true. If it is false, *Jcond* has no effect.

If the operand size attribute (*os*) is 16, only the low-order WORD of *broff* is used as the branch offset; otherwise, all 32 bits are used. The ability to use only the low-order WORD of the branch offset allows compatible execution of 80286 and 8086 code.

OPERATION

```
if ( cnd )
{   if ( os == 32 )        /* Execute next instruction at broff */
      EIP = broff;
    else                   /* os == 16: use low 16 bits only */
      EIP = broff⟨15:0⟩;
}
```

EXAMPLES

```
; Jump to label below if EAX <ᵤ var
SUB      EAX, var              ; Flag CF set if EAX <ᵤ var
JB       below                 ; goto below if CF set

; Jump to label less if EAX < var [signed compare]
SUB      EAX, var              ; SF and OF set based on result
JL       less                  ; goto less if SF != OF (i.e., EAX < var)

; Jump to oddPar if register AL's bits have odd parity
ADD      AL, 0                 ; Do add simply to set parity flag PF
JNP      oddPar                ; goto parOK if PF == 0 (i.e., odd parity)
```

ASSEMBLER USAGE NOTES

1. *Jcond* always inherits the os attribute of the code segment containing it. So, if *Jcond* appears in a USE16 code segment the branch offset is always truncated to the 16 least significant bits. If this is not desired, an explicit operand size override byte should be placed; for example,

```
cseg    segment   use16

        DB   66h       ; operand size override (use EIP)
        JG   lab       ; most significant WORD of EIP is not zeroed out
```

2. For instruction encoding efficiency, each conditional jump instruction has two forms: one with an 8 bit only offset (*rel8*) operand type and one where the offset size matches the operand size attribute (*rel* operand.) The *rel* operand form of the instruction is only available on the 80376, 80386, and i486.

JCXZ/JECXZ: Jump if CX/ECX is zero

INSTRUCTION	PARAMETERS	OPCODE
JCXZ rel8	broff = EIP + signex(rel8), as = 16, os ∈ *{16,32}*	E3
JECXZ rel8	broff = EIP + signex(rel8), as = 32, os ∈ *{16,32}*	E3

SUMMARY
JCXZ transfers control to the branch address *broff* if CX's value is zero. Similarly, JECXZ transfers control to *broff* if ECX's value is zero. The address size attribute (*as*) selects whether CX or ECX is used. In both cases the branch target displacement (*rel8*) can only be a byte value. The operand size attribute determines whether IP (*os* == 16) or EIP (*os* == 32) is used.

OPERATION
```
DWORD val = (as==32) ? ECX : (DWORD) CX;
if ( val == 0 )
{   if ( os == 32 )  /* Execute next instruction at broff */
      EIP = broff;
    else  /* os == 16: use low 16 bits only, clear high bits */
      EIP = broff⟨15:0⟩;
}
```

EXAMPLES
```
JCXZ    done                ; goto done if CX's value is zero
JECXZ   done                ; goto done if ECX's value is zero
```

ASSEMBLER USAGE NOTES
1. J[E]CXZ always inherits the os attribute of the code segment containing it. So, if J[E]CXZ appears in a USE16 code segment the branch offset is always truncated to the sixteen least significant bits. If this is not desired, an explicit operand size override byte should be placed; for example,

```
cseg    segment   use16

        DB      66h         ; operand size override (use EIP)
        JCXZ    lab         ; most significant WORD of EIP is not zeroed out
```

JMP (near): Jump within same segment

INSTRUCTION	PARAMETERS	OPCODE
JMP rel	broff = EIP + signex(rel), os ∈ *{16,32}*	E9
JMP rel8	broff = EIP + signex(rel8), os ∈ *{16,32}*	EB
JMP r/m	broff = r/m, os ∈ *{16,32}*	FF /4

SUMMARY

The "near" JMP instruction transfers control to location *broff*. Since *broff* is an offset value, the transfer point must be within the same code segment. Use the far JMP or gated JMP instructions to transfer control to a different segment, or to switch to a new task.

OPERATION

```
if ( os == 32 )  /* Execute next instruction at broff */
    EIP = broff;
else  /* os == 16: use low 16 bits only */
    EIP = broff⟨15:0⟩;
```

EXAMPLES

```
; Jump to DWORD offset within current code segment, where the offset is stored at
DS:[123].
JMP       DWORD PTR [123]

; Jump to routine at offset AX of current code segment.
JMP       AX

; Jump to code labelled go. Assumes go is encoded as a rel type operand
; (i.e., as an EIP-relative displacement). If the relative displacement is within
; -128 .. +127, the assembler automatically chooses the rel8 form.
JMP       go
```

NOTES

1. Unlike many instructions, the operand size (*os*) attribute of a *direct* near JMP assembly language instruction cannot be determined by its operand. Direct near JMPs always inherits the os attribute of the code segment containing it. Thus, in a USE16 code segment a direct near JMP has an *os* attribute of 16; it has an *os* attribute of 32 in a USE32 code segment.

2. When the *os* attribute is 16, the upper sixteen bits of the new EIP are forced to zeros. This allows proper handling of a 16-bit JMP followed by a 32-bit JMP.

JMP (far): Jump to any segment at the same privilege level

INSTRUCTION	PARAMETERS	OPCODE
JMP sel:off	os ∈ {16,32}	EA
JMP m	os ∈ {16,32}	FF /5

SUMMARY

The far JMP instruction branches to offset *off* of the code segment named by the SELECTOR *sel*. In the indirect variant of this instruction (shown as "JMP m") the offset *off* is stored in location *m* in memory, and *sel* is stored in location *m* + 4 (if the operand size is 32) or *m* + 2 (if the operand size is 16.) Instruction operation depends on the current execution mode, as follows. In either case, the CS segment register is loaded with the SELECTOR value specified.

In REAL *or* VM86 *modes:* The Base of the CS descriptor register is set to *sel* * 16. (This is in accordance with normal REAL/VM86 mode segment access rules.) Then, a branch to offset *off* is executed.

In PROTECTED *mode: sel* is used to index into a descriptor table; see the description of the read_descr routine (on page 63) for details. If the descriptor that is read is for a code segment and has the appropriate access rights, control is transferred to offset *off* of the code segment. The access rights checked are detailed in the description of the load_CS routine. Note for the moment though that far JMPs can only be to segments whose privilege level matches the current privilege level.

If in PROTECTED mode and the descriptor selected by *sel* is not a code segment, it can (validly) either be a CALL gate, a TASK gate, or a task state segment. If a task gate or a task state segment, a task switch is performed; see the description of the JMP (task) instruction on page 458 for details. If *sel* selects a CALL gate the selector and offset specified in the CALL gate (call them *gSel* and *gOff*) are used as the target of the far JMP. Thus, assuming the descriptor selected by *gSel* is a code segment with the approriate access rights (as checked by routine load_CS), control is transferred to offset *gOff* of this code segment. If *gSel* does not select a code segment a protection fault is signaled, thus disallowing long chains of CALL gates. Note that when *sel* references a CALL gate only *gSel* and *gOff* participate in the transfer; the *off* value specified by the instruction is ignored.

OPERATION

```
WORD mem16[] = memVec;        /* Memory accessed as WORDs */
DWORD mem32[] = memVec;       /* Memory accessed as DWORDs */

/* == Get selector and offset values == */
if ( « JMP sel:off » ) /* [direct jump] */
{   offset = off;
    selector = sel;
}
else /* « JUMP m » [indirect jump] */
{   if ( os == 32 )  /* DWORD offset; WORD selector */
    {   mem32 = &m;
        offset = mem32[0];
        selector = mem32[1];
    }
    else  /* WORD offset; WORD selector */
    {   mem16 = &m;
        offset = mem16[0];
        selector = mem16[1];
    }
}

CS = selector;

/* == Check execution mode, and execute accordingly == */
if ( mode == REAL || mode == VM86 )  /* use REAL-mode style segment base */
    CS_desc.Base = CS * 16;

else /* mode == PROTECTED: read descriptor named by SELECTOR */
{   CS_desc = load_CS(CS, FALSE);        /* see page 69 */
    if ( !CS_desc.CDSeg ) /* check control descriptor type */
    {   if ( CS_desc.Type == CALLGATE16 || CS_desc.Type == CALLGATE32 )  /* gated
        JMP */
        {   if ( CPL > CS_desc.DPL || CPL > selector.RPL )  /* insufficient privilege */
                signal_fault(GP, CS & 0xFFFC);

            if ( !CS_desc.Valid )                /* "Present" flag not set in call gate */
                signal_fault(NP, CS & 0xFFFC);
```

```
            selector = CS_desc.Selector;      /* Read SELECTOR named by gate */
            CS = selector & 0xFFFC;           /* RPL bits are ignored here */
            offset = CS_desc.offset;
            CS_desc = load_CS(CS, FALSE);
            if ( !CS_desc.CDSeg )  /* call gates cannot be nested */
               signal_fault(GP, CS & 0xFFFC);
         }
         else if ( CS_desc.Type == TASKGATE || CS_desc.Type == NOTBUSY_TSS16 ||
         CS_desc.Type == NOTBUSY_TSS32 )  /* task switch */
            « see JMP (task) definition on page 458 »
         else signal_fault(GP, CS & 0xFFFC);
      }
      CS.RPL = CPL;
}

/* == Operand size determines whether IP or EIP is used. == */
if ( os == 32 )  /* Execute next instruction at offset */
   EIP = offset;
else  /* os == 16: use low 16 bits only */
   EIP = offset⟨15:0⟩;
```

EXAMPLES
```
; Jump to sel:off, where sel is fetched from the WORD at DS:[122]
; and off is fetched from the WORD at DS:[124].  (Indirect far JMP)
JMP        WORD PTR [123]

; Jump to sel:off, where sel is the label stop's SELECTOR and ; off is stop's OFFSET.
JMP        far ptr stop;
```

NOTES

1. The direct far jump instruction (opcode EA) executes in $12+n$ clocks in REAL and VM86 modes and in $27+n$ clocks in PROTECTED mode. The indirect far jump instruction executes in $17+n$ clocks in REAL and VM86 modes and in $31+n$ clocks in PROTECTED mode. n is the number of bytes in the instruction at the branch target.

2. If it is known that the JMP's target is in the same segment the more efficient, near JMP instruction can be used.

3. Unlike many instructions, the operand size (os) attribute a *direct* far JMP assembly language instruction cannot be determined by its operand. Direct far JMPs always inherit the os attribute of the code segment referenced by the operand. Thus, if in the instruction
JMP stop

stop is a label in a USE16 code segment the *os* attribute is 16; it has an *os* attribute of 32 if stop is in a USE32 code segment.

4. When the operand size is 16, the upper sixteen bits of the new EIP are forced to zeros. This allows proper handling of a 16-bit JMP followed by a 32-bit JMP.

5. The indirect far JMP instruction ("JMP m") can only be used with a memory operand. If a register operand is specified, an INVALID_INSTR fault is signaled.

JMP (task): Invoke a new task (286, 376, 386, 486 only)

INSTRUCTION	PARAMETERS	OPCODE
JMP sel:off	os ∈ *{16,32}*	EA
JMP m	os ∈ *{16,32}*	FF /5

SUMMARY
The task JMP instruction is available only in PROTECTED mode. Its instruction encoding is the same as that of a far JMP. If the SELECTOR specified in the instruction selects a task gate, a TSS16, or a TSS32 descriptor it is assumed to be a task JMP. Since SELECTORs access descriptors only in PROTECTED mode, an 80x86 operating in REAL or VM86 modes can never execute a task JMP.

If the SELECTOR points to a TSS16 or a TSS32 and the TSS descriptor is marked "not busy," the current task state is saved in the existing TSS and the task state named by the TSS16 or TSS32 is loaded. If the selector points to a task gate, the TSS16 or TSS32 referenced by the task gate is used in the operation just described. The task switch operation is specified in detail in §2.11 on page 128.

OPERATION
```
DESCR desc;                          /* Holding tank for gate descriptor */

if ( mode == REAL || mode == VM86 )
   « see far JMP instruction on page 456 »

/* PROTECTED mode task JMP description: */
/* == Get selector and offset values == */
if ( « JMP sel:off » ) /* direct jump */
{   offset = off;
    selector = sel;
}
else /* « JUMP m »: indirect jump */
{   if ( os == 32 )  /* DWORD offset; WORD selector */
    {   DWORD *mem32 = &m;
        offset = mem32[0];
        selector = mem32[1];
    }
    else  /* WORD offset; WORD selector */
    {   WORD *mem16 = &m;
        offset = mem16[0];
        selector = mem16[1];
    }
}
```

```
/* == Load descriptor and check its type == */
desc = load_CS(selector, FALSE);
if ( desc.CDSeg ) /* not a control descriptor */
  « see JMP (far) definition on page 456 »

else /* desc.CDSeg == 0: check control descriptor type */
{  if ( desc.Type == CALLGATE16 || desc.Type == CALLGATE32 )
     « see JMP (far) definition on page 456 »

  /* == Ensure its a task gate or TSS descriptor == */
  else if ( desc.Type == TASKGATE || desc.Type == NOTBUSY_TSS16 ||
         desc.Type == NOTBUSY_TSS32 ) /* task switch */
  {  if ( CPL > descr.DPL || CPL > selector.RPL ) /* insufficient privilege */
       signal_fault(GP,  (selector & 0xFFFC));

     if ( !desc.Valid )
       signal_fault(NP,  (selector & 0xFFFC));

     if ( desc.Type == TASKGATE )
     {  selector = desc.Selector; /* Read SELECTOR named by gate */
        /* Ensure selector named in task gate is not NULL, or in the LDT */
        if ( nullSel(selector) || selector.TI == 1 )
          signal_fault(GP,  (selector & 0xFFFC));
        /* Ensure task gate selector names a not-busy TSS16 or TSS32 */
        desc = readDescr(selector);
        if ( desc.Type != NOTBUSY_TSS16 && desc.Type != NOTBUSY_TSS32 )
          signal_fault(GP,  (selector & 0xFFFC));

        if ( !desc.Valid )
          signal_fault(NP,  (selector, 0xFFFC));
     }

     /* == Do the task switch as a nonnested switch (first "FALSE" parameter), and do
           not report an error code (second "FALSE" parameter).  See page 134 for
           details. == */
     enter_new_task(selector, desc, FALSE, FALSE);
  }

  /* == Invalid gate type: report exception == */
  else signal_fault(GP, (selector & 0xFFFC));
}
```

LAHF: Load flags into AH register

INSTRUCTION	PARAMETERS	OPCODE
LAHF		9F

SUMMARY
LAHF copies the low byte of EFLAGS into the AH register. The low byte contains all the arithmetic flags, except OF.

OPERATION
AH⟨7⟩ = SF;
AH⟨6⟩ = ZF;
AH⟨5⟩ = *undefined*;
AH⟨4⟩ = AF;
AH⟨3⟩ = *undefined*;
AH⟨2⟩ = PF;
AH⟨1⟩ = *undefined*;
AH⟨0⟩ = CF;

EXAMPLE
LAHF

LAR: Load access rights byte (286, 376, 386, 486 only)

INSTRUCTION	PARAMETERS	OPCODE
LAR r, r/m16	dst ≡ r, sel = r/m16, os ∈ *{16,32}*	0F 02

SUMMARY
LAR reads into the general register named by dst the access rights field of the selector sel. The access rights are located in the second byte of the second DWORD of the descriptor corresponding to sel. If the operand size is 32, the granularity bit (G), the default attribute bit (D), and the Intel-reserved and user definable bits are also read. LAR makes sure that a valid descriptor type is referenced by sel. If not, or if the selector is out of the bound of the descriptor table, ZF is cleared. If the descriptor type is valid, ZF is set.

If executed in REAL or VM86 modes, LAR signals an INVALID_INSTR fault. In PROTECTED mode, LAR is executable at all privilege levels.

OPERATION
```
if ( mode == REAL || mode == VM86 )
  signal_fault(INVALID_INSTR);

/* Always executable in PROTECTED mode */
if ( nullSel(sel) || ! inBounds(sel) )  /* not readable: clear ZF */
  ZF = 0;
else
{ desc = read_descr(sel, FALSE, FALSE);  /* see page 63 */
  if ( desc.Conforming ||
     ( ( CPL <= desc.DPL  &&  sel.RPL <= desc.DPL ) &&
       ( desc.Readable ||                      /* Data segment */
       ( ! desc.Conforming && desc.Executable ) ||/* Code segment */
       desc.Type == BUSY_TSS16 || desc.Type == BUSY_TSS32 ||
       desc.Type == NOTBUSY_TSS16 || desc.Type == NOTBUSY_TSS32 ||
       desc.Type == CALLGATE16 || desc.Type == CALLGATE32 ||
       desc.Type == TASKGATE ||
       desc.Type == LDT_SEG ) ) )  /* Checks pass: set ZF and access rights */
  { dst⟨31:24⟩ = 0;                         /* set only if os == 32 */
    dst⟨23:20⟩ = desc.GDField;              /* set only if os == 32 */
    dst⟨19:16⟩ = undefined;                 /* set only if os == 32 */
    dst⟨15⟩ = desc.Valid;
    dst⟨14:13⟩ = desc.DPL;
    dst⟨12⟩ = desc.CDSeg;
    if ( desc.CDSeg ) /* format bits 11 to 8 using segment attrs */
    { dst⟨11⟩ = desc.Executable;
      if ( desc.Executable )
      { dst⟨10⟩ = desc.Conforming;
```

```
            dst⟨9⟩ = desc.Readable;
        }
        else
        {   dst⟨10⟩ = desc.ExpandDown;
            dst⟨9⟩ = desc.Writable;
        }
        dst⟨8⟩ = desc.Accessed;
        dst⟨7:0⟩ = 0;
    }
    else /* load control descriptor type into bits 11 to 8 */
        dst⟨11:8⟩ = desc.Type;

    ZF = 1;
  }

  else /* unacceptable descriptor type: clear ZF */
    ZF = 0;
}
```

EXAMPLES
; Load into EAX the access rights of the selector stored at the WORD *msel*.
```
LAR       EAX, msel
JNZ       arErr                    ; goto arErr if invalid selector or descriptor
```

; Load into CX the access rights of the segment named by selector 1000h.
```
MOV       AX, 1000h
LAR       CX, AX
JNZ       arErr                    ; goto arErr if invalid selector or descriptor
```

LDS: Load pointer into DS and register

INSTRUCTION	PARAMETERS	OPCODE
LDS r, m	dst ≡ r, src ≡ m, os ∈ {8,16,32}	C5

SUMMARY

LDS loads the far pointer stored at the memory location named by *src* into the register pair DS:*dst*. If the operand size attribute (*os*) is 32, the far pointer occupies six bytes (a SELECTOR and a 4-byte OFFSET). If *os* is 16, the far pointer occupies four bytes (a SELECTOR and a 2-byte OFFSET). The size of the *dst* register also matches *os*.

OPERATION
```
SELECTOR sel;
OFFSET off;

/* == Read SELECTOR and OFFSET based on operand size. == */
if ( os == 2 )
{   WORD *mem16 = &src;        /* reference memory as WORDs */
    off = mem16[0];
    sel = mem16[1];
}
else /* os == 4 */
{   DWORD *mem32 = &src;       /* reference memory as DWORDs */
    off = mem32[0];
    sel = mem32[1];
}

/* == Load DS_desc descriptor register based on execution mode. == */
if ( mode == REAL || mode == VM86 ) /* REAL-mode style segment base */
    DS_desc.Base = DS * 16;
else /* load PROTECTED mode descriptor */
    DS_desc = load_data_seg(sel, FALSE); /* see page 71 */

/* == Initialize DS and specified general register. == */
dst = off;
DS = sel;
```

EXAMPLE
```
LDS     AX, [ESI+4]            ;Load DS:AX with SELECTOR and OFFSET
                               ; stored at DS:[ESI+4].
```

NOTES
1. The ES, SS, FS, and GS segment registers can be loaded using similar instructions with a prefixed "L"; for example, LES loads the pair ES:r, where *r* is a general register. Loading the CS segment register only makes sense in conjunction with an EIP load. The far and gated JMP instructions do this.

2. The scheme used to encode the memory operand *src* storing the pointer is of the general *r/m* type, and so can be used to encode a register. If this is attempted, an INVALID_INSTR fault is signaled when the instruction is executed.

LEA: Load effective address

INSTRUCTION	PARAMETERS	OPCODE
LEA r, m	dst ≡ r, src = m, os ∈ {16,32}, as ∈ {16,32}	8D

SUMMARY
LEA computes the effective address (i.e., offset) specified by the src operand and copies the result into the destination register. This is done by adding the base, index, and displacement values specified in the memory address; on the 80376, 80386, and i486, a scale factor for the index register may also be specified.

The memory address at the effective address location is not accessed, nor is a check made to see whether the offset is in a valid part of the data segment. (Since no memory reference is made, segment override prefixes play no role either; if specified, they are ignored.) As always, the address size (*as*) attribute controls whether WORD or DWORD registers and displacements are used to specify the effective address components. Thus the width of the effective address computed is determined by *as*.

The effective address value computed is stored in a WORD or DWORD register depending on the operand size (*os*) attribute. If *os* is less than *as*, only the least significant *os* bits of the offset are stored. If *as* is less than *os*, the offset value is zero-extended to *os* bits.

OPERATION
result = « effective address of *src* »;   /* see ı2.18 (starting on page 185) */
dst = *result*;   /* Store result */

EXAMPLES
```
LEA     EAX, [BX+12]            ; EAX = (BX + 12) & 0xFFFF
LEA     BX, [ESI+EDI*2]         ; BX = (WORD) (ESI+EDI*2)
LEA     EAX, [233146]           ; EAX = 233146
LEA     SI, [SI+DI]             ; SI = SI + DI
LEA     EBX, [EAX*8+EAX+10]     ; EBX = EAX*9 + 10
```

NOTES
1. The *src* can only be a memory operand. If a register operand is encoded for *src*, an attempt to execute the instruction signals an INVALID_INSTR exception. Invalid operation checks are not performed on the 8086.

Executing an invalid **LEA** instruction on an 8086 has an *undefined* effect on the state of the general registers.

2. Since an effective address on a 80376, 80386, and i486 is formed by adding up to two **DWORD** general registers and a constant value, the **LEA** instruction can be used for register to register additions. The ability to scale can also be used to perform restricted types of multiplication. Note that flags are not set by **LEA**; use the **ADD** instruction if flag settings are needed. Similar additions can be done on the 80286 and its predecessors. However, only limited combination of registers are available.

LEAVE: Leave nested procedure (unavailable on the 8086)

INSTRUCTION	PARAMETERS	OPCODE
LEAVE	fptr ≡ BP, os = *16*	C9
LEAVE	fptr ≡ EBP, os = *32*	C9

SUMMARY

LEAVE removes the stack frame created by the ENTER instruction (or equivalent instruction sequence) and restores the caller's frame pointer in EBP or BP. (EBP is used if the operand size is 32; otherwise, BP is used.)

OPERATION

```
/* Delete frame */
if ( SS_desc.DefaultAttr )  /* Stack pointer is 32-bits */
   ESP = EBP;
else
   SP = BP;

/* Restore frame pointer */
if ( os == 32 )
   EBP = pop4();
else
   BP = pop2();
```

EXAMPLE

```
LEAVE
```

NOTE

1. Unlike many instructions, the operand size (os) attribute of a LEAVE assembly language instruction cannot be determined by its operand. LEAVE always inherits the os attribute of the code segment containing it. Thus, in a USE16 code segment LEAVE uses BP as the frame pointer (since os is 16) and in a USE32 it uses EBP. This is merely an artifact of assembly language notation: if desired, the programmer can "hand-code" an operand size override prefix to generate a frame pointer that does not match the code segment's USE attribute.

LES: Load pointer into ES and a register

INSTRUCTION	PARAMETERS	OPCODE
LES r, m	dst ≡ r, src = m, os ∈ *{16,32}*	C4

SUMMARY
LES loads the far pointer stored at the memory location named by *src* into the register pair ES:*dst*. If the operand size attribute (*os*) is 32, the far pointer occupies six bytes (a SELECTOR and a 4-byte OFFSET). If *os* is 16, the far pointer occupies four bytes (a SELECTOR and a 2-byte OFFSET). The size of the *dst* register also matches *os*.

OPERATION
```
SELECTOR sel;
OFFSET off;

/* == Read SELECTOR and OFFSET based on operand size. == */
if ( os == 2 )
{   WORD *mem16 = &src;        /* reference memory as WORDs */
    off = mem16[0];
    sel = mem16[1];
}
else /* os == 4 */
{   DWORD *mem32 = &src;       /* reference memory as DWORDs */
    off = mem32[0];
    sel = mem32[1];
}

/* == Load ES_desc descriptor register based on execution mode. == */
if ( mode == REAL || mode == VM86 )  /* REAL-mode style segment base */
    ES_desc.Base = ES * 16;
else  /* load PROTECTED mode descriptor */
    ES_desc = load_data_seg(sel, FALSE); /* see page 71 */

/* == Initialize ES and specified general register. == */
dst = off;
ES = sel;
```

EXAMPLE
```
LES     EBX, ptr
```

NOTES
1. The SS, DS, FS, and GS segment registers can be loaded using similar instructions with a prefixed "L"; for example, LFS loads the pair FS:r, where

r is a general register. Loading the CS segment register only makes sense in conjunction with an EIP load. The far and gated JMP instructions do this.

2. The scheme used to encode the memory operand *src* storing the pointer is of the general *r/m* type, and so can be used to encode a register. If this is attempted, an INVALID_INSTR fault is signaled when the instruction is executed.

LFS: Load pointer into FS and a register (376, 386, 486 only)

INSTRUCTION	PARAMETERS	OPCODE
LFS r, m	dst ≡ r, src = m, os ∈ {16,32}	0F B4

SUMMARY
LFS loads the far pointer stored at the memory location named by *src* into the register pair FS:*dst*. If the operand size attribute (*os*) is 32, the far pointer occupies six bytes (a SELECTOR and a 4-byte OFFSET). If *os* is 16, the far pointer occupies four bytes (a SELECTOR and a 2-byte OFFSET). The size of the *dst* register also matches *os*.

OPERATION
```
SELECTOR sel;
OFFSET off;

/* == Read SELECTOR and OFFSET based on operand size. == */
if ( os == 2 )/
{   WORD *mem16 = &src;        /* reference memory as WORDs */
    off = mem16[0];
    sel = mem16[1];
}
else /* os == 4 */
{   DWORD *mem32 = &src;       /* reference memory as DWORDs */
    off = mem32[0];
    sel = mem32[1];
}

/* == Load FS_desc descriptor register based on execution mode. == */
if ( mode == REAL || mode == VM86 )  /* REAL-mode style segment base */
    FS_desc.Base = FS * 16;
else  /* load PROTECTED mode descriptor */
    FS_desc = load_data_seg(sel, FALSE);  /* see page 71 */

/* == Initialize FS and specified general register. == */
dst = off;
FS = sel;
```

EXAMPLE
```
LFS     EBX, ptr
```

NOTES

1. The ES, SS, DS, and GS segment registers can be loaded using similar instructions with a prefixed "L"; for example, LGS loads the pair GS:r, where *r* is a general register. Loading the CS segment register only makes sense in conjunction with an EIP load. The far and gated JMP instructions do this.

2. The scheme used to encode the memory operand *src* storing the pointer is of the general *r/m* type, and so can be used to encode a register. If this is attempted, an INVALID_INSTR fault is signaled when the instruction is executed.

LGDT: Load global descriptor table (286, 376, 386, 486 only)

INSTRUCTION	PARAMETERS	OPCODE
LGDT m	src ≡ m, os ∈ {8,16,32}	0F 01 /2

SUMMARY
LGDT interprets src to be a six byte memory area, with addresses src and src+1 storing a WORD-sized limit field and the next four bytes storing a base field. The GDT descriptor is initialized using these base and limit fields. LGDT is a privileged instruction.

OPERATION
```
struct { WORD Limit;
       DWORD Base;
     } * GDTVal;

if ( CPL != 0 )
   signal_fault(GP, 0);

GDTVal = &src;  /* Setup limit and base access */
GDT_desc.Limit = GDTVal->Limit;
if ( os == 16 )
   GDT_desc.Base = GDTVal->Base & 0x00FFFFFF;  /* clear high byte */
else  /* os == 32 */
   GDT_desc.Base = GDTVal->Base;

GDT_desc.Valid = 1;
```

EXAMPLE
```
LGDT      initGDT
```

NOTE
1. The scheme used to encode the memory operand src storing the GDT limit and base is of the general r/m type, and so can be used to encode a register. If this is done, an INVALID_INSTR fault is signaled when the instruction is executed.

LGS: Load pointer into GS and a register (376, 386, 486 only)

INSTRUCTION	PARAMETERS	OPCODE
LGS r, m	dst ≡ r, src = m, os ∈ {16,32}	0F B5

SUMMARY

LGS loads the far pointer stored at the memory location named by *src* into the register pair GS:*dst*. If the operand size attribute (*os*) is 32, the far pointer occupies six bytes (a SELECTOR and a 4-byte OFFSET). If *os* is 16, the far pointer occupies four bytes (a SELECTOR and a 2-byte OFFSET). The size of the *dst* register also matches *os*.

OPERATION

```
SELECTOR sel;
OFFSET off;

/* == Read SELECTOR and OFFSET based on operand size. == */
if ( os == 2 )/
{   WORD *mem16 = &src;          /* reference memory as WORDs */
    off = mem16[0];
    sel = mem16[1];
}
else /* os == 4 */
{   DWORD *mem32 = &src;         /* reference memory as DWORDs */
    off = mem32[0];
    sel = mem32[1];
}

/* == Load GS_desc descriptor register based on execution mode. == */
if ( mode == REAL || mode == VM86 )  /* REAL-mode style segment base */
    GS_desc.Base = GS * 16;
else  /* load PROTECTED mode descriptor */
    GS_desc = load_data_seg(sel, FALSE);  /* see page 71 */

/* == Initialize GS and specified general register. == */
dst = off;
GS = sel;
```

EXAMPLE

```
LGS      EBX, ptr
```

NOTES

1. The ES, SS, DS, and FS segment registers can be loaded using similar instructions with a prefixed "L"; for example, LSS loads the pair SS:*r*, where *r* is a general register. Loading the CS segment register only makes sense in conjunction with an EIP load. The far and gated JMP instructions do this.

2. The scheme used to encode the memory operand *src* storing the pointer is of the general *r/m* type, and so can be used to encode a register. If this is attempted, an INVALID_INSTR fault is signaled when the instruction is executed.

LIDT: Load interrupt descriptor table (286, 376, 386, 486 only)

INSTRUCTION	PARAMETERS	OPCODE
LIDT m	src ≡ m, os ∈ {8,16,32}	0F 01 /3

SUMMARY
LIDT interprets src to be a six byte memory area, with addresses src and src+1 storing a WORD-sized limit field and the next four bytes storing a base field. The IDT descriptor is initialized using these base and limit fields. LIDT is a privileged instruction.

OPERATION
```
struct { WORD Limit;
      DWORD Base;
      } * IDTVal;

if ( CPL != 0 )
   signal_fault(GP, 0);

IDTVal = &src;  /* Setup limit and base access */
IDT_desc.Limit = IDTVal->Limit;
GDT_desc.Limit = GDTVal->Limit;
if ( os == 16 )
   IDT_desc.Base = IDTVal->Base & 0x00FFFFFF;  /* clear high byte */
else  /* os == 32 */
   IDT_desc.Base = IDTVal->Base;
```

EXAMPLE
```
LIDT       initIDT
```

NOTE
1. The scheme used to encode the memory operand src storing the IDT limit and base is of the general r/m type, and so can be used to encode a register. If this is done, an INVALID_INSTR fault is signaled when the instruction is executed.

LLDT: Load local descriptor table (286, 376, 386, 486 only)

INSTRUCTION	PARAMETERS	OPCODE
LLDT r/m16	sel ≡ r/m16	0F 00 /2

SUMMARY
LLDT loads the LDT table descriptor with the descriptor named by the selector sel. The load succeeds only if the descriptor read is a valid LDT table descriptor. To avoid self-reference, LDT table descriptors can reside in the GDT only. Since the GDT is only meaningful in PROTECTED mode, LLDT is not available in REAL or VM86 modes. Furthermore, it is a privileged instruction.

OPERATION
```
DESCR desc;

/* == Make instruction and SELECTOR validity checks. == */
if ( mode == REAL || mode == VM86 )
   signal_fault(INVALID_INSTR);

if ( CPL != 0 )
   signal_fault(GP, 0);

if ( sel.TI == 1 )              /* SELECTOR must be in GDT */
   signal_fault(GP, (sel & 0xFFFC));

/* == Initial checks pass: read descriptor and load LDT_desc. == */
if ( nullSel(sel) )             /* Null LDT pointer: disable descriptor */
   desc.Valid = FALSE;
else
{  lock(DESCR_TABLE);     /* disallow descriptor table access to other system agents */
   desc = read_descr(sel, FALSE, FALSE);  /* see page 63 */
   if ( desc.Type != LDT_SEG )
      signal_fault(GP, (sel & 0xFFFC));
   else if ( ! desc.Valid )
      signal_fault(NP, (sel & 0xFFFC));
   unlock(DESCR_TABLE);  /* reallow other agents to access descriptor tables */
}

LDT_desc = desc;            /* Initialize LDT descriptor */
LDT = sel;                  /* Initialize LDT selector */
```

EXAMPLE
```
; Use entry 5 of the GDT to define the LDT table.
MOV      AX, 40               ; Entry 5 of GDT is 5*8 = 40
LLDT     AX                   ; Load selector in AX as LDT table
```

LMSW: Load machine status word (286, 376, 386, 486 only)

INSTRUCTION	PARAMETERS	OPCODE
LMSW r/m16	src = r/m16	0F 01 /6

SUMMARY
LMSW loads the Machine Status Word (MSW). The MSW is the low order
WORD of the DWORD control register CR0. All low order bits can be modified,
except that the PE bit, once set to 1, cannot be reset to 0. LMSW is an artifact of
the 80286; its use is not recommended in new code (see *Notes* below.) LMSW is
a privileged instruction.

OPERATION
```
if ( CPL != 0 )
   signal_fault(GP, 0);

/* ET, TS, EM, MP, PE are bits in low area of CR0. */
CR0⟨15:4⟩ = undefined;
TS = src⟨3⟩;
EM = src⟨2⟩;
MP = src⟨1⟩;
if ( PE == 0 )   /* LMSW cannot reset PE (80286 compatibility) */
   PE = src⟨0⟩;
```

EXAMPLE
```
; Enable protected mode (set PE); clear other MSW flags.
MOV      CX, 1                     ; Set PE enable mask in CX
LMSW     CX                        ; Load CR0<15:0> with CX.
```

NOTES
1. LMSW is a subset of the MOV CR0, ... instruction. It is provided only for
   backward compatibility with the 80286.

2. LMSW cannot be used to revert to REAL mode from PROTECTED or VM86
   modes. Use MOV CR0, ... to do this.

3. A 80286/80287 system must issue an FNSETPM after setting the PE flag.

LOADALL286: Load 80286 state (286 only)

INSTRUCTION	PARAMETERS	OPCODE
LOADALL286		0F 05

SUMMARY

LOADALL286 is a 80286-specific instruction that loads all on-chip registers of the 80286. Data is loaded from a structure stored at physical address 0x800.

LOADALL286 is a privileged instruction. Since REAL mode operates with an effective CPL of 0, LOADALL286 is available in REAL mode, and in PROTECTED mode when CPL is 0.

LOADALL286 takes about 195 clock cycles to execute. This performance penalty makes the instruction useful only in very specific situations.

OPERATION

```
WORD *ld_base;

if ( CPL != 0 )
    signal_fault(GP, 0);

/* == Access memory starting at physical address 0x800 as a sequence of WORDs. == */
ld_base = (WORD *) &mem_vec[0x800];

/* == Load 80286 registers from memory.  Note that indices are WORD indices. == */
CR0⟨15:0⟩ = ld_base[3];
TSS = ld_base[11];
FLAGS = ld_base[12];
IP = ld_base[13];
LDT = ld_base[14];
DS = ld_base[15];
SS = ld_base[16];
CS = ld_base[17];
ES = ld_base[18];
DI = ld_base[19];
SI = ld_base[20];
BP = ld_base[21];
SP = ld_base[22];
BX = ld_base[23];
DX = ld_base[24];
CX = ld_base[25];
AX = ld_base[26];
```

```
/* == Load descriptor registers.  The  loadall_read_descr  routine is defined on the next
     page. == */
base = ((ld_base[28] & 0xFF) << 16) + ld_base[27];
ar = ld_base[28] >> 8;
limit = ld_base[29];
ES_desc = loadall_read_descr(base, ar, limit);  /* see below */

base = ((ld_base[31] & 0xFF) << 16) + ld_base[30];
ar = ld_base[31] >> 8;
limit = ld_base[32];
CS_desc = loadall_read_descr(base, ar, limit);

base = ((ld_base[34] & 0xFF) << 16) + ld_base[33];
ar = ld_base[34] >> 8;
limit = ld_base[35];
SS_desc = loadall_read_descr(base, ar, limit);

base = ((ld_base[37] & 0xFF) << 16) + ld_base[36];
ar = ld_base[37] >> 8;
limit = ld_base[38];
DS_desc = loadall_read_descr(base, ar, limit);

base = ((ld_base[40] & 0xFF) << 16) + ld_base[39];
ar = ld_base[40] >> 8;
limit = ld_base[41];
GDT_desc = loadall_read_descr(base, ar, limit);

base = ((ld_base[43] & 0xFF) << 16) + ld_base[42];
ar = ld_base[43] >> 8;
limit = ld_base[44];
LDT_desc = loadall_read_descr(base, ar, limit);

base = ((ld_base[46] & 0xFF) << 16) + ld_base[45];
ar = ld_base[46] >> 8;
limit = ld_base[47];
IDT_desc = loadall_read_descr(base, ar, limit);

base = ((ld_base[49] & 0xFF) << 16) + ld_base[48];
ar = ld_base[49] >> 8;
limit = ld_base[50];
TSS_desc = loadall_read_descr(base, ar, limit);
```

Field	Address
reserved	0x800
reserved	0x802
reserved	0x804
MSW	0x806
reserved	0x808
reserved	0x80A
reserved	0x80C
reserved	0x80E
reserved	0x810
reserved	0x812
reserved	0x814
TSS	0x816
FLAGS	0x818
IP	0x81A
LDT	0x81C
DS	0x81E
SS	0x820
CS	0x822
ES	0x824
DI	0x826
SI	0x828
BP	0x82A
SP	0x82C
BX	0x82E
DX	0x830
CX	0x832
AX	0x834
ES_desc.Base	0x836
Acc. Rts.	0x838
ES_desc.Limit	0x83A
CS_desc.Base	0x83C
Acc. Rts.	0x83E
CS_desc.Limit	0x840
SS_desc.Base	0x842
Acc. Rts.	0x844
SS_desc.Limit	0x846
DS_desc.Base	0x848
Acc. Rts.	0x84A
DS_desc.Limit	0x84C
GDT_desc.Base	0x84E
Acc. Rts.	0x850
GDT_desc.Limit	0x852
LDT_desc.Base	0x854
Acc. Rts.	0x856
LDT_desc.Limit	0x858
IDT_desc.Base	0x85A
Acc. Rts.	0x85C
IDT_desc.Limit	0x85E
TSS_desc.Base	0x860
Acc. Rts.	0x862
TSS_desc.Limit	0x864

/* == A special descriptor read routine, described below, is used by LOADALL286. This routine handles differences in the descriptor storage format, and also the fact that the descriptors are stored in fixed memory locations (rather than in the GDT or LDT). == */

```
DESCR loadall_read_descr(base, ar, limit)
DWORD base; /* use 24 bits only */
BYTE ar;
WORD limit;
{  DESCR desc;

    desc.Base = base⟨23:0⟩;  /* High order byte is 0 */
    desc.Limit = limit;
    desc.GDField = 0;

    desc.Valid = ar⟨7⟩;
    desc.DPL = ar⟨6:5⟩;
    desc.CDSeg = ar⟨4⟩;
    if ( desc.CDSeg )
    {   desc.DefaultAttr = 0;  /* 80286 segments are always USE16 */
    desc.Executable = ar⟨3⟩;
    if ( desc.Executable )   /* Code seg. descr. */
    {   desc.Conforming = ar⟨2⟩;
        desc.Readable = ar⟨1⟩;
        desc.Writable = FALSE;  /* Code seg never writable */
        desc.ExpandDown = FALSE;  /* "ExpandDown" is a data seg attr */
    }
    else   /* Data seg. descr. */
    {   desc.ExpandDown = ar⟨2⟩;
        desc.Writable = ar⟨1⟩;
        desc.Readable = TRUE;  /* Data seg always readable */
        desc.Conforming = FALSE;  /* "Conforming" is a code seg attr */
    }
    desc.Accessed = ar⟨0⟩;  /* Save for LAR instruction only */
    desc.Type = 0;  /* Type is Code or data descriptor */
    }
}
```

EXAMPLE
LOADALL286   ; See *Assembler Usage Note* below

NOTES
1. The LOADALL286 instruction, though implemented in all 80286s, is not documented in Intel literature. This is because its original intent was for use in system test products, and not general programming. This description of the instruction is derived from a description provided in the October 1987 issue of *Microprocessor Report*, an industry newsletter based in Palo Alto, California.

2. LOADALL286 is *only available on the 80286.* On the 8086, executing the opcode causes an undefined action. On the 80386 and i486 executing the opcode signals an INVALID_INSTR fault.

3. The primary use of LOADALL286 is for extending addressability in REAL mode, and loading REAL-mode-style SELECTORs in PROTECTED mode. Both these goals can be achieved on the 80386 and i486 by using VM86 mode. Partial simulation of LOADALL286 behavior in REAL mode can also be achieved on these newer processors by loading descriptors in PROTECTED mode, then switching back to REAL mode.

ASSEMBLER USAGE NOTE
1. The LOADALL286 is not supported by assemblers like Microsoft MASM and Borland TASM. To use it the user must either create a macro defining the mnemonic, or encode it directly using the following statement

```
db 0Fh, 05h        ; Encoding for LOADALL286
```

LOCK (prefix): "Lock bus" prefix

INSTRUCTION	PARAMETERS	OPCODE
LOCK		F0

SUMMARY

LOCK is not an instruction. Rather, it is a prefix that, if placed before certain instructions that update (i.e., read, modify, then write back) memory, guarantees that the update occurs without interference from other agents that also have access to the same memory area. Hence, the LOCK prefix is useful for implementing atomic operations (e.g., semaphores) in multimaster environments.

The list of LOCKable instructions is as follows:

BT/BTS/BTR/BTC m, r: Bit test operations on memory with register offset

BT/BTS/BTR/BTC m, imm8: Bit test operations on memory with constant offset

ADC/ADD/AND/SBB/SUB/OR/XOR m, r: Arithmetic/logical operation with memory

ADC/ADD/AND/SBB/SUB/OR/XOR m, imm: Arithmetic/logical operation with memory

DEC/INC/NEG/NOT m: Unary aritmetic/logical with memory

XCHG r, m: Exchange register contents with memory

XADD m, r: Exchange register contents with memory and add (i486 only)

CMPXCHG m, r: Compare and exchange register contents with memory (i486 only)

On the 80376, 80386, and i486, all instructions not in the list above will signal an INVALID_INSTR fault if attempted with the LOCK prefix. This includes nonmemory operand variants of the instructions listed. For example,

LOCK ADD EAX, EBX   ; ** INVALID **

will signal INVALID_INSTR.

OPERATION
lock(MEM);
« execute attached instruction »
unlock(MEM);

EXAMPLE
```
; Acquire semaphore using busy-wait loop
MOV      AH, 1            ; Set to "acquired" value
LOCK XCHG AH, sema        ; Try and get it
CMP      AH, 1            ; Was sema already acquired?
JE       wait            ; Yes: wait till free, then try again
```

NOTES
1. The read and write sequence of operations needed to implement the XCHG instruction is always locked, regardless of whether a LOCK prefix is specified.

2. In the 80286, the ability to execute a LOCKed instruction is IOPL-sensitive. On the 32-bit versions of the 80x86 (the 80376, 80386, and i486), however, instructions can be LOCKed at any privilege level. (This permits high-performance implementations of application-defined semaphores in multiprocessor environments.) The 80286 allows the LOCK prefix on string instructions (e.g., LOCK REP MOVSB is valid.) The 32-bit 80x86's do not allow string instructions to be LOCKed, for doing so would allow application programs (at CPL==3) to lock up the bus practically indefinitely. If a LOCKed string instruction is attempted on on of these machines, an INVALID_INSTR fault is signaled.

3. Memory update is automatically locked by the 80x86 when setting "accessed" or other flags in segment descriptors and page table and directory table enntries. See §2.7.11 on page 111 for more on this.

4. The 8086 ignores the LOCK prefix on unlockable instructions. Hence, 8086 code executed on the 80376, 80386, and i486 may generate INVALID_INSTR faults if it contains spurious LOCKs.

LODSB/LODSD/LODSW: Load string operands

INSTRUCTION	PARAMETERS	OPCODE
LODSB	os = *8*, as ∈ {16,32}	AC
LODSW	os = *16*, as ∈ {16,32}	AD
LODSD	os = *32*, as ∈ {16,32}	AD

SUMMARY

LODS*x* loads into AL, AX, or EAX the contents of the BYTE, WORD, or DWORD pointed at by ESI or SI. ESI is used if the address size attribute is 32; if it is 16, SI participates. After the load [E]SI is incremented by 2 or 4, depending on the operand size. No flags are modified by this instruction.

Offset [E]SI is relative to the segment referenced by the DS segment register, unless it is explicitly overriden by an segment override prefix.

OPERATION

```
src = ( (as == 16) ? SI : ESI );
/* Load src operand */
switch (os)
{   case 8:    AL = *( (char *) src );
               break;
    case 16:   AX = *( (short *) src );
               break;
    case 32:   EAX = *( (int *) src );
               break;
}

/* Increment SI or ESI, as appropriate */
src += (DF ? -os/8 : os/8);
if ( as == 32 )   /* 32-bit addressing */
    ESI = src;
else /* as == 16 : 16-bit addressing */
    SI = src;
```

EXAMPLES

```
LODSB
LODSW
```

NOTES

1. LODS*x* instructions are used mainly to read (within a loop) successive elements of a string. (The corresponding store action is done by STOS.)

Although a REP prefix is not very useful with a LODS it is supported nonetheless. See REP LODS for a description.

ASSEMBLER USAGE NOTE
1. Address register selection (i.e., SI vs. ESI) depends on the address size attribute. To ensure that an address size override prefix is generated (if needed), the assembler notation where explicit operands to LODSx are provided is recommended. For example, a repeated LODSB to SS:SI should be encoded as follows
REP MOVS SS:BYTE PTR [SI]

This also provides a convenient way to specify segment overrides.

LOOP: Jump if CX/ECX not zero

INSTRUCTION	PARAMETERS	OPCODE
LOOP rel8	brad = EIP + rel8, cnt ≡ CX, as = 16	E2
LOOP rel8	brad = EIP + rel8, cnt ≡ ECX, as = 32	E2

SUMMARY
LOOP executed with an address size (as) of 16 transfers control to the branch address brad if CX's value, decremented by 1, is not zero. Similarly, LOOP with an as of 32 transfers control to brad if the decremented ECX value is not zero. In both cases the branch target displacement can only be a byte value.

OPERATION
```
cnt = cnt - 1;
if ( cnt != 0 )
{   if ( os == 32 )  /* Execute next instruction at brad */
       EIP = brad;
   else  /* os == 16: use low 16 bits only */
       EIP = brad<15:0>;
}
```

EXAMPLE
```
LOOP      cont                         ; goto cont if E/CX's value is not zero
```

NOTE
1. Neither the os attribute nor the as attribute of a LOOP assembly language instruction can be determined by its operand. LOOP always inherits the os and as attributes of the code segment containing it. Thus, in a USE16 code segment a LOOP has os and as attributes of 16; they are both 32 in a USE32 code segment. The architecture does not enforce these assembly language restrictions. A programmer may override the defaults by "manually" coding an operand size or address size prefix, as desired.

LOOPE/LOOPZ: Jump if ZF set and CX/ECX not zero

INSTRUCTION	PARAMETERS	OPCODE
LOOPE/LOOPZ rel8	brad = EIP + rel8, cnt ≡ CX, as = 16	E1
LOOPE/LOOPZ rel8	brad = EIP + rel8, cnt ≡ ECX, as = 32	E1

SUMMARY
LOOPE executed with an address size (as) of 16 transfers control to the branch address brad if the zero detect flag (ZF) is set and CX's value, decremented by one, is not zero. Similarly, LOOPE with an as of 32 transfers control to brad if ZF is set and the decremented ECX value is not zero. In both cases the branch target displacement can only be a byte value. LOOPZ is a synonym of LOOPE.

OPERATION
```
cnt = cnt - 1;
if ( ZF == 1  &&  cnt != 0 )
{   if ( os == 32 )  /* Execute next instruction at brad */
      EIP = brad;
   else  /* os == 16: use low 16 bits only */
      EIP = brad<15:0>;
}
```

EXAMPLE
LOOPE   lp   ; goto *lp* if ZF and E/CX's value is not zero

NOTE
1. Neither the os attribute nor the as attribute of a LOOPE assembly language instruction can be determined by its operand. LOOPE always inherits the os and as attributes of the code segment containing it. Thus, in a USE16 code segment a LOOPE has os and as attributes of 16; they are both 32 in a USE32 code segment. The architecture does not enforce these assembly language restrictions. A programmer may override the defaults by "manually" coding an operand size or address size prefix, as desired.

LOOPNE/LOOPNZ: Jump if ZF clear and CX/ECX not zero

INSTRUCTION	PARAMETERS	OPCODE
LOOPNE/LOOPNZ rel8	brad = EIP + rel8, cnt ≡ CX, as = 16	E0
LOOPE/LOOPZ rel8	brad = EIP + rel8, cnt ≡ ECX, as = 32	E0

SUMMARY
LOOPNE executed with an address size (as) of 16 transfers control to the branch
address brad if the zero detect flag (ZF) is clear and CX's value, decremented by
one, is not zero. Similarly, LOOPE with an as of 32 transfers control to brad if
ZF is clear and the decremented ECX value is not zero. In both cases the branch
target displacement can only be a byte value. LOOPNZ is a synonym of
LOOPNE.

OPERATION
```
cnt = cnt - 1;
if ( ZF == 0  && cnt != 0 )
{   if ( os == 32 )  /* Execute next instruction at brad */
      EIP = brad;
   else  /* os == 16: use low 16 bits only */
      EIP = brad<15:0>;
}
```

EXAMPLE
LOOPNZ lp   ; goto lp if ZF cleared and E/CX's value is not
                                    zero

NOTE
1. Neither the os attribute nor the as attribute of a LOOPNE assembly language
instruction can be determined by its operand. LOOPNE always inherits the
os and as attributes of the code segment containing it. Thus, in a USE16
code segment a LOOPNE has os and as attributes of 16; they are both 32 in a
USE32 code segment. The architecture does not enforce these assembly
language restrictions. A programmer may override the defaults by
"manually" coding an operand size or address size prefix, as desired.

LSL: Load segment limit (286, 376, 386, 486 only)

INSTRUCTION	PARAMETERS	OPCODE
LSL r, r/m	dst ≡ r, sel = r/m, os ∈ *{16,32}*	0F 03

SUMMARY
LSL reads into general register dst the segment limit of the segment named by
selector sel. If the segment named is page granular, it is converted to the
corresponding byte value before storing into dst. If the operand size is 32, the
instruction generates a DWORD limit value; otherwise, the limit value is
unconditionally truncated to the low-order 16 bits. No indication is given if the
truncation results in the loss of significant bits. LSL makes sure that a valid
descriptor type is referenced by sel. If not, or if the selector is out of the bound
of the descriptor table, ZF is cleared. If the descriptor type is valid, ZF is set.

If executed in REAL or VM86 modes, LSL signals an INVALID_INSTR fault. In
PROTECTED mode LSL is executable at all privilege levels.

OPERATION
```
if ( mode == REAL || mode == VM86 )
   signal_fault(INVALID_INSTR);

/* Always executable in PROTECTED mode */
if ( nullSel(sel) || ! inBounds(sel) ) /* not readable: clear ZF */
   ZF = 0;
else
{ desc = read_descr(sel, FALSE, FALSE);  /* see page 63 */
  if ( desc.Conforming ||
     ( ( CPL <= desc.DPL  &&  sel.RPL <= desc.DPL ) &&
       ( desc.Readable ||                           /* Data segment */
       (!desc.Conforming && desc.Executable) ||   /* Code segment */
       desc.Type == NOTBUSY_TSS16 ||
       desc.Type == BUSY_TSS16 ||
       desc.Type == NOTBUSY_TSS32 ||
       desc.Type == BUSY_TSS32 ||
       desc.Type == LDT_SEG ) ) ) /* Checks pass: set ZF and limit */
  { dst = desc.Limit;
     ZF = 1;
  }
  else /* unacceptable descriptor type: clear ZF */
     ZF = 0;
}
```

EXAMPLES
; Load into EBX the limit of the selector stored at the WORD *msel*.
LSL   EBX, msel
JNZ   limErr   ; goto *limErr* if invalid selector or descriptor

; Load into CX the limit of the segment named by selector 1004h.
MOV   AX, 1004h
LSL   CX, AX   ; only low 16 bits of limit loaded (hi WORD of
                                                 ECX left unchanged)
JNZ   limErr   ; goto *limErr* if invalid selector or descriptor

NOTE
1. The limit value reported for expand-down segments is the smallest valid
   offset; for expand-up segments it is the greatest valid offset. To determine
   whether a segment is expand-up or expand-down, use the LAR instruction.

LSS: Load pointer into SS and a register (376, 386, 486 only)

INSTRUCTION	PARAMETERS	OPCODE
LSS r, m	dst ≡ r, src = m, os ∈ {16,32}	0F B2

SUMMARY
LSS, available only on the 80386 and i486, loads the far pointer stored at the memory location named by *src* into the register pair SS:*dst*. If the operand size attribute (*os*) is 32, the far pointer occupies six bytes (a SELECTOR and a 4-byte OFFSET). If *os* is 16, the far pointer occupies four bytes (a SELECTOR and a 2-byte OFFSET). The size of the *dst* register also matches *os*.

If the instruction is executed in PROTECTED mode, stack segment protection checks are made on the segment named by the src selector before the SS load is allowed.

OPERATION
```
SELECTOR sel;
OFFSET off;

/* == Read SELECTOR and OFFSET based on operand size. == */
if ( os == 2 )/
{   WORD *mem16 = &src;        /* reference memory as WORDs */
    off = mem16[0];
    sel = mem16[1];
}
else /* os == 4 */
{   DWORD *mem32 = &src;       /* reference memory as DWORDs */
    off = mem32[0];
    sel = mem32[1];
}

/* == Load SS_desc descriptor register based on execution mode. == */
if ( mode == REAL || mode == VM86 )      /* REAL-mode style segment base */
    SS_desc.Base = SS * 16;
else /* load PROTECTED mode descriptor */
    SS_desc = load_SS(sel, FALSE);       /* see page 70 */
```

/* == Initialize SS and specified general register. == */
dst = off;
SS = sel;

EXAMPLE
LSS   ESP, new_stack

NOTES
1. LSS is the preferred over a sequence of two MOVs as a means of initializing a new stack. This is because it can load both SS and ESP at once, thus avoiding problems if a same level interrupt is detected between the two MOVs.

2. The ES, DS, FS, and GS segment registers can be loaded using similar instructions with a prefixed "L"; e.g., LFS loads the pair FS:r, where *r* is a general register. Loading the CS segment register only makes sense in conjunction with an EIP load. The far and gated JMP instructions do this.

3. The scheme used to encode the *src* memory operand is of the general *r/m* type, and so can be used to encode a register. If this is attempted, an INVALID_INSTR fault is signaled when the instruction is executed.

LTR: Load task register (286, 376, 386, 486 only)

INSTRUCTION	PARAMETERS	OPCODE
LTR r/m16	dst ≡ r, sel = r/m16	0F 00 /3

SUMMARY
LTR loads the TSS segment register and descriptor with the selector sel. The "Busy" bit of the descriptor in memory is set. No task switch occurs; LTR's main use is to establish an initial context so that the first task switch operates correctly (i.e., knows where to save the CPU state). LTR succeeds only if the segment named is a free task state segment. If not, a GP fault is signaled.

OPERATION
```
/* LTR unavailable in REAL and VM86 modes */
if ( mode == REAL || mode == VM86 )
   signal_fault(INVALID_INSTR);

/* == LTR available in PROTECTED mode only if CPL is 0 == */
if ( CPL != 0 )
   signal_fault(GP, 0);

/* == LTR's selector cannot be NULL or LDT-based == */
if ( nullSel(sel) || sel⟨2⟩ == 1 )
   signal_fault(GP, (sel & 0xFFFC));

/* == Basic checks have passed: read descriptor and make sure it is valid. == */
lock(DESCR_TABLE);              /* see page 112 */
desc = read_descr(sel, FALSE, FALSE); /* see page 63 */
if ( desc.Type == NOTBUSY_TSS16 || desc.Type == NOTBUSY_TSS32 )
{ if ( ! desc.Valid )
   signal_fault(NP, (sel & 0xFFFC));

   /* == Set BUSY bit in GDT entry for TSS descriptor, then load TSS and TSS_desc == */
   temp = DTAB_read1(sel, GDT_desc, sel.Index*8+5, FALSE);    /* read Type field */
   DTAB_write1(sel, GDT_desc, sel.Index*8+5, temp | 2, FALSE);  /* and set Busy bit */
   unlock(DESCR_TABLE);         /* see page 112 */

   TSS = sel;
   TSS_desc = desc;
}
```

EXAMPLE
```
LTR       firstTSS
```

MOV: Read/write data from/to general registers

INSTRUCTION	PARAMETERS	OPCODE
MOV r, r/m	dst ≡ r, src = r/m, os ∈ {8,16,32}	8A {8}, 8B {16,32}
MOV r/m, r	dst ≡ r/m, src = r, os ∈ {8,16,32}	88 {8}, 89 {16,32}
MOV r/m, imm	dst ≡ r/m, src = imm, os ∈ {8,16,32}	C6 {8}, C7 {16,32}
MOV reg, imm	dst ≡ reg, src = imm, os ∈ {8,16,32}	B0+reg {8}, B8+reg {16,32}
MOV AL, moff	dst ≡ AL, src = moff, os = 8	A0 {8}
MOV eAX, moff	dst ≡ AX/EAX, src = moff, os ∈ {16,32}	A1 {16,32}
MOV moff, AL	dst ≡ moff, src = AL, os = 8	A2 {8}
MOV moff, eAX	dst ≡ moff, src = AX/EAX, os ∈ {16,32}	A3 {16,32}

SUMMARY

The data MOV instruction copies the value of the source (*src*) operand to the destination (*dst*) operand. No flags are modified. *src* and *dst* can be any combination of general register and memory operands, as long as they are both of the same size and both operands are not memory-based.

The MOV mnemonic is used also for reading and writing segment registers, control registers, debug registers and test registers. See the appropriate MOV instruction category for their definitions.

OPERATION
dst = src

EXAMPLES
```
MOV    EAX, 4                    ; EAX = 4
MOV    AH, BYTE PTR [ESI]        ; AH = *( (BYTE *) ESI )
MOV    AX, BX                    ; AX = BX
MOV    WORD PTR [EAX], DX        ; *( (WORD *) EAX ) = DX
```

NOTE
1. As with most instructions, the number of bytes in *src* must match the number of bytes in *dst*. To move a value from a smaller sized to a larger sized variable, use MOVSX (*src* is treated as a signed value) or MOVZX (*src* is treated as an unsigned value).

MOV: Load segment registers DS, ES, FS or GS

INSTRUCTION	PARAMETERS	OPCODE
MOV DS, r/m	sr ≡ DS, desc ≡ DS_desc, sel = r/m	8E /3
MOV ES, r/m	sr ≡ ES, desc ≡ ES_desc, sel = r/m	8E /0
MOV FS, r/m	sr ≡ FS, desc ≡ FS_desc, sel = r/m	8E /4
MOV GS, r/m	sr ≡ GS, desc ≡ GS_desc, sel = r/m	8E /5

SUMMARY

The data segment register MOV instruction initializes the segment register named *sr* with the SELECTOR value *sel*. *Sel* can be a WORD or DWORD operand. If it is a DWORD, the high order WORD is ignored.

In PROTECTED mode, the instruction also reads the descriptor associated with the selector and loads it into the descriptor register associated with *sr*. The load succeeds only if the descriptor in memory is for a data segment that is no more privileged (i.e., numerically greater than or equal to) *sel*'s RPL value and the CPL. If these conditions are not met, a general protection (GP)fault is signaled.

Protection checks for stack segment register (SS) loads are somewhat different from the checks done for data segment register (DS, ES, FS, GS) loads. See the description of MOV SS, ... for details. It is not possible to load the CS register by itself.

The MOV mnemonic is used also for storing segment registers, and reading and writing general registers, control registers, debug registers and test registers. See the appropriate MOV instruction category for their definitions.

OPERATION
```
if ( mode == PROTECTED )
{  desc = load_data_seg(sel, FALSE);   /* Load descriptor after checks (see page 71) */
   sr = sel;                           /* Load segment register if desciptor load OK */
}
else /* REAL or VM86 modes: simulate 8086-style segment */
{  desc.Valid = TRUE;
   desc.Base = selector * 16;          /* Segment base address is selector * 16 */
   desc.Limit = 0xFFFF;                /* Segment limit is always 64K */
   desc.DefaultAttr = FALSE;           /* USE16 data segment */
   desc.Readable = desc.Writable = TRUE;
   desc.ExpandDown = FALSE;
   desc.Executable = FALSE;
   sr = sel;                           /* Load segment register with selector value */
}
```

EXAMPLES
```
MOV      DS, AX
MOV      FS, WORD PTR [ESI]
```

NOTES

1. In REAL or VM86 modes the instruction executes in 2/5 clocks for the register/memory cases of the selector. In PROTECTED mode, 18/19 clocks are required.

2. If a MOV into segment register instruction is executed with the encoding for CS in the segment register field, an INVALID_INSTR fault is signaled.

MOV: Load SS segment register

INSTRUCTION	PARAMETERS	OPCODE
MOV SS, r/m16	sr ≡ SS, sel = r/m16	8E /2

SUMMARY

The SS load instruction initializes the stack segment register with the SELECTOR value sel. Sel can be a WORD or DWORD operand. If it is a DWORD, the high order WORD is ignored. In PROTECTED mode, it also reads the descriptor associated with the selector and loads it into the on-chip descriptor SS_desc. In PROTECTED mode, the load succeeds only if the descriptor in memory is for a data segment that is of the same privilege as the sel's RPL value and the CPL. If these conditions are not met, a STACK fault is signaled.

Protection checks for data segment register (DS, ES, FS, GS) loads are somewhat different from the checks done for SS loads. See the previous description of the data segment register load instruction for details. It is not possible to load the CS register by itself.

The MOV mnemonic is used also for storing segment registers, and reading and writing general registers, control registers, debug registers and test registers. See the appropriate MOV instruction category for their definitions.

OPERATION
```
/* == Load SS and SS_desc based on execution mode. == */
if ( mode == PROTECTED )
{   desc = load_SS(sel, FALSE);     /* Load descriptor after checks (see page 70) */
    SS = sel;                       /* Load segment register */
}

else /* REAL or VM86 modes: simulate 8086-style segment */
{   SS_desc.Valid = TRUE;
    SS_desc.Base = selector * 16;   /* Segment base address is selector * 16 */
    SS_desc.Limit = 0xFFFF;         /* Segment limit is always 64K */
    SS_desc.DefaultAttr = FALSE;    /* USE16 data segment */
    SS_desc.Readable = desc.Writable = TRUE;
    SS_desc.ExpandDown = FALSE;
    SS_desc.Executable = FALSE;
    sr = sel;                       /* Load segment register with selector value */
}
```

/* == *Disable interrupts for next instruction, provided the programmer doesn't make a habit*
of it! == */
if (prev_instr_loaded_SS)
  prev_instr_loaded_SS = FALSE;
else
  prev_instr_loaded_SS = TRUE;

EXAMPLES
MOV   SS, AX
MOV   SS, WORD PTR [DI]

NOTES

1. In REAL or VM86 modes the instruction executes in 2/5 clocks for the register/memory cases of the selector. In PROTECTED mode, 18/19 clocks are required.

2. It is not possible to initialize a segment register with a constant value directly. Use a general register as a temporary buffer to do this; for example, the sequence below initializes SS to 1022.
MOV AX, 1022
MOV SS, AX

3. If a stack pointer is initialized via the sequence

MOV SS, newStack_Selector
MOV ESP, newStack_Top
there is the danger that a same level interrupt may occur between the two instructions. This would not work since the stack pointer is invalid just after the SS load. To prevent this, the architecture inhibits interrupts for one instruction after the SS segment register is loaded. On the 80386 and i486, it is recommended that stack initialization be done using the LSS instruction.

MOV: Store segment register

INSTRUCTION	PARAMETERS	OPCODE
MOV r/m, CS	dst ≡ r/m, sel = CS, os ∈ {16,32}	8C /1
MOV r/m, DS	dst ≡ r/m, sel = DS, os ∈ {16,32}	8C /3
MOV r/m, ES	dst ≡ r/m, sel = ES, os ∈ {16,32}	8C /0
MOV r/m, FS	dst ≡ r/m, sel = FS, os ∈ {16,32}	8C /4
MOV r/m, GS	dst ≡ r/m, sel = GS, os ∈ {16,32}	8C /5
MOV r/m, SS	dst ≡ r/m, sel = SS, os ∈ {16,32}	8C /2

SUMMARY

The segment register store instruction stores the SELECTOR in any one of the segment registers CS, DS, ES, FS, GS, or SS into a WORD-sized or DWORD-sized general register or memory location. If the destination is DWORD-sized, its the high-order WORD is filled with zeros. The instruction is executable in all modes and at all privilege levels.

The MOV mnemonic is used also for loading segment registers and reading and writing general registers, control registers, debug registers, and test registers. See the appropriate MOV instruction category for their definitions.

OPERATION
dst = sr

EXAMPLES
MOV AX, DS
MOV WORD PTR [ESI], FS

NOTE

1. It is not possible to move the contents of one segment register into another segment register directly. Similarly, it is not possible to initialize a segment register to a constant value directly. Use a general register as a temporary buffer to do either operation; for example, the sequence below loads DS with the SELECTOR 0x12B9.
   MOV AX, 12B9h
   MOV DS, AX

MOV: Load control registers (376, 386, 486 only)

INSTRUCTION	PARAMETERS	OPCODE
MOV CR0, r32	dst ≡ CR0, src = r32	0F 22 /0
MOV CR2, r32	dst ≡ CR2, src = r32	0F 22 /2
MOV CR3, r32	dst ≡ CR3, src = r32	0F 22 /3

SUMMARY

The load control register variant of MOV initializes any one of the three control register CR0, CR2, or CR3 to the input value *src*. CR0 is the extended machine status word, CR2 is the page fault address register and CR3 is the page directory base register. CR1 and CR4 through CR7 are not used (nor defined) by the 80*x*86. Code should not attempt to load them. All control register load instructions are privileged.

The MOV mnemonic is used also for storing control registers and reading and writing general registers, segment registers, debug registers, and test registers. See the appropriate MOV instruction category for their definitions.

OPERATION

```
if ( CPL != 0 )
   signal_fault(GP, 0);
```

dst ≡ CR0: /* extended MSW load */
```
   if ( src⟨31⟩ == 1 && src⟨0⟩ == 0 ) /* PG==1 and PE==0 invalid */
   signal_fault(GP, 0);
```

```
   /* Checks pass: load CR0 */
   CR0⟨31⟩ = src⟨31⟩;    /* PG: paging enable [386, 486] */
   CR0⟨30⟩ = src⟨30⟩;    /* CD: caching disable [486] */
   CR0⟨29⟩ = src⟨29⟩;    /* NW: "writes transparent" control [486] */
   CR0⟨28:19⟩ = undefined;
   CR0⟨18⟩ = src⟨18⟩;    /* AM: enable AC (alignment check) flag [486] */
   CR0⟨17⟩ = undefined;
   CR0⟨16⟩ = src⟨16⟩;    /* WP: enable supervisor write protect [486] */
   CR0⟨5⟩ = src⟨5⟩;      /* NE: floating point ops exception reporting ctl. [486] */
   CR0⟨4⟩ = src⟨4⟩;      /* ET: processor extension type [early 386s] */
   CR0⟨3⟩ = src⟨3⟩;      /* TS: task switch occurred */
   CR0⟨2⟩ = src⟨2⟩;      /* EM: emulate math */
   CR0⟨1⟩ = src⟨1⟩;      /* MP: monitor processor extension */
   CR0⟨0⟩ = src⟨0⟩;      /* PE: segmented protection enable [set to 1 on 376] */
```

dst ≡ CR2: /* page fault address register load */
```
   CR2 = src;
```

dst ≡ **CR3:** /* page directory base register load */
  CR3 = src & 0xFFFFF000; /* page-align the directory base */

EXAMPLES
```
MOV     CR0, ECX
MOV     CR3, EAX
```


NOTES
1. Control registers, and hence control register load instructions, are only available on the 80376, 80386, and i486. Only the lower half of CR0, called MSW, is implemented in the 80286. The 80286 instruction LMSW is used to load MSW.

2. The 80386 and i486 can be set back to REAL mode using MOV CR0, *reg* in a way that set the PE flag to 0. Care should be taken to ensure that the descriptor registers ES_desc, CS_desc, SS_desc, DS_desc, FS_desc, and GS_desc have their Limit field set to 0xFFFF. The access rights of all descriptor registers, except CS_desc should describe writable, expand-up segments; CS_desc should describe an executable segment that is readable also. After entering REAL mode, a direct far JMP should be performed. A sample sequence to switch back from PROTECTED to REAL mode is as follows

```
; Initialize segment registers with DATA_SEL, a descriptor formatted to look
; like a REAL mode descriptor (i.e., Limit = 0xFFFF; Base = sel*16; Writable).
mov     ax, DATA_SEL
mov     es, ax
mov     ss, ax
mov     ds, ax
mov     fs, ax
mov     gs, ax

mov     ax, CODE_SEL              ; CODE_SEL is SELECTOR of a "REAL-
                                    style" code descr.
jmpf    CODE_SEL:CS_lab          ; Pseudo-assembly code for a far JMP

CS_lab:
mov     eax, cr0                 ; Clear PE and PG flags in CR0
and     eax, 7FFFFFFEh
mov     cr0, eax
jmp     flush                    ; Flush instruction queue

flush:
jmp     far ptr cont             ; Direct far JMP to ensure REAL mode

cont:    ; ... now in REAL mode ...
```

3. *src* is always interpreted as a DWORD general register, regardless of the operand size attribute implied by the encoding.

4. The mode bits in the MOD/RM byte for this MOV instruction should always be set to 11_2, to signify a general register *src* operand. In fact, the value in this field is ignored; it is assumed to be 11_2.

MOV: Store control registers (376, 386, 486 only)

INSTRUCTION	PARAMETERS	OPCODE
MOV r32, cr	dst ≡ r32, src = cr	0F 20

SUMMARY

The store control register variant of MOV stores the contents of control register *cr* into the general register named by *dst*. CR0 is the extended machine status word, CR2 is the page fault address register, and CR3 is the page directory base register. CR1 and CR4 through CR8 are not used (nor defined) by the 80x86; code should not attempt to store them. All control register store instructions are privileged; see note 3 for an exception to this rule.

The MOV mnemonic is used also for loading control registers and reading and writing general registers, segment registers, debug registers, and test registers. See the appropriate MOV instruction category for their definitions.

OPERATION
```
if ( CPL != 0 )
   signal_fault(GP, 0);

dst = src
```

EXAMPLES
```
MOV     ECX, CR0
MOV     EAX, CR3
```

NOTES

1. Control registers, and hence control register store instructions, are only available on the 80376, 80386, and i486. The lower half of CR0, called MSW, is implemented in the 80286. The 80286 instruction LMSW is used to load MSW.

2. *dst* is always interpreted as a DWORD general register, regardless of the operand size attribute implied by the encoding.

3. The mode bits in the MOD/RM byte for this MOV instruction should always be set to 11_2, to signify a general register *dst* operand. In fact, the value in this field is ignored; it is assumed to be 11_2.

4. SMSW stores the lower half of CR0 into a general register or memory location. Thus, it can be viewed as a specialized form of the control register store instruction MOV r32, CR0. Since SMSW is not a privileged instruction, it has the "advantage" of being executable from any privilege level.

MOV: Load debug registers (376, 386, 486 only)

INSTRUCTION	PARAMETERS	OPCODE
MOV DR0, r32	dst ≡ DR0, src = r32	0F 23 /0
MOV DR1, r32	dst ≡ DR1, src = r32	0F 23 /1
MOV DR2, r32	dst ≡ DR2, src = r32	0F 23 /2
MOV DR3, r32	dst ≡ DR3, src = r32	0F 23 /3
MOV DR6, r32	dst ≡ DR6, src = r32	0F 23 /6
MOV DR7, r32	dst ≡ DR7, src = r32	0F 23 /7

SUMMARY

The load debug register variant of MOV initializes any one of the four breakpoint address registers DR0 through DR3, the debug status register DR6 or the debug control register DR7. Debug register load instructions can only be executed with CPL set to zero. Even access with CPL set to zero raises a DEBUG fault if the GD bit (in DR7) is set.

The MOV mnemonic is used also for storing debug registers and reading and writing general registers, segment registers, control registers, and test registers. See the appropriate MOV instruction category for their definitions.

OPERATION
```
if ( CPL != 0 )
   signal_fault(GP, 0);

/* == Check if debug register access is disabled == */
if ( GD )
{  DR6⟨13⟩ = 1;  /* set BD flag */
   signal_fault(DEBUG);
}


dst ≡ DR0 .. DR3: /* breakpoint addresses */
   dst = src;


dst ≡ DR6:  /* debug status register */
   DR6⟨31:16⟩ = undefined;
   DR6⟨15:13⟩ = src⟨15:13⟩; /* "Because" bits BT, BS, BD */
   DR6⟨12:4⟩ = undefined;
   DR6⟨3:0⟩ = src⟨3:0⟩;       /* "Because" bits B3, B2, B1, B0 */


dst ≡ DR7:  /* debug control register */
   DR7⟨31:16⟩ = src⟨31:16⟩; /* LENgth and R/W control for DR3..DR0 */
   DR7⟨15:14⟩ = undefined;
   DR7⟨13⟩ = src⟨13⟩;        /* GD bit */
```

DR7⟨12:10⟩ = *undefined*;
DR7⟨9:0⟩ = src⟨9:0⟩;

EXAMPLES
MOV DR0, ECX
MOV CR6, EAX

NOTES
1. Debug registers, and hence debug register load instructions, are only available on the 80376, 80386, and i486.

2. src is always interpreted as a DWORD general register, regardless of the operand size attribute implied by the encoding.

3. The mode bits in the MOD/RM byte for this MOV instruction should always be set to 11_2, to signify a general register src operand. In fact, the value in this field is ignored; it is assumed to be 11_2.

4. The GD (global disable) bit is initially clear. Once it is set (via a "MOV DR7, ...",) it cannot be cleared since the very instruction used to clear it is no longer executable! This disabling facility allows a debugger to acquire the debug registers for its own use. The GD bit is cleared whenever a DEBUG exception occurs. Thus the DEBUG exception handler itself has access to the debug registers. The handler needs to set the GD flag before exiting if debug register access is to remain restricted.

MOV: Store debug registers (376, 386, 486 only)

INSTRUCTION	PARAMETERS	OPCODE
MOV r32, dr	dst ≡ r32, src = dr	0F 21

SUMMARY

The store debug register variant of MOV stores the contents of any one of the four breakpoint address registers DR0 through DR3, the debug status register DR6, or the debug control register DR7 into a DWORD general register. Debug register store instructions can only be executed with CPL set to zero. Even access with CPL set to zero raises a DEBUG fault if the GD bit (in DR7) is set.

The MOV mnemonic is used also for loading debug registers and reading and writing general registers, segment registers, control registers, and test registers. See the appropriate MOV instruction category for their definitions.

OPERATION

```
if ( CPL != 0 )
   signal_fault(GP, 0);

/* == Check if debug register access is disabled == */
if ( GD )
{   DR6⟨13⟩ = 1;  /* set BD flag */
   signal_fault(DEBUG);
}

/* == If access allowed, store debug register contents == */
dst = src;
```

EXAMPLES

```
MOV      EAX, DR2
MOV      ESI, DR7
```

NOTES

1. Debug registers, and hence debug register store instructions, are only available on the 80376, 80386, and i486.

2. *src* is always interpreted as a DWORD general register, regardless of the operand size attribute implied by the encoding.

3. The mode bits in the MOD/RM byte for this MOV instruction should always be set to 11_2, to signify a general register *src* operand. In fact, the value in this field is ignored; it is assumed to be 11_2.

4. The GD (global disable) bit is initially clear. Once it is set (via a "MOV DR7, ...",) it cannot be cleared since the very instruction used to clear it is no longer executable! This disabling facility allows a debugger to acquire the debug registers for its own use. The GD bit is cleared automatically whenever a DEBUG exception occurs. Thus the DEBUG exception handler itself has access to the debug registers. The handler needs to set the GD flag before exiting if debug register access is to remain restricted.

MOV: Load test registers (386 and 486 only)

INSTRUCTION	PARAMETERS	OPCODE
MOV TR6, r32	dst ≡ TR6, src = r32	0F 26 /6
MOV TR7, r32	dst ≡ TR7, src = r32	0F 26 /7

SUMMARY

The load test register variant of MOV performs an implementation-defined chip test function. On the 80386 and i486, TR6 and TR7 are used to test the operation of the paging TLB. On the i486, TR3, TR4, and TR5 provide access to the on-chip cache; see §2.7.9.1 (starting on page 103) for a discussion of the i486's cache. TR0 through TR2 inclusive are unused, and are inaccessible. Test capabilities accessed via test registers complement the 80386 and i486's power-on self test features.

The TLB on the 80386 and i486 is a 32 entry cache organized into eight sets, with a set size of four. Each entry contains a linear address, a corresponding physical address, and access rights. The TLB accepts a linear address and an access type (i.e., "read" or "write") as input, looks them up in the cache entries, and generates the corresponding physical address if a match is found. When testing the TLB, a store into TR6 either initializes one of the entries in the cache, or performs a lookup operation (based on the setting of the C bit.) TR7 stores the physical address corresponding to a linear address during a write operation, and returns the physical address corresponding to the input linear address during a lookup operation. See §2.7.10 (starting on page 108) for a discussion of TLBs.

Note that the 80x86 architecture only supports the notion of a test register bank; it does not specify their function. Thus, test features provided by the 80386 and i486 are specific to them. In particular, the features need not be compatibly implemented across different versions of the 80x86. In particular, the test registers and associated instructions are unavailable on the 8086, 80186, 80286, and 80376.

The MOV mnemonic is used also for reading test registers, and reading and writing general registers, segment registers, control registers and debug registers. See the appropriate MOV instruction category for their definitions.

OPERATION

/* TR6 fields */

```
#define TLB_LA      TR6⟨31:15⟩   /* TLB_LA and TLB_SET (bits 31 to 12) */
#define TLB_SET     TR6⟨14:12⟩   /* form the input page address */
#define V           TR6⟨11⟩
#define D           TR6⟨10⟩
#define D_bar       TR6⟨9⟩
#define U           TR6⟨8⟩
#define U_bar       TR6⟨7⟩
#define W           TR6⟨6⟩
#define W_bar       TR6⟨5⟩
#define C           TR6⟨0⟩

/* TR7 fields */
#define TLB_PA      TR7⟨31:12⟩
#define PL          TR7⟨4⟩
#define REP         TR7⟨3:2⟩

/* TLB entry structure */
typedef struct {
    unsigned LinAddr: 17;              /* linear address high bits */
    unsigned V: 1;                     /* Entry valid */
    unsigned D: 1;                     /* Dirty */
    unsigned U: 1;                     /* User page */
    unsigned W: 1;                     /* Writable page */
    unsigned PhysAddr: 20;             /* physical address */
    } TLB_ENTRY;

TLB_ENTRY TLB_x86[8][4];               /* 32 entry TLB */

if ( CPL != 0 )
    signal_fault(GP, 0);

dst ≡ TR6:  /* TLB command register */
    TR6⟨31:5⟩ = src⟨31:5⟩;
    TR6⟨4:1⟩ = undefined;
    TR6⟨0⟩ = src⟨0⟩;

    if ( C == 1 )  /* write into TLB entry */
    {  if ( PL == 1 )  /* REP specifies entry in set to be modified */
            ent = REP;
        else  /* PL == 0: let 80386 choose entry */
            ent = i386Choice();
        TLB_x86[TLB_SET][ent].LinAddr = TLB_LA;
        TLB_x86[TLB_SET][ent].V = V;
        TLB_x86[TLB_SET][ent].D = D;
        TLB_x86[TLB_SET][ent].U = U;
        TLB_x86[TLB_SET][ent].W = W;
    }
    else /* C == 0:  perform TLB lookup */
    {  for ( i = 0;  i < 4;  i++ )
        {  ce = TLB_x86[TLB_SET][i];
            if ( ce.LinAddr == TLB_LA  &&  (ce.V & V)  &&
                ((ce.D & D) | (~ce.D & D_bar)) &&
```

```
                ((ce.U & U) | (~ce.U & U_bar)) &&
                ((ce.W & W) | (~ce.W & W_bar)) )  /* match found */
            {  TLB_PA = ce.PhysAddr;
               break;
            }
        }
    if ( i < 4 )  /* match was found */
        PL = 1;
    else  /* no match found */
        PL = 0;
}
```

dst ≡ **TR7:** /* TLB data output register */
  TR7⟨31:12⟩ = src⟨31:12⟩; /* assign TLB_PA */
  TR7⟨11:5⟩ = *undefined*;
  TR7⟨4:2⟩ = src⟨4:2⟩;
  TR7⟨1:0⟩ = *undefined*;

EXAMPLES
```
; Initialize entry 0 in set 2 with TLB_LA = 20₁₆
; TLB_PA = 1B3₁₆, not Dirty, Writable User page
MOV  EAX, 001B3018h  ; Setup phys. addr. and entry info
MOV  TR7, EAX        ; and load TR7 with it.
MOV  EAX, 00020B40h  ; Setup lin. addr., acc. rights and command.
MOV  TR6, EAX        ; Load data and execute write
```

NOTES
1. Since the TLB participates in every memory access when paging is enabled, writes to the TLB using TR6 and TR7 should be done only with paging disabled (i.e., with PG reset.)

2. When initializing a TLB entry, the access rights pairs (D, D_bar), (U, U_bar), and (W, W_bar) must be set such that one entry of a pair is the inverse of the other entry; for example, if D is set to 0, D_bar must be set to 1. If this is not done, the TLB entry is updated unpredicatably.

3. *src* is always interpreted as a DWORD general register, regardless of the operand size attribute implied by the encoding.

4. The mode bits in the MOD/RM byte for this MOV instruction should always be set to 11_2, to signify a general register *src* operand. In fact, the value in this field is ignored; it is assumed to be 11_2.

MOV: Store test registers (386 and 486 only)

INSTRUCTION	PARAMETERS	OPCODE
MOV r32, tr	dst ≡ r32, src = tr	0F 24 /6

SUMMARY
The store test register variant of MOV performs an implementation defined chip test function. On the 80386, TR6 and TR7 are defined for use in TLB testing. Either of these two registers' value can be stored into a DWORD general register. See the definition of the test register load MOV instruction for more information on test register usage.

The 80x86 architecture only supports the notion of a test register bank; it does not specify their function. Thus, all test features provided by the 80386 are specific to it. They need not be compatibly implemented across different versions of the 80x86; for example, they are unavailable on the 80286. Therefore, instruction that access the test registers should be isolated in a machine-specific area of code.

The MOV mnemonic is used also for reading and writing general registers, segment registers, control registers and debug registers. See the appropriate MOV instruction category for their definitions.

OPERATION
dst = src

EXAMPLES
```
; Check if a valid mapping for a Writable User page at linear
; address 0x20000 is in the TLB. ("Dirty" setting is a don't-care.)
MOV      EAX, 00020F41h          ; Setup lookup command
MOV      TR6, EAX                ; and issue command
MOV      EAX, TR7                ; Get lookup result
BT       EAX, 4                  ; Is PL bit set?
JC       ok                      ; Yes: lookup found a match. TR7⟨31:12⟩ has
                                    physical addr.
; Reaches here if no match found
```

NOTES
1. *src* is always interpreted as a DWORD general register, regardless of the operand size attribute implied by the encoding.

2. The mode bits in the MOD/RM byte for this MOV instruction should always be set to 11_2, to signify a general register *src* operand. In fact, the value in this field is ignored; it is assumed to be 11_2.

MOVSB/MOVSD/MOVSW: Move string element

INSTRUCTION	PARAMETERS	OPCODE
MOVSB	os = *8*, as ∈ {16,32}	A4
MOVSW	os = *16*, as ∈ {16,32}	A5
MOVSD	os = *32*, as ∈ {16,32}	A5

SUMMARY

MOVS*x* copies one location in memory to another. Both the source and destination locations must be a BYTE, WORD, or DWORD. MOVSB copies a BYTE, MOVSW a WORD, and MOVSD a DWORD. The source operand is pointed at by ESI or SI and the destination operand is pointed at by EDI or DI. ESI and EDI are used if the address size attribute is 32; if it is 16, SI and DI participate. After the copy both [E]SI and [E]DI are incremented or decremented by 2 or 4, depending on the operand size. If DF is clear, the values are incremented; otherwise, they are decremented. No flags are modified.

The source offset [E]SI is relative to the segment referenced by the DS segment register, unless it is overridden by the segment override prefix. The destination offset [E]DI is always relative to the segment referenced by thc ES segment register; it cannot be overriden.

OPERATION

```
src = ( (as == 16) ? SI : ESI );
dst = ( (as == 16) ? DI : EDI );
/* Perform copy operation */
switch (os)
{   case 8:    *( (char *) dst ) = *( (char *) src );
            break;
    case 16:   *( (short *) dst ) = *( (short *) src );
            break;
    case 32:   *( (int *) dst ) = *( (int *) src );
            break;
}
```

```
/* Update ESI and EDI */
if ( as == 32 )  /* 32-bit addressing */
{   ESI = src + (DF ? -os/8 : os/8);
    EDI = src + (DF ? -os/8 : os/8);
}
else /* as == 16 :  16-bit addressing */
{   SI = src + (DF ? -os/8 : os/8);
    DI = src + (DF ? -os/8 : os/8);
}
```

EXAMPLES
MOVSB
MOVSW

NOTE
1. The MOVS*x* instructions are restricted forms of the REP MOVS*x* instructions. The REP form of the instructions repeatedly execute the specified MOVS*x* operation until ECX's value becomes zero. This provides a single instruction implementation of 80*x*86 string move. See the discussion of the REP prefix for more details.

ASSEMBLER USAGE NOTE
1. Address register selection (i.e., SI and DI versus ESI and EDI) depends on the address size attribute. To ensure that an address size override prefix is generated (if needed), the assembler notation where explicit operands to MOVS*x* are provided is recommended. For example, a repeated MOVSB from FS:ESI to ES:EDI should be encoded as follows

REP MOVS ES:BYTE PTR [EDI], FS:BYTE PTR [ESI]

This also provides a convenient way to specify segment overrides.

MOVSX: Copy data with sign extension (376, 386, 486 only)

INSTRUCTION	PARAMETERS	OPCODE
MOVSX r, r/m8	dst ≡ r, src = r/m8, os ∈ *{16,32}*	0F BE
MOVSX r, r/m16	dst ≡ r, src = r/m16, os ∈ *{16,32}*	0F BF

SUMMARY
MOVSX loads the sign-extended value of its source operand (*src*) into the destination (*dst*). The size of the source operand must be less than the size of the destination. Therefore, source can be a BYTE or WORD general register or memory location whereas the destination can be a WORD or DWORD. The destination is always constrained to be a general register.

OPERATION
dst = signex(src)   /* *src* is sign extended */

EXAMPLE
```
; Add the signed BYTE value in BL to EDI.
MOVSX   ECX, BL                  ; ECX = sign_extension(BL)
ADD     EDI, ECX                 ; EDI = EDI + ECX
```

NOTE
1. If both *src* and *dst* are WORDs MOVSX degenerates to a simple copy operation. In this case, the (faster and more compact) MOV instruction is recommended.

MOVZX: Copy data with zero extension (376, 386, 486 only)

INSTRUCTION	PARAMETERS	OPCODE
MOVZX r, r/m8	dst ≡ r, src = r/m8, os ∈ *{16,32}*	0F B6
MOVZX r, r/m16	dst ≡ r, src = r/m16, os ∈ *{16,32}*	0F B7

SUMMARY

MOVSX extends its source operand (*src*) with enough high-order zeros as to match the size of the destination. This zero-extended value is loaded into the destination (*dst*). The source can be a BYTE or WORD general register or memory location, but the destination is constrained to be a WORD or DWORD general register.

OPERATION

dst = src;   /* *src* is zero-extended */

EXAMPLES

```
; Subtract the unsigned BYTE value in DH from the WORD in AX.
MOVZX   SI, DH              ; SI = zero_extension(DH)
SUB     AX, SI             ; AX = AX - SI
```

NOTE

1. MOVZX is similar to the data MOV instruction, except that it requires the source operand to have fewer bits than the destination operand. If both *src* and *dst* are WORDs (i.e., *src* of type *r/m16* and *dst* of type *r16*) MOVSX degenerates to a simple data MOV. In this case, the (faster and more compact) MOV instruction is recommended.

MUL: Unsigned multiply

INSTRUCTION	PARAMETERS	OPCODE
MUL r/m8	prd ≡ AX, mnd = AL, mpr = r/m8, os = 8	F6 /4
MUL r/m16	prd ≡ DX:AX, mnd = AX, mpr = r/m16, os = 16	F7 /4
MUL r/m32	prd ≡ EDX:EAX, mnd = EAX, mpr = r/m32, os = 32	F7 /4

SUMMARY

MUL generates the product of an unsigned multiplicand (mnd) and an unsigned multiplier (mpr) and stores the result in the product prd. prd is AX if the operands are BYTEs. prd is the register pair DX:AX if the operands are WORDs and the register pair EDX:EAX if the operands are DWORDs. In these cases, DX and EDX hold the most significant bits of the product.

OPERATION

$result$ = mnd $*_u$ mpr;
if ($result > 2^{os}-1$)
{   CF = 1;
    OF = 1;
}
else
{   CF = 0;
    OF = 0;
}

/* Set remaining flags */
SF = $undefined$
ZF = $undefined$
AF = $undefined$
PF = $undefined$
/* Store result */
prd = $result$;

EXAMPLES

MUL	EAX	; EDX:EAX = EAX $\times_u$ EAX
MUL	BYTE PTR [ESI]	; AX = AL $\times_u$ *((BYTE *) ESI)

NEG: Negate using two's complement

INSTRUCTION	PARAMETERS	OPCODE
NEG r/m	dst ≡ r/m, os ∈ {8,16,32}	F6 /3 {8}, F7 /3 {16,32}

SUMMARY

NEG negates the value of the dst operand, using two's complement arithmetic. All arithmetic flags are modified. Nonarithmetic flags are not affected. A NEG instruction with a memory operand is LOCKable.

OPERATION

result = 0 − dst
/* Set arithmetic flags */
OF = *result* < −2^{os-1} || *result* > 2^{os-1}-1
SF = dst⟨os-1⟩
ZF = *result* == 0
AF = 0 <$_u$ dst⟨3:0⟩
PF = evenParity(*result*)
CF = 0 <$_u$ dst
/* Store result */
dst = *result*

EXAMPLES

NEG   AX   ; AX = -AX
NEG   BYTE PTR [ESI]   ; *((BYTE *) ESI) = 0 - *((BYTE *) ESI)

NOTES

1. Since the flag settings after a NEG operation is the same as that after a subtract with the minuend set to zero, settings of the unsigned comparison flags AF and CF can be rewritten as

   AF = dst⟨3:0⟩ >$_u$ 0
      = dst % 16 >$_u$ 0
   CF = dst >$_u$ 0

   Thus, NEG can be used to check whether a value is nonzero, as follows:
   ; Negate *var* and branch to label *positive* if prenegated value is nonzero
   NEG   var
   JC   positive

NOP: No operation

INSTRUCTION	PARAMETERS	OPCODE
NOP		90

SUMMARY

NOP is a one byte instruction that performs no operation. No CPU state is modified except EIP. The instruction is actually an assembly language alias for the instruction XCHG EAX, EAX (or XCHG AX, AX if used in a USE16 segment).

OPERATION
/* no operation */
continue;

EXAMPLES
NOP

NOT: Bitwise complement

INSTRUCTION	PARAMETERS	OPCODE
NOT r/m	dst ≡ r/m, os ∈ {8,16,32}	F6 /2 {8}, F7 /2 {16,32}

SUMMARY
NOT inverts the value of dst. Thus, every 1 bit becomes a 0 and every 0 bit becomes a 1. No flags are modified by the instruction. A NOT instruction with a memory operand is LOCKable.

OPERATION
result = ~dst
dst = result

EXAMPLES
```
NOT     AX              ; AX = ~AX
NOT     BYTE PTR [ESI]  ; *( (BYTE *) ESI ) = ~ *( (BYTE *) ESI )
```

operand size override (prefix): Toggle operand size attribute of following instruction (376, 386, 486 only)

INSTRUCTION	PARAMETERS	OPCODE
see *ASM USAGE NOTE* below		66

SUMMARY

The 80376, 80386, and i486 support both 16 bit (i.e., WORD) and 32-bit (i.e., DWORD) operations on data. In general, WORD and DWORD operations share the same opcode; the size of the operation actually performed is determined by its *operand size attribute*. Normally, a WORD/DWORD instruction's operand size attribute is determined by the *default* operand size attribute stored in the code segment's descriptor register (i.e., via the flag CS_desc.DefaultAttr). However, this default can be changed for any particular instruction by placing the "operand override" prefix in front of it. If the default operand size is 32, use of the prefix makes it 16. Conversely, if it is 16, use of the prefix makes it 32. See §2.18.4 on page 198 for more details.

Since 32-bit operands are only available on the 80376, 80386, and i486, only these implementations of the 80x86 define the operand size override.

NOTE

1. On a 80376, 80386, and i486, the operand size override prefix is ignored if placed in front of an instruction that operates on BYTEs, or an instruction that has no meaningful operand size attribute (e.g., HLT). On a 80186 and 80286, use of this prefix generates an INVALID_INSTR fault. Its effect on the 8086 is undefined.

ASSEMBLER USAGE NOTE

1. An operand size override prefix is automatically generated by an assembler whenever the operand size implied by the instruction does not match the default operand size for the segment in which the instruction appears. Hence, no explicit "operand size override" mnemonic is required. The assembly language segment attribute USE16 specifies a default operand size of 16; the attribute USE32 specifies a default operand size of 32.

OR: Bitwise inclusive OR

INSTRUCTION	PARAMETERS	OPCODE
OR r, r/m	dst ≡ r, src = r/m, os ∈ {8,16,32}	0A {8}, 0B {16,32}
OR r/m, r	dst ≡ r/m, src = r, os ∈ {8,16,32}	08 {8}, 09 {16,32}
OR r/m, imm	dst ≡ r/m, src = imm, os ∈ {8,16,32}	80 /1 {8}, 81 /1 {16,32}
OR r/m, imm8	dst ≡ r/m, src = signex(imm8), os ∈ {16,32}	83 /1 {16,32}
OR AL, imm8	dst ≡ AL, src = imm8, os = 8	0C {8}
OR eAX, imm	dst ≡ AX/EAX, src = imm, os ∈ {16,32}	0D {16,32}

SUMMARY

OR performs a bitwise inclusive-OR on the source and destination operands and writes the value back into the destination. Thus, if either bit of the operands at a given bit position is set to 1, the corresponding bit in the result is also set. All arithmetic flags except AF are set based on the result; AF's value after the operation is undefined. Nonarithmetic flags are left unmodified. An OR instruction with a memory operand is LOCKable.

OPERATION

```
/* Compute result */
result = dst | src
dst = result

/* Set arithmetic flags */
OF = 0
SF = dst⟨os-1⟩
ZF = (dst == 0)
AF = undefined
PF = evenParity(dst)
CF = 0
```

EXAMPLES

```
OR      EAX, 4                 ; EAX = EAX | 4
OR      AH, BYTE PTR [ESI]     ; AH = AH | *( (BYTE *) ESI )
```

OUT: Output to I/O port

INSTRUCTION	PARAMETERS	OPCODE
OUT imm8, AL	port = imm8, src = AL, os = *8*	E6
OUT imm8, *e*AX	port = imm8, src = AX/EAX, os ∈ *{16,32}*	E7
OUT DX, AL	port = DX, src = AL, os = *8*	EE
OUT DX, *e*AX	port = DX, src = AX/EAX, os ∈ *{16,32}*	EF

SUMMARY
OUT writes AL, AX, or EAX (depending on *os*) to the I/O port addressed by *port*.

OUT is an IOPL-sensitive instruction; that is, in PROTECTED or VM86 modes, the I/O port write is done only if CPL ≤ IOPL. If CPL > IOPL a general protection fault is signaled if the active TSS is a TSS16. If the active TSS is a TSS32 (and CPL > IOPL), the I/O permission map entry for the I/O port named by DX determines whether the I/O port write is allowed. See §2.9 (page 118) for a description of the I/O permission map check algorithm.

OPERATION
```
/* == Check if instruction execution is permitted. == */
if ( CPL > IOPL  &&  mode != REAL )
{   if ( !IOPermission(port, os) )
        signal_fault(GP, 0);
}
/* == Perform I/O write == */
switch (os)
{   case 8:         *( (BYTEPORT *) port ) = AL;
                    break;
    case 16:        *( (WORDPORT *) port ) = AX;
                    break;
    case 32:        *( (DWORDPORT *) port ) = EAX;
                    break;
}
```

EXAMPLES
```
OUT     DX, EAX          ; *( (DWORDPORT *) DX ) = EAX
OUT     200, AL          ; *( (BYTEPORT *) 200 ) = AL
```

OUTSB/OUTSD/OUTSW: Output to I/O port from string element (unavailable on the 8086)

INSTRUCTION	PARAMETERS	OPCODE
OUTSB	os = *8*, as ∈ {16,32}	6E
OUTSW	os = *16*, as ∈ {16,32}	6F
OUTSD	os = *32*, as ∈ {16,32}	6F

SUMMARY

OUTS*x* writes to the I/O port whose address is in register DX the BYTE, WORD, or DWORD in memory pointed at by ESI or SI. The operand size (*os*) attribute selects whether a BYTE, WORD, or DWORD is written, and the address size (*as*) attribute selects whether SI (*as* set to 16) or ESI (*as* set to 32) is used. After the write, [E]SI is incremented or decremented by 1, 2, or 4, depending on the operand size and the current setting of the DF flag. Thus, repeated use of an OUTS*x* instruction copies data from a string in memory to a given I/O port.

Unless overriden by a segment prefix, the [E]SI offset value is relative to the segment referenced by the DS segment register. Any other segment register may be chosen by selecting the appropriate segment override prefix.

The OUTS*x* instructions are IOPL-sensitive; that is, in PROTECTED or VM86 modes, the write to the I/O port is done only if CPL ≤ IOPL. If CPL > IOPL a general protection fault is signaled if the active TSS is a TSS16. If the active TSS is a TSS32 (and CPL > IOPL), the I/O permission map entry for the I/O port named by DX determines whether the I/O port write is allowed. See §2.9 (page 118) for a description of the I/O permission map check algorithm.

OPERATION

```
/* == Check if instruction execution is permitted. == */
if ( CPL > IOPL  &&  mode != REAL )
{   if ( !IOPermission(port, os) )
      signal_fault(GP, 0);
}
src = ( (as == 16) ? SI : ESI );
```

```
/* == Read from memory address src and write to I/O address port == */
switch (os)
{  case 8:          *( (BYTEPORT *) port ) = *( (BYTE *) src ) ;
                    break;
   case 16:         *( (WORDPORT *) port ) = *( (WORD *) src ) ;
                    break;
   case 32:         *( (DWORDPORT *) port ) = *( (DWORD *) src ) ;
                    break;
}

if ( as == 32 )  /* 32-bit addressing */
   ESI = src + (DF ? -os/8 : os/8);
else /* as == 16 : 16-bit addressing */
   SI = src + (DF ? -os/8 : os/8);
```

EXAMPLES
OUTSB
OUTS DWORD PTR [ESI]

NOTES
1. The execution time of OUTS*x* depends on the current mode of the 80386, as follows. REAL mode: 14 clocks; VM86 mode: 28 clocks; PROTECTED mode: 8 clocks if CPL ≤ IOPL, 28 clocks if CPL > IOPL.

2. The OUTS*x* instructions are restricted forms of the REP OUTS*x* instructions. The REP form of the instructions repeatedly execute the specified OUTS*x* operation until ECX's value becomes zero. See the discussion of the REP prefix for more details.

ASSEMBLER USAGE NOTE
1. Address register selection (i.e., SI versus ESI) depends on the address size attribute. To ensure that an address size override prefix is generated (if needed), the assembler notation where explicit operands to OUTS*x* are provided is recommended. For example, a repeated OUTSW from ES:ESI should be encoded as follows

REP OUTS ES:WORD PTR [ESI]

This also provides a convenient way to specify segment overrides.

POP: Pop data into register or memory

INSTRUCTION	PARAMETERS	OPCODE
POP r/m	dst ≡ r/m, os ∈ {16,32}	8F /0
POP reg	dst ≡ reg, os ∈ {16,32}	58+*reg*

SUMMARY
POP removes the top WORD or DWORD from the stack (based on the operand size attribute) and stores it into a same size general register or memory location.

OPERATION
dst = pop*OS*();   /* see page 118 */

EXAMPLES
POP   EAX   ; EAX = pop4()
POP   WORD PTR [ESI]   ; *((WORD *) ESI) = pop2()

NOTES
1. It is not possible to POP a BYTE quantity. This is done to ensure that the stack pointer (ESP or SP) is always at a WORD or DWORD aligned address. Thus, in a 32-bit code environment, it is best to use DWORD-sized POPs (and PUSHes).

2. The POP mnemonic can be used to load a segment register with the contents of the top stack element. See the next instruction description for details.

3. On the 80376, 80386, and i486 an instruction like
   pop   word ptr [esp+12]

   copies the top of stack back into an element of the stack. In such cases the memory reference made (e.g., ESP+12) uses the postincremented value of ESP.

POP: Pop selector into segment register

INSTRUCTION	PARAMETERS	OPCODE
POP DS	dst ≡ DS, desc ≡ DS_desc, os ∈ {16,32}	1F
POP ES	dst ≡ ES, desc ≡ ES_desc, os ∈ {16,32}	07
POP SS	dst ≡ SS, desc ≡ SS_desc, os ∈ {16,32}	17
POP FS	dst ≡ FS, desc ≡ FS_desc, os ∈ {16,32}	0F A1
POP GS	dst ≡ GS, desc ≡ GS_desc, os ∈ {16,32}	0F A9

SUMMARY

POP loads the segment register named by *dst* with the SELECTOR at the top of stack. The top of stack element is removed after the load. Although a SELECTOR is a WORD-sized quantity, a DWORD is removed from the stack top if the operand size attribute *os* is 32. (If *os* is 16, only a WORD is removed.)

The POP mnemonic can be used to load a general register or memory location with the contents of the top stack element. See the previous instruction description for details.

OPERATION

dst ∈ {DS, ES, FS, GS} : /* data segment register load */

```
dst = (WORD) popOS();                  /* Discard upper part of data if os==32 */
if ( mode == PROTECTED )
    desc = load_data_seg(dst, FALSE);   /* see page 71 */
else /* REAL or VM86 modes:  load base appropriately */
    desc.Base = dst * 16;              /* Segment base address is SELECTOR*16 */
```

dst ≡ SS : /* stack segment register load */

```
SS = (WORD) popOS();                   /* Discard upper part of data if os==32 */
if ( mode == PROTECTED )
    SS_desc = load_SS(SS, FALSE);      /* see page 70 */
else /* REAL or VM86 modes:  load base appropriately */
    SS_desc.Base = SS * 16;           /* Stack base address is SELECTOR*16 */
```

```
/* == Loading SS disables interrupts until the next instruction completes, provided the
      previous instruction did not load SS also. == */
if ( prev_instr_loaded_SS )
   prev_instr_loaded_SS = FALSE;
else
   prev_instr_loaded_SS = TRUE;
```

EXAMPLES

```
POP  DS   ; DS = WORD/DWORD from top-of-stack; load DS_desc
POP  SS   ; SS = WORD/DWORD from top-of-stack; load SS_desc
```

NOTES

1. It is not possible to POP a selector into the CS register, since doing so would change the code segment from which the next instruction would be fetched, but not the offset into it (i.e., EIP). It is meaningful to pop data into both the CS and EIP registers in one instruction. The same-level, far RETurn instruction performs just this function.

2. The number of bytes removed by the segment register POP instruction is based on the operand size attribute, even though only the least significant WORD is the element popped is loaded into the segment register. This is done to ensure that the stack pointer ESP (or SP) is always at a DWORD (or WORD) aligned address. Thus, in a 32 bit code environment, it is best to use DWORD-sized POPs (and PUSHes).

3. There is no way to determine the *os* attribute of an assembly language segment register POP instruction from its operands. Therefore, unless an operand size prefix is coded explicitly, *os* is set to 16 if a POP appears in a USE16 segment; it is set to 32 in a USE32 segment.

POPA/POPAD: Pop into all general registers

INSTRUCTION	PARAMETERS	OPCODE
POPA	os = *16*	61
POPAD	os = *32*	61

SUMMARY
POPAD loads all DWORD-sized general registers by performing a series of eight
DWORD-sized stack pops. Similarly, POPA loads all WORD-sized general
registers by performing WORD-sized pops.

OPERATION
```
if ( os == 16 )
{   DI = pop2();
    SI = pop2();
    BP = pop2();
    pop2();                 /* Discard SP */
    BX = pop2();
    DX = pop2();
    CX = pop2();
    AX = pop2();
}
else  /* os == 32 :  DWORD register loads */
{   EDI = pop4();
    ESI = pop4();
    EBP = pop4();
    pop4();                 /* Discard ESP */
    EBX = pop4();
    EDX = pop4();
    ECX = pop4();
    EAX = pop4();
}
```

EXAMPLES
POPA
POPAD

NOTE
1. It is not possible to POPA (or PUSHA) the BYTE-sized general registers AL,
   AH, BL, BH, CL, CH, DL, or DH.

POPF/POPFD: Pop into flags register

INSTRUCTION	PARAMETERS	OPCODE
POPF	os = 16	9D
POPFD	os = 32	9D

SUMMARY
POPFD removes the top DWORD from the stack and stores its low order WORD into the low order WORD of EFLAGS. On the i486, the AC flag is also updated. POPF removes the top WORD from the stack and stores it into the low order WORD of EFLAGS.

The IOPL field in EFLAGS is updated only if the instruction is executed with CPL set to 0. The IF field is updated only if the instruction is executed with IOPL-privilege (i.e., with CPL <= IOPL.) Neither POPF nor POPFD update the RF or VM bits. To allow 8086 virtualization, the PUSHF/PUSHFD instructions are made IOPL-sensitive while executing in VM86 mode.

OPERATION
```
/* == POPF/POPFD are IOPL-sensitive in VM86 mode == */
if ( mode == VM86  &&  CPL > IOPL )
   signal_fault(GP, 0);

/* == Pop flags image into a temporary register == */
flg = popOS();
```

```
/* == Except for the AC flag on the i486, the most significant WORD of EFLAGS is not
        updated by POPF[D]. The remaining bits are updated as follows. == */
if ( « CPU is i486 » )
    AC = flg⟨18⟩        /* "Alignment Check" flag */
    EFLAGS⟨15⟩ = 0;     /* Bit 15 of EFLAGS is always 0 */
    NT = flg⟨14⟩;       /* See Notes below */
    if ( CPL == 0 )     /* IOPL update is privileged */
        IOPL = flg⟨13:12⟩;
    OF = flg⟨11⟩;
    DF = flg⟨10⟩;
    if ( CPL <= IOPL )  /* "Interrupt Enable" flag update is IOPL-sensitive */
        IF = flg⟨9⟩;
    TF = flg⟨8⟩;
    SF = flg⟨7⟩;
    ZF = flg⟨6⟩;
    EFLAGS⟨5⟩ = 0;      /* Bit 5 of EFLAGS is always 0 */
    AF = flg⟨4⟩;
    EFLAGS⟨3⟩ = 0;      /* Bit 3 of EFLAGS is always 0 */
    PF = flg⟨2⟩;
    EFLAGS⟨1⟩ = 1;      /* Bit 1 of EFLAGS is always 1 */
    CF = flg⟨0⟩;
```

EXAMPLES
POPF
POPFD

NOTES

1. Both POPF and POPFD update only the low order 16 bits in the EFLAGS register. However, POPFD removes a DWORD from the stack, thus retaining DWORD alignment of the stack address. POPF is provided mainly for compatibility with the 80286 and its predecessors.

2. The NT and IOPL flags are not updated in REAL mode on a 80286. However, they are updated in the REAL mode of the 80386. This quirk is often used by software to determine if it is running on a 80286. Also note that since only the i486 updates the AC flag, this fact can be used to differentiate between a 80386 and a i486.

3. The unused bits in the high order WORD of EFLAGS are *reserved*. See §1.3.2 on page 8 for a discussion of reserved fields.

PUSH: Push general register, memory data, or immediate

INSTRUCTION	PARAMETERS	OPCODE
PUSH r/m	src = r/m, os ∈ {16,32}	FF /6
PUSH reg	src = reg, os ∈ {16,32}	50+*reg*
PUSH imm	src = imm, os ∈ {16,32}	68
PUSH imm8	src = signex(imm8), os ∈ {16,32}	6A

SUMMARY
PUSH pushes the source operand (*src*) onto the stack by subtracting 2 (*os*==16) or 4 (*os*==32) from the stack pointer and writing *src* at the updated stack pointer address.

OPERATION
push*OS*(src)   /* see page 118 */

EXAMPLES
```
PUSH    EAX                  ; push4(EAX)
PUSH    WORD PTR [ESI]       ; push4( *( (WORD *) ESI ) )
```

NOTES
1. On the 80386 and i486 an instruction like
   PUSH   WORD PTR [ESP+12]
   copies a stack element onto the top of stack. In such cases the memory reference made (e.g., ESP+12) uses the ESP value prior to the predecrement implied by the PUSH operation.

2. On the 80286, 80376, 80386, and i486 PUSH [E]SP pushes the value of [E]SP *prior* to the [E]SP decrement implied by the PUSH. On the 8086 and 80186, the value *after* SP is decremented is pushed.

3. It is not possible to PUSH from (or POP into) a BYTE register or memory location. The PUSH imm8 instruction accepts a BYTE-sized immediate operand but sign extends it based on os. This sign-extended WORD or DWORD is then pushed. This ensures that the stack pointer (ESP or SP) is always at a WORD or DWORD aligned address. Thus, in a 32 bit code environment, it is best to use DWORD-sized PUSHes (and POPs).

4. The assembly language PUSH instruction can also be used to push onto the stack the SELECTOR stored in a segment register. See the next instruction description for details.

PUSH: Push segment register

INSTRUCTION	PARAMETERS	OPCODE
PUSH DS	sr = DS, os ∈ {16,32}	1E
PUSH ES	sr = ES, os ∈ {16,32}	06
PUSH CS	sr = CS, os ∈ {16,32}	0E
PUSH SS	sr = SS, os ∈ {16,32}	16
PUSH FS	sr = FS, os ∈ {16,32}	0F A0
PUSH GS	sr = GS, os ∈ {16,32}	0F A8

SUMMARY
The segment register PUSH instruction pushes the contents of the segment register sr onto the stack. Although a segment register is a WORD-sized quantity, a DWORD is pushed if the operand size attribute (*os*) is 32. In this case the value of the high-order 16 bits of the DWORD is *undefined*.

The PUSH mnemonic can also be used to push the contents of a general register or memory location. See the previous instruction description for details.

OPERATION
```
if ( os == 32 )
    push4( (DWORD) sr );
else /* os == 16 : WORD-sized stack */
    push2( sr );
```

EXAMPLES
```
PUSH    DS
PUSH    SS
```

NOTE
1. The number of bytes pushed by the segment register POP instruction is based on the operand size attribute, even though the SELECTOR only occupies the least significant WORD of the pushed element. This is done to ensure that the stack pointer ESP (or SP) is always at a DWORD (or WORD) aligned address. Thus, in a 32-bit code environment, it is best to use DWORD-sized PUSHes (and POPs.)

ASSEMBLER USAGE NOTE
1. There is no way to determine the os attribute of an assembly language segment register PUSH instruction from its operands. Therefore, unless an

operand size prefix is coded explicitly, os is set to 16 if a PUSH appears in a USE16 segment; it is set to 32 in a USE32 segment.

PUSHA/PUSHAD: Push all general register contents

INSTRUCTION	PARAMETERS	OPCODE
PUSHA	os = *16*	60
PUSHAD	os = *32*	60

SUMMARY
PUSHAD pushes the contents of all DWORD-sized general registers by performing a series of eight DWORD-sized stack pushes. Similarly, PUSHA pushes the contents of all WORD-sized general registers by performing WORD-sized pushes.

OPERATION
```
if ( os == 16 )
{   WORD sp0 = SP;
    push2(AX);
    push2(CX);
    push2(DX);
    push2(BX);
    push2(sp0);          /* Push value that SP had at instruction's start */
    push2(BP);
    push2(SI);
    push2(DI);
}

else  /* os == 32 :  DWORD register pushes */
{   DWORD esp0 = ESP;
    push4(EAX);
    push4(ECX);
    push4(EDX);
    push4(EBX);
    push4(esp0);         /* Push value that ESP had at instruction's start */
    push4(EBP);
    push4(ESI);
    push4(EDI);
}
```

EXAMPLES
PUSHA
PUSHAD

NOTE
1. It is not possible to PUSHA (or POPA) the BYTE-sized general registers AL, AH, BL, BH, CL, CH, DL, or DH.

PUSHF/PUSHFD: Push flags register

INSTRUCTION	PARAMETERS	OPCODE
PUSHF	os = 16	9C
PUSHFD	os = 32	9C

SUMMARY

PUSHFD pushes the contents of EFLAGS onto the stack. PUSHF pushes the contents of the low-order WORD of EFLAGS onto the stack.

The EFLAGS image pushed by PUSHFD always shows the VM bit as set to zero (although the actual VM bit setting is left unchanged). Thus, the behavior of PUSHFD (and PUSHF) is the same in both VM86 and REAL modes.

To allow 8086 virtualization, the PUSHF/PUSHFD instructions are made IOPL-sensitive while executing in VM86 mode.

OPERATION

```
/* == PUSHF/PUSHFD are IOPL-sensitive in VM86 mode == */
if ( mode == VM86 && CPL > IOPL )
   signal_fault(GP, 0);

/* == Push [E]FLAGS image. == */
if ( os == 32 )
{   eflg = EFLAGS;
    /* Clear VM and RF flags before pushing onto stack */
    eflg⟨17⟩ = 0;
    eflg⟨16⟩ = 0;
    push4( eflg );
}
else /* os == 16 : push low-order WORD of EFLAGS */
   push2( EFLAGS⟨15:0⟩ );
```

EXAMPLES

PUSHF
PUSHFD

NOTE

1. To retain stack alignment, 32-bit code should always use the PUSHFD instruction. PUSHF is provided mainly for compatibility with the 80286 and its predecessors.

RCL: Rotate left through carry flag

INSTRUCTION	PARAMETERS	OPCODE
RCL r/m, CL	dst ≡ r/m, shft = CL, os ∈ {8,16,32}	D2 /2 {8}, D3 /2 {16,32}
RCL r/m, imm8	dst ≡ r/m, shft = imm8, os ∈ {8,16,32}	C0 /2 {8}, C1 /2 {16,32}
RCL r/m, 1	dst ≡ r/m, shft = 1, os ∈ {8,16,32}	D0 /2 {8}, D1 /2 {16,32}

SUMMARY

RCL rotates left by *shft* bits the bit pattern formed by concatenating the carry flag (CF) with *dst*. On implementations other than the 8086, *shft* is treated a five bit unsigned quantity (i.e., with range 0 .. 31). If a larger quantity is specified, the higher-order bits are unconditionally ignored. On the 8086, all eight bits of *shft* are used; however, the instruction with the *imm8* form of shift count is unavailable on it.

Since CF participates in the rotate, it is modified accordingly. OF is set if, after a one-bit rotate, the most significant bit of dst does not match CF. The architecture does not define the value of OF if the rotate is for more than one bit. Flags other than CF and OF are not modified.

OPERATION

```
for ( i = 0; i < (shft & 0x1F); i++ )
{   newCF = dst⟨os-1⟩;
    result = ( dst << 1 ) | CF;
    dst = result;
    CF = newCF;
}

if ( (shft & 0x1F) == 1 )  /* OF defined only for one bit rotates */
    OF = ( dst⟨os-1⟩ != CF );
else
    OF = undefined;
```

EXAMPLE
RCL   EAX, 4   ; CF:EAX = (CF:EAX << 4) | ((CF:EAX >> 29) & 0xF)

NOTE
1. RCL rotates an *os* + 1 bit quantity. Therefore, unlike ROL, a RCL by some shift amount *s* is not the same as a RCL by *s* % *os*.

RCR: Rotate right through carry flag

INSTRUCTION	PARAMETERS	OPCODE
RCR r/m, CL	dst ≡ r/m, shft = CL, os ∈ *{8,16,32}*	D2 /3 *{8}*, D3 /3 *{16,32}*
RCR r/m, imm8	dst ≡ r/m, shft = imm8, os ∈ *{8,16,32}*	C0 /3 *{8}*, C1 /3 *{16,32}*
RCR r/m, 1	dst ≡ r/m, shft = 1, os ∈ *{8,16,32}*	D0 /3 *{8}*, D1 /3 *{16,32}*

SUMMARY

RCR rotates right by *shft* bits the bit pattern formed by concatenating the carry flag (CF) with *dst*. On implementations other than the 8086, *shft* is treated a five bit unsigned quantity (i.e., with range $0..31$). If a larger quantity is specified, the higher-order bits are unconditionally ignored. On the 8086, all eight bits of *shft* are used; however, the instruction with the *imm8* form of shift count is unavailable on it.

Since CF participates in the rotate, it is modified accordingly. OF is set if, after a one-bit rotate, the most significant bit of dst does not match the next to most significant bit; that is, if dst⟨os-1⟩ != dst⟨os-2⟩. The architecture does not define the value of OF if the rotate is for more than one bit. Flags other than CF and OF are not modified.

OPERATION

```
for ( i = 0; i < (shft & 0x1F); i++ )
{   newCF = dst⟨0⟩;
    result = ( CF << (os-1) ) | ( dst >> 1 ) ;
    dst = result;
    CF = newCF;
}

if ( (shft & 0x1F) == 1 )   /* OF defined only for one bit rotates */
    OF = ( dst⟨os-1⟩ != dst⟨os-2⟩ );
else
    OF = undefined;
```

EXAMPLES

```
RCR     EAX, 4              ; CF:EAX = (CF:EAX >> 4) |
                                ((CF:EAX << 29) & 0x1E0000000)
```

NOTES

1. RCR rotates an *os* + 1 bit quantity. Therefore, unlike ROR, a RCR by some shift amount *s* is not the same as a RCR by *s* % *os*.

REP/REPE/REPZ/REPNE/REPNZ (prefix): Repeat following string instruction

INSTRUCTION	PARAMETERS	OPCODE
REPE CMPx	func ≡ CMPSx, as ∈ {16,32}, os ∈ {8,16,32}	F3 A6 {8}, F3 A7 {16,32}
REPNE CMPx	func ≡ CMPSx, as ∈ {16,32}, os ∈ {8,16,32}	F2 A6 {8}, F2 A7 {16,32}
REP INSx	func ≡ INSx, as ∈ {16,32}, os ∈ {8,16,32}	F3 6C {8}, F3 6D {16,32}
REP LODSx	func ≡ LODSx, as ∈ {16,32}, os ∈ {8,16,32}	F3 AC {8}, F3 AD {16,32}
REP MOVSx	func ≡ MOVSx, as ∈ {16,32}, os ∈ {8,16,32}	F3 A4 {8}, F3 A5 {16,32}
REP OUTSx	func ≡ OUTSx, as ∈ {16,32}, os ∈ {8,16,32}	F3 6E {8}, F3 6F {16,32}
REPE SCASx	func ≡ SCASx, as ∈ {16,32}, os ∈ {8,16,32}	F3 AE {8}, F3 AF {16,32}
REPNE SCASx	func ≡ SCASx, as ∈ {16,32}, os ∈ {8,16,32}	F2 AE {8}, F2 AF {16,32}
REP STOSx	func ≡ STOSx, as ∈ {16,32}, os ∈ {8,16,32}	F3 AA {8}, F3 AB {16,32}

SUMMARY

REP, REPE, and REPNE are used to construct string operations. They operate by repeatedly executing the instruction they prefix, until a termination condition is satisfied. Every time the subject instruction is executed, the count register is decremented by one. The count register is ECX if the address size attribute *as* is 32; otherwise, CX is used.

REP's termination condition is that the value of ECX or CX be zero; REPE's termination condition is that [E]CX be zero or ZF be set TRUE; REPNE's termination condition is that [E]CX be zero or ZF be set FALSE. REPZ is a synonym for REPE, and REPNZ is a synonym for REPNE.

OPERATION
if prefix is REP: repeat [E]CX times

```
if ( ECX⟨as-1 : 0⟩ != 0 ) /* Use CX or ECX based on as attribute */
do
{ func();                   /* Perform string operation once */
  ECX⟨as-1 : 0⟩ −= 1;       /* Decrement CX or ECX */
  prev = curr;              /* Save current CPU state, except for EIP */
} while ( ECX⟨as-1 : 0⟩ != 0  &&  ! external_interrupt() && ! brkpt_detected() );
```

/* *NOTE: external interrupt is defined on page 166, and brkpt detected is defined on page 167. If an external interrupt is active, EIP is restored to point at the REP instruction (so that it can be resumed after the interrupt is serviced).* */
```
if ( external_interrupt() )
  EIP = prev_EIP;
```

if prefix is REPE: repeat [E]CX times or until ZF flag set

```
if ( ECX⟨as-1 : 0⟩ != 0 ) /* Use CX or ECX based on as attribute */
do
{ func();                    /* Perform string operation once */
  ECX⟨as-1 : 0⟩ -= 1;        /* Decrement CX or ECX */
  prev = curr;               /* Save current CPU state, except for EIP */
} while ( !ZF && ECX⟨as-1 : 0⟩ != 0  &&  ! external_interrupt() && ! brkpt_detected() );

if ( external_interrupt() )
  EIP = prev_EIP;
```

if prefix is REPNE: repeat [E]CX times or until ZF flag cleared

```
if ( ECX⟨as-1 : 0⟩ != 0 ) /* Use CX or ECX based on as attribute */
do
{ func();                    /* Perform string operation once */
  ECX⟨as-1 : 0⟩ -= 1;        /* Decrement CX or ECX */
  prev = curr;               /* Save current CPU state, except for EIP */
} while ( ZF && ECX⟨as-1 : 0⟩ != 0  &&  ! external_interrupt() && ! brkpt_detected() );

if ( external_interrupt() )
  EIP = prev_EIP;
```

EXAMPLES
```
; Copy 5 DWORDs from location in ESI to location in EDI.
MOV      ECX, 5
MOVSD

; Scan for the first newline character (ASCII value 10) in string EDI
MOV      AL, 10
SCASB
```

NOTES

1. If REP, REPE, or REPNE is used to prefix any instruction other than as shown above, an INVALID_INSTR fault is signaled on the 80376, 80386, and i486.

2. On the 80376, 80386, and i486, the REP MOVS*x* instructions may not be LOCKed. If attempted, an INVALID_INSTR fault is signaled. They were allowed to be LOCKed in the 80286 and its predecessors. See the *Notes* on the LOCK instruction (page 485) for more information on this topic.

RET (near), RETN: Return to subroutine in same segment

INSTRUCTION	PARAMETERS	OPCODE
RET/RETN imm16	params = imm16, os ∈ {16,32}	C2
RET/RETN	params = 0, os ∈ {16,32}	C3

SUMMARY
RETN is used to return from a subroutine that was invoked via a near CALL, that is, a call from within the same segment. Thus, RETN pops a DWORD or WORD address from the stack (based on the operand size attribute) and branches to the popped address. See the description of RETF if an intersegment procedure return is required.

If the RETN imm16 form is used, imm16 bytes are popped from the stack after the return address is popped. The popped bytes are discarded; this is useful for removing parameters pushed onto the stack by the caller.

RET is a convenience provided by most 80x86 assemblers. It is equivalent to either a RETN or a RETF (described on page 545). The opcode generated depends on the type of proc in which the RET appears. If it is a "proc near," RETN is generated; however, if it is a "proc far," RETF is generated.

OPERATION
/* == Pop return address: instruction execution resumes at new EIP == */
EIP = pop*OS*();

/* == Pop and discard *params* bytes from stack == */
if (SS_desc.DefaultAttr == 1) /* Stack pointer uses 32 bit addresses */
    ESP = ESP - params;
else /* Stack pointer uses 16 bit addresses */
    SP = SP - params;

EXAMPLES
RET
RE   12

NOTES
1. The *params* parameter is used to remove parameter data that the caller pushed onto the stack prior to the call. This feature is not always usable, however, because some high-level languages (notably C) a given functions to be invoked with a variable numbers of parameters.

RET (far), RETF: Return to subroutine in any segment

INSTRUCTION	PARAMETERS	OPCODE
RET/RETF imm16	params = imm16, os ∈ {16,32}	CA
RET/RETF	params = 0, os ∈ {16,32}	CB

SUMMARY

RETF is used to return from a subroutine that was invoked via a far CALL. A far CALL can originate from any code segment including the segment that stores the corresponding RETF. However, far CALLs and far RETs take substantially longer to execute than their "near" conterparts. Thus, near CALL — RETN should be used to implement procedure calls whenever possible.

The action performed by RETF depends on the current execution mode. In REAL and VM86 modes, the far return address is popped off the stack, and a branch to this address is executed. In PROTECTED mode the action taken depends on whether the procedure was called from the same privilege level or from an environment with less privilege (i.e., via an interlevel call). In both cases the far return address is popped off the stack as in the REAL and VM86 cases. However, a PROTECTED mode branch is made to this address. Also, for the interlevel RET case, the stack is switched back to the caller's stack. (Recall that an interlevel CALL pushes the current stack pointer onto the stack belonging to the called procedure.)

Regardless of execution modes, if the RETF imm16 form is used, imm16 bytes are popped from the caller's stack after the return address (and caller stack address, in the case of an interlevel RETF) is popped. The popped bytes are discarded; this is useful for removing parameters pushed onto the stack by the caller.

RET is a convenience provided by most 80*x*86 assemblers. It is equivalent to either a RETF or a RETN (described on page 544). The opcode generated depends on the type of proc in which the RET appears. If it is a "proc near," RETN is generated; however, if it is a "proc far," RETF is generated.

OPERATION

```
/* == Pop CS:(E)IP off stack == */
if ( os == 32 )  /* Execute next instruction at offset */
   EIP = popOS();
else  /* os == 16: use low 16 bits only */
   EIP = popOS() & 0xFFFF;
CS = popOS();
```

```
/* == Pop and discard params bytes from stack == */
if ( SS_desc.DefaultAttr == 1 )  /* Stack pointer uses 32 bit addresses */
   ESP = ESP - params;
else  /* Stack pointer uses 16 bit addresses */
   SP = SP - params;

/* Now setup branch if in REAL or VM86 modes, or do PROTECTED mode checks. */
if ( mode == REAL || mode == VM86 )  /* REAL mode far RET */
   CS_desc.Base = selector * 16;  /* REAL mode style CS base */

else  /* PROTECTED mode far RET */
{  /* Check if caller's selector is NULL or has bad CPL */
   if ( nullSel(CS) || CPL > CS.RPL )
      signal_fault(GP,  CS & 0xFFFC);

   if ( CS⟨1:0⟩ == CPL )  /* RETurn to caller at same privilege level */
      CS_desc = load_CS(CS, FALSE);
   else /* interlevel RETurn */
   {  DWORD callerESP;

      /* Setup caller's CPL, then check caller's CS's validity */
      CPL = CS.RPL;
      CS_desc = load_CS(CS, FALSE);

      /* Read caller's SS:(E)SP off current stack, and check it */
      callerESP = popOS();  /* save in temp so that SS can be popped */
      SS = popOS()
      SS_desc = load_SS(SS, FALSE);

      /* Setup caller's ESP, taking inot account the "B" bit */
      if ( SS_desc.DefaultAttr )  /* 32-bit addressing */
         ESP = callerESP;
      else
         SP = (WORD) callerESP;

      /* Invalidate ES, DS, FS, GS if they are too privileged for caller's environment */
      if ( ES_desc.DPL < CPL )
         ES_desc.Valid = FALSE;
      if ( DS_desc.DPL < CPL )
         DS_desc.Valid = FALSE;
      if ( FS_desc.DPL < CPL )
         FS_desc.Valid = FALSE;
      if ( GS_desc.DPL < CPL )
         GS_desc.Valid = FALSE;
   }
}
```

EXAMPLES

```
RETF     12
RET      12
RETF
```

NOTE
1. The width (i.e., WORD or DWORD) of all values popped off the return stack is determined by the operand size (os) attribute of RETF. Therefore, in PROTECTED mode, the RETF's os must match the type of call gate (i.e., CALLGATE16 or CALLGATE32) used to activate the procedure. Similarly, if the procedure was activated via a nongated CALL (i.e., a conforming call or a same level call) the os attributes of the CALL and the RETF must match.

ROL: Rotate left

INSTRUCTION	PARAMETERS	OPCODE
ROL r/m, CL	dst ≡ r/m, shft = CL, os ∈ {8,16,32}	D2 /0 {8}, D3 /0 {16,32}
ROL r/m, imm8	dst ≡ r/m, shft = imm8, os ∈ {8,16,32}	C0 /0 {8}, C1 /0 {16,32}
ROL r/m, 1	dst ≡ r/m, shft = 1, os ∈ {8,16,32}	D0 /0 {8}, D1 /0 {16,32}

SUMMARY
ROL rotates the bit pattern in *dst* left by *shft* bits. On implementations other than the 8086, *shft* is treated a five bit unsigned quantity (i.e., with range 0 .. 31). If a larger quantity is specified, the higher-order bits are unconditionally ignored. On the 8086, all eight bits of *shft* are used; however, the instruction with the *imm8* form of shift count is unavailable on it.

Flags settings for ROL are somewhat specialized! The CF and OF flags are updated, but only when the shift amount is nonzero. CF is set to the same value as the least significant bit of *dst* after the rotate. If the rotate count is 1, OF is set if the most significant bit of *dst* does not match CF; that is, if there is numeric overflow. If the rotate count is greater than 1, OF's value after the rotate is *undefined*. Flags other than CF and OF are not modified.

OPERATION
```
int shift_amt = (shft & 0x1F);

for ( i = 0;  i < shift_amt;  i++ )
{   CF = dst⟨os-1⟩;
    dst = ( dst << 1 ) | CF;
}

if ( shift_amt > 0 )
{   if ( shift_amt == 1 )   /* OF defined only for one bit rotates */
      OF = ( dst⟨os-1⟩ != CF );
    else
      OF = undefined;
}
```

EXAMPLE
```
ROL      EAX, 4                    ; EAX = (EAX << 4) | ((EAX >> 28) & 0xF)
```

ROR: Rotate right

INSTRUCTION	PARAMETERS	OPCODE
ROR r/m, CL	dst ≡ r/m, shft = CL, os ∈ *{8,16,32}*	D2 /1 *{8}*, D3 /1 *{16,32}*
ROR r/m, imm8	dst ≡ r/m, shft = imm8, os ∈ *{8,16,32}*	C0 /1 *{8}*, C1 /1 *{16,32}*
ROR r/m, 1	dst ≡ r/m, shft = 1, os ∈ *{8,16,32}*	D0 /1 *{8}*, D1 /1 *{16,32}*

SUMMARY

ROR rotates the bit pattern in *dst* right by *shft* bits. On implementations other than the 8086, *shft* is treated a five bit unsigned quantity (i.e., with range 0 .. 31). If a larger quantity is specified, the higher-order bits are unconditionally ignored. On the 8086, all eight bits of *shft* are used; however, the instruction with the *imm8* form of shift count is unavailable on it.

Flags settings for ROR are somewhat specialized! The CF and OF flags are updated, but only when the shift amount is nonzero. CF is set to the same value as the least significant bit of *dst* after the rotate. If the rotate count is 1, OF is set if the most significant bit of *dst* does not match the next to most significant bit; that is, if $dst\langle os\text{-}1\rangle$!= $dst\langle os\text{-}2\rangle$. If the rotate count is greater than 1, OF's value after the rotate is *undefined*. Flags other than CF and OF are not modified.

OPERATION

```
int shift_amt = (shft & 0x1F);
for ( i = 0; i < shift_amt; i++ )
{   CF = dst⟨0⟩;
    dst = ( CF << (os-1) ) | ( dst >>ᵤ 1 ) ;
}

if ( shift_amt == 0 )
{   if ( shift_amt == 1 )  /* OF defined only for one bit rotates */
      OF = ( dst⟨os-1⟩ != dst⟨os-2⟩ );
    else
      OF = undefined;
}
```

EXAMPLE

```
ROR      EAX, 4              ; CF:EAX = (CF:EAX >> 4) |
                                       ((CF:EAX << 29) & 0x1E0000000)
```

SAHF: Store AH register into flags

INSTRUCTION	PARAMETERS	OPCODE
SAHF		9E

SUMMARY
SAHF copies the contents of AH into the active flags in the low byte of EFLAGS. The low byte contains all the arithmetic flags, except OF.

OPERATION
SF = AH⟨7⟩;
ZF = AH⟨6⟩;
AF = AH⟨4⟩;
PF = AH⟨2⟩;
CF = AH⟨0⟩;

EXAMPLE
SAHF

NOTE
1. The following instruction sequence is an efficient method of transferring condition code settings from the 80x87 status word **FSW** to the 80x86:
   FSTSW   AX
   SAHF

SAL: Shift arithmetic left

INSTRUCTION	PARAMETERS	OPCODE
SAL r/m, CL	dst ≡ r/m, shft = CL, os ∈ {8,16,32}	D2 /4 {8}, D3 /4 {16,32}
SAL r/m, imm8	dst ≡ r/m, shft = imm8, os ∈ {8,16,32}	C0 /4 {8}, C1 /4 {16,32}
SAL r/m, 1	dst ≡ r/m, shft = 1, os ∈ {8,16,32}	D0 /4 {8}, D1 /4 {16,32}

SUMMARY

SAL shifts the bit pattern in *dst* left by *shft* bits, filling the vacated bits with zeros. On implementations other than the 8086, *shft* is treated a five bit unsigned quantity (i.e., with range 0 .. 31). If a larger quantity is specified, the higher-order bits are unconditionally ignored. On the 8086, all eight bits of *shft* are used; however, the instruction with the *imm8* form of shift count is unavailable on it.

CF is set to the value of the last bit that was shifted out (i.e., bit *dst⟨os-shft⟩* prior to the shift). OF is set if, after a one-bit shift, the most significant bit of *dst* does not match CF. The architecture does not define the value of OF if the shift is for more than one bit. The flags SF, ZF, and CF are set to reflect the arithmetic result of the shift, as usual. The value of the AF flag is *undefined*. No flags are modified if the shift amount is zero.

OPERATION
```
int shift_amt = shft & 0x1F;

if ( shift_amt > 0 )
{   if ( shift_amt <= os )
    {   CF = dst⟨os - shift_amt⟩;
        dst = ( dst << shift_amt );
    }
    else
    {   CF = 0;
        dst = 0;
    }

    if ( s == 1 )  /* OF defined only for one-bit shifts */
        OF = ( dst⟨os-1⟩ != CF );
    else
        OF = undefined;
```

```
    SF = dst⟨os-1⟩
    ZF = (dst == 0)
    AF = undefined
    PF = evenParity(dst)
}
```

EXAMPLES
```
SAL     EAX, CL                  ; EAX = (EAX << CL)
SAL     BYTE PTR [ESI], 4        ; *( (BYTE *) ESI ) = *( (BYTE *) ESI ) << 4
```

NOTES
1. On the 80376, 80386, and i486, each of the BYTE shift instructions
```
    SAL     b, 16
    SAL     b, 24
    SAL     b, CL                ; with CL set to 16 or 24
```
set CF if $b\langle 0\rangle$ is set to 1. This anomalous behavior does not occur on the 8086 or 80286.

2. SAL can be used to multiply a value by an integer power of 2; that is,
$$val = val \times 2^n$$
can be computed as
```
    SAL val, n
```

SAR: Shift arithmetic right

INSTRUCTION	PARAMETERS	OPCODE
SAR r/m, CL	dst ≡ r/m, shft = CL, os ∈ {8,16,32}	D2 /7 {8}, D3 /7 {16,32}
SAR r/m, imm8	dst ≡ r/m, shft = imm8, os ∈ {8,16,32}	C0 /7 {8}, C1 /7 {16,32}
SAR r/m, 1	dst ≡ r/m, shft = 1, os ∈ {8,16,32}	D0 /7 {8}, D1 /7 {16,32}

SUMMARY

SAR shifts the bit pattern in *dst* right by *shft* bits. The vacated bits are filled the sign bit's value prior to the shift. Therefore, the sign of the result is always preserved. (The instruction SHR fills the vacated bits with zeros.) On implementations other than the 8086, *shft* is treated a five bit unsigned quantity (i.e., with range 0 .. 31). If a larger quantity is specified, the higher-order bits are unconditionally ignored. On the 8086, all eight bits of *shft* are used; however, the instruction with the *imm8* form of shift count is unavailable on it.

CF is set to the value of the last bit that was shifted out (i.e., bit dst⟨shft-1⟩ prior to the shift.) OF is always set to zero if a one-bit shift is done. OF is left unmodified if the shift is for more than one bit. The flags SF, ZF, and CF are set to reflect the arithmetic result of the shift, as usual. The value of the AF flag is *undefined*. No flags are modified if the shift amount is zero.

OPERATION
```
int shift_amt = shft & 0x1F;

if ( shift_amt > 0 )
{   if ( shift_amt <= os )
    {   CF = dst⟨shift_amt-1⟩;
        dst = ( dst >> shift_amt );
    }
    else
    {   CF = 0;
        dst = 0;
    }
```

```
    if ( shift_amt == 1 )  /* OF zeroed for one-bit shifts */
        OF = 0;
    SF = dst⟨os-1⟩
    ZF = (dst == 0)
    AF = undefined
    PF = evenParity(dst)
}
```

EXAMPLE
SAR   EAX, 4   ; EAX = EAX >> 4

NOTE
  1. Applying SAR with a shift count of n to some value *val* divides *val* by 2^n.
     Note however, that the quotient generated is rounded toward $-\infty$. This
     results in a situation where (for example) -1 divided by 2 yields -1. To
     correct this situation, add $2^n\text{-}1$ to negative dividends before doing the SAR.

SBB: Signed and unsigned integer subtract with borrow

INSTRUCTION	PARAMETERS	OPCODE
SBB r, r/m	dst ≡ r, src = r/m, os ∈ {8,16,32}	1A {8}, 1B {16,32}
SBB r/m, r	dst ≡ r/m, src = r, os ∈ {8,16,32}	18 {8}, 19 {16,32}
SBB r/m, imm	dst ≡ r/m, src = imm, os ∈ {8,16,32}	80 /3 {8}, 81 /3 {16,32}
SBB r/m, imm8	dst ≡ r/m, src = signex(imm8), os ∈ {16,32}	83 /3 {16,32}
SBB AL, imm8	dst ≡ AL, src = imm8, os = 8	1C {8}
SBB eAX, imm	dst ≡ AX/EAX, src = imm, os ∈ {16,32}	1D {16,32}

SUMMARY
SBB subtracts the value of the source operand and CF from the destination operand, leaving the result in the destination. All arithmetic flags are set; nonarithmetic flags are left unmodified. A SBB instruction with a memory operand is LOCKable.

OPERATION
$result$ = dst − src − CF
/* Set arithmetic flags */
OF = $result < -2^{os-1}$ || $result > 2^{os-1}-1$
SF = dst⟨os-1⟩
ZF = $result$ == 0
AF = dst⟨3:0⟩ $<_u$ src⟨3:0⟩
PF = evenParity($result$)
CF = dst $<_u$ src
/* Store result */
dst = $result$

EXAMPLES
SBB EAX, 4   ; EAX = EAX - 4 - CF
SBB AH, BYTE PTR [ESI]   ; AH = AH - *((BYTE *) ESI) - CF

SCASB/SCASD/SCASW: Scan string for value

INSTRUCTION	PARAMETERS	OPCODE
SCASB	sval = AL, os = *8*, as ∈ {16,32}	AE
SCASW	sval = AX, os = *16*, as ∈ {16,32}	AF
SCASD	sval = EAX, os = *32*, as ∈ {16,32}	AF

SUMMARY

SCAS*x* compares the contents of AL, AX, or EAX against the BYTE (*os*==8), WORD (*os*==16), or DWORD (*os*==32) in the memory location pointed at by [E]DI. EDI is used if the address size attribute is 32; if it is 16, DI participates. After the comparison [E]DI is incremented (DF set to 0) or decremented (DF set to 1) by 2 or 4, depending on the operand size. The comparison sets flags just like the CMP and CMPS instructions.

Offset EDI is always relative to the segment referenced by the ES segment register; it cannot be overriden. An override prefix, if specified, is ignored.

OPERATION

```
src = ( (as == 16) ? DI : EDI );

/* Compare AL/AX/EAX against src, and set AF and CF */
switch (os)
{ case 8:  result = AL − *( (char *) src );      /* Signed BYTE quantity */
           AF = (AL⟨3:0⟩ <ᵤ *( (char *) src ));
           CF = (AL <ᵤ *( (char *) src ));
           break;

  case 16: result = AX − *( (short *) src );     /* Signed WORD quantity */
           AF = (AX⟨3:0⟩ <ᵤ *( (short *) src ));
           CF = (AX <ᵤ *( (short *) src ));
           break;

  case 32: result = EAX − *( (int *) src );      /* Signed DWORD quantity */
           AF = (EAX⟨3:0⟩ <ᵤ *( (int *) src ));
           CF = (EAX <ᵤ *( (int *) src ));
           break;
}

/* Increment string pointer */
src += (DF ? −os/8 : os/8);
if ( as == 32 )  /* 32-bit addressing */
  EDI = src;
else /* as == 16 : 16-bit addressing */
  DI = src;
```

```
/* Set remaining arithmetic flags */
```
$OF = result < -2^{os-1} \mathbin{||} result > 2^{os-1}\text{-}1$
$SF = result\langle os\text{-}1\rangle$
$ZF = result\langle os\text{-}1 : 0\rangle == 0$
$PF = \text{evenParity}(result)$

EXAMPLES
SCASB
SCASD

NOTE
1. The SCAS*x* instructions are restricted forms of the REP*x* SCAS*x* instructions. The REP*x* form of the instructions repeatedly execute the specified SCAS*x* operation until one of a variety of flags is set. This way, a single instruction can be used to scan a string for a specified value.

ASSEMBLER USAGE NOTE
1. Address register selection (i.e., DI versus EDI) depends on the address size attribute. To ensure that an address size override prefix is generated (if needed), the assembler notation where explicit operands to OUTS*x* are provided is recommended. For example, a repeated SCASW of ES:EDI should be encoded as follows
REPE SCAS WORD PTR [EDI]

SET*cond*: Set byte on condition (376, 386, 486 only)

INSTRUCTION	PARAMETERS	OPCODE
SETE/SETZ r/m8	cnd = (ZF==1)	0F 94
SETNE/SETNZ r/m8	cnd = (ZF==0)	0F 95
SETA/SETNBE r/m8	cnd = (CF==0 & ZF==0)	0F 97
SETBE/SETNA r/m8	cnd = (CF==1 | ZF==1)	0F 96
SETB/SETNAE r/m8	cnd = (CF==1)	0F 92
SETAE/SETNB r/m8	cnd = (CF==0)	0F 93
SETG/SETNLE r/m8	cnd = (SF==OF & ZF==0)	0F 9F
SETGE/SETNL r/m8	cnd = (SF==OF)	0F 9D
SETL/SETNGE r/m8	cnd = (SF!=OF)	0F 9C
SETLE/SETNG r/m8	cnd = (SF!=OF | ZF==1)	0F 9E
SETS r/m8	cnd = (SF==1)	0F 98
SETNS r/m8	cnd = (SF==0)	0F 99
SETO r/m8	cnd = (OF==1)	0F 90
SETNO r/m8	cnd = (OF==0)	0F 91
SETP r/m8	cnd = (PF==1)	0F 9A
SETNP r/m8	cnd = (PF==0)	0F 9B

SUMMARY
The SET*cond* class of instructions sets the BYTE in memory the BYTE-sized general register to 1 if cnd is true. If not, the byte is set to 0.

OPERATION
```
if ( cnd )
   dst = 1;
else
   dst = 0;
```

EXAMPLES
```
SETB     bt                    ; bt = ( (CF == 1) ? 1 : 0 )
SETNP    pOK                   ; pOK = ( (PF == 0) ? 1 : 0 )
```

NOTE
1. The *r/m8* operand is encoded in a MOD/RM byte (following the opcode). The REG field in the MOD/RM byte is not needed and is ignored.

SGDT: Load global descriptor table (286, 376, 386, 486 only)

INSTRUCTION	PARAMETERS	OPCODE
SGDT m	dst ≡ m, os ∈ {16,32}	0F 01 /0

SUMMARY
SGDT interprets *dst* as a six-byte memory area. At addresses *src* and *src+1* it stores the WORD-sized limit field of the current GDT. In the next four bytes it stores the linear address of the GDT's base. If *os* is 16, a zero is stored in the most significant byte of the base address. SGDT is *not* a privileged instruction.

OPERATION
```
struct { WORD Limit;
      DWORD Base;
    } * GDTVal;

GDTVal = &src;  /* Setup limit and base access */
GDTVal->Limit = GDT_desc.Limit;
if ( os == 32 )
  GDTVal->Base = GDT_desc.Base;
else  /* os == 16: simulate 80286 base address */
  GDTVal->Base = GDT_desc.Base & 0x00FFFFFF
```

EXAMPLE
```
SGDT      initGDT
```

NOTES
1. The scheme used to encode the dst memory operand is of the general r/m type, and so can be used to encode a register. If this is attempted, an INVALID_INSTR fault is signaled when the instruction is executed.

2. The 80286 sets the upper byte of the DWORD base field to all ones (i.e., 0xFF). The 80376, 80386, and i486 set this byte to zero.

SHL: Shift logical left

INSTRUCTION	PARAMETERS	OPCODE
SHL r/m, CL	dst ≡ r/m, shft = CL, os ∈ {8,16,32}	D2 /4 {8}, D3 /4 {16,32}
SHL r/m, imm8	dst ≡ r/m, shft = imm8, os ∈ {8,16,32}	C0 /4 {8}, C1 /4 {16,32}
SHL r/m, 1	dst ≡ r/m, shft = 1, os ∈ {8,16,32}	D0 /4 {8}, D1 /4 {16,32}

SUMMARY
SHL is an assembly language synonym for SAL; see page 551 for a description of
SAL.

SHLD: Shift left double precision (376, 386, 486 only)

INSTRUCTION	PARAMETERS	OPCODE
SHLD r/m, r, CL	dst ≡ r/m, vb = r, shft = CL, os ∈ {16,32}	0F A5
SHLD r/m, r, imm8	dst ≡ r/m, vb= r, shft = imm8, os ∈ {16,32}	0F A4

SUMMARY

SHLD shifts the bit pattern in *dst* left by *shft* bits, filling the vacated bits with the most significant *shft* bits of general register *vb*. The contents of *vb* remain unaltered. *shft* is treated a five bit unsigned quantity (i.e., with range 0 .. 31). If a larger quantity is specified, the higher order bits are unconditionally ignored. Furthermore, if the truncated shift amount is not less than the operand size (possible only when *os* is 16), the value stored in the destination and all the arithmetic flags is *undefined*.

CF is set to the value of the last bit that was shifted out (i.e., bit *dst⟨os-shft⟩* prior to the shift, if *shft* is positive). OF is set if, after the shift, the most significant bit of *dst* does not match the carry flag. The flags SF, ZF, and CF are set to reflect the arithmetic result of the shift, as usual. The value of the AF flag is *undefined*. No flags are modified if the shift amount is zero.

Because SHLD can be used to select an *n*-bit field from a 2*n*-bit input, its operation is known as a funnel shift. SHLD is available only on the 80376, 80386, and i486.

OPERATION

```
int shift_amt = shft & 0x1F;
DWORD vbits = vb;  /* Allow vb and dst to be the same */

if ( shift_amt > 0  &&  shift_amt < os )
{   CF = dst⟨os - shift_amt⟩;
    dst = ( dst << shift_amt ) | ( vb >>ᵤ (os - shift_amt) );
    OF = ( dst⟨os-1⟩ != CF );
    SF = dst⟨os-1⟩
    ZF = (dst == 0)
    AF = undefined
    PF = evenParity(dst)
}
```

/* *SHLD has no effect if shift amount is 0; if greater than operand size, the results are* */
   undefined */
else if (shift_amt >= os) /* results are undefined */
{   dst = *undefined*;
    OF = *undefined*; SF = *undefined*; ZF = *undefined*;
    AF = *undefined*; PF = *undefined*; CF = *undefined*;
}

EXAMPLES
```
SHLD     EAX, EBP, CL              ; EAX = (EAX << CL) + EBP⟨31:31-CL⟩
SHLD     WORD PTR [ESI], AX, 4     ; *( (BYTE *) ESI ) = *( (BYTE *) ESI ) << 4 +
                                                          AX⟨15:12⟩
```

NOTE
   1. It is not possible to "double shift" two BYTE quantities.

SHR: Shift arithmetic right

INSTRUCTION	PARAMETERS	OPCODE
SHR r/m, CL	dst ≡ r/m, shft = CL, os ∈ *{8,16,32}*	D2 /5 *{8}*, D3 /5 *{16,32}*
SHR r/m, imm8	dst ≡ r/m, shft = imm8, os ∈ *{8,16,32}*	C0 /5 *{8}*, C1 /5 *{16,32}*
SHR r/m, 1	dst ≡ r/m, shft = 1, os ∈ *{8,16,32}*	D0 /5 *{8}*, D1 /5 *{16,32}*

SUMMARY

SHR shifts the bit pattern in *dst* right by *shft* bits, filling the vacated bits with zeros. (The instruction SAR fills the vacated bits with the sign bit's value.) On implementations other than the 8086, *shft* is treated a five-bit unsigned quantity (i.e., with range 0 .. 31). If a larger quantity is specified, the higher-order bits are unconditionally ignored. On the 8086, all eight bits of *shft* are used; however, the instruction with the *imm8* form of shift count is unavailable on it.

CF is set to the value of the last bit that was shifted out (i.e., bit *dst*⟨*shft*-1⟩ prior to the shift, if *shft* is positive). For one-bit shifts, OF is set to the value of the most significant bit of *dst* prior to the shift. The architecture does not define the value of OF if the shift is for more than one bit. The flags SF, ZF, and CF are set to reflect the arithmetic result of the shift. The value of the AF flag is *undefined*. No flags are modified if the shift amount is zero.

OPERATION

```
int shft_amt = shft & 0x1F;

if ( shft_amt > 0 )
{if ( shft_amt <= os )
    CF = dst⟨shft_amt - 1⟩;
    dst = ( dst >>ᵤ shft_amt ); /* ">>ᵤ" does logical right shifts */
  else
  {  CF = 0;
     dst = 0;
  }

  if ( shft_amt == 1 )  /* OF defined only for one-bit shifts */
    OF = dst⟨os-2⟩;
  else
    OF = undefined;
```

```
    SF = dst⟨os-1⟩
    ZF = (dst == 0)
    AF = undefined
    PF = evenParity(dst)
}
```

EXAMPLE
SHR   EAX, 4   ; EAX = (EAX >> 4) & 0x0FFFFFFF

SHRD: Shift right double precision (376, 386, 486 only)

INSTRUCTION	PARAMETERS	OPCODE
SHRD r/m, r, CL	dst ≡ r/m, vb = r, shft = CL, os ∈ *{16,32}*	0F AD
SHRD r/m, r, imm8	dst ≡ r/m, vb= r, shft = imm8, os ∈ *{16,32}*	0F AC

SUMMARY
SHRD shifts the bit pattern in *dst* right by *shft* bits, filling the vacated bits with the least significant *shft* bits of general register *vb*. The contents of *vb* remain unaltered. *shft* is treated a five-bit unsigned quantity (i.e., with range 0 .. 31). If a larger quantity is specified, the higher order bits are unconditionally ignored. Furthermore, if the truncated shift amount is not less than the operand size (possible only when *os* is 16), the value stored in the destination and all the arithmetic flags is *undefined*.

CF is set to the value of the last bit that was shifted out (i.e., bit $dst\langle shft\text{-}1\rangle$ prior to the shift, if *shft* is positive.) Nonarithmetic flags are not modified.

Because SHRD can be used to select an *n*-bit field from a 2*n*-bit input, its operation is known as a funnel shift. SHRD is available only on the 80376, 80386, and i486.

OPERATION
```
int shift_amt = shft & 0x1F;
DWORD vbits = vb;  /* Allow vb and dst to be the same */

if ( shift_amt > 0  &&  shift_amt < os )
{   CF = dst⟨shift_amt - 1⟩;
    dst = ( vb << (os - shft_amt) ) | ( dst >>ᵤ shft_amt );
    OF = ( dst⟨os-1⟩ != dst⟨os-2⟩ );
    SF = dst⟨os-1⟩
    ZF = (dst == 0)
    AF = undefined
    PF = evenParity(dst)
}
```

/* *SHRD has no effect if shift amount is 0; if greater than operand size, the results are*
  undefined */
else if (shift_amt >= os) /* results are undefined */
{   dst = *undefined*;
    OF = *undefined*; SF = *undefined*; ZF = *undefined*;
    AF = *undefined*; PF = *undefined*; CF = *undefined*;
}

EXAMPLES
SHRD   EAX, EBP, CL   ; EAX = (EAX >> CL) + EBP⟨CL-1:0⟩ << (32-s)
SHRD   WORD PTR [ESI], AX, 4

NOTE
  1. It is not possible to "double shift" two **BYTE** quantities.

SIDT: Load interrupt descriptor table (286, 376, 386, 486 only)

INSTRUCTION	PARAMETERS	OPCODE
SIDT m	dst ≡ m, os ∈ {16,32}	0F 01 /1

SUMMARY
SIDT interprets *dst* as a six-byte memory area. At addresses *src* and *src*+1 it stores the WORD-sized limit field of the current IDT. In the next four bytes it stores the linear address of the IDT's base. If *os* is 16, the most significant byte of the base address is stored as a zero. SIDT is *not* a privileged instruction.

OPERATION
```
struct { WORD Limit;          /* Limit occupies bytes 0 and 1 */
         DWORD Base;          /* Base occupies bytes 2, 3, 4, and 5 */
       } * IDTVal;

IDTVal = &src;  /* Setup limit and base access */
IDTVal->Limit = IDT_desc.Limit;
if ( os == 32 )
    IDTVal->Base = IDT_desc.Base;
else  /* os == 16:  simulate 80286 base address */
    IDTVal->Base = IDT_desc.Base & 0x00FFFFFF
```

EXAMPLE
```
SIDT        saveIDT
```

NOTES
1. The scheme used to encode the *dst* memory operand is of the general *r/m* type, and so can be used to encode a register. If this is attempted, an INVALID_INSTR fault is signaled when the instruction is executed.

2. The 80286 sets the upper byte of the DWORD base field to all ones (i.e., 0xFF.) The 80376, 80386, and i486 set this byte to zero.

SLDT: Store local descriptor table (286, 376, 386, 486 only)

INSTRUCTION	PARAMETERS	OPCODE
SLDT r/m16	sel ≡ r/m16	0F 00 /0

SUMMARY
SLDT stored the current LDT table descriptor's SELECTOR in *sel*. SLDT is *not* a privileged instruction; however, is not available in REAL or VM86 modes.

OPERATION
```
if ( mode == PROTECTED )
   sel = LDT;
else  /* unavailable in REAL and VM86 modes */
   signal_fault(INVALID_INSTR);
```

EXAMPLE
```
SLDT    AX                    ; Store LDT selector in AX
```

SMSW: Store machine status word (286, 376, 386, 486 only)

INSTRUCTION	PARAMETERS	OPCODE
SMSW r/m16	dst ≡ r/m16	0F 01 /4

SUMMARY
SMSW stores the Machine Status Word (MSW.) The MSW is the low order WORD of the DWORD control register CR0. SMSW is an artifact of the 80286; its use is not recommended in new code (see *Note* below). SMSW is *not* a privileged instruction.

OPERATION
```
/* ET, TS, EM, MP, PE are bits in low area of CR0. */
dst⟨15:5⟩ = undefined;
dst⟨4⟩ = ET;
src⟨3⟩ = TS;
src⟨2⟩ = EM;
src⟨1⟩ = MP;
src⟨0⟩ = PE;
```

EXAMPLE
```
SMSW    AX              ; Store all CR0 bits except PG
```

NOTE
1. SMSW is a subset of the MOV r, CR0 instruction. It is provided only for backward compatibility with the 80286.

SS: (prefix): Use SS for memory access

INSTRUCTION	PARAMETERS	OPCODE
SS:		36

SUMMARY

An instruction making a memory reference always uses an implied segment register. The segment register implied depends on the way the memory offset is generated (see §2.18 on page 185 for more on this). Specifying the SS: override prefix changes the segment register used to SS (and the segment descriptor register to SS_desc). This change is effective *only* for the instruction immediately following the SS: prefix.

Some string operations (e.g., MOVS*x*) have two memory operands. The override prefix only changes the DS in the source operand; that is, the source operand becomes CS:[E]SI. The implied use of ES for the destination operand is not changeable.

EXAMPLE
```
; Use SS instead of DS (the default) in the following SUB.
SUB     AX, SS:[EBX]              ; EAX = EAX - « WORD at SS:EBX »
```

NOTES
1. Segment override prefixes apply only to memory data references; instruction fetches are always done with respect to CS. Furthermore, the stack manipulation instructions (i.e., PUSH, PUSHA, POP, POPA, PUSHF, POPF, CALL, RET, INT, and IRET) always reference the stack via SS. (The segment used by a PUSH or POP whose *operand* is a memory variable can be overridden, as can the pointer operand in an *indirect* CALL or JMP.) Segment override prefix use in front of instructions where it is not meaningful is unconditionally ignored.

2. Segment override prefixes for each of the other segment registers (CS, DS, ES, FS, and GS) are also supported. Apart from these prefixes the 80*x*86 has prefixes that implement string instructions (REP*x*) and perform atomic read-modify-write of memory locations (LOCK). Two additional prefixes, the "address size prefix" and "operand size prefix," are also used on the 80376, 80386, and i486 to encode these later processors' 32-bit instruction extensions.

STC: Set carry flag

INSTRUCTION	PARAMETERS	OPCODE
STC		F9

SUMMARY
STC set CF (the carry flag) to 1. No other flags are modified.

OPERATION
CF = 1

EXAMPLE
STC

STD: Set direction flag

INSTRUCTION	PARAMETERS	OPCODE
STD		FD

SUMMARY

STD sets DF (the direction flag) to 1. No other flags are modified. The direction flag determines whether the source and destination counters in string operations (e.g., MOVS, LODS) are incremented or decremented after each operation. If DF is set, the counters decrement; otherwise they increment.

OPERATION

DF = 1

EXAMPLE

STD

STI: Set interrupt flag

INSTRUCTION	PARAMETERS	OPCODE
STI		FB

SUMMARY
STI sets IF (the interrupt flag) to 1. The instruction can only be executed if the task has I/O privilege (i.e., CPL <= IOPL.) If not, a general protection fault is signaled. No flags other than IF are modified.

OPERATION
```
if ( CPL <= IOPL )
   IF = 1;
else
   signal_fault(GP, 0);
```

EXAMPLE
STI

NOTE
1. STI is always executable in REAL mode, since REAL mode code can be viewed as executing with a CPL of 0. STI is executable in VM86 mode only if IOPL is set to 3.

STOSB/STOSD/STOSW: Load string operands

INSTRUCTION	PARAMETERS	OPCODE
STOSB	os = 8, as ∈ {16,32}	AA
STOSW	os = 16, as ∈ {16,32}	AB
STOSD	os = 32, as ∈ {16,32}	AB

SUMMARY
STOS*x* loads into the BYTE, WORD, or DWORD pointed at by EDI or DI the
contents of AL, AX, or EAX, respectively. EDI is used if the address size attribute
is 32; if it is 16, DI participates. After the load [E]DI is incremented (if DF is 0)
or decremented (if DF is 1) by 2 or 4, depending on the operand size attribute.
No flags are modified by this instruction.

Offset [E]DI is always relative to the segment referenced by the ES segment
register; it cannot be overriden.

OPERATION
```
dst = ( (as == 16) ? DI : EDI );

/* Store into dst operand */
switch (os)
{ case 8:  *( (char *) dst ) = AL;
          break;
  case 16: *( (short *) src ) = AX;
          break;
  case 32: *( (int *) src ) = EAX;
          break;
}

/* Update string pointer */
if ( as == 32 )  /* 32-bit addressing */
  EDI += (DF ? −os/8 : os/8);
else /* as == 16 : 16-bit addressing */
  DI += (DF ? −os/8 : os/8);
```

EXAMPLES
STOSB
STOSB

NOTE
1. The STOS*x* instructions are restricted forms of the REP STOS*x* instructions.
   The REP form of the instructions execute the specified STOS*x* operation the

number of times specified by ECX. This way, a single instruction can be used to initialize all elements of a string to some fixed value.

STR: Store task register (286, 376, 386, 486 only)

INSTRUCTION	PARAMETERS	OPCODE
STR r/m16	dst ≡ r, sel = r/m16	0F 00 /1

SUMMARY
STR stores into dst the selector corresponding to the current TSS segment. STR is *not* a privileged instruction. However, it is only available in PROTECTED mode.

OPERATION
```
if ( mode == PROTECTED )
    dst = TSS;
else  /* unavailable in REAL and VM86 modes */
    signal_fault(INVALID_INSTR);
```

EXAMPLE
```
STR       tssSel
```

SUB: Signed and unsigned integer add

INSTRUCTION	PARAMETERS	OPCODE
SUB r, r/m	dst ≡ r, src = r/m, os ∈ {8,16,32}	2A {8}, 2B {16,32}
SUB r/m, r	dst ≡ r/m, src = r, os ∈ {8,16,32}	28 {8}, 29 {16,32}
SUB r/m, imm	dst ≡ r/m, src = imm, os ∈ {8,16,32}	80 /5 {8}, 81 /5 {16,32}
SUB r/m, imm8	dst ≡ r/m, src = signex(imm8), os ∈ {16,32}	83 /5 {16,32}
SUB AL, imm8	dst ≡ AL, src = imm8, os = 8	2C
SUB AX/EAX, imm	dst ≡ eAX, src = imm, os ∈ {16,32}	2D {16,32}

SUMMARY

SUB subtracts the value of the source from the destination and stores the result in the destination. All arithmetic flags are set. The remaining flags are left unmodified. A SUB instruction with a memory operand is LOCKable. On the 80376, 80386, and i486, specifying LOCK with other SUB instruction formats signals the INVALID_INSTR fault on the 80286 and 80386.

OPERATION

```
/* Compute result */
result = dst − src
dst = result

/* Set arithmetic flags */
```
$OF = result < -2^{os-1} \;||\; result > 2^{os-1}-1$
$SF = dst\langle os-1\rangle$
$ZF = (dst == 0)$
$AF = dst\langle 3:0\rangle <_u src\langle 3:0\rangle$
$PF = evenParity(dst)$
$CF = dst <_u src$

EXAMPLES

```
SUB     EAX, EBX          ; EAX = EAX - EBX
SUB     AH, BYTE PTR [ESI]   ; AH = AH - *( (BYTE *) ESI )
```

TEST: Bitwise logical TEST

INSTRUCTION	PARAMETERS	OPCODE
TEST r/m, r	src$_1$ = r/m, src$_2$ = r, os ∈ {8,16,32}	84 {8}, 85 {16,32}
TEST r/m, imm	src$_1$ = r/m, src$_2$ = imm, os ∈ {8,16,32}	F6 /0 {8}, F7 /0 {16,32}
TEST AL, imm8	src$_1$ = AL, src$_2$ = imm8, os ∈ {16,32}	A8
TEST AX/EAX, imm	src$_1$ = AX/EAX, src$_2$ = imm, os ∈ {16,32}	A9 {16,32}

SUMMARY

TEST performs a bitwise AND-ing of the two input operands *src$_1$ src$_2$* and sets all arithmetic flags except AF based on the result. The result itself is discarded. AF's value is *undefined*; the nonarithmetic flags are left unmodified. Since this is a logical operation, there can never be a carry or overflow. Hence, the instruction always clears CF and OF.

OPERATION

result = src$_1$ & src$_2$

```
/* Set arithmetic flags */
OF = 0
SF = result⟨os-1⟩
ZF = result⟨os-1 : 0⟩ == 0
AF = undefined
PF = evenParity(result)
CF = 0
```

EXAMPLE

```
; Check if low-order 5 bits of AX have either bits 4, 3, or 0 set
TEST    AX, 16h              ; Mask for bits 4, 3, 0 set is 16h
JNZ     bitSet               ; Branch to bitSet if bit 4, 3, or 0 is set
```

VERR: Verify segment for read (286, 376, 386, 486 only)

INSTRUCTION	PARAMETERS	OPCODE
VERR r/m16	sel = r/m16	0F 00 /4

SUMMARY

VERR verifies that the segment referenced by SELECTOR *sel* is valid (i.e., its descriptor is within the table's bounds), that it is a readable segment, and that the current task is executing at a sufficiently great privilege level for the read to occur. If all these conditions are met ZF is set; otherwise it is cleared. No other flags or registers are affected. VERR is not available in REAL or VM86 modes.

OPERATION

```
if ( mode == PROTECTED )
{ DESCR tab_desc = sel⟨2⟩ == 0 ? GDT_desc : LDT_desc;

  /* If null SELECTOR or out of bounds, set ZF. Function in_limits defined on page 78 */
  if ( nullSel(sel)  ||  ! in_limits(tab_desc, sel & 0xFFF8, 8) )
    ZF = 0;

  else /* read descriptor and verify contents */
  { dsc = read_descr(sel);            /* see page 63 */
    if ( ( ( (dsc.Readable || dsc.Writable) && CPL <= dsc.DPL && RPL <= dsc.DPL ) ||
         ( dsc.Executable && dsc.Readable && CPL <= dsc.DPL && RPL <= dsc.DPL ) ||
         ( dsc.Conforming && dsc.Readable ) )
      ZF = 1;
    else /* not a readable data segment: clear ZF */
      ZF = 0;
  }
}

else  /* instruction unavailable in REAL and VM86 modes */
  signal_fault(INVALID_INSTR);
```

EXAMPLE

```
; Check if segment named by selector 23A4₁₆ is readable.
MOV      BX, 23A4h
VERR     BX
JZ       readable
```

VERW: Verify segment for write (286, 376, 386, 486 only)

INSTRUCTION	PARAMETERS	OPCODE
VERW r/m16	sel = r/m16	0F 00 /5

SUMMARY
VERW verifies that the segment referenced by selector *sel* is valid (i.e., its descriptor is within the table's bounds), that it is a writable segment, and that the current task is executing at a sufficiently great privilege level for the write to occur. If all these conditions are met ZF is set; otherwise it is cleared. No other flags or registers are affected. VERW is not available in REAL or VM86 modes.

OPERATION
```
if ( mode == PROTECTED )
{ DESCR tab_desc = sel⟨2⟩ == 0 ? GDT_desc : LDT_desc;

  /* If null SELECTOR or out of bounds, set ZF. Function in_limits defined on page 78 */
  if ( nullSel(sel)  ||  ! in_limits(tab_desc, sel & 0xFFF8, 8) )
    ZF = 0;

  else  /* read descriptor and verify contents for writability */
  { dsc = read_descr(sel);          /* see page 63 */
    if ( dsc.Writable && CPL <= dsc.DPL && RPL <= dsc.DPL )
      ZF = 1;
    else /* not a writable data segment: clear ZF */
      ZF = 0;
  }
}

else /* unavailable in REAL and VM86 modes */
  signal_fault(INVALID_INSTR);
```

EXAMPLE
```
; Check if segment named by selector 23A4₁₆ is writable.
MOV    BX, 23A4h
VERW   BX
JZ     writable
```

WAIT: Wait until BUSY pin inactive

INSTRUCTION	PARAMETERS	OPCODE
WAIT		9B

SUMMARY

The primary purpose of WAIT is to make sure that a numerics (typically a version of the 80x87) is free to accept a new command. WAIT accomplishes on the 8086 by suspending 80x86 instruction execution until the BUSY pin is deactivated.

On the 80286 and its successors, the following checks are performed prior to waiting for BUSY to deactivate. If the task-switched flag TS and the monitor-processor-extension flag MP are both set, the PE_UNAVAILABLE fault is signaled. Then the 80x86 waits until BUSY deactivates. Once this occurs, any 80x87 errors that have occurred during the execution of the previous numerics operation are reported by checking the status of the ERROR pin. If this pin is active, a PE_ERROR exception is signaled. See §3.9 on page 251, however, for a discussion of how the PC/AT reports 80287 errors.

OPERATION

```
/* == TS and MP flag checks only done on the 80286, 80376, 80386, and i486.  This
      check is not done on the 8086 and 80186. == */
if ( TS && MP )  /* Check CR0(3) and CR0(1) */
   signal_fault(PE_UNAVAILABLE);

/* == Wait for BUSY to deactivate, but exit if hardware interrupt occurs.  This keeps
      interrupt latency to a manageable length. == */
while ( « BUSY pin active » )
{   if ( external_interrupt() )           /* see page 166 */
    {   EIP = prev_EIP;                    /* restore EIP to point at WAIT */
        goto NEXT_INSTR;                   /* retry WAIT after interrupt service */
    }
}

/* == Signal "processor extension error" if ERROR pin active.  This check is not done on
      the 8086 and 80186 (since these processors do not have an ERROR pin). == */
check_ERROR();                            /* see page 249 */
```

EXAMPLE
WAIT

NOTES

1. A WAIT should always be executed before referencing data stored by a floating point store instruction using an 80x86 instruction. This is because the architecture allows 80x87 implementations to store data into memory in parallel with 80x86 execution. For example,

```
FISTP    mem32              ; Store into an integer, and pop
WAIT                        ; Make sure store is complete
CMP      mem32, EAX         ; mem32 contents are valid here
JG       exit
```

2. A WAIT should be executed at the end of any program that makes use of the 80x87. This final WAIT ensures that all 80x87 exceptions are serviced in the context of the program using the 80x87.

3. BUSY is an input pin to 80x86 processors. The 80x87 numerics coprocessors activate BUSY whenever they are unable to accept a new command from the 80x86. The 80x86 architecture permits this external BUSY input to be used for purposes other than a numerics coprocessor. In particular, BUSY can be activated by any external device, provided the system does not have an 80x87. In such cases, the WAIT instruction can be used to poll for the activation to occur.

4. WAIT checks the TS flag but not the EM flag because the instruction should normally not have any effect when the 80x87 is being emulated. The task-switched (TS) flag check is only done if MP is set because the architecture allows the BUSY pin to be used for synchronizing an arbitrary external device. Setting the MP flag says "configure the BUSY pin to monitor the processor extension." This in turn configures the behavior of WAIT after a task switch to match the behavior of 80x87 instuctions. Since virtually all 80x86 systems use BUSY only for 80x87 synchronization, the MP flag is somewhat of an anachronism today. In fact, the i486 has dispensed with the BUSY pin altogether (although the MP flags still remains).

ASSEMBLER USAGE NOTE

1. The assembler mnemonics WAIT and FWAIT are equivalent.

WBINVD: Write back and invalidate instruction/data cache (486 only)

INSTRUCTION	PARAMETERS	OPCODE
WBINVD		0F 09

SUMMARY
WBINVD, defined only on the i486, writes back all dirty (i.e., modified but not written back) cache entries. Then it unconditionally invalidates the entire on-chip cache. The i486 also signals the external memory system to flush external caches (if any). Since the i486 always operates in write-through mode (see §2.7.9.1 on page 103), the i486's on-chip cache never has any dirty entries. Hence, WBINVD operates exactly like INVD. See page 445 for a description of the INVD instruction.

WBINVD is a privileged instruction. Defining this instruction on the i486 simplifies systems code migration to future implementations of the 80x86 that may support write-back caches.

OPERATION
```
if ( CPL != 0 )
    signal_fault(GP, 0);

/* == Clear all valid bits in the i486 cache. The i486 cache is described on page 103.
      There is no need for this instruction to write back data on the i486, since the i486
      cache is write-through. == */
for ( set_sel = 0;  set_sel <= 127;  set_sel++ )
    for ( set_elem = 0;  set_elem <= 3;  set_elem++ )
        cache_486[set_sel][set_elem].Valid = 0;
```

EXAMPLE
```
WBINVD
```

XADD: Exchange and add (486 only)

INSTRUCTION	PARAMETERS	OPCODE
XADD r/m, r	$op_1 \equiv$ r/m, $op_2 \equiv$ r	0F C0 *{8}*, 0F C1 *{16,32}*

SUMMARY

XADD, available only on the i486, increments op_1 by the contents of op_2 and stores the preincremented value of op_1 in op_2. The XADD instruction with a memory operand is LOCKable. All arithmetic flags are set based on the result of the addition.

The LOCK XADD instruction can be used to implement counting semaphores in multiprocessor systems.

OPERATION

```
/* Increment and exchange data */
temp = op₂;
op₂ = op₁;
result = op₁ + temp;
op₁ = result;
```

/* Set arithmetic flags */
$OF = result < -2^{os-1} \ || \ result > 2^{os-1}-1$
$SF = op_1\langle os-1\rangle$
$ZF = (op_1\langle os-1 : 0\rangle == 0)$
$AF = op_1\langle 3:0\rangle + op_2\langle 3:0\rangle >_u 15$
$PF = evenParity(result)$
$CF = result >_u 2^{os}-1$

EXAMPLE

```
; implementation of a counting semaphore
mov       ax, 1
lock xadd csem, ax          ; add 1 to csem, returning its original
cmp       ax, 0             ; value in ax
jz        haveit            ; if ax==0, resource is available
```

XCHG: Exchange register or memory with register

INSTRUCTION	PARAMETERS	OPCODE
XCHG r, r/m	dst ≡ r, src ≡ r/m, os ∈ {8,16,32}	86 {8}, 87 {16,32}
XCHG eAX, reg	dst ≡ AX/EAX, src ≡ reg, os ∈ {16,32}	90+reg

SUMMARY
XCHG swaps the contents of src and dst. No flags are modified. If one of the operands is memory based, the exchange is done indivisibly (i.e., as if the LOCK prefix were specified).

Since the LOCK action is already implied the LOCK prefix, if specified, has no effect when exchanging with a memory location. If LOCK is used and both operands are registers, an INVALID_INSTR fault is signaled.

OPERATION
temp = src;
src = dst;
dst = tmp;

EXAMPLES
```
XCHG  EAX, EBX          ; t = EAX;  EAX = EBX;  EBX = t
XCHG  AH, BYTE PTR [ESI]  ; t = *((BYTE *) ESI);  *((BYTE *) ESI) = AH;  AH = t
```

NOTE
1. The NOP instruction is simply an assembly language alias for

   ```
   XCHG AX, AX   ; opcode 90h
   ```

ASSEMBLER USAGE NOTE
1. Since XCHG is a symmetric operation, assemblers allow its operands to be specified in any order. That is, the two instructions that follow have the same binary encoding:
   ```
   XCHG  EDI, DWORD PTR [EBP+4]
   XCHG  DWORD PTR [EBP+4], EDI
   ```

XLATB: Translate byte in AL via table lookup

INSTRUCTION	PARAMETERS	OPCODE
XLATB	as ∈ {16,32}	D7

SUMMARY
XLAT replaces the contents of AL by the byte at index AL of the table pointed at by EBX or BX. The default segment register used is DS. If the address size attribute *as* is 32, EBX is used; otherwise BX is used. No flags are modified.

OPERATION
base = (as==32) ? EBX : BX ;
AL = *((char *) (base + AL));

EXAMPLE
XLATB

NOTES
1. XLATB is equivalent to the instruction

   MOV AL, BYTE PTR [EBX+EAX]

   if it is assumed that 32-bit addressing is used and that the high order 24 bits of EAX are set to zero. Since the MOV executes in the same number of clocks as XLATB and is more flexible (any general register pair can be used instead of EAX and EBX), its use is recommended in new code. The only disadvantage with the MOV is that the instruction requires two more bytes to encode. XLATB is provided for compatibility with the 80286 and 8086.

XOR: Bitwise exclusive-OR

INSTRUCTION	PARAMETERS	OPCODE
XOR r, r/m	dst ≡ r, src = r/m, os ∈ {8,16,32}	32 {8}, 33 {16,32}
XOR r/m, r	dst ≡ r/m, src = r, os ∈ {8,16,32}	30 {8}, 31 {16,32}
XOR r/m, imm	dst ≡ r/m, src = imm, os ∈ {8,16,32}	80 /6 {8}, 81 /6 {16,32}
XOR r/m, imm8	dst ≡ r/m, src = signex(imm8), os ∈ {16,32}	83 /6 {16,32}
XOR AL, imm8	dst ≡ AL, src = imm, os = 8	34 {8}
XOR *e*AX, imm	dst ≡ AX/EAX, src = imm, os ∈ {8,16,32}	35 {16,32}

SUMMARY

XOR performs a bitwise exclusive-OR of the source and destination operands and stores the result in dst. All arithmetic flags (except AF) are set based on the result. AF's value is undefined; the nonarithmetic flags are left unmodified. Since this is a logical operation, there can never be a carry or overflow. Hence, the instruction always clears CF and OF.

A XOR instruction with a memory operand is LOCKable. Specifying LOCK with other XOR instruction formats signals the INVALID_INSTR fault on the 80376, 80386, and i486.

OPERATION

```
/* Compute result */
result = dst ^ src;   /* "^" is the bitwise-exclusive-OR operator */
dst = result

/* Set arithmetic flags */
OF = 0
SF = dst⟨os-1⟩
ZF = (dst == 0)
AF = undefined
PF = evenParity(dst)
CF = 0
```

EXAMPLES

```
XOR     EAX, 4              ; EAX = EAX ^ 4
XOR     BYTE PTR [ESI], BL  ; *( (BYTE *) ESI ) = *( (BYTE *) ESI ) ^ BL
```

References

Bach, Maurice J. [1986], *The Design of the UNIX Operating System*, Englewood Cliffs, NJ: Prentice Hall.

Goodman, J. R. [1983], Using cache memory to reduce processor-memory traffic, *Proc. Tenth International Symposium on Computer Architecture.*

IEEE [1985], *IEEE Standard for Binary Floating Point Arithmetic*, ANSI/IEEE Standard 754-1985, IEEE, New York, NY 10017.

Intel [1986], *iAPX 86/88/186/188 Programmer's Reference Manual*, Santa Clara, CA: Intel Books.

Kernighan, Brian W., and D. M. Ritchie [1978], *The C Programming Language*, Prentice-Hall, Englewood Cliffs, NJ.

Smith, Alan J. [1982], Cache Memories, *ACM Computing Surveys* **14**, 3 (September 1982), 473-530.

Appendix A

Instructions Sorted by Opcode

OPC	MNEMONIC	DESCRIPTION
00	ADD r/m8,r8	Add *r8* to *r/m8* [BYTE operation]
01	ADD r/m,r	Add *r* to *r/m* [(D)WORD operation]
02	ADD r8,r/m8	Add *r/m8* to *r8* [BYTE operation]
03	ADD r,r/m	Add *r/m* to *r* [(D)WORD operation]
04	ADD AL,imm8	Add *imm8* to AL [BYTE operation]
05	ADD *e*AX,imm	Add *imm* to AX/EAX [(D)WORD operation]
06	PUSH ES	Push ES register onto stack
07	POP ES	Pop stack-top to ES register
08	OR r/m8,r8	Inclusive-OR *r8* into *r/m8* [BYTE operation]
09	OR r/m,r	Inclusive-OR *r* into *r/m* [(D)WORD operation]
0A	OR r8,r/m8	Inclusive-OR *r/m8* into *r8* [BYTE operation]
0B	OR r,r/m	Inclusive-OR *r/m* into *r* [(D)WORD operation]
0C	OR AL,imm8	Inclusive-OR *imm8* into AL [BYTE operation]
0D	OR *e*AX,imm	Inclusive-OR *imm* into AX/EAX [(D)WORD operation]
0E	PUSH CS	Push CS register onto stack

0F   ALTERNATE OPCODES GROUP

0F 00   0F00 subgroup

0F 00 /0	SLDT r/m16	Store LDT SELECTOR in *r/m16* (286, 376, 386, 486 only)
0F 00 /1	STR r/m16	Store TSS SELECTOR in *r/m16* (286, 376, 386, 486 only)
0F 00 /2	LLDT r/m16	Load LDT with SELECTOR in *r/m16* (286, 376, 386, 486 only)
0F 00 /3	LTR r/m16	Load TSS with SELECTOR in *r/m16* (286, 376, 386, 486 only)
0F 00 /4	VERR r/m16	Verify segment named by SELECTOR *r/m16* for readability (286, 376, 386, 486 only)
0F 00 /5	VERW r/m16	Verify segment named by SELECTOR *r/m16* for writability (286, 376, 386, 486 only)
0F 00 /6	*unassigned*	*reserved opcode*
0F 00 /7	*unassigned*	*reserved opcode*

0F 01   0F01 subgroup

0F 01 /0	SGDT m	Store GDT descriptor in memory block starting at *m* (286, 376, 386, 486 only)

0F 01 /1	SIDT m	Store IDT descriptor in memory block starting at *m* (286, 376, 386, 486 only)
0F 01 /2	LGDT m	Load GDT descriptor from memory block starting at *m* (286, 376, 386, 486 only)
0F 01 /3	LIDT m	Load IDT descriptor from memory block starting at *m* (286, 376, 386, 486 only)
0F 01 /4	SMSW r/m16	Store MSW in *r/m16* (286, 376, 386, 486 only)
0F 01 /5	*unassigned*	*reserved opcode*
0F 01 /6	LMSW r/m16	Load MSW with *r/m16* (286, 376, 386, 486 only)
0F 01 /7	INVLPG m	Invalidate TLB entry for operand at address *m* (486 only)
0F 02	LAR r,r/m16	Load into *r* the access rights of SELECTOR in *r/m16* (286, 376, 386, 486 only)
0F 03	LSL r,r/m16	Load into *r* the segment of SELECTOR in *r/m16* (286, 376, 386, 486 only)
0F 04	*unassigned*	*reserved opcode*
0F 05	LOADALL286	Load all 80286 state from memory (*specific to the 80286*)
0F 06	CLTS	Clear TS ("task switched") flag (286, 376, 386, 486 only)
0F 07	*unassigned*	*reserved opcode*
0F 08	INVD	Invalidate instruction/data cache (486 only)
0F 09	WBINVD	Write-back, then invalidate instruction/data cache (486 only)
0F 0A	*unassigned*	*reserved opcode*
:	:	:
0F 1F	*unassigned*	*reserved opcode*
0F 20	MOV r32, cr	Store control register *cr* into general register *r32* (376, 386, 486 only)
0F 21	MOV r32, dr	Store debug register *dr* into general register *r32* (376, 386, 486 only)
0F 22	MOV cr, r32	Load control register *cr* with general register *r32* (376, 386, 486 only)
0F 23	MOV dr, r32	Load debug register *dr* with general register *r32* (376, 386, 486 only)
0F 24	MOV r32, tr	Store test register *tr* into general register *r32* (386 and 486 only)
0F 25	*unassigned*	*reserved opcode*
0F 26	MOV tr, r32	Load test register *tr* with general register *r32* (386 and 486 only)
0F 27	*unassigned*	*reserved opcode*
:	:	:
0F 7F	*unassigned*	*reserved opcode*
0F 80	JO rel	Jump (near) if OF flag set (376, 386, 486 only)
0F 81	JNO rel	Jump (near) if OF flag clear (376, 386, 486 only)
0F 82	JB rel	Jump (near) if unsigned result is below 0 (376, 386, 486 only)
0F 83	JAE rel	Jump (near) if unsigned result is above or equal to 0 (376, 386, 486 only)
0F 84	JZ rel	Jump (near) if zero result (376, 386, 486 only)
0F 85	JNZ rel	Jump (near) if nonzero result (376, 386, 486 only)
0F 86	JBE rel	Jump (near) if unsigned result is below or equal to 0 (376, 386, 486 only)
0F 87	JA rel	Jump (near) if unsigned result is above 0 (376, 386, 486 only)
0F 88	JS rel	Jump (near) if sign flag (SF) set (376, 386, 486 only)

0F 89	JNS rel	Jump (near) if sign flag (SF) clear (376, 386, 486 only)
0F 8A	JP rel	Jump (near) if parity flag (PF) set (376, 386, 486 only)
0F 8B	JNP rel	Jump (near) if parity flag (PF) clear (376, 386, 486 only)
0F 8C	JL rel	Jump (near) if signed result is less than 0 (376, 386, 486 only)
0F 8D	JGE rel	Jump (near) if signed result is greater than or equal to 0 (376, 386, 486 only)
0F 8E	JLE rel	Jump (near) if signed result is less than or equal to 0 (376, 386, 486 only)
0F 8F	JG rel	Jump (near) if signed result is greater than 0 (376, 386, 486 only)
0F 90	SETO r/m8	Set r/m8 if OF==1; clear otherwise *(REG field in MOD/RM is ignored)* (376, 386, 486 only)
0F 91	SETNO r/m8	Set r/m8 if OF==0; clear otherwise (376, 386, 486 only)
0F 92	SETB r/m8	Set r/m8 if unsigned result is below 0; clear otherwise (376, 386, 486 only)
0F 93	SETAE r/m8	Set r/m8 if unsigned result is above or equal to 0; clear otherwise (376, 386, 486 only)
0F 94	SETZ r/m8	Set r/m8 if zero result; clear on nonzero result (376, 386, 486 only)
0F 95	SETNZ r/m8	Set r/m8 if nonzero result; clear on zero result (376, 386, 486 only)
0F 96	SETBE r/m8	Set r/m8 if unsigned result is below or equal to 0; clear otherwise (376, 386, 486 only)
0F 97	SETA r/m8	Set r/m8 if unsigned result is above 0; clear otherwise (376, 386, 486 only)
0F 98	SETS r/m8	Set r/m8 if sign flag (SF==1); clear otherwise (376, 386, 486 only)
0F 99	SETNS r/m8	Set r/m8 if sign flag (SF==0); clear otherwise (376, 386, 486 only)
0F 9A	SETP r/m8	Set r/m8 if parity flag (PF==1); clear otherwise (376, 386, 486 only)
0F 9B	SETNP r/m8	Set r/m8 if parity flag (PF==0); clear otherwise (376, 386, 486 only)
0F 9C	SETL r/m8	Set r/m8 if signed result is less than 0; clear otherwise (376, 386, 486 only)
0F 9D	SETGE r/m8	Set r/m8 if signed result is greater than or equal to 0; clear otherwise (376, 386, 486 only)
0F 9E	SETLE r/m8	Set r/m8 if signed result is less than or equal to 0; clear otherwise (376, 386, 486 only)
0F 9F	SETG r/m8	Set r/m8 if signed result is greater than 0; clear otherwise (376, 386, 486 only)
0F A0	PUSH FS	Push FS register onto stack (376, 386, 486 only)
0F A1	POP FS	Pop into FS register (376, 386, 486 only)
0F A2	*unassigned*	*reserved opcode*
0F A3	BT m,r	Bit test (376, 386, 486 only)
0F A4	SHLD r/m,r,imm8	Shift left r/m by *imm8* bits, using r for fill bits (376, 386, 486 only)
0F A5	SHLD r/m,r,CL	Shift left r/m by CL bits, using r for fill bits (376, 386, 486 only)
0F A6	CMPXCHG r/m8,r8	Compare and exchange if unequal [BYTE operation] (486 only)

0F A7	CMPXCHG r/m,r	Compare and exchange if unequal [(D)WORD operation] (486 only)
0F A8	PUSH GS	Push GS register onto stack (376, 386, 486 only)
0F A9	POP GS	Pop into GS register (376, 386, 486 only)
0F AA	*unassigned*	*reserved opcode*
0F AB	BTS m,r	Bit test and set (376, 386, 486 only)
0F AC	SHRD r/m,r,imm8	Shift right *r/m* by *imm8* bits, using *r* for fill bits (376, 386, 486 only)
0F AD	SHRD r/m,r,CL	Shift right *r/m* by CL bits, using *r* for fill bits (376, 386, 486 only)
0F AE	*unassigned*	*reserved opcode*
0F AF	IMUL r,r/m	Multiply *r* by *r/m* (376, 386, 486 only)
0F B0	*unassigned*	*reserved opcode*
0F B1	*unassigned*	*reserved opcode*
0F B2	LSS r,m	Load pointer into SS and a register (376, 386, 486 only)
0F B3	BTR m,r	Bit test and reset (376, 386, 486 only)
0F B4	LFS r,m	Load pointer into FS and a register (376, 386, 486 only)
0F B5	LGS r,m	Load pointer into GS and a register (376, 386, 486 only)
0F B6	MOVZX r, r/m8	Load *r* with zero-extended BYTE *r/m8* (376, 386, 486 only)
0F B7	MOVZX r, r/m16	Load *r* with zero-extended WORD *r/m16* (376, 386, 486 only)
0F B8	*unassigned*	*reserved opcode*
0F B9	*unassigned*	*reserved opcode*

0F BA   Bit test with immediate index subgroup

0F BA /0	*unassigned*	*reserved opcode*
0F BA /1	*unassigned*	*reserved opcode*
0F BA /2	*unassigned*	*reserved opcode*
0F BA /3	*unassigned*	*reserved opcode*
0F BA /4	BT r/m, imm8	Test bit index *imm8* of *r/m* (376, 386, 486 only)
0F BA /5	BTS r/m, imm8	Test bit index *imm8* of *r/m*, then set it (376, 386, 486 only)
0F BA /6	BTR r/m, imm8	Test bit index *imm8* of *r/m*, then reset it (376, 386, 486 only)
0F BA /7	BTC r/m, imm8	Test bit index *imm8* of *r/m*, then complement it (376, 386, 486 only)
0F BB	BTC m,r	Bit test and complement (376, 386, 486 only)
0F BC	BSF r,r/m	Bit scan forward (376, 386, 486 only)
0F BD	BSR r,r/m	Bit scan reverse (376, 386, 486 only)
0F BE	MOVSX r, r/m8	Load *r* with sign-extended BYTE *r/m8* (376, 386, 486 only)
0F BF	MOVSX r, r/m16	Load *r* with sign-extended WORD *r/m16* (376, 386, 486 only)
0F C0	*unassigned*	*reserved opcode*
:	:	:
0F C7	*unassigned*	*reserved opcode*
0F C8	BSWAP EAX	Reverse order of bytes in EAX (486 only)
0F C9	BSWAP ECX	Reverse order of bytes in ECX (486 only)
0F CA	BSWAP EDX	Reverse order of bytes in EDX (486 only)
0F CB	BSWAP EBX	Reverse order of bytes in EBX (486 only)
0F CC	BSWAP ESP	Reverse order of bytes in ESP (486 only)
0F CD	BSWAP EBP	Reverse order of bytes in EBP (486 only)
0F CE	BSWAP ESI	Reverse order of bytes in ESI (486 only)
0F CF	BSWAP EDI	Reverse order of bytes in EDI (486 only)
10	ADC r/m8,r8	Add *r8* and Carry (CF) to *r/m8* [BYTE operation]

11	ADC r/m,r	Add r and Carry (CF) to r/m [(D)WORD operation]
12	ADC r8,r/m8	Add r/m8 and Carry (CF) to r8 [BYTE operation]
13	ADC r,r/m	Add r/m and Carry (CF) to r [(D)WORD operation]
14	ADC AL,imm8	Add imm8 and Carry (CF) to AL [BYTE operation]
15	ADC eAX,imm	Add imm and Carry (CF) to AX/EAX [(D)WORD operation]
16	PUSH SS	Push SS register onto stack
17	POP SS	Pop stack-top to SS register
18	SBB r/m8,r8	Subtract r8 and Borrow (CF) from r/m8 [BYTE operation]
19	SBB r/m,r	Subtract r and Borrow (CF) from r/m [(D)WORD operation]
1A	SBB r8,r/m8	Subtract r/m8 and Borrow (CF) from r8 [BYTE operation]
1B	SBB r,r/m	Subtract r/m and Borrow (CF) from r [(D)WORD operation]
1C	SBB AL,imm8	Subtract imm8 and Borrow (CF) from AL [BYTE operation]
1D	SBB eAX,imm	Subtract imm and Borrow (CF) from AX/EAX [(D)WORD operation]
1E	PUSH DS	Push DS register onto stack
1F	POP DS	Pop stack-top to DS register
20	AND r/m8,r8	Bitwise-AND r8 into r/m8 [BYTE operation]
21	AND r/m,r	Bitwise-AND r into r/m [(D)WORD operation]
22	AND r8,r/m8	Bitwise-AND r/m8 into r8 [BYTE operation]
23	AND r,r/m	Bitwise-AND r/m into r [(D)WORD operation]
24	AND AL,imm8	Bitwise-AND imm8 into AL [BYTE operation]
25	AND eAX,imm	Bitwise-AND imm into AX/EAX [(D)WORD operation]
26	ES:	Override memory access using ES (prefix)
27	DAA	Decimal adjust AL after (binary) add
28	SUB r/m8,r8	Subtract r8 from r/m8 [BYTE operation]
29	SUB r/m,r	Subtract r from r/m [(D)WORD operation]
2A	SUB r8,r/m8	Subtract r/m8 from r8 [BYTE operation]
2B	SUB r,r/m	Subtract r/m from r [(D)WORD operation]
2C	SUB AL,imm8	Subtract imm8 from AL [BYTE operation]
2D	SUB eAX,imm	Subtract imm from AX/EAX [(D)WORD operation]
2E	CS:	Override memory access using CS (prefix)
2F	DAS	Decimal adjust AL after (binary) subtract
30	XOR r/m8,r8	Bitwise-XOR r8 into r/m8 [BYTE operation]
31	XOR r/m,r	Bitwise-XOR r into r/m [(D)WORD operation]
32	XOR r8,r/m8	Bitwise-XOR r/m8 into r8 [BYTE operation]
33	XOR r,r/m	Bitwise-XOR r/m into r [(D)WORD operation]
34	XOR AL,imm8	Bitwise-XOR imm8 into AL [BYTE operation]
35	XOR eAX,imm	Bitwise-XOR imm into AX/EAX [(D)WORD operation]
36	SS:	Override memory access using CS (prefix)
37	AAA	ASCII adjust AL after (binary) add
38	CMP r/m8,r8	Compare r/m8 against r8, and set flags [BYTE operation]
39	CMP r/m,r	Compare r/m against r, and set flags [(D)WORD operation]
3A	CMP r8,r/m8	Compare r8 against r/m8, and set flags [BYTE operation]
3B	CMP r,r/m	Compare r against r/m, and set flags [(D)WORD operation]
3C	CMP AL,imm8	Compare AL against imm8, and set flags [BYTE operation]
3D	CMP eAX,imm	Compare AX/EAX against imm, and set flags [(D)WORD operation]
3E	DS:	Override memory access using DS (prefix)
3F	AAS	ASCII adjust AL after (binary) subtract
40	INC eAX	Increment AX/EAX by 1
41	INC eCX	Increment CX/ECX by 1
42	INC eDX	Increment DX/EDX by 1
43	INC eBX	Increment BX/EBX by 1
44	INC eSP	Increment SP/ESP by 1
45	INC eBP	Increment BP/EBP by 1

46	INC *e*SI	Increment SI/ESI by 1
47	INC *e*DI	Increment DI/EDI by 1
48	DEC *e*AX	Decrement AX/EAX by 1
49	DEC *e*CX	Decrement CX/ECX by 1
4A	DEC *e*DX	Decrement DX/EDX by 1
4B	DEC *e*BX	Decrement BX/EBX by 1
4C	DEC *e*SP	Decrement SP/ESP by 1
4D	DEC *e*BP	Decrement BP/EBP by 1
4E	DEC *e*SI	Decrement SI/ESI by 1
4F	DEC *e*DI	Decrement DI/EDI by 1
50	PUSH *e*AX	Push AX/EAX
51	PUSH *e*CX	Push CX/ECX
52	PUSH *e*DX	Push DX/EDX
53	PUSH *e*BX	Push BX/EBX
54	PUSH *e*SP	Push SP/ESP
55	PUSH *e*BP	Push BP/EBP
56	PUSH *e*SI	Push SI/ESI
57	PUSH *e*DI	Push DI/EDI
58	POP *e*AX	Pop into AX/EAX
59	POP *e*CX	Pop into CX/ECX
5A	POP *e*DX	Pop into DX/EDX
5B	POP *e*BX	Pop into BX/EBX
5C	POP *e*SP	Pop into SP/ESP
5D	POP *e*BP	Pop into BP/EBP
5E	POP *e*SI	Pop into SI/ESI
5F	POP *e*DI	Pop into DI/EDI
60	PUSHA	Push all general registers as WORDs (if *os==16*) or DWORDs (if *os==32*) (unavailable on the 8086)
61	POPA	Pop into all WORD general registers (if *os==16*), or into all DWORD general registers (if *os==32*) (unavailable on the 8086)
62	BOUND r,r/m	Bounds check (unavailable on the 8086)
63	ARPL r/m16,r16	Adjust RPL field of *r/m16* operand (286, 376, 386, 486 only)
64	FS:	Override memory access using FS segment (prefix) (376, 386, 486 only)
65	GS:	Override memory access using GS segment (prefix) (376, 386, 486 only)
66	<osp>	Operand size prefix (toggles between WORD/DWORD sizes) (376, 386, 486 only)
67	<asp>	Address size prefix (toggles between WORD/DWORD offsets) (376, 386, 486 only)
68	PUSH imm	Push *imm* onto stack (unavailable on the 8086)
69	IMUL r,r/m,imm	Multiply *r/m* by *imm*, store result in *r* (unavailable on the 8086)
6A	PUSH imm8	Push sign-extended BYTE quantity as WORD or DWORD (unavailable on the 8086)
6B	IMUL r,r/m,imm8	Multiply *r/m* by *imm8* (a BYTE constant), store result in *r* (unavailable on the 8086)
6C	INSB ES:*e*DI,DX	Read from I/O port DX into BYTE at ES:*e*DI; increment *e*DI by 1 (unavailable on the 8086)
6D	INSW/INSD ES:aDI,DX	Read from I/O port DX into (D)WORD at ES:*e*DI; increment *e*DI by 2 or 4 (unavailable on the 8086)

6E	OUTSB ES:*e*DI,DX	Write to I/O port DX from BYTE at ES:*e*DI; increment *e*DI by 1 (unavailable on the 8086)
6F	OUTSW/OUTSD ES:a*DI,DX	Write to I/O port DX from (D)WORD at ES:*e*DI; increment *e*DI by 2 or 4 (unavailable on the 8086)
70	JO rel8	Jump (short) if OF flag set
71	JNO rel8	Jump (short) if OF flag clear
72	JB rel8	Jump (short) if unsigned result is below 0
73	JAE rel8	Jump (short) if unsigned result is above or equal to 0
74	JZ rel8	Jump (short) if zero result
75	JNZ rel8	Jump (short) if nonzero result
76	JBE rel8	Jump (short) if unsigned result is below or equal to 0
77	JA rel8	Jump (short) if unsigned result is above 0
78	JS rel8	Jump (short) if sign flag (SF) set
79	JNS rel8	Jump (short) if sign flag (SF) clear
7A	JP rel8	Jump (short) if parity flag (PF) set
7B	JNP rel8	Jump (short) if parity flag (PF) clear
7C	JL rel8	Jump (short) if signed result is less than 0
7D	JGE rel8	Jump (short) if signed result is greater than or equal to 0
7E	JLE rel8	Jump (short) if signed result is less than or equal to 0
7F	JG rel8	Jump (short) if signed result is greater than 0

80	**Destination is *r/m8*, inputs are *r/m8* and BYTE immediate**	
80 /0	ADD r/m8,imm8	Add *imm8* into *r/m8*
80 /1	OR r/m8,imm8	Bitwise-OR *imm8* into *r/m8*
80 /2	ADC r/m8,imm8	Add carry flag and *imm8* into *r/m8*
80 /3	SBB r/m8,imm8	Subtract carry flag and *imm8* from *r/m8*
80 /4	AND r/m8,imm8	Bitwise-AND *imm8* into *r/m8*
80 /5	SUB r/m8,imm8	Subtract *imm8* from *r/m8*
80 /6	XOR r/m8,imm8	Bitwise-XOR *imm8* into *r/m8*
80 /7	CMP r/m8,imm8	Compare *imm8* against *r/m8*, and set flags

81	**Destination is *r/m*, inputs are *r/m* and (D)WORD immediate**	
81 /0	ADD r/m,imm	Add *imm* into *r/m*
81 /1	OR r/m,imm	Bitwise-OR *imm* into *r/m*
81 /2	ADC r/m,imm	Add carry flag and *imm* into *r/m*
81 /3	SBB r/m,imm	Subtract carry flag and *imm* from *r/m*
81 /4	AND r/m,imm	Bitwise-AND *imm* into *r/m*
81 /5	SUB r/m,imm	Subtract *imm* from *r/m*
81 /6	XOR r/m,imm	Bitwise-XOR *imm* into *r/m*
81 /7	CMP r/m,imm	Compare *imm* against *r/m*, and set flags

82	**Destination is *r/m8*, inputs are *r/m8* and BYTE immediate (same as 0x80)**	
82 /0	ADD r/m8,imm8	Add *imm8* into *r/m8*
82 /1	OR r/m8,imm8	Bitwise-OR *imm8* into *r/m8*
82 /2	ADC r/m8,imm8	Add carry flag and *imm8* into *r/m8*
82 /3	SBB r/m8,imm8	Subtract carry flag and *imm8* from *r/m8*
82 /4	AND r/m8,imm8	Bitwise-AND *imm8* into *r/m8*
82 /5	SUB r/m8,imm8	Subtract *imm8* from *r/m8*
82 /6	XOR r/m8,imm8	Bitwise-XOR *imm8* into *r/m8*
82 /7	CMP r/m8,imm8	Compare *imm8* against *r/m8*, and set flags

83	**Destination is *r/m*, inputs are *r/m* and a BYTE immediate that is sign-extended to a (D)WORD**	
83 /0	ADD r/m,imm8	Add *sign_ext(imm8)* into *r/m*
83 /1	OR r/m,imm8	Bitwise-OR *sign_ext(imm8)* into *r/m*

83 /2	ADC r/m,imm8	Add carry flag and *sign_ext(imm8)* into *r/m*
83 /3	SBB r/m,imm8	Subtract carry flag and *sign_ext(imm8)* from *r/m*
83 /4	AND r/m,imm8	Bitwise-AND *sign_ext(imm8)* into *r/m*
83 /5	SUB r/m,imm8	Subtract *sign_ext(imm8)* from *r/m*
83 /6	XOR r/m,imm8	Bitwise-XOR *sign_ext(imm8)* into *r/m*
83 /7	CMP r/m,imm8	Compare *sign_ext(imm8)* against *r/m*, and set flags
84	TEST r/m8,r8	Bitwise-AND *r/m8* and *r8*, and set flags
85	TEST r/m,r	Bitwise-AND *r/m* and *r*, and set flags
86	XCHG r/m8,r8	Exchange *r/m8* and *r8* contents
87	XCHG r/m,r	Exchange *r/m* and *r* contents
88	MOV r/m8,r8	Move *r8*'s contents to *r/m8*
89	MOV r/m,r	Move *r*'s contents to *r/m*
8A	MOV r8,r/m8	Move *r/m8*'s contents to *r8*
8B	MOV r,r/m	Move *r/m*'s contents to *r*
8C	MOV r/m,sr	Store segment register *sr* into *r/m*
8D	LEA r,m	Load *r* with effective address of *m*
8E	MOV sr,r/m16	Load segment register *sr* with *r/m*
8F	POP r/m	Pop stack-top into *r/m*
90	XCHG eAX,eAX	Exchange AX/EAX with AX/EAX (i.e. NOP)
91	XCHG eAX,eCX	Exchange AX/EAX with CX/ECX
92	XCHG eAX,eDX	Exchange AX/EAX with DX/EDX
93	XCHG eAX,eBX	Exchange AX/EAX with BX/EBX
94	XCHG eAX,eSP	Exchange AX/EAX with SP/ESP
95	XCHG eAX,eBP	Exchange AX/EAX with BP/EBP
96	XCHG eAX,eSI	Exchange AX/EAX with SI/ESI
97	XCHG eAX,eDI	Exchange AX/EAX with DI/EDI
98	CBW/CWDE	Convert BYTE to WORD (*os* == 16), or WORD to DWORD (*os* == 32)
99	CWD/CDQ	Convert WORD to DWORD (*os* == 16), or DWORD to quadword (*os* == 32)
9A	CALLF	Far call
9B	WAIT	Wait till BUSY pin inactive
9C	PUSHF/PUSHFD	Push FLAGS (*os* == 16), or EFLAGS (*os* == 32)
9D	POPF/POPFD	Pop stack into FLAGS (*os* == 16), or EFLAGS (*os* == 32)
9E	SAHF	Store AH register into low BYTE of FLAGS
9F	LAHF	Load low BYTE of FLAGS into AH
A0	MOV AL,moff	Load AL with BYTE at offset *moff*
A1	MOV AX,moff	Load AX/EAX with (D)WORD at offset *moff*
A2	MOV moff,AL	Store AL into BYTE at offset *moff*
A3	MOV moff,AX	Store AX/EAX into (D)WORD at offset *moff*
A4	MOVSB [eDI],[eSI]	Copy BYTE at DS:eSI to BYTE at ES:eDI; increment eSI and eDI by 1
A5	MOVSW/MOVSD [eDI],[eSI]	Copy (D)WORD at DS:eSI to (D)WORD at ES:eDI; increment eSI and eDI by 2 (if *os*==16) or 4 (if *os*==32)
A6	CMPSB [eSI],[eDI]	Compare BYTE at DS:eSI to BYTE at ES:eDI and set flags; increment eSI and eDI by 1
A7	CMPSW/CMPSD [eSI],[eDI]	Compare (D)WORD at DS:eSI to (D)WORD at ES:eDI and set flags; increment eSI and eDI by 2 (if *os*==16) or 4 (if *os*==32)
A8	TEST AL,imm8	Bitwise-AND AL and *imm8*, and set flags
A9	TEST eAX,imm	Bitwise-AND AX/EAX and *imm*, and set flags
AA	STOSB [eDI],AL	Store AL into BYTE at ES:eDI; increment eDI by 1

AB	STOSW/STOSD [eDI],AX	Store AX/EAX into (D)WORD at ES:eDI; increment eDI by 2 or 4
AC	LODSB AL,[eSI]	Load AL with BYTE at DS:eSI; increment eSI by 1
AD	LODSW/LODSD AX,[eSI]	Load AX/EAX with (D)WORD at DS:eSI; increment eSI by 2 or 4
AE	SCASB [eDI],AL	Compare AL against BYTE at ES:eDI; increment eDI by 1
AF	SCASW/SCASD [eDI],AX	Compare AX/EAX against (D)WORD at ES:eDI; increment eDI by 2 or 4
B0	MOV AL,imm8	Load AL with imm8
B1	MOV CL,imm8	Load CL with imm8
B2	MOV DL,imm8	Load DL with imm8
B3	MOV BL,imm8	Load BL with imm8
B4	MOV AH,imm8	Load AH with imm8
B5	MOV CH,imm8	Load CH with imm8
B6	MOV DH,imm8	Load DH with imm8
B7	MOV BH,imm8	Load BH with imm8
B8	MOV eAX,imm	Load AX/EAX with imm
B9	MOV eCX,imm	Load CX/ECX with imm
BA	MOV eDX,imm	Load DX/EDX with imm
BB	MOV eBX,imm	Load BX/EBX with imm
BC	MOV eSP,imm	Load SP/ESP with imm
BD	MOV eBP,imm	Load BP/EBP with imm
BE	MOV eSI,imm	Load SI/ESI with imm
BF	MOV eDI,imm	Load DI/EDI with imm

C0	**Shift/rotate r/m8 by imm8 (unavailable on the 8086)**	
C0 /0	ROL r/m8,1	Rotate left r/m8 by imm8 bits
C0 /1	ROR r/m8,1	Rotate right r/m8 by imm8 bits
C0 /2	RCL r/m8,1	Rotate left through CF r/m8 by imm8 bits
C0 /3	RCR r/m8,1	Rotate right through CF r/m8 by imm8 bits
C0 /4	SHL/SAL r/m8,1	Shift left r/m8 by imm8 bits
C0 /5	SHR r/m8,1	Shift right logical r/m8 by imm8 bits
C0 /6	*unassigned*	*reserved opcode*
C0 /7	SAR r/m8,1	Shift right arithmetic r/m8 by imm8 bits

C1	**Shift/rotate r/m by imm8 (unavailable on the 8086)**	
C1 /0	ROL r/m8,1	Rotate left r/m by imm8 bits
C1 /1	ROR r/m8,1	Rotate right r/m by imm8 bits
C1 /2	RCL r/m8,1	Rotate left through CF r/m by imm8 bits
C1 /3	RCR r/m8,1	Rotate right through CF r/m by imm8 bits
C1 /4	SHL/SAL r/m8,1	Shift left r/m by imm8 bits
C1 /5	SHR r/m8,1	Shift right logical r/m by imm8 bits
C1 /6	*unassigned*	*reserved opcode*
C1 /7	SAR r/m8,1	Shift right arithmetic r/m by imm8 bits
C2	RETN imm16	Pop parameters, and return from near procedure call
C3	RETN	Return from near procedure call
C4	LES r,m	Load pointer into ES and a register
C5	LDS r,m	Load pointer into DS and a register
C6	MOV r/m8,imm8	Load imm8 into r/m8
C7	MOV r/m,imm	Load imm into r/m [(D)WORD operation]
C8	ENTER imm16,imm8	Enter level imm8 procedure, with imm16 byte frame (unavailable on the 8086)
C9	LEAVE	Leave nested procedure (unavailable on the 8086)
CA	RETF imm16	Pop parameters, and return from far procedure call
CB	RETF	Return from far procedure call

CC	INT3	Signal code breakpoint (via software interrupt 3)
CD	INT imm8	Signal software interrupt *imm8*
CE	INTO	Signal software interrupt 4 on overflow (OF flag set)
CF	IRET/IRETD	Return from interrupt service routine or task

D0	**Shift/rotate *r/m8* by 1**	
D0 /0	ROL r/m8,1	Rotate left *r/m8* by 1 bits
D0 /1	ROR r/m8,1	Rotate right *r/m8* by 1 bits
D0 /2	RCL r/m8,1	Rotate left through CF *r/m8* by 1 bits
D0 /3	RCR r/m8,1	Rotate right through CF *r/m8* by 1 bits
D0 /4	SHL/SAL r/m8,1	Shift left *r/m8* by 1 bits
D0 /5	SHR r/m8,1	Shift right logical *r/m8* by 1 bits
D0 /6	*unassigned*	*reserved opcode*
D0 /7	SAR r/m8,1	Shift right arithmetic *r/m8* by 1 bits

D1	**Shift/rotate *r/m* by 1**	
D1 /0	ROL r/m8,1	Rotate left *r/m* by 1 bits
D1 /1	ROR r/m8,1	Rotate right *r/m* by 1 bits
D1 /2	RCL r/m8,1	Rotate left through CF *r/m* by 1 bits
D1 /3	RCR r/m8,1	Rotate right through CF *r/m* by 1 bits
D1 /4	SHL/SAL r/m8,1	Shift left *r/m* by 1 bits
D1 /5	SHR r/m8,1	Shift right logical *r/m* by 1 bits
D1 /6	*unassigned*	*reserved opcode*
D1 /7	SAR r/m8,1	Shift right arithmetic *r/m* by 1 bits

D2	**Shift/rotate *r/m8* by CL**	
D2 /0	ROL r/m8,1	Rotate left *r/m8* by CL bits
D2 /1	ROR r/m8,1	Rotate right *r/m8* by CL bits
D2 /2	RCL r/m8,1	Rotate left through CF *r/m8* by CL bits
D2 /3	RCR r/m8,1	Rotate right through CF *r/m8* by CL bits
D2 /4	SHL/SAL r/m8,1	Shift left *r/m8* by CL bits
D2 /5	SHR r/m8,1	Shift right logical *r/m8* by CL bits
D2 /6	*unassigned*	*reserved opcode*
D2 /7	SAR r/m8,1	Shift right arithmetic *r/m8* by CL bits

D3	**Shift/rotate *r/m* by CL**	
D3 /0	ROL r/m8,1	Rotate left *r/m* by CL bits
D3 /1	ROR r/m8,1	Rotate right *r/m* by CL bits
D3 /2	RCL r/m8,1	Rotate left through CF *r/m* by CL bits
D3 /3	RCR r/m8,1	Rotate right through CF *r/m* by CL bits
D3 /4	SHL/SAL r/m8,1	Shift left *r/m* by CL bits
D3 /5	SHR r/m8,1	Shift right logical *r/m* by CL bits
D3 /6	*unassigned*	*reserved opcode*
D3 /7	SAR r/m8,1	Shift right arithmetic *r/m* by CL bits

D4 0A	AAM	ASCII adjust AX after binary multiply
D5 0A	AAD	ASCII adjust AX before binary divide
D6	*unassigned*	*reserved opcode*
D7	XLATB	Translate byte in AL using lookup table

D8	**ESC0**	**Processor extension opcode group 0 (x87 required)**

Memory operand subgroup (MOD ∈ {0,1,2})

D8 /0	FADD m32	Add SINGLE *m32* to 80x87 stack-top
D8 /1	FMUL m32	Multiply 80x87 stack-top by SINGLE *m32*

D8 /2	FCOM m32	Compare SINGLE *m32* to 80*x*87 stack-top
D8 /3	FCOMP m32	Compare SINGLE *m32* to 80*x*87 stack-top, then pop stack
D8 /4	FSUB m32	Subtract SINGLE *m32* from 80*x*87 stack-top
D8 /5	FSUBR m32	Store difference of SINGLE *m32* and 80*x*87 stack-top into the stack-top
D8 /6	FDIV m32	Divide 80*x*87 stack-top by SINGLE *m32*
D8 /7	FDIVR m32	Store into the 80*x*87 stack-top the quotient of SINGLE *m32* divided by the 80*x*87 stack-top

Register operand subgroup (MOD == 3)

D8 C0+*n*	FADD ST,ST(*n*)	Add ST(*n*) to 80*x*87 stack-top
D8 C8+*n*	FMUL ST,ST(*n*)	Multiply 80*x*87 stack-top by ST(*n*)
D8 D0+*n*	FCOM ST(*n*)	Compare ST(*n*) to 80*x*87 stack-top
D8 D8+*n*	FCOMP ST(*n*)	Compare ST(*n*) to 80*x*87 stack-top, then pop stack
D8 E0+*n*	FSUB ST,ST(*n*)	Subtract ST(*n*) from 80*x*87 stack-top
D8 E8+*n*	FSUBR ST,ST(*n*)	Store difference of ST(*n*) and 80*x*87 stack-top into the stack-top
D8 F0+*n*	FDIV ST,ST(*n*)	Divide 80*x*87 stack-top by ST(*n*)
D8 F8+*n*	FDIVR ST,ST(*n*)	Store into the 80*x*87 stack-top the quotient of ST(*n*) divided by the 80*x*87 stack-top

| **D9** | **ESC1** | **Processor extension opcode group 1 (x87 required)** |

Memory operand subgroup (MOD ∈ {0,1,2})

D9 /0	FLD m32	Push SINGLE *m32* onto 80*x*87 stack
D9 /1	*unassigned*	*reserved opcode*
D9 /2	FST m32	Store 80*x*87 stack-top into the SINGLE *m32*
D9 /3	FSTP m32	Store 80*x*87 stack-top into the SINGLE *m32*, then pop stack
D9 /4	FLDENV m	Load 80*x*87 environment from *m*. If *os==16*, *m*'s size is 14 bytes; if *os==32*, *m* is 28 bytes
D9 /5	FLDCW m16	Load *m16* into 80*x*87 control word
D9 /6	FSTENV m	Store 80*x*87 environment into *m*. If *os==16*, *m*'s size is 14 bytes; if *os==32*, *m* is 28 bytes
D9 /7	FSTCW m16	Store 80*x*87 control word into *m16*

Register operand subgroup (MOD == 3)

D9 C0+*n*	FLD ST(*n*)	Push ST(*n*) onto 80*x*87 stack
D9 C8+*n*	FXCH ST(*n*)	Exchange contents of ST(*n*) and 80*x*87 stack-top
D9 D0	FNOP	No operation (processor extension)
D9 D1	*unassigned*	*reserved opcode*
:	:	:
D9 DF	*unassigned*	*reserved opcode*
D9 E0	FCHS	Change sign of 80*x*87 stack-top
D9 E1	FABS	Absolute value of 80*x*87 stack-top
D9 E2	*unassigned*	*reserved opcode*
D9 E3	*unassigned*	*reserved opcode*
D9 E4	FTST	Compare 80*x*87 stack-top against 0.0
D9 E5	FXAM	Examine 80*x*87 stack-top's contents
D9 E6	*unassigned*	*reserved opcode*
D9 E7	*unassigned*	*reserved opcode*
D9 E8	FLD1	Push +1.0 onto 80*x*87 stack-top
D9 E9	FLDL2T	Push $\log_2 10$ onto 80*x*87 stack-top
D9 EA	FLDL2E	Push $\log_2 e$ onto 80*x*87 stack-top
D9 EB	FLDPI	Push pi onto 80*x*87 stack-top
D9 EC	FLDLG2	Push $\log_{10} 2$ onto 80*x*87 stack-top

D9 ED	FLDLN2	Push $\log_e 2$ onto 80x87 stack-top
D9 EE	FLDZ	Push 0.0 onto 80x87 stack-top
D9 EF	*unassigned*	*reserved opcode*
D9 F0	F2XM1	Replace 80x87 stack-top with 2ST-1
D9 F1	FYL2X	Pop ST (80x87 stack-top) and ST(1) and push ST(1) * $\log_2$ST
D9 F2	FPTAN	Pop ST (80x87 stack-top) and push tan(ST) and the constant 1.0
D9 F3	FPATAN	Pop ST (80x87 stack-top) and ST(1) and push arctan(ST(1)/ST)
D9 F4	FXTRACT	Extract exponent and significand of 80x87 stack-top
D9 F5	FPREM1	Compute IEEE compatible partial remainder (387 and 486 only)
D9 F6	FDECSTP	Decrement 80x87 stack pointer
D9 F7	FINCSTP	Increment 80x87 stack pointer
D9 F8	FPREM	Compute partial remainder (not IEEE-754 compatible)
D9 F9	FYL2XP1	Pop ST (80x87 stack-top) and ST(1) and push ST(1) * $\log_2$(ST+1.0)
D9 FA	FSQRT	Replace 80x87 stack-top with its square root
D9 FB	FSINCOS	Pop 80x87 stack-top, then push its sine and cosine values (387 and 486 only)
D9 FC	FRNDINT	Replace 80x87 stack-top with its value rounded to an integer
D9 FD	FSCALE	Scale the 80x87 stack-top by an integer power of 2
D9 FE	FSIN	Replace the 80x87 stack-top with its sine (387 and 486 only)
D9 FF	FCOS	Replace the 80x87 stack-top with its cosine (387 and 486 only)
DA	**ESC2**	**Processor extension opcode group 2 (x87 required)**

Memory operand subgroup (MOD ∈ {0,1,2})

DA /0	FIADD m32	Add the DWORD-sized int *m32* to 80x87 stack-top
DA /1	FIMUL m32	Multiply 80x87 stack-top by the DWORD-sized int *m32*
DA /2	FICOM m32	Compare the DWORD-sized int *m32* to 80x87 stack-top
DA /3	FICOMP m32	Compare the DWORD-sized int *m32* to 80x87 stack-top, then pop stack
DA /4	FISUB m32	Subtract the DWORD-sized int *m32* from 80x87 stack-top
DA /5	FISUBR m32	Store difference of the DWORD-sized int *m32* and 80x87 stack-top into the stack-top
DA /6	FIDIV m32	Divide 80x87 stack-top by the DWORD-sized int *m32*
DA /7	FIDIVR m32	Store into the 80x87 stack-top the quotient of the DWORD-sized int *m32* divided by the 80x87 stack-top

Register operand subgroup (MOD == 3)

DA C0	*unassigned*	*reserved opcode*
:	:	:
DA E8	*unassigned*	*reserved opcode*
DA E9	FUCOMPP	Pop ST (80x87 stack-top) and ST(1) and perform an unordered compare of ST with ST(1)
DA EA	*unassigned*	*reserved opcode*
:	:	:
DA FF	*unassigned*	*reserved opcode*

DB   ESC3   **Processor extension opcode group 3 (x87 required)**

Memory operand subgroup (MOD ∈ {0,1,2})

DB /0	FILD m16	Push the WORD-sized int *m16* onto 80*x*87 stack
DB /1	*unassigned*	*reserved opcode*
DB /2	FIST m16	Store the 80*x*87 stack-top into the WORD-sized int *m16*
DB /3	FISTP m16	Pop the 80*x*87 stack-top into the WORD-sized int *m16*
DB /4	*unassigned*	*reserved opcode*
DB /5	FLD m80	Push the EXTENDED *m80* operand onto 80*x*87 stack
DB /6	*unassigned*	*reserved opcode*
DB /7	FSTP m80	Pop the 80*x*87 stack-top into the EXTENDED *m80*

Register operand subgroup (MOD == 3)

DB C0	*unassigned*	*reserved opcode*
:	:	:
DB DF	*unassigned*	*reserved opcode*
DB E0	FENI	Enable 8087 interrupt generation (NOP on non-8087 processor extensions)
DB E1	FDISI	Disable 8087 interrupt generation (NOP on non-8087 processor extensions)
DB E2	FCLEX	Clear all 80*x*87 exceptions
DB E3	FINIT	Initialize 80*x*87
DB E4	FSETPM	Inform 80287 that PROTECTED mode has been entered (*reserved* opcode on 8087, treated as a NOP on the 80387 and the i486)
DB E5	*unassigned*	*reserved opcode*
:	:	:
DB FF	*unassigned*	*reserved opcode*

DC   ESC4   **Processor extension opcode group 4 (x87 required)**

Memory operand subgroup (MOD ∈ {0,1,2})

DC /0	FADD m64	Add DOUBLE *m64* to 80*x*87 stack-top
DC /1	FMUL m64	Multiply 80*x*87 stack-top by DOUBLE *m64*
DC /2	FCOM m64	Compare DOUBLE *m64* to 80*x*87 stack-top
DC /3	FCOMP m64	Compare DOUBLE *m64* to 80*x*87 stack-top, then pop stack
DC /4	FSUB m64	Subtract DOUBLE *m64* from 80*x*87 stack-top
DC /5	FSUBR m64	Store difference of DOUBLE *m64* and 80*x*87 stack-top into the stack-top
DC /6	FDIV m64	Divide 80*x*87 stack-top by DOUBLE *m64*
DC /7	FDIVR m64	Store into the 80*x*87 stack-top the quotient of DOUBLE *m64* divided by the 80*x*87 stack-top

Register operand subgroup (MOD == 3)

DC C0+*n*	FADD ST(*n*),ST	Add 80*x*87 stack-top to ST(*n*)
DC C8+*n*	FMUL ST(*n*),ST	Multiply ST(*n*) by 80*x*87 stack-top
DC D0	*unassigned*	*reserved opcode*
:	:	:
DC DF	*unassigned*	*reserved opcode*
DC E0+*n*	FSUBR ST(*n*),ST	Store difference of 80*x*87 stack-top and ST(*n*) into ST(*n*)
DC E8+*n*	FSUB ST(*n*),ST	Subtract from ST(*n*) the 80*x*87 stack-top value
DC F0+*n*	FDIVR ST(*n*),ST	Store into ST(*n*) the quotient of the 80*x*87 stack-top divided by ST(*n*)
DC F8+*n*	FDIV ST(*n*),ST	Divide ST(*n*) by 80*x*87 stack-top value

DD　　ESC5　　　　　　　　　　**Processor extension opcode group 5 (x87 required)**

Memory operand subgroup (MOD ∈ {0,1,2})

DD /0	FLD m64	Push the DOUBLE *m64* operand onto 80*x*87 stack
DD /1	*unassigned*	*reserved opcode*
DD /2	FST m64	Store the 80*x*87 stack-top into the DOUBLE *m64*
DD /3	FSTP m64	Pop the 80*x*87 stack-top into the DOUBLE *m64*
DD /4	FRESTOR m	Load 80*x*87 environment and stack from save area *m*. If *os==16*, *m*'s size is 94 bytes; if *os==32*, *m* is 108 bytes.
DD /5	*unassigned*	*reserved opcode*
DD /6	FSAVE m	Store 80*x*87 environment and stack into save area *m*. If *os==16*, *m*'s size is 94 bytes; if *os==32*, *m* is 108 bytes.
DD /7	FSTSW m16	Store 80*x*87 status word into *m16*

Register operand subgroup (MOD == 3)

DD C0+*n*	FFREE ST(*n*)	Free 80*x*87 stack entry *n*
DD C8	*unassigned*	*reserved opcode*
:	:	:
DD CF	*unassigned*	*reserved opcode*
DD D0+*n*	FST ST(*n*)	Store 80*x*87 stack-top into ST(*n*)
DD D8+*n*	FSTP ST(*n*)	Pop 80*x*87 stack-top into ST(*n*)
DD E0+*n*	FUCOM ST(*n*)	Compare (unordered) 80*x*87 stack-top against ST(*n*) (387 and 486 only)
DD E8+*n*	FUCOMP ST(*n*)	Compare (unordered) 80*x*87 stack-top against ST(*n*), then pop stack (387 and 486 only)
DD F0	*unassigned*	*reserved opcode*
:	:	:
DD FF	*unassigned*	*reserved opcode*

DE　　ESC6　　　　　　　　　　**Processor extension opcode group 6 (x87 required)**

Memory operand subgroup (MOD ∈ {0,1,2})

DE /0	FIADD m16	Add the WORD-sized int *m16* to 80*x*87 stack-top
DE /1	FIMUL m16	Multiply 80*x*87 stack-top by the WORD-sized int *m16*
DE /2	FICOM m16	Compare the WORD-sized int *m16* to 80*x*87 stack-top
DE /3	FICOMP m16	Compare the WORD-sized int *m16* to 80*x*87 stack-top, then pop stack
DE /4	FISUB m16	Subtract the WORD-sized int *m16* from 80*x*87 stack-top
DE /5	FISUBR m16	Store difference of the WORD-sized int *m16* and 80*x*87 stack-top into the stack-top
DE /6	FIDIV m16	Divide 80*x*87 stack-top by the WORD-sized int *m16*
DE /7	FIDIVR m16	Store into the 80*x*87 stack-top the quotient of the WORD-sized int *m16* divided by the 80*x*87 stack-top

Register operand subgroup (MOD == 3)

DE C0+*n*	FADDP ST(*n*),ST	Increment ST(*n*) by 80*x*87 stack-top, then pop stack
DE C8+*n*	FMULP ST(*n*),ST	Multiply ST(*n*) by 80*x*87 stack-top, then pop stack
DE D0	*unassigned*	*reserved opcode*
:	:	:
DE D7	*unassigned*	*reserved opcode*
DE D8	*unassigned*	*reserved opcode*
DE D9	FCOMPP	Pop ST (80*x*87 stack-top) and ST(1) and compare ST to ST(1)
DE DA	*unassigned*	*reserved opcode*

	:	:
DE DF	*unassigned*	*reserved opcode*
DE E0+*n*	FSUBRP ST(*n*),ST	Compute difference between 80*x*87 stack-top and ST(*n*), store result in ST(*n*), then pop stack
DE E8+*n*	FSUBP ST(*n*),ST	Subtract 80*x*87 stack-top from ST(*n*), then pop stack
DE F0+*n*	FDIVRP ST(*n*),ST	Compute quotient of 80*x*87 stack-top divided by ST(*n*), store result in ST(*n*), then pop stack
DE F8+*n*	FDIVP ST(*n*),ST	Divide ST(*n*) by 80*x*87 stack-top, then pop stack

DF	**ESC7**	**Processor extension opcode group 7 (x87 required)**

Memory operand subgroup (MOD ∈ {0,1,2})

DF /0	FILD m32	Push the DWORD-sized int *m32* onto 80*x*87 stack
DF /1	*unassigned*	*reserved opcode*
DF /2	FIST m32	Store the 80*x*87 stack-top into the DWORD-sized int *m32*
DF /3	FISTP m32	Pop the 80*x*87 stack-top into the DWORD-sized int *m32*
DF /4	FBLD m80	Push PACKED_BCD *m80* onto 80*x*87 stack
DF /5	FILD m64	Push the QWORD-sized int *m64* onto 80*x*87 stack
DF /6	FBSTP m80	Pop 80*x*87 stack-top, and store as a PACKED_BCD into *m80*
DF /7	FISTP m64	Pop the 80*x*87 stack-top into the QWORD-sized int *m64*

Register operand subgroup (MOD == 3)

DF C0	*unassigned*	*reserved opcode*
:	:	:
DF DF	*unassigned*	*reserved opcode*
DF E0	FSTSW AX	Store 80*x*87 status word into AX register
DF E1	*unassigned*	*reserved opcode*
:	:	:
DF FF	*unassigned*	*reserved opcode*

E0	LOOPNE d8	Jump if ZF clear and CX/ECX is not zero
E1	LOOPE d8	Jump if ZF set and CX/ECX is not zero
E2	LOOP d8	Jump if CX/ECX is not zero
E3	JCXZ/JECXZ d8	Jump if CX/ECX is zero
E4	IN AL,imm8	Load AL with BYTE from port *imm8*
E5	IN *e*AX,imm8	Load AX/EAX with (D)WORD from port *imm8*
E6	OUT AL,imm8	Store AL into BYTE port *imm8*
E7	OUT AX,imm8	Store AX/EAX into (D)WORD port *imm8*
E8	CALLN rel	Near procedure call
E9	JMPN rel	Near jump
EA	JMPF sel:off	Far jump
EB	JMPN rel8	Short jump (a near jump with a BYTE displacement
EC	IN AL,DX	Load AL with BYTE port addressed by DX
ED	IN *e*AX,DX	Load AX/EAX with (D)WORD port addressed by DX
EE	OUT AL,DX	Store AL into BYTE port addressed by DX
EF	OUT *e*AX,DX	Store AX/EAX into (D)WORD port addressed by DX
F0	LOCK	"Locked transaction" prefix
F1	*unassigned*	*reserved opcode*
F2	REPNE	"Repeat till unequal" prefix
F3	REPE	"Repeat till equal" prefix
F4	HLT	Wait for interrupt
F5	CMC	Complement carry flag (CF) setting

F6	**F6 opcodes group**

F6 /0	TEST r/m8,imm8	Bitwise-AND *r/m8* and *imm8*, and set flags
F6 /1	*unassigned*	*reserved opcode*
F6 /2	NOT r/m8	Bitwise-NOT *r/m8*
F6 /3	NEG r/m8	Negate *r/m8*
F6 /4	MUL AL,r/m8	Unsigned multiply AL with *r/m8*
F6 /5	IMUL AL,r/m8	Signed multiply AL with *r/m8*
F6 /6	DIV AL,r/m8	Unsigned divide AX by *r/m8*
F6 /7	IDIV AL,r/m8	Signed divide AX by *r/m8*

F7	**F7 opcodes group**	
F7 /0	TEST r/m,imm	Bitwise-AND *r/m* and *imm*, and set flags (((D)WORD operation)
F7 /1	*unassigned*	*reserved opcode*
F7 /2	NOT r/m	Bitwise-NOT *r/m* ((D)WORD operation)
F7 /3	NEG r/m	Negate *r/m* ((D)WORD operation)
F7 /4	MUL *e*AX,r/m	Unsigned multiply AX/EAX by *r/m* ((D)WORD operation)
F7 /5	IMUL *e*AX,r/m	Signed multiply AX/EAX by *r/m* ((D)WORD operation)
F7 /6	DIV *e*AX,r/m	Unsigned divide DX:AX/EDX:EAX by *r/m* ((D)WORD operation)
F7 /7	IDIV *e*AX,r/m	Signed divide DX:AX/EDX:EAX by *r/m* ((D)WORD operation)

F8	CLC	Clear carry flag (CF)
F9	STC	Set carry flag (CF)
FA	CLI	Clear interrupt flag (IF)
FB	STI	Set interrupt flag (IF)
FC	CLD	Clear direction flag (DF)
FD	STD	Set direction flag (DF)

FE	**FE opcodes group**	
FE /0	INC r/m8	Increment *r/m8* by 1
FE /1	DEC r/m8	Decrement *r/m8* by 1
FE /2	*unassigned*	*reserved opcode*
FE /3	*unassigned*	*reserved opcode*
FE /4	*unassigned*	*reserved opcode*
FE /5	*unassigned*	*reserved opcode*
FE /6	*unassigned*	*reserved opcode*
FE /7	*unassigned*	*reserved opcode*

FF	**FF opcodes group**	
FF /0	INC r/m	Increment *r/m* by 1 ((D)WORD operation)
FF /1	DEC r/m	Decrement *r/m* by 1 ((D)WORD operation)
FF /2	CALLN r/m	Indirect near call using OFFSET stored at (D)WORD *r/m*
FF /3	CALLF mP	Indirect far call using SELECTOR:OFFSET stored at memory location *mP*
FF /4	JMPN r/m	Indirect near jump using OFFSET stored at (D)WORD *r/m*
FF /5	JMPF mP	Indirect far jump using SELECTOR:OFFSET stored at memory location *mP*
FF /6	PUSH r/m	Push (D)WORD at *r/m* onto stack
FF /7	*unassigned*	*reserved opcode*

Index

.287 250
.387 250
8080 200
8086 2, 178
  detection method 201
  reset 178
8087 251
  754 conformance 210
  FPREM bug 394
8088 52
8259 202
  See interrupt controller
80186 178
  control block 203
  relocation register 203
80188 52
80286 2, 180
  detection method 534
  reset 180
80287 252
  754 conformance 210
  FPREM bug 394
80376 241
  reset 184
  stack addressing 114
80386 2
  detection method 534
  reset 182
80387 252
80486
  See i486
32000 (CPU) 17
68000 (CPU) 17
80386SX 52
80x87 19, **209**
  administrative instructions
    232
  control word
    See FCW
  detection method 260
  environment **238**, 249
  initialization 257-258, 384
  instruction encoding 259
  nonadministrative
    instructions **232**

  state **238**
  status word
    See FSW
80x87 exception
  DENORMAL 230, 255
  F_OVERFLOW 229, 255
  F_UNDERFLOW 229, 255
  INVALID_FOP 227, 228,
    237, 246, 247, 255, 337,
    338, 408, 420, 428, 430,
    431
  PRECISION 230, 256, 372,
    373, 374, 375, 376
  ZERO_FOP 228, 255, 428
80x86 state
  See CPU state

A

A20 masking 198
A20M (pin) 198
AAA (instr) 18, 275
AAD (instr) 18, 276
AAM (instr) 18, 277
AAS (instr) 18, 278
aborts **145**
AC (flag) 25, 205, 533, 534
access
  misaligned **15**, 25, 53, 115
  misaligned I/O 119
access rights 56
access rule **40**
  for memory 43
  I/O access 42
Accessed (flag) 66, 79, 80,
  141
  See also PAcessed,
  PTAccessed
ADC (instr) 279
ADD (instr) 280, 468
addition using LEA 468
address
  aliasing **103**
  cache tag 103
  linear 37, 44
  logical 37, 44, 59

physical 37, 44
synonyms **103**
address size 44
address size attribute
    See attribute, address size
address size override (prefix)
    190, 281
addressing mode
    80*x*87 stack 232
administrative instructions
    232
AF (flag) 24, 550, 553
AH (register) 323
AHOLD (pin) 182
AL (register) 272, 323
alignment 48
    cache data line 104
    of data 15
    of directory table 84
    of instructions 187
    of page-granular Limits 59
    on natural boundary 98
alignment check flag
    See AC
    See also AM
AM (flag) 25, 27, 183, 205
AND (instr) 282
arithmetic flags **24**
ARPL (instr) 46, 283
as **196**
ASCII 15
assembler directive
    .287 250
    .387 250
    proc 544
    USE16 196, 200
    USE32 196, 200
associativity **102**
attribute
    address size 59, 113, 191,
        192, **195**, 281
    operand size 59, 114, 191,
        192, **198**, 241, 524
auxiliary carry flag
    See AF
AX (register) 272, 323, 391

B

BackLink (field) 133, 134,
    142, 143, 303
Base (field) 54, 56, 58, 59,
    68, 129, 180, 204, 297,
    456
base register **194**
BCD **18**
    and 80*x*87 211, 223
    unpacked **18**

zone format **18**
BD (flag) 507, 509
benign exception 150, **152**
biased exponent **212**
Big (flag) 59, 114, 115, 196
Big Endian **16**, 287
binary arithmetic 15
binary coded decimal **18**
BIST
    See self-test
BOOLEAN (type) 33
BOUND (exception) 203
BOUND (instr) 201, 203, 284
BP (register) 187, 194, 195,
    326
breakpoint
    data 166, 171
    exact 14, 144
    I/O address 169
    instruction 170, 171, 443
    region 171, 174
brkpt_active (flag) 35, 166,
    171, 175, 176, 180, 181,
    184, 185
brkpt_detected **167**, 542
BSF (instr) 285
BSR (instr) 286
BSWAP (instr) 2, 17, 201,
    202, 205, 287
BSY (flag) 258
BT (flag) 135, 139, 142
BT (instr) 288
BTC (instr) 290
BTR (instr) 292
BTS (instr) 294
bug
    in FPREM 394
    in SAL 552
bus
    lock 169
    master **111**
    slaves **111**
    watch **104**
bus cycle
    halt 168
bus lock
    See LOCK
bus size **52**
BUSY (pin) 182, 231, 248,
    250, 253, 381, 382, 383,
    581, 582
BUSY latch 253
BUSY_TSS16 (descr. type)
    132
BUSY_TSS32 (descr. type)
    132
BX (register) 187, 194
BYTE **15**

BYTEPORT **118**
BYTEPORT (type) 118, 526

C

C0 (flag) 236, 258, 341, 344,
   356, 421, 424, 426
C1 (flag) 230, 236, 258, 369,
   372, 373, 374, 375, 376,
   377, 380, 426
C2 (flag) 236, 258, 341, 344,
   356, 393, 395, 421, 424,
   426
C3 (flag) 236, 258, 341, 344,
   356, 421, 424, 426
cache 198, 445, 583
   coherency 100
   deactivation 106
   external 28
   hit **102**
   hit rate **102**
   internal 1
   miss **102**
   miss rate **102**
   replacement policy 100,
      103
   second-level **107**
   set associative **100**
   set size **102**
   Valid flag 101
   write-back **104**, 108, 583
   write-through **104**, 108
cache_486 103, 445, 583
caching disable flag
   See CD
CALL
   indirect 297
   inter-level 298, 300
   interlevel 545
   same level 300, 545
call
   inter-level 283
CALL (far) (instr) 123, 129,
   162, 297
CALL (instr) 63, 195, 325
CALL (near) (instr) 296
CALL (task) (instr) 143, 303
call gate 121-128
CALLF (instr) 297
CALLGATE16 (descr. type)
   115, 124
CALLGATE32 (descr. type)
   115, 124
carry flag
   See CF
CBW (instr) 306
CD (flag) 27, 105, 106, 183
CDQ (instr) 307

CF (flag) 24, 288, 290, 292,
   294, 341, 344, 356, 421,
   424, 548, 549, 550, 552,
   553
characterization
   of registers 187
check_brkpt 91, 95, **175**
check_interrupts 11, 13, **151**
checkpoint 11, 12, **168**
chop (func) 404
CL (register) 192
CLC (instr) 308
CLD (instr) 309
clear_active_brkpts **176**
CLI (instr) 42, 310
CLTS (instr) 251, 311
CMC (instr) 312
CMP (instr) 313
CMPSB/CMPSD/CMPSW
   (instr) 314
CMPS*x* (instr) 24
CMP*x* (instr) 190
CMPXCHG (instr) 316
collating sequence 15
conforming segment
   See segment, conforming
contributory exception **152**
control register **26**
   CR0 26, 28, 88, 94, 104,
      105, 253, 381, 479
   CR2 28, 90, 148
   CR3 28, 51, 84, 87, 105,
      106, 136
   CR7 26
   MSW **26**
   store 505
control registers 502, 505
control word
   See FCW
coprocessor
   See processor extension
copy-on-write 167
CPL **41**, 88, 110, 297
   level 0 override 74
CPL (field) 36, 183, 185
CPL (register) 154, 158
CPU state
   curr 21
   prev 21, 31
CR0 502, 505
CR2 502, 505
CR3 502, 505
CR0 (ctl. reg.) 26, 28, 88, 94,
   104, 105, 253, 381, 479
CR2 (ctl. reg.) 28, 90, 148
CR3 (ctl. reg.) 28, 51, 84, 87,
   105, 106, 136
CR7 (ctl. reg.) 26

CR0 (flag) 25
CR0 (register) 569
CR4 (register) 8
critical section 112
cross-checking **104**
CS: (prefix) 190, 317
CS (register) 124, 159
CS (seg. reg.) 26, 69, 82, 83,
202, 249, 297, 456
CS_desc 59, 199, 317, 524
curr 21, 31
current privilege level **41**
See CPL
CWD (instr) 318
CWDE (instr) 319
CX (register) 196

D

D (flag) **59**
DAA (instr) 19, 320
DAS (instr) 19, 321
data alignment 15
data structures 14
data wraparound
on 8086 201
debug
fault 171
trap 172
DEBUG (exception) 136,
139, 144, 152, 169, 170,
171, 172, 173, 176, 177,
202, 508, 510
debug register 28
DR0 174
DR1 174
DR2 174
DR3 174
DR6 172, 173, 176
DR7 172, 173
field
BD 173
B*i* 173
BS 173
BT 173
See also flag
debug registers 507, 509
DEC (instr) 322
decimal arithmetic 287
See also BCD
decode_instruction 11, 12,
185
DefaultAttr (field) 199
DefaultAttr (flag) 59, 113,
115, 195, 196, 199, 204
demand segmentation 68
denormal **216**, 229, 230, 337,
349, 363, 365, 394, 408

DENORMAL (x87 exception)
230, 255
denormal-sensed mask
See DM
DESCR (type) 62, 63
descriptor
SS_desc 115
descriptor register 68
TSS_desc 132
descriptor type
BUSY_TSS16 132
BUSY_TSS32 132
CALLGATE16 115, 124
CALLGATE32 115, 124
INTERRUPT_GATE16 146,
159, 161
INTERRUPT_GATE32 146,
159, 161, 177
LDT_SEG 141, 478
NOTBUSY_TSS16 132,
133, 142
NOTBUSY_TSS32 132,
133, 142
TASKGATE 129, 146, 159,
161
TRAP_GATE16 146, 159,
161
TRAP_GATE32 146, 159,
161, 177
DF (flag) 24, 527
DH (register) 182
DI (register) 187, 194, 196
Digital Equipment Corp. 17
directory table **51**
directory table entry index
See DTE
DirTabBase (flag) 27
Dirty flag
See PDirty
displacement **194**
display (data struct.) 326
DIV (instr) 323
DIVIDE (exception) 144, 202,
436
DL (register) 182
DM (flag) 235, 258
DMA channel 104
DOUBLE **213**
double fault **152**
double_fault **153**
DOUBLE_FAULT (exception)
145, 146, 152
DPL **44**
DPL (field) 297
DR0 (debug reg.) 174
DR1 (debug reg.) 174
DR2 (debug reg.) 174
DR3 (debug reg.) 174

DR6 (debug reg.) 172, 173, 176
DR7 (debug reg.) 172, 173
DR7 (register) 144
DR*x* 91
DS: (prefix) 190, 325
DS (seg. reg.) 26, 69, 187, 195, 201, 202, 314, 586
DS_desc 63, 325
DTAB_read*x* (func) 74, 75
DTAB_write*x* (func) 81
DTE **50**, 96
DWORD **15**
DWORDPORT **118**
DWORDPORT (type) 526
DX (register) 527

E

EAX (register) 182, 272
EBCDIC 15
EBP (register) 194, 195, 326
ECX (register) 165, 196
ED (flag) 47
EDI (register) 165, 196
effective address **44**
effective privilege level 45
EFLAGS **23**
EFLAGS (flag) 250
EFLAGS (register) 38, 41, 134, 169, 176, 177
EIP 124
EIP (instr) 12
EIP (register) 20, 69, 82, 123, 153, 154, 158, 186, 196, 248, 297, 542, 581
EM (flag) 27, 248, 257, 381, 479, 569, 582
EMPTY **233**
emulate math flag
    See EM
ENTER (instr) 201, 326
enter_new_task **134**
eP (flag) 148
EPL 45
ERROR (pin) 204, 232, 236, 249, 252, 253, 254, 256, 581
error code 90, 133, 146, 188
    IDT flag 77
ERS (flag) 236, 258
ES: (prefix) 190
ES (prefix) 328
ES (seg. reg.) 26, 69, 187, 195, 201, 202, 314
ES_desc 328
ESC (instr) 329
ESI (register) 165, 187, 196

ESP (register) 35, 59, 113, 114, 117, 187, 194, 195, 196, 197, 326, 529, 535
ET (80186 flag) 250, 257
ET (flag) 27, 28, 569
eU_S (flag) 148
evenParity **271**
eW_R (flag) 148
exception **144**
    benign **152**
    BOUND 203
    classes 144
    contributory **152**
    DEBUG 136, 139, 144, 152, 169, 170, 171, 172, 173, 176, 177, 202, 508, 510
    DIVIDE 144, 202, 436
    DOUBLE_FAULT 145, 146, 152
    double fault **152**
    error code 146
    GP 60, 68, 69, 73, 75, 88, 119, 123, 145, 188, 197, 206, 256, 257, 497
    IF 145
    imprecise 144
    INVALID_INSTR 191, 202, 203, 281, 446, 468, 483, 524, 543, 559, 567, 577, 585, 587
    invalid operation in 80*x*87 220
    NMI 149, 450
    NP 68, 88, 141, 152
    OVERFLOW 152
    overflow in 80*x*87 218
    PAGE 9, 90, 93, 110, 146, 152, 177, 256
    PE_ERROR 144, 145, 202, 204, 249, 381
    PE_OVERRUN 144, 256, 257, 384
    PE_UNAVAILABLE 248, 251, 257, 581
    priority 149
    REAL mode 145
    See also 80*x*87 exception
    SHUTDOWN 145
    simultaneous 149
    STACK 73, 499
    TASK 69, 75, 141, 145
    underflow in 80*x*87 218
exception_count (field) 36, 157
exception_count (register) 168
exceptions 11

exclusive-OR 587
Executable (flag) 46, 83
execute 11, 12, 13, **261**
execution mode
   See mode
exit_task **142**
expand-down segment
   See segment, expand-down
exponent **212**
EXT (error code field)
   See XHE
EXTENDED **213**
extension field
   See opcode, extension
external_interrupt **166**, 542
external_interrupt (func) 248,
   581

F

F_OVERFLOW (x87
   exception) 229, 255
F_UNDERFLOW (x87
   exception) 229, 255
F2XM1 (instr) 330
FABS (instr) 222, 331
FADD (instr) 332
FADDP (instr) 334
far operand 186
far pointer **44**, 186, 297
fault 44, 171
   ALIGN 98
   memory access 46
   page 49, 51
   segment 51
   segmentation 68
faults **144**
FBLD (instr) 224, 335
FBSTP (instr) 224, 336
FCHS (instr) 222, 338
FCLEX (instr) 339
FCOM (instr) 228, 340
FCOMP (instr) 228
FCOMP[P] (instr) 342
FCOMPP (instr) 228
FCOS (instr) 345
FCW 232
FCW (register) 219, 226, **234**,
   238, 242, 243, 244, 257,
   370, 372, 373, 374, 375,
   376, 389
FDE (flag) 230, 236, 255, 258
FDECSTP (instr) 346
FDISI (instr) 347
FDIV[R] (instr) 348
FDIV[R]P (instr) 350
FENI (instr) 352
FERR (pin) 254

fetch_code1 **83**
FFREE (instr) 353
FIADD (instr) 354
FICOM (instr) 228, 355
FICOMP (instr) 228, 357
FIDIV[R] (instr) 358
FIE (flag) 236, 255, 258, 334,
   350, 359, 364, 367, 413,
   414, 416
field
   BackLink 133, 134, 142,
   143, 303
   Base 54, 56, 58, 59, 68,
   129, 180, 204, 297, 456
   CPL 36, **41**, 183, 185
   DefaultAttr 199
   DPL **44**, 297
   exception_count 36, 157
   FTAG 353
   FTOP 237
   IDTIndex 147
   Index 67, 147
   IOPL **41**
   LEN 173
   Limit 46, 56, 58, 78, 129,
   204, 504
   ParamCount 124
   PC 258, 372, 373, 374,
   375, 376
   prev_CPL 157, 158
   PTBase 87
   RC 226, 236, 258, 336,
   363, 364, 372, 373, 374,
   375, 376
   RPL **45**, 283
   RW 173
   TI 147
   TOP 232, 234, 246, 346,
   361, 381
   Type 132, 135
FILD (instr) 359
FIMUL (instr) 360
FINCSTP (instr) 361
FINIT (instr) 362
first_page_fault_seen (flag)
   36, 157, 168
FIST (instr) 363
FISTP (instr) 364
FISUB[R] (instr) 366
flag
   AC 25, 205, 533, 534
   Accessed 66, 79, 80, 141
   AF 24, 521, 550, 553
   AM 25, 27, 183, 205
   arithmetic **24**
   BD 507, 509
   Big 59, 114, 115, 196

brkpt_active 35, 166, 171, 175, 176, 180, 181, 184, 185
BSY 258
BT 135, 139, 142
C0 236, 258, 341, 344, 356, 421, 424, 426
C1 230, 236, 258, 369, 372, 373, 374, 375, 376, 377, 380, 426
C2 236, 258, 341, 344, 356, 393, 395, 421, 424, 426
C3 236, 258, 341, 344, 356, 421, 424, 426
CD 27, 105, 106, 183
CF 24, 288, 290, 292, 294, 341, 344, 356, 421, 424, 521, 548, 549, 550, 552, 553
CR0 25
D **59**
DefaultAttr 59, 113, 115, 195, 196, 199, 204
DF 24, 527
DirTabBase 27
DM 235, 258
ED 47
EFLAGS **23**, 250
EM 27, 248, 257, 381, 479, 569, 582
eP 148
ERS 236, 258
ET 27, 28, 569
eU_S 148
eW_R 148
Executable 46, 83
FDE 230, 236, 255, 258
FIE 236, 255, 258, 334, 350, 359, 364, 367, 413, 414, 416
first_page_fault_seen 36, 157, 168
FLAGS **23**
FOE 236, 255, 258
FPE 236, 256, 258
FUE 236, 255, 258
FZE 236, 255, 258
G **58**
G0 173
G1 173
G2 173
G3 173
GD 172, 173, 508, 509, 510
GE 173
IC 219, 236, 258
IDT 147

IEM 235, 256, 258, 382
IF 24, 37, 42, 149, 150, 160, 161, 166, 573
IM 235, 258
IOPL 25, 118, 533, 539, 573
L0 173
L1 173
L2 173
L3 173
ICD 105, 107
LE 173
limit granularity **58**
MP 27, 479, 569, 581, 582
NE 27, 253
NMI_handler_active 35, 179, 181, 184, 185, 447, 450
NT 25, 129, 134, 143, 162, 303, 447
NW 27, 104, 108, 183
OF 24, 444, 548, 549
OM 235, 258
PAccessed 87, 112
PCD 87, 105, 106, 107
PDirty 87, 95, 110, 112
PE 25, 27, 38, 40, 72, 83, 183, 184, 479, 504, 569
PF 24, 341, 344, 356, 421, 424, 550
PG 27, 53, 83, 106, 178, 183, 184
PM 235, 258
PPresent 87
Present 68, 87
prev_instr_loaded_SS 35, 181, 183, 185, 500, 531
prev_TF 35, 135, 142, 160, 162, 163, 164, 170, 175, 181, 183, 185
PTAccessed 87, 112
PTCD 87, 105, 106, 107
PTPresent 87
PTWT 87, 107
PWT 87, 107
Readable 46, 50, 73
reserved 7
RF 25, 155, 158, 163, 164, 166, 175, 176, 177, 180, 181, 449, 451, 539
SF 24, 550, 553
STF 258, 334, 350, 359, 364, 367, 372, 374, 375, 376, 413, 414, 416
T 137, 139, 172, 174
task_switch_in_progress 35, 134, 138, 139, 183, 185

TF 24, 35, 160, 162, 163,
     164, 169, 170, 176
TI 62
TOP 258
TS 27, 248, 250, 257, 381,
     479, 569, 581, 582
U_S 49, 88, 89
UCD 27, 87, 105, 106, 107
UM 235, 258
undefined 7
UWT 27, 87, 107
Valid 67, 68, 73
VM 25, 38, 40, 126, 139,
     164, 184, 539
W_R 49, 88, 89, 94, 96
W_R, simplification on
     80386 88
WP 27, 88, 89, 94, 205
Writable 46
XH_flag 35, 135, 148, 163,
     165
XHE 147, 148, 150
ZF 24, 316, 341, 344, 356,
     421, 424, 550, 553, 579,
     580
ZM 235, 258
FLAGS **23**
FLAGS (register) 159, 177,
     201, 230
FLD1 (instr) 369
FLD (instr) 367
FLDCW (instr) 234, 370
FLDENV (instr) 234, 238, 371
FLDL2E (instr) 372
FLDL2T (instr) 373
FLDLG2 (instr) 374
FLDLN2 (instr) 375
FLDPI (instr) 376
FLDZ (instr) 377
floating point 19
     denormal **216**
     exponent bias **212**
     IEEE standard 210
     infinity **218**
     normalized **214**
     pseudozero **216**
     unnormal 214
     zero **216**
floating point stack
     See FSTK
FMIN 216
FMUL (instr) 378
FMULP (instr) 380
FNCLEX (instr) 381
FNDISI (instr) 382
FNENI (instr) 383
FNINIT (instr) 177, 257, 384,
     386

FNOP (instr) 385
FNSAVE (instr) 386
FNSETPM (instr) 388, 479
FNSTCW (instr) 389
FNSTENV (instr) 390
FNSTSW (instr) 391
FOE (flag) 236, 255, 258
FPATAN (instr) 392
FPE (flag) 236, 256, 258
FPREM1 (instr) 395
FPREM (instr) 393
FPTAN (instr) 397
FRESTOR (instr) 234, 238
FRNDINT (instr) 227, 398
FRSTOR (instr) 234, 238,
     399
FS: (prefix) 190, 401
FS (seg. reg.) 26, 69, 201
FS_desc 401
FSAVE (instr) 234, 238, 403
FSCALE (instr) 404
FSETPM (instr) 250, 405
FSIN (instr) 406
FSINCOS (instr) 407
FSQRT (instr) 408
FST (instr) 409
FSTCW (instr) 234, 410
FSTENV (instr) 234, 238, 411
FSTK **232**
FSTK (register) 238, 242, 246
FSTP (instr) 413
FSTSW (instr) 234, 412
FSUB[R] (instr) 414
FSUB[R]P (instr) 416
FSW **232**
FSW (register) 230, **234**, 238,
     242, 243, 244, 246, 254,
     257, 260, 341, 344, 356,
     381, 391, 394, 421, 424,
     550
FTAG **232**
FTAG (field) 353
FTAG (register) 234, 238,
     242, 243, 244, 257, 258
FTOP (field) 237
FTST (instr) 418
FUCOM (instr) 228, 420
FUCOMP (instr) 228
FUCOMP[P] (instr) 422
FUCOMPP (instr) 228
FUE (flag) 236, 255, 258
function
     brkpt_detected **167**, 542
     check_brkpt 91, 95, **175**
     check_interrupts 11, 13,
          151
     checkpoint 11, 12, **168**
     chop 404

clear_active_brkpts **176**
decode_instruction 11, 12, **185**
double_fault **153**
DTAB_read*x* 74, 75
DTAB_write*x* 81
enter_new_task **134**
evenParity **271**
execute 11, 12, 13, **261**
exit_task **142**
external_interrupt **166**, 248, 542, 581
fetch_code1 **83**
handle_intr_xcp **160**
IDT_read 147
IDT_read*x* 77
IDT_write 147
in_limits **78**, 197
inBounds 463, 491
init_VM_desc() **140**
int_via_task_gate **133**
IOPermission **120**
LA_rdChk **93**
LA_read1 **91**
LA_read2 **92**
LA_read4 **92**
LA_read*x* 73
LA_wrChk **96**
LA_write1 **95**
LA_write2 **95**
LA_write4 **96**
load_CS 69
load_data_seg 71, 530
load_env_16 **242**
load_env_32 **243**
load_LDT **141**
load_protected_descr **140**
load_SS **70**, 530
lock 70, 106, **112**, 113, 134, 141, 160, 162, **478**, **495**
logb **428**
mark_accessed **66**
new_stk_push **126**
nullSel **68**
pop2 **117**
pop4 **117**
pop_FSTK **247**
pop*OS* **118**
push2 **116**
push4 **116**
push_FSTK **247**
push*OS* **118**
read_descr **63**
read_TSS16 **137**
read_TSS32 **138**
read*x* 73, 74, 273

report_brkpts 11, 13, 170, **175**
reset_86 **178**
reset_286 **180**
reset_376 **184**
reset_386_486 **182**
reset_cpu 11, **178**
save_task_state **136**
signal_87 **255**
signal_abort **158**
signal_fault **155**
signal_imprecise **157**
signal_trap **157**
signex **271**, 319
software_interrupt **151**
store_env_16 **244**
store_env_32 **244**
TSS_read*x* 76
TSS_write*x* 81, 82
unlock 71, **112**, 113, 134, 141, 160, 163, **478**, **495**
write*x* 79, 80, 274
funnel shift 561, 565
FWAIT (instr) 425
FXAM (instr) 426
FXCH (instr) 222, 427
FXTRACT (instr) 428
FYL2X (instr) 430
FYL2XP1 (instr) 431
FZE (flag) 236, 255, 258

G

G0 (flag) 173
G1 (flag) 173
G2 (flag) 173
G3 (flag) 173
G (flag) **58**
gate 41, **121**
    interrupt 145
    task 145
    trap 145
GD (flag) 172, 173, 508, 509, 510
GDT **56**, 61, 88
GDT (table) 122
GE (flag) 173
General Electric
    645 computer 43
general purpose register
    See general register
general register **21**
global descriptor table
    See GDT
GP (exception) 60, 68, 69, 73, 75, 88, 119, 123, 145, 188, 197, 206, 256, 257, 497

gradual underflow **216**
GS: (prefix) 190, 432
GS (seg. reg.) 26, 69, 201
GS_desc 432

H

halt **168**
handle_intr_xcp **160**
hardware interrupt 13, 24, 42,
   144, 252
hit rate **102**
hit ratio **102**
HLT (instr) 168, 434

I

i486 2, 582
   detection method 534
   reset 182
I/O address 14, 118
I/O permission map 42, 118,
   119, 206
I/O privilege level
   See IOPL
I/O space 118, 120, 203
IBM 17
   AT 204, 253, 581
   PC 3, 202, 204
   XT 251
IC (flag) 219, 236, 258
IDIV (instr) 435
IDT 77
IDT (flag) 147
IDT (table) 122
IDT flag 77
IDT_read 147
IDT_read*x* (func) 77
IDT_write 147
IDTIndex (field) 147
IEEE Std. 754 211-230
IEM (flag) 235, 256, 258, 382
IF (exception) 145
IF (flag) 24, 37, 42, 149, 150,
   160, 161, 166, 573
IGNNE (pin) 254
IM (flag) 235, 258
immediate 186
implementation
   variations in 52
imprecise exceptions **144**
IMUL (instr) 186, 201, 437
IN (instr) 37, 42, 438
in_limits **78**, 197
inBounds (func) 463, 491
INC (instr) 439
indefinite 228
   packed BCD 224, 247, 335
   real 222, 246, 247

Index (field) 67, 147
index register **194**
infinity **218**
   affine 227, 236
   affine model **219**
   comparison with 228
   projective 228, 236
   projective model **219**
infinity control flag
   See IC
init_VM_desc() **140**
initialization 12
   of tables 79
INSB/INSD/INSW (instr) 440
instruction
   AAA 18, 275
   AAD 18, 276
   AAM 18, 277
   AAS 18, 278
   ADC 279
   ADD 280, 468
   AND 282
   ARPL 46, 283
   BOUND 201, 203, 284
   BSF 285
   BSR 286
   BSWAP 2, 17, 201, 202,
   205, 287
   BT 288
   BTC 290
   BTR 292
   BTS 294
   CALL 63, 195, 325
   CALL (far) 123, 129, 162,
   297
   CALL (near) 296
   CALL (task) 143, 303
   CALLF 297
   CBW 306
   CDQ 307
   CLC 308
   CLD 309
   CLI 42, 310
   CLTS 251, 311
   CMC 312
   CMP 313
   CMPSB/CMPSD/CMPSW
   314
   CMPS*x* 24
   CMP*x* 190
   CMPXCHG 316
   CWD 318
   CWDE 319
   DAA 19, 320
   DAS 19, 321
   DEC 322
   DIV 323
   EIP 12

ENTER 201, 326
ESC 329
F2XM1 330
FABS 222, 331
FADD 332
FADDP 334
FBLD 224, 335
FBSTP 224, 336
FCHS 222, 338
FCLEX 339
FCOM 228, 340
FCOMP 228
FCOMP[P] 342
FCOMPP 228
FCOS 345
FDECSTP 346
FDISI 347
FDIV[R] 348
FDIV[R]P 350
FENI 352
FFREE 353
FIADD 354
FICOM 228, 355
FICOMP 228, 357
FIDIV[R] 358
FILD 359
FIMUL 360
FINCSTP 361
FINIT 362
FIST 363
FISTP 364
FISUB[R] 366
FLD 367
FLD1 369
FLDCW 234, 370
FLDENV 234, 238, 371
FLDL2E 372
FLDL2T 373
FLDLG2 374
FLDLN2 375
FLDPI 376
FLDZ 377
FMUL 378
FMULP 380
FNCLEX 381
FNDISI 382
FNENI 383
FNINIT 177, 257, 384, 386
FNOP 385
FNSAVE 386
FNSETPM 388, 479
FNSTCW 389
FNSTENV 390
FNSTSW 391
FPATAN 392
FPREM 393
FPREM1 395
FPTAN 397

FRESTOR 234, 238
FRNDINT 227, 398
FRSTOR 234, 238, 399
FSAVE 234, 238, 403
FSCALE 404
FSETPM 250, 405
FSIN 406
FSINCOS 407
FSQRT 408
FST 409
FSTCW 234, 410
FSTENV 234, 238, 411
FSTP 413
FSTSW 234, 412
FSUB[R] 414
FSUB[R]P 416
FTST 418
FUCOM 228, 420
FUCOMP 228
FUCOMP[P] 422
FUCOMPP 228
FWAIT 425
FXAM 426
FXCH 222, 427
FXTRACT 428
FYL2X 430
FYL2XP1 431
HLT 168, 434
IDIV 435
IMUL 186, 201, 437
IN 37, 42, 438
INC 439
INSB/INSD/INSW 440
INS*x* 24, 42, 190, 201
INT 129, 191, 195, 325, 442
INT3 170, 202
INT 3 443
interruptable 177
INTO 202, 444
INVD 106, 445
INVLPG 446
IOPL-sensitive **40**, 533, 539
IRET 129, 134, 139, 143, 169, 170, 176, 195, 325
IRET/IRETD (protected) 447
IRET/IRETD (REAL/VM86) 450
IRET*x* 42
Jcond 313, 314, 452
JCXZ/JECXZ 454
JMP (far) 127, 129, 456
JMP (near) 455
JMP (task) 143, 460
LAHF 462
LAR 463, 492

LDS 197, 465
LEA 467
LEAVE 201, 469
LES 470
LFS 472
LGDT 59, 60, 474
LGS 475
LIDT 477
LLDT 57, 61, 141, 478
LMSW 38, 41, 201, 479, 504, 506
LOADALL286 205, 480
LODSB/LODSD/LODSW 486
LODS*x* 24, 190
long running 144
LOOP 488
LOOPE/LOOPZ 489
LOOPNE/LOOPNZ 490
LSL 491
LSS 36, 493, 500
LTR 143, 495
MOV 29, 106, 172, 496, 497, 499, 501, 502, 505, 507, 509, 511, 514
MOVSB 165
MOVSX 192, 518
MOVS*x* 24, 190, 516
MOVZX 519
MUL 520
NEG 521
NOP 522
NOT 523
OR 525
OUT 37, 42, 526
OUTS*x* 24, 42, 190, 201, 527
POP 195, 325, 529, 530
POPA 195, 201, 325
POPA/POPAD 532
POPF 170, 195, 325
POPF/POPFD 533
POPF*x* 42
privileged **40**, 41
PUSH 195, 201, 325, 535, 536
PUSHA 195, 201, 325
PUSHA/PUSHAD 538
PUSHF 195, 325
PUSHF/PUSHFD 539
PUSHF*x* 42
RCL 540
RCR 541
restartability 31
restartable **167**
RET 195, 325
RET (far) 545

RET (near) 544
RETF 122, 302, 545
RETN 544
ROL 540, 548
ROR 287, 541, 549
SAHF 550
SAL 551
SAR 553
SBB 555
SCASB/SCASD/SCASW 556
SCAS*x* 24, 190
SET*cond* 313, 314, 558
SGDT 559
SHL 560
SHLD 186, 201, 202, 561
SHR 563
SHRD 186, 201, 202, 565
SIDT 567
SLDT 568
SMSW 506, 569
STC 571
STD 572
STI 42, 573
STOSB/STOSD/STOSW 574
STOS*x* 24, 190
STR 576
SUB 577
TEST 578
VERR 201, 579
VERW 580
WAIT 202, 204, 250, 252, 581
WBINVD 106, 583
XADD 584
XCHG 17, 585
XLATB 586
XOR 587
instruction encoding 22, 185-200
80*x*87 259
instruction length
maximum 187
instruction pointer
See EIP
INS*x* (instr) 24, 42, 190, 201
INT 3 (instr) 443
INT3 (instr) 170, 202
INT (instr) 129, 191, 195, 325, 442
INT (pin) 204, 251, 256
int_via_task_gate **133**
integers
in 80*x*87 222
Intel 1
interrupt
external 169

hardware 24, 42, **144**, 165, 248
  latency **165**, 581
  non-maskable
    See NMI
  REAL mode 145
  software 24, **143**, 170
interrupt controller 149, 251, 253
interrupt flag
  See IF
INTERRUPT_GATE16 (descr. type) 146, 159, 161
INTERRUPT_GATE32 (descr. type) 146, 159, 161, 177
interrupt vector 37, **145**, 152
Interrupts **143**
interrupts 11
  simultaneous 149
INTO (instr) 202, 444
INTR (pin) 166
INVALID_FOP (x87 exception) 227, 228, 237, 246, 247, 255, 337, 338, 408, 420, 428, 430, 431
INVALID_INSTR (exception) 191, 202, 203, 281, 446, 468, 483, 524, 543, 559, 567, 577, 585, 587
invalid operation mask
  See IM
invalidate cycles **104**
INVD (instr) 106, 445
invisible registers **30**
INVLPG (instr) 446
io_vec **118**
IOPermission **120**
IOPL **41**
IOPL (flag) 25, 118, 533, 539, 573
IOPL-sensitive 37, **40**, 442, 443, 450, 485, 533, 539, 573
IP (register) 82, 159, 196, 297
IRET (instr) 129, 134, 139, 143, 169, 170, 176, 195, 325
IRET/IRETD (protected) (instr) 447
IRET/IRETD (REAL/VM86) (instr) 450
IRET*x* (instr) 42

J

J*cond* (instr) 313, 314, 452
JCXZ/JECXZ (instr) 454

JMP (far) (instr) 127, 129, 456
JMP (near) (instr) 455
JMP (task) (instr) 143, 460

K

KEN (pin) 105, 106, 107

L

L0 (flag) 173
L1 (flag) 173
L2 (flag) 173
L3 (flag) 173
LA_rdChk **93**
LA_read1 **91**
LA_read2 **92**
LA_read4 **92**
LA_read*x* 73
LA_wrChk **96**
LA_write1 **95**
LA_write2 **95**
LA_write4 **96**
label
  NEXT_INSTR **11**, 160, 163, 165
LAHF (instr) 462
LAR (instr) 463, 492
lCD (flag) 105, 107
LDS (instr) 197, 465
LDT 26, **56**, 61, 88
LDT (seg. reg.) 201
LDT (table) 122
LDT_desc 140
LDT_SEG (descr. type) 141, 478
LDTS (register) 26
LDTS (seg. reg.) 26
LE (flag) 173
LEA (instr) 467
LEAVE (instr) 201, 469
LEN (field) 173
LES (instr) 470
LFS (instr) 472
LGDT (instr) 59, 60, 474
LGS (instr) 475
LIDT (instr) 477
Limit (field) 46, 56, 58, 78, 129, 204, 504
Limit granularity **58**
LIN_ADDR (type) 83, **84**, 91
linear address 37, 73
  See address, linear
  wraparound 198
LISP 98
Little Endian 5, **16**, 191, 222, 287
LLDT (instr) 57, 61, 141, 478

LMSW (instr) 38, 41, 201, 479, 504, 506
load_CS 69, 297, 456
load_data_seg 71, 530
load_env_16 **242**
load_env_32 **243**
load_LDT **141**
load_protected_descr **140**
load_SS **70**, 530
LOADALL286 (instr) 205, 480
local descriptor table
  See LDT
lock 69, 70, 71, 105, 106, **112**, 113, 134, 137, 139, 141, 142, 159, 160, 162, 300, **478**, **495**
  DIR_TABLE 93
  PAGE_TABLE 93
LOCK (pin) 112, 113
LOCK (prefix) 12, 106, 112, 190, 191, 484, 577, 585, 587
LODSB/LODSD/LODSW (instr) 486
LODS*x* (instr) 24, 190
logb **428**
logical address 37, **44**
  See address, logical
LOOP (instr) 488
LOOPE/LOOPZ (instr) 489
LOOPNE/LOOPNZ (instr) 490
LSL (instr) 491
LSS (instr) 36, 493, 500
LTR (instr) 143, 495

M

Mach 128
machine status word
  See MSW
main memory
  See mem_vec
mark_accessed **66**
master device **111**
mem_vec **51**, 83, 84, 91, 93, 94, 95, 97, 480
memory operand 186
misaligned access
  See access, misaligned
miss rate **102**
miss ratio **102**
MOD/RM 191, 259, 329
  SET*x* usage 558
mode 26, 159, 388
  effect on 80*x*87 238
  privileged **41**
  PROTECTED 36, 67

REAL 36, 179, 195
  switch 38
  UNREAL 72
  VM86 36, 136, 141, 195
monitor processor extension flag
  See MP
Motorola 17
MOV (instr) 29, 106, 172, 496, 497, 499, 501, 502, 505, 507, 509, 511, 514
MOVSB (instr) 165
MOVSX (instr) 192, 518
MOVS*x* (instr) 24, 190, 516
MOVZX (instr) 519
MP (flag) 27, 479, 569, 581, 582
MS-DOS 206
  A20 enable 198
MSW **26**, 502, 505
MSW (register) 38, 180, 203, 479, 504, 506, 569
MUL (instr) 520
Multics 43
multiplication using LEA 468
multiprocessor 93

N

NaN **220**
  comparison with 227
NaNs 338
National Semiconductor 17
natural boundary **15**, 98
NE (flag) 27, 253
near operand 186
near pointer **44**, 186
NEG (instr) 521
nested task flag
  See NT
new_stk_push **126**
NEXT_INSTR **11**, 160, 163, 165
nibble **18**
NMI **150**, 169, 202
NMI (exception) 149, 450
NMI (pin) 151, 166, 202, 204, 251, 447
NMI_handler_active (flag) 35, 179, 181, 184, 185, 447, 450
non-maskable interrupt
  See NMI
nonadministrative instructions **232**
NOP (instr) 522
NOT (instr) 523

not-a-number
    See NaN
notation
    [E]SI 196
    instruction description 5
NOTBUSY_TSS16 (descr.
    type) 132, 133, 142
NOTBUSY_TSS32 (descr.
    type) 132, 133, 142
NP (exception) 68, 88, 141,
    152
NT (flag) 25, 129, 134, 143,
    162, 303, 447
null SELECTOR **67**
nullSel **68**
numerics exception flag
    See NE
NW (flag) 27, 104, 108, 183

O

OF (flag) 24, 444, 548, 549
OFFSET **44**, 53, 186, 192
    wraparound **196**
offset **44**, 281
    within page **50**
OM (flag) 235, 258
opcode 188, 191
    extension 189, 191
operand size attribute
    See attribute, operand size
operand size override (prefix)
    190, 524
OR (instr) 525
os **200**
OS/2 128
OUT (instr) 37, 42, 526
OUTS*x* (instr) 24, 42, 190,
    201, 527
overflow
    and 80*x*87 218
OVERFLOW (exception) 152
overflow flag
    See OF
overflow mask
    See OM

P

PAccessed (flag) 87, 112
PACKED_BCD **224**
packed BCD **18**, 224
    in 80*x*87 212
packed BCD indefinite **224**
page 40, **48**
PAGE (exception) 9, 90, 93,
    110, 146, 152, 177, 256
page byte index **50**
page fault 49

page table 49, **51**, 133, 148
page table entry index
    See PTE
paging 26, 38, 43
    and TLBs 108
    of exception handlers 152
    of GDT 61
    of LDT 61
paging enable flag
    See PG
ParamCount (field) 124
parity flag
    See PF
PC (field) 258, 372, 373, 374,
    375, 376
PC/AT 204
    80*x*87 interface 253
PC/XT 204, 206
PCD (flag) 87, 105, 106, 107
PDirty (flag) 87, 95, 110, 112
PE (flag) 25, 27, 38, 40, 72,
    83, 183, 184, 479, 504,
    569
PE_ERROR (exception) 144,
    145, 202, 204, 249, 381
PE_OVERRUN (exception)
    144, 256, 257, 384
PE_UNAVAILABLE
    (exception) 248, 251, 257,
    581
performance 4
peripheral device 14
    memory mapped 107
permission map
    See I/O permission map
PF (flag) 24, 341, 344, 356,
    421, 424, 550
PG (flag) 27, 53, 83, 106,
    178, 183, 184
physical address 37
    See address, physical
    wraparound 198
physical memory
    See mem_vec
pin
    A20M 198
    AHOLD 182
    BUSY 182, 231, 248, 250,
    253, 381, 382, 383, 581,
    582
    ERROR 204, 232, 236,
    249, 252, 253, 254, 256,
    581
    FERR 254
    IGNNE 254
    INT 204, 251, 256
    INTR 166
    KEN 105, 106, 107

LOCK 112, 113
NMI 151, 166, 202, 204, 251, 447
RESET 182
PM (flag) 235, 258
pointer
far 197
pop2 **117**
pop4 **117**
POP (instr) 195, 325, 529, 530
pop_FSTK **247**
POPA (instr) 195, 201, 325
POPA/POPAD (instr) 532
POPF (instr) 170, 195, 325
POPF/POPFD (instr) 533
POPF*x* (instr) 42
pop*OS* **118**
PORT (type) 40
POST 29
PPresent (flag) 87
PRECISION (x87 exception) 230, 256, 372, 373, 374, 375, 376
precision control flag
See PC
precision mask
See PM
prefix 190
address override 196
address size 488, 489, 490
address size override 190, 281
CS: 190, 317
DS: 190, 325
ES 328
ES: 190
FS: 190, 401
GS: 190, 432
LOCK 12, 106, 112, 190, 191, 484, 577, 585, 587
operand size 488, 489, 490
operand size override 190, 524
REP 190
REPE 190
REPNE 190
REPNZ 542
REP*x* 165, 191, 542
REPZ 542
segment override 195, 274
SS: 190, 570
Present (flag) 68, 87
segment vs. page 87
prev 31
prev_CPL (field) 157, 158
prev_CPL (register) 154, 158

prev_EIP (register) 31, 154, 158, 248, 249, 542, 581
prev_instr_loaded_SS (flag) 35, 181, 183, 185, 500, 531
prev_TF (flag) 35, 135, 142, 160, 162, 163, 164, 170, 175, 181, 183, 185
priority
exceptions 149
interrupts 149
privilege level 37
changes in 121
Supervisor level 50
User level 50
privileged instruction **40**
privileged mode **41**
proc 544
procedure
far 544
near 544
nested 326
processor
8088 52
80188 52
80386SX 52
processor extension 581
PROTECTED mode
See mode, PROTECTED
protection enable flag
See PE
pseudozero **217**
PTAccessed (flag) 87, 112
PTBase (field) 87
PTCD (flag) 87, 105, 106, 107
PTE **50**, 96
PTPresent (flag) 87
PTWT (flag) 87, 107
push2 **116**
push4 **116**
PUSH (instr) 195, 201, 325, 535, 536
push_FSTK **247**
PUSHA (instr) 195, 201, 325
PUSHA/PUSHAD (instr) 538
PUSHF (instr) 195, 325
PUSHF/PUSHFD (instr) 539
PUSHF*x* (instr) 42
push*OS* **118**
PWT (flag) 87, 107

Q

QNaN **220**
See also NaN
quiet NaN **220**
See QNaN

QWORD (type) 359, 364

R

RC (field) 226, 236, 258, 336, 363, 364, 372, 373, 374, 375, 376
RCL (instr) 540
RCR (instr) 541
read_descr **63**, 297, 456
read_TSS16 **137**
read_TSS32 **138**
Readable (flag) 46, 50, 73
read*x* (func) 73, 74, 273
real indefinite **222**
REAL mode
  See mode, REAL
register 186
  AH 323
  AL 272, 323
  AX 272, 323, 391
  base **194**
  BP 187, 194, 195, 326
  BX 187, 194
  characteriztion **187**
  CL 192
  control
    See control register
  CPL 154, 158
  CR0 569
  CR4 8
  CS 124, 159
  CX 196
  debug
    See debug register
  DH 182
  DI 187, 194, 196
  DL 182
  DR7 144
  DX 527
  EAX 182, 272
  EBP 194, 195, 326
  ECX 165, 196
  EDI 165, 196
  EFLAGS 38, 41, 134, 169, 176, 177
  EIP 20, 69, 82, 123, 153, 154, 158, 186, 196, 248, 297, 542, 581
  encoding 22
  ESI 165, 187, 196
  ESP 35, 59, 113, 114, 117, 187, 194, 195, 196, 197, 326, 529, 535
  exception_count 168
  FCW 219, 226, **234**, 238, 242, 243, 244, 257, 370,
    372, 373, 374, 375, 376, 389
  FLAGS 159, 177, 201, 230
  FSTK 238, 242, 246
  FSW 230, **232**, **234**, 238, 242, 243, 244, 246, 254, 257, 260, 341, 344, 356, 381, 391, 394, 421, 424, 550
  FTAG 234, 238, 242, 243, 244, 257, 258
  general purpose 21
  index **194**
  invisible **30**
  IP 82, 159, 196, 297
  LDTS 26
  MSW 38, 180, 203, 479, 504, 506, 569
  prev_CPL 154, 158
  prev_EIP 31, 154, 158, 248, 249, 542, 581
  segment 21
    See segment register
  SI 187, 194, 196
  SP 35, 59, 113, 117, 196, 197, 201, 326
  test
    See test register
  TSS 26
  visible **20**
  X87CS 242, 243, 244, 258, 385
  X87DOFF 242, 243, 244, 249, 258
  X87DSEL 242, 243, 244, 249, 258
  X87EIP 242, 243, 244, 249, 258, 385
  X87OPER 242, 243, 246, 258, 385
  X87SEL 249
REP (prefix) 190
REPE (prefix) 190
replacement policy **103**
REPNE (prefix) 190
REPNZ (prefix) 542
report_brkpts 11, 13, 170, **175**
REP*x* (prefix) 165, 191, 542
REPZ (prefix) 542
requestor's privilege level
  See RPL
reserved fields 7
reset 12, 28
  TLB state 109
reset_86 **178**
reset_286 **180**
reset_376 **184**

reset_386_486 **182**
RESET (pin) 182
reset_cpu 11, **178**
restart flag
    See RF
restartability **31**
restartable instruction
    See instruction, restartable
result **6**
RET (far) (instr) 545
RET (instr) 195, 325
RET (near) (instr) 544
RETF (instr) 122, 302, 545
RETN (instr) 544
REXX 98
RF (flag) 25, 155, 158, 163,
    164, 166, 175, 176, 177,
    180, 181, 449, 451, 539
ROL (instr) 540, 548
ROM 443
ROR (instr) 287, 541, 549
rotate
    by a constant 201
rounding 226-227
rounding control flag
    See RC
RPL **45**, 56
RPL (field) 283
RW (field) 173

S

SAHF (instr) 550
SAL (instr) 551
SAR (instr) 553
save_task_state **136**
SBB (instr) 555
scale factor 194
SCASB/SCASD/SCASW
    (instr) 556
SCAS*x* (instr) 24, 190
second-level cache **107**
segment 32, 40, 44
    conforming 41, 123, **128**
    expand-down **47**, 78, 115,
        492
    expand-up **47**
    limit 78
    task state 123
segment descriptor
    Base 33
    CDSeg 33
    Conforming 33
    DefaultAttr 33
    DPL 33
    Executable 33
    ExpandDown 33
    gate Offset 33

gate Selector 33
Limit 33
Readable 33
register **32**
Type 33
Valid 33
Writable 33
segment descriptor table
    See table, segment
    descriptor
    See also GDT,LDT
segment limit 58
segment register 21, **25**, 32,
    192
    CS 26, 69, 82, 83, 201,
        202, 249, 297, 456
    DS 26, 69, 187, 195, 201,
        202, 314, 586
    ES 26, 69, 187, 195, 201,
        202, 314
    FS 26, 69, 201
    GS 26, 69, 201
    LDT 201
    LDTS 26
    SS 26, 35, 69, 113, 115,
        195, 201, 202
    TSS 26, 134, 135, 142,
        143, 201
segmentation 43
SELECTOR 21, 186, 192,
    194
    null **67**
selector 36
    Index (field) 56
    tables index 56
SELECTOR (type) 20, 25, 32,
    44, 45, 56, 122
self-test 181
semaphore 112
sensitive instruction
    See IOPL-sensitive
set size **102**
SET*cond* (instr) 313, 314,
    558
SF (flag) 24, 550, 553
SGDT (instr) 559
shift
    by a constant 201
SHL (instr) 560
SHLD (instr) 186, 201, 202,
    561
SHR (instr) 563
SHRD (instr) 186, 201, 202,
    565
shutdown 153, **168**
SHUTDOWN (exception) 145
SI (register) 187, 194, 196
SIB byte **194**

SIDT (instr) 567
sign extension 5
sign flag
  See SF
signal_87 **255**
signal_abort **158**
signal_fault **155**
signal_imprecise **157**
signal_trap **157**
signaling NaN **220**
  See SNaN
signex 5, **271**, 319
significand **212**
simultaneous exceptions 149
simultaneous interrupts 149
SINGLE **213**
single precision 210
single step **169**
single step flag
  See TF
slave device **111**
SLDT (instr) 568
Smalltalk 98
SMSW (instr) 506, 569
SNaN **220**, 338
  See also NaN
software interrupt 24, **144**
software_interrupt **151**
SP (register) 35, 59, 113,
  117, 196, 197, 201, 326
SPECIAL **233**
special segment
  TSS 129
split reference
  See access, misaligned
SS: (prefix) 190, 570
SS (seg. reg.) 26, 35, 69, 113,
  115, 195, 201, 202
SS_desc 195, 570
SS_desc (descriptor) 115
ST 232
stack 13, 59, **113**
  16 vs. 32 bit address 114
  add op 334
  alignment 115
  big 197
  divide op 351
  ESP usage 196
  multiply op 380
  SS usage 328
  subtract op 417
  top 113
STACK (exception) 73, 499
stack segment 69
stack-top (80x87)
  See ST
status word
  See FSW

STC (instr) 571
STD (instr) 572
stepping id 28, 182
STF (flag) 258, 334, 350,
  359, 364, 367, 372, 374,
  375, 376, 413, 414, 416
STI (instr) 42, 573
store_env_16 **244**
store_env_32 **244**
STOSB/STOSD/STOSW
  (instr) 574
STOS*x* (instr) 24, 190
STR (instr) 576
string direction flag
  See DF
string instruction
  and DF 24
SUB (instr) 577
supervisor write protect flag
  See WP

T

T (flag) 137, 139, 172, 174
table
  segment descriptor 36
TASK (exception) 69, 75,
  141, 145
task gate 143
task state segment 123, **129**
task switch 58
  LDT load 61
  nested 133
task_switch_in_progress
  (flag) 35, 134, 138, 139,
  183, 185
task switched flag
  See TS
TASKGATE 298
TASKGATE (descr. type) 129,
  146, 159, 161
TEST (instr) 578
test register 29
  TR3 511
  TR4 106, 511
  TR5 106, 511
testability
  of cache 29
  of TLB 29
TF (flag) 24, 35, 160, 162,
  163, 164, 169, 170, 176
TI 56
TI (field) 147
TI (flag) 62
tiny numbers **216**, 229
TLB 94, **108**, 182, 446, 511,
  514
  replacement policy 110

testing 511
TLB miss **110**
TLB_x86 109, 446, 512
TOP (field) 232, 234, 246,
   346, 361, 381
TOP (flag) 258
TR3 (test reg.) 511
TR4 (test reg.) 106, 511
TR5 (test reg.) 106, 511
translation lookaside buffer
   See TLB
trap 172
trap flag
   See TF
TRAP_GATE16 (descr. type)
   146, 159, 161
TRAP_GATE32 (descr. type)
   146, 159, 161, 177
traps **144**
Trojan horse 45, 128
TS (flag) 27, 248, 250, 257,
   381, 479, 569, 581, 582
TSS 26, **129**
   286-style
      See TSS16
   386-style
      See TSS32
   486-style
      See TSS32
   busy 132
   CALL via 298
   not busy 132
TSS32 172
TSS (register) 26
TSS (seg. reg.) 26, 134, 135,
   142, 143, 201
TSS_desc 132, 134, 135,
   142, 143
TSS_INDEX 121
TSS_read*x* (func) 76
TSS_write*x* (func) 81, 82
two's-complement 15, 191
type
   BOOLEAN 33
   BYTE **15**
   BYTEPORT 118, 526
   DESCR 62, 63
   DWORD **15**
   DWORDPORT 526
   LIN_ADDR 83, **84**, 91
   PACKED_BCD **224**
   PORT 40
   QWORD 359, 364
   SELECTOR 20, 25, 32, 44,
      45, 56, 122
   WORD **15**
   WORDPORT 526

X86_REGISTERS **20**, 31
Type (field) 132, 135

U

U_S (flag) 49, 88, 89
UCD (flag) 27, 87, 105, 106,
   107
UM (flag) 235, 258
unaligned access **15**
   See access, misaligned
undefined fields 7
underflow
   and 80*x*87 218
underflow mask
   See UM
unlock 70, 71, **112**, 113, 134,
   137, 139, 141, 142, 160,
   163, 301, **478**, **495**
unnormal **214**, 230
UNREAL mode 72
USE16 196, 200, 281, 302,
   524
USE32 196, 200, 281, 524
UWT (flag) 27, 87, 107

V

VALID **234**
Valid (flag) 67, 68, 73
VAX 17
VERR (instr) 201, 579
VERW (instr) 580
virtual-86 flag
   See VM
virtual address
   See address, logical
visible registers **20**
VM86 mode
   See mode, VM86
VM (flag) 25, 38, 40, 126,
   139, 164, 184, 539

W

W_R (flag) 49, 88, 89, 94, 96
W_R, simplification on 80386
   (flag) 88
WAIT (instr) 202, 204, 250,
   252, 581
WBINVD (instr) 106, 583
WORD **15**
WORDPORT **118**
WORDPORT (type) 526
WP (flag) 27, 88, 89, 94, 205
wraparound
   of data **197**
   of linear address 198
   of physical address 198

Writable (flag) 46
write-back **104**
write protect flag
    See WP
write-through **104**, 108
writes transparent flag
    See NW
write*x* (func) 79, 80, 274

X

X86_REGISTERS (type) 31
X87CS **237**
X87CS (register) 242, 243,
    244, 258, 385
X87DOFF **237**
X87DOFF (register) 242, 243,
    244, 249, 258
X87DSEL **237**
X87DSEL (register) 242, 243,
    244, 249, 258
X87EIP **237**
X87EIP (register) 242, 243,
    244, 249, 258, 385
X87OPER **237**

X87OPER (register) 242,
    243, 246, 258, 385
X87SEL (register) 249
XADD (instr) 584
XCHG (instr) 17, 585
XH_flag (flag) 35, 135, 148,
    163, 165
XHE (flag) 147, 148, 150
XLATB (instr) 586
XOR (instr) 587

Z

ZERO **234**
zero-divide mask
    See ZM
zero flag
    See ZF
ZERO_FOP (x87 exception)
    228, 255, 428
ZF (flag) 24, 316, 341, 344,
    356, 421, 424, 550, 553,
    579, 580
ZM (flag) 235, 258